2024/25
FACTS AND FIGURES

TABLES FOR THE CALCULATION OF DAMAGES

2024/25
FACTS AND FIGURES

TABLES FOR THE CALCULATION OF DAMAGES

Compiled and Edited by:

Members of the Professional Negligence Bar Association

General Editor: William Latimer-Sayer KC

Editors:

Chris Daykin CB FIA
Vitek Frenkel FCA MAE
Peter Jennings
Tejina Mangat
Emily Read
James Rowley KC
Olinga Tahzib
and
Harry Trusted

Sweet & Maxwell

Thomson Reuters™

Published in 2024 by Thomson Reuters, trading as Sweet & Maxwell.
Thomson Reuters is registered in England and Wales. Company number 1679046.
Registered Office and address for service: 5 Canada Square, Canary Wharf, London E14 5AQ.

For further information on our products and services, visit *http://www.sweetandmaxwell.co.uk.*

Typeset by YHT 2018 Ltd, Ashford, Middlesex
Printed and bound by CPI Group (UK) Ltd, Croydon, CR0 4YY.

A CIP catalogue record for this book is available from the British Library.

ISBN (print) 978-0-414-12095-2
ISBN (e-book) 978-0-414-12099-0
ISBN (print and e-book) 978-0-414-12098-3

ACKNOWLEDGEMENTS

We are very grateful to the following contributors:

- Professor Victoria Wass formerly of Cardiff Business School for updating *B6: Step-by-step guide to finding the annual estimates for hourly pay in ASHE SOC 2000 6115* and for providing the guide to the ASHE earnings tables at *F8: Average earning statistics.*

- Rodney Nelson Jones formerly of Field Fisher Waterhouse and Lexis Nexis for allowing us to use and to develop his table for the calculation of special damages interest in *C4: Special and general damages interest.*

- Charlotte Cato at KCA (formerly Keith Carter & Associates) for the research undertaken for the preparation of the tables F5 on Regional Unemployment Statistics and *F6* and *F7* on average weekly earnings.

- The Family Law Bar Association for their permission to use table I1 & I2 and Gary Vaux, Head of Money Advice, Hertfordshire County Council for updating *I1: Social security benefits (non means-tested)* and *I2: Social security benefits and tax credits (means-tested).*

- Lynne Bradey & Janice Jefferies FCILEX at Wrigleys, for updating *I4: Personal injury trusts.*

- Christine Bunting, Partner at Hugh James, for her contribution to *J1, J2* and *J3* on Court of Protection and Deputyship Costs.

- James Rowley KC of Byrom Street Chambers and Matthew White of St John's Chambers for *H1: Notes on pension losses.*

- Jessica Thurston, Managing Director, of Somek & Associates Ltd and James Rowley KC of Byrom Street Chambers, for their work on *K1: Care and attendance.*

- Nicholas Leviseur for preparing the notes for *L3: The Motability Scheme.*

- Margaret McDonald, specialist costs counsel of Kenworthy's Chambers, for updating *M1: Senior Court Costs Office Guideline Rates for Summary Assessment.*

- Rory Donaghy and Brian Fee for reviewing the section *C10 on Rates of interest on damages (Northern Ireland).*

We are very grateful to the following organisations for kindly granting us permission to use their material:

- The HMSO for their permission to use *Table C2: Real and nominal interest rates and price inflation.* Crown Copyright is reproduced with the permission of HMSO.

- The Office for National Statistics for the data reported in *A3: Life Tables and Projected Life Tables, B6: Hourly Pay ASHE 6115, E1: Retail Prices Index, E2: Inflation table, E4: How prices have changed over 18 years, F6: Average earnings index; F7: Average weekly earnings* and *F8: Average earnings statistics.*

- www.gov.uk for their permission to use their figures in *I6: Foster Care Allowances.*
- HM Revenue & Customs and HMSO for their permission to use the material in *L2: Taxation of car and fuel benefits.*
- W. Green for their permission to use *C9: Judicial rates of interest (Scotland).*
- FTSE Russell for their permission to use the FTSE 100 Index at *D1: Share price index.*
- HM Land Registry for the use of the UK House Price Index (HPI) for *E3: House price indices.*
- Intuition Communication Ltd for their permission to reproduce figures from their website www.privatehealth.co.uk at *K4: Hospital self-pay (uninsured) charges.*
- National Health Services for data reported in *K5: NHS charges.*
- APIL, FOIL and the Serious Injury Guide Steering Committee for permission to publish the Serious Injury Guide at K7.
- The RAC Motoring Services in conjunction with Emmerson Hill Associates, who compiled the illustrative running costs at *L1: Motoring costs.*
- Bauer Media, publishers of Parker's Car Price Guide, upon whose figures the calculations in *L4: The costs of buying and replacing cars* are based.
- Collins Debden Australia for their permission to reproduce the perpetual calendar, as featured in the International Management Diary, at *M3: Perpetual calendar.*

INTRODUCTION TO THE TWENTY-NINTH EDITION

Well so far this year, Donald Trump was found guilty on 34 counts of falsifying business records but remains the 2024 presidential nominee for the Republican Party, England lost to Spain in the final of the Euros, Djokovic completed a career Golden Slam furthering his claim to be the undisputed GOAT, there's been a General Election, the Olympics, and on the last date allowed by the Civil Liability Act 2018, the new Lord Chancellor, Shabana Mahmood, announced her review of the Personal Injury Discount Rate (PIDR). Despite the distractions, like Oasis, we managed to get the old band back together to produce the latest edition of Facts & Figures. This time we warmly welcome Olinga Tahzib to the editorial team, who amongst other things, has updated the section on benefits including adding details of the historical amounts of Carer's Allowance and has written a helpful section on CRU recoupment.

This edition is the product of hard work from a number of dedicated editors and practitioners. I am indebted to my fellow editors and contributors who put significant time and effort into checking and double-checking that all the relevant data has been fully updated. I am also very grateful to the publishing team at Sweet & Maxwell for keeping things on track, making sure that deadlines are met and ensuring that the material is presented in the clearest and most user-friendly way possible.

Perhaps the most exciting development in the world of quantum, is that due to the concerted efforts of members of the Ogden Working Party, funding has been secured from various firms and organisations across the personal and clinical negligence sector in order to update the discount factors for contingencies other than mortality. Dr Sule Sahin, a Senior Lecturer in Actuarial Science at York University, will be leading the research team, under the watchful eye of Professor Victoria Wass. The results, which are expected in 2026, should enable more accurate assessment of individual loss of earnings claims by using up-to-date data on how disability affects employment prospects that can be adjusted to reflect the extent of a claimant's disability. The current reduction factors are based upon underlying data collected from the Labour Force Survey from 1998–2003. It is hoped that the third-generation reduction factors will be a significant improvement, allowing for greater detail and including suggested contingency discounts for individuals older than 54 where the current reduction factors are truncated.

By the time of the next edition, the wait regarding the new PIDR will be over and we will know whether a single or dual rate will apply. In the meantime, there continues to be significant speculation regarding the outcome of the review. However, the world keeps turning, and almost counter-intuitively, many cases are still resolving, perhaps because of the increased certainty—clearly, a bird in the hand is worth more than two in the bush or half a bird in six months' time.

No doubt Robin de Wilde KC has been following Bernie Ecclestone's criminal proceedings with interest. For others that have not kept up with the news, in October 2023 the 92-year-old pleaded guilty to fraud. He was sentenced to 17 months in prison, which was suspended for two years on the basis that he repaid almost £653m to the HM Revenue and Customs.

Finally, for those who haven't discovered this function yet, some not insignificant amusement can be found from using AI to roast things on your behalf. Obviously, I am not talking about Sunday lunch. Social media accounts are often a rich source of potential entertainment, however, by way of example, the following is Chat GPT's roast of our beloved tome:

"Sweet & Maxwell's 'Facts & Figures' is like the encyclopaedic tome that every law student dreads and every practitioner pretends to have read cover to cover. It's the literary equivalent of a really dense fruitcake: heavy, packed with details nobody asked for, and only enjoyable if you have absolutely nothing better to do.

Let's face it—calling them 'facts and figures' is generous. It's more like 'obscure minutiae and mind-numbing statistics.' You know it's bad when even the footnotes have footnotes. If there were an award for the most efficient sleep aid disguised as a legal reference book, this would win, hands down. And the formatting? Let's just say it's got all the aesthetic appeal of a 1980s VCR manual.

You can always tell when someone's trying to look smart in a meeting—they casually toss out a 'fact' from Sweet & Maxwell like it's the gospel, but you know they're praying no one asks them to elaborate. The real trick is how this tome manages to be both bloated and dry—like a legal textbook on a diet of nothing but bread and water.

In the end, Sweet & Maxwell's 'Facts & Figures' is the perfect companion for those long nights when insomnia just won't quit, and you're desperate for something to bore you to tears. Because nothing says 'engaging reading' like a book that could double as a paperweight for your entire legal library."

WILLIAM LATIMER-SAYER KC
August 2024

CONTENTS

Group M—Other Information

A

Group A
Ogden Tables and Related Materials

A1: -0.25 per cent discount tables "at a glance"

The following tables comprise the -0.25 per cent columns from Ogden Tables 1–34. However, we now include columns for loss of earnings to, and loss of pension from, ages 66, 67, 68 and 69, which have been obtained from the Ogden 8th edition Additional Tables.

The Ogden Tables for loss of earnings are not extended below age 16.

Readers are reminded that the figures for loss of earnings must be adjusted in accordance with Section B of the Explanatory Notes to the Ogden Tables (Contingencies other than mortality) reproduced in Table A8. Multipliers already adjusted for these contingencies are set out in Table A4.

The multiplier for loss of pension commencing at ages 66 to 69 is calculated as the difference between the multiplier for life, as set out in tables 1 and 2 of the Ogden Tables, and the calculated multiplier to pension age.

Multipliers for loss of earnings/loss of pension to and from ages 66 to 69 are shown at the back of Table A1 for a -0.25 per cent discount rate and at the back of Table A2 for a Nil discount rate.

-0.25 per cent discount tables "at a glance"? MALE

Age at date of trial	Table 1 Pecuniary loss for life	Table 3 Loss of earnings to age 50	Table 5 Loss of earnings to age 55	Table 7 Loss of earnings to age 60	Table 9 Loss of earnings to age 65	Table 13 Loss of earnings to age 70	Table 15 Loss of earnings to age 75	Table 19 Loss of pension from age 50	Table 21 Loss of pension from age 55	Table 23 Loss of pension from age 60	Table 25 Loss of pension from age 65	Table 29 Loss of pension from age 70	Table 31 Loss of pension from age 75
0	98.93							46.17	40.64	35.11	29.60	24.16	18.85
1	97.90							46.09	40.56	35.02	29.51	24.06	18.76
2	96.56							45.86	40.35	34.82	29.33	23.90	18.61
3	95.19							45.61	40.11	34.61	29.13	23.72	18.45
4	93.83							45.38	39.89	34.40	28.94	23.55	18.30
5	92.47							45.14	39.67	34.19	28.75	23.38	18.15
6	91.11							44.90	39.44	33.98	28.56	23.20	18.00
7	89.76							44.66	39.22	33.78	28.37	23.04	17.85
8	88.40							44.41	38.99	33.57	28.17	22.86	17.69
9	87.05							44.17	38.77	33.36	27.98	22.69	17.54
10	85.71							43.94	38.55	33.16	27.80	22.52	17.40
11	84.36							43.70	38.32	32.94	27.60	22.34	17.24
12	83.02							43.46	38.10	32.74	27.41	22.17	17.09
13	81.68							43.22	37.87	32.53	27.22	22.00	16.94
14	80.35							42.99	37.66	32.33	27.04	21.84	16.80
15	79.02							42.75	37.44	32.12	26.85	21.67	16.65
16	77.70	35.18	40.48	45.78	51.03	56.20	61.20	42.52	37.22	31.92	26.67	21.50	16.50
17	76.38	34.09	39.38	44.66	49.90	55.05	60.02	42.29	37.00	31.72	26.48	21.33	16.36
18	75.07	33.01	38.28	43.55	48.77	53.90	58.86	42.06	36.79	31.52	26.30	21.17	16.21
19	73.76	31.93	37.19	42.44	47.65	52.76	57.70	41.83	36.57	31.32	26.11	21.00	16.06
20	72.46	30.86	36.10	41.34	46.53	51.62	56.54	41.60	36.36	31.12	25.93	20.84	15.92
21	71.17	29.79	35.02	40.24	45.42	50.49	55.39	41.38	36.15	30.93	25.75	20.68	15.78
22	69.89	28.72	33.94	39.15	44.31	49.36	54.24	41.17	35.95	30.74	25.58	20.53	15.65
23	68.60	27.66	32.86	38.06	43.20	48.24	53.10	40.94	35.74	30.54	25.40	20.36	15.50
24	67.33	26.60	31.79	36.97	42.10	47.12	51.96	40.73	35.54	30.36	25.23	20.21	15.37
25	66.05	25.54	30.72	35.88	41.00	46.00	50.82	40.51	35.33	30.17	25.05	20.05	15.23
26	64.78	24.48	29.65	34.80	39.90	44.89	49.69	40.30	35.13	29.98	24.88	19.89	15.09
27	63.52	23.43	28.58	33.72	38.80	43.78	48.56	40.09	34.94	29.80	24.72	19.74	14.96
28	62.26	22.38	27.52	32.65	37.71	42.67	47.44	39.88	34.74	29.61	24.55	19.59	14.82
29	61.00	21.34	26.46	31.57	36.63	41.57	46.32	39.66	34.54	29.43	24.37	19.43	14.68
30	59.75	20.29	25.41	30.51	35.55	40.47	45.20	39.46	34.34	29.24	24.20	19.28	14.55
31	58.51	19.25	24.36	29.44	34.47	39.38	44.09	39.26	34.15	29.07	24.04	19.13	14.42
32	57.28	18.22	23.31	28.38	33.40	38.29	42.98	39.06	33.97	28.90	23.88	18.99	14.30
33	56.05	17.18	22.27	27.33	32.33	37.21	41.88	38.87	33.78	28.72	23.72	18.84	14.17
34	54.82	16.15	21.23	26.28	31.26	36.13	40.78	38.67	33.59	28.54	23.56	18.69	14.04
35	53.61	15.13	20.19	25.23	30.20	35.05	39.69	38.48	33.42	28.38	23.41	18.56	13.92
36	52.40	14.10	19.15	24.18	29.15	33.98	38.60	38.30	33.25	28.22	23.25	18.42	13.80
37	51.19	13.08	18.12	23.14	28.09	32.92	37.52	38.11	33.07	28.05	23.10	18.27	13.67
38	50.00	12.06	17.10	22.11	27.05	31.86	36.45	37.94	32.90	27.89	22.95	18.14	13.55
39	48.81	11.05	16.07	21.07	26.00	30.80	35.38	37.76	32.74	27.74	22.81	18.01	13.43
40	47.63	10.03	15.05	20.05	24.97	29.75	34.31	37.60	32.58	27.58	22.66	17.88	13.32
41	46.46	9.02	14.04	19.02	23.93	28.71	33.26	37.44	32.42	27.44	22.53	17.75	13.20
42	45.30	8.02	13.02	18.00	22.90	27.67	32.20	37.28	32.28	27.30	22.40	17.63	13.10
43	44.14	7.01	12.01	16.98	21.88	26.63	31.16	37.13	32.13	27.16	22.26	17.51	12.98
44	42.99	6.01	11.00	15.97	20.86	25.60	30.11	36.98	31.99	27.02	22.13	17.39	12.88
45	41.85	5.00	10.00	14.96	19.84	24.58	29.08	36.85	31.85	26.89	22.01	17.27	12.77
46	40.71	4.00	8.99	13.95	18.83	23.56	28.05	36.71	31.72	26.76	21.88	17.15	12.66
47	39.59	3.00	7.99	12.95	17.82	22.54	27.02	36.59	31.60	26.64	21.77	17.05	12.57
48	38.46	2.00	6.99	11.94	16.81	21.53	26.00	36.46	31.47	26.52	21.65	16.93	12.46
49	37.35	1.00	5.99	10.94	15.81	20.52	24.98	36.35	31.36	26.41	21.54	16.83	12.37
50	36.24		4.99	9.94	14.81	19.51	23.96	36.24	31.25	26.30	21.43	16.73	12.28
51	35.14		3.99	8.95	13.81	18.51	22.95		31.15	26.19	21.33	16.63	12.19
52	34.05		3.00	7.95	12.81	17.51	21.95		31.05	26.10	21.24	16.54	12.10
53	32.96		2.00	6.96	11.82	16.52	20.95		30.96	26.00	21.14	16.44	12.01
54	31.89		1.00	5.96	10.83	15.53	19.96		30.89	25.93	21.06	16.36	11.93

-0.25 per cent discount tables "at a glance"—MALE *continued*

Age at date of trial	Table 1 Pecuniary loss for life	Table 3 Loss of earnings to age 50	Table 5 Loss of earnings to age 55	Table 7 Loss of earnings to age 60	Table 9 Loss of earnings to age 65	Table 13 Loss of earnings to age 70	Table 15 Loss of earnings to age 75	Table 19 Loss of pension from age 50	Table 21 Loss of pension from age 55	Table 23 Loss of pension from age 60	Table 25 Loss of pension from age 65	Table 29 Loss of pension from age 70	Table 31 Loss of pension from age 75
55	30.82			4.97	9.84	14.54	18.97		30.82	25.85	20.98	16.28	11.85
56	29.77			3.98	8.86	13.56	17.98			25.79	20.91	16.21	11.79
57	28.72			2.99	7.87	12.58	17.01			25.73	20.85	16.14	11.71
58	27.69			1.99	6.89	11.61	16.04			25.70	20.80	16.08	11.65
59	26.68			1.00	5.91	10.64	15.08			25.68	20.77	16.04	11.60
60	25.68				4.93	9.68	14.12			25.68	20.75	16.00	11.56
61	24.69				3.95	8.71	13.17				20.74	15.98	11.52
62	23.72				2.97	7.75	12.23				20.75	15.97	11.49
63	22.76				1.99	6.80	11.29				20.77	15.96	11.47
64	21.81				1.00	5.84	10.36				20.81	15.97	11.45
65	20.88					4.88	9.43				20.88	16.00	11.45
66	19.97					3.92	8.50					16.05	11.47
67	19.07					2.95	7.57					16.12	11.50
68	18.19					1.98	6.65					16.21	11.54
69	17.33					0.99	5.72					16.34	11.61
70	16.48						4.79					16.48	11.69
71	15.64						3.85						11.79
72	14.83						2.91						11.92
73	14.03						1.96						12.07
74	13.26						0.99						12.27
75	12.50												12.50
76	11.77												
77	11.05												
78	10.36												
79	9.70												
80	9.06												
81	8.45												
82	7.86												
83	7.31												
84	6.78												
85	6.28												
86	5.82												
87	5.37												
88	4.96												
89	4.57												
90	4.21												
91	3.88												
92	3.57												
93	3.29												
94	3.03												
95	2.80												
96	2.58												
97	2.38												
98	2.20												
99	2.04												
100	1.89												

-0.25 per cent discount tables "at a glance"—FEMALE

Age at date of trial	Table 2 Pecuniary loss for life	Table 4 Loss of earnings to age 50	Table 6 Loss of earnings to age 55	Table 8 Loss of earnings to age 60	Table 10 Loss of earnings to age 65	Table 14 Loss of earnings to age 70	Table 16 Loss of earnings to age 75	Table 20 Loss of pension from age 50	Table 22 Loss of pension from age 55	Table 24 Loss of pension from age 60	Table 26 Loss of pension from age 65	Table 30 Loss of pension from age 70	Table 32 Loss of pension from age 75
0	102.08							49.17	43.58	37.97	32.35	26.75	21.22
1	101.01							49.08	43.49	37.88	32.25	26.66	21.13
2	99.67							48.86	43.28	37.68	32.07	26.49	20.98
3	98.31							48.62	43.06	37.47	31.88	26.32	20.83
4	96.96							48.40	42.85	37.28	31.70	26.15	20.68
5	95.61							48.17	42.63	37.08	31.52	25.98	20.53
6	94.26							47.93	42.41	36.87	31.33	25.82	20.38
7	92.92							47.71	42.20	36.68	31.15	25.65	20.24
8	91.57							47.47	41.98	36.47	30.96	25.48	20.08
9	90.23							47.24	41.76	36.27	30.77	25.31	19.93
10	88.90							47.01	41.56	36.08	30.60	25.15	19.79
11	87.56							46.78	41.33	35.87	30.41	24.98	19.64
12	86.23							46.55	41.12	35.67	30.22	24.81	19.49
13	84.91							46.33	40.91	35.48	30.05	24.65	19.35
14	83.59							46.10	40.70	35.28	29.87	24.49	19.21
15	82.27							45.87	40.49	35.08	29.68	24.33	19.06
16	80.95	35.31	40.68	46.07	51.45	56.79	62.04	45.64	40.27	34.88	29.50	24.16	18.91
17	79.65	34.22	39.58	44.95	50.32	55.65	60.87	45.43	40.07	34.70	29.33	24.00	18.78
18	78.34	33.14	38.48	43.84	49.20	54.50	59.71	45.20	39.86	34.50	29.14	23.84	18.63
19	77.04	32.06	37.39	42.74	48.07	53.37	58.56	44.98	39.65	34.30	28.97	23.67	18.48
20	75.75	30.99	36.30	41.63	46.95	52.23	57.40	44.76	39.45	34.12	28.80	23.52	18.35
21	74.45	29.91	35.21	40.53	45.84	51.10	56.25	44.54	39.24	33.92	28.61	23.35	18.20
22	73.17	28.84	34.13	39.43	44.72	49.97	55.10	44.33	39.04	33.74	28.45	23.20	18.07
23	71.88	27.77	33.05	38.34	43.61	48.84	53.96	44.11	38.83	33.54	28.27	23.04	17.92
24	70.60	26.71	31.97	37.25	42.51	47.72	52.82	43.89	38.63	33.35	28.09	22.88	17.78
25	69.32	25.65	30.90	36.16	41.40	46.60	51.68	43.67	38.42	33.16	27.92	22.72	17.64
26	68.05	24.59	29.82	35.07	40.30	45.48	50.54	43.46	38.23	32.98	27.75	22.57	17.51
27	66.78	23.53	28.75	33.99	39.20	44.36	49.41	43.25	38.03	32.79	27.58	22.42	17.37
28	65.52	22.48	27.69	32.91	38.11	43.25	48.28	43.04	37.83	32.61	27.41	22.27	17.24
29	64.26	21.43	26.63	31.83	37.02	42.15	47.16	42.83	37.63	32.43	27.24	22.11	17.10
30	63.00	20.38	25.57	30.76	35.93	41.05	46.04	42.62	37.43	32.24	27.07	21.95	16.96
31	61.75	19.34	24.51	29.69	34.85	39.95	44.92	42.41	37.24	32.06	26.90	21.80	16.83
32	60.51	18.30	23.46	28.62	33.77	38.85	43.81	42.21	37.05	31.89	26.74	21.66	16.70
33	59.27	17.26	22.41	27.56	32.69	37.76	42.71	42.01	36.86	31.71	26.58	21.51	16.56
34	58.04	16.22	21.36	26.50	31.62	36.68	41.60	41.82	36.68	31.54	26.42	21.36	16.44
35	56.81	15.19	20.32	25.45	30.55	35.59	40.50	41.62	36.49	31.36	26.26	21.22	16.31
36	55.59	14.16	19.28	24.39	29.49	34.51	39.41	41.43	36.31	31.20	26.10	21.08	16.18
37	54.37	13.14	18.24	23.35	28.43	33.44	38.32	41.23	36.13	31.02	25.94	20.93	16.05
38	53.16	12.11	17.20	22.30	27.37	32.37	37.23	41.05	35.96	30.86	25.79	20.79	15.93
39	51.95	11.09	16.17	21.26	26.32	31.30	36.15	40.86	35.78	30.69	25.63	20.65	15.80
40	50.75	10.07	15.15	20.22	25.27	30.24	35.07	40.68	35.60	30.53	25.48	20.51	15.68
41	49.56	9.06	14.12	19.19	24.22	29.18	34.00	40.50	35.44	30.37	25.34	20.38	15.56
42	48.37	8.04	13.10	18.15	23.18	28.13	32.93	40.33	35.27	30.22	25.19	20.24	15.44
43	47.19	7.03	12.08	17.12	22.14	27.07	31.87	40.16	35.11	30.07	25.05	20.12	15.32
44	46.01	6.02	11.06	16.10	21.10	26.03	30.80	39.99	34.95	29.91	24.91	19.98	15.21
45	44.84	5.01	10.05	15.08	20.07	24.98	29.75	39.83	34.79	29.76	24.77	19.86	15.09
46	43.68	4.01	9.03	14.05	19.04	23.95	28.70	39.67	34.65	29.63	24.64	19.73	14.98
47	42.52	3.00	8.02	13.04	18.02	22.91	27.65	39.52	34.50	29.48	24.50	19.61	14.87
48	41.37	2.00	7.01	12.02	16.99	21.88	26.61	39.37	34.36	29.35	24.38	19.49	14.76
49	40.22	1.00	6.01	11.01	15.97	20.85	25.57	39.22	34.21	29.21	24.25	19.37	14.65
50	39.09		5.00	10.00	14.96	19.83	24.54	39.09	34.09	29.09	24.13	19.26	14.55
51	37.96		4.00	9.00	13.95	18.81	23.51		33.96	28.96	24.01	19.15	14.45
52	36.84		3.00	7.99	12.94	17.80	22.49		33.84	28.85	23.90	19.04	14.35
53	35.72		2.00	6.99	11.93	16.79	21.47		33.72	28.73	23.79	18.93	14.25
54	34.62		1.00	5.99	10.93	15.78	20.46		33.62	28.63	23.69	18.84	14.16

-0.25 per cent discount tables "at a glance"—FEMALE *continued*

Age at date of trial	Table 2 Pecuniary loss for life	Table 4 Loss of earnings to age 50	Table 6 Loss of earnings to age 55	Table 8 Loss of earnings to age 60	Table 10 Loss of earnings to age 65	Table 14 Loss of earnings to age 70	Table 16 Loss of earnings to age 75	Table 20 Loss of pension from age 50	Table 22 Loss of pension from age 55	Table 24 Loss of pension from age 60	Table 26 Loss of pension from age 65	Table 30 Loss of pension from age 70	Table 32 Loss of pension from age 75
55	33.53			4.99	9.93	14.78	19.45		33.53	28.54	23.60	18.75	14.08
56	32.44			3.99	8.94	13.78	18.45			28.45	23.50	18.66	13.99
57	31.37			2.99	7.94	12.79	17.45			28.38	23.43	18.58	13.92
58	30.30			2.00	6.95	11.80	16.46			28.30	23.35	18.50	13.84
59	29.25			1.00	5.96	10.81	15.47			28.25	23.29	18.44	13.78
60	28.20				4.97	9.82	14.49			28.20	23.23	18.38	13.71
61	27.17				3.98	8.84	13.52				23.19	18.33	13.65
62	26.15				2.98	7.86	12.55				23.17	18.29	13.60
63	25.14				1.99	6.88	11.58				23.15	18.26	13.56
64	24.14				1.00	5.91	10.61				23.14	18.23	13.53
65	23.15					4.93	9.65				23.15	18.22	13.50
66	22.17					3.95	8.69					18.22	13.48
67	21.21					2.97	7.73					18.24	13.48
68	20.26					1.99	6.78					18.27	13.48
69	19.33					1.00	5.82					18.33	13.51
70	18.41						4.86					18.41	13.55
71	17.50						3.91						13.59
72	16.62						2.94						13.68
73	15.75						1.97						13.78
74	14.90						0.99						13.91
75	14.07												14.07
76	13.27												
77	12.48												
78	11.72												
79	10.98												
80	10.27												
81	9.58												
82	8.92												
83	8.28												
84	7.68												
85	7.10												
86	6.55												
87	6.03												
88	5.55												
89	5.10												
90	4.68												
91	4.30												
92	3.95												
93	3.63												
94	3.34												
95	3.08												
96	2.84												
97	2.61												
98	2.40												
99	2.21												
100	2.04												

A1: -0.25 per cent discount tables for retirement ages 66 to 69—MALE

	Loss of earnings to age 66	Loss of earnings to age 67	Loss of earnings to age 68	Loss of earnings to age 69	Loss of pension from age 66	Loss of pension from age 67	Loss of pension from age 68	Loss of pension from age 69
16	52.08	53.11	54.15	55.17	25.62	24.59	23.55	22.53
17	50.94	51.97	53.00	54.03	25.44	24.41	23.38	22.35
18	49.81	50.84	51.86	52.88	25.26	24.23	23.21	22.19
19	48.68	49.71	50.73	51.75	25.08	24.05	23.03	22.01
20	47.56	48.58	49.60	50.61	24.90	23.88	22.86	21.85
21	46.44	47.46	48.48	49.49	24.73	23.71	22.69	21.68
22	45.33	46.35	47.36	48.36	24.56	23.54	22.53	21.53
23	44.22	45.23	46.24	47.24	24.38	23.37	22.36	21.36
24	43.11	44.12	45.13	46.13	24.22	23.21	22.20	21.20
25	42.01	43.02	44.02	45.01	24.04	23.03	22.03	21.04
26	40.91	41.91	42.91	43.90	23.87	22.87	21.87	20.88
27	39.81	40.81	41.81	42.80	23.71	22.71	21.71	20.72
28	38.72	39.71	40.71	41.69	23.54	22.55	21.55	20.57
29	37.63	38.62	39.61	40.59	23.37	22.38	21.39	20.41
30	36.54	37.53	38.52	39.50	23.21	22.22	21.23	20.25
31	35.46	36.45	37.43	38.41	23.05	22.06	21.08	20.10
32	34.39	35.37	36.35	37.32	22.89	21.91	20.93	19.96
33	33.31	34.30	35.27	36.24	22.74	21.75	20.78	19.81
34	32.25	33.23	34.20	35.17	22.57	21.59	20.62	19.65
35	31.18	32.16	33.13	34.10	22.43	21.45	20.48	19.51
36	30.12	31.10	32.07	33.03	22.28	21.30	20.33	19.37
37	29.07	30.04	31.01	31.97	22.12	21.15	20.18	19.22
38	28.02	28.99	29.95	30.91	21.98	21.01	20.05	19.09
39	26.98	27.94	28.90	29.86	21.83	20.87	19.91	18.95
40	25.94	26.90	27.86	28.81	21.69	20.73	19.77	18.82
41	24.90	25.86	26.82	27.77	21.56	20.60	19.64	18.69
42	23.87	24.83	25.78	26.73	21.43	20.47	19.52	18.57
43	22.84	23.80	24.75	25.70	21.30	20.34	19.39	18.44
44	21.82	22.78	23.73	24.67	21.17	20.21	19.26	18.32
45	20.80	21.76	22.71	23.65	21.05	20.09	19.14	18.20
46	19.79	20.74	21.69	22.63	20.92	19.97	19.02	18.08
47	18.78	19.73	20.67	21.61	20.81	19.86	18.92	17.98
48	17.77	18.72	19.66	20.60	20.69	19.74	18.80	17.86
49	16.76	17.71	18.66	19.59	20.59	19.64	18.69	17.76
50	15.76	16.71	17.65	18.59	20.48	19.53	18.59	17.65
51	14.76	15.71	16.65	17.59	20.38	19.43	18.49	17.55
52	13.77	14.72	15.66	16.59	20.28	19.33	18.39	17.46
53	12.77	13.72	14.66	15.60	20.19	19.24	18.30	17.36
54	11.78	12.73	13.67	14.60	20.11	19.16	18.22	17.29
55	10.80	11.75	12.69	13.62	20.02	19.07	18.13	17.20
56	9.81	10.76	11.70	12.64	19.96	19.01	18.07	17.13
57	8.83	9.78	10.73	11.66	19.89	18.94	17.99	17.06
58	7.85	8.81	9.75	10.68	19.84	18.88	17.94	17.01
59	6.88	7.83	8.78	9.71	19.80	18.85	17.90	16.97
60	5.90	6.86	7.81	8.75	19.78	18.82	17.87	16.93
61	4.92	5.89	6.84	7.78	19.77	18.80	17.85	16.91
62	3.95	4.91	5.87	6.82	19.77	18.81	17.85	16.90
63	2.97	3.94	4.90	5.86	19.79	18.82	17.86	16.90
64	1.98	2.96	3.93	4.89	19.83	18.85	17.88	16.92
65	1.00	1.98	2.96	3.92	19.88	18.90	17.92	16.96
66		1.00	1.98	2.95	19.97	18.97	17.99	17.02
67			0.99	1.98		19.07	18.08	17.09
68				0.99			18.19	17.20
69								17.33

See notes at the start of section A1 for details of methodology

A1: -0.25 per cent discount tables for retirement ages 66 to 69—FEMALE

	Loss of earnings to age 66	Loss of earnings to age 67	Loss of earnings to age 68	Loss of earnings to age 69	Loss of pension from age 66	Loss of pension from age 67	Loss of pension from age 68	Loss of pension from age 69
16	52.52	53.60	54.66	55.73	28.43	27.35	26.29	25.22
17	51.39	52.46	53.53	54.59	28.26	27.19	26.12	25.06
18	50.26	51.33	52.39	53.45	28.08	27.01	25.95	24.89
19	49.14	50.20	51.26	52.31	27.90	26.84	25.78	24.73
20	48.01	49.07	50.13	51.18	27.74	26.68	25.62	24.57
21	46.89	47.95	49.00	50.05	27.56	26.50	25.45	24.40
22	45.78	46.83	47.88	48.92	27.39	26.34	25.29	24.25
23	44.66	45.71	46.76	47.80	27.22	26.17	25.12	24.08
24	43.55	44.60	45.64	46.68	27.05	26.00	24.96	23.92
25	42.45	43.49	44.53	45.56	26.87	25.83	24.79	23.76
26	41.34	42.38	43.42	44.45	26.71	25.67	24.63	23.60
27	40.24	41.28	42.31	43.34	26.54	25.50	24.47	23.44
28	39.14	40.18	41.21	42.23	26.38	25.34	24.31	23.29
29	38.05	39.08	40.11	41.13	26.21	25.18	24.15	23.13
30	36.96	37.99	39.01	40.03	26.04	25.01	23.99	22.97
31	35.87	36.90	37.92	38.94	25.88	24.85	23.83	22.81
32	34.79	35.81	36.83	37.84	25.72	24.70	23.68	22.67
33	33.71	34.73	35.75	36.76	25.56	24.54	23.52	22.51
34	32.64	33.65	34.67	35.67	25.40	24.39	23.37	22.37
35	31.57	32.58	33.59	34.59	25.24	24.23	23.22	22.22
36	30.50	31.51	32.52	33.52	25.09	24.08	23.07	22.07
37	29.44	30.44	31.45	32.44	24.93	23.93	22.92	21.93
38	28.38	29.38	30.38	31.38	24.78	23.78	22.78	21.78
39	27.32	28.32	29.32	30.31	24.63	23.63	22.63	21.64
40	26.27	27.27	28.26	29.25	24.48	23.48	22.49	21.50
41	25.22	26.22	27.21	28.20	24.34	23.34	22.35	21.36
42	24.17	25.17	26.16	27.14	24.20	23.20	22.21	21.23
43	23.13	24.12	25.11	26.10	24.06	23.07	22.08	21.09
44	22.10	23.08	24.07	25.05	23.91	22.93	21.94	20.96
45	21.06	22.05	23.03	24.01	23.78	22.79	21.81	20.83
46	20.03	21.02	22.00	22.97	23.65	22.66	21.68	20.71
47	19.00	19.99	20.97	21.94	23.52	22.53	21.55	20.58
48	17.98	18.96	19.94	20.91	23.39	22.41	21.43	20.46
49	16.96	17.94	18.92	19.89	23.26	22.28	21.30	20.33
50	15.94	16.92	17.90	18.87	23.15	22.17	21.19	20.22
51	14.93	15.91	16.88	17.85	23.03	22.05	21.08	20.11
52	13.92	14.90	15.87	16.84	22.92	21.94	20.97	20.00
53	12.91	13.89	14.86	15.83	22.81	21.83	20.86	19.89
54	11.91	12.89	13.86	14.82	22.71	21.73	20.76	19.80
55	10.91	11.89	12.86	13.82	22.62	21.64	20.67	19.71
56	9.91	10.89	11.86	12.82	22.53	21.55	20.58	19.62
57	8.92	9.89	10.86	11.83	22.45	21.48	20.51	19.54
58	7.93	8.90	9.87	10.84	22.37	21.40	20.43	19.46
59	6.94	7.91	8.88	9.85	22.31	21.34	20.37	19.40
60	5.95	6.93	7.90	8.86	22.25	21.27	20.30	19.34
61	4.96	5.94	6.91	7.88	22.21	21.23	20.26	19.29
62	3.97	4.95	5.93	6.90	22.18	21.20	20.22	19.25
63	2.98	3.97	4.95	5.92	22.16	21.17	20.19	19.22
64	1.99	2.98	3.96	4.94	22.15	21.16	20.18	19.20
65	1.00	1.99	2.98	3.96	22.15	21.16	20.17	19.19
66		1.00	1.99	2.97	22.17	21.17	20.18	19.20
67			1.00	1.99		21.21	20.21	19.22
68				1.00			20.26	19.26
69								19.33

See notes at the start of section A1 for details of methodology

A2: Nil discount tables "at a glance"

Tables at 0.0%

MALE

Age at date of trial	Table 1 Pecuniary loss for life	Table 3 Loss of earnings to age 50	Table 5 Loss of earnings to age 55	Table 7 Loss of earnings to age 60	Table 9 Loss of earnings to age 65	Table 13 Loss of earnings to age 70	Table 15 Loss of earnings to age 75	Table 19 Loss of pension from age 50	Table 21 Loss of pension from age 55	Table 23 Loss of pension from age 60	Table 25 Loss of pension from age 65	Table 29 Loss of pension from age 70	Table 31 Loss of pension from age 75
0	88.13							38.59	33.75	28.95	24.24	19.64	15.22
1	87.34							38.63	33.77	28.96	24.24	19.63	15.19
2	86.26							38.54	33.68	28.87	24.15	19.54	15.11
3	85.16							38.43	33.58	28.77	24.05	19.45	15.02
4	84.05							38.32	33.47	28.67	23.95	19.35	14.93
5	82.95							38.23	33.37	28.57	23.85	19.26	14.85
6	81.84							38.12	33.26	28.46	23.75	19.16	14.75
7	80.74							38.02	33.16	28.37	23.66	19.07	14.67
8	79.63							37.91	33.06	28.26	23.56	18.98	14.58
9	78.53							37.81	32.96	28.17	23.47	18.89	14.50
10	77.42							37.70	32.85	28.06	23.36	18.80	14.41
11	76.31							37.59	32.75	27.96	23.26	18.70	14.33
12	75.20							37.49	32.64	27.86	23.16	18.60	14.24
13	74.09							37.38	32.53	27.75	23.06	18.51	14.15
14	72.98							37.27	32.43	27.65	22.96	18.41	14.06
15	71.87							37.16	32.32	27.54	22.86	18.32	13.97
16	70.76	33.71	38.55	43.32	48.00	52.54	56.88	37.05	32.21	27.44	22.76	18.22	13.88
17	69.66	32.71	37.55	42.32	46.99	51.53	55.86	36.95	32.11	27.34	22.67	18.13	13.80
18	68.56	31.71	36.55	41.32	45.99	50.52	54.85	36.85	32.01	27.24	22.57	18.04	13.71
19	67.46	30.71	35.55	40.32	44.99	49.51	53.83	36.75	31.91	27.14	22.47	17.95	13.63
20	66.36	29.72	34.55	39.32	43.99	48.51	52.82	36.64	31.81	27.04	22.37	17.85	13.54
21	65.27	28.73	33.56	38.33	42.99	47.51	51.81	36.54	31.71	26.94	22.28	17.76	13.46
22	64.17	27.73	32.57	37.33	41.99	46.51	50.81	36.44	31.60	26.84	22.18	17.66	13.36
23	63.08	26.74	31.57	36.34	41.00	45.51	49.80	36.34	31.51	26.74	22.08	17.57	13.28
24	61.99	25.75	30.58	35.34	40.00	44.50	48.79	36.24	31.41	26.65	21.99	17.49	13.20
25	60.90	24.75	29.59	34.35	39.00	43.50	47.79	36.15	31.31	26.55	21.90	17.40	13.11
26	59.81	23.76	28.59	33.35	38.01	42.50	46.78	36.05	31.22	26.46	21.80	17.31	13.03
27	58.72	22.77	27.60	32.36	37.01	41.51	45.77	35.95	31.12	26.36	21.71	17.21	12.95
28	57.63	21.78	26.61	31.37	36.02	40.51	44.77	35.85	31.02	26.26	21.61	17.12	12.86
29	56.55	20.78	25.62	30.38	35.02	39.51	43.77	35.77	30.93	26.17	21.53	17.04	12.78
30	55.46	19.79	24.63	29.39	34.03	38.52	42.77	35.67	30.83	26.07	21.43	16.94	12.69
31	54.38	18.80	23.64	28.40	33.04	37.52	41.77	35.58	30.74	25.98	21.34	16.86	12.61
32	53.31	17.81	22.65	27.41	32.05	36.53	40.77	35.50	30.66	25.90	21.26	16.78	12.54
33	52.23	16.82	21.66	26.42	31.07	35.54	39.78	35.41	30.57	25.81	21.16	16.69	12.45
34	51.16	15.83	20.68	25.44	30.08	34.55	38.78	35.33	30.48	25.72	21.08	16.61	12.38
35	50.09	14.85	19.69	24.45	29.10	33.57	37.79	35.24	30.40	25.64	20.99	16.52	12.30
36	49.02	13.86	18.71	23.47	28.11	32.58	36.80	35.16	30.31	25.55	20.91	16.44	12.22
37	47.96	12.87	17.72	22.49	27.13	31.60	35.82	35.09	30.24	25.47	20.83	16.36	12.14
38	46.90	11.88	16.74	21.51	26.16	30.62	34.84	35.02	30.16	25.39	20.74	16.28	12.06
39	45.85	10.90	15.76	20.53	25.18	29.65	33.85	34.95	30.09	25.32	20.67	16.20	12.00
40	44.80	9.91	14.77	19.55	24.20	28.67	32.88	34.89	30.03	25.25	20.60	16.13	11.92
41	43.75	8.92	13.79	18.58	23.23	27.70	31.90	34.83	29.96	25.17	20.52	16.05	11.85
42	42.71	7.94	12.81	17.60	22.26	26.73	30.93	34.77	29.90	25.11	20.45	15.98	11.78
43	41.68	6.95	11.83	16.63	21.29	25.76	29.96	34.73	29.85	25.05	20.39	15.92	11.72
44	40.65	5.96	10.85	15.66	20.32	24.80	29.00	34.69	29.80	24.99	20.33	15.85	11.65
45	39.62	4.97	9.87	14.68	19.36	23.83	28.03	34.65	29.75	24.94	20.26	15.79	11.59
46	38.59	3.98	8.89	13.71	18.39	22.87	27.07	34.61	29.70	24.88	20.20	15.72	11.52
47	37.57	2.99	7.91	12.74	17.43	21.91	26.11	34.58	29.66	24.83	20.14	15.66	11.46
48	36.55	1.99	6.93	11.77	16.46	20.95	25.16	34.56	29.62	24.78	20.09	15.60	11.39
49	35.54	1.00	5.94	10.79	15.50	19.99	24.20	34.54	29.60	24.75	20.04	15.55	11.34

Nil discount tables "at a glance"—MALE *continued*

Age at date of trial	Table 1 Pecuniary loss for life	Table 3 Loss of earnings to age 50	Table 5 Loss of earnings to age 55	Table 7 Loss of earnings to age 60	Table 9 Loss of earnings to age 65	Table 13 Loss of earnings to age 70	Table 15 Loss of earnings to age 75	Table 19 Loss of pension from age 50	Table 21 Loss of pension from age 55	Table 23 Loss of pension from age 60	Table 25 Loss of pension from age 65	Table 29 Loss of pension from age 70	Table 31 Loss of pension from age 75
50	34.53		4.96	9.82	14.53	19.04	23.25	34.53	29.57	24.71	20.00	15.49	11.28
51	33.52		3.97	8.85	13.57	18.08	22.29		29.55	24.67	19.95	15.44	11.23
52	32.52		2.98	7.87	12.61	17.13	21.35		29.54	24.65	19.91	15.39	11.17
53	31.52		1.99	6.90	11.64	16.18	20.40		29.53	24.62	19.88	15.34	11.12
54	30.53		1.00	5.92	10.68	15.22	19.45		29.53	24.61	19.85	15.31	11.0
55	29.55			4.94	9.72	14.27	18.51		29.55	24.61	19.83	15.28	11.04
56	28.57			3.96	8.76	13.33	17.57			24.61	19.81	15.24	11.00
57	27.60			2.97	7.79	12.38	16.64			24.63	19.81	15.22	10.96
58	26.64			1.99	6.83	11.44	15.71			24.65	19.81	15.20	10.93
59	25.70			1.00	5.87	10.50	14.79			24.70	19.83	15.20	10.91
60	24.76				4.90	9.56	13.87			24.76	19.86	15.20	10.89
61	23.84				3.93	8.62	12.95				19.91	15.22	10.89
62	22.93				2.96	7.68	12.04				19.97	15.25	10.89
63	22.02				1.98	6.74	11.13				20.04	15.28	10.89
64	21.13				0.99	5.79	10.22				20.14	15.34	10.91
65	20.25					4.85	9.31				20.25	15.40	10.94
66	19.39					3.90	8.41					15.49	10.98
67	18.54					2.94	7.50					15.60	11.04
68	17.70					1.97	6.59					15.73	11.11
69	16.88					0.99	5.68					15.89	11.20
70	16.07						4.76					16.07	11.31
71	15.27						3.83						11.44
72	14.49						2.90						11.59
73	13.73						1.95						11.78
74	12.98						0.99						11.99
75	12.25												12.25
76	11.54												
77	10.85												
78	10.19												
79	9.54												
80	8.92												
81	8.33												
82	7.76												
83	7.22												
84	6.70												
85	6.21												
86	5.75												
87	5.32												
88	4.91												
89	4.53												
90	4.18												
91	3.85												
92	3.55												
93	3.27												
94	3.01												
95	2.78												
96	2.57												
97	2.37												
98	2.19												
99	2.03												
100	1.88												

Nil discount tables "at a glance"—FEMALE

Age at date of trial	Table 2 Pecuniary loss for life	Table 4 Loss of earnings to age 50	Table 6 Loss of earnings to age 55	Table 8 Loss of earnings to age 60	Table 10 Loss of earnings to age 65	Table 14 Loss of earnings to age 70	Table 16 Loss of earnings to age 75	Table 20 Loss of pension from age 50	Table 22 Loss of pension from age 55	Table 24 Loss of pension from age 60	Table 26 Loss of pension from age 65	Table 30 Loss of pension from age 70	Table 32 Loss of pension from age 75
0	90.69							41.02	36.12	31.26	26.45	21.72	17.11
1	89.87							41.06	36.14	31.27	26.45	21.71	17.09
2	88.80							40.98	36.06	31.19	26.37	21.63	17.01
3	87.71							40.88	35.97	31.09	26.28	21.54	16.93
4	86.62							40.79	35.88	31.01	26.19	21.46	16.85
5	85.54							40.71	35.80	30.93	26.11	21.38	16.78
6	84.45							40.62	35.71	30.84	26.03	21.30	16.70
7	83.36							40.53	35.62	30.75	25.94	21.22	16.62
8	82.27							40.44	35.53	30.66	25.85	21.13	16.54
9	81.17							40.34	35.43	30.57	25.76	21.04	16.45
10	80.08							40.25	35.34	30.48	25.67	20.96	16.38
11	78.99							40.16	35.26	30.39	25.59	20.88	16.30
12	77.90							40.07	35.17	30.30	25.50	20.79	16.22
13	76.80							39.97	35.07	30.21	25.41	20.70	16.13
14	75.71							39.88	34.98	30.12	25.32	20.62	16.06
15	74.62							39.79	34.89	30.03	25.24	20.54	15.98
16	73.53	33.83	38.73	43.59	48.38	53.08	57.63	39.70	34.80	29.94	25.15	20.45	15.90
17	72.44	32.83	37.73	42.59	47.38	52.07	56.62	39.61	34.71	29.85	25.06	20.37	15.82
18	71.35	31.83	36.74	41.59	46.38	51.07	55.61	39.52	34.61	29.76	24.97	20.28	15.74
19	70.26	30.84	35.74	40.59	45.38	50.07	54.61	39.42	34.52	29.67	24.88	20.19	15.65
20	69.17	29.84	34.74	39.59	44.38	49.06	53.60	39.33	34.43	29.58	24.79	20.11	15.57
21	68.09	28.84	33.74	38.60	43.38	48.06	52.59	39.25	34.35	29.49	24.71	20.03	15.50
22	67.00	27.85	32.75	37.60	42.38	47.06	51.58	39.15	34.25	29.40	24.62	19.94	15.42
23	65.91	26.85	31.75	36.60	41.38	46.05	50.58	39.06	34.16	29.31	24.53	19.86	15.33
24	64.83	25.85	30.75	35.60	40.38	45.05	49.57	38.98	34.08	29.23	24.45	19.78	15.26
25	63.74	24.86	29.75	34.60	39.38	44.05	48.56	38.88	33.99	29.14	24.36	19.69	15.18
26	62.65	23.86	28.76	33.61	38.38	43.05	47.56	38.79	33.89	29.04	24.27	19.60	15.09
27	61.57	22.86	27.76	32.61	37.38	42.05	46.55	38.71	33.81	28.96	24.19	19.52	15.02
28	60.48	21.87	26.77	31.61	36.39	41.05	45.55	38.61	33.71	28.87	24.09	19.43	14.93
29	59.40	20.87	25.77	30.62	35.39	40.05	44.54	38.53	33.63	28.78	24.01	19.35	14.86
30	58.32	19.88	24.78	29.62	34.39	39.05	43.54	38.44	33.54	28.70	23.93	19.27	14.78
31	57.24	18.88	23.78	28.63	33.40	38.05	42.54	38.36	33.46	28.61	23.84	19.19	14.70
32	56.16	17.89	22.79	27.64	32.41	37.06	41.54	38.27	33.37	28.52	23.75	19.10	14.62
33	55.09	16.90	21.80	26.65	31.41	36.06	40.54	38.19	33.29	28.44	23.68	19.03	14.55
34	54.01	15.90	20.81	25.65	30.42	35.07	39.54	38.11	33.20	28.36	23.59	18.94	14.47
35	52.94	14.91	19.81	24.66	29.43	34.08	38.55	38.03	33.13	28.28	23.51	18.86	14.39
36	51.87	13.92	18.82	23.67	28.44	33.09	37.55	37.95	33.05	28.20	23.43	18.78	14.32
37	50.80	12.92	17.83	22.68	27.45	32.10	36.56	37.88	32.97	28.12	23.35	18.70	14.24
38	49.73	11.93	16.84	21.70	26.46	31.11	35.57	37.80	32.89	28.03	23.27	18.62	14.16
39	48.67	10.94	15.85	20.71	25.48	30.12	34.58	37.73	32.82	27.96	23.19	18.55	14.09
40	47.61	9.95	14.86	19.72	24.49	29.13	33.59	37.66	32.75	27.89	23.12	18.48	14.02
41	46.55	8.95	13.88	18.74	23.51	28.15	32.60	37.60	32.67	27.81	23.04	18.40	13.95
42	45.49	7.96	12.89	17.75	22.52	27.16	31.62	37.53	32.60	27.74	22.97	18.33	13.87
43	44.44	6.97	11.90	16.76	21.54	26.18	30.63	37.47	32.54	27.68	22.90	18.26	13.81
44	43.39	5.98	10.91	15.78	20.56	25.20	29.65	37.41	32.48	27.61	22.83	18.19	13.74
45	42.34	4.98	9.92	14.80	19.58	24.22	28.67	37.36	32.42	27.54	22.76	18.12	13.67
46	41.29	3.99	8.93	13.81	18.60	23.24	27.69	37.30	32.36	27.48	22.69	18.05	13.60
47	40.25	2.99	7.94	12.83	17.62	22.27	26.71	37.26	32.31	27.42	22.63	17.98	13.54
48	39.21	2.00	6.95	11.84	16.64	21.29	25.74	37.21	32.26	27.37	22.57	17.92	13.47
49	38.17	1.00	5.96	10.86	15.66	20.32	24.76	37.17	32.21	27.31	22.51	17.85	13.41
50	37.14		4.97	9.88	14.68	19.34	23.79	37.14	32.17	27.26	22.46	17.80	13.35
51	36.12		3.98	8.90	13.71	18.37	22.83		32.14	27.22	22.41	17.75	13.29
52	35.09		2.99	7.91	12.73	17.40	21.86		32.10	27.18	22.36	17.69	13.23
53	34.08		1.99	6.93	11.76	16.44	20.90		32.09	27.15	22.32	17.64	13.18
54	33.07		1.00	5.94	10.78	15.47	19.94		32.07	27.13	22.29	17.60	13.13

Nil discount tables "at a glance"—FEMALE *continued*

Age at date of trial	Table 2 Pecuniary loss for life	Table 4 Loss of earnings to age 50	Table 6 Loss of earnings to age 55	Table 8 Loss of earnings to age 60	Table 10 Loss of earnings to age 65	Table 14 Loss of earnings to age 70	Table 16 Loss of earnings to age 75	Table 20 Loss of pension from age 50	Table 22 Loss of pension from age 55	Table 24 Loss of pension from age 60	Table 26 Loss of pension from age 65	Table 30 Loss of pension from age 70	Table 32 Loss of pension from age 75
55	32.06			4.96	9.81	14.51	18.98		32.06	27.10	22.25	17.55	13.08
56	31.06			3.97	8.84	13.54	18.02			27.09	22.22	17.52	13.04
57	30.07			2.98	7.86	12.58	17.07			27.09	22.21	17.49	13.00
58	29.08			1.99	6.89	11.62	16.12			27.09	22.19	17.46	12.96
59	28.11			1.00	5.91	10.66	15.17			27.11	22.20	17.45	12.94
60	27.14				4.93	9.70	14.23			27.14	22.21	17.44	12.91
61	26.18				3.96	8.74	13.29				22.22	17.44	12.89
62	25.22				2.97	7.79	12.35				22.25	17.43	12.87
63	24.27				1.99	6.83	11.41				22.28	17.44	12.86
64	23.34				1.00	5.86	10.47				22.34	17.48	12.87
65	22.41					4.90	9.53				22.41	17.51	12.88
66	21.49					3.93	8.60					17.56	12.89
67	20.58					2.96	7.66					17.62	12.92
68	19.68					1.98	6.72					17.70	12.96
69	18.80					0.99	5.78					17.81	13.02
70	17.92						4.83					17.92	13.09
71	17.06						3.89						13.17
72	16.21						2.93						13.28
73	15.38						1.97						13.41
74	14.57						0.99						13.58
75	13.77												13.77
76	13.00												
77	12.24												
78	11.50												
79	10.79												
80	10.10												
81	9.43												
82	8.79												
83	8.17												
84	7.58												
85	7.01												
86	6.48												
87	5.97												
88	5.49												
89	5.05												
90	4.64												
91	4.26												
92	3.92												
93	3.61												
94	3.32												
95	3.06												
96	2.82												
97	2.60												
98	2.39												
99	2.20												
100	2.03												

A2: Nil discount tables for retirement ages 66 to 69 – MALE

	Loss of earnings to age 66	Loss of earnings to age 67	Loss of earnings to age 68	Loss of earnings to age 69	Loss of pension from age 66	Loss of pension from age 67	Loss of pension from age 68	Loss of pension from age 69
16	48.92	49.84	50.74	51.65	21.84	20.92	20.02	19.11
17	47.91	48.83	49.74	50.64	21.75	20.83	19.92	19.02
18	46.91	47.82	48.73	49.63	21.65	20.74	19.83	18.93
19	45.91	46.82	47.72	48.62	21.55	20.64	19.74	18.84
20	44.91	45.82	46.72	47.62	21.45	20.54	19.64	18.74
21	43.91	44.82	45.72	46.62	21.36	20.45	19.55	18.65
22	42.91	43.82	44.72	45.62	21.26	20.35	19.45	18.55
23	41.91	42.82	43.72	44.62	21.17	20.26	19.36	18.46
24	40.91	41.82	42.72	43.62	21.08	20.17	19.27	18.37
25	39.92	40.83	41.73	42.62	20.98	20.07	19.17	18.28
26	38.92	39.83	40.73	41.62	20.89	19.98	19.08	18.19
27	37.92	38.83	39.73	40.62	20.80	19.89	18.99	18.10
28	36.93	37.84	38.73	39.63	20.70	19.79	18.90	18.00
29	35.94	36.84	37.74	38.63	20.61	19.71	18.81	17.92
30	34.94	35.85	36.75	37.64	20.52	19.61	18.71	17.82
31	33.95	34.86	35.75	36.64	20.43	19.52	18.63	17.74
32	32.97	33.87	34.76	35.65	20.34	19.44	18.55	17.66
33	31.98	32.88	33.78	34.66	20.25	19.35	18.45	17.57
34	30.99	31.89	32.79	33.68	20.17	19.27	18.37	17.48
35	30.01	30.91	31.80	32.69	20.08	19.18	18.29	17.40
36	29.02	29.93	30.82	31.71	20.00	19.09	18.20	17.31
37	28.04	28.95	29.84	30.73	19.92	19.01	18.12	17.23
38	27.06	27.97	28.86	29.75	19.84	18.93	18.04	17.15
39	26.09	26.99	27.88	28.77	19.76	18.86	17.97	17.08
40	25.11	26.02	26.91	27.80	19.69	18.78	17.89	17.00
41	24.14	25.04	25.94	26.82	19.61	18.71	17.81	16.93
42	23.17	24.07	24.97	25.85	19.54	18.64	17.74	16.86
43	22.20	23.11	24.00	24.89	19.48	18.57	17.68	16.79
44	21.24	22.14	23.04	23.92	19.41	18.51	17.61	16.73
45	20.27	21.17	22.07	22.96	19.35	18.45	17.55	16.66
46	19.30	20.21	21.11	21.99	19.29	18.38	17.48	16.60
47	18.34	19.25	20.15	21.03	19.23	18.32	17.42	16.54
48	17.38	18.29	19.18	20.07	19.17	18.26	17.37	16.48
49	16.42	17.32	18.23	19.12	19.12	18.22	17.31	16.42
50	15.45	16.36	17.27	18.16	19.08	18.17	17.26	16.37
51	14.49	15.41	16.31	17.20	19.03	18.11	17.21	16.32
52	13.53	14.45	15.35	16.25	18.99	18.07	17.17	16.27
53	12.57	13.49	14.39	15.29	18.95	18.03	17.13	16.23
54	11.61	12.53	13.44	14.34	18.92	18.00	17.09	16.19
55	10.65	11.57	12.48	13.39	18.90	17.98	17.07	16.16
56	9.69	10.62	11.53	12.44	18.88	17.95	17.04	16.13
57	8.73	9.66	10.58	11.49	18.87	17.94	17.02	16.11
58	7.77	8.71	9.63	10.54	18.87	17.93	17.01	16.10
59	6.82	7.75	8.68	9.59	18.88	17.95	17.02	16.11
60	5.86	6.80	7.73	8.65	18.90	17.96	17.03	16.11
61	4.89	5.84	6.78	7.71	18.95	18.00	17.06	16.13
62	3.93	4.88	5.83	6.76	19.00	18.05	17.10	16.17
63	2.96	3.92	4.87	5.81	19.06	18.10	17.15	16.21
64	1.98	2.95	3.91	4.86	19.15	18.18	17.22	16.27
65	0.99	1.98	2.95	3.90	19.26	18.27	17.30	16.35
66		0.99	1.98	2.94	19.39	18.40	17.41	16.45
67			0.99	1.97		18.54	17.55	16.57
68				0.99			17.70	16.71
69								16.88

See notes at the start of section A1 for details of methodology

A2: Nil discount tables for retirement ages 66 to 69 – FEMALE

	Loss of earnings to age 66	Loss of earnings to age 67	Loss of earnings to age 68	Loss of earnings to age 69	Loss of pension from age 66	Loss of pension from age 67	Loss of pension from age 68	Loss of pension from age 69
16	49.33	50.27	51.21	52.15	24.20	23.26	22.32	21.38
17	48.33	49.27	50.21	51.14	24.11	23.17	22.23	21.30
18	47.33	48.27	49.21	50.14	24.02	23.08	22.14	21.21
19	46.32	47.27	48.20	49.14	23.94	22.99	22.06	21.12
20	45.32	46.27	47.20	48.14	23.85	22.90	21.97	21.03
21	44.32	45.26	46.20	47.13	23.77	22.83	21.89	20.96
22	43.32	44.26	45.20	46.13	23.68	22.74	21.80	20.87
23	42.32	43.26	44.20	45.13	23.59	22.65	21.71	20.78
24	41.32	42.26	43.20	44.13	23.51	22.57	21.63	20.70
25	40.32	41.26	42.20	43.13	23.42	22.48	21.54	20.61
26	39.32	40.26	41.20	42.13	23.33	22.39	21.45	20.52
27	38.33	39.26	40.20	41.13	23.24	22.31	21.37	20.44
28	37.33	38.27	39.20	40.13	23.15	22.21	21.28	20.35
29	36.33	37.27	38.20	39.13	23.07	22.13	21.20	20.27
30	35.34	36.27	37.20	38.13	22.98	22.05	21.12	20.19
31	34.34	35.28	36.21	37.13	22.90	21.96	21.03	20.11
32	33.35	34.28	35.21	36.14	22.81	21.88	20.95	20.02
33	32.35	33.29	34.22	35.14	22.74	21.80	20.87	19.95
34	31.36	32.30	33.23	34.15	22.65	21.71	20.78	19.86
35	30.37	31.31	32.24	33.16	22.57	21.63	20.70	19.78
36	29.38	30.32	31.24	32.17	22.49	21.55	20.63	19.70
37	28.39	29.33	30.26	31.18	22.41	21.47	20.54	19.62
38	27.40	28.34	29.27	30.19	22.33	21.39	20.46	19.54
39	26.42	27.35	28.28	29.20	22.25	21.32	20.39	19.47
40	25.43	26.37	27.29	28.22	22.18	21.24	20.32	19.39
41	24.45	25.38	26.31	27.23	22.10	21.17	20.24	19.32
42	23.46	24.40	25.33	26.25	22.03	21.09	20.16	19.24
43	22.48	23.42	24.34	25.27	21.96	21.02	20.10	19.17
44	21.50	22.43	23.36	24.29	21.89	20.96	20.03	19.10
45	20.52	21.45	22.38	23.31	21.82	20.89	19.96	19.03
46	19.54	20.47	21.40	22.33	21.75	20.82	19.89	18.96
47	18.56	19.50	20.43	21.35	21.69	20.75	19.82	18.90
48	17.58	18.52	19.45	20.37	21.63	20.69	19.76	18.84
49	16.60	17.54	18.47	19.40	21.57	20.63	19.70	18.77
50	15.63	16.57	17.50	18.43	21.51	20.57	19.64	18.71
51	14.65	15.59	16.53	17.45	21.47	20.53	19.59	18.67
52	13.68	14.62	15.56	16.48	21.41	20.47	19.53	18.61
53	12.71	13.65	14.59	15.52	21.37	20.43	19.49	18.56
54	11.73	12.68	13.62	14.55	21.34	20.39	19.45	18.52
55	10.76	11.71	12.65	13.58	21.30	20.35	19.41	18.48
56	9.79	10.74	11.68	12.62	21.27	20.32	19.38	18.44
57	8.82	9.77	10.72	11.65	21.25	20.30	19.35	18.42
58	7.85	8.80	9.75	10.69	21.23	20.28	19.33	18.39
59	6.88	7.83	8.79	9.73	21.23	20.28	19.32	18.38
60	5.90	6.87	7.82	8.77	21.24	20.27	19.32	18.37
61	4.93	5.89	6.85	7.80	21.25	20.29	19.33	18.38
62	3.95	4.92	5.89	6.84	21.27	20.30	19.33	18.38
63	2.97	3.95	4.92	5.87	21.30	20.32	19.35	18.40
64	1.99	2.97	3.94	4.91	21.35	20.37	19.40	18.43
65	1.00	1.98	2.97	3.94	21.41	20.43	19.44	18.47
66		1.00	1.98	2.96	21.49	20.49	19.51	18.53
67			1.00	1.98		20.58	19.58	18.60
68				1.00			19.68	18.68
69								18.80

See notes at the start of section A1 for details of methodology.

A3: Life tables and projected life tables

National Life Tables, United Kingdom

Period expectation of life **Office for National Statistics**

Based on data for the years 2020–2022

Age	Males					Females				
x	m_x	q_x	l_x	d_x	e_x	m_x	q_x	l_x	d_x	e_x
0	0.004323	0.004314	100000.0	431.4	78.57	0.003526	0.003519	100000.0	351.9	82.57
1	0.000224	0.000224	99568.6	22.3	77.91	0.000201	0.000201	99648.1	20.0	81.86
2	0.000146	0.000146	99546.4	14.5	76.93	0.000124	0.000124	99628.0	12.3	80.88
3	0.000117	0.000117	99531.9	11.7	75.94	0.000081	0.000081	99615.7	8.1	79.89
4	0.000081	0.000081	99520.2	8.0	74.95	0.000069	0.000069	99607.6	6.8	78.90
5	0.000072	0.000072	99512.2	7.2	73.96	0.000066	0.000066	99600.8	6.5	77.90
6	0.000069	0.000069	99505.0	6.8	72.96	0.000059	0.000059	99594.2	5.9	76.91
7	0.000080	0.000080	99498.2	7.9	71.97	0.000055	0.000055	99588.4	5.5	75.91
8	0.000075	0.000075	99490.2	7.4	70.97	0.000057	0.000057	99582.9	5.7	74.92
9	0.000074	0.000074	99482.8	7.4	69.98	0.000054	0.000054	99577.2	5.4	73.92
10	0.000059	0.000059	99475.4	5.8	68.98	0.000051	0.000051	99571.8	5.1	72.92
11	0.000075	0.000075	99469.6	7.5	67.99	0.000065	0.000065	99566.7	6.5	71.93
12	0.000103	0.000103	99462.1	10.2	66.99	0.000067	0.000067	99560.2	6.7	70.93
13	0.000110	0.000110	99451.9	11.0	66.00	0.000098	0.000098	99553.5	9.7	69.94
14	0.000115	0.000115	99440.9	11.5	65.01	0.000092	0.000092	99543.8	9.1	68.94
15	0.000167	0.000167	99429.5	16.6	64.01	0.000121	0.000121	99534.6	12.0	67.95
16	0.000212	0.000212	99412.9	21.1	63.02	0.000115	0.000115	99522.6	11.4	66.96
17	0.000304	0.000304	99391.8	30.2	62.04	0.000167	0.000167	99511.2	16.6	65.97
18	0.000405	0.000405	99361.6	40.2	61.06	0.000171	0.000171	99494.5	17.0	64.98
19	0.000482	0.000482	99321.3	47.8	60.08	0.000204	0.000204	99477.5	20.3	63.99
20	0.000500	0.000500	99273.5	49.6	59.11	0.000222	0.000222	99457.2	22.1	63.00
21	0.000528	0.000527	99223.9	52.3	58.14	0.000215	0.000215	99435.1	21.4	62.01
22	0.000497	0.000497	99171.5	49.3	57.17	0.000221	0.000221	99413.7	22.0	61.03
23	0.000576	0.000576	99122.2	57.1	56.20	0.000236	0.000236	99391.7	23.4	60.04
24	0.000537	0.000537	99065.1	53.2	55.23	0.000230	0.000230	99368.3	22.8	59.06
25	0.000587	0.000587	99011.9	58.1	54.26	0.000249	0.000249	99345.5	24.7	58.07
26	0.000667	0.000666	98953.7	65.9	53.29	0.000270	0.000270	99320.8	26.8	57.08
27	0.000652	0.000652	98887.8	64.5	52.33	0.000314	0.000314	99294.0	31.2	56.10
28	0.000684	0.000684	98823.3	67.6	51.36	0.000310	0.000310	99262.8	30.7	55.12
29	0.000746	0.000746	98755.8	73.7	50.39	0.000339	0.000339	99232.1	33.6	54.13
30	0.000773	0.000773	98682.1	76.3	49.43	0.000361	0.000361	99198.5	35.8	53.15
31	0.000845	0.000844	98605.8	83.3	48.47	0.000383	0.000383	99162.7	38.0	52.17
32	0.000935	0.000934	98522.6	92.1	47.51	0.000457	0.000457	99124.7	45.3	51.19
33	0.000981	0.000980	98430.5	96.5	46.55	0.000503	0.000503	99079.4	49.9	50.21
34	0.001024	0.001024	98334.0	100.7	45.60	0.000589	0.000588	99029.6	58.3	49.24
35	0.001109	0.001109	98233.3	108.9	44.65	0.000603	0.000603	98971.3	59.7	48.27
36	0.001239	0.001239	98124.4	121.5	43.69	0.000660	0.000660	98911.6	65.3	47.30
37	0.001342	0.001341	98002.9	131.5	42.75	0.000740	0.000740	98846.4	73.1	46.33
38	0.001435	0.001434	97871.4	140.3	41.81	0.000900	0.000900	98773.2	88.9	45.36
39	0.001633	0.001631	97731.1	159.4	40.86	0.000914	0.000914	98684.4	90.2	44.40
40	0.001697	0.001696	97571.7	165.5	39.93	0.000989	0.000988	98594.2	97.4	43.44
41	0.001881	0.001879	97406.2	183.1	39.00	0.001082	0.001082	98496.8	106.6	42.48
42	0.001937	0.001936	97223.1	188.2	38.07	0.001184	0.001183	98390.2	116.4	41.53
43	0.002098	0.002096	97035.0	203.4	37.14	0.001254	0.001253	98273.8	123.2	40.58
44	0.002279	0.002276	96831.6	220.4	36.22	0.001393	0.001392	98150.6	136.7	39.63
45	0.002561	0.002558	96611.2	247.1	35.30	0.001494	0.001493	98014.0	146.3	38.68
46	0.002774	0.002770	96364.0	267.0	34.39	0.001656	0.001654	97867.6	161.9	37.74
47	0.002947	0.002943	96097.1	282.8	33.48	0.001913	0.001912	97705.7	186.8	36.80
48	0.003269	0.003264	95814.3	312.8	32.58	0.002057	0.002055	97519.0	200.4	35.87
49	0.003553	0.003546	95501.5	338.7	31.69	0.002154	0.002151	97318.5	209.4	34.94
50	0.003863	0.003855	95162.8	366.9	30.80	0.002359	0.002356	97109.1	228.8	34.02

Period expectation of life

Based on data for the years 2020–2022

Age	Males					Females				
x	m_x	q_x	l_x	d_x	e_x	m_x	q_x	l_x	d_x	e_x
51	0.004112	0.004103	94796.0	389.0	29.92	0.002565	0.002562	96880.3	248.2	33.10
52	0.004503	0.004493	94407.0	424.2	29.04	0.002739	0.002735	96632.1	264.3	32.18
53	0.004704	0.004693	93982.8	441.1	28.17	0.002991	0.002987	96367.8	287.8	31.27
54	0.005181	0.005168	93541.7	483.4	27.30	0.003200	0.003194	96080.0	306.9	30.36
55	0.005529	0.005514	93058.4	513.1	26.43	0.003499	0.003493	95773.0	334.5	29.46
56	0.006017	0.005999	92545.2	555.1	25.58	0.003820	0.003813	95438.5	363.9	28.56
57	0.006522	0.006501	91990.1	598.0	24.73	0.004104	0.004095	95074.6	389.4	27.66
58	0.007020	0.006996	91392.1	639.4	23.89	0.004514	0.004504	94685.3	426.5	26.78
59	0.007695	0.007665	90752.7	695.7	23.05	0.004866	0.004854	94258.8	457.5	25.89
60	0.008473	0.008437	90057.0	759.8	22.23	0.005419	0.005405	93801.3	506.9	25.02
61	0.009217	0.009175	89297.3	819.3	21.41	0.005762	0.005745	93294.3	536.0	24.15
62	0.010109	0.010058	88478.0	889.9	20.61	0.006563	0.006541	92758.3	606.7	23.29
63	0.011053	0.010992	87588.1	962.7	19.81	0.007158	0.007132	92151.6	657.2	22.44
64	0.011876	0.011806	86625.3	1022.7	19.03	0.007818	0.007788	91494.4	712.5	21.60
65	0.013106	0.013021	85602.7	1114.6	18.25	0.008401	0.008366	90781.8	759.5	20.76
66	0.014626	0.014519	84488.0	1226.7	17.48	0.009364	0.009321	90022.4	839.1	19.93
67	0.015887	0.015762	83261.3	1312.4	16.73	0.010194	0.010142	89183.3	904.5	19.12
68	0.017384	0.017234	81948.9	1412.3	15.99	0.011332	0.011268	88278.8	994.7	18.31
69	0.018962	0.018784	80536.6	1512.8	15.26	0.012217	0.012143	87284.0	1059.9	17.51
70	0.020609	0.020399	79023.8	1612.0	14.54	0.013658	0.013565	86224.1	1169.7	16.72
71	0.022502	0.022252	77411.8	1722.6	13.84	0.014707	0.014600	85054.5	1241.8	15.94
72	0.024846	0.024541	75689.2	1857.5	13.14	0.016189	0.016059	83812.7	1346.0	15.17
73	0.026677	0.026326	73831.7	1943.7	12.46	0.017659	0.017504	82466.7	1443.5	14.41
74	0.029382	0.028956	71888.1	2081.6	11.78	0.019865	0.019669	81023.2	1593.7	13.66
75	0.032969	0.032434	69806.5	2264.1	11.12	0.022465	0.022216	79429.5	1764.6	12.92
76	0.037983	0.037275	67542.3	2517.6	10.47	0.025565	0.025242	77664.9	1960.4	12.20
77	0.041464	0.040622	65024.7	2641.4	9.86	0.028555	0.028153	75704.5	2131.3	11.51
78	0.046869	0.045796	62383.3	2856.9	9.26	0.032196	0.031685	73573.2	2331.2	10.83
79	0.052987	0.051619	59526.4	3072.7	8.68	0.036765	0.036102	71242.0	2571.9	10.16
80	0.060193	0.058434	56453.7	3298.8	8.12	0.041861	0.041003	68670.0	2815.6	9.53
81	0.066585	0.064440	53154.8	3425.3	7.60	0.047944	0.046822	65854.4	3083.4	8.91
82	0.074965	0.072256	49729.6	3593.3	7.08	0.053228	0.051848	62771.0	3254.6	8.32
83	0.082944	0.079641	46136.3	3674.4	6.60	0.059995	0.058248	59516.4	3466.7	7.75
84	0.093451	0.089279	42461.9	3791.0	6.12	0.068248	0.065996	56049.7	3699.1	7.20
85	0.105026	0.099786	38671.0	3858.8	5.68	0.077819	0.074904	52350.6	3921.3	6.67
86	0.118657	0.112011	34812.2	3899.4	5.25	0.089172	0.085366	48429.3	4134.2	6.17
87	0.135358	0.126777	30912.8	3919.0	4.85	0.101352	0.096463	44295.1	4272.9	5.70
88	0.152007	0.141270	26993.8	3813.4	4.48	0.116391	0.109990	40022.2	4402.0	5.26
89	0.170359	0.156987	23180.4	3639.0	4.14	0.132798	0.124530	35620.2	4435.8	4.85
90	0.192960	0.175981	19541.3	3438.9	3.81	0.150007	0.139541	31184.4	4351.5	4.47
91	0.215039	0.194163	16102.4	3126.5	3.52	0.171160	0.157667	26832.9	4230.7	4.11
92	0.240004	0.214289	12975.9	2780.6	3.25	0.193424	0.176368	22602.3	3986.3	3.78
93	0.269943	0.237842	10195.3	2424.9	3.00	0.219942	0.198151	18616.0	3688.8	3.49
94	0.297716	0.259141	7770.5	2013.6	2.78	0.240756	0.214888	14927.2	3207.7	3.23
95	0.332517	0.285114	5756.8	1641.4	2.57	0.269735	0.237680	11719.5	2785.5	2.97
96	0.357154	0.303039	4115.5	1247.1	2.40	0.300654	0.261364	8934.0	2335.0	2.74
97	0.394554	0.329543	2868.3	945.2	2.22	0.333306	0.285694	6599.0	1885.3	2.54
98	0.422358	0.348716	1923.1	670.6	2.07	0.372851	0.314264	4713.7	1481.3	2.35
99	0.480690	0.387546	1252.5	485.4	1.91	0.397053	0.331284	3232.4	1070.8	2.20
100	0.501891	0.401209	767.1	307.8	1.80	0.438023	0.359327	2161.5	776.7	2.04

Source: Office for National Statistics licensed under the Open Government licence V.I.O.

Expectations of life table

Expectations of life for age attained in 2024 allowing for projected changes in mortality assumed in the 2020-based population projections produced by the Office for National Statistics.

United Kingdom					
Age	**Males**	**Females**	**Age**	**Males**	**Females**
0	87.8	90.6	**51**	33.2	36.0
1	87.0	89.8	**52**	32.2	35.0
2	85.9	88.7	**53**	31.2	34.0
3	84.8	87.6	**54**	30.2	33.0
4	83.7	86.5	**55**	29.3	31.9
5	82.6	85.4	**56**	28.3	31.0
6	81.5	84.3	**57**	27.3	30.0
7	80.4	83.3	**58**	26.4	29.0
8	79.3	82.2	**59**	25.4	28.0
9	78.1	81.1	**60**	24.5	27.0
10	77.0	80.0	**61**	23.6	26.1
11	75.9	78.9	**62**	22.7	25.1
12	74.8	77.8	**63**	21.8	24.2
13	73.7	76.7	**64**	20.9	23.3
14	72.6	75.6	**65**	20.1	22.3
15	71.5	74.5	**66**	19.2	21.4
16	70.4	73.4	**67**	18.4	20.5
17	69.3	72.3	**68**	17.5	19.6
18	68.2	71.2	**69**	16.7	18.8
19	67.0	70.1	**70**	15.9	17.9
20	66.0	69.0	**71**	15.1	17.0
21	64.9	67.9	**72**	14.4	16.2
22	63.8	66.9	**73**	13.6	15.4
23	62.7	65.8	**74**	12.9	14.6
24	61.6	64.7	**75**	12.2	13.8
25	60.5	63.6	**76**	11.5	13.0
26	59.4	62.5	**77**	10.8	12.3
27	58.3	61.4	**78**	10.1	11.5
28	57.2	60.3	**79**	9.5	10.8
29	56.1	59.2	**80**	8.9	10.1
30	55.0	58.2	**81**	8.3	9.5
31	54.0	57.1	**82**	7.7	8.8
32	52.9	56.0	**83**	7.2	8.2
33	51.8	54.9	**84**	6.7	7.6
34	50.7	53.8	**85**	6.2	7.1
35	49.7	52.8	**86**	5.8	6.6
36	48.6	51.7	**87**	5.3	6.1
37	47.6	50.6	**88**	4.9	5.6
38	46.5	49.6	**89**	4.6	5.2
39	45.5	48.5	**90**	4.2	4.8
40	44.4	47.5	**91**	3.9	4.4
41	43.4	46.4	**92**	3.6	4.0
42	42.3	45.3	**93**	3.3	3.7
43	41.3	44.3	**94**	3.1	3.4
44	40.3	43.2	**95**	2.8	3.1
45	39.3	42.2	**96**	2.6	2.9
46	38.2	41.2	**97**	2.4	2.6
47	37.2	40.1	**98**	2.2	2.4
48	36.2	39.1	**99**	2.0	2.2
49	35.2	38.1	**100**	1.9	2.0
50	34.2	37.0			

Source: Office for National Statistics

Notes:

1. National life tables of various kinds and population projections have been produced for a considerable period, formerly by the Government Actuary's Department and, since February 2006, by the Office for National Statistics. The Decennial Life Tables for England and Wales combined and for Scotland are based on data for the three-year period around a Census. Between Censuses, life tables known as National Life Tables (formerly named Interim Life Tables) are produced, which are based on data for the numbers in the population and the deaths by age and sex for the latest three-year period available. These National Life Tables are produced for the United Kingdom as a whole, Great Britain, England & Wales and also for each individual country of the United Kingdom. It is intended to update the life tables in *Facts and Figures* every year, using the latest data then available.

The historical life tables

2. The latest published Decennial Life Tables are the English Life Tables No.17 (ELT No.17). These are based on data on the numbers in the population and the numbers of deaths by age and sex for 2010–2012 (the three years around the 2011 Census). The latest published decennial life tables for Scotland are the Scottish Life Tables 2000–2002.

3. Data from the Decennial Life Table, ELT No.15, based on data for 1990–1992, formed the mortality assumptions underlying the calculations of the multipliers in Tables 1–18 of the 4th edition of the Ogden Tables. Tables of multipliers using mortality from the Decennial Life Tables are no longer reproduced in the Ogden Tables.

4. The tables reproduced on pages 16 and 17 are the latest available National Life Tables for the United Kingdom (based on data for 2020–2022). These life tables are based on historical data (and expectations of life which are calculated using these data), and effectively assume that the mortality rate for a given age and sex will remain constant in future years. They provide a measure of mortality for that particular period but are not a good indication of how long someone of a given age now may be expected to live.

5. There have been large improvements in mortality rates over the last 100 years or so. For estimating how long someone of a given age is expected to live it is reasonable to assume that mortality rates will continue to improve in future.

Projected mortality

6. The table reproduced on page 18 is the latest available official projection of expectations of life for the United Kingdom making allowance for expected future changes in mortality for individuals of specified ages in 2024. This table allows for the projected changes in mortality assumed in the 2020-based population projections produced by the Office for National Statistics. There were no changes to the mortality assumptions for the 2021-based interim population projections. The mortality assumptions are slightly higher than those used to prepare the 8th edition of the Ogden Tables. As a result, cohort expectations of life shown on page 18 are of the order of 0.4 years lower for males up to around age 50 and about 0.1 years lower for females up to around age 70 compared to the figures in Tables 1 and 2 of the Ogden Tables, getting closer at higher ages. This reflects a slowdown in the rate of fall of mortality rates and is not directly as a result of Covid-19.

7. At Appendix A to the Introduction to the 4th edition of the Ogden Tables there is an extract from ELT No.15, which shows graphs indicating rates of mortality expressed in percentages of the 1911 rates of mortality on a logarithmic scale. They demonstrate in stark fashion the improvement in longevity which has taken place since 1911.

8. An exception in some recent years has been small increases in the mortality of young males in their 30s due to increases in deaths caused by HIV infection and AIDS; suicide rates and alcohol-related mortality have also increased for men at young ages in some years. However, even if this slight worsening of mortality were to continue, the effects on the tables of multipliers (in the Ogden Tables) would not be significant.

9. Unusually high mortality was experienced at all ages in 2020–2022 as a result of the Covid-19 pandemic and its aftereffects. Some impact of this can be seen in the published life table for 2020–22 on pages 16-17, with period expectations of life down about 0.7 years for males and 0.4 years for females up to around age 50 compared to pre-Covid-19 figures for 2017–19. The Office for National Statistics is currently reviewing long-term mortality improvement assumptions in preparation for the 2022-based population projections, due to be published in late 2024.

10. The Office for National Statistics carries out official population projections for the United Kingdom and constituent countries, usually every two years. In particular, these projections include assumptions of improving mortality rates at most ages in the years following the base year of the projections. The latest projections were based on the 2021 population, without updating the mortality assumptions from the 2020-based projections, and were published in January 2024.

11. Tables 1–34 of the 8th edition of the Ogden Tables give multipliers based on the projected mortality rates underlying the 2018-based principal population projections for the United Kingdom. These take as their base the estimated numbers in the population by sex and age in the constituent countries of the United Kingdom in mid-2018. The projections and the underlying assumptions are available on the website of the Office for National Statistics.

12. Multipliers in earlier editions of the Ogden Tables were based on historical or projected mortality rates for the population of England & Wales combined. However, the Ogden Tables are used extensively in Scotland and Northern Ireland. Although it would be possible to produce separate Tables based on projected mortality rates for Scotland and for Northern Ireland, it was agreed for the 6th edition that rather than have three separate sets of tables there should be one set calculated using mortality rates from the population projections of the United Kingdom as a whole and this was continued in the 7th and 8th editions.

13. The Ogden Tables take account of the possibilities that a claimant may live for different periods, e.g. die soon or live to be very old. As mentioned above, the mortality assumptions for the 8th edition relate to the general population of the United Kingdom. Although comparable expectations of life are available for the constituent countries of the United Kingdom (and statistics are available which give a measure of variations in mortality between regions and local authority areas), the Ogden Tables are recommended for use unadjusted regardless of location within the United Kingdom or for other potentially relevant factors such as earnings level, educational background, lifestyle or health status. Unless there is clear evidence in an individual case to support the view that the claimant concerned is "atypical" and can be expected to experience a significantly shorter or longer than average lifespan, to an extent greater than would be encompassed by variations in place of residence, lifestyle, educational level, occupation and general health status, no further increase or reduction should be made for mortality alone. Examples of an atypical claimant might be a lifelong heavy smoker, someone suffering from a traumatic brain

injury, an immobile patient or more likely a combination of such adverse factors, without off-setting favourable factors.

14. Where a claimant is thought to be atypical, medical, actuarial or other relevant expert evidence should be sought on the possible overall impact of all relevant factors on life expectancy. For large cases where it is thought appropriate to argue, on medical evidence or for other reasons, that the situation of the claimant is atypical, an actuary should be consulted on how an appropriate adjustment may be made to the Ogden Tables.

15. The mortality tables in this section and those underlying the Ogden Tables do not make any allowance for contingencies other than mortality. Appropriate adjustments for such contingencies are considered in section A4.

A4: Loss of earnings multipliers adjusted for education, disability and employment status

The Ogden Tables dealing with loss of earnings (Ogden tables 3–18) are subject to adjustment for contingencies other than mortality (Ogden section B). The tables which follow incorporate those factors without the need for further calculation.

The contingencies are whether the claimant was in employment or not, whether he or she was disabled or not, and his or her educational or skill level. Earlier editions (1st–5th) of the Ogden Tables and of *Facts & Figures,* based on earlier research, made adjustments for the general state of the economy; the nature of the claimant's employment, whether clerical or manual; and for different geographical areas of the country. These are not used now as more recent research has shown that when adjustments are made for employment status, disability and educational attainment the difference made by these other factors is small.

Employment

Employed
Those who at the time of injury (or, as the case may be, of trial/assessment) are employed, self-employed or on a government training scheme.

Not employed
All others (including those temporarily out of work, full-time students and unpaid family workers).

Disability

Disabled
A person is classified as being disabled if all three of the following conditions in relation to the ill-health or disability are met:

(i) he or she has either a progressive illness, or an illness or disability which has lasted or is expected to last for over a year,

and

(ii) he or she satisfies the Disability Discrimination Act 1995 definition that the impact of the disability has a substantial adverse effect on the person's ability to carry out normal day-to-day activities,

and

(iii) the effects of impairment limit either the kind **or** the amount of paid work he or she can do.

Not disabled.
All others.

Section B of the Ogden notes (in section A8 in this book) gives examples of the ways in which a disability may affect one's day-to-day activities, and on the interpretation of "normal" and "substantial". Note that this is not the definition in the Equality Act 2010.

Educational attainment means the highest level of education attained by the claimant. It is a shorthand for the level of skill and includes equivalent non-academic qualifications.

Level 3 Higher degree, degree or equivalent, higher education qualification below degree level. This includes professional qualifications, for example as a nurse.

Level 2 A-level or equivalent (at least one at pass level E).
GCSE or equivalent (at least one at pass level A* to C / 9 to 4)

Level 1 Low level qualifications below GCSE grade C, no qualifications and other qualifications.

There are 12 tables each for men and women arranged in the following order.

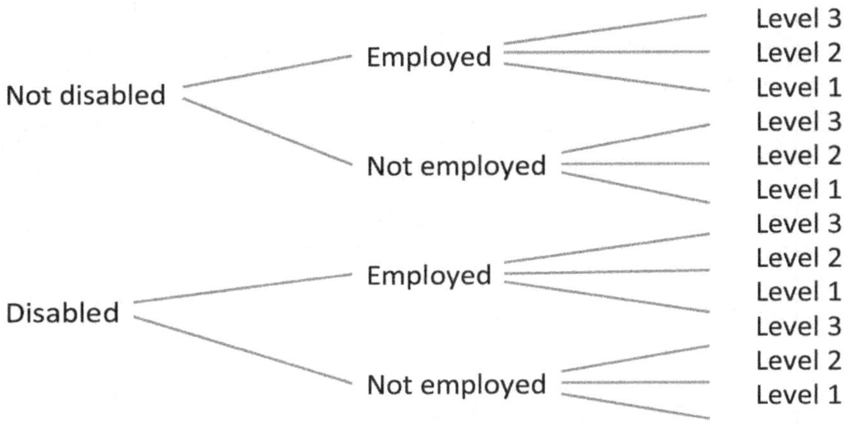

Thus, if the claimant is a 32-year-old male solicitor, employed before the accident at a salary of

£40,000, not disabled and proposing to retire at 65, the first table on the next page gives the multiplier for loss of earnings to age 65 as 30.06.

By using the tables for disabled claimants it is possible to obtain an estimate of the claimant's residual earning capacity, with an "inbuilt" allowance for employment risks which would otherwise require a separate *Smith v Manchester* award. Thus, if the accident has seriously affected the solicitor's ability to work as a solicitor, and he is now employed at a salary of £25,000, the seventh table gives a multiplier of 19.04 for his new earning capacity to age 65. This approach will not always be suitable and there will be cases where a *Smith v Manchester* or *Blamire* award is still needed.

In the case of someone who has not yet reached the age at which it is likely that he or she would start work, there should be an assessment of the level of education he or she would have attained, the age he or she would have started work, and whether he or she would have been employed or not. The multiplier appropriate to that age and those conditions should then be adjusted for early receipt (for the period between the date of trial and the putative date of starting work). A similar approach should be taken with those who have not completed their education/skills training at the date of trial.

The notes to the Ogden Tables do not provide specific adjustment factors for ages above 54 on the basis that, above that age, the likely course of someone's employment will depend on individual circumstances and the use of statistical averages may be inappropriate.

If it is proposed to depart from a strict application of the reduction factors, attention should be paid to the matters set out in section B(g) of the Ogden Tables.

The tables use the -0.25 per cent discount rate.

ND E Level 3

Loss of earnings: not disabled; employed; degree level education or equivalent

Age	Male to retiring age								
	55	60	65	66	67	68	69	70	75
16									
17	See introductory notes								
18									
19									
20	32.85	37.62	42.34	43.28	44.21	45.14	46.06	46.97	51.45
21	31.87	36.62	41.33	42.26	43.19	44.12	45.04	45.95	50.40
22	30.89	35.63	40.32	41.25	42.18	43.10	44.01	44.92	49.36
23	29.90	34.63	39.31	40.24	41.16	42.08	42.99	43.90	48.32
24	28.93	33.64	38.31	39.23	40.15	41.07	41.98	42.88	47.28
25	27.96	32.65	37.31	38.23	39.15	40.06	40.96	41.86	46.25
26	26.98	31.67	36.31	37.23	38.14	39.05	39.95	40.85	45.22
27	26.01	30.69	35.31	36.23	37.14	38.05	38.95	39.84	44.19
28	25.04	29.71	34.32	35.24	36.14	37.05	37.94	38.83	43.17
29	24.08	28.73	33.33	34.24	35.14	36.05	36.94	37.83	42.15
30	22.87	27.46	32.00	32.89	33.78	34.67	35.55	36.42	40.68
31	21.92	26.50	31.02	31.91	32.81	33.69	34.57	35.44	39.68
32	20.98	25.54	30.06	30.95	31.83	32.72	33.59	34.46	38.68
33	20.04	24.60	29.10	29.98	30.87	31.74	32.62	33.49	37.69
34	19.11	23.65	28.13	29.03	29.91	30.78	31.65	32.52	36.70
35	17.77	22.20	26.58	27.44	28.30	29.15	30.01	30.84	34.93
36	16.85	21.28	25.65	26.51	27.37	28.22	29.07	29.90	33.97
37	15.95	20.36	24.72	25.58	26.44	27.29	28.13	28.97	33.02
38	15.05	19.46	23.80	24.66	25.51	26.36	27.20	28.04	32.08
39	14.14	18.54	22.88	23.74	24.59	25.43	26.28	27.10	31.13
40	12.94	17.24	21.47	22.31	23.13	23.96	24.78	25.59	29.51
41	12.07	16.36	20.58	21.41	22.24	23.07	23.88	24.69	28.60
42	11.20	15.48	19.69	20.53	21.35	22.17	22.99	23.80	27.69
43	10.33	14.60	18.82	19.64	20.47	21.29	22.10	22.90	26.80
44	9.46	13.73	17.94	18.77	19.59	20.41	21.22	22.02	25.89
45	8.30	12.42	16.47	17.26	18.06	18.85	19.63	20.40	24.14
46	7.46	11.58	15.63	16.43	17.21	18.00	18.78	19.55	23.28
47	6.63	10.75	14.79	15.59	16.38	17.16	17.94	18.71	22.43
48	5.80	9.91	13.95	14.75	15.54	16.32	17.10	17.87	21.58
49	4.97	9.08	13.12	13.91	14.70	15.49	16.26	17.03	20.73
50	4.04	8.05	12.00	12.77	13.54	14.30	15.06	15.80	19.41
51	3.19	7.16	11.05	11.81	12.57	13.32	14.07	14.81	18.36
52	2.34	6.20	9.99	10.74	11.48	12.21	12.94	13.66	17.12
53	1.54	5.36	9.10	9.83	10.56	11.29	12.01	12.72	16.13
54	0.76	4.53	8.23	8.95	9.67	10.39	11.10	11.80	15.17

See introductory notes as regards claimants over 54 at date of trial

Age	Female to retiring age								
	55	60	65	66	67	68	69	70	75
16									
17	See introductory notes								
18									
19									
20	31.94	36.63	41.32	42.25	43.18	44.11	45.04	45.96	50.51
21	30.98	35.67	40.34	41.26	42.20	43.12	44.04	44.97	49.50
22	30.03	34.70	39.35	40.29	41.21	42.13	43.05	43.97	48.49
23	29.08	33.74	38.38	39.30	40.22	41.15	42.06	42.98	47.48
24	28.13	32.78	37.41	38.32	39.25	40.16	41.08	41.99	46.48
25	27.19	31.82	36.43	37.36	38.27	39.19	40.09	41.01	45.48
26	26.24	30.86	35.46	36.38	37.29	38.21	39.12	40.02	44.48
27	25.30	29.91	34.50	35.41	36.33	37.23	38.14	39.04	43.48
28	24.37	28.96	33.54	34.44	35.36	36.26	37.16	38.06	42.49
29	23.43	28.01	32.58	33.48	34.39	35.30	36.19	37.09	41.50
30	22.50	27.07	31.62	32.52	33.43	34.33	35.23	36.12	40.52
31	21.57	26.13	30.67	31.57	32.47	33.37	34.27	35.16	39.53
32	20.64	25.19	29.72	30.62	31.51	32.41	33.30	34.19	38.55
33	19.72	24.25	28.77	29.66	30.56	31.46	32.35	33.23	37.58
34	18.80	23.32	27.83	28.72	29.61	30.51	31.39	32.28	36.61
35	17.88	22.40	26.88	27.78	28.67	29.56	30.44	31.32	35.64
36	16.97	21.46	25.95	26.84	27.73	28.62	29.50	30.37	34.68
37	16.05	20.55	25.02	25.91	26.79	27.68	28.55	29.43	33.72
38	15.14	19.62	24.09	24.97	25.85	26.73	27.61	28.49	32.76
39	14.23	18.71	23.16	24.04	24.92	25.80	26.67	27.54	31.81
40	13.33	17.79	22.24	23.12	24.00	24.87	25.74	26.61	30.86
41	12.43	16.89	21.31	22.19	23.07	23.94	24.82	25.68	29.92
42	11.53	15.97	20.40	21.27	22.15	23.02	23.88	24.75	28.98
43	10.63	15.07	19.48	20.35	21.23	22.10	22.97	23.82	28.05
44	9.73	14.17	18.57	19.45	20.31	21.18	22.04	22.91	27.10
45	8.74	13.12	17.46	18.32	19.18	20.04	20.89	21.73	25.88
46	7.86	12.22	16.56	17.43	18.29	19.14	19.98	20.84	24.97
47	6.98	11.34	15.68	16.53	17.39	18.24	19.09	19.93	24.06
48	6.10	10.46	14.78	15.64	16.50	17.35	18.19	19.04	23.15
49	5.23	9.58	13.89	14.76	15.61	16.46	17.30	18.14	22.25
50	4.25	8.50	12.72	13.55	14.38	15.22	16.04	16.86	20.86
51	3.36	7.56	11.72	12.54	13.36	14.18	14.99	15.80	19.75
52	2.49	6.63	10.74	11.55	12.37	13.17	13.98	14.77	18.67
53	1.64	5.73	9.78	10.59	11.39	12.19	12.98	13.77	17.61
54	0.82	4.91	8.96	9.77	10.57	11.37	12.15	12.94	16.78

See introductory notes as regards claimants over 54 at date of trial

ND E Level 2

Loss of earnings: not disabled; employed; good GCSE level education or equivalent

Age	Male to retiring age								
	55	60	65	66	67	68	69	70	75
16	36.03	40.74	45.42	46.35	47.27	48.19	49.10	50.02	54.47
17	35.05	39.75	44.41	45.34	46.25	47.17	48.09	48.99	53.42
18	34.07	38.76	43.41	44.33	45.25	46.16	47.06	47.97	52.39
19	33.10	37.77	42.41	43.33	44.24	45.15	46.06	46.96	51.35
20	32.85	37.62	42.34	43.28	44.21	45.14	46.06	46.97	51.45
21	31.87	36.62	41.33	42.26	43.19	44.12	45.04	45.95	50.40
22	30.89	35.63	40.32	41.25	42.18	43.10	44.01	44.92	49.36
23	29.90	34.63	39.31	40.24	41.16	42.08	42.99	43.90	48.32
24	28.93	33.64	38.31	39.23	40.15	41.07	41.98	42.88	47.28
25	27.96	32.65	37.31	38.23	39.15	40.06	40.96	41.86	46.25
26	26.98	31.67	36.31	37.23	38.14	39.05	39.95	40.85	45.22
27	26.01	30.69	35.31	36.23	37.14	38.05	38.95	39.84	44.19
28	25.04	29.71	34.32	35.24	36.14	37.05	37.94	38.83	43.17
29	24.08	28.73	33.33	34.24	35.14	36.05	36.94	37.83	42.15
30	22.87	27.46	32.00	32.89	33.78	34.67	35.55	36.42	40.68
31	21.92	26.50	31.02	31.91	32.81	33.69	34.57	35.44	39.68
32	20.98	25.54	30.06	30.95	31.83	32.72	33.59	34.46	38.68
33	20.04	24.60	29.10	29.98	30.87	31.74	32.62	33.49	37.69
34	19.11	23.65	28.13	29.03	29.91	30.78	31.65	32.52	36.70
35	17.97	22.45	26.88	27.75	28.62	29.49	30.35	31.19	35.32
36	17.04	21.52	25.94	26.81	27.68	28.54	29.40	30.24	34.35
37	16.13	20.59	25.00	25.87	26.74	27.60	28.45	29.30	33.39
38	15.22	19.68	24.07	24.94	25.80	26.66	27.51	28.36	32.44
39	14.30	18.75	23.14	24.01	24.87	25.72	26.58	27.41	31.49
40	13.09	17.44	21.72	22.57	23.40	24.24	25.06	25.88	29.85
41	12.21	16.55	20.82	21.66	22.50	23.33	24.16	24.98	28.94
42	11.33	15.66	19.92	20.77	21.60	22.43	23.26	24.07	28.01
43	10.45	14.77	19.04	19.87	20.71	21.53	22.36	23.17	27.11
44	9.57	13.89	18.15	18.98	19.82	20.65	21.46	22.27	26.20
45	8.50	12.72	16.86	17.68	18.50	19.30	20.10	20.89	24.72
46	7.64	11.86	16.01	16.82	17.63	18.44	19.24	20.03	23.84
47	6.79	11.01	15.15	15.96	16.77	17.57	18.37	19.16	22.97
48	5.94	10.15	14.29	15.10	15.91	16.71	17.51	18.30	22.10
49	5.09	9.30	13.44	14.25	15.05	15.86	16.65	17.44	21.23
50	4.14	8.25	12.29	13.08	13.87	14.65	15.43	16.19	19.89
51	3.27	7.34	11.32	12.10	12.88	13.65	14.42	15.18	18.82
52	2.43	6.44	10.38	11.15	11.92	12.68	13.44	14.18	17.78
53	1.60	5.57	9.46	10.22	10.98	11.73	12.48	13.22	16.76
54	0.79	4.71	8.56	9.31	10.06	10.80	11.53	12.27	15.77

See introductory notes as regards claimants over 54 at date of trial

Age	Female to retiring age								
	55	60	65	66	67	68	69	70	75
16	32.95	37.32	41.67	42.54	43.42	44.27	45.14	46.00	50.25
17	32.06	36.41	40.76	41.63	42.49	43.36	44.22	45.08	49.30
18	31.17	35.51	39.85	40.71	41.58	42.44	43.29	44.15	48.37
19	30.29	34.62	38.94	39.80	40.66	41.52	42.37	43.23	47.43
20	29.77	34.14	38.50	39.37	40.24	41.11	41.97	42.83	47.07
21	28.87	33.23	37.59	38.45	39.32	40.18	41.04	41.90	46.13
22	27.99	32.33	36.67	37.54	38.40	39.26	40.11	40.98	45.18
23	27.10	31.44	35.76	36.62	37.48	38.34	39.20	40.05	44.25
24	26.22	30.55	34.86	35.71	36.57	37.42	38.28	39.13	43.31
25	25.65	30.01	34.36	35.23	36.10	36.96	37.81	38.68	42.89
26	24.75	29.11	33.45	34.31	35.18	36.04	36.89	37.75	41.95
27	23.86	28.21	32.54	33.40	34.26	35.12	35.97	36.82	41.01
28	22.98	27.32	31.63	32.49	33.35	34.20	35.05	35.90	40.07
29	22.10	26.42	30.73	31.58	32.44	33.29	34.14	34.98	39.14
30	21.48	25.84	30.18	31.05	31.91	32.77	33.63	34.48	38.67
31	20.59	24.94	29.27	30.13	31.00	31.85	32.71	33.56	37.73
32	19.71	24.04	28.37	29.22	30.08	30.94	31.79	32.63	36.80
33	18.82	23.15	27.46	28.32	29.17	30.03	30.88	31.72	35.88
34	17.94	22.26	26.56	27.42	28.27	29.12	29.96	30.81	34.94
35	17.48	21.89	26.27	27.15	28.02	28.89	29.75	30.61	34.83
36	16.58	20.98	25.36	26.23	27.10	27.97	28.83	29.68	33.89
37	15.69	20.08	24.45	25.32	26.18	27.05	27.90	28.76	32.96
38	14.79	19.18	23.54	24.41	25.27	26.13	26.99	27.84	32.02
39	13.91	18.28	22.64	23.50	24.36	25.22	26.07	26.92	31.09
40	12.88	17.19	21.48	22.33	23.18	24.02	24.86	25.70	29.81
41	12.00	16.31	20.59	21.44	22.29	23.13	23.97	24.80	28.90
42	11.14	15.43	19.70	20.54	21.39	22.24	23.07	23.91	27.99
43	10.27	14.55	18.82	19.66	20.50	21.34	22.19	23.01	27.09
44	9.40	13.69	17.94	18.79	19.62	20.46	21.29	22.13	26.18
45	8.44	12.67	16.86	17.69	18.52	19.35	20.17	20.98	24.99
46	7.59	11.80	15.99	16.83	17.66	18.48	19.29	20.12	24.11
47	6.74	10.95	15.14	15.96	16.79	17.61	18.43	19.24	23.23
48	5.89	10.10	14.27	15.10	15.93	16.75	17.56	18.38	22.35
49	5.05	9.25	13.41	14.25	15.07	15.89	16.71	17.51	21.48
50	4.15	8.30	12.42	13.23	14.04	14.86	15.66	16.46	20.37
51	3.32	7.47	11.58	12.39	13.21	14.01	14.82	15.61	19.51
52	2.49	6.63	10.74	11.55	12.37	13.17	13.98	14.77	18.67
53	1.66	5.80	9.90	10.72	11.53	12.33	13.14	13.94	17.82
54	0.83	4.97	9.07	9.89	10.70	11.50	12.30	13.10	16.98

See introductory notes as regards claimants over 54 at date of trial

ND E Level 1

Loss of earnings: not disabled; employed; education below good GCSE level

Age	Male to retiring age								
	55	60	65	66	67	68	69	70	75
16	34.81	39.37	43.89	44.79	45.67	46.57	47.45	48.33	52.63
17	33.87	38.41	42.91	43.81	44.69	45.58	46.47	47.34	51.62
18	32.92	37.45	41.94	42.84	43.72	44.60	45.48	46.35	50.62
19	31.98	36.50	40.98	41.86	42.75	43.63	44.51	45.37	49.62
20	31.41	35.97	40.48	41.38	42.26	43.15	44.03	44.91	49.19
21	30.47	35.01	39.52	40.40	41.29	42.18	43.06	43.93	48.19
22	29.53	34.06	38.55	39.44	40.32	41.20	42.07	42.94	47.19
23	28.59	33.11	37.58	38.47	39.35	40.23	41.10	41.97	46.20
24	27.66	32.16	36.63	37.51	38.38	39.26	40.13	40.99	45.21
25	27.03	31.57	36.08	36.97	37.86	38.74	39.61	40.48	44.72
26	26.09	30.62	35.11	36.00	36.88	37.76	38.63	39.50	43.73
27	25.15	29.67	34.14	35.03	35.91	36.79	37.66	38.53	42.73
28	24.22	28.73	33.18	34.07	34.94	35.82	36.69	37.55	41.75
29	23.28	27.78	32.23	33.11	33.99	34.86	35.72	36.58	40.76
30	22.36	26.85	31.28	32.16	33.03	33.90	34.76	35.61	39.78
31	21.44	25.91	30.33	31.20	32.08	32.94	33.80	34.65	38.80
32	20.51	24.97	29.39	30.26	31.13	31.99	32.84	33.70	37.82
33	19.60	24.05	28.45	29.31	30.18	31.04	31.89	32.74	36.85
34	18.68	23.13	27.51	28.38	29.24	30.10	30.95	31.79	35.89
35	17.57	21.95	26.27	27.13	27.98	28.82	29.67	30.49	34.53
36	16.66	21.04	25.36	26.20	27.06	27.90	28.74	29.56	33.58
37	15.76	20.13	24.44	25.29	26.13	26.98	27.81	28.64	32.64
38	14.88	19.24	23.53	24.38	25.22	26.06	26.89	27.72	31.71
39	13.98	18.33	22.62	23.47	24.31	25.14	25.98	26.80	30.78
40	12.94	17.24	21.47	22.31	23.13	23.96	24.78	25.59	29.51
41	12.07	16.36	20.58	21.41	22.24	23.07	23.88	24.69	28.60
42	11.20	15.48	19.69	20.53	21.35	22.17	22.99	23.80	27.69
43	10.33	14.60	18.82	19.64	20.47	21.29	22.10	22.90	26.80
44	9.46	13.73	17.94	18.77	19.59	20.41	21.22	22.02	25.89
45	8.50	12.72	16.86	17.68	18.50	19.30	20.10	20.89	24.72
46	7.64	11.86	16.01	16.82	17.63	18.44	19.24	20.03	23.84
47	6.79	11.01	15.15	15.96	16.77	17.57	18.37	19.16	22.97
48	5.94	10.15	14.29	15.10	15.91	16.71	17.51	18.30	22.10
49	5.09	9.30	13.44	14.25	15.05	15.86	16.65	17.44	21.23
50	4.19	8.35	12.44	13.24	14.04	14.83	15.62	16.39	20.13
51	3.31	7.43	11.46	12.25	13.04	13.82	14.60	15.36	19.05
52	2.49	6.60	10.63	11.43	12.22	13.00	13.77	14.53	18.22
53	1.64	5.71	9.69	10.47	11.25	12.02	12.79	13.55	17.18
54	0.81	4.83	8.77	9.54	10.31	11.07	11.83	12.58	16.17

See introductory notes as regards claimants over 54 at date of trial

Age	Female to retiring age								
	55	60	65	66	67	68	69	70	75
16	26.85	30.41	33.96	34.66	35.38	36.08	36.78	37.48	40.95
17	26.12	29.67	33.21	33.92	34.62	35.33	36.03	36.73	40.17
18	25.40	28.93	32.47	33.17	33.88	34.58	35.28	35.97	39.41
19	24.68	28.21	31.73	32.43	33.13	33.83	34.52	35.22	38.65
20	25.05	28.72	32.40	33.13	33.86	34.59	35.31	36.04	39.61
21	24.29	27.97	31.63	32.35	33.09	33.81	34.53	35.26	38.81
22	23.55	27.21	30.86	31.59	32.31	33.04	33.75	34.48	38.02
23	22.80	26.45	30.09	30.82	31.54	32.26	32.98	33.70	37.23
24	22.06	25.70	29.33	30.05	30.77	31.49	32.21	32.93	36.45
25	22.25	26.04	29.81	30.56	31.31	32.06	32.80	33.55	37.21
26	21.47	25.25	29.02	29.76	30.51	31.26	32.00	32.75	36.39
27	20.70	24.47	28.22	28.97	29.72	30.46	31.20	31.94	35.58
28	19.94	23.70	27.44	28.18	28.93	29.67	30.41	31.14	34.76
29	19.17	22.92	26.65	27.40	28.14	28.88	29.61	30.35	33.96
30	19.18	23.07	26.95	27.72	28.49	29.26	30.02	30.79	34.53
31	18.38	22.27	26.14	26.90	27.68	28.44	29.21	29.96	33.69
32	17.60	21.47	25.33	26.09	26.86	27.62	28.38	29.14	32.86
33	16.81	20.67	24.52	25.28	26.05	26.81	27.57	28.32	32.03
34	16.02	19.88	23.72	24.48	25.24	26.00	26.75	27.51	31.20
35	15.65	19.60	23.52	24.31	25.09	25.86	26.63	27.40	31.19
36	14.85	18.78	22.71	23.49	24.26	25.04	25.81	26.57	30.35
37	14.04	17.98	21.89	22.67	23.44	24.22	24.98	25.75	29.51
38	13.24	17.17	21.07	21.85	22.62	23.39	24.16	24.92	28.67
39	12.45	16.37	20.27	21.04	21.81	22.58	23.34	24.10	27.84
40	11.97	15.97	19.96	20.75	21.54	22.33	23.11	23.89	27.71
41	11.15	15.16	19.13	19.92	20.71	21.50	22.28	23.05	26.86
42	10.35	14.34	18.31	19.09	19.88	20.67	21.44	22.22	26.01
43	9.54	13.52	17.49	18.27	19.05	19.84	20.62	21.39	25.18
44	8.74	12.72	16.67	17.46	18.23	19.02	19.79	20.56	24.33
45	8.04	12.06	16.06	16.85	17.64	18.42	19.21	19.98	23.80
46	7.22	11.24	15.23	16.02	16.82	17.60	18.38	19.16	22.96
47	6.42	10.43	14.42	15.20	15.99	16.78	17.55	18.33	22.12
48	5.61	9.62	13.59	14.38	15.17	15.95	16.73	17.50	21.29
49	4.81	8.81	12.78	13.57	14.35	15.14	15.91	16.68	20.46
50	4.00	8.00	11.97	12.75	13.54	14.32	15.10	15.86	19.63
51	3.20	7.20	11.16	11.94	12.73	13.50	14.28	15.05	18.81
52	2.40	6.39	10.35	11.14	11.92	12.70	13.47	14.24	17.99
53	1.62	5.66	9.66	10.46	11.25	12.04	12.82	13.60	17.39
54	0.81	4.85	8.85	9.65	10.44	11.23	12.00	12.78	16.57

See introductory notes as regards claimants over 54 at date of trial

Loss of earnings: not disabled; not employed; degree level education or equivalent

Age	Male to retiring age								
	55	60	65	66	67	68	69	70	75
16	See introductory notes								
17									
18									
19									
20	31.77	36.38	40.95	41.85	42.75	43.65	44.54	45.43	49.76
21	30.82	35.41	39.97	40.86	41.76	42.66	43.54	44.43	48.74
22	29.87	34.45	38.99	39.88	40.78	41.67	42.56	43.44	47.73
23	28.92	33.49	38.02	38.90	39.80	40.69	41.57	42.45	46.73
24	27.98	32.53	37.05	37.93	38.82	39.71	40.59	41.47	45.72
25	27.03	31.57	36.08	36.96	37.85	38.74	39.61	40.48	44.72
26	26.09	30.62	35.11	35.99	36.87	37.76	38.63	39.50	43.73
27	25.15	29.67	34.14	35.03	35.91	36.79	37.66	38.53	42.73
28	24.22	28.73	33.18	34.06	34.94	35.82	36.69	37.55	41.75
29	23.28	27.78	32.23	33.11	33.98	34.86	35.72	36.58	40.76
30	22.11	26.54	30.93	31.79	32.65	33.51	34.36	35.21	39.32
31	21.19	25.61	29.99	30.85	31.71	32.57	33.41	34.26	38.36
32	20.28	24.69	29.06	29.91	30.77	31.63	32.47	33.31	37.39
33	19.37	23.78	28.13	28.98	29.83	30.69	31.53	32.37	36.44
34	18.47	22.86	27.20	28.05	28.90	29.75	30.59	31.43	35.48
35	17.16	21.45	25.67	26.50	27.33	28.16	28.98	29.79	33.74
36	16.28	20.55	24.78	25.60	26.43	27.26	28.07	28.88	32.81
37	15.40	19.67	23.88	24.70	25.53	26.36	27.17	27.98	31.89
38	14.54	18.79	22.99	23.81	24.64	25.46	26.27	27.08	30.98
39	13.66	17.91	22.10	22.93	23.75	24.57	25.37	26.18	30.07
40	12.34	16.44	20.48	21.26	22.05	22.84	23.62	24.40	28.13
41	11.51	15.60	19.62	20.41	21.20	21.99	22.77	23.54	27.27
42	10.68	14.76	18.78	19.57	20.36	21.14	21.92	22.69	26.40
43	9.85	13.92	17.94	18.73	19.51	20.30	21.07	21.84	25.55
44	9.02	13.10	17.11	17.89	18.67	19.46	20.23	20.99	24.69
45	7.70	11.52	15.28	16.01	16.75	17.48	18.21	18.93	22.39
46	6.92	10.74	14.50	15.23	15.97	16.70	17.42	18.14	21.60
47	6.15	9.97	13.72	14.45	15.19	15.92	16.64	17.36	20.81
48	5.38	9.19	12.94	13.68	14.41	15.14	15.86	16.58	20.02
49	4.61	8.42	12.17	12.90	13.64	14.37	15.08	15.80	19.23
50	3.59	7.16	10.66	11.35	12.03	12.71	13.38	14.05	17.25
51	2.75	6.18	9.53	10.18	10.84	11.49	12.13	12.77	15.84
52	2.01	5.33	8.58	9.22	9.86	10.49	11.11	11.73	14.71
53	1.28	4.45	7.56	8.17	8.78	9.38	9.98	10.57	13.41
54	0.60	3.58	6.50	7.07	7.64	8.20	8.76	9.32	11.98

See introductory notes as regards claimants over 54 at date of trial

Age	Female to retiring age								
	55	60	65	66	67	68	69	70	75
16	See introductory notes								
17									
18									
19									
20	31.22	35.80	40.38	41.29	42.20	43.11	44.01	44.92	49.36
21	30.28	34.86	39.42	40.32	41.23	42.14	43.04	43.95	48.38
22	29.35	33.91	38.46	39.36	40.27	41.18	42.07	42.97	47.39
23	28.42	32.97	37.50	38.41	39.31	40.21	41.11	42.00	46.41
24	27.49	32.04	36.56	37.45	38.35	39.25	40.14	41.04	45.43
25	25.96	30.37	34.78	35.65	36.53	37.40	38.27	39.14	43.41
26	25.05	29.46	33.85	34.72	35.60	36.47	37.33	38.20	42.45
27	24.15	28.55	32.93	33.80	34.67	35.54	36.40	37.26	41.50
28	23.26	27.64	32.01	32.88	33.74	34.61	35.47	36.33	40.56
29	22.37	26.74	31.10	31.96	32.82	33.69	34.55	35.41	39.61
30	20.97	25.22	29.46	30.30	31.15	31.99	32.82	33.66	37.75
31	20.10	24.35	28.58	29.41	30.25	31.09	31.92	32.76	36.83
32	19.24	23.47	27.69	28.53	29.36	30.20	31.03	31.86	35.92
33	18.38	22.60	26.81	27.64	28.48	29.31	30.14	30.96	35.02
34	17.52	21.73	25.93	26.76	27.59	28.43	29.25	30.08	34.11
35	16.46	20.61	24.75	25.57	26.39	27.21	28.02	28.83	32.81
36	15.62	19.76	23.89	24.70	25.52	26.34	27.15	27.95	31.92
37	14.77	18.91	23.03	23.84	24.65	25.47	26.28	27.09	31.04
38	13.93	18.06	22.17	22.98	23.79	24.61	25.41	26.22	30.16
39	13.10	17.22	21.32	22.13	22.94	23.75	24.55	25.35	29.28
40	11.97	15.97	19.96	20.75	21.54	22.33	23.11	23.89	27.71
41	11.15	15.16	19.13	19.92	20.71	21.49	22.27	23.05	26.86
42	10.35	14.34	18.31	19.09	19.88	20.67	21.44	22.22	26.01
43	9.54	13.52	17.49	18.27	19.05	19.84	20.61	21.39	25.18
44	8.74	12.72	16.67	17.45	18.23	19.02	19.79	20.56	24.33
45	7.34	11.01	14.65	15.37	16.09	16.81	17.53	18.24	21.72
46	6.59	10.26	13.90	14.62	15.34	16.06	16.77	17.48	20.95
47	5.85	9.52	13.15	13.87	14.59	15.31	16.01	16.72	20.18
48	5.12	8.77	12.40	13.12	13.84	14.56	15.26	15.97	19.43
49	4.39	8.04	11.66	12.38	13.09	13.81	14.52	15.22	18.67
50	3.25	6.50	9.72	10.36	11.00	11.63	12.26	12.89	15.95
51	2.48	5.58	8.65	9.25	9.86	10.47	11.06	11.66	14.58
52	1.71	4.55	7.38	7.93	8.49	9.05	9.59	10.15	12.82
53	1.02	3.56	6.08	6.58	7.08	7.58	8.07	8.56	10.95
54	0.45	2.70	4.92	5.36	5.80	6.24	6.67	7.10	9.21

See introductory notes as regards claimants over 54 at date of trial

Loss of earnings: not disabled; not employed; good GCSE level education or equivalent

Age	Male to retiring age								
	55	60	65	66	67	68	69	70	75
16	35.22	39.83	44.40	45.30	46.20	47.11	48.00	48.89	53.24
17	34.26	38.85	43.41	44.31	45.21	46.11	47.00	47.89	52.22
18	33.30	37.89	42.43	43.33	44.22	45.12	46.01	46.89	51.21
19	32.36	36.92	41.46	42.35	43.24	44.14	45.02	45.90	50.20
20	31.77	36.38	40.95	41.85	42.75	43.65	44.54	45.43	49.76
21	30.82	35.41	39.97	40.86	41.76	42.66	43.54	44.43	48.74
22	29.87	34.45	38.99	39.88	40.78	41.67	42.56	43.44	47.73
23	28.92	33.49	38.02	38.90	39.80	40.69	41.57	42.45	46.73
24	27.98	32.53	37.05	37.93	38.82	39.71	40.59	41.47	45.72
25	26.73	31.22	35.67	36.54	37.42	38.29	39.16	40.02	44.21
26	25.80	30.28	34.71	35.58	36.46	37.33	38.19	39.05	43.23
27	24.86	29.34	33.76	34.63	35.50	36.37	37.23	38.09	42.25
28	23.94	28.41	32.81	33.68	34.55	35.41	36.27	37.12	41.27
29	23.02	27.47	31.87	32.73	33.60	34.46	35.31	36.17	40.30
30	21.85	26.24	30.57	31.42	32.27	33.13	33.97	34.80	38.87
31	20.95	25.32	29.64	30.49	31.34	32.19	33.03	33.87	37.92
32	20.05	24.41	28.72	29.57	30.41	31.26	32.10	32.93	36.96
33	19.15	23.50	27.80	28.64	29.49	30.34	31.17	32.00	36.02
34	18.26	22.60	26.88	27.73	28.57	29.41	30.24	31.07	35.07
35	16.96	21.19	25.37	26.19	27.01	27.83	28.64	29.44	33.34
36	16.09	20.31	24.49	25.30	26.12	26.94	27.74	28.54	32.42
37	15.22	19.44	23.60	24.41	25.23	26.05	26.85	27.65	31.52
38	14.36	18.57	22.72	23.53	24.35	25.16	25.96	26.76	30.62
39	13.50	17.70	21.84	22.66	23.47	24.28	25.08	25.87	29.72
40	12.19	16.24	20.23	21.00	21.78	22.57	23.33	24.10	27.79
41	11.37	15.41	19.38	20.17	20.94	21.72	22.49	23.26	26.94
42	10.55	14.58	18.55	19.33	20.11	20.89	21.65	22.41	26.08
43	9.73	13.75	17.72	18.50	19.28	20.05	20.81	21.57	25.24
44	8.91	12.94	16.90	17.67	18.45	19.22	19.98	20.74	24.39
45	7.70	11.52	15.28	16.01	16.75	17.48	18.21	18.93	22.39
46	6.92	10.74	14.50	15.23	15.97	16.70	17.42	18.14	21.60
47	6.15	9.97	13.72	14.45	15.19	15.92	16.64	17.36	20.81
48	5.38	9.19	12.94	13.68	14.41	15.14	15.86	16.58	20.02
49	4.61	8.42	12.17	12.90	13.64	14.37	15.08	15.80	19.23
50	3.64	7.26	10.81	11.50	12.20	12.89	13.57	14.24	17.49
51	2.79	6.27	9.67	10.33	11.00	11.66	12.31	12.96	16.07
52	2.01	5.33	8.58	9.22	9.86	10.49	11.11	11.73	14.71
53	1.28	4.45	7.56	8.17	8.78	9.38	9.98	10.57	13.41
54	0.60	3.58	6.50	7.07	7.64	8.20	8.76	9.32	11.98

See introductory notes as regards claimants over 54 at date of trial

Age	Female to retiring age								
	55	60	65	66	67	68	69	70	75
16	31.73	35.93	40.13	40.97	41.80	42.64	43.47	44.30	48.39
17	30.87	35.06	39.25	40.08	40.91	41.75	42.58	43.41	47.48
18	30.01	34.20	38.38	39.20	40.03	40.86	41.69	42.51	46.57
19	29.16	33.34	37.49	38.32	39.15	39.98	40.80	41.63	45.68
20	28.31	32.47	36.62	37.45	38.27	39.10	39.92	40.74	44.77
21	27.46	31.61	35.76	36.57	37.40	38.22	39.04	39.86	43.88
22	26.62	30.76	34.88	35.70	36.52	37.35	38.16	38.98	42.98
23	25.78	29.91	34.02	34.83	35.65	36.47	37.28	38.10	42.09
24	24.94	29.06	33.16	33.97	34.78	35.60	36.41	37.22	41.20
25	23.79	27.84	31.88	32.68	33.48	34.29	35.08	35.88	39.79
26	22.96	27.00	31.03	31.83	32.63	33.43	34.22	35.02	38.92
27	22.14	26.17	30.18	30.98	31.78	32.58	33.37	34.16	38.05
28	21.32	25.34	29.34	30.14	30.93	31.73	32.52	33.30	37.18
29	20.51	24.51	28.51	29.29	30.09	30.88	31.67	32.46	36.31
30	19.69	23.69	27.67	28.46	29.25	30.04	30.82	31.61	35.45
31	18.87	22.86	26.83	27.62	28.41	29.20	29.98	30.76	34.59
32	18.06	22.04	26.00	26.79	27.57	28.36	29.14	29.91	33.73
33	17.26	21.22	25.17	25.96	26.74	27.52	28.30	29.08	32.89
34	16.45	20.41	24.35	25.13	25.91	26.69	27.47	28.24	32.03
35	15.44	19.34	23.22	23.99	24.76	25.53	26.29	27.05	30.78
36	14.65	18.54	22.41	23.18	23.94	24.71	25.47	26.23	29.95
37	13.86	17.75	21.61	22.37	23.13	23.90	24.66	25.41	29.12
38	13.07	16.95	20.80	21.56	22.33	23.09	23.84	24.60	28.29
39	12.29	16.16	20.00	20.76	21.52	22.28	23.04	23.79	27.47
40	11.06	14.76	18.45	19.17	19.90	20.63	21.35	22.08	25.60
41	10.31	14.01	17.68	18.41	19.13	19.86	20.58	21.30	24.82
42	9.56	13.25	16.92	17.64	18.37	19.10	19.81	20.53	24.04
43	8.82	12.50	16.16	16.88	17.61	18.33	19.05	19.76	23.27
44	8.07	11.75	15.40	16.13	16.85	17.57	18.29	19.00	22.48
45	6.53	9.80	13.05	13.69	14.33	14.97	15.61	16.24	19.34
46	5.87	9.13	12.38	13.02	13.66	14.30	14.93	15.57	18.66
47	5.21	8.48	11.71	12.35	12.99	13.63	14.26	14.89	17.97
48	4.56	7.81	11.04	11.68	12.32	12.96	13.59	14.22	17.30
49	3.91	7.16	10.38	11.02	11.66	12.29	12.92	13.55	16.62
50	2.75	5.50	8.23	8.77	9.30	9.84	10.37	10.91	13.50
51	2.04	4.59	7.11	7.61	8.11	8.61	9.10	9.59	11.99
52	1.38	3.68	5.95	6.40	6.85	7.30	7.74	8.19	10.35
53	0.80	2.80	4.77	5.16	5.55	5.94	6.33	6.72	8.59
54	0.34	2.04	3.72	4.05	4.38	4.71	5.04	5.37	6.96

See introductory notes as regards claimants over 54 at date of trial

ND NE Level 1

Loss of earnings: not disabled; not employed; education below good GCSE level

Age	Male to retiring age								
	55	60	65	66	67	68	69	70	75
16	33.60	38.00	42.35	43.22	44.08	44.94	45.79	46.65	50.80
17	32.69	37.07	41.42	42.27	43.13	43.99	44.84	45.69	49.82
18	31.77	36.15	40.48	41.33	42.19	43.05	43.89	44.74	48.85
19	30.87	35.23	39.55	40.40	41.25	42.11	42.95	43.79	47.89
20	30.32	34.73	39.09	39.94	40.80	41.67	42.51	43.36	47.49
21	29.42	33.80	38.15	39.00	39.86	40.72	41.57	42.41	46.53
22	28.51	32.89	37.22	38.07	38.92	39.78	40.62	41.46	45.56
23	27.60	31.97	36.29	37.14	37.99	38.84	39.68	40.52	44.60
24	26.70	31.05	35.36	36.21	37.06	37.91	38.74	39.58	43.65
25	25.50	29.78	34.03	34.86	35.70	36.53	37.36	38.18	42.18
26	24.61	28.88	33.12	33.95	34.78	35.62	36.44	37.26	41.24
27	23.72	27.99	32.20	33.04	33.87	34.70	35.52	36.34	40.30
28	22.84	27.10	31.30	32.13	32.96	33.79	34.60	35.42	39.38
29	21.96	26.20	30.40	31.23	32.05	32.88	33.69	34.50	38.45
30	20.84	25.02	29.15	29.96	30.77	31.59	32.39	33.19	37.06
31	19.98	24.14	28.27	29.07	29.88	30.70	31.49	32.29	36.15
32	19.11	23.27	27.39	28.19	29.00	29.81	30.60	31.40	35.24
33	18.26	22.41	26.51	27.31	28.12	28.92	29.72	30.51	34.34
34	17.41	21.55	25.63	26.44	27.24	28.04	28.83	29.63	33.44
35	16.35	20.44	24.46	25.25	26.04	26.84	27.61	28.39	32.15
36	15.51	19.59	23.61	24.40	25.18	25.97	26.75	27.52	31.27
37	14.68	18.74	22.75	23.54	24.33	25.12	25.89	26.67	30.39
38	13.85	17.91	21.91	22.69	23.48	24.26	25.03	25.81	29.52
39	13.02	17.07	21.06	21.85	22.63	23.41	24.18	24.95	28.66
40	11.89	15.84	19.73	20.49	21.25	22.01	22.76	23.50	27.10
41	11.09	15.03	18.90	19.67	20.43	21.19	21.93	22.68	26.28
42	10.29	14.22	18.09	18.85	19.61	20.37	21.11	21.86	25.44
43	9.49	13.41	17.29	18.04	18.80	19.56	20.30	21.04	24.62
44	8.69	12.62	16.48	17.23	17.99	18.75	19.49	20.22	23.79
45	7.50	11.22	14.88	15.60	16.31	17.03	17.73	18.44	21.81
46	6.74	10.46	14.12	14.84	15.55	16.27	16.97	17.67	21.04
47	5.99	9.71	13.37	14.08	14.79	15.51	16.21	16.91	20.27
48	5.24	8.96	12.61	13.32	14.04	14.75	15.45	16.15	19.50
49	4.49	8.21	11.86	12.57	13.28	13.99	14.69	15.39	18.74
50	3.54	7.06	10.52	11.19	11.86	12.53	13.19	13.85	17.01
51	2.75	6.18	9.53	10.18	10.84	11.49	12.13	12.77	15.84
52	2.01	5.33	8.58	9.22	9.86	10.49	11.11	11.73	14.71
53	1.28	4.45	7.56	8.17	8.78	9.38	9.98	10.57	13.41
54	0.60	3.58	6.50	7.07	7.64	8.20	8.76	9.32	11.98

See introductory notes as regards claimants over 54 at date of trial

Age	Female to retiring age								
	55	60	65	66	67	68	69	70	75
16	25.63	29.02	32.41	33.09	33.76	34.44	35.11	35.78	39.09
17	24.94	28.32	31.70	32.37	33.05	33.72	34.39	35.06	38.35
18	24.24	27.62	31.00	31.66	32.33	33.01	33.67	34.34	37.62
19	23.56	26.93	30.28	30.95	31.62	32.29	32.95	33.62	36.89
20	22.87	26.23	29.58	30.25	30.91	31.58	32.24	32.90	36.16
21	22.18	25.53	28.88	29.54	30.20	30.87	31.53	32.19	35.44
22	21.50	24.84	28.17	28.84	29.50	30.16	30.82	31.48	34.71
23	20.82	24.15	27.47	28.14	28.80	29.46	30.11	30.77	33.99
24	20.14	23.47	26.78	27.44	28.09	28.75	29.41	30.06	33.28
25	19.78	23.14	26.50	27.16	27.83	28.50	29.16	29.82	33.08
26	19.08	22.44	25.79	26.46	27.12	27.79	28.45	29.11	32.35
27	18.40	21.75	25.09	25.75	26.41	27.08	27.74	28.39	31.62
28	17.72	21.06	24.39	25.05	25.71	26.37	27.03	27.68	30.90
29	17.04	20.37	23.69	24.35	25.01	25.67	26.32	26.98	30.18
30	16.62	19.99	23.35	24.02	24.69	25.36	26.02	26.68	29.93
31	15.93	19.30	22.65	23.32	23.98	24.65	25.31	25.97	29.20
32	15.25	18.60	21.95	22.61	23.28	23.94	24.60	25.25	28.48
33	14.57	17.91	21.25	21.91	22.57	23.23	23.89	24.54	27.76
34	13.88	17.23	20.55	21.21	21.87	22.53	23.19	23.84	27.04
35	13.21	16.54	19.86	20.52	21.17	21.83	22.48	23.13	26.33
36	12.53	15.85	19.17	19.82	20.48	21.13	21.78	22.43	25.62
37	11.86	15.18	18.48	19.13	19.78	20.44	21.09	21.74	24.91
38	11.18	14.50	17.79	18.44	19.09	19.75	20.39	21.04	24.20
39	10.51	13.82	17.11	17.76	18.41	19.06	19.70	20.35	23.50
40	9.39	12.54	15.67	16.28	16.90	17.52	18.13	18.75	21.74
41	8.75	11.90	15.02	15.63	16.25	16.87	17.48	18.09	21.08
42	8.12	11.25	14.37	14.99	15.60	16.22	16.83	17.44	20.42
43	7.49	10.61	13.73	14.34	14.95	15.57	16.18	16.78	19.76
44	6.86	9.98	13.08	13.70	14.31	14.92	15.53	16.14	19.10
45	5.33	7.99	10.64	11.16	11.68	12.21	12.72	13.24	15.77
46	4.79	7.45	10.09	10.61	11.14	11.66	12.17	12.69	15.21
47	4.25	6.91	9.55	10.07	10.59	11.11	11.63	12.14	14.65
48	3.72	6.37	9.00	9.53	10.05	10.57	11.08	11.60	14.10
49	3.19	5.84	8.46	8.99	9.51	10.03	10.54	11.05	13.55
50	2.20	4.40	6.58	7.01	7.44	7.87	8.30	8.73	10.80
51	1.60	3.60	5.58	5.97	6.36	6.75	7.14	7.52	9.40
52	1.08	2.88	4.66	5.01	5.36	5.71	6.06	6.41	8.10
53	0.64	2.24	3.82	4.13	4.44	4.76	5.06	5.37	6.87
54	0.28	1.68	3.06	3.33	3.61	3.88	4.15	4.42	5.73

See introductory notes as regards claimants over 54 at date of trial

D E Level 3

Loss of earnings: disabled; employed; degree level education or equivalent

Age	Male to retiring age								
	55	60	65	66	67	68	69	70	75
16									
17	See introductory notes								
18									
19									
20	19.49	22.32	25.13	25.68	26.23	26.78	27.33	27.87	30.53
21	18.91	21.73	24.53	25.07	25.63	26.18	26.72	27.26	29.91
22	18.33	21.14	23.93	24.47	25.02	25.57	26.11	26.65	29.29
23	17.74	20.55	23.33	23.87	24.42	24.97	25.51	26.05	28.67
24	17.17	19.96	22.73	23.28	23.82	24.37	24.91	25.44	28.06
25	17.51	20.45	23.37	23.94	24.51	25.09	25.65	26.22	28.97
26	16.90	19.84	22.74	23.31	23.88	24.46	25.02	25.59	28.32
27	16.29	19.22	22.12	22.69	23.26	23.83	24.39	24.95	27.68
28	15.69	18.61	21.49	22.06	22.63	23.20	23.76	24.32	27.04
29	15.08	17.99	20.88	21.44	22.01	22.58	23.14	23.69	26.40
30	14.48	17.39	20.26	20.83	21.39	21.96	22.51	23.07	25.76
31	13.89	16.78	19.65	20.21	20.77	21.34	21.89	22.45	25.13
32	13.29	16.18	19.04	19.60	20.16	20.72	21.27	21.83	24.50
33	12.69	15.58	18.43	18.99	19.55	20.11	20.66	21.21	23.87
34	12.10	14.98	17.82	18.38	18.94	19.49	20.04	20.59	23.24
35	11.10	13.88	16.61	17.15	17.68	18.22	18.75	19.28	21.83
36	10.53	13.30	16.03	16.57	17.10	17.64	18.16	18.69	21.23
37	9.97	12.73	15.45	15.99	16.52	17.05	17.58	18.11	20.64
38	9.41	12.16	14.88	15.41	15.94	16.47	17.00	17.52	20.05
39	8.84	11.59	14.30	14.83	15.37	15.90	16.42	16.94	19.46
40	8.28	11.03	13.73	14.26	14.79	15.32	15.84	16.36	18.87
41	7.72	10.46	13.16	13.69	14.22	14.75	15.27	15.79	18.29
42	7.16	9.90	12.60	13.13	13.65	14.18	14.70	15.22	17.71
43	6.61	9.34	12.03	12.56	13.09	13.61	14.13	14.65	17.14
44	6.05	8.78	11.47	12.00	12.52	13.05	13.57	14.08	16.56
45	5.30	7.93	10.52	11.02	11.53	12.03	12.53	13.03	15.41
46	4.76	7.39	9.98	10.48	10.99	11.50	11.99	12.49	14.87
47	4.23	6.86	9.44	9.95	10.45	10.96	11.45	11.95	14.32
48	3.70	6.33	8.91	9.41	9.92	10.42	10.92	11.41	13.78
49	3.17	5.80	8.38	8.88	9.39	9.89	10.38	10.88	13.24
50	2.59	5.17	7.70	8.19	8.69	9.18	9.66	10.15	12.46
51	2.07	4.65	7.18	7.67	8.17	8.66	9.14	9.63	11.93
52	1.56	4.13	6.66	7.16	7.65	8.14	8.62	9.11	11.41
53	1.06	3.69	6.26	6.77	7.27	7.77	8.26	8.76	11.10
54	0.54	3.22	5.85	6.36	6.87	7.38	7.89	8.39	10.78

See introductory notes as regards claimants over 54 at date of trial

Age	Female to retiring age								
	55	60	65	66	67	68	69	70	75
16									
17	See introductory notes								
18									
19									
20	21.78	24.98	28.17	28.80	29.44	30.08	30.71	31.34	34.44
21	21.13	24.32	27.50	28.13	28.77	29.40	30.03	30.66	33.75
22	20.48	23.66	26.83	27.46	28.09	28.73	29.35	29.98	33.06
23	19.83	23.00	26.17	26.80	27.42	28.06	28.68	29.30	32.38
24	19.18	22.35	25.51	26.13	26.76	27.39	28.01	28.63	31.69
25	18.23	21.33	24.43	25.04	25.65	26.27	26.88	27.49	30.49
26	17.59	20.69	23.78	24.39	25.00	25.62	26.22	26.83	29.82
27	16.96	20.05	23.13	23.74	24.35	24.96	25.57	26.17	29.15
28	16.34	19.42	22.48	23.09	23.70	24.31	24.92	25.52	28.49
29	15.71	18.78	21.84	22.45	23.05	23.66	24.26	24.87	27.82
30	15.09	18.15	21.20	21.80	22.41	23.02	23.62	24.22	27.16
31	14.46	17.52	20.56	21.16	21.77	22.37	22.97	23.57	26.50
32	13.84	16.89	19.92	20.52	21.13	21.73	22.33	22.92	25.85
33	13.22	16.26	19.29	19.89	20.49	21.09	21.68	22.28	25.20
34	12.60	15.64	18.66	19.25	19.85	20.45	21.05	21.64	24.54
35	11.99	15.02	18.02	18.62	19.22	19.82	20.41	21.00	23.90
36	11.38	14.39	17.40	17.99	18.59	19.18	19.77	20.36	23.25
37	10.76	13.78	16.77	17.36	17.96	18.55	19.14	19.73	22.61
38	10.15	13.16	16.15	16.74	17.33	17.92	18.51	19.10	21.97
39	9.54	12.54	15.53	16.12	16.71	17.30	17.88	18.47	21.33
40	8.79	11.73	14.66	15.23	15.81	16.39	16.96	17.54	20.34
41	8.19	11.13	14.05	14.62	15.20	15.78	16.35	16.92	19.72
42	7.60	10.53	13.44	14.02	14.59	15.17	15.74	16.32	19.10
43	7.01	9.93	12.84	13.41	13.99	14.57	15.13	15.70	18.48
44	6.41	9.34	12.24	12.81	13.39	13.96	14.53	15.10	17.86
45	5.83	8.75	11.64	12.21	12.79	13.36	13.92	14.49	17.26
46	5.24	8.15	11.04	11.62	12.19	12.76	13.32	13.89	16.65
47	4.65	7.56	10.45	11.02	11.59	12.16	12.72	13.29	16.04
48	4.07	6.97	9.85	10.43	11.00	11.56	12.13	12.69	15.43
49	3.49	6.39	9.26	9.83	10.40	10.97	11.53	12.09	14.83
50	2.95	5.90	8.83	9.40	9.98	10.56	11.13	11.70	14.48
51	2.36	5.31	8.23	8.81	9.38	9.96	10.53	11.10	13.87
52	1.80	4.79	7.76	8.35	8.94	9.52	10.10	10.68	13.49
53	1.22	4.26	7.28	7.88	8.47	9.06	9.65	10.24	13.10
54	0.62	3.71	6.78	7.38	7.99	8.59	9.19	9.78	12.69

See introductory notes as regards claimants over 54 at date of trial

D E Level 2

Loss of earnings: disabled; employed; good GCSE level education or equivalent

Age	Male to retiring age								
	55	60	65	66	67	68	69	70	75
16	20.24	22.89	25.52	26.03	26.55	27.07	27.59	28.10	30.60
17	19.69	22.33	24.95	25.47	25.98	26.50	27.01	27.53	30.01
18	19.14	21.78	24.39	24.90	25.42	25.93	26.44	26.95	29.43
19	18.60	21.22	23.83	24.34	24.85	25.36	25.87	26.38	28.85
20	18.05	20.67	23.27	23.78	24.29	24.80	25.31	25.81	28.27
21	17.51	20.12	22.71	23.22	23.73	24.24	24.74	25.25	27.70
22	16.97	19.58	22.16	22.66	23.17	23.68	24.18	24.68	27.12
23	16.43	19.03	21.60	22.11	22.61	23.12	23.62	24.12	26.55
24	15.90	18.49	21.05	21.55	22.06	22.56	23.06	23.56	25.98
25	15.36	17.94	20.50	21.00	21.50	22.01	22.50	23.00	25.41
26	14.83	17.40	19.95	20.45	20.95	21.46	21.95	22.45	24.85
27	14.29	16.86	19.40	19.90	20.40	20.90	21.40	21.89	24.28
28	13.76	16.33	18.86	19.36	19.85	20.35	20.84	21.34	23.72
29	13.23	15.79	18.32	18.81	19.31	19.81	20.29	20.79	23.16
30	11.69	14.03	16.35	16.81	17.26	17.72	18.17	18.62	20.79
31	11.21	13.54	15.86	16.31	16.76	17.22	17.67	18.11	20.28
32	10.72	13.05	15.36	15.81	16.27	16.72	17.17	17.61	19.77
33	10.24	12.57	14.87	15.32	15.77	16.23	16.67	17.12	19.26
34	9.77	12.09	14.38	14.83	15.28	15.73	16.17	16.62	18.76
35	8.68	10.85	12.99	13.41	13.83	14.25	14.66	15.07	17.07
36	8.23	10.40	12.53	12.95	13.37	13.79	14.20	14.61	16.60
37	7.79	9.95	12.08	12.50	12.92	13.33	13.74	14.16	16.13
38	7.35	9.51	11.63	12.05	12.46	12.88	13.29	13.70	15.67
39	6.91	9.06	11.18	11.60	12.01	12.43	12.84	13.24	15.21
40	6.47	8.62	10.74	11.15	11.56	11.98	12.39	12.79	14.75
41	6.04	8.18	10.29	10.71	11.12	11.53	11.94	12.35	14.30
42	5.60	7.74	9.85	10.26	10.67	11.09	11.49	11.90	13.85
43	5.16	7.30	9.41	9.82	10.23	10.64	11.05	11.45	13.40
44	4.73	6.87	8.97	9.38	9.79	10.20	10.61	11.01	12.95
45	4.40	6.58	8.73	9.15	9.57	9.99	10.40	10.82	12.80
46	3.96	6.14	8.29	8.70	9.12	9.54	9.95	10.37	12.34
47	3.52	5.70	7.84	8.26	8.68	9.10	9.51	9.92	11.89
48	3.08	5.25	7.40	7.82	8.23	8.65	9.06	9.47	11.44
49	2.64	4.81	6.96	7.37	7.79	8.21	8.62	9.03	10.99
50	2.30	4.57	6.81	7.25	7.68	8.12	8.55	8.97	11.02
51	1.84	4.12	6.35	6.79	7.23	7.66	8.09	8.51	10.56
52	1.38	3.66	5.89	6.33	6.77	7.20	7.63	8.05	10.10
53	0.92	3.20	5.44	5.87	6.31	6.75	7.17	7.60	9.64
54	0.47	2.80	5.09	5.54	5.98	6.43	6.86	7.30	9.38

See introductory notes as regards claimants over 54 at date of trial

Age	Female to retiring age								
	55	60	65	66	67	68	69	70	75
16	15.87	17.97	20.07	20.48	20.90	21.32	21.73	22.15	24.20
17	15.44	17.53	19.62	20.04	20.46	20.87	21.29	21.70	23.74
18	15.01	17.10	19.19	19.60	20.02	20.43	20.84	21.26	23.29
19	14.58	16.67	18.75	19.16	19.58	19.99	20.40	20.81	22.84
20	14.52	16.65	18.78	19.20	19.63	20.05	20.47	20.89	22.96
21	14.08	16.21	18.34	18.76	19.18	19.60	20.02	20.44	22.50
22	13.65	15.77	17.89	18.31	18.73	19.15	19.57	19.99	22.04
23	13.22	15.34	17.44	17.86	18.28	18.70	19.12	19.54	21.58
24	12.79	14.90	17.00	17.42	17.84	18.26	18.67	19.09	21.13
25	12.98	15.19	17.39	17.83	18.26	18.70	19.14	19.57	21.71
26	12.52	14.73	16.93	17.36	17.80	18.24	18.67	19.10	21.23
27	12.08	14.28	16.46	16.90	17.33	17.77	18.20	18.63	20.75
28	11.63	13.82	16.01	16.44	16.87	17.31	17.74	18.17	20.28
29	11.18	13.37	15.55	15.98	16.41	16.84	17.27	17.70	19.81
30	10.74	12.92	15.09	15.52	15.95	16.38	16.81	17.24	19.34
31	10.29	12.47	14.64	15.07	15.50	15.93	16.35	16.78	18.87
32	9.85	12.02	14.18	14.61	15.04	15.47	15.89	16.32	18.40
33	9.41	11.58	13.73	14.16	14.59	15.01	15.44	15.86	17.94
34	8.97	11.13	13.28	13.71	14.13	14.56	14.98	15.41	17.47
35	8.94	11.20	13.44	13.89	14.33	14.78	15.22	15.66	17.82
36	8.48	10.73	12.98	13.42	13.86	14.31	14.75	15.18	17.34
37	8.03	10.27	12.51	12.95	13.39	13.84	14.27	14.71	16.86
38	7.57	9.81	12.04	12.48	12.93	13.37	13.80	14.24	16.38
39	7.11	9.35	11.58	12.02	12.46	12.90	13.34	13.77	15.91
40	7.27	9.71	12.13	12.61	13.09	13.57	14.04	14.52	16.83
41	6.78	9.21	11.63	12.10	12.58	13.06	13.53	14.01	16.32
42	6.29	8.71	11.13	11.60	12.08	12.56	13.03	13.50	15.81
43	5.80	8.22	10.63	11.10	11.58	12.05	12.52	12.99	15.30
44	5.31	7.73	10.13	10.60	11.08	11.55	12.02	12.49	14.78
45	5.13	7.69	10.24	10.74	11.24	11.75	12.24	12.74	15.17
46	4.61	7.17	9.71	10.21	10.72	11.22	11.72	12.21	14.64
47	4.09	6.65	9.19	9.69	10.19	10.69	11.19	11.68	14.10
48	3.58	6.13	8.66	9.17	9.67	10.17	10.66	11.16	13.57
49	3.07	5.62	8.14	8.65	9.15	9.65	10.14	10.63	13.04
50	2.70	5.40	8.08	8.61	9.14	9.66	10.19	10.71	13.25
51	2.24	5.04	7.81	8.36	8.91	9.45	9.99	10.53	13.17
52	1.74	4.63	7.51	8.07	8.64	9.20	9.76	10.32	13.04
53	1.22	4.26	7.28	7.88	8.47	9.06	9.65	10.24	13.10
54	0.64	3.83	7.00	7.62	8.25	8.87	9.48	10.10	13.09

See introductory notes as regards claimants over 54 at date of trial

D E Level 1

Loss of earnings: disabled; employed; education below good GCSE level

Age	Male to retiring age								
	55	60	65	66	67	68	69	70	75
16	11.74	13.28	14.80	15.10	15.40	15.70	16.00	16.30	17.75
17	11.42	12.95	14.47	14.77	15.07	15.37	15.67	15.96	17.41
18	11.10	12.63	14.14	14.44	14.74	15.04	15.34	15.63	17.07
19	10.79	12.31	13.82	14.12	14.41	14.71	15.01	15.30	16.73
20	12.27	14.06	15.82	16.17	16.52	16.86	17.21	17.55	19.22
21	11.91	13.68	15.44	15.79	16.13	16.48	16.82	17.17	18.83
22	11.54	13.31	15.07	15.41	15.75	16.10	16.44	16.78	18.44
23	11.17	12.94	14.69	15.03	15.38	15.72	16.06	16.40	18.05
24	10.81	12.57	14.31	14.66	15.00	15.34	15.68	16.02	17.67
25	11.37	13.28	15.17	15.54	15.91	16.29	16.65	17.02	18.80
26	10.97	12.88	14.76	15.13	15.50	15.88	16.24	16.61	18.39
27	10.57	12.48	14.36	14.73	15.10	15.47	15.83	16.20	17.97
28	10.18	12.08	13.95	14.32	14.69	15.06	15.42	15.79	17.55
29	9.79	11.68	13.55	13.92	14.29	14.66	15.02	15.38	17.14
30	8.89	10.68	12.44	12.79	13.13	13.48	13.82	14.16	15.82
31	8.53	10.30	12.06	12.41	12.76	13.10	13.44	13.78	15.43
32	8.16	9.93	11.69	12.03	12.38	12.72	13.06	13.40	15.04
33	7.79	9.57	11.32	11.66	12.00	12.35	12.68	13.02	14.66
34	7.43	9.20	10.94	11.28	11.63	11.97	12.31	12.65	14.27
35	7.07	8.83	10.57	10.91	11.25	11.60	11.93	12.27	13.89
36	6.70	8.46	10.20	10.54	10.88	11.22	11.56	11.89	13.51
37	6.34	8.10	9.83	10.17	10.51	10.85	11.19	11.52	13.13
38	5.99	7.74	9.47	9.81	10.14	10.48	10.82	11.15	12.76
39	5.62	7.37	9.10	9.44	9.78	10.12	10.45	10.78	12.38
40	5.27	7.02	8.74	9.08	9.41	9.75	10.08	10.41	12.01
41	4.91	6.66	8.38	8.71	9.05	9.39	9.72	10.05	11.64
42	4.56	6.30	8.02	8.35	8.69	9.02	9.35	9.68	11.27
43	4.20	5.94	7.66	7.99	8.33	8.66	8.99	9.32	10.91
44	3.85	5.59	7.30	7.64	7.97	8.30	8.63	8.96	10.54
45	3.60	5.39	7.14	7.49	7.83	8.17	8.51	8.85	10.47
46	3.24	5.02	6.78	7.12	7.47	7.81	8.14	8.48	10.10
47	2.88	4.66	6.42	6.76	7.10	7.44	7.78	8.11	9.73
48	2.52	4.30	6.05	6.39	6.74	7.08	7.41	7.75	9.36
49	2.16	3.94	5.69	6.03	6.38	6.72	7.05	7.39	8.99
50	1.90	3.78	5.63	5.99	6.35	6.71	7.06	7.41	9.10
51	1.52	3.40	5.25	5.61	5.97	6.33	6.68	7.03	8.72
52	1.17	3.10	5.00	5.37	5.74	6.11	6.47	6.83	8.56
53	0.80	2.78	4.73	5.11	5.49	5.87	6.24	6.61	8.38
54	0.41	2.44	4.44	4.83	5.22	5.61	5.99	6.37	8.18

See introductory notes as regards claimants over 54 at date of trial

Age	Female to retiring age								
	55	60	65	66	67	68	69	70	75
16	8.95	10.14	11.32	11.55	11.79	12.03	12.26	12.49	13.65
17	8.71	9.89	11.07	11.31	11.54	11.78	12.01	12.24	13.39
18	8.47	9.64	10.82	11.06	11.29	11.53	11.76	11.99	13.14
19	8.23	9.40	10.58	10.81	11.04	11.28	11.51	11.74	12.88
20	7.99	9.16	10.33	10.56	10.79	11.03	11.26	11.49	12.63
21	7.75	8.92	10.08	10.32	10.55	10.78	11.01	11.24	12.38
22	7.51	8.67	9.84	10.07	10.30	10.53	10.76	10.99	12.12
23	7.27	8.43	9.59	9.82	10.06	10.29	10.52	10.74	11.87
24	7.03	8.20	9.35	9.58	9.81	10.04	10.27	10.50	11.62
25	7.11	8.32	9.52	9.76	10.00	10.24	10.48	10.72	11.89
26	6.86	8.07	9.27	9.51	9.75	9.99	10.22	10.46	11.62
27	6.61	7.82	9.02	9.25	9.49	9.73	9.97	10.20	11.36
28	6.37	7.57	8.77	9.00	9.24	9.48	9.71	9.95	11.10
29	6.12	7.32	8.51	8.75	8.99	9.22	9.46	9.69	10.85
30	6.90	8.31	9.70	9.98	10.26	10.53	10.81	11.08	12.43
31	6.62	8.02	9.41	9.68	9.96	10.24	10.51	10.79	12.13
32	6.33	7.73	9.12	9.39	9.67	9.94	10.22	10.49	11.83
33	6.05	7.44	8.83	9.10	9.38	9.65	9.92	10.20	11.53
34	5.77	7.16	8.54	8.81	9.09	9.36	9.63	9.90	11.23
35	6.30	7.89	9.47	9.78	10.10	10.41	10.72	11.03	12.56
36	5.98	7.56	9.14	9.45	9.77	10.08	10.39	10.70	12.22
37	5.65	7.24	8.81	9.12	9.44	9.75	10.06	10.37	11.88
38	5.33	6.91	8.48	8.80	9.11	9.42	9.73	10.03	11.54
39	5.01	6.59	8.16	8.47	8.78	9.09	9.40	9.70	11.21
40	5.15	6.87	8.59	8.93	9.27	9.61	9.94	10.28	11.92
41	4.80	6.52	8.23	8.57	8.91	9.25	9.59	9.92	11.56
42	4.45	6.17	7.88	8.22	8.56	8.89	9.23	9.56	11.20
43	4.11	5.82	7.53	7.86	8.20	8.54	8.87	9.20	10.84
44	3.76	5.47	7.17	7.51	7.85	8.18	8.52	8.85	10.47
45	4.02	6.03	8.03	8.42	8.82	9.21	9.60	9.99	11.90
46	3.61	5.62	7.62	8.01	8.40	8.80	9.19	9.58	11.48
47	3.21	5.22	7.21	7.60	7.99	8.39	8.78	9.16	11.06
48	2.80	4.81	6.80	7.19	7.58	7.98	8.36	8.75	10.64
49	2.40	4.40	6.39	6.78	7.17	7.57	7.95	8.34	10.23
50	2.25	4.50	6.73	7.17	7.61	8.05	8.49	8.92	11.04
51	1.88	4.23	6.56	7.02	7.47	7.93	8.39	8.84	11.05
52	1.50	4.00	6.47	6.96	7.45	7.93	8.42	8.90	11.25
53	1.06	3.70	6.32	6.84	7.36	7.88	8.39	8.90	11.38
54	0.57	3.41	6.23	6.79	7.34	7.90	8.45	8.99	11.66

See introductory notes as regards claimants over 54 at date of trial

D NE Level 3

Loss of earnings: disabled; not employed; degree level education or equivalent

Age	Male to retiring age 55	60	65	66	67	68	69	70	75
16	See introductory notes								
17									
18									
19									
20	18.05	20.67	23.27	23.78	24.29	24.80	25.31	25.81	28.27
21	17.51	20.12	22.71	23.22	23.73	24.24	24.74	25.25	27.70
22	16.97	19.58	22.16	22.66	23.17	23.68	24.18	24.68	27.12
23	16.43	19.03	21.60	22.11	22.61	23.12	23.62	24.12	26.55
24	15.90	18.49	21.05	21.55	22.06	22.56	23.06	23.56	25.98
25	11.67	13.63	15.58	15.96	16.34	16.73	17.10	17.48	19.31
26	11.27	13.22	15.16	15.54	15.92	16.31	16.68	17.06	18.88
27	10.86	12.81	14.74	15.13	15.51	15.89	16.26	16.64	18.45
28	10.46	12.41	14.33	14.71	15.09	15.47	15.84	16.21	18.03
29	10.05	12.00	13.92	14.30	14.67	15.05	15.42	15.80	17.60
30	9.91	11.90	13.86	14.25	14.64	15.02	15.40	15.78	17.63
31	9.50	11.48	13.44	13.83	14.21	14.60	14.98	15.36	17.20
32	9.09	11.07	13.03	13.41	13.79	14.18	14.55	14.93	16.76
33	8.69	10.66	12.61	12.99	13.37	13.76	14.13	14.51	16.33
34	8.28	10.25	12.19	12.57	12.96	13.34	13.71	14.09	15.90
35	8.08	10.09	12.08	12.47	12.86	13.25	13.64	14.02	15.88
36	7.66	9.67	11.66	12.05	12.44	12.83	13.21	13.59	15.44
37	7.25	9.26	11.24	11.63	12.01	12.40	12.78	13.17	15.01
38	6.84	8.84	10.82	11.21	11.59	11.98	12.36	12.74	14.58
39	6.43	8.43	10.40	10.79	11.17	11.56	11.94	12.32	14.15
40	5.12	6.82	8.49	8.82	9.14	9.47	9.79	10.12	11.67
41	4.77	6.47	8.14	8.46	8.79	9.12	9.44	9.76	11.31
42	4.43	6.12	7.79	8.11	8.44	8.77	9.09	9.41	10.95
43	4.08	5.77	7.44	7.77	8.09	8.42	8.74	9.05	10.59
44	3.74	5.43	7.09	7.42	7.74	8.07	8.39	8.70	10.24
45	2.70	4.04	5.36	5.62	5.87	6.13	6.38	6.64	7.85
46	2.43	3.77	5.08	5.34	5.60	5.86	6.11	6.36	7.57
47	2.16	3.50	4.81	5.07	5.33	5.58	5.83	6.09	7.30
48	1.89	3.22	4.54	4.80	5.05	5.31	5.56	5.81	7.02
49	1.62	2.95	4.27	4.52	4.78	5.04	5.29	5.54	6.74
50	1.25	2.49	3.70	3.94	4.18	4.41	4.65	4.88	5.99
51	0.96	2.15	3.31	3.54	3.77	4.00	4.22	4.44	5.51
52	0.69	1.83	2.95	3.17	3.38	3.60	3.81	4.03	5.05
53	0.44	1.53	2.60	2.81	3.02	3.23	3.43	3.63	4.61
54	0.20	1.19	2.17	2.36	2.55	2.73	2.92	3.11	3.99

See introductory notes as regards claimants over 54 at date of trial

Age	Female to retiring age 55	60	65	66	67	68	69	70	75
16	See introductory notes								
17									
18									
19									
20	19.97	22.90	25.82	26.40	26.99	27.57	28.15	28.73	31.57
21	19.37	22.29	25.21	25.79	26.37	26.95	27.53	28.11	30.94
22	18.77	21.69	24.60	25.17	25.75	26.33	26.91	27.48	30.31
23	18.18	21.09	23.99	24.56	25.14	25.72	26.29	26.86	29.68
24	17.58	20.49	23.38	23.95	24.53	25.10	25.67	26.25	29.05
25	15.14	17.72	20.29	20.80	21.31	21.82	22.32	22.83	25.32
26	14.61	17.18	19.75	20.26	20.76	21.27	21.78	22.29	24.76
27	14.09	16.66	19.21	19.72	20.22	20.73	21.23	21.74	24.21
28	13.57	16.13	18.67	19.18	19.68	20.19	20.69	21.19	23.66
29	13.05	15.60	18.14	18.64	19.15	19.65	20.15	20.65	23.11
30	11.25	13.53	15.81	16.26	16.71	17.16	17.61	18.06	20.26
31	10.78	13.06	15.33	15.78	16.23	16.68	17.13	17.58	19.76
32	10.32	12.59	14.86	15.31	15.76	16.21	16.65	17.09	19.28
33	9.86	12.13	14.38	14.83	15.28	15.73	16.17	16.61	18.79
34	9.40	11.66	13.91	14.36	14.81	15.25	15.69	16.14	18.30
35	8.33	10.43	12.53	12.94	13.36	13.77	14.18	14.59	16.61
36	7.90	10.00	12.09	12.50	12.92	13.33	13.74	14.15	16.16
37	7.48	9.57	11.66	12.07	12.48	12.89	13.30	13.71	15.71
38	7.05	9.14	11.22	11.63	12.04	12.46	12.86	13.27	15.26
39	6.63	8.72	10.79	11.20	11.61	12.02	12.43	12.83	14.82
40	5.30	7.08	8.84	9.19	9.54	9.89	10.24	10.58	12.27
41	4.94	6.72	8.48	8.83	9.17	9.52	9.87	10.21	11.90
42	4.59	6.35	8.11	8.46	8.81	9.16	9.50	9.85	11.53
43	4.23	5.99	7.75	8.09	8.44	8.79	9.13	9.47	11.15
44	3.87	5.64	7.39	7.73	8.08	8.42	8.77	9.11	10.78
45	2.61	3.92	5.22	5.47	5.73	5.99	6.24	6.49	7.74
46	2.35	3.65	4.95	5.21	5.46	5.72	5.97	6.23	7.46
47	2.09	3.39	4.69	4.94	5.20	5.45	5.70	5.96	7.19
48	1.82	3.13	4.42	4.67	4.93	5.18	5.44	5.69	6.92
49	1.56	2.86	4.15	4.41	4.66	4.92	5.17	5.42	6.65
50	1.05	2.10	3.14	3.35	3.55	3.76	3.96	4.16	5.15
51	0.76	1.71	2.65	2.84	3.02	3.21	3.39	3.57	4.47
52	0.54	1.44	2.33	2.51	2.68	2.86	3.03	3.20	4.05
53	0.34	1.19	2.03	2.19	2.36	2.53	2.69	2.85	3.65
54	0.15	0.90	1.64	1.79	1.93	2.08	2.22	2.37	3.07

See introductory notes as regards claimants over 54 at date of trial

D NE Level 2

Loss of earnings: disabled; not employed; good GCSE level education or equivalent

Age	Male to retiring age								
	55	60	65	66	67	68	69	70	75
16	19.03	21.52	23.98	24.47	24.96	25.45	25.93	26.41	28.76
17	18.51	20.99	23.45	23.94	24.42	24.91	25.39	25.87	28.21
18	17.99	20.47	22.92	23.41	23.89	24.38	24.85	25.33	27.66
19	17.48	19.95	22.40	22.88	23.36	23.84	24.32	24.80	27.12
20	16.25	18.60	20.94	21.40	21.86	22.32	22.77	23.23	25.44
21	15.76	18.11	20.44	20.90	21.35	21.81	22.27	22.72	24.93
22	15.27	17.62	19.94	20.39	20.85	21.31	21.76	22.21	24.41
23	14.79	17.13	19.44	19.89	20.35	20.81	21.26	21.71	23.90
24	14.31	16.64	18.95	19.40	19.85	20.31	20.75	21.20	23.38
25	12.29	14.35	16.40	16.80	17.20	17.61	18.00	18.40	20.33
26	11.86	13.92	15.96	16.36	16.76	17.16	17.56	17.96	19.88
27	11.43	13.49	15.52	15.92	16.32	16.72	17.12	17.51	19.42
28	11.01	13.06	15.08	15.48	15.88	16.28	16.68	17.07	18.98
29	10.58	12.63	14.65	15.05	15.45	15.84	16.24	16.63	18.53
30	8.13	9.76	11.38	11.69	12.01	12.33	12.64	12.95	14.46
31	7.80	9.42	11.03	11.35	11.66	11.98	12.29	12.60	14.11
32	7.46	9.08	10.69	11.00	11.32	11.63	11.94	12.25	13.75
33	7.13	8.75	10.35	10.66	10.97	11.29	11.60	11.91	13.40
34	6.79	8.41	10.00	10.32	10.63	10.94	11.25	11.56	13.05
35	5.05	6.31	7.55	7.79	8.04	8.28	8.52	8.76	9.92
36	4.79	6.05	7.29	7.53	7.77	8.02	8.26	8.50	9.65
37	4.53	5.79	7.02	7.27	7.51	7.75	7.99	8.23	9.38
38	4.28	5.53	6.76	7.00	7.25	7.49	7.73	7.97	9.11
39	4.02	5.27	6.50	6.74	6.98	7.23	7.46	7.70	8.85
40	3.16	4.21	5.24	5.45	5.65	5.85	6.05	6.25	7.21
41	2.95	3.99	5.03	5.23	5.43	5.63	5.83	6.03	6.98
42	2.73	3.78	4.81	5.01	5.21	5.41	5.61	5.81	6.76
43	2.52	3.57	4.59	4.80	5.00	5.20	5.40	5.59	6.54
44	2.31	3.35	4.38	4.58	4.78	4.98	5.18	5.38	6.32
45	1.70	2.54	3.37	3.54	3.70	3.86	4.02	4.18	4.94
46	1.53	2.37	3.20	3.36	3.53	3.69	3.85	4.01	4.77
47	1.36	2.20	3.03	3.19	3.35	3.51	3.67	3.83	4.59
48	1.19	2.03	2.86	3.02	3.18	3.34	3.50	3.66	4.42
49	1.02	1.86	2.69	2.85	3.01	3.17	3.33	3.49	4.25
50	0.80	1.59	2.37	2.52	2.67	2.82	2.97	3.12	3.83
51	0.60	1.34	2.07	2.21	2.36	2.50	2.64	2.78	3.44
52	0.39	1.03	1.67	1.79	1.91	2.04	2.16	2.28	2.85
53	0.26	0.90	1.54	1.66	1.78	1.91	2.03	2.15	2.72
54	0.12	0.72	1.30	1.41	1.53	1.64	1.75	1.86	2.40

See introductory notes as regards claimants over 54 at date of trial

Age	Female to retiring age								
	55	60	65	66	67	68	69	70	75
16	13.83	15.66	17.49	17.86	18.22	18.59	18.95	19.31	21.09
17	13.46	15.28	17.11	17.47	17.83	18.20	18.56	18.92	20.70
18	13.08	14.91	16.73	17.09	17.45	17.81	18.17	18.53	20.30
19	12.71	14.53	16.34	16.70	17.07	17.43	17.79	18.15	19.91
20	11.25	12.91	14.55	14.88	15.21	15.54	15.86	16.19	17.79
21	10.92	12.56	14.21	14.54	14.86	15.19	15.51	15.84	17.44
22	10.58	12.22	13.86	14.19	14.52	14.84	15.17	15.49	17.08
23	10.25	11.89	13.52	13.84	14.17	14.50	14.82	15.14	16.73
24	9.91	11.55	13.18	13.50	13.82	14.15	14.47	14.79	16.37
25	9.58	11.21	12.83	13.16	13.48	13.80	14.12	14.45	16.02
26	9.24	10.87	12.49	12.81	13.14	13.46	13.78	14.10	15.67
27	8.91	10.54	12.15	12.47	12.79	13.12	13.43	13.75	15.32
28	8.58	10.20	11.81	12.13	12.45	12.77	13.09	13.41	14.97
29	8.26	9.87	11.48	11.79	12.11	12.43	12.75	13.07	14.62
30	7.93	9.54	11.14	11.46	11.77	12.09	12.41	12.73	14.27
31	7.60	9.20	10.80	11.12	11.44	11.75	12.07	12.38	13.93
32	7.27	8.87	10.47	10.78	11.10	11.42	11.73	12.04	13.58
33	6.95	8.54	10.13	10.45	10.77	11.08	11.39	11.71	13.24
34	6.62	8.22	9.80	10.12	10.43	10.75	11.06	11.37	12.90
35	5.69	7.13	8.55	8.84	9.12	9.40	9.69	9.97	11.34
36	5.40	6.83	8.26	8.54	8.82	9.10	9.38	9.66	11.03
37	5.11	6.54	7.96	8.24	8.52	8.80	9.08	9.36	10.73
38	4.82	6.24	7.66	7.94	8.23	8.51	8.78	9.06	10.42
39	4.53	5.95	7.37	7.65	7.93	8.21	8.49	8.76	10.12
40	3.64	4.85	6.06	6.30	6.54	6.78	7.02	7.26	8.42
41	3.39	4.61	5.81	6.05	6.29	6.53	6.77	7.00	8.16
42	3.14	4.36	5.56	5.80	6.04	6.28	6.51	6.75	7.90
43	2.90	4.11	5.31	5.55	5.79	6.03	6.26	6.50	7.65
44	2.65	3.86	5.06	5.30	5.54	5.78	6.01	6.25	7.39
45	1.91	2.87	3.81	4.00	4.19	4.38	4.56	4.75	5.65
46	1.72	2.67	3.62	3.80	3.99	4.18	4.36	4.55	5.45
47	1.52	2.48	3.42	3.61	3.80	3.98	4.17	4.35	5.25
48	1.33	2.28	3.23	3.42	3.60	3.79	3.97	4.16	5.06
49	1.14	2.09	3.03	3.22	3.41	3.59	3.78	3.96	4.86
50	0.75	1.50	2.24	2.39	2.54	2.68	2.83	2.97	3.68
51	0.56	1.26	1.95	2.09	2.23	2.36	2.50	2.63	3.29
52	0.36	0.96	1.55	1.67	1.79	1.90	2.02	2.14	2.70
53	0.22	0.77	1.31	1.42	1.53	1.63	1.74	1.85	2.36
54	0.09	0.54	0.98	1.07	1.16	1.25	1.33	1.42	1.84

See introductory notes as regards claimants over 54 at date of trial

D NE Level 1

Loss of earnings: disabled; not employed; education below good GCSE level

Age	Male to retiring age									Age	Female to retiring age								
	55	60	65	66	67	68	69	70	75		55	60	65	66	67	68	69	70	75
16	10.12	11.45	12.76	13.02	13.28	13.54	13.79	14.05	15.30	**16**	7.32	8.29	9.26	9.45	9.65	9.84	10.03	10.22	11.17
17	9.85	11.17	12.48	12.73	12.99	13.25	13.51	13.76	15.01	**17**	7.12	8.09	9.06	9.25	9.44	9.63	9.83	10.02	10.96
18	9.57	10.89	12.19	12.45	12.71	12.97	13.22	13.48	14.72	**18**	6.93	7.89	8.86	9.05	9.24	9.43	9.62	9.81	10.75
19	9.30	10.61	11.91	12.17	12.43	12.68	12.94	13.19	14.43	**19**	6.73	7.69	8.65	8.84	9.03	9.23	9.42	9.61	10.54
20	8.66	9.92	11.17	11.41	11.66	11.90	12.15	12.39	13.57	**20**	5.81	6.66	7.51	7.68	7.85	8.02	8.19	8.36	9.18
21	8.40	9.66	10.90	11.14	11.39	11.63	11.88	12.12	13.29	**21**	5.63	6.48	7.33	7.50	7.67	7.84	8.01	8.18	9.00
22	8.15	9.40	10.63	10.88	11.12	11.37	11.61	11.85	13.02	**22**	5.46	6.31	7.16	7.32	7.49	7.66	7.83	8.00	8.82
23	7.89	9.13	10.37	10.61	10.85	11.10	11.34	11.58	12.74	**23**	5.29	6.13	6.98	7.15	7.31	7.48	7.65	7.81	8.63
24	7.63	8.87	10.10	10.34	10.59	10.83	11.07	11.31	12.47	**24**	5.12	5.96	6.80	6.97	7.13	7.30	7.47	7.64	8.45
25	7.07	8.25	9.43	9.66	9.89	10.12	10.35	10.58	11.69	**25**	4.94	5.79	6.62	6.79	6.96	7.12	7.29	7.46	8.27
26	6.82	8.00	9.18	9.41	9.64	9.87	10.10	10.32	11.43	**26**	4.77	5.61	6.45	6.61	6.78	6.95	7.11	7.28	8.09
27	6.57	7.76	8.92	9.15	9.38	9.62	9.84	10.07	11.17	**27**	4.60	5.44	6.27	6.44	6.60	6.77	6.93	7.10	7.91
28	6.33	7.51	8.67	8.90	9.13	9.36	9.59	9.81	10.91	**28**	4.43	5.27	6.10	6.26	6.43	6.59	6.76	6.92	7.72
29	6.09	7.26	8.42	8.65	8.88	9.11	9.34	9.56	10.65	**29**	4.26	5.09	5.92	6.09	6.25	6.42	6.58	6.74	7.55
30	5.59	6.71	7.82	8.04	8.26	8.47	8.69	8.90	9.94	**30**	3.84	4.61	5.39	5.54	5.70	5.85	6.00	6.16	6.91
31	5.36	6.48	7.58	7.80	8.02	8.24	8.45	8.66	9.70	**31**	3.68	4.45	5.23	5.38	5.53	5.69	5.84	5.99	6.74
32	5.13	6.24	7.35	7.56	7.78	8.00	8.21	8.42	9.46	**32**	3.52	4.29	5.07	5.22	5.37	5.52	5.68	5.83	6.57
33	4.90	6.01	7.11	7.33	7.54	7.76	7.97	8.19	9.21	**33**	3.36	4.13	4.90	5.06	5.21	5.36	5.51	5.66	6.41
34	4.67	5.78	6.88	7.09	7.31	7.52	7.74	7.95	8.97	**34**	3.20	3.98	4.74	4.90	5.05	5.20	5.35	5.50	6.24
35	3.84	4.79	5.74	5.92	6.11	6.29	6.48	6.66	7.54	**35**	2.84	3.56	4.28	4.42	4.56	4.70	4.84	4.98	5.67
36	3.64	4.59	5.54	5.72	5.91	6.09	6.27	6.46	7.33	**36**	2.70	3.41	4.13	4.27	4.41	4.55	4.69	4.83	5.52
37	3.44	4.40	5.34	5.52	5.71	5.89	6.07	6.25	7.13	**37**	2.55	3.27	3.98	4.12	4.26	4.40	4.54	4.68	5.36
38	3.25	4.20	5.14	5.32	5.51	5.69	5.87	6.05	6.93	**38**	2.41	3.12	3.83	3.97	4.11	4.25	4.39	4.53	5.21
39	3.05	4.00	4.94	5.12	5.31	5.49	5.67	5.85	6.72	**39**	2.26	2.98	3.68	3.82	3.96	4.10	4.24	4.38	5.06
40	2.26	3.01	3.75	3.89	4.03	4.18	4.32	4.46	5.15	**40**	1.97	2.63	3.29	3.41	3.54	3.67	3.80	3.93	4.56
41	2.11	2.85	3.59	3.73	3.88	4.02	4.16	4.31	4.99	**41**	1.84	2.49	3.15	3.28	3.41	3.54	3.67	3.79	4.42
42	1.95	2.70	3.44	3.58	3.72	3.87	4.01	4.15	4.83	**42**	1.70	2.36	3.01	3.14	3.27	3.40	3.53	3.66	4.28
43	1.80	2.55	3.28	3.43	3.57	3.71	3.85	3.99	4.67	**43**	1.57	2.23	2.88	3.01	3.14	3.26	3.39	3.52	4.14
44	1.65	2.40	3.13	3.27	3.42	3.56	3.70	3.84	4.52	**44**	1.44	2.09	2.74	2.87	3.00	3.13	3.26	3.38	4.00
45	1.10	1.65	2.18	2.29	2.39	2.50	2.60	2.70	3.20	**45**	1.11	1.66	2.21	2.32	2.42	2.53	2.64	2.75	3.27
46	0.99	1.53	2.07	2.18	2.28	2.39	2.49	2.59	3.09	**46**	0.99	1.55	2.09	2.20	2.31	2.42	2.53	2.63	3.16
47	0.88	1.42	1.96	2.06	2.17	2.27	2.38	2.48	2.97	**47**	0.88	1.43	1.98	2.09	2.20	2.31	2.41	2.52	3.04
48	0.77	1.31	1.85	1.95	2.06	2.16	2.27	2.37	2.86	**48**	0.77	1.32	1.87	1.98	2.09	2.19	2.30	2.41	2.93
49	0.66	1.20	1.74	1.84	1.95	2.05	2.15	2.26	2.75	**49**	0.66	1.21	1.76	1.87	1.97	2.08	2.19	2.29	2.81
50	0.45	0.89	1.33	1.42	1.50	1.59	1.67	1.76	2.16	**50**	0.50	1.00	1.50	1.59	1.69	1.79	1.89	1.98	2.45
51	0.36	0.81	1.24	1.33	1.41	1.50	1.58	1.67	2.07	**51**	0.36	0.81	1.26	1.34	1.43	1.52	1.61	1.69	2.12
52	0.24	0.64	1.02	1.10	1.18	1.25	1.33	1.40	1.76	**52**	0.24	0.64	1.04	1.11	1.19	1.27	1.35	1.42	1.80
53	0.14	0.49	0.83	0.89	0.96	1.03	1.09	1.16	1.47	**53**	0.14	0.49	0.84	0.90	0.97	1.04	1.11	1.18	1.50
54	0.06	0.36	0.65	0.71	0.76	0.82	0.88	0.93	1.20	**54**	0.06	0.36	0.66	0.71	0.77	0.83	0.89	0.95	1.23

See introductory notes as regards claimants over 54 at date of trial

See introductory notes as regards claimants over 54 at date of trial

A5: Multipliers for fixed periods and at intervals

Introductory notes

1. The purpose of the table is to provide a means of calculating an appropriate multiplier which will produce the present day equivalent of a cost recurring, either continuously or at fixed intervals, over a given number of years. It does not allow for mortality or contingencies.

2. The tables are based on discount rates of -0.25, -0.75 and -1.5 per cent per annum. The Lord Chancellor fixed the discount rate, for England and Wales, under the Damages Act 1996 (from 5 August 2019) at -0.25 per cent, leaving open the possibility of a different rate in exceptional cases such as the effect of tax on large sums. In recent editions of this book, the range of discount rates was extended as a result of the decision in *Helmot v Simon.*[1] Readers requiring tables at 1 per cent per annum should refer to the 2013/14 edition, for tables at 2.5 per cent per annum to the 2016/17 edition and for tables at -1.75 per cent to the 2021/22 edition. In Scotland the rate is -0.75 per cent and in Northern Ireland from 22 March 2022 -1.5 per cent.

3. It is assumed that yearly loss is incurred at the *end* of each year in which the loss arises. (Continuous loss obviously accrues from day to day throughout the period. Weekly and monthly losses can in practice be treated as continuous.) For example:

   For expenditure assumed to recur every seven years the expenditure is shown as arising at the end of years seven, 14, and so on.

4. The table contains a number of columns: the number of years; the multiplier for a single payment in *n* years' time; that for a continuous loss over a period of *n* years; that for annual payments in the sense of a series of payments at intervals of one year; and those for payments at intervals of two, three, four and so on years.

5. The figures in the continuous column reproduce those in Table 36 of the Ogden Tables at a discount rate of -0.25 per cent, and hence make no allowance for mortality. For continuous loss for rest of life or up to a particular age, where due allowance should be made for mortality, the multiplier should be derived from Tables 1 to 18 of the Ogden Tables. In large and complex cases, where allowance for mortality could be material to the value of payments at fixed intervals, the advice of an actuary should be sought. Multipliers allowing for mortality are provided in A6 for situations where there is a payment for life but deferred for a number of years.

6. The multiplier for a single payment in *n* years' time (second column) is the same as the discount factor for deferment for the next *n* years.

7. The table shows a multiplier appropriate to each year in which expenditure is to be incurred, and also cumulative multipliers for expenditure up to the end of that year. For example, at -0.25 per cent discount:

   The multiplier for expenditure at the end of year 10 is 1.025. Thus the current lump sum required to provide £100 in 10 years' time is £102.50.

And similarly:

[1] [2020] EWCA Civ 1295.

- £100 a year continuously over the next 10 years has a present value of £1,013;
- £100 payable at the end of each of the next 10 years has a present value of £1,014;
- £100 payable at the end of two, four, six, eight and 10 years a present value of £508 (row 10, two-yearly column); and
- £100 payable at the end of three, six and nine years a present value of £305 (row nine, three-yearly column).

The cumulative multipliers do not include an immediate payment; where one is needed in addition to the recurring payments add 1.00 to the multiplier.

8. The multipliers have been rounded to two places of decimals. To use the table to value payments *for life* for a given periodicity, find the expectation of life from Table 1 or 2 of the Ogden Tables at 0.0 per cent. Then take the value in the relevant frequency column at this duration or at the nearest duration shorter than this duration which has a non-zero entry. If a different expectation of life is advised by an actuary or medical expert for an atypical case then that expectation of life should be used. As an example, for a 40 year-old female, the Ogden Table 2 expectation of life is 47.61 (also available from the table on page 12). The value of payments every four years would be 12.81, for every seven years would be 7.51 and for every 10 years would be 4.26.

Multipliers for life where there is evidence of life expectancy

9. In some cases there is medical evidence of the particular claimant's life expectancy. As more distant losses have higher present value, the possibility of dying earlier than expected has less effect on the multiplier than that of dying later than expected. The multiplier for life of someone whose life expectancy is *n* years will therefore be higher than the multiplier for a fixed period of *n* years. The difference varies with sex and age and can be quite significant at a discount rate of -0.25[2] per cent. It is recommended to find the equivalent age for the specified life expectancy, as recommended in paragraph 20 of the notes to the 7th edition of the Ogden Tables (Section A8 of the 2019/20 edition), and use the appropriate Ogden Tables at -0.25 per cent for that age.

10. If the conditions set out in the cases of *Sarwar v Ali*[3] and *Burton v Kingsbury*[4] for the estimation of life expectancy are met, then it is appropriate to adopt a multiplier from term certain tables (such as the tables in this section and in Tables 35 and 36 of the Ogden Tables) with no further adjustment for mortality. In all other cases an adjustment to the fixed term multipliers should be adopted for mortality.

Reduction of fixed term multipliers for mortality

11. For the reasons discussed above in relation to cases where there is evidence of life expectancy, in all cases where the period of loss is dependent on someone's life the multiplier for a fixed period will be lower than the true multiplier. In appropriate cases the fixed term multipliers can be increased by the method discussed in paragraph 20 of the notes to the 7th edition of the Ogden Tables (Section A8 of the 2019/20 edition), which calculates an equivalent age based on reduced life expectation.

[2] This relation holds only for life multipliers. Multipliers for fixed periods or up to a specified age will be lower if allowance is made for survival than if Tables 35 and 36 are used. It is still recommended to proceed by finding the equivalent age for the specified life expectancy but ensuring that the period for which the calculation is made is maintained.

[3] [2007] EWHC 2091 (QB).

[4] [2007] EWHC 2091 (QB).

12. For example:

The claimant is aged 53 and seven months. On the basis of evidence his life expectancy has been determined to be 30 years. For the first 12 years he will need care at £10,000 a year and will incur expenditure on equipment of £5,000 at the end of every four years (i.e. after four, eight and 12 years). For the remaining 18 years he will need care at £20,000 a year and will incur expenditure on equipment of £6,000 at the end of every three years (i.e. after 15, 18, 21, 24, 27 and 30 years).

For a continuous loss of 30 years (e.g. required to value the future care expenditure) the multipliers—from the continuous loss column of Table A5 at -0.25 per cent—are:

	First 12 years	Remaining 18 years[5]	30 years
Care:	12.18	18.98	31.16

The equivalent age to be adopted is calculated from interpolation of the 0% column in the life multipliers shown at Table 1 of the Ogden Tables, as follows:

54 year old multiplier for life at 0%	30.53
55 year old multiplier for life at 0%	29.55

$$\left(\frac{30.53 - 30.00}{30.53 - 29.55}\right) \times 55 + \left(\frac{30.00 - 29.55}{30.53 - 29.55}\right) \times 54 = 54.54$$

The life multiplier at a discount rate of -0.25 per cent for a male aged 54.54 is shown at Table 1 of the Ogden Tables to be 31.31. It is not 31.16 (the multiplier for a continuous loss for 30 years allowing only for compound interest), because the possibility of dying later than expected affects the multiplier more than the possibility of dying earlier. The fixed term multipliers for care are therefore too low and need to be increased by a factor of 31.31/31.16 = 100.48 per cent.

Multipliers for care (as set out above) adjusted for mortality (that is multiplied by 100.48 per cent):

	First 12 years	Remaining 18 years	30 years
Care:	12.24	19.07	31.31

For expenditure at fixed intervals (i.e. non-continuous) over a period of 30 years (i.e. required to value the future equipment expenditure) the multipliers—from the appropriate frequency of loss columns of Table A5 at -0.25 per cent—are:

	First 12 years[6]	Remaining 18 years[7]	30 years[8]
Equipment:	3.06	6.34	31.19

To allow for mortality these multipliers must be increased by 100.48 per cent as above.

[5] Calculated by subtraction, taking 12.18 for the first 12 years from 31.16 for 30 years.

[6] 12-year multiplier for four-yearly replacements.

[7] Calculated by subtraction: 30-year multiplier for three-yearly replacements 10.42 (Table A5) less 12-year multiplier for three-yearly replacements 4.08 (Table A5)—see point 13.

[8] 30-year multiplier for a one-yearly frequency of loss.

Multipliers for equipment adjusted for mortality (that is multiplied by 100.48 per cent):

	First 12 years	Remaining 18 years	30 years
Equipment:	3.07	6.37	31.34

Modifications

13. Multipliers for continuous loss for periods other than entire years can be obtained by interpolation:

    For continuous payments for 10 and 11 years the multipliers are 10.13 and 11.15. So, for weekly or monthly payments for 10 years three months (i.e. 10.25 years) the multiplier is:

    $10.13 + (10.25 - 10.00) \times (11.15 - 10.13) = 10.13 + (0.25 \times 1.02) = 10.38$

14. Multipliers for payments beginning after a deferred period can be derived by subtraction or by multiplying by a factor from the single payment column;

    multipliers for five-yearly payments for 15 and for 50 years are 3.08 and 10.72;

    so the multiplier for five-yearly payments from years 20 to 50 inclusive is $10.72 - 3.08 = 7.64$; multiplier for one payment after 18 years is 1.046;

    so the multiplier for five-yearly payments from years 38–68 inclusive is $7.64 \times 1.046 = 7.99$;

    multipliers allowing for mortality are provided in A6 for situations where there is a payment for life but deferred for a number of years.

15. Multipliers for irregular payments can be found by adding individual figures from the single payment column.

Multipliers at -0.25 per cent discount

n	Single payment	Continuous loss	Frequency of payments in years: 1	2	3	4	5	6	7	8	10	12	15	20
1	1.003	1.00	1.00											
2	1.005	2.01	2.01	1.01										
3	1.008	3.01	3.02		1.01									
4	1.010	4.02	4.03	2.02		1.01								
5	1.013	5.03	5.04				1.01							
6	1.015	6.05	6.05	3.03	2.02			1.02						
7	1.018	7.06	7.07						1.02					
8	1.020	8.08	8.09	4.05		2.03				1.02				
9	1.023	9.10	9.11		3.05									
10	1.025	10.13	10.14	5.08			2.04				1.03			
11	1.028	11.15	11.17											
12	1.030	12.18	12.20	6.11	4.08	3.06		2.05				1.03		
13	1.033	13.21	13.23											
14	1.036	14.25	14.27	7.14					2.05					
15	1.038	15.29	15.30		5.11		3.08						1.04	
16	1.041	16.32	16.35	8.18		4.10				2.06				
17	1.043	17.37	17.39											
18	1.046	18.41	18.43	9.23	6.16			3.09						
19	1.049	19.46	19.48											
20	1.051	20.51	20.53	10.28		5.15	4.13				2.08			1.05
21	1.054	21.56	21.59		7.21				3.11					
22	1.057	22.62	22.65	11.34										
23	1.059	23.67	23.70											
24	1.062	24.74	24.77	12.40	8.28	6.21		4.15		3.12		2.09		
25	1.065	25.80	25.83				5.19							
26	1.067	26.86	26.90	13.47										
27	1.070	27.93	27.97		9.35									
28	1.073	29.00	29.04	14.54		7.29			4.18					
29	1.075	30.08	30.12											
30	1.078	31.16	31.19	15.62	10.42		6.27	5.23			3.15		2.12	
31	1.081	32.23	32.27											
32	1.083	33.32	33.36	16.70		8.37				4.21				
33	1.086	34.40	34.44		11.51									
34	1.089	35.49	35.53	17.79										
35	1.092	36.58	36.62				7.36		5.27					
36	1.094	37.67	37.72	18.88	12.60	9.47		6.33				3.19		
37	1.097	38.77	38.82											
38	1.100	39.87	39.92	19.98										
39	1.103	40.97	41.02		13.71									
40	1.105	42.07	42.12	21.09		10.57	8.47			5.31	4.26			2.16
41	1.108	43.18	43.23											
42	1.111	44.29	44.34	22.20	14.82			7.44	6.38					
43	1.114	45.40	45.46											
44	1.116	46.51	46.57	23.32		11.69								
45	1.119	47.63	47.69		15.94		9.59						3.24	
46	1.122	48.75	48.81	24.44										
47	1.125	49.88	49.94											
48	1.128	51.00	51.07	25.57	17.06	12.81		8.56		6.44		4.31		
49	1.130	52.13	52.20						7.51					
50	1.133	53.26	53.33	26.70			10.72				5.39			
51	1.136	54.40	54.47		18.20									
52	1.139	55.54	55.61	27.84		13.95								
53	1.142	56.68	56.75											
54	1.145	57.82	57.89	28.98	19.35			9.71						
55	1.148	58.97	59.04				11.87							
56	1.150	60.11	60.19	30.13		15.10			8.66	7.59				
57	1.153	61.27	61.34		20.50									
58	1.156	62.42	62.50	31.29										
59	1.159	63.58	63.66											
60	1.162	64.74	64.82	32.45	21.66	16.27	13.03	10.87			6.56	5.48	4.40	3.32

Multipliers at -0.25 per cent discount

n	Single payment	Continuous loss	1	2	3	4	5	6	7	8	10	12	15	20
			Frequency of payments in years											
61	1.165	65.90	65.99											
62	1.168	67.07	67.15	33.62										
63	1.171	68.24	68.32		22.83				9.83					
64	1.174	69.41	69.50	34.79		17.44				8.76				
65	1.177	70.59	70.68				14.21							
66	1.180	71.76	71.85	35.97	24.01			12.05						
67	1.183	72.95	73.04											
68	1.186	74.13	74.22	37.16		18.63								
69	1.189	75.32	75.41		25.20									
70	1.192	76.51	76.60	38.35			15.40		11.03		7.75			
71	1.194	77.70	77.80											
72	1.197	78.90	78.99	39.55	26.40	19.82		13.25		9.96		6.67		
73	1.200	80.10	80.20											
74	1.203	81.30	81.40	40.75										
75	1.207	82.50	82.61		27.60		16.60						5.60	
76	1.210	83.71	83.81	41.96		21.03								
77	1.213	84.92	85.03						12.24					
78	1.216	86.14	86.24	43.18	28.82			14.46						
79	1.219	87.35	87.46											
80	1.222	88.57	88.68	44.40		22.25	17.83			11.18	8.97			4.54
81	1.225	89.80	89.91		30.04									
82	1.228	91.02	91.14	45.63										
83	1.231	92.25	92.37											
84	1.234	93.48	93.60	46.86	31.28	23.49		15.70	13.47			7.91		
85	1.237	94.72	94.84				19.06							
86	1.240	95.96	96.08	48.10										
87	1.243	97.20	97.32		32.52									
88	1.246	98.44	98.57	49.35		24.73				12.43				
89	1.250	99.69	99.82											
90	1.253	100.94	101.07	50.60	33.77		20.32	16.95			10.22		6.86	
91	1.256	102.20	102.33						14.73					
92	1.259	103.46	103.59	51.86		25.99								
93	1.262	104.72	104.85		35.04									
94	1.265	105.98	106.11	53.12										
95	1.268	107.25	107.38				21.58							
96	1.272	108.52	108.65	54.39	36.31	27.27		18.22		13.70		9.18		
97	1.275	109.79	109.93											
98	1.278	111.07	111.21	55.67					16.01					
99	1.281	112.35	112.49		37.59									
100	1.284	113.63	113.77	56.96		28.55	22.87				11.51			5.82

1. The single payment column is the appropriate multiplier for one payment in n years' time.
2. The continuous loss column is for loss accruing from day to day: in practice it is appropriate for weekly and monthly losses as well.
3. The column headed "1" is for a series of payments at yearly intervals at the end of each year for n years. If you want an immediate payment as well, add 1.
4. The remaining columns similarly show the multiplier for a series of payments at intervals of two, three, four and so on years.
5. Thus at -0.25 per cent discount £100 paid after 10 years has a present value of £102.50;
   - £100 a year continuously over the next 10 years has a present value of £1,013;
   - £100 at the end of each of the next 10 years has a present value of £1,014;
   - £100 at the end of two, four, six, eight and 10 years has a present value of £508 (row 10, two-yearly column);
   - £100 at the end of three, six and nine years has a present value of £305 (row 9, three-yearly column); and
   - £100 now and after two, four, six and eight years (but not the 10th year) has a present value of £505 (row 8, two-yearly column, plus one).

Multipliers at -0.75 per cent discount

	Single payment	Continuous loss	Frequency of payments in years											
n			1	2	3	4	5	6	7	8	10	12	15	20
1	1.008	1.00	1.01											
2	1.015	2.02	2.02	1.02										
3	1.023	3.03	3.05		1.02									
4	1.031	4.06	4.08	2.05		1.03								
5	1.038	5.10	5.11				1.04							
6	1.046	6.14	6.16	3.09	2.07			1.05						
7	1.054	7.19	7.21						1.05					
8	1.062	8.25	8.28	4.15		2.09				1.06				
9	1.070	9.31	9.35		3.14									
10	1.078	10.39	10.43	5.23			2.12				1.08			
11	1.086	11.47	11.51											
12	1.095	12.56	12.61	6.33	4.23	3.19		2.14				1.09		
13	1.103	13.66	13.71											
14	1.111	14.76	14.82	7.44					2.17					
15	1.120	15.88	15.94		5.35		3.24						1.12	
16	1.128	17.00	17.07	8.57		4.32				2.19				
17	1.137	18.14	18.20											
18	1.145	19.28	19.35	9.71	6.50			3.29						
19	1.154	20.43	20.50											
20	1.162	21.58	21.67	10.87		5.48	4.40				2.24			1.16
21	1.171	22.75	22.84		7.67				3.34					
22	1.180	23.93	24.02	12.05										
23	1.189	25.11	25.21											
24	1.198	26.30	26.40	13.25	8.87	6.68		4.48		3.39		2.29		
25	1.207	27.51	27.61				5.61							
26	1.216	28.72	28.83	14.47										
27	1.225	29.94	30.05		10.09									
28	1.235	31.17	31.29	15.70		7.91			4.57					
29	1.244	32.41	32.53											
30	1.253	33.66	33.78	16.96	11.35		6.86	5.74			3.49		2.37	
31	1.263	34.92	35.05											
32	1.272	36.18	36.32	18.23		9.18				4.66				
33	1.282	37.46	37.60		12.63									
34	1.292	38.75	38.89	19.52										
35	1.301	40.04	40.20				8.16		5.87					
36	1.311	41.35	41.51	20.83	13.94	10.49		7.05				3.60		
37	1.321	42.67	42.83											
38	1.331	43.99	44.16	22.16										
39	1.341	45.33	45.50		15.28									
40	1.351	46.68	46.85	23.51		11.85	9.51			6.01	4.85			2.51
41	1.362	48.03	48.21											
42	1.372	49.40	49.58	24.89	16.65			8.42	7.24					
43	1.382	50.78	50.97											
44	1.393	52.16	52.36	26.28		13.24								
45	1.403	53.56	53.76		18.06		10.92						3.78	
46	1.414	54.97	55.18	27.69										
47	1.425	56.39	56.60											
48	1.435	57.82	58.04	29.13	19.49	14.67		9.86		7.45		5.04		
49	1.446	59.26	59.48						8.69					
50	1.457	60.71	60.94	30.58			12.37				6.30			
51	1.468	62.17	62.41		20.96									
52	1.479	63.65	63.89	32.06		16.15								
53	1.490	65.13	65.38											
54	1.502	66.63	66.88	33.57	22.46			11.36						
55	1.513	68.14	68.39				13.89							
56	1.524	69.65	69.92	35.09		17.68			10.22	8.97				
57	1.536	71.18	71.45		24.00									
58	1.547	72.73	73.00	36.64										
59	1.559	74.28	74.56											
60	1.571	75.84	76.13	38.21	25.57	19.25	15.46	12.93			7.87	6.61	5.35	4.08

Multipliers at -0.75 per cent discount

	Single payment	Continuous loss	Frequency of payments in years											
n			**1**	**2**	**3**	**4**	**5**	**6**	**7**	**8**	**10**	**12**	**15**	**20**
61	1.583	77.42	77.71											
62	1.595	79.01	79.31	39.80										
63	1.607	80.61	80.91		27.17				11.82					
64	1.619	82.22	82.53	41.42		20.87				10.59				
65	1.631	83.85	84.16				17.09							
66	1.644	85.49	85.81	43.07	28.82			14.57						
67	1.656	87.14	87.46											
68	1.668	88.80	89.13	44.73		22.54								
69	1.681	90.47	90.81		30.50									
70	1.694	92.16	92.51	46.43			18.78		13.52		9.57			
71	1.707	93.86	94.21											
72	1.720	95.57	95.93	48.15	32.22	24.25		16.29		12.31		8.33		
73	1.732	97.30	97.67											
74	1.746	99.04	99.41	49.89										
75	1.759	100.79	101.17		33.98		20.54						7.11	
76	1.772	102.56	102.94	51.67		26.03								
77	1.785	104.33	104.73						15.30					
78	1.799	106.13	106.53	53.46	35.78			18.09						
79	1.813	107.93	108.34											
80	1.826	109.75	110.17	55.29		27.85	22.37			14.14	11.39			5.91
81	1.840	111.59	112.01		37.62									
82	1.854	113.43	113.86	57.14										
83	1.868	115.29	115.73											
84	1.882	117.17	117.61	59.03	39.50	29.74		19.97	17.18			10.21		
85	1.896	119.06	119.51				24.26							
86	1.911	120.96	121.42	60.94										
87	1.925	122.88	123.34		41.42									
88	1.940	124.81	125.28	62.88		31.67				16.08				
89	1.954	126.76	127.24											
90	1.969	128.72	129.20	64.85	43.39		26.23	21.94			13.36		9.07	
91	1.984	130.70	131.19						19.17					
92	1.999	132.69	133.19	66.84		33.67								
93	2.014	134.69	135.20		45.41									
94	2.029	136.72	137.23	68.87										
95	2.045	138.75	139.28				28.28							
96	2.060	140.80	141.34	70.93	47.47	35.73		24.00		18.14		12.27		
97	2.076	142.87	143.41											
98	2.091	144.96	145.50	73.02					21.26					
99	2.107	147.06	147.61		49.57									
100	2.123	149.17	149.73	75.15		37.86	30.40				15.49			8.03

1. The single payment column is the appropriate multiplier for one payment in *n* years' time.
2. The continuous loss column is for loss accruing from day to day: in practice it is appropriate for weekly and monthly losses as well.
3. The column headed "1" is for a series of payments at yearly intervals *at the end of each year* for *n* years. If you want an immediate payment as well, add 1.
4. The remaining columns similarly show the multiplier for a series of payments at intervals of two, three, four and so on years.
5. Thus at -0.75 per cent discount £100 paid after 10 years has a present value of £107.80;
   - £100 a year continuously over the next 10 years has a present value of £1,039;
   - £100 at the end of each of the next 10 years has a present value of £1,043;
   - £100 at the end of two, four, six, eight and 10 years has a present value of £523 (row 10, two-yearly column);
   - £100 at the end of three, six and nine years has a present value of £314 (row 9, three-yearly column); and
   - £100 now and after two, four, six and eight years (but not the 10th year) has a present value of £515 (row 8, two-yearly column, plus one).

Multipliers at -1.5 per cent discount

	Single payment	Continuous loss	Frequency of payments in years											
n			1	2	3	4	5	6	7	8	10	12	15	20
1	1.015	1.01	1.02											
2	1.031	2.03	2.05	1.03										
3	1.046	3.07	3.09		1.05									
4	1.062	4.12	4.15	2.09		1.06								
5	1.078	5.19	5.23				1.08							
6	1.095	6.28	6.33	3.19	2.14			1.09						
7	1.112	7.38	7.44						1.11					
8	1.129	8.50	8.57	4.32		2.19				1.13				
9	1.146	9.64	9.71		3.29									
10	1.163	10.80	10.88	5.48			2.24				1.16			
11	1.181	11.97	12.06											
12	1.199	13.16	13.26	6.68	4.49	3.39		2.29				1.20		
13	1.217	14.37	14.47											
14	1.236	15.59	15.71	7.91					2.35					
15	1.254	16.84	16.96		5.74		3.50						1.25	
16	1.274	18.10	18.24	9.19		4.66				2.40				
17	1.293	19.38	19.53											
18	1.313	20.69	20.84	10.50	7.05			3.61						
19	1.333	22.01	22.18											
20	1.353	23.35	23.53	11.85		6.02	4.85				2.52			1.35
21	1.374	24.71	24.90		8.43				3.72					
22	1.394	26.10	26.30	13.25										
23	1.416	27.50	27.71											
24	1.437	28.93	29.15	14.68	9.86	7.45		5.04		3.84		2.64		
25	1.459	30.38	30.61				6.31							
26	1.481	31.85	32.09	16.17										
27	1.504	33.34	33.59		11.37									
28	1.527	34.86	35.12	17.69		8.98			5.25					
29	1.550	36.40	36.67											
30	1.574	37.96	38.24	19.27	12.94		7.88	6.62			4.09		2.83	
31	1.598	39.54	39.84											
32	1.622	41.15	41.46	20.89		10.60				5.46				
33	1.647	42.79	43.11		14.59									
34	1.672	44.45	44.78	22.56										
35	1.697	46.13	46.48				9.58		6.94					
36	1.723	47.84	48.20	24.28	16.31	12.33		8.34				4.36		
37	1.749	49.58	49.95											
38	1.776	51.34	51.73	26.06										
39	1.803	53.13	53.53		18.11									
40	1.830	54.95	55.36	27.89		14.16	11.41			7.29	5.92			3.18
41	1.858	56.79	57.22											
42	1.887	58.66	59.11	29.78	20.00			10.23	8.83					
43	1.915	60.56	61.02											
44	1.944	62.49	62.97	31.72		16.10								
45	1.974	64.45	64.94		21.97		13.38						4.80	
46	2.004	66.44	66.94	33.73										
47	2.035	68.46	68.98											
48	2.066	70.51	71.04	35.79	24.04	18.17		12.29		9.36		6.42		
49	2.097	72.59	73.14						10.93					
50	2.129	74.70	75.27	37.92			15.51				8.05			
51	2.161	76.85	77.43		26.20									
52	2.194	79.03	79.63	40.11		20.36								
53	2.228	81.24	81.85											
54	2.262	83.48	84.12	42.38	28.46			14.55						
55	2.296	85.76	86.41				17.81							
56	2.331	88.08	88.74	44.71		22.69			13.26	11.69				
57	2.367	90.43	91.11		30.83									
58	2.403	92.81	93.51	47.11										
59	2.439	95.23	95.95											
60	2.476	97.69	98.43	49.59	33.31	25.17	20.29	17.03			10.53	8.90	7.28	5.66

Multipliers at -1.5 per cent discount

n	Single payment	Continuous loss	Frequency of payments in years 1	2	3	4	5	6	7	8	10	12	15	20
61	2.514	100.18	100.94											
62	2.552	102.72	103.50	52.14										
63	2.591	105.29	106.09		35.90				15.85					
64	2.631	107.90	108.72	54.77		27.80				14.32				
65	2.671	110.55	111.39				22.96							
66	2.711	113.24	114.10	57.48	38.61			19.74						
67	2.753	115.97	116.85											
68	2.795	118.75	119.65	60.28		30.59								
69	2.837	121.56	122.48		41.45									
70	2.880	124.42	125.36	63.16			25.84		18.73		13.41			
71	2.924	127.32	128.29											
72	2.969	130.27	131.26	66.12	44.42	33.56		22.71		17.29		11.87		
73	3.014	133.26	134.27											
74	3.060	136.30	137.33	69.18										
75	3.107	139.38	140.44		47.52		28.94						10.39	
76	3.154	142.51	143.59	72.34		36.72								
77	3.202	145.69	146.79						21.93					
78	3.251	148.92	150.05	75.59	50.77			25.96						
79	3.300	152.19	153.35											
80	3.350	155.52	156.70	78.94		40.07	32.29			20.64	16.76			9.01
81	3.401	158.89	160.10		54.17									
82	3.453	162.32	163.55	82.39										
83	3.506	165.80	167.06											
84	3.559	169.33	170.62	85.95	57.73	43.63		29.52	25.49			15.43		
85	3.613	172.92	174.23				35.91							
86	3.668	176.56	177.90	89.62										
87	3.724	180.26	181.62		61.46									
88	3.781	184.01	185.40	93.40		47.41				24.42				
89	3.839	187.82	189.24											
90	3.897	191.69	193.14	97.30	65.35		39.80	33.42			20.65		14.28	
91	3.956	195.61	197.10						29.45					
92	4.017	199.60	201.11	101.32		51.42								
93	4.078	203.65	205.19		69.43									
94	4.140	207.76	209.33	105.46										
95	4.203	211.93	213.53				44.01							
96	4.267	216.16	217.80	109.72	73.70	55.69		37.69		28.69		19.70		
97	4.332	220.46	222.13											
98	4.398	224.83	226.53	114.12					33.85					
99	4.465	229.26	230.99		78.16									
100	4.533	233.76	235.53	118.65		60.22	48.54				25.19			13.54

1. The single payment column is the appropriate multiplier for one payment in *n* years' time.
2. The continuous loss column is for loss accruing from day to day: in practice it is appropriate for weekly and monthly losses as well.
3. The column headed "1" is for a series of payments at yearly intervals *at the end of each year* for *n* years. If you want an immediate payment as well, add 1.
4. The remaining columns similarly show the multiplier for a series of payments at intervals of two, three, four and so on years.
5. Thus at -1.5 per cent discount £100 paid after 10 years has a present value of £116.30;
   - £100 a year continuously over the next 10 years has a present value of £1,080;
   - £100 at the end of each of the next 10 years has a present value of £1,088;
   - £100 at the end of two, four, six, eight and 10 years has a present value of £548 (row 10, two-yearly column);
   - £100 at the end of three, six and nine years has a present value of £329 (row 9, three-yearly column); and
   - £100 now and after two, four, six and eight years (but not the 10th year) has a present value of £532 (row 8, two-yearly column, plus one).

A6: Tables of deferred loss

Introductory notes

Part 1

1. The first table that follows is intended for use when a claimant will suffer a loss over a specified number of years, but that loss will not start to run immediately. The figures in the table have been derived from first principles, but they are the same as combining Ogden Tables 35 and 36 at -0.25 per cent per annum.

2. For example:

   a. The claimant is now 30 years old. The Court has decided that he has a reduced expectation of life of 30 years, to the age of 60. For the last 20 years of his life he is expected to need nursing care at a cost of £7,500 a year. His nursing needs will therefore start in 10 years' time.

   b. At -0.25 per cent per annum discount, the multiplier for a period of 20 years is 20.51 [Ogden Table 36].

   c. At -0.25 per cent per annum discount, a loss that will not occur for another 10 years should be adjusted by multiplying it by 1.0253 [Ogden Table 35].

   d. The appropriate multiplier is therefore (20.51 × 1.0253) = 21.03 (to two decimal places).

   e. Compare the figure in the table that follows for 20 years of loss and 10 years before the loss starts to run.[1]

3. The following points should also be remembered:

   a. Ogden Table 35 (Discounting Factors for Term Certain) gives the discount factor for a period of complete years. So, in the example above, where the date of trial is 23 August 2023, the need for nursing care is assumed to start on 23 August 2033.

   b. Ogden Table 36 (Multipliers for Pecuniary Loss for Term Certain) assumes that the loss will occur continuously throughout the year, e.g. weekly or monthly bills for nursing care.

[1] Note that sometimes the result of making the calculation using Table 35 and Table 36 and multiplying together the rounded figures from each will differ in the second decimal place from the figures in the table which follows, which is calculated exactly without rounding at the intermediate stages.

Combination grid for different terms certain and different deferment periods (Discount rate -0.25% per annum)

Years of loss	Years before loss starts to run 1	2	3	4	5	6	7	8	9	10	12.5	15	20	25	30	35	40	Years of loss
1	1.00	1.01	1.01	1.01	1.01	1.02	1.02	1.02	1.02	1.03	1.03	1.04	1.05	1.07	1.08	1.09	1.11	1
2	2.01	2.02	2.02	2.03	2.03	2.04	2.04	2.05	2.05	2.06	2.07	2.08	2.11	2.13	2.16	2.19	2.22	2
3	3.02	3.03	3.03	3.04	3.05	3.06	3.06	3.07	3.08	3.09	3.11	3.13	3.17	3.21	3.25	3.29	3.33	3
4	4.03	4.04	4.05	4.06	4.07	4.08	4.09	4.10	4.11	4.12	4.15	4.17	4.23	4.28	4.33	4.39	4.44	4
5	5.04	5.06	5.07	5.08	5.09	5.11	5.12	5.13	5.15	5.16	5.19	5.22	5.29	5.36	5.42	5.49	5.56	5
6	6.06	6.08	6.09	6.11	6.12	6.14	6.15	6.17	6.18	6.20	6.24	6.28	6.36	6.44	6.52	6.60	6.68	6
7	7.08	7.10	7.11	7.13	7.15	7.17	7.19	7.20	7.22	7.24	7.29	7.33	7.42	7.52	7.61	7.71	7.81	7
8	8.10	8.12	8.14	8.16	8.18	8.20	8.22	8.24	8.26	8.29	8.34	8.39	8.50	8.60	8.71	8.82	8.93	8
9	9.12	9.15	9.17	9.19	9.22	9.24	9.26	9.29	9.31	9.33	9.39	9.45	9.57	9.69	9.81	9.94	10.06	9
10	10.15	10.18	10.20	10.23	10.25	10.28	10.31	10.33	10.36	10.38	10.45	10.51	10.65	10.78	10.92	11.05	11.19	10
11	11.18	11.21	11.24	11.27	11.29	11.32	11.35	11.38	11.41	11.44	11.51	11.58	11.73	11.87	12.02	12.17	12.33	11
12	12.21	12.24	12.27	12.30	12.34	12.37	12.40	12.43	12.46	12.49	12.57	12.65	12.81	12.97	13.13	13.30	13.46	12
13	13.25	13.28	13.31	13.35	13.38	13.41	13.45	13.48	13.51	13.55	13.63	13.72	13.89	14.07	14.24	14.42	14.61	13
14	14.28	14.32	14.36	14.39	14.43	14.46	14.50	14.54	14.57	14.61	14.70	14.79	14.98	15.17	15.36	15.55	15.75	14
15	15.32	15.36	15.40	15.44	15.48	15.52	15.56	15.59	15.63	15.67	15.77	15.87	16.07	16.27	16.48	16.68	16.89	15
16	16.37	16.41	16.45	16.49	16.53	16.57	16.61	16.65	16.70	16.74	16.84	16.95	17.16	17.38	17.60	17.82	18.04	16
17	17.41	17.45	17.50	17.54	17.59	17.63	17.67	17.72	17.76	17.81	17.92	18.03	18.26	18.49	18.72	18.96	19.20	17
18	18.46	18.50	18.55	18.60	18.64	18.69	18.74	18.78	18.83	18.88	19.00	19.12	19.36	19.60	19.85	20.10	20.35	18
19	19.51	19.56	19.61	19.65	19.70	19.75	19.80	19.85	19.90	19.95	20.08	20.20	20.46	20.72	20.98	21.24	21.51	19
20	20.56	20.61	20.66	20.72	20.77	20.82	20.87	20.92	20.98	21.03	21.16	21.29	21.56	21.83	22.11	22.39	22.67	20
21	21.62	21.67	21.72	21.78	21.83	21.89	21.94	22.00	22.05	22.11	22.25	22.39	22.67	22.95	23.24	23.54	23.83	21
22	22.67	22.73	22.79	22.84	22.90	22.96	23.02	23.07	23.13	23.19	23.34	23.48	23.78	24.08	24.38	24.69	25.00	22
23	23.73	23.79	23.85	23.91	23.97	24.03	24.09	24.15	24.21	24.28	24.43	24.58	24.89	25.20	25.52	25.84	26.17	23
24	24.80	24.86	24.92	24.98	25.05	25.11	25.17	25.24	25.30	25.36	25.52	25.68	26.01	26.33	26.66	27.00	27.34	24
25	25.86	25.93	25.99	26.06	26.12	26.19	26.25	26.32	26.39	26.45	26.62	26.79	27.12	27.46	27.81	28.16	28.52	25
26	26.93	27.00	27.07	27.14	27.20	27.27	27.34	27.41	27.48	27.55	27.72	27.89	28.24	28.60	28.96	29.32	29.69	26
27	28.00	28.07	28.14	28.21	28.29	28.36	28.43	28.50	28.57	28.64	28.82	29.00	29.37	29.74	30.11	30.49	30.87	27
28	29.08	29.15	29.22	29.30	29.37	29.44	29.52	29.59	29.67	29.74	29.93	30.11	30.49	30.88	31.27	31.66	32.06	28
29	30.15	30.23	30.31	30.38	30.46	30.53	30.61	30.69	30.76	30.84	31.03	31.23	31.62	32.02	32.42	32.83	33.25	29
30	31.23	31.31	31.39	31.47	31.55	31.63	31.71	31.79	31.86	31.94	32.15	32.35	32.75	33.17	33.58	34.01	34.44	30
31	32.32	32.40	32.48	32.56	32.64	32.72	32.80	32.89	32.97	33.05	33.26	33.47	33.89	34.32	34.75	35.19	35.63	31
32	33.40	33.48	33.57	33.65	33.74	33.82	33.91	33.99	34.08	34.16	34.38	34.59	35.03	35.47	35.91	36.37	36.83	32
33	34.49	34.57	34.66	34.75	34.83	34.92	35.01	35.10	35.19	35.27	35.49	35.72	36.17	36.62	37.08	37.55	38.02	33
34	35.58	35.67	35.76	35.85	35.94	36.03	36.12	36.21	36.30	36.39	36.62	36.85	37.31	37.78	38.26	38.74	39.23	34
35	36.67	36.76	36.85	36.95	37.04	37.13	37.23	37.32	37.41	37.51	37.74	37.98	38.46	38.94	39.43	39.93	40.43	35
36	37.77	37.86	37.96	38.05	38.15	38.24	38.34	38.43	38.53	38.63	38.87	39.11	39.61	40.10	40.61	41.12	41.64	36
37	38.86	38.96	39.06	39.16	39.26	39.35	39.45	39.55	39.65	39.75	40.00	40.25	40.76	41.27	41.79	42.32	42.85	37
38	39.97	40.07	40.17	40.27	40.37	40.47	40.57	40.67	40.77	40.88	41.13	41.39	41.91	42.44	42.97	43.52	44.06	38
39	41.07	41.17	41.28	41.38	41.48	41.59	41.69	41.80	41.90	42.01	42.27	42.53	43.07	43.61	44.16	44.72	45.28	39
40	42.18	42.28	42.39	42.49	42.60	42.71	42.81	42.92	43.03	43.14	43.41	43.68	44.23	44.79	45.35	45.92	46.50	40
41	43.29	43.39	43.50	43.61	43.72	43.83	43.94	44.05	44.16	44.27	44.55	44.83	45.39	45.97	46.54	47.13	47.72	41
42	44.40	44.51	44.62	44.73	44.84	44.96	45.07	45.18	45.30	45.41	45.69	45.98	46.56	47.15	47.74	48.34	48.95	42
43	45.51	45.63	45.74	45.86	45.97	46.09	46.20	46.32	46.43	46.55	46.84	47.14	47.73	48.33	48.94	49.56	50.18	43
44	46.63	46.75	46.87	46.98	47.10	47.22	47.34	47.46	47.57	47.69	47.99	48.29	48.90	49.52	50.14	50.77	51.41	44
45	47.75	47.87	47.99	48.11	48.23	48.35	48.47	48.60	48.72	48.84	49.15	49.45	50.08	50.71	51.35	51.99	52.65	45
Years of loss	1	2	3	4	5	6	7	8	9	10	12.5	15	20	25	30	35	40	Years of loss

Part 2

4. The following tables are intended for use when a claimant will suffer a loss for the rest of life, but that loss will not start to run immediately. These tables allow for mortality and are therefore consistent with Ogden Tables 1 to 34. The period of deferment is represented by *m*. When *m* is zero the factors correspond to Tables 1 and 2 of the Ogden Tables at the relevant ages. Some other combinations correspond to other tables in the Ogden Tables. Thus, the multiplier for a male age 40 with a 20 year period of deferment is 27.58. This is the same as Table 23 of the Ogden Tables at age 40.

5. For example, the claimant is a female aged 30 and a payment of £5,000 a year is expected to start after 15 years. The multiplier from the female tables at -0.25 per cent per annum for age 30 at the start and a period of deferment of 15 years is 47.78. The value of this loss is thus £5,000 × 47.78 = £238,900.

6. In another example the claimant is a male aged 45, who would have a normal expectation of life of 39.62 (from Table 1 of the Ogden Tables at 0.0 per cent per annum). On the basis of medical evidence he is deemed to have an expectation of life of only 25 years. His deemed age is thus 59.74 (from Table 1 of Ogden at 0.0 per cent). A multiplier is required for a continuous payment for the rest of life starting 10 years from now. The multipliers from the table below are 26.30 for a male aged 50 at the date of calculation and 16.00 for a male aged 60 at the date of calculation. For a male aged 61 at the date of calculation the multiplier required is 26.30 × 0.26/10 + 16.00 × 9.74/10 = 16.27.

7. If a multiplier is required for a specific number of payments after a period of deferment, the combination table on the previous page can be used with mortality ignored.

8. If there is medical evidence of the particular claimant's life expectancy, it may be appropriate to follow the approach set out in paragraph 20 of the Explanatory Notes to the 7th edition of the Ogden Tables to find the effective age for which the expectation of life in accordance with the mortality tables underlying the Ogden Tables (from the 0.0% per annum column of Table 1 or 2 of the Ogden Tables as appropriate) would be equal to the deemed life expectancy. This effective age can then be used as the starting age in order to apply the following table to find a multiplier for a series of payments for life which is deferred for a given period. Expectation of life for impaired lives is discussed in more detail in paragraphs 15-17 of the Explanatory Notes to the 8th edition of the Ogden Tables.

9. The following points should also be remembered:

   a. When applying the multipliers to claims for loss of earnings, this table (along with the Ogden Tables themselves) only take into account the discount rate and mortality. They do not take into accounts other factors such as employment status or disability and the impact that such factors may be expected to have on the likelihood of continuing to be employed up to normal retirement age. Where appropriate a discount should be applied for these contingencies other than mortality in accordance with Section B of the Explanatory Notes of the 8th edition of the Ogden Tables.

   b. The multipliers in the tables below assume that payments are made continually (or on a weekly or monthly basis) once they come into payment.

10. If a multiplier at -0.25 per cent per annum is required for future continuous payment for just *m* years, this can be obtained by subtracting the relevant multiplier in the following tables for payments deferred for *m* years from the corresponding whole life multiplier from Table 1 or 2 of the Ogden Tables.

Multipliers at -0.25 per cent for future continuous annual payments for life deferred *m* years (Males)

Starting age

m	0	10	20	30	40	50	60	70	80
0	98.93	85.71	72.46	59.75	47.63	36.24	25.68	16.48	9.06
1	97.93	84.71	71.46	58.75	46.63	35.24	24.68	15.49	8.08
2	96.93	83.71	70.46	57.75	45.63	34.24	23.69	14.51	7.16
3	95.93	82.70	69.45	56.74	44.63	33.24	22.70	13.55	6.29
4	94.92	81.69	68.44	55.74	43.62	32.25	21.72	12.61	5.47
5	93.92	80.68	67.43	54.73	42.62	31.25	20.75	11.69	4.71
6	92.91	79.67	66.42	53.72	41.61	30.25	19.78	10.79	4.01
7	91.89	78.65	65.41	52.71	40.61	29.26	18.82	9.92	3.37
8	90.88	77.63	64.39	51.69	39.61	28.27	17.87	9.07	2.80
9	89.86	76.61	63.37	50.68	38.60	27.28	16.93	8.25	2.29
10	88.84	75.59	62.35	49.66	37.60	26.30	16.00	7.46	1.85
11	87.82	74.56	61.33	48.65	36.59	25.32	15.09	6.70	1.46
12	86.80	73.54	60.31	47.63	35.59	24.34	14.18	5.98	1.13
13	85.77	72.51	59.28	46.61	34.58	23.36	13.29	5.29	0.86
14	84.74	71.47	58.25	45.59	33.58	22.40	12.42	4.64	0.64
15	83.71	70.44	57.22	44.57	32.58	21.43	11.56	4.03	0.46
20	78.51	65.23	52.05	39.46	27.58	16.73	7.57	1.68	0.06
25	73.25	59.97	46.83	34.34	22.66	12.28	4.25	0.46	0.00
30	67.94	54.67	41.60	29.24	17.88	8.23	1.88	0.07	0.00
35	62.56	49.32	36.36	24.20	13.32	4.79	0.56	0.01	0.00
40	57.14	43.94	31.12	19.28	9.11	2.23	0.09	0.00	0.00

Multipliers at -0.25 per cent for future continuous annual payments for life deferred *m* years (Females)

Starting age

m	0	10	20	30	40	50	60	70	80
0	102.08	88.90	75.75	63.00	50.75	39.09	28.20	18.41	10.27
1	101.08	87.90	74.75	62.00	49.75	38.09	27.20	17.41	9.29
2	100.08	86.90	73.75	61.00	48.75	37.09	26.20	16.43	8.34
3	99.08	85.89	72.74	59.99	47.74	36.09	25.21	15.46	7.43
4	98.07	84.88	71.73	58.98	46.74	35.09	24.22	14.49	6.57
5	97.06	83.87	70.72	57.97	45.73	34.09	23.23	13.55	5.75
6	96.05	82.86	69.71	56.96	44.72	33.08	22.25	12.61	4.98
7	95.04	81.84	68.69	55.95	43.71	32.08	21.27	11.70	4.27
8	94.02	80.82	67.68	54.93	42.70	31.08	20.30	10.80	3.61
9	93.01	79.80	66.66	53.92	41.69	30.09	19.34	9.92	3.02
10	91.99	78.78	65.63	52.90	40.68	29.09	18.38	9.07	2.48
11	90.96	77.75	64.61	51.88	39.66	28.09	17.42	8.24	2.00
12	89.94	76.72	63.58	50.85	38.65	27.10	16.48	7.44	1.59
13	88.91	75.69	62.55	49.83	37.64	26.11	15.54	6.67	1.24
14	87.88	74.66	61.52	48.80	36.62	25.12	14.62	5.93	0.94
15	86.85	73.62	60.49	47.78	35.60	24.13	13.71	5.23	0.70
20	81.64	68.41	55.29	42.62	30.53	19.26	9.36	2.36	0.10
25	76.38	63.14	50.05	37.43	25.48	14.55	5.57	0.71	0.01
30	71.05	57.81	44.76	32.24	20.51	10.13	2.64	0.11	0.00
35	65.67	52.44	39.45	27.07	15.68	6.21	0.86	0.01	0.00
40	60.22	47.01	34.12	21.95	11.10	3.08	0.14	0.00	0.00

A7: Table of adjustments to multiplier for Fatal Accidents Acts dependency

These tables deal with the risk in dependency cases that the deceased would not have survived until trial. They are derived from the Explanatory Notes of the Ogden Tables, Section D (approved as correct by the Supreme Court in *Knauer v Ministry of Justice*[1]).

The same principle for calculating the loss applies in Scotland. Section 7(1)(d) of the Damages (Scotland) Act 2011 requires that the multiplier for loss of support applies only to future loss and is to run from the date of the interlocutor awarding damages.

Note that Ogden provides a simplified approach which overstates the future dependency multiplier. An approach using joint life multipliers, as in the table at the end of this section, would be more accurate. In complex cases actuarial evidence should be sought.

PRE-TRIAL damages (factor to be applied to damages from date of accident to trial)

Age of deceased at date of death	Period from date of death to date of trial or date of cessation of dependency, if earlier (years)									
	Male deceased									
	1	2	3	4	5	6	7	8	9	10
Below 40	1.00	1.00	1.00	1.00	1.00	1.00	1.00	1.00	1.00	1.00
40	1.00	1.00	1.00	1.00	1.00	0.99	0.99	0.99	0.99	0.99
45	1.00	1.00	1.00	1.00	0.99	0.99	0.99	0.99	0.99	0.99
50	1.00	1.00	1.00	0.99	0.99	0.99	0.99	0.99	0.98	0.98
55	1.00	1.00	0.99	0.99	0.99	0.98	0.98	0.98	0.97	0.97
60	1.00	0.99	0.99	0.98	0.98	0.98	0.97	0.97	0.96	0.95
65	0.99	0.99	0.98	0.98	0.97	0.96	0.95	0.95	0.94	0.93
70	0.99	0.98	0.97	0.96	0.95	0.94	0.93	0.92	0.90	0.89
75	0.98	0.97	0.95	0.94	0.92	0.90	0.88	0.86	0.84	0.82
80	0.97	0.95	0.92	0.89	0.86	0.83	0.80	0.77	0.74	0.71
85	0.95	0.91	0.86	0.81	0.77	0.72	0.68	0.64	0.60	0.56
90	0.92	0.84	0.77	0.70	0.64	0.58	0.53	0.48	0.44	0.40

Age of deceased at date of death	Period from date of death to date of trial or date of cessation of dependency, if earlier (years)									
	Female deceased									
	1	2	3	4	5	6	7	8	9	10
Below 40	1.00	1.00	1.00	1.00	1.00	1.00	1.00	1.00	1.00	1.00
40	1.00	1.00	1.00	1.00	1.00	1.00	1.00	1.00	1.00	0.99
45	1.00	1.00	1.00	1.00	1.00	1.00	0.99	0.99	0.99	0.99
50	1.00	1.00	1.00	1.00	0.99	0.99	0.99	0.99	0.99	0.99
55	1.00	1.00	1.00	0.99	0.99	0.99	0.99	0.99	0.98	0.98
60	1.00	1.00	0.99	0.99	0.99	0.98	0.98	0.98	0.97	0.97
65	1.00	0.99	0.99	0.98	0.98	0.97	0.97	0.96	0.96	0.95
70	0.99	0.99	0.98	0.97	0.97	0.96	0.95	0.94	0.93	0.92
75	0.99	0.98	0.97	0.95	0.94	0.93	0.91	0.90	0.88	0.87
80	0.98	0.96	0.94	0.92	0.90	0.87	0.85	0.82	0.80	0.77
85	0.96	0.93	0.89	0.85	0.81	0.77	0.73	0.69	0.65	0.62
90	0.93	0.87	0.80	0.74	0.68	0.62	0.57	0.53	0.48	0.44

[1] [2016] UKSC 9.

POST-TRIAL damages (factor to be applied to damages from date of trial to retirement age)

Age of deceased at date of death	Period from date of death to date of trial (years) — Male deceased									
	1	2	3	4	5	6	7	8	9	10
Below 40	1.00	1.00	1.00	1.00	1.00	1.00	1.00	1.00	1.00	1.00
40	1.00	1.00	1.00	0.99	0.99	0.99	0.99	0.98	0.98	0.98
45	1.00	1.00	0.99	0.99	0.99	0.98	0.98	0.98	0.98	0.97
50	1.00	0.99	0.99	0.99	0.98	0.98	0.97	0.97	0.96	0.96
55	1.00	0.99	0.99	0.98	0.97	0.97	0.96	0.95	0.94	0.93
60	0.99	0.98	0.98	0.97	0.96	0.95	0.94	0.92	0.91	0.90
65	0.99	0.98	0.96	0.95	0.93	0.92	0.90	0.88	0.86	0.84
70	0.98	0.96	0.94	0.92	0.90	0.87	0.84	0.81	0.78	0.75
75	0.97	0.94	0.90	0.87	0.83	0.79	0.75	0.70	0.65	0.60
80	0.95	0.89	0.84	0.78	0.72	0.65	0.59	0.52	0.46	0.40
85	0.91	0.81	0.72	0.63	0.54	0.46	0.38	0.31	0.24	0.19
90	0.84	0.69	0.56	0.44	0.33	0.25	0.18	0.13	0.09	0.06

Age of deceased at date of death	Period from date of death to date of trial (years) — Female deceased									
	1	2	3	4	5	6	7	8	9	10
Below 40	1.00	1.00	1.00	1.00	1.00	1.00	1.00	1.00	1.00	1.00
40	1.00	1.00	1.00	1.00	0.99	0.99	0.99	0.99	0.99	0.99
45	1.00	1.00	1.00	0.99	0.99	0.99	0.99	0.99	0.98	0.98
50	1.00	1.00	0.99	0.99	0.99	0.99	0.98	0.98	0.98	0.97
55	1.00	0.99	0.99	0.99	0.98	0.98	0.97	0.97	0.96	0.96
60	1.00	0.99	0.98	0.98	0.97	0.96	0.96	0.95	0.94	0.93
65	0.99	0.98	0.98	0.97	0.96	0.94	0.93	0.92	0.91	0.89
70	0.99	0.97	0.96	0.94	0.93	0.91	0.89	0.87	0.84	0.82
75	0.98	0.96	0.93	0.90	0.88	0.84	0.81	0.77	0.73	0.69
80	0.96	0.92	0.88	0.83	0.78	0.73	0.67	0.61	0.55	0.49
85	0.93	0.85	0.77	0.69	0.61	0.53	0.46	0.38	0.31	0.25
90	0.86	0.73	0.61	0.50	0.39	0.30	0.23	0.17	0.12	0.08

POST-RETIREMENT damages (for the period of dependency after retirement age)

1. ***Either*** A First obtain the multiplier for the whole of life dependency by the following steps:

   (a) determine, from 0 per cent tables, the expectation of life which the deceased would have had at date of trial (or shorter period for which s/he would have provided the dependency);

   (b) determine the expected period for which the dependant would have been able to receive the dependency (for a widow, normally her life expectancy from 0 per cent tables; for a child, normally the period until it reaches adulthood);

   (c) take the lesser of the two periods; and

   (d) treat the resulting period as a term certain and look up the multiplier for that period (Table A5, continuous loss column).

   Or B Obtain the whole of life dependency multiplier from tables of joint life multipliers at -0.25 per cent.

2. Obtain the multiplier for dependency from date of trial to retirement age. Do not adjust it for contingencies other than mortality. Do not apply the factors in the Post-Trial table above.

3. Subtract the multiplier for dependency to retirement age (2) from the whole life multiplier (1). Multiply by the factor in the Post-Trial table above.

Post-retirement multiplier = [Stage 1 figure *minus* Stage 2 figure] × Post-Trial factor.

Table of joint life multipliers at -0.25%

Age of male	Age of female											
	30	35	40	45	50	55	60	65	70	75	80	85
30	53.57	50.49	46.62	42.17	37.38	32.45	27.54	22.75	18.18	13.95	10.20	7.07
35	49.71	47.57	44.58	40.84	36.53	31.92	27.22	22.56	18.07	13.89	10.17	7.06
40	45.22	43.84	41.77	38.89	35.27	31.14	26.74	22.28	17.91	13.80	10.13	7.03
45	40.35	39.51	38.19	36.20	33.42	29.96	26.03	21.87	17.68	13.68	10.07	7.01
50	35.32	34.81	34.02	32.75	30.84	28.21	24.93	21.22	17.32	13.49	9.98	6.96
55	30.26	29.96	29.49	28.74	27.54	25.74	23.26	20.19	16.73	13.17	9.82	6.89
60	25.34	25.16	24.89	24.45	23.75	22.65	20.98	18.67	15.82	12.67	9.56	6.77
65	20.68	20.58	20.43	20.18	19.79	19.15	18.15	16.62	14.50	11.92	9.17	6.59
70	16.36	16.31	16.22	16.09	15.87	15.53	14.97	14.08	12.70	10.80	8.57	6.30
75	12.44	12.41	12.37	12.30	12.18	12.01	11.72	11.25	10.46	9.25	7.64	5.82
80	9.03	9.01	8.99	8.96	8.90	8.81	8.68	8.45	8.05	7.39	6.38	5.09
85	6.27	6.26	6.25	6.24	6.21	6.17	6.11	6.00	5.82	5.49	4.95	4.17

Note to the table of joint life multipliers

To find the appropriate joint life multiplier for a discount rate of -0.25% a year read across in the table above to the column for the age of the woman and down to the row for the age of the man. Thus, the joint life multiplier for a woman of 40 and a man of 45 is 38.19.

The multiplier for ages not found in the table can be obtained by interpolation, using the method in paras 33 and 34 of the notes to the Ogden Tables.

Thus, if A is the multiplier for a woman of 40 and a man of 45 and B is the multiplier for a woman of 45 and a man of 50, the multiplier for a woman of 42 and a man of 47 is (3A + 2B)/5.

From the table, A = 38.19 and B = 32.75. Therefore the joint life multiplier for a woman of 42 and man of 47 = ((3 × 38.19) + (2 × 32.75))/5 = 36.01.

Where the difference in age is not a multiple of five years, the method should be repeated as follows:

Multiplier for woman of 42 and man of 47 = ((3 × 38.19) + (2 × 32.75))/5 = 36.01.
Multiplier for woman of 42 and man of 52 = ((3 × 34.02) + (2 × 28.74))/5 = 31.91.
Joint life multiplier for woman of 42 and man of 48 = ((4 × 36.01) + (1 × 31.91))/5 = 35.19[1]

Tables of joint life multipliers for discount rates of -0.75% and -1.5% a year are set out in the tables below.

[1] The combined calculation can be arranged in more than one way and the result may vary in the second decimal place.

Table of joint life multipliers at -0.75%

Age of male	Age of female											
	30	35	40	45	50	55	60	65	70	75	80	85
30	61.75	57.76	52.83	47.27	41.41	35.52	29.77	24.30	19.20	14.57	10.55	7.25
35	56.79	54.06	50.30	45.65	40.40	34.90	29.41	24.09	19.08	14.50	10.52	7.23
40	51.10	49.39	46.82	43.28	38.90	33.99	28.87	23.78	18.90	14.41	10.47	7.21
45	45.07	44.05	42.45	40.03	36.71	32.62	28.06	23.32	18.65	14.28	10.41	7.18
50	38.97	38.37	37.43	35.93	33.67	30.58	26.80	22.59	18.26	14.08	10.31	7.14
55	32.98	32.63	32.08	31.21	29.83	27.75	24.92	21.45	17.61	13.74	10.14	7.06
60	27.28	27.08	26.77	26.28	25.48	24.23	22.34	19.77	16.62	13.20	9.87	6.94
65	22.01	21.90	21.72	21.45	21.01	20.31	19.19	17.50	15.19	12.39	9.46	6.75
70	17.22	17.16	17.06	16.92	16.68	16.31	15.70	14.73	13.23	11.20	8.82	6.44
75	12.96	12.92	12.88	12.80	12.68	12.49	12.18	11.68	10.84	9.55	7.85	5.94
80	9.32	9.30	9.28	9.24	9.18	9.09	8.94	8.70	8.28	7.58	6.53	5.19
85	6.42	6.41	6.40	6.38	6.36	6.31	6.25	6.14	5.95	5.61	5.05	4.23

Table of joint life multipliers at -1.5%

Age of male	Age of female											
	30	35	40	45	50	55	60	65	70	75	80	85
30	77.57	71.65	64.50	56.68	48.70	40.95	33.66	26.95	20.90	15.59	11.12	7.53
35	70.28	66.33	60.97	54.49	47.39	40.18	33.21	26.70	20.76	15.52	11.08	7.52
40	62.13	59.73	56.15	51.30	45.43	39.03	32.56	26.33	20.56	15.41	11.03	7.49
45	53.74	52.37	50.20	46.96	42.58	37.30	31.56	25.79	20.27	15.27	10.96	7.46
50	45.54	44.76	43.53	41.58	38.67	34.74	30.03	24.92	19.82	15.04	10.85	7.42
55	37.77	37.33	36.65	35.55	33.81	31.22	27.75	23.57	19.07	14.66	10.67	7.33
60	30.64	30.39	30.02	29.42	28.45	26.93	24.66	21.60	17.94	14.06	10.38	7.20
65	24.25	24.12	23.92	23.60	23.08	22.25	20.94	18.97	16.31	13.16	9.93	7.00
70	18.64	18.57	18.46	18.30	18.03	17.60	16.91	15.79	14.10	11.83	9.23	6.67
75	13.80	13.76	13.71	13.62	13.49	13.28	12.94	12.37	11.44	10.03	8.18	6.14
80	9.77	9.76	9.73	9.69	9.63	9.53	9.37	9.11	8.65	7.89	6.77	5.35
85	6.65	6.64	6.63	6.61	6.58	6.54	6.47	6.35	6.15	5.79	5.20	4.34

A8: The Ogden Tables – 8th edition (updated)

(updated August 2022 in light of the change of the Northern Ireland discount rate from -1.75% to -1.5%)

Actuarial tables with explanatory notes for use in personal injury and fatal accident cases.

Prepared by an Inter-Professional Working Party of Actuaries, Lawyers, Accountants and other interested parties.

8th edition prepared by the Government Actuary's Department.

Table of Contents *Page*

Foreword by the Government Actuary

1. Assessing the appropriate amount of damages to pay in personal injury and fatal accident cases is a complex issue which often requires lawyers to work together with actuaries and other experts in order to reach the widely recognised objective of achieving fair levels of compensation to those affected.

2. Actuaries are experts in the evaluation of financial risk and were well represented, including the Government Actuary and the Institute and the Faculty of Actuaries, alongside representatives from the legal profession when a working group was first established in 1984. This group published a set of actuarial tables and explanatory notes to assist the Courts in determining appropriate multipliers for use in assessing lump sum awards for damages to be paid in compensation for financial losses or expenses (such as care costs) directly caused by personal injury or death.

3. These tables have become known as the Ogden Tables, and the working group known as the Ogden Working Party, both named after Sir Michael Ogden QC who instigated the publication of the tables and chaired the original working party. The tables have become widely recognised as the appropriate basis on which to calculate the loss of future earning capacity, and we have now reached the publication of the eighth edition.

4. The original 1984 tables provided multipliers based on retirement ages of 65 for males and 60 for females and did not take account of any contingencies other than mortality. Since then, further editions of the tables and notes have been published providing multipliers for an increasing range of retirement ages based on updated mortality assumptions and providing factors to allow for contingencies other than mortality. There have also been changes in the discount rates tabulated. Over time, the explanatory notes have been expanded and examples provided to assist practitioners. The methods set out in the notes offer a reasonable balance between accuracy and simplicity of application.

5. The Government Actuary currently has a statutory role in the process of setting the personal injury discount rate, in each of England & Wales, Scotland and Northern Ireland. Additionally, the Government Actuary's Department (GAD) has been represented on the Ogden Working Party since its inception and has been commissioned to prepare the tables of multipliers and other factors in all the previous editions of the Ogden Tables. I am very pleased that this involvement has continued, and that we are able to present this new edition of the tables.

July 2020

Martin Clarke, FIA
Government Actuary

Members of the Working Party Responsible for the 8th edition
Chairman: William Latimer-Sayer KC

Harry Trusted, Barrister	Secretary to the Ogden Working Party
Tamar Burton, Barrister	Assistant Secretary to the Ogden Working Party
Cara Guthrie, Barrister	Former Assistant Secretary to the Ogden Working Party
Adrian Gallop, FIA	Government Actuary's Department
Paul Nixon, FIA	Government Actuary's Department
Shahram Sharghy, Barrister	Association of Personal Injury Lawyers representative
John Pollock, FFA	Institute and Faculty of Actuaries representative
Andrew Smith KC	Faculty of Advocates representative
Alistair Kinley	Forum of Insurance Lawyers representative
Julian Chamberlayne	Forum of Complex Injury Solicitors, chairman and representative
Dermot Fee KC	General Council of the Bar of Northern Ireland representative
John Mead	NHS Resolution, Technical Claims Director and representative
Richard Methuen KC	Personal Injuries Bar Association representative
Simon Levene, Barrister	Professional Negligence Bar Association representative
Stephen Webber	Society of Clinical Injury Lawyers, chairman and representative
Kim Leslie	The Law Society of Scotland representative
Richard Cropper, DipPFS	Independent financial adviser, invited by Chairman
Chris Daykin, FIA	Actuary, invited by Chairman
Maurice Faull, FCA	Forensic accountant, invited by Chairman
Hugh Gregory, FCA	Forensic accountant, invited by Chairman
Jon Ramsey	Re-insurance claims manager at Munich Re, invited by Chairman
John Saunders	Director of Technical and Large Loss at Direct Line Group, invited by Chairman
Andrew Underwood, Solicitor	Solicitor, invited by Chairman
Professor Victoria Wass	Labour economist, invited by Chairman
Martin White, FIA	Actuary, invited by Chairman

Chairman's Introduction to the 8th edition of the Ogden Tables

"When it comes to the explanatory notes we must make sure that they are readily comprehensible. We must assume the most stupid circuit judge in the country and before him are the two most stupid advocates. All three of them must be able to understand what we are saying".

Sir Michael Ogden, QC, on his explanatory notes to the 1st edition of the Ogden Tables.[1]

1. Supposedly, good things come to those who wait. It's been nearly a decade since the last edition of the Ogden Tables was published in 2011. A lot has happened since then. We have had three prime ministers, two changes to the discount rate in England and Wales, one Brexit referendum and now a global pandemic.

2. I am extremely grateful to the dedicated, diligent and distinguished members of the Ogden Working Party (OWP) for their combined efforts in the production of these tables. The explanatory notes have been completely re-written. Never content to rest on our laurels, the OWP has striven to prepare tables and accompanying guidance to make the quantification of personal injury claims ever more accurate, efficient and user-friendly.

3. Since the last edition, the OWP has evolved. Sadly, an august former member, Harvey McGregor QC, has passed away. Several others have retired. One former member, Professor Andrew Burrows KC, has been appointed to the Supreme Court and we wish him well with his judicial career. A number of new members have joined, representing the interests of FOCIS, SCIL, general insurers and re-insurers at numerous meetings ably and efficiently organised by the new assistant secretary, Tamar Burton. Stalwart members of the group, such as Chris Daykin and Adrian Gallop, continue to make an enormous contribution to the production of the Tables and the accompanying explanatory notes, which would be inconceivable to produce without their input.

Application of the Tables and different discount rates

4. These tables are designed to assist those concerned with calculating lump sum damages for future losses in personal injury and fatal accident cases in the UK.

5. The methodology is long-established: multipliers are applied to the present-day value of a future annual loss (net of tax in the case of a loss of earnings and pension) with the aim of producing a lump sum equivalent to the capitalised value of the future losses.[2] In essence, the multiplier is the figure by which an annual loss is multiplied in order to calculate a capitalised sum, taking into account accelerated receipt, mortality risks and, in relation to claims for loss of earnings and pension, discounts for contingencies other than mortality. Multipliers are calculated by reference to an annual assumed interest rate after tax and inflation, known as the discount rate.

6. Previously, the discount rate was set by reference to the yields on Index Linked Government Stock. However, following a lengthy consultation process in England and Wales and in Scotland, we now have new statutory discount rates, set by secondary legislation. As explained in Section A, different discount rates now apply in each of the three separate UK jurisdictions. At the time of writing, the applicable discount rates range from -0.75% in Scotland to -0.25% in England and Wales, and

[1] Memoirs of Sir Michael Ogden, QC, "Variety is the Spice of Legal Life", p.182; *The Book Guild,* 2002.
[2] This methodology was endorsed in the leading House of Lords authority *Wells v Wells* [1999] 1 AC 345.

-1.5% in Northern Ireland.[3] When using the Tables care must be taken to ensure that the correct discount rate is applied for the appropriate jurisdiction at the relevant time.

Mortality data

7. Projections of future mortality rates are usually produced on a two-yearly basis by the ONS as part of the production of national population projections for the United Kingdom and its constituent countries. Multipliers published in the 7th edition of the Ogden Tables were calculated using mortality rates from the 2008-based projections; the 8th edition provides multipliers based on mortality rates from the most recent, 2018-based, projections (published at the end of 2019).

8. Somewhat surprisingly, given the previous upward trend in projected life expectancy data, the expectations of life (and hence the multipliers derived from them at all discount rates and ages) in this edition of the Tables are lower than in the 7th edition of the Tables, notwithstanding the 10 year difference in the data. This reflects both the lower decreases in mortality than previously projected between 2008 and 2018 and more pessimistic assumptions adopted by the ONS regarding the future rates of improvement of mortality at some ages over the next few years, but especially at older ages.

9. For younger claimants, the approximate reduction in life expectancy between the 7th and 8th editions of the Tables is about one year for men and two years for women. This reflects a difference in overall predicted life expectancy of 1-2%. However, for older claimants, the difference in predicted life expectancy can be as much as 8-9%.

Changes to the Tables and explanatory notes

10. The main updates and changes in the 8th edition of the Ogden Tables are as follows:

- Section A has been fully updated. In particular, the section on life expectancy has been expanded, and there is new guidance and new examples regarding the interpolation of multipliers and calculating split multipliers for variable losses.
- Section B has been extensively revised and there is new guidance on when and how to depart from the suggested Table A to D reduction factors in appropriate cases.
- There is a new Section C regarding the application of the Tables to pension loss claims together with two examples.
- Following the Supreme Court's decision in *Knauer v Ministry of Justice* [2016] UKSC 9, Section D regarding the application of the Tables to Fatal Accident Act claims has been re-written and simplified, with a number of new examples.
- A new Section E deals with the indexation of loss of earnings periodical payment orders (PPOs), the application of the suggested Table A to D reduction factors and how to update for different earnings-based measures of inflation.
- Four new tables are provided for men and women for loss of earnings to a retirement age of 68 and pension losses from the same age.

[3] The Department of Justice for Northern Ireland increased the discount rate from -1.75% to -1.5% with effect from 22 March 2022.

- Four new tables are provided for men and women for loss of earnings to a retirement age of 80 and pension losses from the same age.
- There are new Additional Tables at discount rates of -0.25%, -0.75%, -1.5% and 0%.

11. A few of the more significant changes are highlighted below.

Additional Tables

12. Perhaps the most significant development in the 8th edition is the provision of several new tables. The Additional Tables allow for the calculation of multipliers from any age at trial to any future age (up to age 125). They were initially suggested by William Chapman (barrister at 7 Bedford Row). These Additional Tables will be published only on the Government Actuary's Department website in Excel format. These are provided for men and women at discount rates of -1.5%, -0.75%, -0.25% and 0%.

13. The key advantage of the Additional Tables is that they allow for accurate interpolation and calculation of split multipliers, especially for retirement ages that are not contained within the main Ogden Tables. Practitioners may find the Additional Tables quicker and easier to use, especially when calculating split multipliers. It should be noted that the multipliers derived from the Additional Tables are more accurate and reliable – and should be treated as definitive – than other previous methods of interpolation such as using the apportionment method.

Contingencies other than mortality

14. Section B has been completely over-hauled by Professor Wass and a small sub-group of Working Party members including myself, Andrew Underwood and Shahram Sharghy. Importantly, the specific Ogden definition of disability is clarified – this requires both the claimant to be disabled under the more restrictive Disability Discrimination Act 1995 (rather than the Equality Act 2010) and for the disability to affect either the type or amount of work that the claimant can do. Guidance is provided regarding the circumstances where it might be appropriate to adjust the suggested Table A to D reduction factors, and how to calculate the size of any such adjustment. The phrase "ready reckoner" has been removed.

15. The Table A to D reduction factors, used for discounting loss of earnings and pension loss multipliers for contingencies other than mortality, continue to be calculated using the original research conducted by Professors Richard Verrall, Zoltan Butt and Victoria Wass based upon the Labour Force Survey data from 1998-2003. At present, this is the best data we have. Unfortunately, the experts from Cass Business School do not have capacity to update their research at this time, although it is hoped that, if the necessary funding is secured, this is something that can be commissioned for a subsequent edition of the Tables.

Pension Loss

16. Maurice Faull led a small sub-group of forensic accountants and actuaries, including Chris Daykin and John Pollock, who drafted new guidance set out in Section C to assist with the calculation of pension loss in straightforward cases. Two practical examples have been provided showing the methodology for using the Ogden Tables and Additional Tables to calculate such claims.

Fatal Accidents Act Guidance

17. Julian Chamberlayne led a small sub-group of committee members including Richard Methuen KC, Harry Trusted and myself who streamlined the explanatory notes for Section D and the application of the Tables to claims brought under the Fatal Accidents Act 1976 (as amended). Examples have been adroitly drafted by Maurice Faull demonstrating the new methodology including use of the Additional Tables.

Loss of Earnings PPO Guidance

18. In a new Section E, Richard Cropper, Professor Wass and Harry Trusted have provided succinct guidance and a suggested formula to use when uprating periodical payments for loss of earnings taking into account post-injury residual earning capacity in a different role.

Tribute to Previous Chairman

19. Before signing off, I would like to pay tribute to Robin de Wilde KC who chaired the Ogden Working Party from 2004 to 2017. He oversaw the publication of four editions of the Tables, which is no mean feat. He deftly steered the committee, whose members naturally come from very different backgrounds and have varying interests and viewpoints, with compassion, warmth and good humour. Every Chairperson will face his or her own challenges. Robin met his with grace and a majestic calmness, always promoting free and open debate on the most intricate and challenging of issues.

Concluding Remarks

20. When we started work on the 8th edition, few, if any, could have predicted recent events.

21. At the time of writing, the UK remains under lockdown and the future remains uncertain. The restrictions are slowly easing. However, there is no doubt that the long-term and far-reaching impact of Covid-19 on life expectancy, employment prospects and the economy will need to be considered in future editions of these Tables.

22. In the meantime, we're keen to continue improving the Tables and would welcome any feedback, good, bad or indifferent, especially regarding the new Additional Tables.

23. I hope the 8th edition was worth the wait.

July 2020 William Latimer-Sayer KC

(updated August 2022 in light of the change of the Northern Ireland discount rate from -1.75% to -1.5%)

Explanatory Notes to the 8th edition

Section A: General

(a) Purpose of the Ogden Tables

1. The Ogden Tables have been prepared by the Government Actuary's Department (GAD). They provide an aid for those assessing lump sum damages for future pecuniary loss in personal injury and fatal accident cases.

(b) Application of the Ogden Tables

2. The Ogden Tables set out multipliers. These multipliers enable the user to assess the present capital value of future annual loss (net of tax) or annual expense calculated on the basis of various assumptions which are explained below. Accordingly, to find the present capital value of a given annual loss or expense (the multiplicand), it is necessary to select the appropriate table, find the appropriate multiplier and then multiply the multiplicand by that figure.

3. The Ogden Tables may be used to obtain multipliers to calculate the following:
   - claims for lifetime losses;
   - claims for periods of loss (especially loss of earnings) until retirement age;
   - claims for losses (especially pension loss) from retirement age;
   - claims for other pecuniary losses for fixed periods of time;
   - claims for losses deferred for fixed periods of time;
   - claims for variable losses, where the loss changes;
   - claims for dependency brought under the Fatal Accidents Act.

4. There are 36 separate Ogden Tables which make up the main Ogden Tables, and a number of sets of Additional Tables. Tables 1 to 34 of the main Ogden Tables deal with annual loss or annual expense extending over three different periods of time (for life, until retirement and post-retirement). In each case there are separate tables for men and women. The last two tables, Tables 35 and 36, assist with assessing losses in respect of deferred and fixed periods of time (the multipliers are the same for men and women, as these two tables make no allowance for mortality). The main Ogden Tables are arranged as follows:
   - Tables 1 and 2 provide multipliers where the loss or expense is assumed to begin immediately (i.e. as at the date of trial or assessment) and to continue for the rest of the claimant's life.
   - Tables 3 to 18 provide multipliers where the loss or expense is assumed to begin immediately (i.e. as at the date of trial or assessment) but to continue only until the claimant's retirement age or earlier death.
   - Tables 19 to 34 provide multipliers where it is assumed that the loss or expense will not begin until the claimant reaches retirement age but will then continue for the whole of the rest of his or her life.

- Tables 35 and 36 provide discount factors and multipliers for fixed periods of time, referred to as "term certain".

(c) The Tables which do and do not take mortality into account

5. Tables 1 to 34 take mortality into account (in accordance with the assumptions under the next sub- heading). In other words, Tables 1 to 2 take account of the age to which the claimant is expected to live; Tables 3 to 18 take account of the chance that the claimant may not live until retirement age; and Tables 19 to 34 make due allowance for the chance that the claimant may not live to reach the age of retirement and thereafter take account of typical life expectancy.

6. Tables 35 and 36 do not take mortality into account. It is assumed that the loss will continue to be deferred for the relevant period (Table 35) or continue for the entirety of the fixed term (Table 36).

(d) Mortality assumptions, impaired life expectancy and calculation of multipliers

7. The Tables are based on a reasonable estimate of the future mortality likely to be experienced by average members of the population alive today and are based on projected mortality rates for the United Kingdom as a whole. The Office for National Statistics (ONS) publishes population projections on a regular basis (usually bi-annually) which include estimates of the extent of future changes in mortality. Tables 1 to 34 show the multipliers which result from the application of projected mortality rates which were derived from the past and projected period and cohort life tables, 2018-based, UK: 1981 to 2068, which were published by the ONS in December 2019.[4]

8. The Tables are based upon average or typical male and female life expectancy, which it is assumed claimants will have unless proved otherwise. The Tables do not assume that the claimant dies after a period equating to the expectation of life, but take account of the possibilities that the claimant will live for different periods, e.g. die soon or live to be very old. The mortality assumptions relate to the general population of the United Kingdom as a whole. Therefore no further increase or reduction is required for mortality alone, unless there is clear evidence in an individual case that the claimant is "atypical" and can be expected to experience a significantly shorter or longer than average lifespan, to an extent greater than would be encompassed by reasonable variations resulting from place of residence, lifestyle, educational level, occupation and general health status.

9. If it is determined that the claimant's life expectancy is atypical and that the standard average life expectancy data does not apply, the court starts with a clean sheet and a bespoke calculation needs to be performed. The court tends to view the assessment of life expectancy as essentially a medical issue[5]. However, that exercise may require medical, statistical, actuarial or other expert evidence.

10. Whilst statistical evidence is a useful starting point and it may be necessary to adduce statistical or actuarial evidence (especially in cases involving multiple or overlapping reasons for impaired or enhanced life expectancy), the normal or primary route through which statistical evidence is put before the court is through medical experts.

[4] Further details of the 2018-based population projections can be found on the ONS website at: *https://www.ons.gov.uk/peoplepopulationandcommunity/birthsdeathsandmarriages/lifeexpectancies/bulletins/pastandprojecteddatafromtheperiodandcohortlifetables/1981to2068.*

[5] *B (a child) v RVI* [2002] P.I.Q.R. Q137, per Tuckey LJ at [20], and Sir Anthony Evans at [39].

11. There may be a variety of reasons why an individual's life expectancy is atypical. The most obvious reason will be a reduction in life expectancy caused by the injuries which are the subject of the claim. However, claimants may also have an atypical life expectancy due to pre-injury or post-injury factors that would have applied whether or not they suffered the injury in question.

12. Whilst there is no definition of what constitutes atypical, the courts have generally been reluctant to admit expert evidence to argue for a different life expectancy solely on the basis of lifestyle factors, since the average in the Tables includes smokers, non-smokers, drinkers, teetotallers, people who are over-weight and people who have an ideal BMI etc.[6]

13. When a claimant's life expectancy is atypical and a bespoke life expectancy assessment is required, the court should take into account not only the consequences of the injury but also all pre- and post-injury positive and negative factors relevant to the individual claimant, including, but not confined to, the claimant's medical history; genetic and hereditary factors; geographical location; educational, professional or vocational status; lifestyle factors such as smoking, drinking and weight (whether of ideal BMI or obese); and whether the claimant is likely to receive the appropriate level and quality of care, accommodation, aids and equipment and other support needed.

14. Having determined that the claimant's life expectancy is atypical, then the court has to determine the appropriate multiplier to be applied for calculating future losses by using either Tables 1 or 2 (that contain an adjustment for mortality) or Table 36 (that contains no adjustment for mortality).

15. In some cases, the court will determine that the reduction in a claimant's life expectancy is equivalent to adding a certain number of years to his or her current age, or to treating the individual as having a specific age different from his or her actual age. A common example of this is the development of epilepsy following a traumatic brain injury which reduces a claimant's life expectancy by a few years compared to the average. In such a case, Table 1 or 2[7] may be used to calculate the claimant's approximate lifetime multiplier by deeming the claimant to be older than his or her actual age by the same number of years by which his or her life expectancy has been reduced. For example, the lifetime multiplier for a claimant who suffers a reduction in life expectancy of five years due to developing epilepsy as a result of a brain injury can be estimated by using the multiplier which would otherwise apply to a person five years older than the claimant's chronological age.[8] However, when using this method, consideration needs to be given to the applicability of the other Ogden Tables (especially for loss of earnings and pension). In particular, if the claimant's working life is not affected by reason of the reduction in life expectancy, the loss of earnings multiplier can be derived from Tables 3 to 18 in the usual way. However, when calculating multipliers from retirement age, such as loss of pension, the relevant multipliers can be calculated by treating the claimant as being five years older for the purposes of Tables 19 to 34 or by using the method set out below which involves deducting the loss of earnings multiplier from the (adjusted) life expectancy multiplier derived from Table 1 or 2. Where the adjustment is not so straightforward, the advice of an actuary should be sought.

16. In other cases the court may make a finding that a claimant has a given life expectancy based upon his or her mortality risks as a whole and that finding will have involved a more extensive and

[6] See further *Edwards v Martin* [2010] EWHC 570 (QB) and *Dodds v Arif and Aviva Insurance* [2019] EWHC 1512 (QB).

[7] Cases in which the court has used Table 1 include *Tinsley v Sarkar* [2005] EWHC 192 (QB); *Crofts v Murton* [2009] EWHC 3538 (QB); *Smith v LC Window Fashions Ltd* [2009] EWHC 1532 (QB); and *Edwards v Martin* [2010] EWHC 570 (QB).

[8] Medical experts often express their opinion as "the claimant is likely to live X years less than the average". Actuarially, however, treating someone as being X years older is not the same as deducting X years from the life expectancy for an average person of the claimant's current age. The life expectancy of someone X years older is likely to be a slightly different figure; and where the deduction to life expectancy is significant, it may be sensible to seek actuarial advice.

refined exercise which examines all of the claimant's mortality risks and therefore renders it inappropriate to regard him or her as one of the class who was subject to the statistical mortality risks for which Tables 1 or 2 provide. In such a case the relevant fixed term multiplier should be derived from Table 36[9] or the advice of an actuary should be sought.

17. At present, when the discount rate is negative in each jurisdiction, the use of Table 36 will understate the applicable multiplier. However, the level of understatement is negligible when the discount rate is close to zero as it is in England and Wales at the moment. In the future, if the discount rate were to reduce to a more significant negative number or to increase to a significant positive number, using fixed term multipliers from Table 36 is likely to result in technically inaccurate multipliers because this does not allow for the distribution of deaths around the expected length of life. In such circumstances, the preferable methodology for calculating actuarially accurate multipliers is set out in paragraph 20 of the Explanatory Notes to the 6th edition of the Ogden Tables.[10]

(e) Selection of the appropriate table

18. To find the appropriate figure for the present value of a particular loss or expense, the user must first select the relevant Table that relates to the period of loss or expense for which the individual claimant is to be compensated and to the sex of the claimant, or, where appropriate, the dependants of the deceased.

19. If, for some reason, the facts in a particular case do not correspond with the assumptions on which one of the Tables is based (e.g. it is known that the claimant will have a different retiring age from that assumed in the Tables), then the Tables can be used if an appropriate allowance is made for this difference by way of interpolation: see Section A (f) below.

20. It should be noted that the Additional Tables provided by GAD for this 8th edition will allow for a greater range of multipliers to be calculated without requiring interpolation.

(f) Interpolation

21. It is often necessary to calculate specific multipliers which are not contained in the main Ogden Tables. For example, it may be necessary to calculate a lifetime multiplier or loss of earnings multiplier for the exact age of a person at trial, which is not a whole number. Alternatively, it may be necessary to calculate a loss of earnings multiplier to a retirement age which is not provided for in the main Ogden Tables. Such multipliers may be calculated by the process of interpolation, usually by interpolating between different columns in the same Tables or by interpolating between multipliers from two different Tables. The four main methods used for interpolation of multipliers are as follows:

[9] Cases in which the courts have used Table 28, now Table 36, include *B (a child) v RVI* [2002] P.I.Q.R. Q137; *Sarwar v Ali* [2007] EWHC 274 (QB); *Burton v Kingsbury* [2007] EWHC 2091 (QB); *Whiten v St George's Healthcare NHS Trust* [2011] EWHC 2066 (QB); *Reaney v University Hospital of North Staffordshire NHS Trust* [2014] EWHC 3016 (QB); and *Manna v Central Manchester University Hospitals NHS Foundation Trust* [2015] EWHC9 (QB).

[10] Although note that the courts have generally been reluctant to adopt the impaired lives approach suggested at paragraph 20 of the explanatory notes to the 6th edition of the Ogden Tables even when the discount rate was +2.5% as it was considered to be inconsistent with the approach of the Court of Appeal in *B (a child) v RVI* [2002] P.I.Q.R. Q137: see further *Whiten v St George's Healthcare NHS Trust* [2011] EWHC 2066 (QB); *Reaney v University Hospital of North Staffordshire NHS Trust* [2014] EWHC 3016 (QB); *Manna v Central Manchester University Hospitals NHS Foundation Trust* [2015] EWHC9 (QB).

- Using a computer programme.
- Manually interpolating using the methods set out in the following paragraph and under "Different retirement ages".
- Using the Additional Tables to calculate loss of earnings or pension loss multipliers involving retirement ages which are not provided for in the main Ogden Tables.
- Using alternative tables such as Table A1 in *Facts & Figures* for calculating multipliers in respect of different retirement ages not provided for in the main Ogden Tables.

22. If interpolating manually, the method described below under "Different retirement ages" is the most accurate. However, when undertaking simple interpolation between two multipliers or two Tables, there is an alternative simpler approach which produces very similar results which are approximate to the more exact figure. This is illustrated in the following two examples.

Example 1 – simple interpolation between two integers at -0.25%

23. A male claimant is aged 21.75 as at the date of trial. The lifetime multiplier for a 21-year-old male at -0.25% is 71.17 (X). The lifetime multiplier for a 22-year-old male is 69.89 (Y). The interpolated multiplier for a male aged 21.75 can be calculated as X – [(X – Y) × 0.75] or Y + [(X – Y) × 0.25]. In either case the result is 70.21.

Example 2 – simple interpolation between two retirement ages at -0.25%

24. A female claimant aged 45 at trial and her state retirement age is 67. The multiplier from Table 10 to a retirement age of 65 at -0.25% is 20.07 (X). The multiplier from Table 12 to a retirement age of 68 at -0.25% is 23.03 (Y). Since 67 is 2/3's of the way between 65 and 68, the interpolated loss of earnings multiplier for a female retiring at age 67, can be estimated as X + [(Y – X) × 2 / 3] or Y – [(Y – X) × 1 / 3]. Both approaches produce the same result of 22.04.

(g) The Additional Tables

25. When there is a need to calculate multipliers between two ages, the Additional Tables to the 8th edition of the Ogden Tables (which can be downloaded from the GAD website[11]) provide a convenient way of identifying multipliers at selected rates of discount that can be used to capitalise multiplicands payable from any age at the date of trial to any future age up to age 125 (i.e. for life). These multipliers have been calculated using the same mortality rates and other assumptions underlying the main Ogden Tables in the 8th edition, namely the projected mortality rates underlying the 2018-based principal population projection for the United Kingdom and assuming a date of trial in 2022.

26. Where multipliers need to be calculated starting or ending at ages which are non-integers, one of the above methods must still be used for interpolating the exact multipliers. Likewise, one of the above methods must still be used to interpolate multipliers at a discount rates not provided by the Additional Tables.

[11] *https://www.gov.uk/government/publications/ogden-tables-actuarial-compensation-tables-for-injury-and-death.*

27. Where there is a need to interpolate multipliers derived from Tables 1 to 34 and there are discrepancies in the results obtained using different interpolation methods, using the Additional Tables will produce the most accurate and reliable multipliers.

(h) The discount rate

28. The basis of the multipliers set out in the Tables is that the lump sum will be invested and yield income (but that over the period in question the claimant will gradually reduce the capital sum, so that at the end of the period it is exhausted). Accordingly, an essential factor in arriving at the right figure is the choice of the appropriate rate of return, known as the discount rate. However, the applicable discount rate (represented by individual columns in each table running from −2% to +2.5% (and to 3% in the standalone tables), depends upon the jurisdiction where the damages are being assessed. Multipliers for discount rates between tabulated rates can be obtained by interpolation. If multipliers are required for discount rates outside the tabulated range the advice of an actuary should be sought or a suitable computer programme used.

29. The table below summarises the currently applicable discount rates, effective legislation and relevant review periods in the UK.[12]

Jurisdiction	Rate	Effective Legislation	Review
England & Wales	-0.25% (from 5 August 2019)	Civil Liability Act 2018 – rate determined by the Lord Chancellor and the Damages (Personal Injury) Order 2019[13]	Rate set by Lord Chancellor – reviewed at least every five years[14]
Scotland	-0.75% (from 27 September 2019)	Damages (Investment Returns and Periodical Payments) (Scotland) Act 2019 – rate determined by the Government Actuary[15]	Rate set by the Government Actuary[16] – reviewed at least every five years
Northern Ireland	-1.5% (from 22 March 2022)	The Damages (Return on Investment) Act (Northern Ireland) 202217	Rate set by the Government Actuary – reviewed at least every five years

30. The figures in the 0% column show the multiplier without any discount for interest and provide the expectations of life (Tables 1 and 2) or the expected period over which a person would have

[12] Other discount rates apply in non-UK parts of the British Isles such as Guernsey and Jersey.
[13] SI 2019 No 1126.
[14] To help him or her set the assumed rate of return (i.e. the applicable discount rate), at the first review (carried out in 2019) the Lord Chancellor was required to consult with the Treasury and the Government Actuary; at all future reviews, the Lord Chancellor must consult with the Treasury and an expert panel consisting of the Government Actuary (who is the chair of the panel), an actuary, a member with experience of managing investments, an economist and a specialist in consumer affairs relating to investments.
[15] See further *The Personal Injury Discount Rate: Review and determination of the rate in Scotland by the Government Actuary* dated 27 September 2019 available from: *https://www.gov.uk/government/publications/the-personal-injury-discount-rate- review-and-determination-of-the- rate-in-scotland-by-the-government-actuary.*
[16] In Scotland the discount rate is set by the official "rate-assessor". This is the Government Actuary or a person appointed in place of the Government Actuary by regulations made by Scottish Ministers.
[17] *http://www.legislation.gov.uk/nia/2022/1/contents.*

provided a dependency (up to retirement age Tables 3 to 18 or from pension age Tables 19 to 34). These are particularly helpful when calculating multipliers in respect of claims brought under the Fatal Accidents Act 1976 (see Section D).

31. Section 1(2) of the Damages Act 1996 makes provision for the courts to make variations to the discount rate if any party to the proceedings shows that it is more appropriate in the case in question. However, this power is limited to exceptional cases involving special circumstances.[18] Section 1(2) will therefore only be exercised in comparatively few cases,[19] and indeed, at the time of writing there have been no reported cases in which the court has been persuaded to invoke the power under this section to apply a different discount rate, although a number of cases have been settled making such assumptions, for example where the claimant or dependants are not resident in the UK.[20]

(i) Different retirement ages

32. Separate Ogden Tables are provided for retirement ages of 50, 55, 60, 65, 68,[21] 70, 75 and 80. The Additional Tables provided by GAD can be used to calculate accurate multipliers outside or between these ages. In addition, where the claimant's actual retiring age would have been between two of the retirement ages for which main Ogden Tables are provided, the multiplier can be calculated by interpolation of the main Ogden Tables for retirement age immediately above and below the actual retirement age, keeping the period to retirement age the same.

Example 3 – more accurate interpolation between two retirement ages at +2.5%

33. Take for example a woman of 42 who would have retired at 58. Her loss of earnings multiplier can be considered as being in-between the multipliers for a woman of 39 with a retirement age of 55 and a woman of 44 with a retirement age of 60. The most accurate method for interpolation is as follows:

    (1) Determine between which retirement ages, for which Tables are provided, the claimant's actual retirement age R lies. Let the lower of these ages be A and the higher be B.

    (2) Determine how many years must be subtracted from the claimant's actual retirement age to get to A and subtract that period from the claimant's age. If the claimant's age is X, the result of this calculation is $(X + A - R)$.

    (3) Look up this new reduced age in the Table corresponding to retirement age A at the appropriate rate of return. Let the resulting multiplier be M.

    (4) Determine how many years must be added to the claimant's actual retirement age to get to B and add that period to the claimant's age. The result of this calculation is $(X + B - R)$.

[18] *Warriner v Warriner* [2002] EWCA Civ 81, [2002] 1 W.L.R 1703 and *Cooke v United Bristol Health Care* [2003] EWCA Civ 1370, [2004] 1 W.L.R 251.

[19] *Warriner v Warriner* [2002] EWCA Civ 81 per Dyson LJ at [35].

[20] Other discount rates have also been adopted in non-UK common law jurisdictions which also use the Ogden Tables, for example Guernsey in the case of *Helmot v Simon* [2012] UKPC 5.

[21] Under the current law, the State Pension age is due to increase to age 68 between 2044 and 2046 (although this may be brought forwards following a recent government review). To check the state retirement age of a particular claimant, there is a helpful calculator at: *https://www.gov.uk/state-pension-age.*

(5) Look up this new increased age in the Table corresponding to retirement age *B* at the appropriate rate of return. Let the resulting multiplier be *N*.

(6) Interpolate between *M* and *N*. In other words, calculate:

$(B - R) \times M + (R - A) \times N$

and divide the result by $[(B - R) + (R - A)]$, (or equivalently $[B - A]$).

34. In the example given in the preceding paragraph, the steps to interpolate the appropriate multiplier are set out below.

(1) R is 58, *A* is 55 and *B* is 60.

(2) Subtracting three years from the claimant's age gives 39.

(3) Looking up age 39 in Table 6 (for retirement age 55) gives 13.11 (*M*) at a rate of return of +2.5%.

(4) Adding two years to the claimant's age gives 44.

(5) Looking up age 44 in Table 8 (for retirement age 60) gives 13.05 (*N*) at a rate of return of +2.5%.

(6) Interpolate between M and N applying the above formula: $2 \times 13.11 + 3 \times 13.05$ and dividing by (60−58) + (58−55) [equals 5] gives 13.07 as the multiplier.

(j) Calculating losses from retirement

35. When the loss or expense to be valued is that from the date of retirement to death, and the claimant's date of retirement differs from that assumed in the main Ogden Tables, the Additional Tables may be used to calculate the appropriate multiplier.

36. Alternatively, to calculate the multiplier using the main Ogden Tables, a different approach is necessary involving the following three steps:

(1) Assume that there is a present loss which will continue for the rest of the claimant's life and from Table 1 or 2 establish the value of that loss or expense over the whole period from the date of assessment until the claimant's death.

(2) Establish the value of such loss or expense over the period from the date of assessment until the claimant's expected date of retirement following the procedure explained in Section A (i) above.

(3) Subtract the second figure from the first. The balance remaining represents the present value of the claimant's loss or expense between retirement and death.

(k) Younger ages

37. Tables 1 and 2, which concern pecuniary loss for life, and Tables 19 to 34, which concern loss of pension from retirement age, have been extended down to age 0. In some circumstances the multiplier at age 0 is slightly lower than that at age 1; this arises because of the relatively high incidence of deaths immediately after birth.

38. Tables for multipliers for loss of earnings (Tables 3 to 18) have not been extended below age 16. In order to determine the multiplier for loss of earnings for someone who has not yet started work, it is first necessary to determine an assumed age at which the claimant would have commenced work and to find the appropriate multiplier for that age from Tables 3 to 18, according to the assumed retirement age. This multiplier should then be multiplied by the discount or deferment factor from Table 35 which corresponds to the prevailing discount rate in the relevant jurisdiction and the period from the date of the trial to the date on which it is assumed that the claimant would have started work.

39. A similar approach can be used for determining a multiplier for pecuniary loss for life where the loss is assumed to commence in a number of years from the date of the trial. For simplicity the factors in Table 35 relate purely to the impact of compound interest and ignore mortality. At ages below 30 this is a reasonable approximation but, at higher ages, and where the losses are significant, it may be appropriate to allow explicitly for mortality and the advice of an actuary should be sought.

(l) Contingencies other than mortality

40. Tables 1 to 34 make reasonable provision for mortality risk i.e. the levels of mortality which members of the population of the United Kingdom alive today may typically expect to experience in future. However, these Tables do not take account of any other risks or vicissitudes of life, such as the possibility that the claimant would have had interruptions in employment due to periods out for reasons including ill-health, childcare and redundancy. Section B suggests ways in which allowance may be made to the multipliers for loss of earnings, to allow for risks other than mortality.

(m) Fixed periods

41. In cases where pecuniary loss is to be valued for a fixed period, the multipliers in Table 36 may be used. These make no allowance for mortality or any other contingency but assume that regular frequent payments (e.g. weekly or monthly) will continue throughout the period. These figures should in principle be adjusted if the periodicity of payment is less frequent, especially if the payments in question are annually in advance or in arrears.

(n) Variable future losses or expenses

42. The Tables do not provide an immediate answer when the annual future loss or expense is likely to change at given points in time in the future (other than increasing with inflation). The most common examples will be where:

(a) The claimant's lost earnings would have increased on a sliding scale or changed due to promotion; or

(b) The claimant's future care needs are likely to change in the future, perhaps because it is anticipated that a family carer will not be able to continue to provide help or because deterioration of the claimant's condition is expected.

43. In such situations it is usually necessary to split the overall multiplier, whether for working life or whole of life, into segments, and then to apply those smaller segmented multipliers to the multiplicand appropriate for each period.

44. Splitting a Table 36 multiplier is relatively straightforward. It is usually easier to use a computer programme or the Additional Tables to split multipliers from Tables 1 to 34. However, split multipliers can also be calculated manually as set out in Example 6 below.

Example 4 – splitting Table 36 multipliers at -0.25%

45. Where the claimant's life expectancy is impaired and the claimant's whole life multiplier is derived using a fixed term multiplier from Table 36, it is common practice to derive the multipliers for each period of loss from the same table.

46. Take, for example, an English male aged 20 years at the date of settlement/trial who requires personal care and assistance for life. He has a reduced life expectancy to age 70. Significant changes in his care regime are anticipated at age 30 and again at age 50.

47. The multiplicands for care costs are set out in the following table.

Period	**Age**	**Annual care costs**
1.	From age 20 to 30	£30,000 per annum
2.	From age 30 to 50	£60,000 per annum
3.	From age 50 for life	£80,000 per annum

48. The whole life multiplier from age 20 to 70 for a fixed term of 50 years derived from Table 36 at a discount rate of -0.25% is 53.26. The split multipliers for each period of loss can be calculated as follows: the multiplier for the first 10 year period (20-30) is the multiplier for a term certain of 10 years derived from Table 36, namely 10.13; for the next period of 20 years (30-50) the Table 36 multiplier is 21.03 (being the fixed term multiplier of 30 years of 31.16 minus the multiplier for a fixed term of 10 years of 10.13); then, the multiplier for the final period of loss (50-70) is the balance of the full multiplier i.e. 22.10 (being the term certain multiplier of 53.26 minus the fixed term multiplier for 30 years of 31.16).

Age (years)	**Table 36 Split multipliers**	**Care costs £ a year**	**Total £**
20 – 30	10.13	30,000	303,900
30 – 50	21.03	60,000	1,261,800
50 – 70	22.10	80,000	1,768,000
Totals	53.26		**3,333,700**

Example 5 – splitting Table 1 multipliers using the Additional Tables at -0.25%

49. Where the claimant has a normal life expectancy, the whole life multiplier is derived from Table 1 for men or Table 2 for women. The easiest and most accurate way to calculate split multipliers for

variable periods of loss derived from Tables 1 to 34 is to use the Additional Tables or a computer programme based on the Additional Tables.

50. Using the same facts and multiplicands as Example 4 above but with the normal life expectancy, the split multipliers for each period at a discount rate of -0.25% can be derived from the Additional Tables as follows. The whole life multiplier for a man aged 20 at a discount rate of -0.25% is 72.46. For the first period from age 20 to 30, the multiplier is 10.11. For the second period from age 30 to 50, the multiplier is 20.75 (being the multiplier from age 20 to 50 of 30.86 minus the multiplier from age 20 to 30 of 10.11). The multiplier for the final period from age 50 for life is 41.60 (being the whole life multiplier of 72.46 minus the multiplier from age 20 to 50 of 30.86).

51. The total claim for care over the claimant's lifetime is £4,876,300, as set out in the following table.

Age (years)	Table 1 Split multipliers	Care costs £ a year	Total £
20 – 30	10.11	30,000	303,300
30 – 50	20.75	60,000	1,245,000
50 till death	41.60	80,000	3,328,000
Totals	72.46		**4,876,300**

Example 6 – splitting Table 1 multipliers using the apportionment method at -0.25%

52. An alternative way to estimate split multipliers for variable periods of loss derived from Tables 1 to 34 is to use the "apportionment method". This method involves apportioning the multiplier that needs to be split by reference to percentages of the fixed term multiplier for the same period derived from Table 36. The apportionment method, which was set out in paras 23 to 24 of the explanatory notes to the 6th edition of the Tables, is less accurate than using the Additional Tables, however, an example of its use is set out below in the event that it is not possible to access the Additional Tables.

53. Using the same facts as in the above examples (with a normal life expectancy), the Table 1 whole life multiplier of 72.46 can be split manually using the main Ogden Tables at a discount rate of -0.25% as follows:

(1) The life expectation will be 66.36 years (from the 0% column of Table 1) and the multiplier for that period taking into account mortality risks (from the -0.25% column of Table 1) will be 72.46.

(2) The multiplier for a term certain of 66.36 years (ignoring mortality risks) from Table 36 at -0.25% lies between 71.76 (for 66 years) and 72.95 (for 67 years) and is calculated thus:

$[(67 - 66.36) \times 71.76] + [(66.36 - 66) \times 72.95] = 72.19.$[22]

(3) The above Table 36 multiplier of 72.19 for a full period of 72.46 years should be split into separate smaller Table 36 fixed term multipliers representing each period of loss. So, the

[22] Using the simpler interpolation method referred to in Section A (f), the calculation is the same i.e. $71.76 + [(72.95 - 71.76) \times 0.36] = 72.19$.

multiplier for the first 10 year period (20-30) is represented by a multiplier for a term certain of 10 years derived from Table 36, namely 10.13; for the next period of 20 years (30-50) the Table 36 multiplier is represented by a multiplier of 21.03 (being the fixed term multiplier of 30 years of 31.16 minus the multiplier for a fixed term of 10 years of 10.13); then, the final period of loss (from 50 to death) is represented by the balance of the full multiplier i.e. 41.03 (being the term certain multiplier of 72.19 minus the fixed term multiplier for 30 years of 31.16).

(4) Each of those smaller segmented multipliers can be shown as a percentage or fraction of the whole: so, for the first 10 years the segmented multiplier of 10.13 is 14.032% of the whole figure of 72.19, and so on for each segment of the life period.

(5) The life multiplier from Table 1 can now be split up in the way in which the Table 36 multiplier was treated above and in identical proportions: thus the first 10 year period is now represented by a multiplier of 10.17 which is calculated by taking 14.032% of 72.46.

(6) The figures (rounded at each step of the calculation) are set out in tabular form below and give a total lump sum award of £4,866,100:

Age (years)	**Table 36 (66.36 years) Split multipliers**	**% Split (of Table 36 figure)**	**Table 1 (multiplier allowing for mortality)**	**Care costs £ a year**	**Total £**
20 - 30	10.13	14.032%	10.17	30,000	305,100
30 - 50	21.03	29.131%	21.11	60,000	1,266,600
50 till death	41.03	56.836%	41.18	80,000	3,294,400
Totals	72.19 (no mortality discount)	100.00%	72.46 life multiplier		**4,866,100**

Section B: Contingencies other than Mortality

(a) Introduction

54. As stated in Section A, Tables 3 to 18 of the main Ogden Tables for calculating loss of earnings take no account of risks other than mortality. Likewise, loss of earnings multipliers derived from the Additional Tables make no allowance for risks other than mortality. This section shows how the multipliers in these Tables may be reduced to take account of risks other than mortality by applying reduction factors in Tables A to D.

55. Tables of reduction factors to be applied to the existing multipliers were first introduced in the 2nd edition of the Ogden Tables. These factors were based on work commissioned by the Institute of Actuaries and carried out by Professor S Haberman and Mrs D S F Bloomfield.[23] Although there was some debate within the actuarial profession about the details of the work, and in particular about the scope for developing it further, the findings were broadly accepted and were adopted by the Government Actuary and the other actuaries who were members of the Ogden Working Party when the 2nd edition of the Tables was published and remained unchanged until the 6th edition.

[23] Work time lost to sickness, unemployment and stoppages: measurement and application (1990), *Journal of the Institute of Actuaries,* 117, 533-595.

56. Some related work was published in 2002 by Lewis, McNabb and Wass.[24] For the publication of the 6th edition of the Ogden Tables, the Ogden Working Party was involved in further research into the impact of contingencies other than mortality carried out by Professor Richard Verrall, Professor Steven Haberman and Mr Zoltan Butt of City University, London and, in a separate exercise, by Dr Victoria Wass of Cardiff University. Their findings were combined to produce the tables of reduction factors, Tables A to D, given in Section B of the 6th edition.

57. The Haberman and Bloomfield paper relied on data from the Labour Force Surveys for 1973, 1977, 1981 and 1985 and English Life Tables No. 14 (1980-82). The Labour Force Survey (LFS) was originally designed to produce a periodic cross-sectional snapshot of the working age population and collects information on an extensive range of socio-economic and labour force characteristics. Since the winter of 1992/3, the LFS has been carried out on a quarterly basis, with respondents being included in the survey over five successive quarters. The research of Professor Verrall *et al* and Dr Wass used panel data from the Labour Force Surveys conducted from 1998 to 2003 to estimate the probabilities of movement of males and females between different employment states, dependent on age, sex, starting employment state and level of disability. These probabilities permit the calculation of the expected periods in employment until retirement age, dependent on the starting employment state, disability status and educational attainment. These working-life expectancies can be compared to the working time to retirement where the person remains in work throughout, to obtain reduction factors which give the expected proportion of time to retirement age which will be spent in employment. The reduction factor is applied to the relevant baseline multiplier from Tables 3 to 18, in order to give a multiplier which takes into account only those periods the claimant would be expected, on average, to be in work. The reduction factors reported in this edition are calculated on the basis of a discount rate of 0%[25] compared to 2.5% in the earlier editions.

58. The factors described in subsequent paragraphs are for use in calculating loss of earnings up to retirement age. The research did not investigate the impact of contingencies other than mortality on the value of future pension rights. Some reduction to the multiplier for loss of pension would often be appropriate when a reduction is being applied for loss of earnings. This may be a smaller reduction than in the case of loss of earnings because the ill-health contingency (as opposed to the unemployment contingency) may give rise to significant ill-health retirement pension rights. A bigger reduction may be necessary in cases where there is significant doubt whether pension rights would have continued to accrue (to the extent not already allowed for in the post-retirement multiplier) or in cases where there may be doubt over the ability of the pension fund to pay promised benefits. In the case of a defined contribution pension scheme, loss of pension rights may be allowed for simply by increasing the future earnings loss (adjusted for contingencies other than mortality) by the percentage of earnings which the employer contributions to the scheme represent. For further details and an example, see under the subheading "Assessing Pension Losses" in Section C of the explanatory notes.

59. The methodology of applying the Table A to D reduction factors described below is the suggested method for dealing with contingencies other than mortality and is applicable in most circumstances. The methodology provides for the separate valuation of pre- and post-injury earnings, where the latter accounts for anticipated residual earnings in cases where the claimant is considered capable of working after the injury, whether on an employed or self-employed basis. This will in the majority of cases enable a more accurate assessment to be made of the mitigation of loss. However, there may be some cases when the *Smith v Manchester*[26] *or Blamire*[27] approach

[24] Methods of calculating damages for loss of future earnings, *Journal of Personal Injury Law,* 2002 No. 2.

[25] The data is not available to provide reduction factors at -0.25% or -0.75%. However, any difference is thought to be negligible compared to the available reduction factors calculated at 0%.

[26] *Smith v Manchester Corporation* (1974) 17 KIR 1.

[27] *Blamire v South Cumbria Health Authority* [1993] P.I.Q.R. Q1.

remains applicable or otherwise where a precise mathematical approach is inapplicable.[28] For example, there may be no real alternative to a *Smith v Manchester* or *Blamire* award where there is insufficient evidence or too many imponderables for the judge to be able to make the findings necessary to support the conventional multiplicand/multiplier approach.[29] But, merely because there are uncertainties about the future does not of itself justify a departure from the well-established multiplicand/multiplier method and judges should therefore be slow to resort to the broad-brush *Blamire* approach, unless they really have no alternative.[30]

60. The reduction factor approach which follows is for guidance and is not prescriptive. However, the Table A to D reduction factors should generally be used unless there is a good reason to disapply or to adjust them. The suggested reduction factors adjust the baseline multiplier to reflect the average pre- and post-injury contingencies according to the employment risks associated with the age, sex, employment status, disability status and educational attainment of the claimant when calculating awards for loss of earnings and for any mitigation of this loss in respect of potential future post-injury earnings. This method of calculation, based as it is on three broadly defined characteristics, will not capture all the factors which might be expected to affect the claimant's future earnings. Neither is the average for a broad category likely to capture the detail of individual circumstances and characteristics. First, employment history is based on employment status at the time of trial or assessment and does not include details of the claimant's career up to that date. Secondly, educational achievement is measured as three broad groups which are an imperfect proxy for individual human capital and skill level. Thirdly, it can be difficult to place a value on the possible mitigating income when considering the potential range of impairments and their effect on post-work capability, even within the Ogden definition of disability set out below. For these reasons it may be appropriate in certain circumstances to depart from the published reduction factors in Tables A to D by increasing or reducing the reduction factor to better account for the individual characteristics of the claimant. Some of the circumstances which warrant departure and a methodology to determine the scale of the departure are described below. The examples at the end of this section illustrate the strict application of the reduction factors and also the circumstances and method for making a departure.

61. The reduction factors have not been updated using more recent data from the LFS. They remain based on the data from 1998-2003. Since the introduction of the Equality Act 2010, there have been major changes in the interpretation of disability which has involved a lowering of the threshold of the disability status classification. This is ongoing and is particularly evident in data collected from 2013 onwards. As the definition of disability gets wider and as awareness and acceptance increase, its prevalence rate in the working-age population increases. This is because more people think of themselves as disabled and self-report disability when questioned in surveys. As the prevalence rate increases, the difference in employment risks between disabled and non-disabled people gets narrower. This is not because people with a specific impairment, for example a visual impairment, suffer less employment disadvantage but rather because people with a lower severity of impairment or activity limitation increasingly classify themselves as disabled rather than non-disabled. The employment chances among this bigger group are higher than for those under the narrower definition of disability. While the expanding definition of disability precludes a consistent measure of the disability employment gap, it is advisable to rely upon older data based on a more stable definition of disability and a definition that more closely matches the needs of the Ogden Tables.

[28] See *Billett v MOD* [2015] EWCA Civ 773; [2016] P.I.Q.R. Q1 at para 99; and *Ward v Allies and Morrison Architects* [2012] EWCA Civ 1287; [2013] P.I.Q.R. Q1 which considered similar wording from the 6th edition of the guidance notes.
[29] See *Irani v Duchon* [2019] EWCA Civ 1846, per Hamblen LJ at [22].
[30] See *Bullock v Atlas Ward Structures Ltd* [2008] EWCA Civ 194, per Lord Keene at [21].

62. Whilst the underlying data remain the same, there are three differences to the suggested reduction factors in the 8th edition of the Tables and the way they are calculated. These are as follows:

(a) Re-calculation of the reduction factors at a discount rate of 0% to reflect the reduction in the personal injury discount rate[31];

(b) Re-labelling of the education classification to Level 1 (below GCSE level qualification, no qualification or other qualification); Level 2 (A level or equivalent, GCSE or equivalent); Level 3 (higher degree, degree and equivalent, higher education qualification below degree level); and

(c) Allocation of new qualifications and newly graded qualifications within a re-labelled three-way education classification.

63. Guidance is provided below regarding when it might be appropriate to consider departing from the strict application of the reduction factors and how to estimate the scale of that departure.

(b) The deduction for contingencies other than mortality

64. Under this method, multipliers for loss of earnings obtained from Tables 3 to 18, or, alternatively derived from the Additional Tables, are multiplied by reduction factors to allow for the risk of periods of non-employment.

65. The research by Professor Verrall *et al* and Dr Wass referred to above demonstrated that the key issues affecting a person's future working life are age, sex, employment status, disability status and educational attainment.

66. The definitions of employed/not employed, disabled/not disabled and educational attainment used in this analysis and which should be used for determining which reduction factors to apply to the baseline multipliers to allow for contingencies other than mortality are as follows.

(c) Definition of Employed

67. *"Employed"*: In respect of Tables A and C – those who were employed, self-employed or on a government training scheme as at the time of injury.

In respect of Tables B and D – those who are employed, self-employed or on a government training scheme as at the date of assessment / trial.

"Not employed": All others (including those temporarily out of work, full-time students and unpaid family workers).

(d) Ogden Definition of Disability

68. It is important to note that the definition of disability used in the Ogden Tables is not the same as that used in the Equality Act 2010. The Ogden definition of disability is based upon the definition of disability set out in the Disability Discrimination Act (DDA) 1995 (supported by the accompanying guidance notes). This is because this is the definition that applied at the time of the underlying LFS research which underpins the suggested Table A to D reduction factors. In addition

[31] In England, Wales and Scotland.

to meeting the DDA 1995 definition of disability, the impairment must also be work-affecting by either limiting the kind or amount of work the claimant is able to do. The Ogden definition of disability is defined as follows.

"Disabled person": A person is classified as being disabled if **all three** of the following conditions in relation to ill-health or disability are met:

(i) The person has an illness or a disability which has or is expected to last for over a year or is a progressive illness; and

(ii) The DDA1995 definition is satisfied in that the impact of the disability has a substantial[32] adverse effect on the person's ability to carry out normal day-to-day activities[33]; and

(iii) The effects of impairment limit either the kind **or** the amount of paid work he/she can do.

"Not disabled": All others

69. Disability is therefore defined as an impairment that has a substantial adverse effect on a respondent's ability to carry out normal day-to-day activities. Both 'normal' and 'substantial' require interpretation. Normal day-to-day activities are those which are carried out by most people on a daily basis and which include those carried out at work. The meaning of the word 'substantial' has changed over time in both law and common understanding such that the threshold whereby an activity-limitation qualifies as 'substantial' (and therefore amounts to a disability) was lower in 2019 than it was when the data were collected. This is reflected in a higher disability prevalence rate in the working-age population which was around 12% in 1998 and is around 19% in 2019, reflecting an increased reporting of qualifying activity-limiting impairments rather than an increase in the number or severity of such impairments.[34] The issue of severity of disability within the reduction factors underpinned the disagreement in the case of *Billett v MOD*[35] *litigated in 2014 and 2015. Mr Billett was disabled under the looser Equality Act 2010 de*finition but arguably he was not disabled under the tighter Ogden definition of disability because his impairment was not sufficiently limiting relative to the criteria set out below.[36]

70. Criteria (i) to (iii) above, which determine disability status, were self-reported. The guidance notes on the meaning of substantial from the DDA 1995 were available to survey respondents to assist them to self-classify. The guidance notes were not intended to be inclusive or exhaustive and it is not clear to what extent respondents referred to them. The guidance notes were dropped from the Equality Act 2010 and from the LFS survey question in 2013 because they were considered to be

[32] Para 3.2 of the DDA Code of Practice defined substantial as being more than minor or trivial.

[33] The reduction factors are based on data from 1998-2003 when disability status was defined by the DDA 1995. Under Sch.1, para 4 of the DDA, an impairment was taken to affect the ability of the person concerned to carry out normal day- to-day activities only if it affects one of the following: (a) mobility; (b) manual dexterity; (c) physical coordination; (d) continence; (e) ability to lift, carry or otherwise move everyday objects; (f) speech, hearing or eyesight; (g) memory or ability to concentrate, learn or understand; or (h) perception of the risk of physical danger.

[34] These prevalence rates are DDA and Equality Act 2010 definitions of disability and not the Ogden Tables definition. They are reported by ONS in Table A08: (*https://www.ons.gov.uk/employmentandlabourmarket/peopleinwork/employmentandemployeetypes/datasets/labo urmarketstatusofdisabledpeoplea08*). The prevalence rate on the Ogden tables definition has increased from 11.3% to 13.5% (Jones, M. and Wass, V. J. (2013). *"Understanding changing disability-related employment gaps in Britain"*, 1998-2011. *Work Employment and Society* 27(6), pp. 982-1003 updated to 2019 using LFS April-June 2019).

[35] *Billett v MOD* [2015] EWCA Civ 773; [2016] P.I.Q.R. Q1.

[36] See further Wass V (2015) "Billett v Ministry of Defence: A second bite", Journal of Personal Injury Law, 4 pp. 243-245; and Wass V (2015) "Billett v Ministry of Defence and the meaning of disability in the Ogden Tables", *Journal of Personal Injury Law*, 1 pp. 37-41.

overly restrictive in the definition of disability. The guidance notes are reproduced here but should be used with the above caveats in mind.

Mobility - for example, unable to travel short journeys as a passenger in a car, unable to walk other than at a slow pace or with jerky movements, difficulty in negotiating stairs, unable to use one or more forms of public transport, unable to go out of doors unaccompanied.

Manual dexterity - for example, loss of functioning in one or both hands, inability to use a knife and fork at the same time, or difficulty in pressing buttons on a keyboard.

Physical co-ordination - for example, the inability to feed or dress oneself; or to pour liquid from one vessel to another except with unusual slowness or concentration.

Problems with bowel/bladder control - for example, frequent or regular loss of control of the bladder or bowel. Occasional bedwetting is not considered a disability.

Ability to lift, carry or otherwise move everyday objects (for example, books, kettles, light furniture) - for example, inability to pick up a weight with one hand but not the other, or to carry a tray steadily.

Speech - for example, unable to communicate (clearly) orally with others, taking significantly longer to say things. A minor stutter, difficulty in speaking in front of an audience, or inability to speak a foreign language would not be considered impairments.

Hearing - for example, not being able to hear without the use of a hearing aid, the inability to understand speech under normal conditions or over the telephone.

Eyesight - for example, while wearing spectacles or contact lenses - being unable to pass the standard driving eyesight test, total inability to distinguish colours (excluding ordinary red/green colour blindness), or inability to read newsprint.

Memory or ability to concentrate, learn or understand - for example, intermittent loss of consciousness or confused behaviour, inability to remember names of family or friends, unable to write a cheque without assistance, or an inability to follow a recipe.

Perception of risk of physical danger - for example, reckless behaviour putting oneself or others at risk, mobility to cross the road safely. This excludes (significant) fear of heights or underestimating risk of dangerous hobbies.

(e) Highest educational qualification

71. Highest educational qualification is used here as a proxy for human capital/skill level, so that those in professional occupations such as law, accountancy, nursing etc who do not have a degree ought to be treated as if they do have one.

72. Three levels of educational attainment are defined for the purposes of Tables A to D as follows:

Level 3 Higher degree, degree or equivalent, higher education qualification below degree level.

Level 2 A level or equivalent (at least one at pass level E), GCSE or equivalent (at least one at pass level A* to C/9 to 4).

Level 1 Low level qualifications below GCSE, no qualifications and other qualifications.

73. The following table gives a more detailed breakdown of the allocation of various types of educational qualification to each of the three categories above and is based on the allocations used in the most recent LFS.

(f) Categories of highest educational attainment[37]

Level 3 Higher degree, degree or equivalent, higher education qualification below degree level

Higher degree; NVQ level 5; Level 8 Diploma; Level 8 Certificate; Level 7 Diploma; Level 7 Certificate; Level 8 Award; First degree/foundation degree; Other degree; NVQ level 4; Level 6 Diploma; Level 6; Level 7 Award; Diploma in higher education; Level 5 Diploma; Level 5 Certificate; Level 6 Award; HNC/HND/BTEC higher etc; Teaching D further education; Teaching D secondary education; Teaching D primary education; Teaching D foundation stage; Teaching D level not stated; Nursing etc; RSA higher diploma; Other higher education below degree.

Level 2 GCSE A level or equivalent, GCSE grade A* to C, 9 to 4 or equivalent

Level 4 Diploma; Level 4 Certificate; Level 5 Award; NVQ level 3; Advanced/Progression (14-19) Diploma; Level 3 Diploma; Advanced Welsh Baccalaureate; International Baccalaureate; Scottish Baccalaureate; GNVQ/GSVQ advanced; A-level or equivalent; RSA advanced diploma; OND/ONC/BTEC/SCOTVEC National etc; City & Guilds Advanced Craft/Part 1; Scottish 6 year certificate/CSYS; SCE higher or equivalent; Access qualifications; AS-level or equivalent; Trade apprenticeship; Level 3 Certificate; Level 4 Award; NVQ level 2 or equivalent; Intermediate Welsh Baccalaureate; GNVQ/GSVQ intermediate; RSA diploma; City & Guilds Craft/Part 2; BTEC/SCOTVEC First or General diploma etc; Higher (14-19) Diploma; Level 2 Diploma; Level 2 Certificate; Scottish National Level 5; O-level, GCSE grade A*-C, 9-4, or equivalent; Level 3 Award.

Level 1 Low level qualifications below GCSE, no or other qualification

NVQ level 1 or equivalent; Foundation Welsh Baccalaureate; GNVQ/GSVQ foundation level; Foundation (14-19) Diploma; Level 1 Diploma; Scottish National Level 4; CSE below grade 1, GCSE below grade C; BTEC/SCOTVEC First or General certificate; SCOTVEC modules; RSA other, Scottish Nationals Level 3; Scottish Nationals below Level 3; City & Guilds foundation/Part 1; Level 1 Certificate; Level 2 Award; YT/YTP certificate; Key skills qualification; Basic skills qualification; Entry level qualification; Entry level Diploma; Entry level Certificate; Level 1 Award; Entry level Award; Other qualification; No qualifications.

74. The research also considered the extent to which a person's future working life expectancy is affected by individual circumstances such as occupation and industrial sector, geographical region and education. The researchers concluded that the most significant consideration was the highest level of education achieved by the claimant and that, if this was allowed for, the effect of the other factors was relatively small. As a result, the Ogden Working Party decided to publish reduction factors which allow for employment status, disability status and educational attainment only. This was a change from the 6th edition of the Ogden Tables compared to previous editions where adjustments were made for types of occupation and for geographical region.

[37] Source: Certificate Labour Force Survey User Guide – Volume 3: Details of LFS variables 2019, Highest Qualification, pp 303-305. *https://www.ons.gov.uk/employmentandlabourmarket/peopleinwork/employmentandemployeetypes/methodologies/labourforcesurveyuserguidance.*

75. A separate assessment is made for (a) the value of earnings the claimant would have received if the injury had not been suffered and (b) the value of the claimant's earnings (if any) taking account of the injuries sustained. The risk of non-employment is significantly higher post-injury where there has been an activity-limiting impairment. The loss is arrived at by deducting (b) from (a).

76. In order to calculate the claimant's loss of earnings had the injury not been suffered, the claimant's employment status and disability status need to be determined as at the date of the injury (or the onset of symptoms resulting in a loss of earnings) giving rise to the claim, so that the correct reduction factor can be selected. For the calculation of future loss of earnings (based on actual pre- injury earnings and also future employment prospects), Tables A and C should be used for claimants who were not disabled at the time of the accident, and Tables B and D should be used for those with a pre-existing disability. In all these tables the three left hand columns are for those who were employed at the time of the accident and the three right hand columns are for those who were not.

77. In order to calculate the value of the actual earnings that a claimant is likely to receive in the future (i.e. after settlement or trial), the employment status and the disability status need to be determined as at the date of settlement or trial. For claimants who meet the Ogden definition of disability defined above at that point in time, Tables B and D should be used. The three left hand columns will apply in respect of claimants actually in employment at the date of settlement or trial and the three right hand columns will apply in respect of those who remain unemployed at that point in time.

78. The factors in Tables A to D allow for the interruption of employment for bringing up children and caring for other dependants.

79. In the case of those who, at the date of the injury, have not yet reached the age at which it is likely they would have started work, the relevant factor will be chosen based on a number of assessments of the claimant's likely employment had the injury not occurred. The relevant reduction factor from the tables needs to be selected on the basis of the level of education the claimant would have been expected to attain, the age at which it is likely the claimant would have started work, together with an assessment as to whether the claimant would have become employed or not. The overall multiplier will also have to be discounted for early receipt by applying the appropriate discount factor from Table 35 to reflect the number of years between the claimant's age at the date of trial and the age at which it is likely that he/she would have started work.

80. In the case of those who at the date of trial have not completed their education/skills acquisition, the relevant education level will be chosen on an assessment of the claimant's likely highest qualification that he/she is likely to have achieved (pre-injury) and is now likely to be achieved (post-injury). It is for this reason that the reduction factors are not available before an individual is old enough to have achieved them, namely aged 16-19 for a degree.

81. In the case of those who, as a result of injury can no longer work in an area which makes use of their qualifications, these qualifications may need to be ignored (see below).

82. Tables A to D include reduction factors up to age 54 only. For older ages the reduction factors tend to increase towards 1 at retirement age for those who are employed and fall towards 0 for those who are not employed. Where the claimant is older than 54, it is anticipated that the likely future course of employment status will be particularly dependent on individual circumstances, so that the use of factors based on averages would not be appropriate. Hence reduction factors are not provided for these older ages.

Table A Loss of earnings to pension age 65: Males – Not disabled

Age at trial	Employed			Non-employed		
	Level 3	Level 2	Level 1	Level 3	Level 2	Level 1
16-19		0.89	0.86		0.87	0.83
20-24	0.91	0.91	0.87	0.88	0.88	0.84
25-29	0.91	0.91	0.88	0.88	0.87	0.83
30-34	0.90	0.90	0.88	0.87	0.86	0.82
35-39	0.88	0.89	0.87	0.85	0.84	0.81
40-44	0.86	0.87	0.86	0.82	0.81	0.79
45-49	0.83	0.85	0.85	0.77	0.77	0.75
50	0.81	0.83	0.84	0.72	0.73	0.71
51	0.80	0.82	0.83	0.69	0.70	0.69
52	0.78	0.81	0.83	0.67	0.67	0.67
53	0.77	0.80	0.82	0.64	0.64	0.64
54	0.76	0.79	0.81	0.60	0.60	0.60

Table B Table B Loss of earnings to pension age 65: Males – Disabled

Age at trial	Employed			Non-employed		
	Level 3	Level 2	Level 1	Level 3	Level 2	Level 1
16-19		0.50	0.29		0.47	0.25
20-24	0.54	0.50	0.34	0.50	0.45	0.24
25-29	0.57	0.50	0.37	0.38	0.40	0.23
30-34	0.57	0.46	0.35	0.39	0.32	0.22
35-39	0.55	0.43	0.35	0.40	0.25	0.19
40-44	0.55	0.43	0.35	0.34	0.21	0.15
45-49	0.53	0.44	0.36	0.27	0.17	0.11
50	0.52	0.46	0.38	0.25	0.16	0.09
51	0.52	0.46	0.38	0.24	0.15	0.09
52	0.52	0.46	0.39	0.23	0.13	0.08
53	0.53	0.46	0.40	0.22	0.13	0.07
54	0.54	0.47	0.41	0.20	0.12	0.06

Table C Loss of earnings to pension age 60: Females – Not disabled

Age at trial	Employed			Non-employed		
	Level 3	Level 2	Level 1	Level 3	Level 2	Level 1
16-19		0.81	0.66		0.78	0.63
20-24	0.88	0.82	0.69	0.86	0.78	0.63
25-29	0.88	0.83	0.72	0.84	0.77	0.64
30-34	0.88	0.84	0.75	0.82	0.77	0.65
35-39	0.88	0.86	0.77	0.81	0.76	0.65
40-44	0.88	0.85	0.79	0.79	0.73	0.62
45-49	0.87	0.84	0.80	0.73	0.65	0.53
50	0.85	0.83	0.80	0.65	0.55	0.44
51	0.84	0.83	0.80	0.62	0.51	0.40
52	0.83	0.83	0.80	0.57	0.46	0.36
53	0.82	0.83	0.81	0.51	0.40	0.32
54	0.82	0.83	0.81	0.45	0.34	0.28

Table D Loss of earnings to pension age 60: Females – Disabled

Age at trial	Employed			Non-employed		
	Level 3	Level 2	Level 1	Level 3	Level 2	Level 1
16-19		0.39	0.22		0.34	0.18
20-24	0.60	0.40	0.22	0.55	0.31	0.16
25-29	0.59	0.42	0.23	0.49	0.31	0.16
30-34	0.59	0.42	0.27	0.44	0.31	0.15
35-39	0.59	0.44	0.31	0.41	0.28	0.14
40-44	0.58	0.48	0.34	0.35	0.24	0.13
45-49	0.58	0.51	0.40	0.26	0.19	0.11
50	0.59	0.54	0.45	0.21	0.15	0.10
51	0.59	0.56	0.47	0.19	0.14	0.09
52	0.60	0.58	0.50	0.18	0.12	0.08
53	0.61	0.61	0.53	0.17	0.11	0.07
54	0.62	0.64	0.57	0.15	0.09	0.06

(g) Departures from a strict application

83. Adjustments to the reduction factors since they were introduced in the 6th edition (2007) have proved to be difficult and controversial. It is in the nature of assessing damages that a single estimate based on a group average will be inaccurate for an individual claimant and a certain degree of inaccuracy must be accepted.

84. There will be many reasons to argue for a departure, but it is important that the departure is made with the following three cautions in mind:

(i) Reduction factors are based upon group averages which are statistically verifiable;

(ii) The average is a central estimate and there will be a distribution of observations either side; and

(iii) In the data, most departures will be modest because observations will cluster closely around the central estimate.

85. The need to depart from a strict application of the reduction factors might arise from characteristics which are relevant to the future loss of earnings but which are not included in the set of characteristics which determine the published estimate, namely age, sex, employment status, highest educational achievement and disability status or because the included characteristics are too broadly defined so that the average does not reasonably represent the claimant.

86. Characteristics included in the reduction factors are measured at the average, so for example a claimant who dropped out of the education system before reaching their potential highest qualification for positive reasons (such as an offer of employment) might be better represented by a higher educational category. Similarly, claimants whose qualifications are close to the border, for example they may just meet the threshold for a category (for example they are in the GCSE qualification category because they have a single GCSE at the minimum grade for a pass) might be better represented by a lower educational category. However, a full category change may not be required, in which case interpolation between the suggested reduction factors for adjacent categories would facilitate a partial change of category. In such a case the parties may wish to take advice on an adjustment based on outcomes from a more detailed classification.

87. Employment status is measured at the date of injury and at the date of settlement. A claimant who changed employment status around either of these dates, for example through recruitment to a new position or suffering a job loss from a previous position, perhaps a position of long duration, may require a departure. Claimants who are established in employment in an expanding niche market or in a thriving family firm will face lower than average employment risks for their group. Likewise, claimants who are in temporary work, who have had a chequered employment history or who are restricted by injury to employment in a declining occupation or skill set will face higher than average employment risks for their group.

88. Where injury precludes use of an educational qualification or skill, a claimant may be better represented by a lower qualification group. For example, a nurse who is now restricted to a basic clerical role would no longer have the employment risks of a graduate. Alternatively, a nurse who was able to transfer to a sedentary role using her nursing skills, for example working as a General Practice nurse or providing telephone or online medical advice, would probably continue to face similar graduate level employment risks.

89. Disability is perhaps the characteristic where at least one of the parties (sometimes both and in opposite directions) is most likely to seek a departure from a strict application of the reduction factors. Disability is measured as either disabled or not disabled and both categories include different levels of severity of impairment and activity-limitation. The defining characteristics are subjective and context specific. There is often a misconception that impairment and activity-limitation must be severe or at least moderately severe to qualify as a disability. The best available evidence on the severity of impairment which underlies disability in the data used to estimate the reduction factors is reported in Berthoud (2006)[38] and discussed in Wass (2008)[39] and Latimer-Sayer and Wass (2013).[40] On a severity scale of 1 to 10 in a sample collected in the Health and Disability Survey 1996-7 and with a disability prevalence rate that matches that found in the data

[38] Berthoud R (2006) "The employment rates of disabled people", Department for Work and Pensions, Research Paper No 298.

[39] Wass V (2008) "Discretion in the Application of the New Ogden Six Multipliers: The case of *Connor v Bradman*", *Journal of Personal Injury Law*, 2 pp. 155-164.

[40] Latimer-Sayer, W. and Wass, V. (2013) "Ask the Expert: William Latimer-Sayer asks Victoria Wass some questions about the practical application of the Ogden Reduction Factors", *Journal of Personal Injury Law*, 1, 35-44.

underlying the reduction factors (12%), the median level of severity is 4, 43% lie in the range 1 to 3 (mild), 44% lie in the range 4 to 7 (moderate) and 13% score in the range 7 to 10 (severe). The message here is that the norm for severity is not severe: it is at the mild end of the mild to moderate category. In the circumstances, as long as the claimant meets the above Ogden definition of disability, a departure on the basis of a perceived mild impairment / activity-limitation might not be appropriate (see further under Section B (d) above).

90. When considering whether it is appropriate to depart from the suggested Table A to D reduction factors, it is important to consider how the degree of residual disability may have a different effect on residual earnings depending upon its relevance to the claimant's likely field of work. In this regard there is a distinction between impairment and disability. For example, a lower limb amputation may have less effect on a sedentary worker's earnings than on the earnings of a manual worker. Likewise, cognitive problems may prevent someone from continuing to work in a professional or "knowledge" capacity where the same problems may not prevent continuing employment in job roles with low cognitive demands. In this context, disability is defined in relation to work and is specific to the skills that are required in a particular job and also to the outstanding effects of the impairment where barriers have not been overcome. Disability is more closely related to employment outcomes than is impairment. So, whilst occupation is irrelevant to impairment (an amputation is the same regardless of the occupation), it is crucial to disability. Disability is the better predictor of employment prospects than the impairment itself and close regard must be given to the effects of the claimant's impairments on his or her future intended occupation.

91. Where a departure is considered to be appropriate, it could be in either direction and it would normally be expected to be modest. Interpolation using a mid-point between the disabled and non-disabled reduction factors is not advised.[41] Disability results in substantial employment disadvantage and therefore applying a mid-point between the pre-and post-injury reduction factors will normally be too great a departure. Professor Victoria Wass, a co-author of the reduction factors, has published advice on when and how to consider an adjustment on the basis of severity of disability.[42] This advice involves using the reduction factors for different employment or educational categories as a guide to the size of the departure rather than the difference between disability categories.

92. All departures will be case-specific. In some cases, it may be difficult to determine the scale of the departure and it may be helpful to consult expert opinion. Expert opinion may also be required to advise upon how the suggested reduction factors should be applied and/or adjusted when the claimant was already disabled at the time of the injury which forms the subject of the claim.

(h) Distinction between Wage Effect and Disability Effect

93. It should be noted that injury causing disability (as defined above) has two separate and distinct effects:

(i) The first, known as the wage effect, is the reduction in earnings caused by injury, which may result from changing role, working less hours or missing out on promotions. This effect is usually captured by using a different multiplicand for pre- and post-injury net annual earnings, reflecting the change or expected change as a consequence of the injury.

[41] See further Wass V (2008) "Discretion in the Application of the New Ogden Six Multipliers: The case of *Connor v Bradman*", *Journal of Personal Injury Law*, 2 pp. 155-164.

[42] See footnotes 39, 40 and 41 above.

(ii) The second, known as the employment effect, is the impact of the person's disability on their long-term employment prospects. In particular, disability is known to increase job search periods, cause longer periods out of work and is associated with a greater risk of early retirement. Tables A to D seek to capture the disadvantage that the second effect, i.e. a claimant's disability, has on employment prospects.

94. It is a mistake to conflate these two separate and distinct effects.[43] A lower post-injury multiplicand to account for a reduction in earnings following injury does not make any allowance for reduced employment prospects. Assuming that the claimant meets the Ogden definition of disability, then the application of the disability-adjusted reduction factor is also required. There is extensive literature on the impact of both effects of disability, with the employment effect being the most important.[44]

(i) Different pension ages

95. The factors in Tables A to D assume retirement at age 65 for males and age 60 for females. It is not possible to calculate expected working lifetimes, assuming alternative retirement ages from the LFS data, since the employment data in the LFS were collected only for the working age population, assumed aged between 16 and 64 for males and between 16 and 59 for females. Where the retirement age is different from age 65 for males or age 60 for females, it is suggested that this should be ignored and the reduction factor and the adjustments thereto be taken from the above tables for the age of the claimant as at the date of trial with no adjustment i.e. assume that the retirement age is age 65 for males and age 60 for females. However, if the retirement age is close to the age at the date of trial, then it may be more appropriate to take into account the circumstances of the individual case.

96. It should be noted that the reduction factors in Tables A to D are based on data for the period 1998 to 2003. Whilst the reduction factors and adjustments allow for the age-specific probabilities of moving into, or out of, employment over a future working lifetime, based on data for the period 1998 to 2003, the methodology assumes that these probabilities remain constant over time; there is no allowance for changes in these age-specific probabilities in future cohorts. Future changes in the probabilities of moving into, and out of, employment are especially difficult to predict. It is also assumed that there will be no change in disability status or educational achievement after the date of the accident.

(j) Early Retirement

97. It should be noted that the lower reduction factors for disabled people in Tables B and D already include an allowance for retiring earlier than the assumed retirements of 65 (for men) and 60 (for women). Sometimes medical evidence will suggest that a claimant who may be able to return to work following injury will now need to retire earlier as a result of the injury than he or she otherwise would have done in the absence of the injury. Since some allowance has already been made in the Table B and D reduction factors to reflect the average increased risk of early retirement post-injury, adopting a base multiplier to calculate residual earnings with an earlier retirement age

[43] As occurred in the case of *Clarke v Maltby* [2010] EWHC 1201 (QB): see further the commentary in Latimer- Sayer, W. and Wass, V. (2012) Ogden Reduction Factor adjustments since *Conner v Bradman*: Part 1 *Journal of Personal Injury Law*, 2012, No 4, pp 219-230.

[44] The disability employment gap in 2019 was 29 percentage points whereas the disability pay gap is between 10% and 20%. Both are based on the Equality Act 2010 definition of disability: *https://www.disabilityatwork.co.uk/*.

than the base multiplier used to calculate but for the injury earnings may amount to a double discount.

(k) Summary

98. In summary to perform a loss of earnings calculation applying the methodology set out in this section, the process is as follows:

(1) Choose the table relating to the appropriate sex of the claimant and retirement age. Where the claimant's retirement age differs from that assumed in Tables 1 to 34, the Additional Tables can be used to calculate the appropriate multiplier or the procedure set out under the "interpolation" and "Different retirement ages" subheadings of Section A of the explanatory notes should be followed.

(2) Choose the appropriate discount rate column (currently -0.25% in England and Wales; -0.75% in Scotland; and -1.5% in Northern Ireland.

(3) In that column find the appropriate figure for the claimant's age at trial ("the basic multiplier").

(4) When calculating loss of earnings, Tables 3 to 18 or the Additional Tables should be used when a multiplier/multiplicand approach is appropriate. If it is, the basic multiplier should be adjusted to take account of contingencies other than mortality. These contingencies include the claimant's employment and disability status and educational qualifications. The basic multiplier should be multiplied by the appropriate figure taken from Tables A to D to give the employment risks adjusted multiplier. If there is a good reason to depart from the suggested reduction factor, it may be necessary at this stage to modify the resulting figure further to allow for circumstances specific to the claimant.

(5) Multiply the net annual loss (the multiplicand) by the employment risks adjusted multiplier to arrive at a figure which represents the capitalised value of the future loss of earnings.

(6) If the claimant has a residual earning capacity, allowance should be made for any post-accident vulnerability on the labour market: the following paragraphs show the suggested way of doing this, although there may still be cases where a *Smith v Manchester* award is appropriate.

Where it is appropriate to do so, repeat steps 1 to 5 above, replacing the pre-injury employment and disability status with the post-injury employment and disability status in step 4 and replacing the net annual loss by the assumed new level of net earnings at step 5. It will only be necessary to reconsider the claimant's educational attainments if these have changed between the accident and the date of trial or settlement.

The result will represent the capitalised value of the claimant's likely post-accident earnings

(7) Deduct the sum yielded by step 6 from that yielded by step 5 to obtain the net amount of loss of earnings allowing for residual earning capacity. Where the above methodology is used there will usually be no need for a separate *Smith v Manchester* award.

(I) Worked Examples of Discounts for Contingencies Using Tables A to D Reduction Factors

99. The following are examples of the use of the Ogden Tables and Tables A to D in illustrative personal injury cases with simplified assumptions.

Example 7 – loss of earnings to a retirement age of 68 using Table 12 at -0.25%

100. The claimant is a Welsh female aged 35 at the date of the trial who brings her claim in Cardiff. She has three A levels, but not a degree, and was in employment at the date of the accident at a salary of £25,000 a year net of tax. She was not disabled (as defined in Section B) before the accident. As a result of her injuries, she is now disabled and has lost her job but has found part-time employment at a salary of £5,000 a year net of tax. She expected to retire at age 68 pre-accident and still intends to retire at this age, if she can, following her injuries. Her future loss of earnings is assessed as shown below.

(1) Look up Table 12 for loss of earnings to pension age 68 for females.

(2) At present, the discount rate for those living in England and Wales is -0.25%.

(3) Table 12 shows that, on the basis of a -0.25% rate of return, the multiplier for a female aged 35 is 33.59.

(4) Now take account of risks other than mortality: allowing for the claimant being employed, having achieved A-levels and not being disabled at the date of trial, Table C (Level 2) indicates 33.59 should be multiplied by a reduction factor of 0.86, resulting in a revised multiplier of 28.89.

(5) The claimant's expected earnings in the absence of the accident are therefore £722,250 (£25,000 × 28.89).

(6) Allow for mitigation of loss of earnings in respect of post-injury residual earnings. As before, Table 12 shows that, using a discount rate of -0.25%, the multiplier for a female aged 35 is 33.59.

(7) Now take account of risks other than mortality: allowing for the claimant being employed, having achieved A-levels and being disabled at the date of trial, Table D (Level 2) would require 33.59 to be multiplied by a reduction factor of 0.44, resulting in a revised multiplier of 14.78.

(8) The amount of mitigation for post-injury earnings is therefore £73,900 (£5,000 × 14.78).

(9) Overall, the claimant's future loss of earnings after allowing for her anticipated residual earnings capacity is £722,250 minus £73,900, giving a total of £648,350.

Example 8 – loss of earnings to a retirement age of 65 using Table 9 at -0.75%

101. The claimant is a 48-year-old Scottish male at the date of the trial. He pursues his claim in Glasgow. He has no educational qualifications. He was employed at the time of the accident earning £20,000 annually net of tax. He intended to retire at age 65. He was not disabled before the accident. As a result of his injuries, he is now disabled and has lost his job. The multiplicand

for costs of care is deemed to be £50,000 a year. He is unemployed at the date of trial but has been assessed as capable of finding work with possible future earnings of £5,000 a year net of tax up to normal retirement age. His loss of earnings to retirement age of 65 is assessed as set out below.

(1) Look up Table 9 for loss of earnings to pension age 65 for males.

(2) At present, the appropriate discount rate for claims brought in Scotland is -0.75%.

(3) Table 9 shows that, using a discount rate of -0.75%, the multiplier for a male aged 48 is 17.55.

(4) Now to take account of risks other than mortality: allowing for the claimant being employed, not disabled and having no educational qualifications at the date of trial, Table A (Level 1) would require 17.55 to be multiplied by a reduction factor of 0.85, resulting in a revised multiplier of 14.92.

(5) Therefore, the subtotal of the claimant's expected earnings in the absence of his injuries is £298,400 (£20,000 × 14.92).

(6) Allowing for mitigation of loss of earnings in respect of anticipated post-injury residual earnings: as before, Table 9 shows that, on the basis of a -0.75% discount rate, the multiplier for a male aged 48 is 17.55.

(7) Taking account of risks other than mortality in respect of residual earnings capacity: allowing for the claimant being unemployed and disabled with no educational qualifications at the date of trial, Table B (Level 1) would require 17.55 to be multiplied by a reduction factor of 0.11, resulting in a revised multiplier of 1.93.

(8) Therefore, the subtotal for mitigation in respect of post-injury residual earnings is £9,650 (£5,000 × 1.93).

(9) Hence, the claimant's total award for future loss of earnings after allowing for his anticipated residual earnings is: £298,400 – £9,650 = £288,750.

102. The damages for cost of care are assessed as follows:

(1) Look up Table 1 for the lifetime multiplier for a male aged 48.

(2) The appropriate discount rate is -0.75%.

(3) Table 1 shows that, on the basis of a -0.75% rate of return, the multiplier at age 48 is 42.75.

(4) No adjustment is made for risks other than mortality.

(5) The damages for cost of care are assessed at £2,137,500 (£50,000 × 42.75).

Example 9 – loss of earnings to a retirement age of 70 using Table 14 at -0.25%

103. The claimant is female, aged 14 at the date of the trial. She lives in Milton Keynes and brings proceedings in England. She is expected to achieve a degree and to be in employment thereafter on an average salary, in current terms, of £30,000 a year net of tax. She was not disabled before

the accident. As a result of her injuries, she is now disabled – she is still expected to achieve a degree and to be in employment, but with an average annual salary for part-time work in current terms of £15,000 net of tax. She will be aged 21 when she completes her degree. She expected to retire at age 70 before the accident and hopes to still be able to retire at the same age notwithstanding her injuries. Using the main Ogden Tables,[45] her future loss of earnings claim is assessed as set out below.

(1) Look up Table 14 for loss of earnings to pension age 70 for females.

(2) At present, the discount rate for those living in England and Wales is -0.25%.

(3) Table 14 shows that, on the basis of a -0.25% rate of return, the multiplier for a female aged 21 is 51.10.

(4) Now take account of risks other than mortality: allowing for the claimant at age 21 assessed as achieving a degree, being employed and not disabled, Table C (Level 3) would require 51.10 to be multiplied by a reduction factor of 0.88. However, since the loss does not arise until age 21, a discount factor must be applied for accelerated receipt. The appropriate Table 35 discount factor for seven years early receipt at a discount rate of -0.25% is 1.0177. Therefore, the adjusted multiplier is calculated as follows: 51.10 × 0.88 × 1.0177 = 45.76.

(5) The subtotal for the claimant's expected earnings but for her injury is £1,372,800 (£30,000 × 45.76).

(6) Allow for mitigation of loss of earnings in respect of post-injury earnings: as before, Table 14 shows that, on the basis of a -0.25% discount rate, the multiplier for a female graduate aged 21 is 51.10.

(7) Taking account of risks other than mortality: allowing for the claimant at age 21 assessed as achieving a degree, being employed and disabled, Table D (Level 3) indicates that the base multiplier of 51.10 should be multiplied by a reduction factor of 0.60. However, again, since the loss does not arise until age 21, a discount factor must be applied for accelerated receipt. The appropriate Table 35 discount factor for seven years early receipt at a discount rate of -0.25% is 1.0177. Therefore, the adjusted multiplier is 51.10 × 0.60 × 1.0177 = 31.20.

(8) Therefore, the subtotal in respect of anticipated residual earnings is £468,000 (£15,000 × 31.20).

(9) Hence the total award for future loss of earnings after allowing for mitigation in respect of anticipated residual earnings is: £1,372,800 – £468,000 = £904,800.

Example 10 – loss of earnings to a retirement age of 67 using Additional Tables at -0.25%

104. The claimant is male, aged 55 at the date of the trial. He lives in London and pursues his claim in England. He has achieved O-levels. He was unemployed at the time of the accident. His potential pre-retirement multiplicand has been assessed at £15,000 a year net of tax. He was

[45] The applicable multiplier can also be calculated using the Additional Tables. The pre-injury multiplier for age 14 at trial starting from age 21 in seven years' time at -0.25% is 59.10 minus 7.06 i.e. 52.04 × 0.88 = 45.80. The post- injury multiplier is 52.04 × 0.6 = 31.22. These compare to the pre and post injury multipliers in this example of 45.76 and 31.20 respectively. Whilst the multiplier derived from the Additional Tables is more accurate, access to the Additional Tables may not always be possible and they are not available for all discount rates.

disabled before the accident. As a result of his injuries, he has been assessed as having no future prospect of employment. His future loss of earnings to retirement age of 67 is shown as follows.

(1) Select the appropriate discount rate: at present, the discount rate for those living in England and Wales is -0.25%.

(2) Using the Additional Tables for Males at a discount rate of minus 0.25%, the appropriate multiplier for loss of earnings from age 55 to 67 is 11.75, derived by scrolling across from the age 55 row in the first column until age 67.[46]

(3) Take account of risks other than mortality: allowing for the claimant being unemployed, disabled and having achieved O-levels at the date of trial, Table B (Level 2) indicates that 11.75 should be multiplied by a reduction factor of 0.12, resulting in a revised multiplier of 1.41.

(4) Pre-injury damages for loss of earnings are assessed as £21,150 (£15,000 × 1.41).

(5) As the claimant has been assessed as having no realistic prospect of future employment following his injury, no credit needs to be given in respect of post-injury residual earnings.

(6) Therefore, the claimant's award for loss of earnings is £21,150.

Example 11 – variable earnings with split multiplier using the Additional Tables at -0.75%

105. The claimant is female, a graduate with a degree, aged 25 at date of settlement / trial. She suffers a road traffic accident resulting in catastrophic injuries. But for her injuries, her probable career progression, in the absence of injury, would have provided her with salary increases at ages 30, 35 and 40. Thereafter she would have continued earning at the same level to age 60, when she would have stepped down from full-time work to work part-time until 70. Post-accident, by reason of her injuries, there is no realistic prospect of her returning to paid employment. She is living in Edinburgh and pursues her claim for personal injuries in Scotland, where at present the discount rate is -0.75%.

106. The working life multiplier from age 25 to 70, is derived from the Females -0.75% table by reading across from the age 25 row in the first column until age 70. This gives a working life multiplier of 52.33.[47] The working life multiplier needs to be discounted for contingencies other than mortality. Using the column for a female, not disabled, with degree level education, the applicable reduction factor from Table C (Level 3) is 0.88. The adjusted working life multiplier is therefore 52.33 × 0.88 = 46.05. The multiplicands for lost future age earnings are set out in the following table.

[46] Using the Additional Tables is the most accurate way of deriving multipliers involving non-standard retirement ages which do not have a specific table in the Ogden Tables. However, the loss of earnings multiplier to age 67 can be estimated by using one of the interpolation methods and Tables 9 and 11 of the numbered Ogden Tables: see further Section A (h) "different retirement ages". The age-adjusted interpolation method gives an estimate as follows: [(11.82 [Table 9] × 1) + (11.70 [Table 11] × 2)] / 3 = 11.74. The simple interpolation method gives an estimate as follows: [(9.84 [Table 9] × 1) + (12.69 [Table 11] × 2] / 3 = 11.74. The more precise multiplier derived from the Additional Tables is 11.75.

[47] This is the same as the multiplier for a 25-year-old woman retiring at 70 derived from Table 14 at a discount rate of -0.75%.

Period	Annual Net Earnings
From age 25 to 30	£20,000 a year
From age 30 to 35	£25,000 a year
From age 35 to 40	£35,000 a year
From age 40 to 60	£40,000 a year
From age 60 to 70	£20,000 a year

107. The split multipliers for each period at a discount rate of -0.75% can be calculated as follows. For the first period from age 25 to 30, the multiplier is 5.09. For the second period from age 30 to 35, the multiplier is 5.28 (being the multiplier from age 25 to 35 of 10.37 minus the multiplier from age 25 to 30 of 5.09). For the third period from age 35 to 40, the multiplier is 5.47 (being the multiplier from age 25 to 40 of 15.84 minus the multiplier from age 25 to 35 of 10.37). For the fourth period from age 40 to 60, the multiplier is 23.72 (being the multiplier from age 25 to 60 of 39.56 minus the multiplier from age 25 to 40 of 15.84). The multiplier for the final period from age 60 to 70 is 12.77 (being the whole working life multiplier of 52.33 minus the multiplier from age 25 to 60 of 39.56). Each of these multipliers needs to be multiplied by the Table C reduction factor of 0.88 (Level 3).

108. The total claim for loss of earnings over the claimant's working lifetime is £1,433,800 as set out in the following table.

Age (years)	**Table 14 Split multipliers**	**Final multiplier (× 0.88)**	**Annual earnings £ a year**	**Total £**
25 – 30	5.09	4.48	20,000	89,600
30 – 35	5.28	4.65	25,000	116,250
35 – 40	5.47	4.81	35,000	168,350
40 – 60	23.72	20.87	40,000	834,800
60 – 70	12.77	11.24	20,000	224,800
Totals	52.33	46.05		**1,433,800**

Example 12 – variable earnings with split multiplier using the apportionment method at -0.75%

109. An alternative way to estimate split multipliers for variable periods of loss derived from Tables 1 to 34 is to use the "apportionment method". This method involves apportioning the multiplier that needs to be split by reference to percentages of the fixed term multiplier for the same period derived from Table 36. The apportionment method, which was set out in paras 23 to 24 of the explanatory notes to the 6th edition of the Tables, is less accurate than using the Additional Tables, however, an example of its use is set out below in the event that it is not possible to access the Additional Tables.

110. Using the same facts as in Example 11 above, the working life multiplier can be split manually using the main Ogden Tables at a discount rate of -0.75% and the apportionment method as follows:

(1) The working-life will be 45 years and the multiplier from Table 14 for that period taking into account mortality risks but without any discounts for any other contingencies is 52.33.

(2) The Table 14 working life multiplier needs to be discounted for contingencies other than mortality. Using the column for a female, not disabled, with degree level education, the applicable reduction factor from Table C (Level 3) is 0.88.

(3) The adjusted working life multiplier is therefore 52.33 × 0.88 = 46.05.

(4) The multiplier for a term certain of 45 years (Table 36) is 53.56.

(5) The fixed term multiplier from Table 36 for 45 years should be split using Table 36 multipliers for the partial periods making up the whole working life period of 45 years. So, the first five year period is represented by a multiplier for a term certain of five years, namely 5.10; the next five years is represented by a multiplier of 5.29 (being the multiplier for a term certain of 10 years, namely 10.39 minus the multiplier for a term certain of five years, namely 5.10); the next five years by 5.49 (being the fixed term multiplier for 15 years of 15.88 minus the fixed term multiplier for 10 years of 10.39); the next 20 years by 24.16 (being the fixed term multiplier for 35 years of 40.04 minus the fixed term multiplier for 15 years of 15.88); then, the final 10 years by the balance of 13.52 (bring the difference between the Table 36 multiplier for the whole period of 53.56 minus the fixed term multiplier for 35 years of 40.04).

(6) Each of those smaller segmented multipliers can be shown as a percentage or fraction of the whole: so, for the first five years the segmented multiplier of 5.10 is 9.52% of the multiplier for the whole period of 53.56, and so on for each segment of the 45 year period.

(7) The working life multiplier from Table 14 can now be split up in identical proportions to the way in which the Table 36 multiplier has been treated above: thus the first five year period is now represented by a multiplier of 4.38, which is calculated by taking 9.52% of 46.05. Each segmented multiplier is calculated in the same way.

(8) The multiplicand for each segment of working life is now multiplied by the appropriate segmented multiplier to calculate the loss for that period. The sum total of those losses represents the full sum for loss of future earnings but for the injuries.

(9) The lump sum award as set out in tabular form below totals £1,429,750.

Age	**Period (years)**	**Table 36**	**% Split**	**Table 14**	**Net Annual Earnings £**	**Total £**
25 – 30	5	5.10	9.52	4.38	20,000	87,600
30 – 35	5	5.29	9.88	4.55	25,000	113,750
35 – 40	5	5.49	10.25	4.72	35,000	165,200
40 – 60	20	24.16	45.11	20.77	40,000	830,800
60 – 70	10	13.52	25.24	11.62	20,000	232,400
Totals:	45 years	53.56	100.0	46.05		**1,429,750**

NB the figures in the above table have been rounded at each step of the calculation so the totals shown are not necessarily the sum of the individual multipliers in the columns.

Section C: Quantification of Pension Loss

(a) Introduction

111. Where there is a claim for loss of earnings, pension losses now frequently also arise, given the required auto-enrolment of employees into, as a minimum, a Workplace Pension (explained later in this section). The quantification of pension loss is, however, a complex matter, as there is both a variety of types of occupational pension provision and a substantial variation in the level of employer contribution within each type of scheme.

112. There are two types of pension scheme: Defined Benefit schemes (where the pension benefit is defined at retirement, usually by level of earnings before retirement and length of service) and Defined Contribution schemes (where only the contributions into the scheme are defined). In the private sector there are very few Defined Benefit schemes still accruing new pension benefits, having largely been replaced by Defined Contribution schemes.

113. Defined Benefit schemes historically provided a pension of a fraction of final pay for each year of service, with either an automatic tax-free lump sum or one available by commutation.[48] In the public sector these arrangements have mostly been replaced by career average schemes[49] where members accrue a fraction of pay each year, which is revalued to retirement age and becomes payable as a pension from that time. The public sector contains a number of different schemes with varying rates of accrual and rates of revaluation. Care should be taken to source the member's entitlements as he or she may have benefits in more than one arrangement with the same employer, although normally there will not be any loss in respect of service accrued in periods prior to the injury in a previous scheme. In the broadest of terms pension loss in Defined Benefit schemes is assessed by first calculating the expected net of tax pension from retirement age had the accident not happened and from this deducting the net of tax pension he or she will now receive from retirement age. To this multiplicand will be applied a multiplier from Tables 19 to 34, suitably discounted for contingencies other than mortality. An adjustment may then be needed to allow for contingent spouse's benefits. If the member has not been awarded an ill-health pension and the issue of promotion does not arise, the loss can be assessed by valuing the additional pension that would have been earned but for the accident.

114. Most Defined Benefit schemes also offer a continuing pension to a surviving spouse or civil partner. None of the Ogden Tables are suitable for valuing survivorship benefits on the future death of the claimant, although an approximation can be made using the simplified methodology for fatal accident claims. An alternative approximation is to follow the method adopted by the trial judge in *Auty and others v National Coal Board* [1985] 1 W.L.R. 784, which is to calculate the multiplier for life of the surviving spouse or civil partner, deduct from that the multiplier for life of the claimant, apply the percentage for survivor pension benefits (usually 50% or two-thirds) and add that to the annual pension loss multiplier. If pension loss is a significant element of an award, consideration should be given to taking advice from an actuary or suitably qualified forensic accountant.

115. Defined Contribution pension schemes are now the main type of pension provision in the private sector. Member and employer contributions accumulate and grow in an individual fund, without taxation on the returns. On retirement the resulting fund is used, according to the individual's choice (subject to HM Revenue & Customs constraints), to provide either an ongoing source of taxable income or a reduced level of ongoing taxable income and a tax-free lump sum, through annuity purchase or more commonly flexible drawdown, or, in certain circumstances, a lump

[48] The acceptance of a reduced level of annual pension in exchange for a lump sum.
[49] Career Average Revalued Earnings ("CARE") schemes.

sum only. Tax may be payable on all or part of the lump sum if it exceeds the level permitted by HMRC.

116. Defined Contribution pensions do not generally include any continuing benefit to a surviving spouse or civil partner, although many employers do provide separate life insurance cover with a lump sum payable on the death of the employee, at least up to retirement age.

(b) Automatic Enrolment

117. By virtue of the Pensions Act 2008, every employer in the UK must now put certain staff into a workplace pension scheme and contribute towards it. This is called "automatic enrolment". This can be done through a pension scheme already in place if it meets appropriate standards, or by the employer choosing a master trust to join in order to fulfil the auto-enrolment requirements. All employers are required to auto-enrol their employees earning over £10,000 a year into a Workplace Pension if they are aged between 22 and State pension age, and must make pension contributions on, as a minimum,[50] "Qualifying Earnings". Qualifying Earnings are the band of earnings between the Lower Earnings Limit (£6,240 in 2020/21) and the Upper Earnings Limit (£50,000 in 2020/21).[51]

118. Statutory auto-enrolment workplace pensions are Defined Contribution schemes, under which from 6 April 2019[52] (ongoing until any new rate is announced):

- the employer must contribute a minimum[53] of 3% of Qualifying Earnings;
- the employee must contribute a minimum of 5% of Qualifying Earnings;
- the employee contributions are paid from gross earnings but are eligible for Income Tax relief at the employee's marginal rate;
- employers and/or employees may opt to contribute at a higher level than the minimum required under auto-enrolment; and
- employees may opt out, but the employer is obliged to contribute for as long as the employee chooses to remain a member by not opting out.

119. Where members contribute to the pension scheme, which is usually the case, care should be taken to ensure consistency with any associated loss of earnings calculation. If the loss of earnings calculation has been based on the member's net income after pension contribution deductions, then his or her contributions must be included in the pension loss assessment. Similar consistency is needed in the choice of retirement age and any assumed promotion or increments in pay.

(c) Case Law and Applicable Principles

120. The leading case regarding the assessment of pension loss is *Auty and others v National Coal Board* [1985] 1 W.L.R. 784. Other cases of interest include:

[50] Some employer schemes pay contributions on total earnings, not just Qualifying Earnings.
[51] These Limits change each tax year and are readily available on the Internet or in publications such as *Facts & Figures*.
[52] For the rates which applied before 6 April 2019 consult the Pensions Advisory Service (*https://www.pensionsadvisoryservice.org.uk*), *Facts & Figures* or a pensions specialist.
[53] Some employers, particularly larger employers, pay in excess of the minimum level of contribution obligated by statute: see further data available from the ONS, such as the Occupational Pension Schemes Survey, UK: 2018 (published on 20 June 2019).

- *Parry v Cleaver* [1970] AC 1 – confirming that any immediately payable ill-health pension award is only offset against the pre-injury pension in the period after normal retirement age;
- *Longden v National Coal Corporation* [1997] UKHL 52; [1998] AC 653 – which addressed the treatment of lump sum awards on ill-health retirement;
- *Page v Sheerness Steel Company Ltd* [1999] 1 AC 345 – which considered the discount for contingencies other than mortality in a pension loss claim;
- *Pidduck v Eastern Scottish Omnibus Ltd* [1990] 1 W.L.R. 993 – regarding a widow's pension entitlement following the death of her husband; and
- *Brown v MOD* [2006] P.I.Q.R. Q9; EWCA Civ 546 – on how to deal with the prospects of promotion.

121. Where pension loss is complex, the amounts involved are material in the context of the claim for loss of earnings/benefits/pension as a whole or when dealing with pensions when assessing loss of dependency/support in fatal accident cases, advice should be sought from an actuary or forensic accountant with appropriate experience. The following examples, however, illustrate the broad principles involved.

(d) Worked Examples

Example 13 – auto-enrolment pension using Table 12 of the main Ogden Tables at -0.25%

122. The claimant is female, aged 35, degree-educated, lived in England (so a -0.25% discount rate is appropriate) and up to the date of the accident was earning £40,000 gross per annum. She is a member of a Workplace (auto-enrolment) Pension scheme, with minimum statutory contributions. Since the accident the claimant has moved to a part-time role with the same company earning £20,000 gross per annum and is considered "disabled". A simplistic[54] calculation of her loss of pension is to treat the lost employer pension contributions as a tax-free benefit during the period of expected employment.

(1) The "but for" employer pension contributions are (£40,000 − £6,240) × 3% = £1,013 p.a.

(2) The residual employer pension contributions are (£20,000 − £6,240) × 3% = £413 p.a.

(3) The multiplier for valuing contributions to her State Pension Age of 68 is 33.59 (Table 12) and allowing for other contingencies this reduces to 33.59 × 0.88 (Table C, Employed, Level 3) = 29.56 in the "but for" calculation and 33.59 × 0.59 (Table D, Employed, Level 3) = 19.82 in the credit for residual pension calculation.

(4) The approximate pension loss is then (£1,013 × 29.56) − (£413 × 19.82) = £21,759.

[54] This method is considered simplistic by many pension experts as: (i) it does not value the actual loss suffered by the claimant (which will be her reduced pension from retirement and her reduced lump sum at retirement); (ii) it takes no account of the tax benefits of pension contributions; (iii) it takes no account of any higher pension fund management charges that may be incurred post-accident (potentially on the whole of the fund, not just on post- accident contributions), and (iv) it takes no account of expected real (i.e. above inflation) pension fund growth, so tends to understate (perhaps significantly) the value of the claim. However, this was the method put forward (without expert pension assistance) by the claimant in *Manna v Central Manchester University Hospitals NHS Foundation Trust* [2015] EWHC 2279 (QB) and was accepted by the Judge and no appeal was raised on that element of the award in the Court of Appeal.

(5) The expected employee contributions should not be deducted in the loss of earnings calculations, if this method is adopted.[55]

Example 14 – Local Government Pension Scheme using the Additional Tables at -0.25%

123. The claimant is male and before the accident was a member of the Local Government Pension Scheme accruing a pension of 1/49th of pay each year he worked to be payable from age 67, his State Pension Age. He is aged 50 at the date of the trial and left employment three years ago without an ill-health award. He earned £30,000 p.a., had a degree, lived in England (so a -0.25% discount rate is appropriate) and was not disabled at the time of the accident. He is not married. He will not work again. Differences between the revaluation rate and CPI or RPI are ignored in this example, which assumes the future rate of inflation implicit in the statutory discount rate.

(1) There are three past lost years of service and 17 future lost years of service. The total lost service can be estimated as follows: 17 × 0.81 (Table A, Employed, Level 3)[56] + 3 = 16.77 years.

(2) The lost pension is then 16.77 × £30,000 ÷ 49 = £10,267 p.a. in today's terms.

(3) On retirement the claimant could exchange part of his pension for a lump sum at a rate of 12:1. Assuming a 15% commutation rate gives a lost taxable pension of 0.85 × £10,267 = £8,727 p.a. and a lost tax-free lump sum of (£10,267 – £8,727) × 12 = £18,480, both in today's terms.

(4) The multiplier for valuing pension payable from age 67 is derived from the Additional Tables. For a 50-year-old male at a -0.25% discount rate the multiplier for life is 36.24 and the multiplier to age 67 is 16.71. By subtraction the multiplier from age 67 is 19.53.

(5) Assuming tax at 20% on the lost annual pension gives an approximate pension loss of (0.8 × £8,727 × 19.53) + (£18,480 × 1.0435) = £155,635.

(6) The expected employee contributions (net of tax relief) should be deducted in the loss of earnings calculations.

Section D: Application of Tables to Dependency Claims Resulting From Fatal Accidents/Incidents

(a) Introduction

124. For several decades following *Cookson v Knowles* [1979] AC 556 the approach of the courts in England was to assess the multiplier for dependency claims as at the date of death.

[55] Some practitioners claim the basic rate tax relief on the employee contributions (i.e. 1%, being 20% of 5%) as an additional loss, but that may not be a valid loss because after trial or settlement a claimant may invest those additional gross earnings in a stakeholder pension (and up to £3,600 per annum even without any income) and gain similar basic rate tax relief.

[56] In this example the Table A contingency factor has been adopted and applied to the future service, as no ill-health pension benefits are assumed. An alternative method is to apply the discount for contingencies other than mortality to the loss of future pension benefits in accordance with the decision of the House of Lords in *Page v Sheerness Steel Company Ltd* [1999] 1 AC 345, where a 10% discount was applied, effectively equating to a discount for contingencies of 0.294% for each year of future loss of service. However, such an approach may require adjustment where the claimant is disabled post-injury, so that a higher discount for contingencies should be applied to the residual pension than the "but for the injury" pension.

125. That approach was criticised by the Law Commission in their Report 263 (*Claims for Wrongful Death*). The Law Commission recommended that multipliers should be assessed as at the date of trial and that the multipliers derived from the Ogden Tables should only take effect from the date of trial.

126. The Working Party, then under the Chairmanship of the late Sir Michael Ogden QC, considered that the Law Commission's criticism was valid. In the Fourth Edition of the Tables published in August 2000, the Working Party set out guidance in Section D of the Explanatory Notes on how damages should be calculated in such cases. That recommended approach was adopted in Scotland by the Damages (Scotland) Act 2011.

127. Finally, in 2016 the Supreme Court corrected this anomaly for the remainder of the UK. *Cookson v Knowles* was overruled by *Knauer v Ministry of Justice* [2016] UKSC 9 in which the recommended approach was approved. All English, Welsh and Northern Irish courts must now apply multipliers calculated from the date of trial when assessing the value of future dependency claims brought under the Fatal Accidents Act 1976 (as amended).

(b) The law of dependency claims

128. Under the Fatal Accidents Act 1976[57] (as amended) (the "FAA") the loss is that of the dependants, i.e. those who relied upon the deceased for support. They may claim that part of the deceased's income (whether earnings,[58] unearned income or state benefits) and/or pension that the deceased would have spent on them.[59] They may also claim the loss of the services such as DIY, domestic/household or childcare which the deceased would have undertaken and from which they would have benefited. The position of each dependant, and each head of dependency for each dependant, may need to be considered separately.

129. For pre-trial losses, the actual loss to the date of trial[60] is calculated (taking into account any expected increases in losses, for example, by way of salary increases or increases in the level of services provided). Interest is added. Post-trial losses are calculated as at the date of trial.[61] For each head of future dependency for each dependant the court determines a multiplicand.

130. A multiplier for the period of post-trial dependency is applied to the multiplicand to arrive at an overall lump sum for each head of dependency.

(c) The simplified approach

131. Whereas in personal injury cases the problem to be solved is that of setting a value on an income stream during the potential life of one person (the claimant), the situation is generally more

[57] The FAA is the relevant statute for claims brought in England and Wales. In Scotland the relevant act is the Damages (Scotland) Act 2011 and in Northern Ireland it is the Fatal Accidents (Northern Ireland) Order 1977.

[58] Including the cost of replacing the deceased's skills and contribution to a business: see *Williams v Welsh Ambulance Services NHS Trust* [2008] EWCA Civ 81.

[59] The rule of thumb for couples with one or more dependent children is that the court will adopt as a starting point the assumption that 25% is spent individually by each of the partners, 25% collectively on the children, and 25% on joint expenses (house etc). As the joint expenditure is part of the dependency, this gives 75% as the combined dependency of a partner and one of more dependent children. Where there are no children or they have ceased to be dependent, the corresponding proportions become one-thirds, giving 66.67% as the combined dependency of a partner with no dependent children. Alternatively, a bespoke calculation of the actual amounts spent by the deceased can be undertaken. See further *Harris v Empress Motors* [1984] 1 W.L.R. 212 and *Coward v Comex Houlder Diving Ltd* [1988] EWCA Civ 18. Note the position is codified in Scotland under s.7 of the Damages (Scotland) Act 2011.

[60] For cases being prepared for a settlement meeting or mediation that is a long way in advance of any trial date it may be appropriate to calculate the losses as if the date of that meeting/mediation were the notional trial date.

[61] *Knauer v Ministry of Justice* [2016] UKSC 9.

complicated in fatal accident cases. Here the compensation is intended to reflect the value of an income stream during the lifetime of one or more dependants of the deceased (or the expected period for which the dependants would have expected to receive the dependency, if shorter) but limited according to the expectation of how long the deceased would have been able to provide the financial support, had he or she not sustained fatal injuries.

132. Firstly, there should be compensation for the period between the date of the death and the date of trial. Secondly, in principle, the compensation for post-trial dependency should be based on the present value at the date of the trial of the dependency during the expected future joint lifetime of the deceased and the dependant or claimant, subject to any limitations on the period of dependency and any expected future changes in the level of dependency, notably for the post-retirement period. Both pre- and post-trial periods are subject to an adjustment for the small risk of the deceased having died pre-trial in any event.

133. A set of actuarial tables to make such calculations accurately would require tables similar to Tables 1 to 34 but for each combination of ages as at the date of the trial of the deceased and the dependant to whom compensation is to be paid. The Working Party since the Fourth Edition have concluded that this would not meet the criterion of simplicity of application which was a central objective of these tables and recommends that, in complex cases, or cases where the accuracy of the multiplier is of critical importance and material to the resulting amount of compensation, the expert advice of an actuary should be sought. However, for the majority of cases, a certain amount of approximation will be appropriate, bearing in mind the need for a simple and streamlined process, and taking into consideration the other uncertainties in the determination of an appropriate level of compensation. The following paragraphs describe a methodology based on the principles endorsed by the Supreme Court in *Knauer v Ministry of Justice,* which uses Tables 1 to 34 and will yield reasonably accurate outcomes for most cases.

(d) Calculating the dependency for the period from the fatal incident to the date of trial

134. The period of pre-trial dependency is the period from the commencement of the dependency loss up to the date of trial. The dependency loss will normally run from the date of the incident causing the fatal injuries. However, sometimes this date may be later, for example when there is more than a brief period between the date of the incident and the date of death and the deceased continues to be paid by his employer until he passes away.[62] Account must also be taken of any likely reduction in dependency prior to the date of assessment or trial. For example, the claim for earnings dependency on behalf of a child would be reduced if the dependent child had been expected to become fully financially independent before the trial date.

135. A discount may be made for the risk that the deceased might have died anyway, in the period between the date of death and the date at which the trial takes place. In many cases this adjustment will be small and may in some cases, notably if the deceased was under 40, may be regarded as negligible.[63] An adjustment becomes more necessary the longer the period from the date of death to the date of trial and the older the deceased at the date of death. As an illustration of the order of magnitude of the adjustment, Table E[64] shows some factors by which the pre-trial

[62] Where the estate sustains losses between the date of the fatal incident and the date of death, these may be claimed under the Law Reform (Miscellaneous Provisions) Act 1934.

[63] The Supreme Court in *Knauer* indicated this type of discount would usually be modest but there will be rare cases in which a larger discount would be appropriate.

[64] Note Tables E and F are based on an assumption of a date of death of 2020, which is likely to prove reasonably accurate (with any difference being circa 0.01 or less) for most fatal incident cases reaching trial between 2020 and 2025.

damages should be discounted for different ages of the deceased and for different periods from the date of death to the date of the trial.

TABLE E
Factor by which pre-trial damages should be discounted to allow for the risk that the deceased would not in any case have survived to provide the dependency for the full period to the date of trial or cessation of dependency, if earlier.

Age of deceased at date of death	Period from date of accident to date of trial or date of cessation of dependency, if earlier (years)									
	Male deceased									
	1	2	3	4	5	6	7	8	9	10
Below 40	1.00	1.00	1.00	1.00	1.00	1.00	1.00	1.00	1.00	1.00
40	1.00	1.00	1.00	1.00	1.00	0.99	0.99	0.99	0.99	0.99
45	1.00	1.00	1.00	1.00	0.99	0.99	0.99	0.99	0.99	0.99
50	1.00	1.00	1.00	0.99	0.99	0.99	0.99	0.99	0.98	0.98
55	1.00	1.00	0.99	0.99	0.99	0.98	0.98	0.98	0.97	0.97
60	1.00	0.99	0.99	0.98	0.98	0.98	0.97	0.97	0.96	0.95
65	0.99	0.99	0.98	0.98	0.97	0.96	0.95	0.95	0.94	0.93
70	0.99	0.98	0.97	0.96	0.95	0.94	0.93	0.92	0.90	0.89
75	0.98	0.97	0.95	0.94	0.92	0.90	0.88	0.86	0.84	0.82
80	0.97	0.95	0.92	0.89	0.86	0.83	0.80	0.77	0.74	0.71
85	0.95	0.91	0.86	0.81	0.77	0.72	0.68	0.64	0.60	0.56
90	0.92	0.84	0.77	0.70	0.64	0.58	0.53	0.48	0.44	0.40

Age of deceased at date of death	Period from date of death to date of trial or date of cessation of dependency, if earlier (years)									
	Female deceased									
	1	2	3	4	5	6	7	8	9	10
Below 40	1.00	1.00	1.00	1.00	1.00	1.00	1.00	1.00	1.00	1.00
40	1.00	1.00	1.00	1.00	1.00	1.00	1.00	1.00	1.00	0.99
45	1.00	1.00	1.00	1.00	1.00	1.00	0.99	0.99	0.99	0.99
50	1.00	1.00	1.00	1.00	0.99	0.99	0.99	0.99	0.99	0.99
55	1.00	1.00	1.00	0.99	0.99	0.99	0.99	0.99	0.98	0.98
60	1.00	1.00	0.99	0.99	0.99	0.98	0.98	0.98	0.97	0.97
65	1.00	0.99	0.99	0.98	0.98	0.97	0.97	0.96	0.96	0.95
70	0.99	0.99	0.98	0.97	0.97	0.96	0.95	0.94	0.93	0.92
75	0.99	0.98	0.97	0.95	0.94	0.93	0.91	0.90	0.88	0.87
80	0.98	0.96	0.94	0.92	0.90	0.87	0.85	0.82	0.80	0.77
85	0.96	0.93	0.89	0.85	0.81	0.77	0.73	0.69	0.65	0.62
90	0.93	0.87	0.80	0.74	0.68	0.62	0.57	0.53	0.48	0.44

136. Interest should then be added to the date of trial on the same basis as for special damages.

(e) Types of post-trial dependency

137. There are three main classes of dependency (earnings, pension and services) which result in at least five common types of dependency claims:

(1) Loss of earnings to retirement age.

(2) Loss of earnings for a shorter period (e.g. because the dependency or earnings would have changed or ended).

(3) Loss of pension for life of the deceased (or the dependant, if shorter).

(4) Loss of services for life of the deceased (or the dependant, if shorter).

(5) Loss of services for a shorter period than the life of the deceased or dependant.

138. Each type of dependency will require separate calculation using a different multiplier. However, the methodology is very similar and so this guidance should be followed for each dependency that requires calculation.

(f) Calculating the duration of dependency

139. The first step in calculating the multiplier is to work out the duration of the dependency. This may be limited by the deceased or by the dependant, factoring in any likely limiting factors due to health or life expectancy. Normal life expectancy can be derived using the 0% column in Tables 1 or 2, depending on gender, unless medical expert evidence proves either has an impaired life expectancy.

140. There are two periods to be determined:

(i) The expected period from the date of the trial for which the deceased would have provided the dependency in question.

(ii) The expected period from the date of the trial for which the dependant(s) would have received the dependency.

141. The shorter of those two periods provides the basis for the multiplier for the dependency. However, see Section D (i) below for the approach when there are a number of dependants to a single type of loss.

(g) Discounting for Contingencies

142. Next, consider what, if any, discount should be made for contingencies. Avoid double discounting with any assumptions already made when defining the period of loss, other adjustments and the underlying UK-wide mortality predictions that are within Tables 1 to 34. Also, consider the scale and duration of the contingency especially if it is not equally applicable throughout the period (e.g. deterioration in arthritis leading to a 50% risk of being unable to continue to provide services but only for the last five years of a 20 year period). Contingencies usually fall into the following five categories, although in many claims only the first and/or second will apply, as the others are much less common:

(1) Factors relating to the deceased's earnings. The starting point for the adjustment factor should be the figures contained in Tables as further explained in Section B above.

(2) A deduction, if appropriate,[65] for the risk that the deceased might have died anyway before the date of trial. Table F[66] shows factors by which the multiplier, determined as above, should be adjusted for different ages of the deceased and for different periods from the date of death following the fatal incident to the date of trial.

Table F
Factor by which post-trial damages should be multiplied to allow for the risk that the deceased would not in any case have survived to the date of trial in order to provide any post-trial dependency.

Age of deceased at date of death	Period from date of death to date of trial (years)									
	Male deceased									
	1	2	3	4	5	6	7	8	9	10
Below 40	1.00	1.00	1.00	1.00	1.00	1.00	1.00	1.00	1.00	1.00
40	1.00	1.00	1.00	0.99	0.99	0.99	0.99	0.98	0.98	0.98
45	1.00	1.00	0.99	0.99	0.99	0.98	0.98	0.98	0.98	0.97
50	1.00	0.99	0.99	0.99	0.98	0.98	0.97	0.97	0.96	0.96
55	1.00	0.99	0.99	0.98	0.97	0.97	0.96	0.95	0.94	0.93
60	0.99	0.98	0.98	0.97	0.96	0.95	0.94	0.92	0.91	0.90
65	0.99	0.98	0.96	0.95	0.93	0.92	0.90	0.88	0.86	0.84
70	0.98	0.96	0.94	0.92	0.90	0.87	0.84	0.81	0.78	0.75
75	0.97	0.94	0.90	0.87	0.83	0.79	0.75	0.70	0.65	0.60
80	0.95	0.89	0.84	0.78	0.72	0.65	0.59	0.52	0.46	0.40
85	0.91	0.81	0.72	0.63	0.54	0.46	0.38	0.31	0.24	0.19
90	0.84	0.69	0.56	0.44	0.33	0.25	0.18	0.13	0.09	0.06

Age of deceased at date of death	Period from date of death to date of trial (years)									
	Female deceased									
	1	2	3	4	5	6	7	8	9	10
Below 40	1.00	1.00	1.00	1.00	1.00	1.00	1.00	1.00	1.00	1.00
40	1.00	1.00	1.00	1.00	0.99	0.99	0.99	0.99	0.99	0.99
45	1.00	1.00	1.00	0.99	0.99	0.99	0.99	0.99	0.98	0.98
50	1.00	1.00	0.99	0.99	0.99	0.99	0.98	0.98	0.98	0.97
55	1.00	0.99	0.99	0.99	0.98	0.98	0.97	0.97	0.96	0.96
60	1.00	0.99	0.98	0.98	0.97	0.96	0.96	0.95	0.94	0.93
65	0.99	0.98	0.98	0.97	0.96	0.94	0.93	0.92	0.91	0.89
70	0.99	0.97	0.96	0.94	0.93	0.91	0.89	0.87	0.84	0.82
75	0.98	0.96	0.93	0.90	0.88	0.84	0.81	0.77	0.73	0.69
80	0.96	0.92	0.88	0.83	0.78	0.73	0.67	0.61	0.55	0.49
85	0.93	0.85	0.77	0.69	0.61	0.53	0.46	0.38	0.31	0.25
90	0.86	0.73	0.61	0.50	0.39	0.30	0.23	0.17	0.12	0.08

[65] As with Table E above, this reduction will usually be negligible if the deceased was under 40 unless a very long period had elapsed between death and trial.
[66] The simplest way to conceptualise the difference between Table E factors and Table F factors is that the latter represent point to point survival ratios, of a fixed number of years from the date of death, whereas Table E factors are applied to a total figure which has been calculated for pre-trial damages and they therefore represent effectively the average survival period from the date to which an element of damages relates up to the date of trial. Roughly speaking this is half as long an effective period of survival.

(3) Rarely, it may be appropriate to make a further adjustment for atypical health or mortality risks of the deceased or the dependant. See the further guidance in Section A and in the preamble to this paragraph.

(4) An adjustment for contingencies in respect of the damages for the period of dependency on a pension after retirement age will often be less than that required for pre-retirement earnings dependency for the reasons set out in Section B under the subheading "(a) Introduction".

(5) Factors relating to the relationship of the deceased and the dependant; for example, an unmarried couple who were on the point of separation before the deceased died. See also s.3(4) of the FAA, *Drew v Abassi* (Court of Appeal) 24 May 1995 and *Wheatley v Cunningham* [1992] P.I.Q.R. Q100.

(h) Calculating the post-trial dependency

143. Applying the above principles, the assessment of the loss for each type of dependency involves the following steps (as further illustrated in the worked examples in Section D(j) below):

(1) Calculate the annual loss based on the value at the date of the trial.

(2) For earnings and pension (but not services) dependencies, apply the appropriate dependency factor to work out the proportion of the loss which the dependant is entitled to.

(3) Work out whether the duration of the dependency in question is limited by the deceased or the dependant, as described in Section D (f) above.

(4) Translate that figure into a multiplier by using one of the following at the current discount rate:

(i) Life-long losses, using Tables 1 or 2 (according to the gender of the deceased or dependant and using age at the date of the trial).

(ii) Losses to retirement age, using Tables 3 to 18 (according to the gender of the deceased and the expected age at retirement).

(iii) Losses of earnings or services for a fixed lesser period that the deceased would have provided the dependency, using the most applicable of Tables 3 to 18, adjusting if necessary, following the guidance relating to the analogous scenario of different retirement ages in Section A.

(iv) Pension losses post-retirement age, using Tables 19 to 34. This is the same as calculating the multiplier for life-long losses and then deducting the multiplier for losses to retirement age derived from Tables 3 to 18.

(v) Using Table 36 for losses for fixed periods which cannot otherwise be derived from Tables 1 to 34.[67]

(5) Make an adjustment applying Table F, if appropriate, for the risk that the deceased might have died anyway before the date of trial.

[67] Alternatively, it may be possible to calculate such multipliers using a computer programme or the Additional Tables.

(6) For earnings losses only, apply an appropriate adjustment to the above figure to reflect earnings related contingencies, ordinarily using the adjustment factor contained in Tables.

(7) Consider whether there are proven atypical health or mortality risks, and if so, consider applying a contingency factor for this.

(8) For pension losses, consider whether a contingency is required.

(9) On rare occasions it may be appropriate to make a deduction for factors relating to the dependant's relationship to the deceased.

(10) The resulting multiplier is then applied to the multiplicand for the post-trial dependency in question.

(i) Multiple dependants

144. There will be cases where there are several dependants who have different periods of dependency. For example, one dependant may have a shorter life expectancy than another, or children may be dependent for different periods according to their ages. Sometimes a single multiplicand for the dependency in question is determined, which is to be shared among two or more dependants (for example children), as long as at least one of them is expected to remain alive and dependent. For this approach the multiplier will be calculated utilising the longest of the expected periods for which any dependency might last (for example until the youngest child is no longer dependent).

145. Alternatively, if the dependencies are truly independent of each other, separate multiplicands and multipliers should be determined for each dependant. The total amount of dependency damages is then calculated by adding the separate components. In any event calculations of separate multipliers may be required for apportionment of damages between the dependants, even if it does not impact upon the total amount of the damages to be paid by the tortfeasor, notably if there is a claim made on behalf of dependants under the age of 18 or otherwise lacking capacity. Any proposed settlement of such claims will require court approval which will include consideration of the damages payable to each dependant protected by CPR Part 21.

(j) Examples of Fatal Accident Act Claims

Example 15 – FAA claim calculated using the main Ogden Tables 1 to 34 at -0.25%

146. The sole financial dependant is a woman, aged 38 at the date of the trial, which is taking place three years after the date of a fatal accident, which killed her husband, who at that time was aged 37. The deceased would have been age 40 at the date of trial. The deceased had A levels, was in employment, was not disabled (as defined in Section B) and lived and worked in London at the time of the fatal accident (so a -0.25% discount rate is applicable). There was no evidence suggesting that either the deceased or the dependant had atypical mortality risks nor that their relationship was unstable. The court has determined a multiplicand of £30,000 up to the deceased's normal retirement age of 65 and has decided that post-retirement damages should be payable based on a multiplicand of £12,000. The multipliers in this example are taken from Ogden Tables 1 to 34 (although, as no interpolation is required, identical multipliers would be obtained from the Additional Tables).

147. Pre-trial damages are calculated as shown below.

(1) Period between fatal accident and trial: three years.

(2) Adjust for the risk of possible early death (considered negligible as the deceased was under 40): apply an adjustment factor of 1.00 (Ogden Table E for male aged 37 and three years).

(3) Pre-trial damages: £30,000 × three years × 1.00 = £90,000 (plus interest as special damages).

(4) Interest at half rate from date of death to date of trial: three years at 0.25% a year = 0.75%. £90,000 × 0.75% = £675.

148. Post-trial damages are split between pre- and post-retirement damages. Post-trial pre- retirement damages are calculated as set out below.

(1) Expected period for which the dependant would have been able to receive the dependency (Ogden Table 2 at 0% for female aged 38): 49.73. This is when the deceased would have been aged 89.73 (i.e. 40 years + 49.73 years), so the dependency would be for the entire period to the deceased's retirement age 65.

(2) Multiplier for male age 40 retiring at age 65 (Ogden Table 9 at -0.25% rate of return) = 24.97.

(3) Adjust for contingencies other than mortality (in accordance with Section B) for an employed male aged 40 with A levels (Level 2) and who was not disabled: apply a reduction factor of 0.87 to give a multiplier of 24.97 × 0.87 = 21.72.

(4) Adjust for the risk that the deceased might have died anyway before the date of trial (considered negligible as the deceased was under 40): apply an adjustment factor of 1.00 (Ogden Table F for male aged 37 and three years), to give a multiplier of 21.72 × 1.00 = 21.72.

(5) The post-trial pre-retirement damages total: 21.72 × £30,000 = £651,600.

149. Post-trial, post-retirement damages are calculated as set out below.

(1) Expectation of life of deceased at date of trial (Ogden Table 1 at 0% for male aged 40 at the date of trial): 44.80.

(2) Expected period for which the dependant would have been able to receive the dependency (Ogden Table 2 at 0% for female aged 38): 49.73.

(3) Lesser of two periods at (1) and (2) = 44.80 [so based on the life expectancy of the deceased].

(4) Multiplier from age 65 for a male age 40 (Ogden Table 25 at -0.25% for male aged 40): 22.66.

(5) Adjust for the risk that the deceased might have died anyway before the date of trial (considered negligible as the deceased was under 40): apply an adjustment factor of 1.00 (Ogden Table F for male aged 37 and three years) to give a multiplier of 22.66 × 1.00 = 22.66.

(6) Post-retirement damages: £12,000 × 22.66 = £271,920.

150. Total financial dependency is therefore: £90,000 + interest of £675 + £651,600 + £271,920 = £1,014,195.

Example 16 – FAA claim calculated using the main Ogden Tables 1 to 34 at -0.75%

151. The sole dependant is a man, aged 52 at the date of the trial, which is taking place 4 years after the date of the fatal accident, which killed his wife, at that time aged 43, and on whom he was financially dependent. The deceased lived and worked in Edinburgh and would have been aged 47 at the date of trial. She was in employment at the time of the fatal accident, was not disabled and had achieved a Certificate of Sixth Year Studies (''CSYS''). The widower brings his dependency claim in Scotland (so a -0.75% discount rate is appropriate). The court has determined a multiplicand, up to the deceased's normal retirement age of 60, of £50,000 and has decided that post-retirement damages should be payable based on a multiplicand of £30,000. The multipliers in this example use multipliers derived from Ogden Tables 1 to 34 (although, as no interpolation is required, identical multipliers would be obtained from the Additional Tables).

152. Pre-trial damages are calculated as shown below.

(1) Period between fatal accident and trial: four years.

(2) Adjust for risk of possible early death: apply an adjustment factor of 1.00 (Ogden Table E for female aged 43 and four years).

(3) Pre-trial damages: £50,000 × 4 years × 1.00 = £200,000 (plus interest as special damages).

153. Post-trial damages are split between pre- and post-retirement damages. Post-trial, pre-retirement damages are calculated as set out below.

(1) Expected period for which the dependant would have been able to receive the dependency (Ogden Table 1 at 0% for male aged 52): 32.52. This is when the deceased would have been aged 79.52 (i.e. 47 years + 32.52 years), so the dependency would be for the entire period to the deceased's age 60.

(2) Multiplier for female age 47 retiring at age 60 (Ogden Table 8 at -0.75% rate of return) = 13.47.

(3) Adjustment factor for contingencies other than mortality (in accordance with Section B) for an employed female aged 47 with CSYS (Level 2) and who was not disabled = 0.84 to give a multiplier of 13.47 × 0.84 = 11.31.

(4) Adjustment factor for the risk that the deceased might have died anyway before the date of trial (Ogden Table F for female aged 43 and 4 years): 0.99 to give a multiplier of 11.31 × 0.99 = 11.20.

(5) Post-trial pre-retirement damages total: £50,000 × 11.20 = £560,000.

154. Post-trial, post-retirement damages are calculated as set out below.

(1) Expectation of life of deceased at date of trial (Ogden Table 2 at 0% for female aged 47, the age as at the date of trial): 40.25.

(2) Expected period for which the dependant would have been able to receive the dependency (Ogden Table 1 at 0% for male aged 52): 32.52.

(3) Lesser of two periods at (1) and (2) = 32.52 [so based on the dependant].

(4) Multiplier from age 65 (i.e. when the deceased would have been age 60) for a male age 52 at -0.75% rate of return (Ogden Table 25 at -0.75% for a male aged 52): 24.20.

(5) Adjust for the risk that the deceased might have died anyway before the date of trial: apply an adjustment factor of 0.99 (Ogden Table F for female aged 43 and four years) to give a multiplier of 24.20 × 0.99 = 23.96.

(6) Post-retirement damages total: £30,000 × 23.96 = £718,800.

155. Total financial dependency is therefore: £200,000 (plus interest) + £560,000 + £718,800 = £1,478,800.

Example 17 – FAA claim calculated using the Additional Tables at -0.25%

156. A woman has been killed in a road traffic accident, when she was aged 35. She had three financial dependants, her husband aged 40 and two children aged 15 and 11 at the date of the trial, which is taking place three years after the date of the accident. The deceased had a degree, lived and worked in Leeds (so a -0.25% discount rate is applicable). The deceased would have been aged 38 at the date of trial. The court has determined a multiplicand, up to the deceased's normal retirement age of 67 (when the deceased's husband will have reached age 69), of £50,000 when there are dependent children and £40,000 when there are no dependent children (so spouse only) and has decided that post-retirement damages should be payable based on a multiplicand of £20,000. The court has determined that the younger child would have remained financially dependent until at least age 22 (so 11 years from trial). The multipliers in this example use the Additional Tables, but shown in the footnotes are the multipliers using interpolation of Ogden Tables 1 to 34.[68]

157. Pre-trial damages are calculated as follows:

(1) Period between fatal accident and trial: three years.

(2) Adjust for the risk of possible early death (considered negligible as the deceased was under 40: apply a discount factor of 1.00 (Ogden Table E for female aged 35 and three years).

(3) Pre-trial damages = 3 × 1.00 × £50,000 = £150,000 (plus interest as special damages).

158. Post-trial damages are split between pre- and post-retirement damages. Post-trial, pre-retirement damages are calculated as set out below.

(1) Expected period for which the deceased would have provided the dependency should be based on female aged 38 at the date of trial with retirement age of 67 (for female aged 38 to age 67 at 0%), i.e. 28.34.

[68] As explained in Section A (f), where there is any difference between multipliers derived by interpolation from Ogden Tables 1 to 34 and multipliers from the Additional Tables, the latter are to be treated as definitive, although in this example, as it happens, there are no differences.

(2) Expected period for which the male adult dependant would have been able to receive the dependency (in the table for males at 0%, read across the row from age 40 in the first column to age 125 i.e. for life): 44.80.

(3) Lesser of two periods at (1) and (2) = 28.34 [so based on the deceased].

(4) Multiplier for 11 years (for female age 38 to age 49 at -0.25%): 11.10. Multiplier for 29 years (for female age 38 to age 67 at -0.25%): 29.38.[69]

(5) Multiplier from age 49 (i.e. 38 + 11) to age 67 for female age 38 is calculated as: Multiplier to age 67 less multiplier to age 49: 29.38 – 11.10 = 18.28.

(6) Adjust for contingencies other than mortality: apply a reduction factor of 0.88 reflecting an employed female aged 38 with a degree who was not disabled (Table C, Level 3) to give multipliers of 11.10 × 0.88 = 9.77 and 18.28 × 0.88 = 16.09.

(7) Adjust for the risk that the deceased might have died anyway before the date of trial (considered negligible because the deceased was under 40): apply an adjustment factor of 1.00 (Ogden Table F for female aged 35 and three years), so multipliers are 9.77 and 16.09, respectively.

(8) Post-trial pre-retirement damages total: (£50,000 × 9.77) + (£40,000 × 16.09) = £1,132,100.

159. Post-trial, post-retirement damages are calculated as set out below.

(1) Expectation of life of deceased at date of trial (for female aged 38 for life at 0%): 49.73.

(2) Expected period for which the adult dependant would have been able to receive the dependency (for male aged 40 for life at 0%): 44.80 (no post-retirement dependency for the children).

(3) Lesser of two periods at (1) and (2) = 44.80 [so based on the adult dependant].

(4) Multiplier for life for adult dependant (Table for Males at a discount rate of -0.25% for life): 47.63.

(5) Deduct multiplier for the dependants' pre-retirement damages (for a male aged 40 to age 69 at a discount rate of -0.25%): 28.81.[70] This gives a multiplier of: 47.63 – 28.81 = 18.82.

(6) Adjust for the risk that the deceased might have died anyway before the date of trial (considered negligible because the deceased was under 40): apply an adjustment factor of

[69] Multiplier to age 67 years for female age 38 using the age-adjusted interpolation method: first calculate as though deceased was aged 36 and had retirement age of 65 (Ogden Table 10 at -0.25% for female aged 36): 29.49. Then calculate as though deceased was aged 39 and had retirement age of 68 (Ogden Table 12 at -0.25% for female aged 39): 29.32. Interpolate for age 38 with retirement age of 67: [(1 × 29.49) + (2 × 29.32)] / 3 = 29.38. Multiplier to age 67 years for female age 38 using simple interpolation method: 38-year-old female retiring at age 65 (Ogden Table 10 for female age 38 at -0.25%) = 27.37. A 38-year-old female retiring at age 68 (Ogden Table 12 for female age 38 at -0.25%): 30.38. 27.37 + ((30.38 – 27.37) × 2/3) = 29.38.

[70] Multiplier to age 69 years for male age 40 using age-adjusted interpolation method: first calculate as though the male was aged 39 and had retirement age of 68 (Ogden Table 11 at -0.25% for male aged 39): 28.90. Then calculate as though the male was aged 41 and had retirement age of 70 (Ogden Table 13 at -0.25% for male aged 41): 28.71. Interpolate for age 40 with retirement age of 69 = [(1 × 28.90) + (1 × 28.71)] / 2 = 28.81. Using the simple interpolation method gives the same multiplier: the age 40 to age 68 multiplier is 27.86 and age 40 to age 70 is 29.75, so simple interpolation (the midpoint) = 28.81.

1.00 (Ogden Table F for female aged 35 and three years), so multiplier is 18.82 × 1.00 = 18.82.

(7) Post-trial, post-retirement damages total: £20,000 × 18.82 = £376,400.

160. Total financial dependency is therefore: £150,000 (plus interest) + £1,132,100 + £376,400 = £1,658,500.

Section E: Periodical Payments for Loss of Earnings

161. The personal injury discount rate is set by reference to "real" and "net" returns; "real" being relative to price inflation and "net" being after taxation and investment charges and costs.

162. The discount rate in England and Wales, set under the Civil Liability Act 2018, is based on a definition of "damages inflation" as being the Consumer Prices Index (CPI) plus 1%.[71] This is because there is assumed to be,[72] broadly on average across all claimants:

(i) an expectation of earnings growth of CPI+2% on half of the future losses; and

(ii) an expectation of prices growth of CPI on the other half.

163. The discount rate in Scotland, set under the Damages (Investment Returns and Periodical Payments) (Scotland) Act 2019, defines "inflation" as being the Retail Prices Index (RPI).[73] This is similar to CPI+1% as historically over the last 10 years the difference between RPI and CPI has been about +0.8%.[74] The discount rate in Northern Ireland, set under the Damages (Return on Investment) Act 2022, also defines "inflation" as being the Retail Prices Index (RPI).[75]

(a) Form of Award

164. Some claimants prefer the flexibility and clean break provided by a lump sum award. A lump sum calculated assuming that damages inflation will be CPI+1% may or may not match the inflation that in fact occurs. Fortunate claimants who invest their lump sum damages at the right time may be able to meet their needs, the costs of which have escalated in line with earnings growth. However, investment returns are unpredictable and the level of risk required to achieve returns sufficient to meet earnings growth on earnings-based elements of the claim may be unattractive.

[71] See further *Setting the Personal Injury Discount Rate published by the Government Actuary* dated 25 June 2019 and para.14 of the explanatory statement made by the Lord Chancellor, David Gauke, dated 15 July 2019 accepting the Government Actuary's advice and confirming the outcome of the first personal injury discount rate review under the Civil Liability Act 2018 available at: *https://assets.publishing.service.gov.uk/government/uploads/system/uploads/attachment_-data/file/816819/stateme nt-of-reasons.pdf.*

[72] See further paras 8.9 to 8.12 of *Setting the Personal Injury Discount Rate published by the Government Actuary* dated 25 June 2019: *https://assets.publishing.service.gov.uk/government/uploads/system/uploads/attachment_data/file/817236/ Setting_the_Personal_Injury_Discount_Rate web_.pdf*

[73] Paragraph 9(2) of Schedule B1 of the Damages (Investment Returns and Periodical Payments) (Scotland) Act 2019 Act states that the impact of inflation is to be allowed for by reference to the RPI, whether indicating an upward or downward trend.

[74] Source ONS Difference between CPI and RPI rounded: *https://www.ons.gov.uk/economy/inflationandpriceindices/time series/dra2/mm23.*

[75] Paragraph 9(2)(a) of Schedule C1 of the Damages (Return on Investment) Act (Northern Ireland) 2022 states that the impact of inflation is to be allowed for by reference to the RPI, whether indicating an upward or downward trend.

165. In the absence of annuities linked to earnings-based measures, the safest means to track future earnings growth on earnings-based elements of the claim is by way of an award of earnings-linked periodical payments. It should be noted that such tracking can be positive or negative, and periodical payments linked to earnings-based measures may go up or down. Historically wages have increased at a faster rate than prices[76] and periodical payments are the only reliable way to closely match changes in earnings-based losses and expenses which may occur.

166. If loss of earnings claims are to be paid in the form of periodical payments, there are two substantial issues to be considered – namely indexation and accounting for residual earnings capacity through reduced earnings, reduced earnings growth and reduced employment prospects.

(b) Indexation

167. Fundamentally periodical payments are an entirely different character to lump sum awards.[77] In order to keep pace with inflation, they can be uprated by a measure other than the rate of inflation assumed when setting the discount rate. Indexation is the term used to describe the measure that is to be applied under the Damages Act to escalate the periodical payments into the future. The default measure set in the Damages Act 1996 (as amended) is presently the RPI.[78] However, the cases of *Thompstone v Tameside & Glossop Acute Services NHS Trust* [2008] EWCA Civ 5; [2008] 1 W.L.R. 2207 established that, exercising its powers under s.2(9) of the Damages Act 1996, the court could apply an alternative measure for indexation of periodical payments as long as it was more appropriate.

168. The test as to whether a measure is more appropriate, referred to as the Mackay test,[79] is as follows:

(1) accuracy of match of the particular data series to the loss or expenditure being compensated;

(2) authority of the collector of the data;

(3) statistical reliability;

(4) accessibility;

(5) consistency over time;

(6) reproducibility in the future; and

(7) simplicity and consistency in application.

169. In respect of future care and case management, the Court of Appeal held in the *Thompstone* cases that periodical payments should be indexed by reference to the earnings of those within the standard occupational classification (SOC) of the Annual Survey of Hours and Earnings (ASHE) for

[76] *Thompstone v Tameside & Glossop Acute Services NHS Trust & others* [2008] EWCA Civ 5; [2008] 1 W.L.R. 2207.
[77] *Flora v Wakom (Heathrow) Ltd* [2006] EWCA Civ 1103, per Brooke LJ at para.28.
[78] Damages Act 1996, s.2(8).
[79] *RH v United Bristol Healthcare Trust* [2007] EWHC 1441 para.71, approved by the Court of Appeal in *Thompstone v Tameside & Glossop Acute Services NHS Trust & others* [2008] EWCA Civ 5; [2008] 1 W.L.R. 2207.

'care assistants and home carers' (classification "6115").[80] The courts have tended to index future care and case management by reference to the 80th centile (the level of the earnings of the top 20% within the earnings distribution, as this is usually the closest earnings level to that of the carers being employed). ASHE SOC 6115 is statistically reliable because the sample size defined in this role is large. There are many occupational groups where the cell size is too small to produce reliable estimates.

170. Small cell sizes are associated with statistical volatility. There is also a risk that the series will not be published in the future. Whilst the model Schedule to the Order can and does deal with a 'discontinuity of data' (i.e. the non-publication of an estimate), the model Schedule cannot accommodate statistical volatility which can give rise to large swings in the escalation that is applied.

171. For example, ASHE 2412 is the occupational classification for "barristers and judges". Earnings estimates for this occupational classification are not reliable (flagged by shading) due to small numbers. In 2015, the mean earnings level fell by 12.8%. Since there was no clear reason why the earnings of barristers and judges would have fallen in that year, we must assume that the large change was caused by statistical volatility. Interestingly, in 2016 there was a 14.3% increase in earnings; another large swing without an obvious cause.

172. If the closest occupational classification is not statistically reliable, an obvious problem arises. Would it be better to index with reference to a broader SOC, or would an aggregate measure at the appropriate centile of the earnings distribution produce a better measure under the Mackay test? If in doubt, in more substantial cases, it may be advisable to seek expert advice regarding the most suitable measure for indexation.

(c) Residual Earning Capacity

173. Where there is a residual earnings capacity, the lost earnings and the residual earnings may be in two different occupations, at different levels and with different employment risks. For the reasons explained under Section B above, a different reduction factor (RF) will probably need to be applied to capture the post-injury impact of disability on the claimant's employment prospects. In these circumstances, the court may need to consider applying two different indexation measures and two different reduction factors to the two different multiplicands in respect of the estimated net annual earnings "but for" the injury on the one hand and anticipated post-injury residual earnings on the other.

174. Take the example of a 25-year-old female full-time nurse prior to the index accident who is rendered disabled by reason of her injuries. Post-accident, she is restricted to basic entry-level clerical work on a part time basis and with no promotion prospects. The indexation of a periodical payments award for loss of earnings would need to reflect the following factors:

- Pre-injury – the calculation of earnings will be based on nurses' annual net earnings. The assessment will take account of her probable earnings growth from the age-earnings profile, including her prospects of promotion. Additionally, consideration must be given to the likely national wage growth for the occupation. Finally, a deduction will be made for risks other than mortality (in this example, the reduction factor would be 0.88 for 25-year-old, employed, female graduate) (Level 3).

[80] When occupational groups were reclassified in ASHE in 2011, carers were split into two groups (6145 and 6146). The ONS continue to publish the equivalent 2000 classification of SOC 6115 with the title Care Workers in Table 26.

- Post-injury – the earnings calculation will be based on a basic clerical rate for part time work. The probable earnings growth will be derived from the new post-injury age-earnings profile which is likely to be flatter. Promotion prospects are likely to be lower and may be nil. Earnings growth calculations will also take account of national wage growth for the post-injury occupation (which may also be lower). Finally, there will be a significant discount for risks other than mortality. In this example, the reduction factor for a disabled 25-year-old woman restricted to GCSE-level employment (Level 2) would be 0.42 if she is employed at the time of assessment and 0.31 if she is not employed at the time of assessment.

175. Once the pre-and post-injury occupations have been established, ASHE provides a helpful source of information for estimating individual earnings (the annual wage) and earnings growth (the annual escalation) for both pre-and post-injury earnings. However, it should be noted that the indexation of future earnings claims can be more complex than for future commercial costs of care because (i) the occupational earnings measure must be seen to meet the Mackay test, especially point (3) above in view of smaller SOC sample sizes; (ii) differential wages and wages growth pre- and post-injury; (iii) differential employment risks pre- and post-injury; and (iv) the potential application of a part-time pay penalty post-injury. Given the comparatively few reported cases concerning the indexation of periodical payments for loss of earnings and the additional complexity over the indexation of care costs, selecting the appropriate measure for uprating loss of earnings claims may well justify the input of expert advice, in more substantial cases, especially where there is some residual earnings capacity.

176. Where there is a residual earnings capacity to be taken into account, there is a need to draft two separate Schedules to the Order, establishing two separate indexation calculations, applied as follows:

PP = [(a) × (b) × (c)] – [(d) × (e) × (f)]
where
(a) = annual pre-injury loss of earnings.
(b) = the appropriate RF for pre-injury loss of earnings.
(c) = the growth in earnings at the relevant part of the earnings distribution for the pre-injury loss of earnings at the relevant SOC.
(d) = annual post-injury residual earnings.
(e) = the appropriate RF for post-injury residual earnings.
(f) = the growth in earnings at the relevant part of the earnings distribution for the post-injury residual earnings at the relevant SOC.

177. Any differences in the duration of pre-injury earnings compared to post-injury earnings will normally be accounted for in the difference between the respective reduction factors applied to each. It is important to note that promotion/age-earnings growth profiles must be included in the Schedule to the Order at (a) and (d) above. In the same way that there may be steps in the annual periodical payments for care and case management, if a periodical payments order for loss of earnings is to match the claimant's loss as closely as possible, similarly, there may be steps up and down over the course of the claimant's working life.

ASHE provides a guide to annual wages and will normally be used for the annual wage escalation. The reduction factors account for the employment risks. A view must be taken on how to account for earnings growth due to individual effects (age-earnings profile and promotion). There is no statistical evidence on the impact of disability on earnings growth other than through the effects of occupational downgrading, reduced pay due to working less hours and lost promotion opportunities.

Section F: Concluding Remarks

178. The Ogden Tables are designed to assist practitioners and the courts to arrive at suitable multipliers in a range of possible situations and retirement ages. The Additional Tables allow for the calculation of multipliers between different ages. However, not all possibilities are covered and in more complex situations, such as where there are significant pension rights, it may be advisable to seek specialist advice from a Fellow of the Institute and Faculty of Actuaries.

July 2020

William Latimer-Sayer KC
On behalf of the Ogden Working Party
London
(updated August 2022 in light of the change of the Northern Ireland discount rate from -1.75% to -1.5%)

Appendix A – Technical Note

1. The purposes of the tables and the application of the multipliers are set out in Section A of the explanatory notes. The main set of tables provide multipliers at rates of return ranging from -2.0% to +3.0%, in steps of 0.5%, along with inclusion of multipliers at the prescribed rates of discount at the date of publication of -0.25% for England and Wales, -0.75% for Scotland and -1.5% for Northern Ireland.

2. The assumptions underlying the calculation of the multipliers have been set by the Ogden Working Party following detailed consideration of the relevant issues and the latest available data.

3. The multipliers have been calculated assuming the average date of trial, or settlement, is 2022. This date has been chosen as providing multipliers which will be appropriate for award settlements occurring over the next four or five years, after which it is anticipated a new edition of the Ogden Tables will be produced. Further information on the construction of the multipliers are available on request from GAD using *enquiries@gad.gov.uk.*

4. The multipliers are assumed to be applicable to the average member of the United Kingdom population and allow for future projected changes in mortality based on the projected mortality rates underlying the 2018-based principal population projections for the United Kingdom, published by the Office for National Statistics (ONS) in October 2019.[81]

5. The multipliers in the 8th edition are generally lower than those in the 7th edition, especially in respect of losses after retirement age. This is because over the last decade there has been a stalling of mortality improvements at most ages with little increase in projected life expectancies. As a result, the 2008-based population projections (which were used in the 7th edition of the tables) have proved more optimistic over the short term than the actual outturn, and the 2018-based projections assume lower life expectancies for a given age in 2022 than the 2008-based projections had done. Section A of the explanatory notes provides further details on the mortality assumptions and discusses how the multipliers may be amended if the claimant is deemed to have atypical life expectancy.

6. In addition to the main set of tables, Additional Tables have been produced using the same assumptions which can be used to derive multipliers for loss of pension or to split multipliers into shorter periods, for example where variable levels of earnings or care costs are assumed payable over different age periods. These Additional Tables are provided at rates of discount of -0.25%, -0.75%, -1.5% and 0%. These include the rates of discount prescribed for use in England & Wales, in Scotland and in Northern Ireland at the date of publication. If the prescribed rates in any of the jurisdictions are changed in future, further supplementary tables will be provided.

7. In addition to the tables of multipliers we have also derived the factors for Table E (which provides factors for discounting pre-trial damages to allow for the risk the deceased would not have survived to provide a dependency for the full period to the date of trial or cessation of dependency) and Table F (which provides factors to apply to post-trial damages to allow for the risk that the deceased would not have survived to the date of trial). The factors in both of these tables were

[81] The mortality rates used for the calculations are not published directly by ONS but have been derived from data provided by ONS giving the projected death rates assumed for the United Kingdom as a whole at the start of the projections process. These were converted into the format and age definition required for calculating the multipliers. There are a variety of other data sets published by ONS from which the mortality rates required could be derived. These can give slightly different results in some cases to the multipliers calculated for Ogden 8. The mortality rates used for the calculations are available from GAD on request at enquiries@gad.gov.uk.

calculated using the same mortality rates used for calculating the multipliers but assuming the date of death was in 2020, which is believed a reasonable assumption for most fatal accident cases reaching trial between 2020 and 2025.

8. The mortality projections do not include any allowance for the possible effects of the COVID-19 pandemic on future mortality, as the projections used were published before the outbreak of the pandemic. At this stage, the full impact of the COVID-19 pandemic is not known and will remain uncertain until further evidence has been established. In general, whilst pandemics may affect mortality rates in the short term, the effects on longer term rates may be relatively slight. For example, the main result may be the bringing forward of deaths that would have occurred anyway in the next few years so that longer-term mortality rates would be expected to remain relatively unaffected. The position may need to be reviewed in due course once the implications of the COVID-19 pandemic become more apparent to ensure that the mortality rates used in these projections remain fit for purpose.

Limitations and professional compliance

9. The multipliers and other actuarial analysis outlined in this publication have been calculated and carried out in accordance with the applicable Technical Actuarial Standard: TAS 100 issued by the Financial Reporting Council (FRC). The FRC sets technical standards for actuarial work in the UK.

July 2020 Government Actuary's Department

(updated August 2022 in light of the change of the Northern Ireland discount rate from -1.75% to -1.5%)

Table 1: Multipliers for pecuniary loss for life (males)

Age at date of trial	Multipliers calculated with allowance for projected mortality from the 2018-based population projections and rate of return of:													Age at date of trial
	-2.0%	-1.75%	**-1.5%**	-1.0%	**-0.75%**	-0.5%	**-0.25%**	0.0%	0.5%	1.0%	1.5%	2.0%	2.5%	
0	254.93	219.46	**189.83**	144.12	**126.51**	111.60	**98.93**	88.13	70.95	58.19	48.57	41.20	35.48	0
1	249.12	214.91	**186.26**	141.94	**124.81**	110.27	**97.90**	87.34	70.49	57.93	48.43	41.14	35.47	1
2	242.63	209.74	**182.15**	139.32	**122.71**	108.60	**96.56**	86.26	69.79	57.47	48.14	40.95	35.34	2
3	236.22	204.63	**178.06**	136.70	**120.61**	106.90	**95.19**	85.16	69.07	57.00	47.82	40.74	35.20	3
4	229.95	199.60	**174.03**	134.10	**118.51**	105.21	**93.83**	84.05	68.34	56.52	47.50	40.52	35.05	4
5	223.80	194.67	**170.07**	131.52	**116.43**	103.53	**92.47**	82.95	67.61	56.04	47.18	40.30	34.90	5
6	217.79	189.83	**166.17**	128.98	**114.37**	101.86	**91.11**	81.84	66.88	55.54	46.84	40.08	34.75	6
7	211.91	185.09	**162.33**	126.46	**112.33**	100.20	**89.76**	80.74	66.14	55.05	46.51	39.85	34.59	7
8	206.16	180.43	**158.55**	123.96	**110.30**	98.54	**88.40**	79.63	65.40	54.54	46.16	39.61	34.42	8
9	200.53	175.85	**154.83**	121.50	**108.28**	96.89	**87.05**	78.53	64.65	54.03	45.81	39.37	34.26	9
10	195.02	171.37	**151.17**	119.05	**106.28**	95.25	**85.71**	77.42	63.89	53.51	45.46	39.12	34.08	10
11	189.62	166.96	**147.57**	116.63	**104.29**	93.62	**84.36**	76.31	63.13	52.99	45.09	38.87	33.90	11
12	184.35	162.64	**144.03**	114.24	**102.32**	92.00	**83.02**	75.20	62.37	52.46	44.72	38.61	33.72	12
13	179.19	158.40	**140.55**	111.88	**100.37**	90.38	**81.68**	74.09	61.60	51.93	44.35	38.34	33.53	13
14	174.14	154.25	**137.12**	109.54	**98.44**	88.78	**80.35**	72.98	60.83	51.39	43.97	38.07	33.34	14
15	169.20	150.17	**133.75**	107.23	**96.52**	87.18	**79.02**	71.87	60.06	50.84	43.58	37.80	33.14	15
16	164.38	146.18	**130.44**	104.94	**94.61**	85.59	**77.70**	70.76	59.28	50.29	43.19	37.51	32.93	16
17	159.67	142.27	**127.19**	102.69	**92.73**	84.02	**76.38**	69.66	58.50	49.74	42.79	37.23	32.72	17
18	155.06	138.44	**124.00**	100.46	**90.87**	82.46	**75.07**	68.56	57.72	49.18	42.39	36.94	32.51	18
19	150.57	134.68	**120.86**	98.26	**89.02**	80.91	**73.76**	67.46	56.93	48.62	41.98	36.64	32.29	19
20	146.18	131.01	**117.78**	96.09	**87.19**	79.37	**72.46**	66.36	56.15	48.05	41.57	36.34	32.07	20
21	141.89	127.41	**114.76**	93.95	**85.39**	77.84	**71.17**	65.27	55.36	47.48	41.15	36.03	31.85	21
22	137.69	123.88	**111.78**	91.83	**83.60**	76.32	**69.89**	64.17	54.57	46.90	40.73	35.72	31.61	22
23	133.59	120.42	**108.86**	89.73	**81.82**	74.82	**68.60**	63.08	53.77	46.32	40.30	35.40	31.38	23
24	129.58	117.03	**105.99**	87.66	**80.06**	73.32	**67.33**	61.99	52.97	45.73	39.87	35.08	31.13	24
25	125.66	113.70	**103.16**	85.62	**78.31**	71.83	**66.05**	60.90	52.17	45.14	39.42	34.74	30.88	25
26	121.83	110.44	**100.38**	83.59	**76.58**	70.34	**64.78**	59.81	51.36	44.54	38.97	34.41	30.62	26
27	118.08	107.24	**97.65**	81.59	**74.87**	68.87	**63.52**	58.72	50.55	43.93	38.52	34.06	30.36	27
28	114.42	104.11	**94.97**	79.62	**73.17**	67.41	**62.26**	57.63	49.74	43.32	38.05	33.71	30.09	28
29	110.84	101.04	**92.33**	77.67	**71.49**	65.96	**61.00**	56.55	48.92	42.70	37.59	33.35	29.81	29
30	107.35	98.04	**89.74**	75.74	**69.82**	64.52	**59.75**	55.46	48.10	42.08	37.11	32.98	29.53	30
31	103.93	95.09	**87.20**	73.84	**68.18**	63.09	**58.51**	54.38	47.28	41.45	36.63	32.61	29.24	31
32	100.60	92.21	**84.71**	71.96	**66.54**	61.67	**57.28**	53.31	46.46	40.82	36.14	32.23	28.95	32
33	97.34	89.38	**82.25**	70.11	**64.93**	60.26	**56.05**	52.23	45.64	40.19	35.65	31.85	28.65	33
34	94.16	86.62	**79.85**	68.28	**63.33**	58.86	**54.82**	51.16	44.81	39.54	35.15	31.46	28.34	34
35	91.06	83.91	**77.48**	66.47	**61.75**	57.48	**53.61**	50.09	43.98	38.90	34.64	31.06	28.02	35
36	88.02	81.26	**75.16**	64.69	**60.19**	56.10	**52.40**	49.02	43.15	38.25	34.13	30.66	27.70	36
37	85.06	78.67	**72.89**	62.93	**58.64**	54.74	**51.19**	47.96	42.32	37.59	33.62	30.25	27.37	37
38	82.17	76.13	**70.66**	61.20	**57.11**	53.39	**50.00**	46.90	41.49	36.94	33.09	29.83	27.04	38
39	79.36	73.64	**68.47**	59.49	**55.60**	52.05	**48.81**	45.85	40.65	36.28	32.57	29.40	26.70	39
40	76.61	71.21	**66.32**	57.80	**54.10**	50.72	**47.63**	44.80	39.82	35.61	32.03	28.98	26.35	40
41	73.92	68.84	**64.21**	56.14	**52.63**	49.41	**46.46**	43.75	38.99	34.94	31.49	28.54	26.00	41
42	71.30	66.51	**62.14**	54.51	**51.17**	48.11	**45.30**	42.71	38.15	34.27	30.95	28.10	25.64	42
43	68.75	64.24	**60.12**	52.89	**49.72**	46.81	**44.14**	41.68	37.32	33.59	30.40	27.65	25.27	43
44	66.26	62.01	**58.13**	51.30	**48.30**	45.53	**42.99**	40.65	36.48	32.91	29.84	27.19	24.89	44
45	63.82	59.83	**56.18**	49.73	**46.89**	44.27	**41.85**	39.62	35.64	32.23	29.28	26.73	24.51	45
46	61.45	57.70	**54.26**	48.18	**45.49**	43.01	**40.71**	38.59	34.80	31.54	28.71	26.26	24.12	46
47	59.13	55.62	**52.38**	46.65	**44.11**	41.76	**39.59**	37.57	33.96	30.85	28.14	25.78	23.72	47
48	56.86	53.57	**50.54**	45.14	**42.75**	40.52	**38.46**	36.55	33.12	30.15	27.56	25.30	23.31	48
49	54.65	51.58	**48.73**	43.66	**41.40**	39.30	**37.35**	35.54	32.28	29.45	26.97	24.80	22.90	49
50	52.50	49.62	**46.95**	42.19	**40.06**	38.08	**36.24**	34.53	31.44	28.74	26.38	24.30	22.47	50
51	50.39	47.71	**45.21**	40.75	**38.74**	36.88	**35.14**	33.52	30.59	28.03	25.78	23.80	22.04	51
52	48.34	45.83	**43.50**	39.32	**37.44**	35.69	**34.05**	32.52	29.75	27.32	25.17	23.28	21.60	52
53	46.34	44.00	**41.83**	37.92	**36.15**	34.51	**32.96**	31.52	28.90	26.60	24.56	22.76	21.15	53
54	44.38	42.21	**40.19**	36.53	**34.88**	33.34	**31.89**	30.53	28.06	25.88	23.95	22.23	20.70	54

Table 1: Multipliers for pecuniary loss for life (males) *continued*

Age at date of trial	Multipliers calculated with allowance for projected mortality from the 2018-based population projections and rate of return of:													Age at date of trial
	-2.0%	-1.75%	**-1.5%**	-1.0%	**-0.75%**	-0.5%	**-0.25%**	0.0%	0.5%	1.0%	1.5%	2.0%	2.5%	
55	42.48	40.47	**38.58**	35.17	**33.63**	32.18	**30.82**	29.55	27.22	25.16	23.33	21.69	20.23	55
56	40.63	38.76	**37.01**	33.84	**32.40**	31.04	**29.77**	28.57	26.38	24.43	22.70	21.15	19.76	56
57	38.83	37.10	**35.48**	32.53	**31.18**	29.92	**28.72**	27.60	25.55	23.71	22.07	20.61	19.29	57
58	37.09	35.49	**33.98**	31.24	**29.99**	28.81	**27.69**	26.64	24.72	22.99	21.45	20.06	18.81	58
59	35.39	33.92	**32.52**	29.98	**28.82**	27.72	**26.68**	25.70	23.89	22.27	20.82	19.51	18.32	59
60	33.75	32.39	**31.10**	28.75	**27.67**	26.64	**25.68**	24.76	23.07	21.56	20.19	18.95	17.83	60
61	32.15	30.90	**29.71**	27.54	**26.54**	25.59	**24.69**	23.84	22.26	20.84	19.56	18.39	17.34	61
62	30.60	29.45	**28.36**	26.36	**25.43**	24.55	**23.72**	22.93	21.46	20.13	18.93	17.83	16.84	62
63	29.10	28.05	**27.05**	25.20	**24.34**	23.53	**22.76**	22.02	20.66	19.42	18.30	17.27	16.34	63
64	27.65	26.68	**25.76**	24.06	**23.28**	22.53	**21.81**	21.13	19.87	18.72	17.67	16.71	15.83	64
65	26.23	25.35	**24.51**	22.95	**22.23**	21.54	**20.88**	20.25	19.08	18.02	17.04	16.14	15.32	65
66	24.87	24.06	**23.30**	21.87	**21.21**	20.57	**19.97**	19.39	18.31	17.32	16.41	15.58	14.81	66
67	23.55	22.82	**22.12**	20.82	**20.21**	19.63	**19.07**	18.54	17.54	16.63	15.79	15.01	14.30	67
68	22.27	21.61	**20.97**	19.79	**19.23**	18.70	**18.19**	17.70	16.79	15.94	15.17	14.45	13.78	68
69	21.04	20.44	**19.86**	18.78	**18.28**	17.79	**17.33**	16.88	16.04	15.26	14.55	13.88	13.27	69
70	19.84	19.30	**18.78**	17.80	**17.34**	16.90	**16.48**	16.07	15.30	14.59	13.93	13.32	12.75	70
71	18.69	18.20	**17.73**	16.85	**16.43**	16.03	**15.64**	15.27	14.57	13.92	13.32	12.76	12.23	71
72	17.58	17.14	**16.72**	15.92	**15.54**	15.18	**14.83**	14.49	13.86	13.26	12.71	12.20	11.71	72
73	16.51	16.11	**15.73**	15.02	**14.68**	14.35	**14.03**	13.73	13.15	12.61	12.11	11.64	11.20	73
74	15.47	15.12	**14.78**	14.14	**13.84**	13.54	**13.26**	12.98	12.46	11.97	11.52	11.09	10.68	74
75	14.48	14.17	**13.87**	13.29	**13.02**	12.76	**12.50**	12.25	11.78	11.34	10.93	10.54	10.17	75
76	13.53	13.25	**12.98**	12.47	**12.23**	11.99	**11.77**	11.54	11.12	10.73	10.35	10.00	9.67	76
77	12.62	12.37	**12.14**	11.68	**11.47**	11.26	**11.05**	10.85	10.48	10.12	9.79	9.47	9.17	77
78	11.75	11.53	**11.32**	10.92	**10.73**	10.54	**10.36**	10.19	9.85	9.53	9.23	8.95	8.68	78
79	10.92	10.73	**10.55**	10.19	**10.02**	9.86	**9.70**	9.54	9.24	8.96	8.69	8.44	8.19	79
80	10.14	9.97	**9.81**	9.50	**9.35**	9.20	**9.06**	8.92	8.66	8.40	8.16	7.94	7.72	80
81	9.39	9.25	**9.10**	8.83	**8.70**	8.57	**8.45**	8.33	8.09	7.87	7.66	7.45	7.26	81
82	8.69	8.56	**8.44**	8.20	**8.09**	7.97	**7.86**	7.76	7.55	7.35	7.17	6.99	6.82	82
83	8.03	7.92	**7.81**	7.60	**7.50**	7.40	**7.31**	7.22	7.03	6.86	6.70	6.54	6.39	83
84	7.41	7.31	**7.22**	7.04	**6.95**	6.87	**6.78**	6.70	6.54	6.39	6.25	6.11	5.97	84
85	6.83	6.75	**6.67**	6.51	**6.43**	6.36	**6.28**	6.21	6.08	5.94	5.82	5.69	5.58	85
86	6.29	6.22	**6.14**	6.01	**5.94**	5.88	**5.82**	5.75	5.63	5.52	5.41	5.30	5.20	86
87	5.78	5.72	**5.66**	5.54	**5.48**	5.43	**5.37**	5.32	5.22	5.12	5.02	4.93	4.84	87
88	5.31	5.26	**5.20**	5.10	**5.05**	5.01	**4.96**	4.91	4.82	4.74	4.65	4.57	4.49	88
89	4.87	4.83	**4.78**	4.70	**4.65**	4.61	**4.57**	4.53	4.45	4.38	4.31	4.24	4.17	89
90	4.47	4.43	**4.39**	4.32	**4.28**	4.25	**4.21**	4.18	4.11	4.05	3.98	3.92	3.86	90
91	4.10	4.07	**4.03**	3.97	**3.94**	3.91	**3.88**	3.85	3.79	3.74	3.68	3.63	3.58	91
92	3.76	3.73	**3.70**	3.65	**3.62**	3.60	**3.57**	3.55	3.50	3.45	3.40	3.36	3.31	92
93	3.45	3.43	**3.40**	3.36	**3.33**	3.31	**3.29**	3.27	3.23	3.18	3.14	3.11	3.07	93
94	3.17	3.15	**3.13**	3.09	**3.07**	3.05	**3.03**	3.01	2.98	2.94	2.91	2.87	2.84	94
95	2.92	2.90	**2.88**	2.85	**2.83**	2.82	**2.80**	2.78	2.75	2.72	2.69	2.66	2.63	95
96	2.69	2.67	**2.66**	2.63	**2.61**	2.60	**2.58**	2.57	2.54	2.52	2.49	2.47	2.44	96
97	2.47	2.46	**2.45**	2.42	**2.41**	2.40	**2.38**	2.37	2.35	2.33	2.31	2.28	2.26	97
98	2.28	2.26	**2.25**	2.23	**2.22**	2.21	**2.20**	2.19	2.17	2.15	2.13	2.12	2.10	98
99	2.10	2.09	**2.08**	2.06	**2.05**	2.05	**2.04**	2.03	2.01	2.00	1.98	1.96	1.95	99
100	1.94	1.93	**1.93**	1.91	**1.90**	1.90	**1.89**	1.88	1.87	1.85	1.84	1.82	1.81	100

Table 2: Multipliers for pecuniary loss for life (females)

Age at date of trial	Multipliers calculated with allowance for projected mortality from the 2018-based population projections and rate of return of:													Age at date of trial
	-2.0%	-1.75%	**-1.5%**	-1.0%	**-0.75%**	-0.5%	**-0.25%**	0.0%	0.5%	1.0%	1.5%	2.0%	2.5%	
0	268.92	230.71	**198.89**	150.02	**131.29**	115.47	**102.08**	90.69	72.66	59.34	49.35	41.74	35.86	0
1	262.78	225.90	**195.13**	147.74	**129.51**	114.09	**101.01**	89.87	72.18	59.07	49.21	41.67	35.83	1
2	256.07	220.59	**190.92**	145.09	**127.40**	112.41	**99.67**	88.80	71.49	58.63	48.92	41.49	35.72	2
3	249.45	215.34	**186.75**	142.43	**125.28**	110.72	**98.31**	87.71	70.79	58.18	48.63	41.30	35.59	3
4	242.97	210.17	**182.63**	139.81	**123.18**	109.03	**96.96**	86.62	70.09	57.71	48.32	41.10	35.45	4
5	236.62	205.11	**178.58**	137.20	**121.09**	107.35	**95.61**	85.54	69.38	57.25	48.02	40.89	35.32	5
6	230.41	200.13	**174.59**	134.63	**119.02**	105.68	**94.26**	84.45	68.66	56.78	47.70	40.68	35.18	6
7	224.34	195.25	**170.66**	132.08	**116.96**	104.02	**92.92**	83.36	67.94	56.30	47.38	40.47	35.03	7
8	218.39	190.46	**166.80**	129.56	**114.92**	102.37	**91.57**	82.27	67.22	55.82	47.06	40.25	34.88	8
9	212.56	185.76	**163.00**	127.07	**112.89**	100.72	**90.23**	81.17	66.49	55.33	46.73	40.02	34.73	9
10	206.86	181.14	**159.25**	124.60	**110.88**	99.08	**88.90**	80.08	65.76	54.83	46.39	39.79	34.57	10
11	201.29	176.61	**155.57**	122.15	**108.89**	97.45	**87.56**	78.99	65.02	54.33	46.05	39.56	34.41	11
12	195.83	172.17	**151.95**	119.74	**106.91**	95.83	**86.23**	77.90	64.28	53.83	45.70	39.32	34.24	12
13	190.49	167.81	**148.38**	117.35	**104.95**	94.22	**84.91**	76.80	63.54	53.32	45.35	39.07	34.07	13
14	185.27	163.53	**144.88**	114.98	**103.00**	92.62	**83.59**	75.71	62.79	52.80	44.99	38.82	33.89	14
15	180.16	159.34	**141.43**	112.64	**101.08**	91.02	**82.27**	74.62	62.04	52.28	44.63	38.57	33.71	15
16	175.17	155.23	**138.04**	110.33	**99.16**	89.44	**80.95**	73.53	61.28	51.75	44.26	38.31	33.53	16
17	170.28	151.20	**134.71**	108.05	**97.27**	87.87	**79.65**	72.44	60.52	51.22	43.89	38.04	33.34	17
18	165.50	147.24	**131.43**	105.79	**95.39**	86.30	**78.34**	71.35	59.76	50.69	43.51	37.77	33.14	18
19	160.83	143.36	**128.21**	103.56	**93.53**	84.75	**77.04**	70.26	58.99	50.14	43.12	37.50	32.94	19
20	156.26	139.56	**125.04**	101.35	**91.68**	83.20	**75.75**	69.17	58.22	49.60	42.73	37.22	32.74	20
21	151.79	135.83	**121.92**	99.16	**89.85**	81.67	**74.45**	68.09	57.45	49.04	42.33	36.93	32.53	21
22	147.42	132.17	**118.86**	97.01	**88.04**	80.14	**73.17**	67.00	56.67	48.49	41.93	36.63	32.32	22
23	143.14	128.58	**115.84**	94.87	**86.23**	78.62	**71.88**	65.91	55.89	47.92	41.52	36.33	32.10	23
24	138.95	125.06	**112.87**	92.76	**84.45**	77.10	**70.60**	64.83	55.11	47.35	41.10	36.03	31.87	24
25	134.86	121.60	**109.96**	90.67	**82.68**	75.60	**69.32**	63.74	54.32	46.77	40.68	35.72	31.64	25
26	130.85	118.21	**107.09**	88.60	**80.92**	74.11	**68.05**	62.65	53.52	46.19	40.25	35.40	31.40	26
27	126.94	114.89	**104.26**	86.56	**79.18**	72.62	**66.78**	61.57	52.73	45.60	39.81	35.07	31.15	27
28	123.11	111.63	**101.49**	84.54	**77.45**	71.15	**65.52**	60.48	51.93	45.01	39.37	34.74	30.90	28
29	119.36	108.44	**98.76**	82.54	**75.74**	69.68	**64.26**	59.40	51.12	44.41	38.92	34.40	30.65	29
30	115.70	105.31	**96.08**	80.57	**74.05**	68.22	**63.00**	58.32	50.32	43.81	38.47	34.05	30.38	30
31	112.13	102.24	**93.45**	78.62	**72.37**	66.78	**61.75**	57.24	49.51	43.20	38.00	33.70	30.11	31
32	108.63	99.23	**90.86**	76.70	**70.71**	65.34	**60.51**	56.16	48.70	42.58	37.54	33.35	29.84	32
33	105.21	96.29	**88.32**	74.80	**69.07**	63.91	**59.27**	55.09	47.88	41.96	37.06	32.98	29.56	33
34	101.87	93.40	**85.82**	72.92	**67.43**	62.49	**58.04**	54.01	47.06	41.34	36.58	32.61	29.27	34
35	98.61	90.57	**83.36**	71.06	**65.82**	61.09	**56.81**	52.94	46.24	40.71	36.09	32.23	28.97	35
36	95.42	87.79	**80.95**	69.23	**64.22**	59.69	**55.59**	51.87	45.42	40.07	35.60	31.85	28.67	36
37	92.30	85.08	**78.57**	67.42	**62.63**	58.30	**54.37**	50.80	44.59	39.43	35.10	31.45	28.36	37
38	89.25	82.41	**76.24**	65.63	**61.07**	56.92	**53.16**	49.73	43.77	38.78	34.59	31.05	28.05	38
39	86.27	79.80	**73.96**	63.87	**59.51**	55.55	**51.95**	48.67	42.93	38.13	34.08	30.65	27.72	39
40	83.37	77.25	**71.71**	62.12	**57.97**	54.20	**50.75**	47.61	42.10	37.47	33.56	30.23	27.39	40
41	80.52	74.74	**69.50**	60.40	**56.45**	52.85	**49.56**	46.55	41.27	36.81	33.03	29.81	27.06	41
42	77.75	72.29	**67.33**	58.70	**54.94**	51.51	**48.37**	45.49	40.43	36.14	32.50	29.38	26.71	42
43	75.03	69.89	**65.20**	57.02	**53.45**	50.18	**47.19**	44.44	39.59	35.47	31.96	28.95	26.36	43
44	72.38	67.53	**63.11**	55.36	**51.97**	48.87	**46.01**	43.39	38.74	34.79	31.41	28.51	26.00	44
45	69.79	65.23	**61.05**	53.73	**50.51**	47.56	**44.84**	42.34	37.90	34.11	30.86	28.05	25.63	45
46	67.27	62.97	**59.04**	52.11	**49.07**	46.26	**43.68**	41.29	37.05	33.42	30.30	27.59	25.25	46
47	64.80	60.76	**57.06**	50.52	**47.63**	44.97	**42.52**	40.25	36.20	32.73	29.73	27.13	24.86	47
48	62.39	58.60	**55.11**	48.95	**46.22**	43.70	**41.37**	39.21	35.36	32.03	29.16	26.65	24.47	48
49	60.03	56.48	**53.21**	47.40	**44.82**	42.43	**40.22**	38.17	34.50	31.33	28.58	26.17	24.07	49
50	57.74	54.41	**51.33**	45.87	**43.43**	41.18	**39.09**	37.14	33.65	30.63	27.99	25.68	23.66	50
51	55.50	52.38	**49.50**	44.36	**42.07**	39.94	**37.96**	36.12	32.80	29.92	27.40	25.19	23.24	51
52	53.31	50.40	**47.70**	42.88	**40.72**	38.71	**36.84**	35.09	31.95	29.21	26.80	24.69	22.82	52
53	51.18	48.46	**45.94**	41.41	**39.38**	37.49	**35.72**	34.08	31.10	28.49	26.20	24.18	22.39	53
54	49.10	46.57	**44.21**	39.97	**38.06**	36.28	**34.62**	33.07	30.25	27.77	25.59	23.66	21.95	54

Table 2: Multipliers for pecuniary loss for life (females) *continued*

Age at date of trial	Multipliers calculated with allowance for projected mortality from the 2018-based population projections and rate of return of:													Age at date of trial
	-2.0%	-1.75%	**-1.5%**	-1.0%	**-0.75%**	-0.5%	**-0.25%**	0.0%	0.5%	1.0%	1.5%	2.0%	2.5%	
55	47.08	44.72	**42.52**	38.55	**36.76**	35.09	**33.53**	32.06	29.40	27.05	24.98	23.14	21.50	55
56	45.10	42.91	**40.86**	37.16	**35.48**	33.91	**32.44**	31.06	28.55	26.33	24.36	22.61	21.04	56
57	43.18	41.14	**39.24**	35.78	**34.22**	32.75	**31.37**	30.07	27.70	25.60	23.74	22.07	20.58	57
58	41.31	39.42	**37.65**	34.43	**32.97**	31.59	**30.30**	29.08	26.86	24.88	23.11	21.53	20.11	58
59	39.49	37.74	**36.10**	33.11	**31.74**	30.46	**29.25**	28.11	26.02	24.15	22.48	20.98	19.64	59
60	37.72	36.10	**34.58**	31.80	**30.53**	29.33	**28.20**	27.14	25.18	23.42	21.85	20.43	19.15	60
61	35.99	34.50	**33.09**	30.52	**29.34**	28.22	**27.17**	26.18	24.34	22.69	21.21	19.87	18.66	61
62	34.31	32.94	**31.64**	29.26	**28.16**	27.13	**26.15**	25.22	23.51	21.96	20.57	19.31	18.17	62
63	32.68	31.42	**30.22**	28.02	**27.01**	26.05	**25.14**	24.27	22.68	21.23	19.93	18.74	17.66	63
64	31.09	29.93	**28.83**	26.81	**25.87**	24.98	**24.14**	23.34	21.85	20.50	19.28	18.17	17.15	64
65	29.55	28.48	**27.48**	25.61	**24.75**	23.93	**23.15**	22.41	21.03	19.77	18.63	17.59	16.64	65
66	28.05	27.08	**26.15**	24.44	**23.65**	22.89	**22.17**	21.49	20.21	19.05	17.98	17.01	16.12	66
67	26.59	25.70	**24.86**	23.30	**22.57**	21.88	**21.21**	20.58	19.40	18.32	17.33	16.42	15.59	67
68	25.18	24.37	**23.61**	22.18	**21.51**	20.87	**20.26**	19.68	18.59	17.59	16.68	15.84	15.06	68
69	23.81	23.08	**22.38**	21.08	**20.47**	19.89	**19.33**	18.80	17.79	16.87	16.03	15.25	14.52	69
70	22.48	21.82	**21.19**	20.00	**19.45**	18.92	**18.41**	17.92	17.00	16.16	15.38	14.65	13.98	70
71	21.19	20.60	**20.03**	18.96	**18.45**	17.97	**17.50**	17.06	16.22	15.44	14.73	14.06	13.44	71
72	19.95	19.42	**18.90**	17.93	**17.48**	17.04	**16.62**	16.21	15.45	14.74	14.08	13.47	12.90	72
73	18.76	18.28	**17.81**	16.94	**16.53**	16.13	**15.75**	15.38	14.69	14.04	13.44	12.88	12.36	73
74	17.60	17.17	**16.76**	15.97	**15.60**	15.25	**14.90**	14.57	13.94	13.35	12.80	12.29	11.81	74
75	16.49	16.11	**15.74**	15.04	**14.70**	14.38	**14.07**	13.77	13.20	12.67	12.17	11.71	11.27	75
76	15.43	15.09	**14.76**	14.13	**13.83**	13.54	**13.27**	13.00	12.48	12.00	11.55	11.13	10.73	76
77	14.41	14.10	**13.81**	13.25	**12.99**	12.73	**12.48**	12.24	11.78	11.35	10.94	10.56	10.20	77
78	13.43	13.16	**12.90**	12.40	**12.17**	11.94	**11.72**	11.50	11.09	10.70	10.34	10.00	9.67	78
79	12.49	12.25	**12.03**	11.59	**11.38**	11.18	**10.98**	10.79	10.42	10.08	9.75	9.44	9.15	79
80	11.60	11.39	**11.19**	10.80	**10.62**	10.44	**10.27**	10.10	9.77	9.46	9.17	8.90	8.63	80
81	10.75	10.57	**10.39**	10.05	**9.89**	9.73	**9.58**	9.43	9.14	8.87	8.61	8.36	8.13	81
82	9.94	9.78	**9.63**	9.33	**9.19**	9.05	**8.92**	8.79	8.53	8.29	8.06	7.85	7.64	82
83	9.18	9.04	**8.90**	8.65	**8.52**	8.40	**8.28**	8.17	7.95	7.73	7.53	7.34	7.16	83
84	8.45	8.33	**8.22**	7.99	**7.89**	7.78	**7.68**	7.58	7.38	7.20	7.02	6.85	6.69	84
85	7.77	7.67	**7.57**	7.37	**7.28**	7.19	**7.10**	7.01	6.84	6.68	6.53	6.38	6.24	85
86	7.13	7.04	**6.95**	6.79	**6.71**	6.63	**6.55**	6.48	6.33	6.19	6.05	5.92	5.80	86
87	6.53	6.45	**6.38**	6.24	**6.17**	6.10	**6.03**	5.97	5.84	5.72	5.60	5.49	5.38	87
88	5.97	5.91	**5.85**	5.72	**5.66**	5.61	**5.55**	5.49	5.38	5.28	5.18	5.08	4.99	88
89	5.46	5.41	**5.35**	5.25	**5.20**	5.15	**5.10**	5.05	4.96	4.87	4.78	4.69	4.61	89
90	4.99	4.94	**4.90**	4.81	**4.77**	4.72	**4.68**	4.64	4.56	4.48	4.41	4.33	4.26	90
91	4.56	4.52	**4.48**	4.41	**4.37**	4.34	**4.30**	4.26	4.20	4.13	4.06	4.00	3.94	91
92	4.18	4.14	**4.11**	4.04	**4.01**	3.98	**3.95**	3.92	3.86	3.80	3.75	3.70	3.64	92
93	3.83	3.80	**3.77**	3.71	**3.69**	3.66	**3.63**	3.61	3.56	3.51	3.46	3.41	3.37	93
94	3.51	3.48	**3.46**	3.41	**3.39**	3.37	**3.34**	3.32	3.28	3.24	3.20	3.16	3.12	94
95	3.22	3.20	**3.18**	3.14	**3.12**	3.10	**3.08**	3.06	3.03	2.99	2.95	2.92	2.89	95
96	2.96	2.94	**2.92**	2.89	**2.87**	2.85	**2.84**	2.82	2.79	2.76	2.73	2.70	2.67	96
97	2.71	2.70	**2.68**	2.65	**2.64**	2.62	**2.61**	2.60	2.57	2.54	2.52	2.49	2.47	97
98	2.49	2.47	**2.46**	2.44	**2.43**	2.41	**2.40**	2.39	2.37	2.34	2.32	2.30	2.28	98
99	2.29	2.27	**2.26**	2.24	**2.23**	2.22	**2.21**	2.20	2.18	2.16	2.14	2.13	2.11	99
100	2.10	2.09	**2.08**	2.07	**2.06**	2.05	**2.04**	2.03	2.02	2.00	1.98	1.97	1.95	100

Table 3 Multipliers for loss of earnings to pension age 50 (males)

Age at date of trial	Multipliers calculated with allowance for projected mortality from the 2018-based population projections and rate of return of:													Age at date of trial
	-2.0%	-1.75%	**-1.5%**	-1.0%	**-0.75%**	-0.5%	**-0.25%**	0.0%	0.5%	1.0%	1.5%	2.0%	2.5%	
16	48.39	46.14	**44.02**	40.16	**38.40**	36.74	**35.18**	33.71	31.02	28.62	26.48	24.56	22.85	16
17	46.44	44.34	**42.37**	38.76	**37.11**	35.56	**34.09**	32.71	30.17	27.90	25.87	24.05	22.41	17
18	44.52	42.57	**40.74**	37.38	**35.84**	34.38	**33.01**	31.71	29.32	27.18	25.25	23.52	21.96	18
19	42.64	40.84	**39.14**	36.01	**34.58**	33.22	**31.93**	30.71	28.47	26.45	24.63	22.98	21.50	19
20	40.81	39.14	**37.57**	34.66	**33.33**	32.06	**30.86**	29.72	27.61	25.71	23.99	22.44	21.03	20
21	39.01	37.47	**36.02**	33.33	**32.09**	30.91	**29.79**	28.73	26.75	24.97	23.35	21.88	20.54	21
22	37.24	35.83	**34.49**	32.01	**30.86**	29.76	**28.72**	27.73	25.89	24.22	22.70	21.31	20.05	22
23	35.52	34.22	**32.99**	30.70	**29.64**	28.62	**27.66**	26.74	25.02	23.46	22.04	20.74	19.54	23
24	33.83	32.64	**31.51**	29.41	**28.43**	27.49	**26.60**	25.75	24.15	22.70	21.37	20.15	19.03	24
25	32.17	31.09	**30.05**	28.12	**27.22**	26.36	**25.54**	24.75	23.28	21.93	20.69	19.54	18.50	25
26	30.54	29.56	**28.62**	26.86	**26.03**	25.24	**24.48**	23.76	22.40	21.15	19.99	18.93	17.95	26
27	28.95	28.06	**27.20**	25.60	**24.85**	24.13	**23.43**	22.77	21.52	20.36	19.29	18.31	17.39	27
28	27.39	26.59	**25.81**	24.36	**23.67**	23.02	**22.38**	21.78	20.63	19.57	18.58	17.67	16.82	28
29	25.86	25.14	**24.44**	23.13	**22.51**	21.91	**21.34**	20.78	19.74	18.76	17.86	17.02	16.24	29
30	24.37	23.72	**23.09**	21.91	**21.35**	20.81	**20.29**	19.79	18.84	17.96	17.13	16.36	15.64	30
31	22.90	22.32	**21.77**	20.71	**20.21**	19.72	**19.25**	18.80	17.94	17.14	16.39	15.68	15.02	31
32	21.47	20.95	**20.46**	19.52	**19.07**	18.64	**18.22**	17.81	17.04	16.31	15.63	15.00	14.40	32
33	20.06	19.61	**19.17**	18.34	**17.94**	17.56	**17.18**	16.82	16.13	15.48	14.87	14.29	13.75	33
34	18.68	18.29	**17.90**	17.17	**16.82**	16.48	**16.15**	15.83	15.22	14.64	14.10	13.58	13.09	34
35	17.33	16.99	**16.66**	16.02	**15.71**	15.42	**15.13**	14.85	14.31	13.80	13.31	12.85	12.42	35
36	16.01	15.71	**15.43**	14.88	**14.61**	14.35	**14.10**	13.86	13.39	12.94	12.51	12.11	11.73	36
37	14.71	14.46	**14.22**	13.75	**13.52**	13.30	**13.08**	12.87	12.46	12.08	11.71	11.35	11.02	37
38	13.44	13.23	**13.02**	12.63	**12.43**	12.25	**12.06**	11.88	11.54	11.20	10.89	10.58	10.29	38
39	12.20	12.02	**11.85**	11.52	**11.36**	11.20	**11.05**	10.90	10.60	10.32	10.05	9.80	9.55	39
40	10.98	10.84	**10.69**	10.42	**10.29**	10.16	**10.03**	9.91	9.67	9.43	9.21	8.99	8.79	40
41	9.78	9.67	**9.56**	9.34	**9.23**	9.13	**9.02**	8.92	8.73	8.54	8.35	8.18	8.00	41
42	8.61	8.52	**8.43**	8.26	**8.18**	8.10	**8.02**	7.94	7.78	7.63	7.48	7.34	7.20	42
43	7.46	7.39	**7.33**	7.20	**7.13**	7.07	**7.01**	6.95	6.83	6.71	6.60	6.49	6.38	43
44	6.34	6.29	**6.24**	6.14	**6.10**	6.05	**6.01**	5.96	5.87	5.79	5.70	5.62	5.54	44
45	5.23	5.20	**5.16**	5.10	**5.07**	5.03	**5.00**	4.97	4.91	4.85	4.79	4.73	4.68	45
46	4.15	4.12	**4.10**	4.06	**4.04**	4.02	**4.00**	3.98	3.94	3.90	3.86	3.83	3.79	46
47	3.08	3.07	**3.06**	3.03	**3.02**	3.01	**3.00**	2.99	2.97	2.94	2.92	2.90	2.88	47
48	2.04	2.03	**2.03**	2.01	**2.01**	2.00	**2.00**	1.99	1.98	1.97	1.97	1.96	1.95	48
49	1.01	1.01	**1.01**	1.00	**1.00**	1.00	**1.00**	1.00	1.00	0.99	0.99	0.99	0.99	49

Table 4 Multipliers for loss of earnings to pension age 50 (females)

Age at date of trial	Multipliers calculated with allowance for projected mortality from the 2018-based population projections and rate of return of:													Age at date of trial
	-2.0%	-1.75%	**-1.5%**	-1.0%	**-0.75%**	-0.5%	**-0.25%**	0.0%	0.5%	1.0%	1.5%	2.0%	2.5%	
16	48.60	46.33	**44.20**	40.31	**38.54**	36.88	**35.31**	33.83	31.12	28.71	26.56	24.64	22.92	16
17	46.64	44.53	**42.54**	38.92	**37.26**	35.70	**34.22**	32.83	30.28	28.00	25.96	24.12	22.48	17
18	44.72	42.76	**40.91**	37.53	**35.98**	34.52	**33.14**	31.83	29.43	27.27	25.34	23.60	22.03	18
19	42.83	41.02	**39.31**	36.17	**34.72**	33.35	**32.06**	30.84	28.58	26.54	24.71	23.06	21.57	19
20	40.99	39.32	**37.73**	34.81	**33.47**	32.19	**30.99**	29.84	27.72	25.81	24.08	22.52	21.10	20
21	39.19	37.64	**36.18**	33.47	**32.22**	31.04	**29.91**	28.84	26.86	25.06	23.44	21.96	20.61	21
22	37.42	35.99	**34.65**	32.15	**30.99**	29.89	**28.84**	27.85	25.99	24.31	22.78	21.39	20.12	22
23	35.68	34.38	**33.14**	30.83	**29.76**	28.75	**27.77**	26.85	25.12	23.55	22.12	20.81	19.61	23
24	33.98	32.79	**31.65**	29.53	**28.55**	27.61	**26.71**	25.85	24.25	22.79	21.45	20.22	19.09	24
25	32.32	31.23	**30.19**	28.25	**27.34**	26.48	**25.65**	24.86	23.37	22.01	20.76	19.62	18.56	25
26	30.68	29.69	**28.75**	26.97	**26.14**	25.35	**24.59**	23.86	22.49	21.23	20.07	19.00	18.02	26
27	29.09	28.19	**27.33**	25.71	**24.96**	24.23	**23.53**	22.86	21.60	20.44	19.37	18.38	17.46	27
28	27.52	26.71	**25.93**	24.47	**23.78**	23.11	**22.48**	21.87	20.71	19.64	18.66	17.74	16.88	28
29	25.98	25.26	**24.55**	23.23	**22.61**	22.01	**21.43**	20.87	19.82	18.84	17.93	17.09	16.30	29
30	24.48	23.83	**23.20**	22.01	**21.45**	20.90	**20.38**	19.88	18.92	18.03	17.20	16.42	15.70	30
31	23.01	22.43	**21.87**	20.80	**20.30**	19.81	**19.34**	18.88	18.02	17.21	16.45	15.75	15.08	31
32	21.56	21.05	**20.55**	19.60	**19.15**	18.72	**18.30**	17.89	17.11	16.38	15.70	15.06	14.45	32
33	20.15	19.70	**19.26**	18.42	**18.02**	17.63	**17.26**	16.90	16.20	15.55	14.93	14.35	13.81	33
34	18.77	18.37	**17.98**	17.25	**16.90**	16.56	**16.22**	15.90	15.29	14.70	14.15	13.63	13.14	34
35	17.41	17.06	**16.73**	16.09	**15.78**	15.48	**15.19**	14.91	14.37	13.85	13.37	12.90	12.47	35
36	16.08	15.78	**15.49**	14.94	**14.67**	14.41	**14.16**	13.92	13.44	12.99	12.56	12.16	11.77	36
37	14.78	14.52	**14.28**	13.80	**13.58**	13.35	**13.14**	12.92	12.51	12.12	11.75	11.40	11.06	37
38	13.50	13.29	**13.08**	12.68	**12.49**	12.30	**12.11**	11.93	11.58	11.25	10.93	10.62	10.33	38
39	12.25	12.07	**11.90**	11.57	**11.40**	11.25	**11.09**	10.94	10.64	10.36	10.09	9.83	9.58	39
40	11.02	10.88	**10.74**	10.46	**10.33**	10.20	**10.07**	9.95	9.70	9.47	9.24	9.03	8.82	40
41	9.82	9.70	**9.59**	9.37	**9.26**	9.16	**9.06**	8.95	8.76	8.57	8.38	8.20	8.03	41
42	8.64	8.55	**8.46**	8.29	**8.21**	8.12	**8.04**	7.96	7.81	7.65	7.51	7.36	7.23	42
43	7.49	7.42	**7.35**	7.22	**7.16**	7.09	**7.03**	6.97	6.85	6.73	6.62	6.51	6.40	43
44	6.35	6.30	**6.26**	6.16	**6.11**	6.07	**6.02**	5.98	5.89	5.80	5.72	5.64	5.56	44
45	5.24	5.21	**5.18**	5.11	**5.08**	5.05	**5.01**	4.98	4.92	4.86	4.80	4.74	4.69	45
46	4.15	4.13	**4.11**	4.07	**4.05**	4.03	**4.01**	3.99	3.95	3.91	3.87	3.83	3.80	46
47	3.09	3.07	**3.06**	3.04	**3.03**	3.02	**3.00**	2.99	2.97	2.95	2.93	2.91	2.89	47
48	2.04	2.03	**2.03**	2.02	**2.01**	2.01	**2.00**	2.00	1.99	1.98	1.97	1.96	1.95	48
49	1.01	1.01	**1.01**	1.00	**1.00**	1.00	**1.00**	1.00	1.00	0.99	0.99	0.99	0.99	49

Table 5 Multipliers for loss of earnings to pension age 55 (males)

Age at date of trial	Multipliers calculated with allowance for projected mortality from the 2018-based population projections and rate of return of:													Age at date of trial
	-2.0%	-1.75%	**-1.5%**	-1.0%	**-0.75%**	-0.5%	**-0.25%**	0.0%	0.5%	1.0%	1.5%	2.0%	2.5%	
16	58.51	55.36	**52.42**	47.14	**44.76**	42.55	**40.48**	38.55	35.05	31.98	29.29	26.91	24.82	16
17	56.35	53.39	**50.64**	45.67	**43.43**	41.34	**39.38**	37.55	34.22	31.30	28.72	26.44	24.42	17
18	54.23	51.47	**48.89**	44.22	**42.11**	40.13	**38.28**	36.55	33.39	30.61	28.15	25.96	24.02	18
19	52.16	49.58	**47.16**	42.78	**40.80**	38.94	**37.19**	35.55	32.56	29.91	27.56	25.48	23.61	19
20	50.13	47.72	**45.47**	41.37	**39.50**	37.75	**36.10**	34.55	31.72	29.21	26.97	24.98	23.20	20
21	48.14	45.90	**43.80**	39.96	**38.22**	36.57	**35.02**	33.56	30.88	28.50	26.38	24.47	22.77	21
22	46.20	44.12	**42.16**	38.58	**36.94**	35.40	**33.94**	32.57	30.04	27.79	25.77	23.96	22.33	22
23	44.29	42.36	**40.54**	37.20	**35.67**	34.23	**32.86**	31.57	29.20	27.07	25.15	23.43	21.88	23
24	42.42	40.64	**38.95**	35.84	**34.42**	33.07	**31.79**	30.58	28.35	26.34	24.53	22.90	21.42	24
25	40.59	38.94	**37.38**	34.50	**33.17**	31.91	**30.72**	29.59	27.49	25.60	23.90	22.35	20.95	25
26	38.80	37.28	**35.83**	33.16	**31.93**	30.76	**29.65**	28.59	26.63	24.86	23.25	21.79	20.46	26
27	37.04	35.64	**34.31**	31.85	**30.70**	29.62	**28.58**	27.60	25.77	24.11	22.60	21.23	19.97	27
28	35.32	34.04	**32.81**	30.54	**29.49**	28.48	**27.52**	26.61	24.91	23.35	21.94	20.65	19.46	28
29	33.64	32.46	**31.34**	29.25	**28.28**	27.35	**26.46**	25.62	24.04	22.59	21.27	20.06	18.94	29
30	31.99	30.91	**29.89**	27.97	**27.08**	26.23	**25.41**	24.63	23.16	21.82	20.59	19.46	18.41	30
31	30.37	29.39	**28.46**	26.71	**25.89**	25.11	**24.36**	23.64	22.29	21.04	19.90	18.84	17.87	31
32	28.79	27.90	**27.05**	25.46	**24.72**	24.00	**23.31**	22.65	21.41	20.26	19.20	18.22	17.31	32
33	27.24	26.44	**25.67**	24.23	**23.55**	22.89	**22.27**	21.66	20.52	19.47	18.49	17.59	16.74	33
34	25.72	25.00	**24.31**	23.00	**22.39**	21.80	**21.23**	20.68	19.64	18.67	17.77	16.94	16.16	34
35	24.23	23.59	**22.97**	21.79	**21.24**	20.70	**20.19**	19.69	18.75	17.87	17.05	16.28	15.56	35
36	22.77	22.20	**21.65**	20.60	**20.10**	19.62	**19.15**	18.71	17.85	17.05	16.31	15.61	14.95	36
37	21.35	20.84	**20.35**	19.41	**18.97**	18.54	**18.12**	17.72	16.95	16.23	15.56	14.92	14.33	37
38	19.95	19.50	**19.07**	18.24	**17.85**	17.47	**17.10**	16.74	16.05	15.41	14.80	14.23	13.69	38
39	18.58	18.19	**17.81**	17.08	**16.74**	16.40	**16.07**	15.76	15.15	14.57	14.03	13.52	13.03	39
40	17.24	16.90	**16.57**	15.94	**15.64**	15.34	**15.05**	14.77	14.24	13.73	13.25	12.79	12.36	40
41	15.93	15.64	**15.35**	14.81	**14.54**	14.29	**14.04**	13.79	13.33	12.88	12.46	12.06	11.67	41
42	14.64	14.39	**14.15**	13.68	**13.46**	13.24	**13.02**	12.81	12.41	12.02	11.66	11.31	10.97	42
43	13.38	13.17	**12.97**	12.57	**12.38**	12.19	**12.01**	11.83	11.49	11.16	10.84	10.54	10.25	43
44	12.15	11.97	**11.80**	11.47	**11.31**	11.16	**11.00**	10.85	10.56	10.28	10.02	9.76	9.51	44
45	10.94	10.79	**10.65**	10.38	**10.25**	10.12	**10.00**	9.87	9.63	9.40	9.18	8.96	8.75	45
46	9.75	9.63	**9.52**	9.31	**9.20**	9.10	**8.99**	8.89	8.70	8.51	8.32	8.15	7.98	46
47	8.58	8.49	**8.41**	8.24	**8.15**	8.07	**7.99**	7.91	7.76	7.61	7.46	7.32	7.18	47
48	7.44	7.37	**7.31**	7.18	**7.11**	7.05	**6.99**	6.93	6.81	6.69	6.58	6.47	6.37	48
49	6.32	6.27	**6.22**	6.13	**6.08**	6.03	**5.99**	5.94	5.86	5.77	5.69	5.61	5.53	49
50	5.22	5.18	**5.15**	5.09	**5.05**	5.02	**4.99**	4.96	4.90	4.84	4.78	4.72	4.67	50
51	4.14	4.12	**4.10**	4.05	**4.03**	4.01	**3.99**	3.97	3.93	3.90	3.86	3.82	3.78	51
52	3.08	3.06	**3.05**	3.03	**3.02**	3.01	**3.00**	2.98	2.96	2.94	2.92	2.90	2.88	52
53	2.03	2.03	**2.02**	2.01	**2.01**	2.00	**2.00**	1.99	1.98	1.97	1.96	1.95	1.94	53
54	1.01	1.01	**1.01**	1.00	**1.00**	1.00	**1.00**	1.00	1.00	0.99	0.99	0.99	0.99	54

Table 6 Multipliers for loss of earnings to pension age 55 (females)

Age at date of trial	-2.0%	-1.75%	**-1.5%**	-1.0%	**-0.75%**	-0.5%	**-0.25%**	0.0%	0.5%	1.0%	1.5%	2.0%	2.5%	Age at date of trial
	Multipliers calculated with allowance for projected mortality from the 2018-based population projections and rate of return of:													
16	58.85	55.67	**52.71**	47.39	**44.99**	42.76	**40.68**	38.73	35.21	32.12	29.41	27.02	24.91	16
17	56.68	53.70	**50.93**	45.92	**43.66**	41.55	**39.58**	37.73	34.38	31.44	28.85	26.55	24.52	17
18	54.56	51.77	**49.17**	44.47	**42.34**	40.35	**38.48**	36.74	33.56	30.75	28.27	26.07	24.12	18
19	52.48	49.88	**47.44**	43.03	**41.03**	39.15	**37.39**	35.74	32.72	30.06	27.69	25.59	23.71	19
20	50.44	48.02	**45.74**	41.61	**39.73**	37.96	**36.30**	34.74	31.89	29.35	27.10	25.09	23.30	20
21	48.45	46.19	**44.07**	40.20	**38.44**	36.78	**35.21**	33.74	31.05	28.65	26.50	24.59	22.87	21
22	46.49	44.39	**42.42**	38.80	**37.15**	35.60	**34.13**	32.75	30.20	27.93	25.90	24.07	22.43	22
23	44.58	42.63	**40.79**	37.42	**35.88**	34.43	**33.05**	31.75	29.35	27.21	25.28	23.54	21.98	23
24	42.70	40.89	**39.19**	36.06	**34.62**	33.26	**31.97**	30.75	28.50	26.48	24.65	23.01	21.52	24
25	40.86	39.19	**37.61**	34.71	**33.37**	32.10	**30.90**	29.75	27.64	25.74	24.02	22.46	21.05	25
26	39.06	37.52	**36.06**	33.37	**32.13**	30.94	**29.82**	28.76	26.78	24.99	23.37	21.90	20.56	26
27	37.29	35.87	**34.53**	32.04	**30.89**	29.80	**28.75**	27.76	25.92	24.24	22.72	21.33	20.07	27
28	35.56	34.26	**33.03**	30.73	**29.67**	28.65	**27.69**	26.77	25.05	23.48	22.06	20.75	19.56	28
29	33.86	32.68	**31.54**	29.44	**28.46**	27.52	**26.63**	25.77	24.18	22.72	21.39	20.16	19.04	29
30	32.20	31.12	**30.09**	28.15	**27.25**	26.39	**25.57**	24.78	23.30	21.95	20.70	19.56	18.51	30
31	30.58	29.59	**28.65**	26.88	**26.06**	25.27	**24.51**	23.78	22.42	21.17	20.01	18.95	17.97	31
32	28.98	28.09	**27.23**	25.63	**24.87**	24.15	**23.46**	22.79	21.54	20.38	19.31	18.32	17.41	32
33	27.42	26.62	**25.84**	24.38	**23.70**	23.04	**22.41**	21.80	20.65	19.59	18.60	17.69	16.84	33
34	25.89	25.17	**24.47**	23.15	**22.53**	21.94	**21.36**	20.81	19.76	18.78	17.88	17.04	16.25	34
35	24.40	23.75	**23.12**	21.94	**21.38**	20.84	**20.32**	19.81	18.86	17.97	17.15	16.37	15.65	35
36	22.93	22.35	**21.79**	20.73	**20.23**	19.75	**19.28**	18.82	17.96	17.16	16.40	15.70	15.04	36
37	21.49	20.98	**20.48**	19.54	**19.09**	18.66	**18.24**	17.83	17.06	16.33	15.65	15.01	14.41	37
38	20.08	19.63	**19.20**	18.36	**17.96**	17.58	**17.20**	16.84	16.15	15.50	14.89	14.31	13.77	38
39	18.70	18.31	**17.93**	17.19	**16.84**	16.50	**16.17**	15.85	15.24	14.66	14.11	13.60	13.11	39
40	17.35	17.01	**16.68**	16.04	**15.73**	15.44	**15.15**	14.86	14.32	13.81	13.33	12.87	12.43	40
41	16.03	15.73	**15.45**	14.90	**14.63**	14.37	**14.12**	13.88	13.40	12.96	12.53	12.12	11.74	41
42	14.73	14.48	**14.24**	13.76	**13.54**	13.31	**13.10**	12.89	12.48	12.09	11.72	11.37	11.03	42
43	13.46	13.25	**13.04**	12.64	**12.45**	12.26	**12.08**	11.90	11.55	11.22	10.90	10.59	10.30	43
44	12.21	12.04	**11.87**	11.53	**11.37**	11.21	**11.06**	10.91	10.62	10.34	10.07	9.81	9.56	44
45	10.99	10.85	**10.71**	10.44	**10.30**	10.17	**10.05**	9.92	9.68	9.44	9.22	9.00	8.79	45
46	9.79	9.68	**9.57**	9.35	**9.24**	9.14	**9.03**	8.93	8.74	8.55	8.36	8.18	8.01	46
47	8.62	8.53	**8.44**	8.27	**8.19**	8.10	**8.02**	7.94	7.79	7.64	7.49	7.35	7.21	47
48	7.47	7.40	**7.33**	7.20	**7.14**	7.08	**7.01**	6.95	6.83	6.72	6.60	6.49	6.39	48
49	6.34	6.29	**6.24**	6.15	**6.10**	6.05	**6.01**	5.96	5.88	5.79	5.71	5.62	5.54	49
50	5.23	5.20	**5.17**	5.10	**5.07**	5.04	**5.00**	4.97	4.91	4.85	4.79	4.74	4.68	50
51	4.15	4.13	**4.10**	4.06	**4.04**	4.02	**4.00**	3.98	3.94	3.90	3.87	3.83	3.79	51
52	3.08	3.07	**3.06**	3.03	**3.02**	3.01	**3.00**	2.99	2.97	2.95	2.92	2.90	2.88	52
53	2.04	2.03	**2.03**	2.02	**2.01**	2.00	**2.00**	1.99	1.98	1.98	1.97	1.96	1.95	53
54	1.01	1.01	**1.01**	1.00	**1.00**	1.00	**1.00**	1.00	1.00	0.99	0.99	0.99	0.99	54

Table 7 Multipliers for loss of earnings to pension age 60 (males)

Age at date of trial	Multipliers calculated with allowance for projected mortality from the 2018-based population projections and rate of return of:													Age at date of trial
	-2.0%	-1.75%	**-1.5%**	-1.0%	**-0.75%**	-0.5%	**-0.25%**	0.0%	0.5%	1.0%	1.5%	2.0%	2.5%	
16	69.56	65.29	**61.36**	54.38	**51.29**	48.43	**45.78**	43.32	38.93	35.14	31.86	29.01	26.53	16
17	67.17	63.15	**59.44**	52.84	**49.90**	47.18	**44.66**	42.32	38.12	34.49	31.33	28.58	26.18	17
18	64.83	61.05	**57.55**	51.31	**48.53**	45.95	**43.55**	41.32	37.31	33.83	30.80	28.15	25.82	18
19	62.54	58.99	**55.70**	49.81	**47.17**	44.72	**42.44**	40.32	36.49	33.16	30.25	27.70	25.46	19
20	60.30	56.97	**53.87**	48.32	**45.82**	43.50	**41.34**	39.32	35.68	32.49	29.70	27.25	25.09	20
21	58.11	54.98	**52.07**	46.84	**44.49**	42.29	**40.24**	38.33	34.86	31.82	29.14	26.79	24.70	21
22	55.96	53.04	**50.31**	45.38	**43.16**	41.09	**39.15**	37.33	34.03	31.14	28.58	26.32	24.31	22
23	53.86	51.12	**48.56**	43.94	**41.85**	39.89	**38.06**	36.34	33.21	30.45	28.00	25.84	23.91	23
24	51.80	49.24	**46.85**	42.51	**40.54**	38.70	**36.97**	35.34	32.38	29.75	27.42	25.35	23.50	24
25	49.78	47.40	**45.16**	41.10	**39.25**	37.51	**35.88**	34.35	31.54	29.05	26.83	24.85	23.08	25
26	47.80	45.58	**43.50**	39.70	**37.97**	36.34	**34.80**	33.35	30.70	28.34	26.23	24.35	22.65	26
27	45.86	43.80	**41.86**	38.31	**36.69**	35.16	**33.72**	32.36	29.86	27.63	25.62	23.83	22.21	27
28	43.96	42.05	**40.25**	36.94	**35.43**	34.00	**32.65**	31.37	29.01	26.90	25.01	23.30	21.76	28
29	42.10	40.33	**38.66**	35.59	**34.18**	32.84	**31.57**	30.38	28.17	26.18	24.38	22.77	21.30	29
30	40.28	38.65	**37.10**	34.25	**32.93**	31.69	**30.51**	29.39	27.31	25.44	23.75	22.22	20.83	30
31	38.50	36.99	**35.57**	32.92	**31.70**	30.54	**29.44**	28.40	26.46	24.70	23.11	21.66	20.35	31
32	36.76	35.37	**34.05**	31.61	**30.48**	29.41	**28.38**	27.41	25.60	23.95	22.46	21.10	19.85	32
33	35.05	33.78	**32.57**	30.32	**29.27**	28.28	**27.33**	26.42	24.74	23.20	21.80	20.52	19.35	33
34	33.38	32.21	**31.10**	29.03	**28.07**	27.15	**26.28**	25.44	23.87	22.44	21.13	19.93	18.83	34
35	31.74	30.68	**29.66**	27.77	**26.88**	26.04	**25.23**	24.45	23.00	21.67	20.45	19.33	18.30	35
36	30.13	29.17	**28.24**	26.51	**25.70**	24.93	**24.18**	23.47	22.13	20.90	19.77	18.72	17.76	36
37	28.56	27.69	**26.85**	25.27	**24.53**	23.82	**23.14**	22.49	21.26	20.12	19.07	18.10	17.20	37
38	27.03	26.24	**25.48**	24.05	**23.37**	22.73	**22.11**	21.51	20.38	19.34	18.37	17.47	16.64	38
39	25.52	24.81	**24.13**	22.83	**22.23**	21.64	**21.07**	20.53	19.50	18.54	17.66	16.83	16.06	39
40	24.05	23.41	**22.80**	21.64	**21.09**	20.56	**20.05**	19.55	18.62	17.75	16.93	16.17	15.47	40
41	22.61	22.04	**21.49**	20.45	**19.96**	19.48	**19.02**	18.58	17.73	16.94	16.20	15.51	14.86	41
42	21.19	20.69	**20.20**	19.28	**18.84**	18.41	**18.00**	17.60	16.84	16.13	15.46	14.83	14.24	42
43	19.81	19.37	**18.94**	18.12	**17.73**	17.35	**16.98**	16.63	15.95	15.31	14.71	14.14	13.60	43
44	18.46	18.07	**17.69**	16.97	**16.63**	16.29	**15.97**	15.66	15.05	14.48	13.94	13.44	12.96	44
45	17.13	16.79	**16.46**	15.84	**15.54**	15.24	**14.96**	14.68	14.15	13.65	13.17	12.72	12.29	45
46	15.83	15.54	**15.26**	14.71	**14.45**	14.20	**13.95**	13.71	13.25	12.81	12.39	11.99	11.61	46
47	14.55	14.31	**14.07**	13.60	**13.38**	13.16	**12.95**	12.74	12.34	11.95	11.59	11.24	10.91	47
48	13.30	13.09	**12.89**	12.50	**12.31**	12.12	**11.94**	11.77	11.42	11.10	10.78	10.48	10.19	48
49	12.08	11.90	**11.74**	11.41	**11.25**	11.09	**10.94**	10.79	10.50	10.23	9.96	9.71	9.46	49
50	10.88	10.73	**10.60**	10.33	**10.20**	10.07	**9.94**	9.82	9.58	9.35	9.13	8.92	8.71	50
51	9.70	9.58	**9.47**	9.26	**9.15**	9.05	**8.95**	8.85	8.65	8.46	8.28	8.11	7.94	51
52	8.54	8.45	**8.36**	8.19	**8.11**	8.03	**7.95**	7.87	7.72	7.57	7.42	7.28	7.15	52
53	7.40	7.34	**7.27**	7.14	**7.08**	7.02	**6.96**	6.90	6.78	6.66	6.55	6.44	6.34	53
54	6.29	6.24	**6.19**	6.10	**6.05**	6.01	**5.96**	5.92	5.83	5.75	5.66	5.58	5.50	54
55	5.20	5.16	**5.13**	5.06	**5.03**	5.00	**4.97**	4.94	4.88	4.82	4.76	4.70	4.65	55
56	4.12	4.10	**4.08**	4.04	**4.02**	4.00	**3.98**	3.96	3.92	3.88	3.84	3.81	3.77	56
57	3.07	3.05	**3.04**	3.02	**3.01**	3.00	**2.99**	2.97	2.95	2.93	2.91	2.89	2.87	57
58	2.03	2.02	**2.02**	2.01	**2.00**	2.00	**1.99**	1.99	1.98	1.97	1.96	1.95	1.94	58
59	1.01	1.01	**1.00**	1.00	**1.00**	1.00	**1.00**	1.00	0.99	0.99	0.99	0.99	0.98	59

Table 8 Multipliers for loss of earnings to pension age 60 (females)

Age at date of trial	Multipliers calculated with allowance for projected mortality from the 2018-based population projections and rate of return of:													Age at date of trial
	-2.0%	-1.75%	**-1.5%**	-1.0%	**-0.75%**	-0.5%	**-0.25%**	0.0%	0.5%	1.0%	1.5%	2.0%	2.5%	
16	70.09	65.78	**61.81**	54.76	**51.63**	48.74	**46.07**	43.59	39.16	35.34	32.03	29.16	26.65	16
17	67.69	63.63	**59.89**	53.22	**50.25**	47.50	**44.95**	42.59	38.35	34.69	31.50	28.73	26.31	17
18	65.35	61.53	**57.99**	51.69	**48.88**	46.27	**43.84**	41.59	37.54	34.03	30.97	28.30	25.95	18
19	63.05	59.46	**56.13**	50.18	**47.52**	45.04	**42.74**	40.59	36.73	33.37	30.43	27.85	25.59	19
20	60.80	57.43	**54.30**	48.68	**46.16**	43.82	**41.63**	39.59	35.91	32.70	29.88	27.40	25.22	20
21	58.60	55.44	**52.49**	47.20	**44.82**	42.60	**40.53**	38.60	35.09	32.02	29.32	26.94	24.84	21
22	56.44	53.48	**50.72**	45.74	**43.49**	41.40	**39.43**	37.60	34.27	31.34	28.76	26.47	24.45	22
23	54.32	51.55	**48.96**	44.29	**42.17**	40.19	**38.34**	36.60	33.44	30.65	28.18	26.00	24.05	23
24	52.25	49.66	**47.24**	42.85	**40.86**	39.00	**37.25**	35.60	32.60	29.95	27.60	25.51	23.64	24
25	50.21	47.80	**45.54**	41.43	**39.56**	37.81	**36.16**	34.60	31.77	29.25	27.01	25.01	23.22	25
26	48.22	45.98	**43.87**	40.02	**38.27**	36.62	**35.07**	33.61	30.93	28.54	26.41	24.50	22.79	26
27	46.27	44.18	**42.22**	38.63	**36.99**	35.45	**33.99**	32.61	30.08	27.82	25.80	23.99	22.35	27
28	44.36	42.42	**40.60**	37.25	**35.72**	34.27	**32.91**	31.61	29.23	27.10	25.18	23.46	21.90	28
29	42.49	40.70	**39.00**	35.89	**34.46**	33.11	**31.83**	30.62	28.38	26.37	24.56	22.92	21.44	29
30	40.65	39.00	**37.43**	34.54	**33.21**	31.95	**30.76**	29.62	27.53	25.63	23.92	22.38	20.97	30
31	38.86	37.33	**35.89**	33.21	**31.98**	30.80	**29.69**	28.63	26.67	24.89	23.28	21.82	20.49	31
32	37.10	35.70	**34.36**	31.89	**30.75**	29.66	**28.62**	27.64	25.81	24.14	22.63	21.25	19.99	32
33	35.38	34.09	**32.86**	30.59	**29.53**	28.52	**27.56**	26.65	24.94	23.39	21.97	20.67	19.49	33
34	33.69	32.51	**31.39**	29.30	**28.32**	27.39	**26.50**	25.65	24.07	22.62	21.30	20.08	18.97	34
35	32.04	30.96	**29.94**	28.02	**27.12**	26.27	**25.45**	24.66	23.20	21.85	20.62	19.48	18.44	35
36	30.42	29.44	**28.51**	26.75	**25.93**	25.15	**24.39**	23.67	22.32	21.07	19.93	18.87	17.89	36
37	28.84	27.95	**27.10**	25.50	**24.75**	24.04	**23.35**	22.68	21.44	20.29	19.23	18.25	17.34	37
38	27.28	26.48	**25.71**	24.27	**23.58**	22.93	**22.30**	21.70	20.55	19.50	18.52	17.61	16.77	38
39	25.76	25.04	**24.35**	23.04	**22.42**	21.83	**21.26**	20.71	19.67	18.70	17.80	16.96	16.18	39
40	24.27	23.63	**23.01**	21.83	**21.27**	20.74	**20.22**	19.72	18.78	17.89	17.07	16.30	15.59	40
41	22.81	22.24	**21.68**	20.63	**20.13**	19.65	**19.19**	18.74	17.88	17.08	16.33	15.63	14.97	41
42	21.38	20.88	**20.38**	19.45	**19.00**	18.57	**18.15**	17.75	16.98	16.26	15.58	14.95	14.35	42
43	19.98	19.54	**19.10**	18.27	**17.88**	17.50	**17.12**	16.76	16.08	15.43	14.82	14.25	13.71	43
44	18.61	18.22	**17.84**	17.11	**16.76**	16.43	**16.10**	15.78	15.17	14.59	14.05	13.54	13.05	44
45	17.27	16.93	**16.60**	15.96	**15.66**	15.36	**15.08**	14.80	14.26	13.75	13.27	12.81	12.38	45
46	15.95	15.66	**15.37**	14.82	**14.56**	14.30	**14.05**	13.81	13.34	12.90	12.47	12.07	11.69	46
47	14.66	14.41	**14.17**	13.70	**13.47**	13.25	**13.04**	12.83	12.42	12.04	11.67	11.32	10.98	47
48	13.40	13.19	**12.98**	12.58	**12.39**	12.21	**12.02**	11.84	11.50	11.17	10.85	10.55	10.26	48
49	12.16	11.98	**11.81**	11.48	**11.32**	11.16	**11.01**	10.86	10.57	10.29	10.02	9.77	9.52	49
50	10.94	10.80	**10.66**	10.39	**10.26**	10.13	**10.00**	9.88	9.64	9.41	9.18	8.97	8.76	50
51	9.75	9.64	**9.53**	9.31	**9.20**	9.10	**9.00**	8.90	8.70	8.51	8.33	8.15	7.98	51
52	8.58	8.50	**8.41**	8.24	**8.15**	8.07	**7.99**	7.91	7.76	7.61	7.46	7.32	7.18	52
53	7.44	7.37	**7.31**	7.18	**7.11**	7.05	**6.99**	6.93	6.81	6.69	6.58	6.47	6.37	53
54	6.32	6.27	**6.22**	6.13	**6.08**	6.03	**5.99**	5.94	5.86	5.77	5.69	5.61	5.53	54
55	5.22	5.18	**5.15**	5.08	**5.05**	5.02	**4.99**	4.96	4.90	4.84	4.78	4.72	4.67	55
56	4.14	4.11	**4.09**	4.05	**4.03**	4.01	**3.99**	3.97	3.93	3.89	3.86	3.82	3.78	56
57	3.08	3.06	**3.05**	3.03	**3.02**	3.01	**2.99**	2.98	2.96	2.94	2.92	2.90	2.88	57
58	2.03	2.03	**2.02**	2.01	**2.01**	2.00	**2.00**	1.99	1.98	1.97	1.96	1.95	1.94	58
59	1.01	1.01	**1.01**	1.00	**1.00**	1.00	**1.00**	1.00	1.00	0.99	0.99	0.99	0.99	59

Table 9 Multipliers for loss of earnings to pension age 65 (males)

Age at date of trial	Multipliers calculated with allowance for projected mortality from the 2018-based population projections and rate of return of:													Age at date of trial
	-2.0%	-1.75%	**-1.5%**	-1.0%	**-0.75%**	-0.5%	**-0.25%**	0.0%	0.5%	1.0%	1.5%	2.0%	2.5%	
16	81.53	75.93	**70.81**	61.85	**57.93**	54.33	**51.03**	48.00	42.64	38.09	34.21	30.88	28.02	16
17	78.89	73.59	**68.74**	60.23	**56.49**	53.06	**49.90**	46.99	41.85	37.46	33.71	30.48	27.70	17
18	76.31	71.30	**66.71**	58.62	**55.06**	51.79	**48.77**	45.99	41.05	36.83	33.21	30.08	27.38	18
19	73.79	69.06	**64.71**	57.04	**53.65**	50.53	**47.65**	44.99	40.25	36.19	32.70	29.68	27.05	19
20	71.32	66.85	**62.74**	55.47	**52.25**	49.28	**46.53**	43.99	39.45	35.55	32.18	29.26	26.72	20
21	68.90	64.69	**60.81**	53.92	**50.86**	48.03	**45.42**	42.99	38.65	34.90	31.66	28.84	26.38	21
22	66.53	62.57	**58.91**	52.39	**49.49**	46.80	**44.31**	41.99	37.84	34.25	31.13	28.41	26.03	22
23	64.21	60.48	**57.03**	50.87	**48.12**	45.57	**43.20**	41.00	37.03	33.59	30.59	27.97	25.67	23
24	61.94	58.43	**55.18**	49.37	**46.77**	44.35	**42.10**	40.00	36.22	32.93	30.05	27.53	25.31	24
25	59.71	56.42	**53.37**	47.88	**45.42**	43.13	**41.00**	39.00	35.40	32.26	29.50	27.07	24.93	25
26	57.53	54.45	**51.58**	46.41	**44.09**	41.92	**39.90**	38.01	34.58	31.58	28.94	26.61	24.55	26
27	55.39	52.51	**49.81**	44.96	**42.77**	40.72	**38.80**	37.01	33.76	30.89	28.37	26.13	24.15	27
28	53.30	50.60	**48.08**	43.52	**41.46**	39.53	**37.71**	36.02	32.93	30.20	27.79	25.65	23.75	28
29	51.25	48.73	**46.37**	42.10	**40.16**	38.34	**36.63**	35.02	32.10	29.51	27.21	25.16	23.34	29
30	49.25	46.90	**44.70**	40.69	**38.87**	37.16	**35.55**	34.03	31.26	28.81	26.62	24.66	22.91	30
31	47.28	45.10	**43.04**	39.30	**37.59**	35.98	**34.47**	33.04	30.43	28.10	26.02	24.15	22.48	31
32	45.36	43.33	**41.42**	37.92	**36.33**	34.82	**33.40**	32.05	29.59	27.38	25.41	23.64	22.04	32
33	43.48	41.59	**39.82**	36.56	**35.07**	33.66	**32.33**	31.07	28.75	26.66	24.79	23.11	21.59	33
34	41.64	39.89	**38.25**	35.22	**33.83**	32.51	**31.26**	30.08	27.90	25.94	24.17	22.57	21.13	34
35	39.83	38.22	**36.70**	33.89	**32.59**	31.37	**30.20**	29.10	27.05	25.21	23.54	22.03	20.66	35
36	38.07	36.58	**35.18**	32.57	**31.37**	30.23	**29.15**	28.11	26.20	24.47	22.90	21.47	20.17	36
37	36.34	34.98	**33.68**	31.27	**30.16**	29.10	**28.09**	27.13	25.35	23.73	22.25	20.91	19.68	37
38	34.65	33.40	**32.21**	29.99	**28.96**	27.98	**27.05**	26.16	24.49	22.98	21.60	20.33	19.18	38
39	33.00	31.85	**30.76**	28.72	**27.77**	26.87	**26.00**	25.18	23.64	22.23	20.93	19.75	18.66	39
40	31.38	30.33	**29.33**	27.47	**26.60**	25.76	**24.97**	24.20	22.78	21.47	20.26	19.16	18.14	40
41	29.79	28.84	**27.93**	26.23	**25.43**	24.67	**23.93**	23.23	21.91	20.70	19.58	18.55	17.60	41
42	28.24	27.38	**26.55**	25.00	**24.27**	23.58	**22.90**	22.26	21.05	19.93	18.89	17.94	17.05	42
43	26.73	25.95	**25.20**	23.79	**23.13**	22.49	**21.88**	21.29	20.18	19.15	18.20	17.31	16.49	43
44	25.24	24.54	**23.87**	22.59	**21.99**	21.42	**20.86**	20.32	19.31	18.37	17.49	16.67	15.91	44
45	23.79	23.16	**22.55**	21.41	**20.87**	20.35	**19.84**	19.36	18.43	17.58	16.77	16.03	15.33	45
46	22.36	21.80	**21.26**	20.24	**19.75**	19.28	**18.83**	18.39	17.56	16.78	16.05	15.37	14.73	46
47	20.96	20.47	**19.99**	19.08	**18.64**	18.22	**17.82**	17.43	16.68	15.97	15.31	14.69	14.11	47
48	19.60	19.16	**18.74**	17.93	**17.55**	17.17	**16.81**	16.46	15.79	15.16	14.57	14.01	13.48	48
49	18.26	17.87	**17.50**	16.80	**16.46**	16.13	**15.81**	15.50	14.90	14.34	13.81	13.31	12.84	49
50	16.94	16.61	**16.29**	15.67	**15.37**	15.09	**14.81**	14.53	14.01	13.51	13.04	12.60	12.18	50
51	15.66	15.37	**15.09**	14.56	**14.30**	14.05	**13.81**	13.57	13.11	12.68	12.27	11.87	11.50	51
52	14.40	14.15	**13.91**	13.46	**13.24**	13.02	**12.81**	12.61	12.21	11.84	11.48	11.13	10.81	52
53	13.16	12.95	**12.75**	12.37	**12.18**	12.00	**11.82**	11.64	11.31	10.98	10.68	10.38	10.10	53
54	11.95	11.78	**11.61**	11.29	**11.13**	10.98	**10.83**	10.68	10.40	10.12	9.86	9.61	9.37	54
55	10.76	10.62	**10.48**	10.22	**10.09**	9.96	**9.84**	9.72	9.48	9.26	9.04	8.83	8.62	55
56	9.60	9.48	**9.37**	9.16	**9.06**	8.96	**8.86**	8.76	8.57	8.38	8.20	8.03	7.86	56
57	8.45	8.37	**8.28**	8.11	**8.03**	7.95	**7.87**	7.79	7.64	7.50	7.35	7.21	7.08	57
58	7.33	7.27	**7.20**	7.08	**7.01**	6.95	**6.89**	6.83	6.72	6.60	6.49	6.38	6.28	58
59	6.24	6.19	**6.14**	6.05	**6.00**	5.96	**5.91**	5.87	5.78	5.70	5.62	5.54	5.46	59
60	5.16	5.12	**5.09**	5.03	**4.99**	4.96	**4.93**	4.90	4.84	4.78	4.73	4.67	4.61	60
61	4.10	4.07	**4.05**	4.01	**3.99**	3.97	**3.95**	3.93	3.89	3.86	3.82	3.78	3.75	61
62	3.05	3.04	**3.03**	3.00	**2.99**	2.98	**2.97**	2.96	2.94	2.92	2.89	2.87	2.85	62
63	2.02	2.02	**2.01**	2.00	**2.00**	1.99	**1.99**	1.98	1.97	1.96	1.95	1.94	1.93	63
64	1.00	1.00	**1.00**	1.00	**1.00**	1.00	**1.00**	0.99	0.99	0.99	0.99	0.99	0.98	64

Table 10 Multipliers for loss of earnings to pension age 65 (females)

Age at date of trial	Multipliers calculated with allowance for projected mortality from the 2018-based population projections and rate of return of:													Age at date of trial
	-2.0%	-1.75%	**-1.5%**	-1.0%	**-0.75%**	-0.5%	**-0.25%**	0.0%	0.5%	1.0%	1.5%	2.0%	2.5%	trial
16	82.35	76.67	**71.48**	62.41	**58.43**	54.79	**51.45**	48.38	42.96	38.36	34.43	31.07	28.17	16
17	79.71	74.33	**69.41**	60.78	**57.00**	53.52	**50.32**	47.38	42.17	37.73	33.94	30.68	27.87	17
18	77.12	72.03	**67.38**	59.18	**55.57**	52.25	**49.20**	46.38	41.38	37.11	33.44	30.28	27.55	18
19	74.58	69.78	**65.37**	57.59	**54.16**	50.99	**48.07**	45.38	40.58	36.47	32.93	29.88	27.23	19
20	72.10	67.56	**63.39**	56.02	**52.75**	49.74	**46.95**	44.38	39.78	35.83	32.42	29.47	26.90	20
21	69.66	65.39	**61.45**	54.46	**51.36**	48.49	**45.84**	43.38	38.98	35.19	31.90	29.05	26.56	21
22	67.28	63.25	**59.53**	52.92	**49.98**	47.25	**44.72**	42.38	38.17	34.53	31.37	28.62	26.21	22
23	64.94	61.15	**57.65**	51.40	**48.61**	46.02	**43.61**	41.38	37.36	33.88	30.84	28.18	25.86	23
24	62.65	59.09	**55.79**	49.89	**47.25**	44.79	**42.51**	40.38	36.55	33.21	30.29	27.74	25.49	24
25	60.40	57.06	**53.96**	48.39	**45.90**	43.57	**41.40**	39.38	35.73	32.54	29.74	27.28	25.12	25
26	58.20	55.07	**52.16**	46.91	**44.56**	42.36	**40.30**	38.38	34.91	31.86	29.18	26.82	24.73	26
27	56.05	53.12	**50.38**	45.45	**43.23**	41.15	**39.20**	37.38	34.08	31.18	28.62	26.35	24.34	27
28	53.94	51.20	**48.64**	44.00	**41.91**	39.95	**38.11**	36.39	33.25	30.49	28.04	25.87	23.94	28
29	51.88	49.31	**46.92**	42.57	**40.60**	38.75	**37.02**	35.39	32.42	29.79	27.46	25.38	23.53	29
30	49.85	47.47	**45.23**	41.16	**39.31**	37.57	**35.93**	34.39	31.58	29.09	26.86	24.88	23.11	30
31	47.87	45.65	**43.56**	39.76	**38.02**	36.39	**34.85**	33.40	30.74	28.38	26.26	24.37	22.68	31
32	45.93	43.87	**41.92**	38.37	**36.75**	35.21	**33.77**	32.41	29.90	27.66	25.66	23.86	22.24	32
33	44.03	42.12	**40.31**	37.00	**35.48**	34.05	**32.69**	31.41	29.05	26.94	25.04	23.33	21.79	33
34	42.17	40.40	**38.72**	35.64	**34.23**	32.89	**31.62**	30.42	28.21	26.21	24.42	22.79	21.33	34
35	40.35	38.71	**37.16**	34.30	**32.98**	31.74	**30.55**	29.43	27.35	25.48	23.78	22.25	20.86	35
36	38.56	37.05	**35.62**	32.97	**31.75**	30.59	**29.49**	28.44	26.50	24.74	23.14	21.69	20.37	36
37	36.82	35.43	**34.11**	31.66	**30.53**	29.45	**28.43**	27.45	25.64	23.99	22.49	21.12	19.88	37
38	35.11	33.83	**32.62**	30.36	**29.32**	28.32	**27.37**	26.46	24.77	23.23	21.83	20.55	19.37	38
39	33.43	32.26	**31.15**	29.08	**28.12**	27.19	**26.32**	25.48	23.91	22.47	21.16	19.96	18.86	39
40	31.79	30.72	**29.71**	27.81	**26.92**	26.08	**25.27**	24.49	23.04	21.71	20.48	19.36	18.33	40
41	30.18	29.21	**28.29**	26.55	**25.74**	24.96	**24.22**	23.51	22.17	20.93	19.80	18.75	17.78	41
42	28.61	27.73	**26.89**	25.31	**24.57**	23.86	**23.18**	22.52	21.29	20.15	19.10	18.13	17.23	42
43	27.07	26.27	**25.51**	24.08	**23.41**	22.76	**22.14**	21.54	20.41	19.36	18.40	17.50	16.66	43
44	25.56	24.84	**24.16**	22.87	**22.26**	21.67	**21.10**	20.56	19.53	18.57	17.68	16.85	16.08	44
45	24.08	23.44	**22.83**	21.66	**21.11**	20.58	**20.07**	19.58	18.64	17.77	16.95	16.19	15.48	45
46	22.63	22.06	**21.51**	20.47	**19.98**	19.50	**19.04**	18.60	17.75	16.96	16.22	15.52	14.87	46
47	21.21	20.71	**20.22**	19.29	**18.85**	18.43	**18.02**	17.62	16.86	16.14	15.47	14.84	14.25	47
48	19.82	19.38	**18.95**	18.13	**17.74**	17.36	**16.99**	16.64	15.96	15.32	14.72	14.15	13.61	48
49	18.46	18.07	**17.70**	16.98	**16.63**	16.30	**15.97**	15.66	15.06	14.49	13.95	13.44	12.96	49
50	17.13	16.79	**16.46**	15.84	**15.54**	15.24	**14.96**	14.68	14.15	13.65	13.17	12.72	12.29	50
51	15.82	15.53	**15.25**	14.71	**14.45**	14.20	**13.95**	13.71	13.24	12.80	12.38	11.99	11.61	51
52	14.54	14.30	**14.06**	13.59	**13.37**	13.15	**12.94**	12.73	12.33	11.95	11.59	11.24	10.91	52
53	13.29	13.08	**12.88**	12.49	**12.30**	12.12	**11.93**	11.76	11.42	11.09	10.77	10.48	10.19	53
54	12.07	11.89	**11.72**	11.40	**11.24**	11.08	**10.93**	10.78	10.49	10.22	9.95	9.70	9.45	54
55	10.86	10.72	**10.58**	10.32	**10.19**	10.06	**9.93**	9.81	9.57	9.34	9.12	8.91	8.70	55
56	9.68	9.57	**9.46**	9.24	**9.14**	9.04	**8.94**	8.84	8.64	8.45	8.27	8.10	7.93	56
57	8.53	8.44	**8.35**	8.18	**8.10**	8.02	**7.94**	7.86	7.71	7.56	7.41	7.27	7.14	57
58	7.39	7.33	**7.26**	7.13	**7.07**	7.01	**6.95**	6.89	6.77	6.65	6.54	6.43	6.33	58
59	6.28	6.23	**6.19**	6.09	**6.05**	6.00	**5.96**	5.91	5.82	5.74	5.66	5.58	5.50	59
60	5.19	5.16	**5.13**	5.06	**5.03**	5.00	**4.97**	4.93	4.87	4.81	4.76	4.70	4.64	60
61	4.12	4.10	**4.08**	4.04	**4.02**	4.00	**3.98**	3.96	3.92	3.88	3.84	3.80	3.77	61
62	3.07	3.05	**3.04**	3.02	**3.01**	3.00	**2.98**	2.97	2.95	2.93	2.91	2.89	2.87	62
63	2.03	2.02	**2.02**	2.01	**2.00**	2.00	**1.99**	1.99	1.98	1.97	1.96	1.95	1.94	63
64	1.01	1.01	**1.00**	1.00	**1.00**	1.00	**1.00**	1.00	0.99	0.99	0.99	0.99	0.98	64

Table 11 Multipliers for loss of earnings to pension age 68 (males)

Age at date of trial	Multipliers calculated with allowance for projected mortality from the 2018-based population projections and rate of return of:													Age at date of trial
	-2.0%	-1.75%	**-1.5%**	-1.0%	**-0.75%**	-0.5%	**-0.25%**	0.0%	0.5%	1.0%	1.5%	2.0%	2.5%	
16	89.14	82.62	**76.70**	66.41	**61.94**	57.87	**54.15**	50.74	44.78	39.75	35.50	31.89	28.80	16
17	86.35	80.16	**74.53**	64.74	**60.47**	56.57	**53.00**	49.74	43.99	39.14	35.02	31.51	28.51	17
18	83.61	77.75	**72.41**	63.08	**59.01**	55.28	**51.86**	48.73	43.20	38.52	34.54	31.13	28.21	18
19	80.93	75.39	**70.32**	61.45	**57.56**	54.00	**50.73**	47.72	42.41	37.90	34.05	30.74	27.90	19
20	78.31	73.07	**68.26**	59.83	**56.13**	52.73	**49.60**	46.72	41.62	37.27	33.55	30.35	27.59	20
21	75.75	70.79	**66.24**	58.24	**54.71**	51.47	**48.48**	45.72	40.83	36.64	33.05	29.95	27.27	21
22	73.24	68.56	**64.25**	56.66	**53.30**	50.21	**47.36**	44.72	40.03	36.00	32.54	29.54	26.94	22
23	70.78	66.36	**62.29**	55.09	**51.91**	48.96	**46.24**	43.72	39.23	35.36	32.02	29.12	26.60	23
24	68.37	64.21	**60.37**	53.55	**50.52**	47.72	**45.13**	42.72	38.43	34.71	31.50	28.70	26.26	24
25	66.01	62.09	**58.47**	52.02	**49.15**	46.49	**44.02**	41.73	37.62	34.06	30.97	28.27	25.91	25
26	63.70	60.01	**56.60**	50.50	**47.78**	45.26	**42.91**	40.73	36.81	33.40	30.43	27.83	25.55	26
27	61.43	57.97	**54.75**	49.00	**46.43**	44.03	**41.81**	39.73	35.99	32.73	29.88	27.38	25.18	27
28	59.21	55.96	**52.94**	47.52	**45.09**	42.82	**40.71**	38.73	35.17	32.06	29.32	26.92	24.80	28
29	57.04	54.00	**51.16**	46.06	**43.76**	41.61	**39.61**	37.74	34.35	31.38	28.76	26.45	24.41	29
30	54.92	52.07	**49.41**	44.61	**42.44**	40.42	**38.52**	36.75	33.53	30.69	28.19	25.98	24.02	30
31	52.84	50.17	**47.68**	43.17	**41.13**	39.22	**37.43**	35.75	32.70	30.00	27.62	25.50	23.61	31
32	50.80	48.31	**45.98**	41.76	**39.84**	38.04	**36.35**	34.76	31.87	29.31	27.03	25.01	23.20	32
33	48.81	46.49	**44.31**	40.36	**38.56**	36.86	**35.27**	33.78	31.04	28.61	26.44	24.51	22.78	33
34	46.86	44.70	**42.67**	38.97	**37.29**	35.70	**34.20**	32.79	30.20	27.90	25.84	24.00	22.34	34
35	44.95	42.94	**41.06**	37.60	**36.03**	34.54	**33.13**	31.80	29.37	27.19	25.23	23.48	21.90	35
36	43.08	41.22	**39.47**	36.25	**34.78**	33.38	**32.07**	30.82	28.53	26.47	24.62	22.95	21.45	36
37	41.25	39.53	**37.90**	34.91	**33.54**	32.24	**31.01**	29.84	27.69	25.75	24.00	22.42	20.99	37
38	39.46	37.87	**36.37**	33.59	**32.32**	31.10	**29.95**	28.86	26.84	25.02	23.37	21.87	20.52	38
39	37.71	36.25	**34.86**	32.29	**31.10**	29.97	**28.90**	27.88	26.00	24.28	22.73	21.32	20.04	39
40	36.00	34.65	**33.37**	31.00	**29.90**	28.85	**27.86**	26.91	25.15	23.55	22.09	20.76	19.54	40
41	34.33	33.09	**31.91**	29.73	**28.71**	27.74	**26.82**	25.94	24.30	22.80	21.44	20.19	19.04	41
42	32.69	31.56	**30.48**	28.47	**27.53**	26.64	**25.78**	24.97	23.44	22.05	20.78	19.60	18.53	42
43	31.08	30.05	**29.07**	27.22	**26.36**	25.54	**24.75**	24.00	22.59	21.30	20.11	19.01	18.01	43
44	29.51	28.57	**27.68**	25.99	**25.21**	24.45	**23.73**	23.04	21.73	20.53	19.43	18.41	17.47	44
45	27.98	27.13	**26.31**	24.78	**24.06**	23.37	**22.71**	22.07	20.87	19.77	18.75	17.80	16.92	45
46	26.47	25.70	**24.97**	23.58	**22.92**	22.29	**21.69**	21.11	20.01	18.99	18.05	17.18	16.36	46
47	25.00	24.31	**23.64**	22.39	**21.79**	21.22	**20.67**	20.15	19.14	18.21	17.35	16.54	15.79	47
48	23.56	22.94	**22.34**	21.21	**20.68**	20.16	**19.66**	19.18	18.28	17.43	16.64	15.90	15.21	48
49	22.14	21.59	**21.06**	20.05	**19.57**	19.11	**18.66**	18.23	17.40	16.63	15.91	15.24	14.61	49
50	20.76	20.27	**19.80**	18.90	**18.47**	18.05	**17.65**	17.27	16.53	15.83	15.18	14.57	13.99	50
51	19.40	18.97	**18.55**	17.76	**17.38**	17.01	**16.65**	16.31	15.65	15.03	14.44	13.89	13.37	51
52	18.07	17.70	**17.33**	16.63	**16.30**	15.97	**15.66**	15.35	14.76	14.21	13.69	13.19	12.72	52
53	16.77	16.44	**16.13**	15.52	**15.22**	14.94	**14.66**	14.39	13.88	13.39	12.92	12.49	12.07	53
54	15.50	15.21	**14.94**	14.41	**14.16**	13.91	**13.67**	13.44	12.99	12.56	12.15	11.76	11.40	54
55	14.25	14.01	**13.77**	13.32	**13.11**	12.89	**12.69**	12.48	12.10	11.72	11.37	11.03	10.71	55
56	13.03	12.82	**12.63**	12.24	**12.06**	11.88	**11.70**	11.53	11.20	10.88	10.58	10.28	10.00	56
57	11.83	11.66	**11.50**	11.18	**11.02**	10.87	**10.73**	10.58	10.30	10.03	9.77	9.52	9.28	57
58	10.66	10.52	**10.38**	10.12	**10.00**	9.87	**9.75**	9.63	9.40	9.17	8.96	8.75	8.55	58
59	9.51	9.40	**9.29**	9.08	**8.98**	8.88	**8.78**	8.68	8.49	8.31	8.13	7.96	7.80	59
60	8.38	8.30	**8.21**	8.05	**7.96**	7.89	**7.81**	7.73	7.58	7.43	7.29	7.16	7.02	60
61	7.28	7.21	**7.15**	7.02	**6.96**	6.90	**6.84**	6.78	6.66	6.55	6.44	6.34	6.23	61
62	6.19	6.14	**6.10**	6.00	**5.96**	5.91	**5.87**	5.83	5.74	5.66	5.58	5.50	5.42	62
63	5.12	5.09	**5.06**	5.00	**4.96**	4.93	**4.90**	4.87	4.81	4.75	4.70	4.64	4.59	63
64	4.07	4.05	**4.03**	3.99	**3.97**	3.95	**3.93**	3.91	3.87	3.84	3.80	3.76	3.73	64
65	3.04	3.03	**3.01**	2.99	**2.98**	2.97	**2.96**	2.95	2.93	2.90	2.88	2.86	2.84	65
66	2.02	2.01	**2.01**	1.99	**1.99**	1.98	**1.98**	1.98	1.97	1.96	1.95	1.94	1.93	66
67	1.00	1.00	**1.00**	1.00	**1.00**	1.00	**0.99**	0.99	0.99	0.99	0.99	0.98	0.98	67

Table 12 Multipliers for loss of earnings to pension age 68 (females)

Age at date of trial	Multipliers calculated with allowance for projected mortality from the 2018-based population projections and rate of return of:													Age at date of trial
	-2.0%	-1.75%	**-1.5%**	-1.0%	**-0.75%**	-0.5%	**-0.25%**	0.0%	0.5%	1.0%	1.5%	2.0%	2.5%	
16	90.21	83.58	**77.56**	67.11	**62.58**	58.44	**54.66**	51.21	45.16	40.07	35.76	32.11	28.99	16
17	87.40	81.11	**75.39**	65.44	**61.10**	57.15	**53.53**	50.21	44.38	39.46	35.29	31.74	28.70	17
18	84.65	78.69	**73.26**	63.78	**59.65**	55.86	**52.39**	49.21	43.60	38.85	34.81	31.36	28.40	18
19	81.96	76.32	**71.17**	62.15	**58.20**	54.58	**51.26**	48.20	42.81	38.23	34.33	30.98	28.10	19
20	79.32	73.99	**69.10**	60.52	**56.76**	53.31	**50.13**	47.20	42.02	37.61	33.84	30.59	27.79	20
21	76.74	71.69	**67.07**	58.92	**55.34**	52.04	**49.00**	46.20	41.23	36.98	33.34	30.19	27.48	21
22	74.21	69.44	**65.06**	57.33	**53.92**	50.78	**47.88**	45.20	40.43	36.35	32.83	29.79	27.15	22
23	71.73	67.23	**63.09**	55.76	**52.52**	49.53	**46.76**	44.20	39.63	35.71	32.31	29.37	26.82	23
24	69.30	65.06	**61.15**	54.21	**51.13**	48.28	**45.64**	43.20	38.83	35.06	31.79	28.95	26.48	24
25	66.92	62.92	**59.23**	52.67	**49.75**	47.04	**44.53**	42.20	38.02	34.40	31.26	28.52	26.13	25
26	64.59	60.83	**57.35**	51.14	**48.38**	45.81	**43.42**	41.20	37.21	33.74	30.72	28.08	25.77	26
27	62.30	58.77	**55.50**	49.64	**47.02**	44.58	**42.31**	40.20	36.39	33.08	30.18	27.64	25.40	27
28	60.07	56.75	**53.67**	48.15	**45.67**	43.36	**41.21**	39.20	35.57	32.40	29.63	27.18	25.03	28
29	57.87	54.77	**51.87**	46.67	**44.33**	42.15	**40.11**	38.20	34.75	31.73	29.06	26.72	24.64	29
30	55.73	52.82	**50.11**	45.21	**43.00**	40.94	**39.01**	37.20	33.93	31.04	28.50	26.25	24.25	30
31	53.63	50.91	**48.37**	43.77	**41.69**	39.74	**37.92**	36.21	33.10	30.35	27.92	25.77	23.85	31
32	51.57	49.03	**46.65**	42.34	**40.39**	38.55	**36.83**	35.21	32.26	29.65	27.34	25.28	23.44	32
33	49.56	47.19	**44.97**	40.93	**39.09**	37.37	**35.75**	34.22	31.43	28.95	26.75	24.78	23.02	33
34	47.58	45.38	**43.31**	39.53	**37.81**	36.19	**34.67**	33.23	30.59	28.24	26.15	24.27	22.59	34
35	45.65	43.60	**41.68**	38.15	**36.54**	35.02	**33.59**	32.24	29.75	27.53	25.54	23.75	22.15	35
36	43.76	41.86	**40.07**	36.79	**35.28**	33.86	**32.52**	31.24	28.91	26.81	24.92	23.23	21.69	36
37	41.91	40.15	**38.49**	35.43	**34.03**	32.70	**31.45**	30.26	28.06	26.08	24.30	22.69	21.23	37
38	40.09	38.47	**36.93**	34.10	**32.79**	31.55	**30.38**	29.27	27.21	25.35	23.67	22.14	20.76	38
39	38.32	36.82	**35.40**	32.78	**31.56**	30.41	**29.32**	28.28	26.35	24.61	23.02	21.59	20.28	39
40	36.58	35.20	**33.89**	31.47	**30.35**	29.28	**28.26**	27.29	25.50	23.86	22.37	21.02	19.78	40
41	34.88	33.61	**32.41**	30.18	**29.14**	28.15	**27.21**	26.31	24.64	23.11	21.72	20.44	19.28	41
42	33.21	32.05	**30.95**	28.90	**27.94**	27.03	**26.16**	25.33	23.77	22.35	21.05	19.86	18.76	42
43	31.58	30.52	**29.51**	27.63	**26.76**	25.92	**25.11**	24.34	22.90	21.58	20.37	19.26	18.23	43
44	29.98	29.02	**28.10**	26.38	**25.58**	24.81	**24.07**	23.36	22.03	20.81	19.69	18.65	17.69	44
45	28.41	27.54	**26.71**	25.15	**24.41**	23.71	**23.03**	22.38	21.16	20.03	18.99	18.03	17.14	45
46	26.88	26.09	**25.34**	23.92	**23.26**	22.61	**22.00**	21.40	20.28	19.25	18.29	17.40	16.57	46
47	25.38	24.67	**23.99**	22.71	**22.11**	21.53	**20.97**	20.43	19.41	18.46	17.57	16.75	15.99	47
48	23.91	23.28	**22.67**	21.52	**20.97**	20.45	**19.94**	19.45	18.52	17.66	16.85	16.10	15.39	48
49	22.47	21.91	**21.36**	20.33	**19.84**	19.37	**18.92**	18.47	17.64	16.85	16.12	15.43	14.79	49
50	21.06	20.56	**20.08**	19.16	**18.73**	18.30	**17.90**	17.50	16.75	16.04	15.38	14.75	14.17	50
51	19.68	19.24	**18.82**	18.01	**17.62**	17.24	**16.88**	16.53	15.85	15.22	14.62	14.06	13.53	51
52	18.33	17.95	**17.57**	16.86	**16.52**	16.19	**15.87**	15.56	14.96	14.39	13.86	13.36	12.88	52
53	17.01	16.68	**16.35**	15.73	**15.43**	15.14	**14.86**	14.59	14.06	13.56	13.09	12.64	12.22	53
54	15.71	15.43	**15.15**	14.61	**14.35**	14.10	**13.86**	13.62	13.16	12.72	12.31	11.91	11.54	54
55	14.45	14.20	**13.96**	13.50	**13.28**	13.07	**12.86**	12.65	12.25	11.87	11.51	11.17	10.84	55
56	13.20	13.00	**12.80**	12.41	**12.22**	12.04	**11.86**	11.68	11.34	11.02	10.71	10.41	10.13	56
57	11.99	11.82	**11.65**	11.33	**11.17**	11.01	**10.86**	10.72	10.43	10.16	9.89	9.64	9.40	57
58	10.80	10.66	**10.52**	10.25	**10.12**	10.00	**9.87**	9.75	9.51	9.29	9.07	8.86	8.65	58
59	9.63	9.52	**9.41**	9.19	**9.09**	8.98	**8.88**	8.79	8.59	8.41	8.23	8.05	7.89	59
60	8.48	8.39	**8.31**	8.14	**8.06**	7.98	**7.90**	7.82	7.67	7.52	7.38	7.24	7.10	60
61	7.36	7.29	**7.23**	7.10	**7.04**	6.97	**6.91**	6.85	6.74	6.62	6.51	6.40	6.30	61
62	6.25	6.21	**6.16**	6.07	**6.02**	5.97	**5.93**	5.89	5.80	5.71	5.63	5.55	5.47	62
63	5.17	5.14	**5.10**	5.04	**5.01**	4.98	**4.95**	4.92	4.85	4.80	4.74	4.68	4.63	63
64	4.11	4.08	**4.06**	4.02	**4.00**	3.98	**3.96**	3.94	3.90	3.87	3.83	3.79	3.76	64
65	3.06	3.04	**3.03**	3.01	**3.00**	2.99	**2.98**	2.97	2.94	2.92	2.90	2.88	2.86	65
66	2.02	2.02	**2.01**	2.00	**2.00**	1.99	**1.99**	1.98	1.97	1.96	1.95	1.94	1.94	66
67	1.01	1.00	**1.00**	1.00	**1.00**	1.00	**1.00**	1.00	0.99	0.99	0.99	0.99	0.98	67

Table 13 Multipliers for loss of earnings to pension age 70 (males)

Age at date of trial	Multipliers calculated with allowance for projected mortality from the 2018-based population projections and rate of return of:													Age at date of trial
	-2.0%	-1.75%	**-1.5%**	-1.0%	**-0.75%**	-0.5%	**-0.25%**	0.0%	0.5%	1.0%	1.5%	2.0%	2.5%	
16	94.38	87.20	**80.70**	69.47	**64.62**	60.21	**56.20**	52.54	46.15	40.81	36.32	32.52	29.29	16
17	91.48	84.65	**78.47**	67.76	**63.12**	58.90	**55.05**	51.53	45.37	40.21	35.85	32.15	29.01	17
18	88.63	82.16	**76.28**	66.07	**61.64**	57.59	**53.90**	50.52	44.59	39.60	35.38	31.78	28.72	18
19	85.85	79.71	**74.13**	64.41	**60.17**	56.30	**52.76**	49.51	43.81	38.99	34.90	31.41	28.42	19
20	83.12	77.31	**72.01**	62.76	**58.72**	55.01	**51.62**	48.51	43.02	38.37	34.41	31.03	28.12	20
21	80.46	74.96	**69.93**	61.13	**57.27**	53.74	**50.49**	47.51	42.23	37.75	33.92	30.64	27.81	21
22	77.85	72.65	**67.88**	59.52	**55.84**	52.47	**49.36**	46.51	41.44	37.12	33.42	30.24	27.50	22
23	75.29	70.38	**65.87**	57.92	**54.43**	51.21	**48.24**	45.51	40.65	36.49	32.92	29.84	27.18	23
24	72.79	68.15	**63.88**	56.35	**53.02**	49.95	**47.12**	44.50	39.85	35.85	32.41	29.43	26.85	24
25	70.34	65.96	**61.92**	54.78	**51.62**	48.70	**46.00**	43.50	39.05	35.21	31.89	29.01	26.51	25
26	67.93	63.80	**60.00**	53.24	**50.24**	47.46	**44.89**	42.50	38.24	34.56	31.36	28.59	26.16	26
27	65.58	61.69	**58.10**	51.71	**48.86**	46.23	**43.78**	41.51	37.43	33.90	30.83	28.15	25.81	27
28	63.27	59.62	**56.24**	50.20	**47.50**	45.00	**42.67**	40.51	36.62	33.24	30.29	27.71	25.44	28
29	61.02	57.59	**54.40**	48.70	**46.15**	43.78	**41.57**	39.51	35.80	32.57	29.74	27.26	25.07	29
30	58.81	55.59	**52.60**	47.23	**44.81**	42.57	**40.47**	38.52	34.98	31.89	29.18	26.80	24.69	30
31	56.65	53.63	**50.82**	45.76	**43.49**	41.36	**39.38**	37.52	34.16	31.21	28.62	26.33	24.30	31
32	54.53	51.71	**49.08**	44.32	**42.17**	40.17	**38.29**	36.53	33.34	30.53	28.05	25.85	23.91	32
33	52.46	49.82	**47.36**	42.89	**40.87**	38.98	**37.21**	35.54	32.51	29.84	27.47	25.37	23.50	33
34	50.44	47.97	**45.67**	41.48	**39.58**	37.80	**36.13**	34.55	31.69	29.15	26.89	24.88	23.09	34
35	48.45	46.16	**44.00**	40.09	**38.30**	36.63	**35.05**	33.57	30.86	28.44	26.30	24.38	22.66	35
36	46.51	44.38	**42.37**	38.71	**37.04**	35.46	**33.98**	32.58	30.02	27.74	25.70	23.87	22.23	36
37	44.62	42.63	**40.76**	37.35	**35.78**	34.31	**32.92**	31.60	29.19	27.03	25.09	23.35	21.79	37
38	42.76	40.92	**39.18**	36.00	**34.54**	33.16	**31.86**	30.62	28.35	26.31	24.48	22.83	21.34	38
39	40.94	39.24	**37.63**	34.67	**33.31**	32.02	**30.80**	29.65	27.51	25.59	23.86	22.29	20.88	39
40	39.17	37.59	**36.10**	33.36	**32.09**	30.89	**29.75**	28.67	26.67	24.86	23.23	21.75	20.41	40
41	37.43	35.98	**34.60**	32.06	**30.88**	29.77	**28.71**	27.70	25.83	24.13	22.60	21.20	19.92	41
42	35.73	34.39	**33.13**	30.78	**29.69**	28.65	**27.67**	26.73	24.98	23.40	21.95	20.64	19.43	42
43	34.06	32.84	**31.67**	29.51	**28.51**	27.55	**26.63**	25.76	24.14	22.66	21.30	20.07	18.93	43
44	32.43	31.31	**30.25**	28.26	**27.33**	26.45	**25.60**	24.80	23.29	21.91	20.65	19.49	18.42	44
45	30.84	29.82	**28.84**	27.02	**26.17**	25.36	**24.58**	23.83	22.44	21.16	19.98	18.90	17.90	45
46	29.28	28.35	**27.46**	25.80	**25.02**	24.27	**23.56**	22.87	21.58	20.40	19.30	18.30	17.36	46
47	27.75	26.91	**26.10**	24.59	**23.88**	23.20	**22.54**	21.91	20.73	19.63	18.62	17.69	16.82	47
48	26.26	25.50	**24.77**	23.39	**22.75**	22.13	**21.53**	20.95	19.87	18.86	17.93	17.06	16.26	48
49	24.79	24.11	**23.45**	22.21	**21.63**	21.06	**20.52**	19.99	19.00	18.08	17.23	16.43	15.69	49
50	23.36	22.75	**22.16**	21.04	**20.51**	20.00	**19.51**	19.04	18.14	17.30	16.52	15.79	15.10	50
51	21.95	21.41	**20.88**	19.88	**19.41**	18.95	**18.51**	18.08	17.27	16.51	15.80	15.13	14.50	51
52	20.58	20.10	**19.63**	18.74	**18.32**	17.91	**17.51**	17.13	16.40	15.71	15.07	14.46	13.89	52
53	19.23	18.81	**18.39**	17.61	**17.23**	16.87	**16.52**	16.18	15.52	14.91	14.33	13.78	13.27	53
54	17.91	17.54	**17.18**	16.49	**16.16**	15.84	**15.53**	15.22	14.64	14.10	13.58	13.09	12.63	54
55	16.62	16.30	**15.99**	15.38	**15.09**	14.81	**14.54**	14.27	13.76	13.28	12.82	12.39	11.97	55
56	15.36	15.08	**14.81**	14.29	**14.04**	13.80	**13.56**	13.33	12.88	12.46	12.06	11.67	11.31	56
57	14.12	13.89	**13.66**	13.21	**13.00**	12.79	**12.58**	12.38	12.00	11.63	11.28	10.94	10.62	57
58	12.91	12.72	**12.52**	12.14	**11.96**	11.78	**11.61**	11.44	11.11	10.79	10.49	10.20	9.93	58
59	11.73	11.57	**11.40**	11.09	**10.94**	10.79	**10.64**	10.50	10.22	9.95	9.70	9.45	9.22	59
60	10.57	10.44	**10.30**	10.05	**9.92**	9.80	**9.68**	9.56	9.33	9.11	8.89	8.69	8.49	60
61	9.44	9.33	**9.22**	9.01	**8.91**	8.81	**8.71**	8.62	8.43	8.25	8.07	7.91	7.74	61
62	8.32	8.24	**8.15**	7.99	**7.91**	7.83	**7.75**	7.68	7.53	7.39	7.25	7.11	6.98	62
63	7.23	7.17	**7.10**	6.98	**6.92**	6.86	**6.80**	6.74	6.62	6.51	6.40	6.30	6.20	63
64	6.16	6.11	**6.06**	5.97	**5.93**	5.88	**5.84**	5.79	5.71	5.63	5.55	5.47	5.39	64
65	5.10	5.07	**5.03**	4.97	**4.94**	4.91	**4.88**	4.85	4.79	4.73	4.67	4.62	4.56	65
66	4.06	4.04	**4.01**	3.97	**3.95**	3.93	**3.92**	3.90	3.86	3.82	3.78	3.75	3.71	66
67	3.03	3.02	**3.00**	2.98	**2.97**	2.96	**2.95**	2.94	2.92	2.89	2.87	2.85	2.83	67
68	2.01	2.01	**2.00**	1.99	**1.99**	1.98	**1.98**	1.97	1.96	1.95	1.94	1.93	1.92	68
69	1.00	1.00	**1.00**	1.00	**1.00**	0.99	**0.99**	0.99	0.99	0.99	0.98	0.98	0.98	69

Table 14 Multipliers for loss of earnings to pension age 70 (females)

Age at date of trial	Multipliers calculated with allowance for projected mortality from the 2018-based population projections and rate of return of:													Age at date of trial
	-2.0%	-1.75%	**-1.5%**	-1.0%	**-0.75%**	-0.5%	**-0.25%**	0.0%	0.5%	1.0%	1.5%	2.0%	2.5%	
16	95.65	88.33	**81.71**	70.29	**65.35**	60.87	**56.79**	53.08	46.59	41.17	36.61	32.76	29.49	16
17	92.73	85.78	**79.48**	68.58	**63.86**	59.56	**55.65**	52.07	45.82	40.57	36.15	32.41	29.22	17
18	89.87	83.28	**77.29**	66.89	**62.38**	58.26	**54.50**	51.07	45.04	39.97	35.68	32.04	28.93	18
19	87.07	80.82	**75.13**	65.22	**60.91**	56.97	**53.37**	50.07	44.26	39.37	35.21	31.67	28.64	19
20	84.33	78.40	**73.00**	63.57	**59.45**	55.68	**52.23**	49.06	43.48	38.75	34.73	31.30	28.35	20
21	81.64	76.03	**70.90**	61.93	**58.00**	54.40	**51.10**	48.06	42.69	38.13	34.24	30.91	28.04	21
22	79.01	73.70	**68.84**	60.31	**56.57**	53.13	**49.97**	47.06	41.90	37.51	33.75	30.52	27.73	22
23	76.43	71.41	**66.81**	58.71	**55.14**	51.86	**48.84**	46.05	41.11	36.88	33.25	30.12	27.41	23
24	73.90	69.16	**64.81**	57.12	**53.73**	50.60	**47.72**	45.05	40.31	36.24	32.74	29.71	27.09	24
25	71.43	66.95	**62.84**	55.55	**52.33**	49.35	**46.60**	44.05	39.51	35.60	32.22	29.30	26.75	25
26	69.00	64.78	**60.90**	54.00	**50.93**	48.10	**45.48**	43.05	38.70	34.95	31.70	28.87	26.41	26
27	66.62	62.65	**58.99**	52.46	**49.55**	46.86	**44.36**	42.05	37.89	34.29	31.17	28.44	26.06	27
28	64.30	60.56	**57.11**	50.94	**48.18**	45.63	**43.25**	41.05	37.08	33.63	30.63	28.00	25.70	28
29	62.02	58.51	**55.26**	49.43	**46.83**	44.40	**42.15**	40.05	36.26	32.97	30.08	27.56	25.33	29
30	59.79	56.49	**53.43**	47.94	**45.48**	43.19	**41.05**	39.05	35.45	32.29	29.53	27.10	24.96	30
31	57.60	54.52	**51.64**	46.47	**44.15**	41.98	**39.95**	38.05	34.62	31.61	28.97	26.64	24.57	31
32	55.47	52.57	**49.88**	45.02	**42.82**	40.77	**38.85**	37.06	33.80	30.93	28.40	26.16	24.18	32
33	53.37	50.67	**48.14**	43.58	**41.51**	39.58	**37.76**	36.06	32.97	30.24	27.82	25.68	23.78	33
34	51.32	48.80	**46.44**	42.15	**40.21**	38.39	**36.68**	35.07	32.14	29.54	27.24	25.19	23.36	34
35	49.31	46.96	**44.75**	40.74	**38.92**	37.21	**35.59**	34.08	31.30	28.84	26.65	24.69	22.94	35
36	47.34	45.16	**43.10**	39.35	**37.64**	36.03	**34.51**	33.09	30.47	28.13	26.05	24.18	22.51	36
37	45.42	43.39	**41.47**	37.97	**36.37**	34.86	**33.44**	32.10	29.63	27.42	25.44	23.67	22.07	37
38	43.53	41.65	**39.87**	36.61	**35.12**	33.70	**32.37**	31.11	28.78	26.70	24.82	23.14	21.62	38
39	41.69	39.94	**38.29**	35.26	**33.87**	32.55	**31.30**	30.12	27.94	25.97	24.20	22.60	21.15	39
40	39.88	38.27	**36.74**	33.93	**32.63**	31.40	**30.24**	29.13	27.09	25.24	23.57	22.06	20.68	40
41	38.11	36.63	**35.22**	32.61	**31.41**	30.27	**29.18**	28.15	26.23	24.50	22.93	21.50	20.20	41
42	36.38	35.01	**33.72**	31.31	**30.19**	29.13	**28.13**	27.16	25.38	23.76	22.28	20.93	19.70	42
43	34.68	33.43	**32.24**	30.02	**28.99**	28.01	**27.07**	26.18	24.52	23.00	21.62	20.36	19.20	43
44	33.02	31.88	**30.78**	28.75	**27.80**	26.89	**26.03**	25.20	23.66	22.25	20.95	19.77	18.68	44
45	31.40	30.35	**29.35**	27.49	**26.61**	25.78	**24.98**	24.22	22.79	21.48	20.28	19.17	18.15	45
46	29.81	28.85	**27.94**	26.24	**25.44**	24.68	**23.95**	23.24	21.92	20.71	19.59	18.56	17.61	46
47	28.25	27.39	**26.56**	25.01	**24.28**	23.58	**22.91**	22.27	21.05	19.93	18.90	17.94	17.06	47
48	26.72	25.94	**25.20**	23.79	**23.13**	22.49	**21.88**	21.29	20.18	19.15	18.20	17.31	16.49	48
49	25.23	24.53	**23.86**	22.59	**21.99**	21.41	**20.85**	20.32	19.30	18.36	17.49	16.67	15.91	49
50	23.77	23.14	**22.54**	21.39	**20.85**	20.33	**19.83**	19.34	18.42	17.57	16.77	16.02	15.32	50
51	22.34	21.78	**21.24**	20.22	**19.73**	19.26	**18.81**	18.37	17.54	16.76	16.04	15.35	14.71	51
52	20.94	20.44	**19.96**	19.05	**18.62**	18.20	**17.80**	17.40	16.66	15.95	15.30	14.68	14.10	52
53	19.57	19.13	**18.71**	17.90	**17.52**	17.15	**16.79**	16.44	15.77	15.14	14.55	13.99	13.46	53
54	18.22	17.84	**17.47**	16.77	**16.43**	16.10	**15.78**	15.47	14.88	14.32	13.79	13.29	12.82	54
55	16.91	16.58	**16.26**	15.64	**15.35**	15.06	**14.78**	14.51	13.98	13.49	13.02	12.58	12.15	55
56	15.62	15.34	**15.06**	14.53	**14.27**	14.02	**13.78**	13.54	13.09	12.65	12.24	11.85	11.48	56
57	14.36	14.12	**13.89**	13.43	**13.21**	13.00	**12.79**	12.58	12.19	11.81	11.45	11.11	10.79	57
58	13.13	12.93	**12.73**	12.34	**12.16**	11.97	**11.80**	11.62	11.29	10.96	10.65	10.36	10.08	58
59	11.92	11.75	**11.59**	11.27	**11.11**	10.96	**10.81**	10.66	10.38	10.11	9.84	9.59	9.35	59
60	10.74	10.60	**10.47**	10.20	**10.07**	9.95	**9.82**	9.70	9.47	9.24	9.02	8.81	8.61	60
61	9.58	9.47	**9.36**	9.15	**9.04**	8.94	**8.84**	8.74	8.55	8.37	8.19	8.02	7.85	61
62	8.44	8.36	**8.27**	8.10	**8.02**	7.94	**7.86**	7.79	7.63	7.49	7.34	7.21	7.07	62
63	7.33	7.26	**7.20**	7.07	**7.01**	6.95	**6.88**	6.83	6.71	6.60	6.49	6.38	6.27	63
64	6.23	6.18	**6.13**	6.04	**6.00**	5.95	**5.91**	5.86	5.78	5.69	5.61	5.53	5.45	64
65	5.15	5.12	**5.09**	5.02	**4.99**	4.96	**4.93**	4.90	4.84	4.78	4.72	4.67	4.61	65
66	4.09	4.07	**4.05**	4.01	**3.99**	3.97	**3.95**	3.93	3.89	3.85	3.82	3.78	3.74	66
67	3.05	3.04	**3.03**	3.00	**2.99**	2.98	**2.97**	2.96	2.94	2.91	2.89	2.87	2.85	67
68	2.02	2.02	**2.01**	2.00	**1.99**	1.99	**1.99**	1.98	1.97	1.96	1.95	1.94	1.93	68
69	1.00	1.00	**1.00**	1.00	**1.00**	1.00	**1.00**	0.99	0.99	0.99	0.99	0.98	0.98	69

Table 15 Multipliers for loss of earnings to pension age 75 (males)

Age at date of trial	Multipliers calculated with allowance for projected mortality from the 2018-based population projections and rate of return of:													Age at date of trial
	-2.0%	-1.75%	**-1.5%**	-1.0%	**-0.75%**	-0.5%	**-0.25%**	0.0%	0.5%	1.0%	1.5%	2.0%	2.5%	
16	107.97	98.96	**90.89**	77.12	**71.26**	65.97	**61.20**	56.88	49.43	43.28	38.19	33.94	30.37	16
17	104.77	96.20	**88.49**	75.33	**69.70**	64.62	**60.02**	55.86	48.66	42.70	37.75	33.60	30.11	17
18	101.64	93.48	**86.14**	73.55	**68.16**	63.28	**58.86**	54.85	47.89	42.12	37.30	33.26	29.85	18
19	98.58	90.82	**83.82**	71.80	**66.63**	61.95	**57.70**	53.83	47.12	41.52	36.85	32.91	29.58	19
20	95.58	88.21	**81.55**	70.07	**65.12**	60.62	**56.54**	52.82	46.34	40.93	36.39	32.55	29.30	20
21	92.65	85.65	**79.31**	68.35	**63.62**	59.31	**55.39**	51.81	45.56	40.33	35.92	32.19	29.02	21
22	89.78	83.13	**77.11**	66.66	**62.13**	58.01	**54.24**	50.81	44.78	39.73	35.45	31.83	28.74	22
23	86.96	80.66	**74.94**	64.98	**60.66**	56.71	**53.10**	49.80	44.00	39.11	34.98	31.45	28.44	23
24	84.21	78.24	**72.80**	63.32	**59.19**	55.42	**51.96**	48.79	43.21	38.50	34.49	31.07	28.14	24
25	81.51	75.86	**70.70**	61.68	**57.74**	54.13	**50.82**	47.79	42.42	37.88	34.00	30.68	27.83	25
26	78.87	73.52	**68.63**	60.06	**56.30**	52.86	**49.69**	46.78	41.63	37.25	33.50	30.29	27.52	26
27	76.28	71.22	**66.59**	58.45	**54.87**	51.59	**48.56**	45.77	40.83	36.61	33.00	29.89	27.20	27
28	73.75	68.97	**64.59**	56.86	**53.46**	50.33	**47.44**	44.77	40.03	35.97	32.49	29.47	26.87	28
29	71.27	66.76	**62.61**	55.29	**52.06**	49.07	**46.32**	43.77	39.23	35.33	31.97	29.06	26.53	29
30	68.84	64.59	**60.68**	53.74	**50.67**	47.83	**45.20**	42.77	38.42	34.68	31.44	28.63	26.18	30
31	66.46	62.46	**58.77**	52.20	**49.29**	46.59	**44.09**	41.77	37.61	34.02	30.91	28.20	25.83	31
32	64.14	60.37	**56.89**	50.69	**47.92**	45.36	**42.98**	40.77	36.80	33.36	30.37	27.76	25.47	32
33	61.87	58.33	**55.05**	49.19	**46.57**	44.14	**41.88**	39.78	35.99	32.70	29.83	27.31	25.10	33
34	59.64	56.32	**53.23**	47.71	**45.23**	42.93	**40.78**	38.78	35.18	32.03	29.27	26.85	24.72	34
35	57.46	54.35	**51.45**	46.24	**43.90**	41.72	**39.69**	37.79	34.36	31.35	28.72	26.39	24.34	35
36	55.33	52.41	**49.69**	44.80	**42.59**	40.53	**38.60**	36.80	33.54	30.67	28.15	25.92	23.95	36
37	53.25	50.52	**47.97**	43.37	**41.29**	39.34	**37.52**	35.82	32.72	29.99	27.58	25.44	23.55	37
38	51.21	48.66	**46.28**	41.96	**40.00**	38.17	**36.45**	34.84	31.90	29.30	27.00	24.96	23.14	38
39	49.22	46.84	**44.61**	40.56	**38.72**	37.00	**35.38**	33.85	31.07	28.61	26.42	24.46	22.72	39
40	47.27	45.06	**42.98**	39.19	**37.46**	35.84	**34.31**	32.88	30.25	27.91	25.83	23.96	22.29	40
41	45.37	43.31	**41.37**	37.83	**36.21**	34.69	**33.26**	31.90	29.42	27.21	25.23	23.45	21.86	41
42	43.51	41.59	**39.79**	36.49	**34.98**	33.55	**32.20**	30.93	28.59	26.50	24.62	22.94	21.42	42
43	41.68	39.91	**38.23**	35.16	**33.75**	32.42	**31.16**	29.96	27.76	25.79	24.01	22.41	20.96	43
44	39.90	38.26	**36.71**	33.85	**32.54**	31.29	**30.11**	29.00	26.93	25.07	23.40	21.88	20.50	44
45	38.16	36.64	**35.21**	32.56	**31.34**	30.18	**29.08**	28.03	26.10	24.35	22.77	21.34	20.03	45
46	36.45	35.06	**33.73**	31.28	**30.15**	29.07	**28.05**	27.07	25.26	23.63	22.14	20.78	19.55	46
47	34.78	33.50	**32.28**	30.02	**28.97**	27.97	**27.02**	26.11	24.43	22.89	21.50	20.22	19.06	47
48	33.15	31.97	**30.85**	28.77	**27.80**	26.88	**26.00**	25.16	23.59	22.16	20.85	19.65	18.56	48
49	31.55	30.47	**29.45**	27.54	**26.64**	25.79	**24.98**	24.20	22.75	21.41	20.19	19.07	18.05	49
50	29.99	29.01	**28.07**	26.32	**25.50**	24.71	**23.96**	23.25	21.90	20.67	19.53	18.48	17.52	50
51	28.45	27.56	**26.71**	25.11	**24.36**	23.64	**22.95**	22.29	21.05	19.91	18.86	17.89	16.99	51
52	26.96	26.15	**25.37**	23.92	**23.24**	22.58	**21.95**	21.35	20.21	19.15	18.18	17.28	16.44	52
53	25.49	24.76	**24.06**	22.74	**22.12**	21.52	**20.95**	20.40	19.35	18.39	17.49	16.66	15.88	53
54	24.06	23.40	**22.77**	21.58	**21.02**	20.48	**19.96**	19.45	18.50	17.62	16.79	16.03	15.31	54
55	22.65	22.07	**21.50**	20.43	**19.93**	19.44	**18.97**	18.51	17.65	16.84	16.09	15.39	14.73	55
56	21.29	20.76	**20.26**	19.30	**18.85**	18.41	**17.98**	17.57	16.79	16.06	15.38	14.74	14.14	56
57	19.95	19.48	**19.04**	18.19	**17.78**	17.39	**17.01**	16.64	15.94	15.28	14.66	14.08	13.53	57
58	18.64	18.23	**17.84**	17.09	**16.73**	16.38	**16.04**	15.71	15.09	14.50	13.94	13.42	12.92	58
59	17.37	17.01	**16.66**	16.00	**15.68**	15.38	**15.08**	14.79	14.23	13.71	13.21	12.74	12.30	59
60	16.12	15.81	**15.51**	14.93	**14.65**	14.39	**14.12**	13.87	13.38	12.91	12.47	12.06	11.66	60
61	14.90	14.64	**14.38**	13.88	**13.64**	13.40	**13.17**	12.95	12.52	12.12	11.73	11.36	11.01	61
62	13.71	13.49	**13.26**	12.84	**12.63**	12.43	**12.23**	12.04	11.67	11.32	10.98	10.66	10.35	62
63	12.55	12.36	**12.17**	11.81	**11.63**	11.46	**11.29**	11.13	10.81	10.51	10.22	9.94	9.68	63
64	11.41	11.25	**11.09**	10.79	**10.64**	10.50	**10.36**	10.22	9.95	9.70	9.45	9.21	8.99	64
65	10.29	10.16	**10.03**	9.78	**9.66**	9.54	**9.43**	9.31	9.09	8.88	8.67	8.47	8.28	65
66	9.20	9.09	**8.99**	8.79	**8.69**	8.59	**8.50**	8.41	8.23	8.05	7.88	7.72	7.56	66
67	8.12	8.04	**7.96**	7.80	**7.72**	7.65	**7.57**	7.50	7.36	7.22	7.08	6.95	6.82	67
68	7.07	7.01	**6.94**	6.82	**6.76**	6.70	**6.65**	6.59	6.48	6.37	6.27	6.16	6.07	68
69	6.03	5.98	**5.94**	5.85	**5.81**	5.76	**5.72**	5.68	5.60	5.52	5.44	5.36	5.29	69

Table 15 Multipliers for loss of earnings to pension age 75 (males) *continued*

Age at date of trial	Multipliers calculated with allowance for projected mortality from the 2018-based population projections and rate of return of:													Age at date of trial
	-2.0%	-1.75%	**-1.5%**	-1.0%	**-0.75%**	-0.5%	**-0.25%**	0.0%	0.5%	1.0%	1.5%	2.0%	2.5%	
70	5.00	4.97	**4.94**	4.88	**4.85**	4.82	**4.79**	4.76	4.70	4.65	4.59	4.54	4.48	70
71	3.99	3.97	**3.95**	3.91	**3.89**	3.87	**3.85**	3.83	3.80	3.76	3.72	3.69	3.65	71
72	2.99	2.98	**2.97**	2.94	**2.93**	2.92	**2.91**	2.90	2.88	2.86	2.84	2.82	2.80	72
73	1.99	1.99	**1.98**	1.97	**1.97**	1.96	**1.96**	1.95	1.94	1.93	1.92	1.91	1.90	73
74	1.00	1.00	**0.99**	0.99	**0.99**	0.99	**0.99**	0.99	0.98	0.98	0.98	0.98	0.97	74

Table 16 Multipliers for loss of earnings to pension age 75 (females)

Age at date of trial	Multipliers calculated with allowance for projected mortality from the 2018-based population projections and rate of return of:													Age at date of trial
	-2.0%	-1.75%	**-1.5%**	-1.0%	**-0.75%**	-0.5%	**-0.25%**	0.0%	0.5%	1.0%	1.5%	2.0%	2.5%	
16	109.91	100.68	**92.41**	78.32	**72.32**	66.92	**62.04**	57.63	50.03	43.77	38.58	34.25	30.62	16
17	106.69	97.90	**90.01**	76.53	**70.77**	65.57	**60.87**	56.62	49.27	43.19	38.14	33.92	30.37	17
18	103.54	95.17	**87.64**	74.75	**69.23**	64.23	**59.71**	55.61	48.51	42.62	37.70	33.59	30.12	18
19	100.45	92.49	**85.32**	72.99	**67.70**	62.91	**58.56**	54.61	47.74	42.03	37.26	33.25	29.86	19
20	97.43	89.86	**83.03**	71.25	**66.18**	61.58	**57.40**	53.60	46.97	41.44	36.81	32.90	29.59	20
21	94.47	87.28	**80.77**	69.53	**64.68**	60.27	**56.25**	52.59	46.20	40.85	36.35	32.55	29.32	21
22	91.57	84.74	**78.55**	67.83	**63.19**	58.96	**55.10**	51.58	45.42	40.25	35.89	32.19	29.04	22
23	88.72	82.25	**76.36**	66.14	**61.71**	57.66	**53.96**	50.58	44.64	39.64	35.41	31.82	28.75	23
24	85.94	79.80	**74.21**	64.48	**60.24**	56.36	**52.82**	49.57	43.86	39.03	34.94	31.44	28.45	24
25	83.21	77.39	**72.09**	62.82	**58.78**	55.07	**51.68**	48.56	43.07	38.41	34.45	31.06	28.15	25
26	80.54	75.03	**70.00**	61.19	**57.33**	53.79	**50.54**	47.56	42.28	37.79	33.96	30.67	27.84	26
27	77.92	72.71	**67.94**	59.57	**55.90**	52.52	**49.41**	46.55	41.48	37.16	33.46	30.27	27.53	27
28	75.35	70.43	**65.92**	57.97	**54.47**	51.25	**48.28**	45.55	40.68	36.52	32.95	29.87	27.20	28
29	72.84	68.20	**63.93**	56.39	**53.06**	49.99	**47.16**	44.54	39.88	35.88	32.44	29.46	26.87	29
30	70.39	66.00	**61.97**	54.83	**51.66**	48.74	**46.04**	43.54	39.08	35.24	31.92	29.04	26.53	30
31	67.98	63.85	**60.04**	53.28	**50.28**	47.50	**44.92**	42.54	38.27	34.58	31.39	28.61	26.18	31
32	65.62	61.74	**58.15**	51.75	**48.90**	46.26	**43.81**	41.54	37.46	33.93	30.85	28.17	25.83	32
33	63.32	59.66	**56.28**	50.24	**47.54**	45.03	**42.71**	40.54	36.65	33.26	30.31	27.73	25.47	33
34	61.06	57.63	**54.44**	48.74	**46.19**	43.81	**41.60**	39.54	35.83	32.60	29.76	27.28	25.09	34
35	58.85	55.63	**52.63**	47.26	**44.85**	42.60	**40.50**	38.55	35.01	31.92	29.21	26.82	24.71	35
36	56.68	53.67	**50.85**	45.80	**43.52**	41.39	**39.41**	37.55	34.19	31.24	28.64	26.35	24.33	36
37	54.56	51.74	**49.11**	44.35	**42.20**	40.20	**38.32**	36.56	33.37	30.56	28.07	25.88	23.93	37
38	52.49	49.85	**47.38**	42.92	**40.90**	39.01	**37.23**	35.57	32.54	29.86	27.50	25.39	23.52	38
39	50.46	48.00	**45.69**	41.50	**39.61**	37.82	**36.15**	34.58	31.71	29.17	26.91	24.90	23.11	39
40	48.47	46.18	**44.02**	40.11	**38.32**	36.65	**35.07**	33.59	30.88	28.46	26.32	24.40	22.68	40
41	46.53	44.39	**42.39**	38.72	**37.05**	35.48	**34.00**	32.60	30.04	27.76	25.72	23.89	22.25	41
42	44.62	42.64	**40.77**	37.36	**35.79**	34.32	**32.93**	31.62	29.20	27.04	25.11	23.37	21.80	42
43	42.76	40.92	**39.19**	36.01	**34.55**	33.17	**31.87**	30.63	28.36	26.32	24.49	22.84	21.35	43
44	40.94	39.23	**37.63**	34.67	**33.31**	32.02	**30.80**	29.65	27.52	25.60	23.87	22.30	20.89	44
45	39.15	37.58	**36.09**	33.35	**32.08**	30.89	**29.75**	28.67	26.67	24.87	23.23	21.75	20.41	45
46	37.40	35.95	**34.58**	32.04	**30.87**	29.76	**28.70**	27.69	25.82	24.13	22.59	21.20	19.93	46
47	35.69	34.36	**33.10**	30.75	**29.67**	28.63	**27.65**	26.71	24.97	23.39	21.94	20.63	19.43	47
48	34.02	32.80	**31.64**	29.48	**28.47**	27.52	**26.61**	25.74	24.12	22.64	21.29	20.05	18.92	48
49	32.38	31.26	**30.20**	28.22	**27.29**	26.41	**25.57**	24.76	23.26	21.88	20.62	19.47	18.40	49
50	30.78	29.76	**28.79**	26.97	**26.12**	25.31	**24.54**	23.79	22.40	21.12	19.95	18.87	17.88	50
51	29.21	28.29	**27.40**	25.74	**24.97**	24.22	**23.51**	22.83	21.54	20.36	19.27	18.27	17.34	51
52	27.68	26.84	**26.04**	24.53	**23.82**	23.14	**22.49**	21.86	20.68	19.59	18.58	17.65	16.78	52
53	26.18	25.42	**24.70**	23.33	**22.68**	22.06	**21.47**	20.90	19.82	18.81	17.89	17.02	16.22	53
54	24.71	24.03	**23.38**	22.14	**21.56**	21.00	**20.46**	19.94	18.95	18.03	17.18	16.39	15.65	54
55	23.28	22.67	**22.08**	20.97	**20.45**	19.94	**19.45**	18.98	18.08	17.25	16.47	15.74	15.06	55
56	21.87	21.33	**20.81**	19.82	**19.34**	18.89	**18.45**	18.02	17.21	16.46	15.75	15.08	14.46	56
57	20.50	20.02	**19.56**	18.67	**18.25**	17.85	**17.45**	17.07	16.34	15.66	15.02	14.42	13.85	57
58	19.16	18.74	**18.33**	17.55	**17.17**	16.81	**16.46**	16.12	15.47	14.86	14.28	13.74	13.23	58
59	17.85	17.48	**17.12**	16.43	**16.10**	15.78	**15.47**	15.17	14.60	14.05	13.54	13.05	12.59	59
60	16.57	16.24	**15.93**	15.33	**15.05**	14.77	**14.49**	14.23	13.72	13.24	12.78	12.35	11.94	60
61	15.31	15.03	**14.76**	14.25	**14.00**	13.75	**13.52**	13.29	12.84	12.42	12.02	11.64	11.28	61
62	14.08	13.85	**13.62**	13.17	**12.96**	12.75	**12.55**	12.35	11.96	11.60	11.25	10.92	10.60	62
63	12.88	12.68	**12.49**	12.11	**11.93**	11.75	**11.58**	11.41	11.08	10.77	10.47	10.18	9.90	63
64	11.70	11.53	**11.37**	11.06	**10.91**	10.76	**10.61**	10.47	10.19	9.93	9.67	9.43	9.19	64
65	10.54	10.41	**10.28**	10.02	**9.89**	9.77	**9.65**	9.53	9.30	9.08	8.87	8.66	8.47	65
66	9.41	9.30	**9.20**	8.99	**8.89**	8.79	**8.69**	8.60	8.41	8.23	8.05	7.89	7.72	66
67	8.30	8.22	**8.13**	7.97	**7.89**	7.81	**7.73**	7.66	7.51	7.37	7.23	7.09	6.96	67
68	7.21	7.15	**7.08**	6.96	**6.90**	6.84	**6.78**	6.72	6.61	6.49	6.39	6.28	6.18	68
69	6.14	6.09	**6.05**	5.95	**5.91**	5.87	**5.82**	5.78	5.69	5.61	5.53	5.45	5.38	69

Table 16 Multipliers for loss of earnings to pension age 75 (females) *continued*

Age at date of trial	Multipliers calculated with allowance for projected mortality from the 2018-based population projections and rate of return of:													Age at date of trial
	-2.0%	-1.75%	**-1.5%**	-1.0%	**-0.75%**	-0.5%	**-0.25%**	0.0%	0.5%	1.0%	1.5%	2.0%	2.5%	
70	5.08	5.05	**5.02**	4.96	**4.93**	4.90	**4.86**	4.83	4.78	4.72	4.66	4.61	4.55	70
71	4.05	4.02	**4.00**	3.96	**3.94**	3.92	**3.91**	3.89	3.85	3.81	3.77	3.74	3.70	71
72	3.02	3.01	**3.00**	2.97	**2.96**	2.95	**2.94**	2.93	2.91	2.89	2.87	2.85	2.83	72
73	2.01	2.00	**2.00**	1.99	**1.98**	1.98	**1.97**	1.97	1.96	1.95	1.94	1.93	1.92	73
74	1.00	1.00	**1.00**	1.00	**0.99**	0.99	**0.99**	0.99	0.99	0.99	0.98	0.98	0.98	74

Table 17 Multipliers for loss of earnings to pension age 80 (males)

Age at date of trial	Multipliers calculated with allowance for projected mortality from the 2018-based population projections and rate of return of:													Age at date of trial
	-2.0%	-1.75%	**-1.5%**	-1.0%	**-0.75%**	-0.5%	**-0.25%**	0.0%	0.5%	1.0%	1.5%	2.0%	2.5%	
16	121.96	110.93	**101.12**	84.62	**77.68**	71.47	**65.91**	60.92	52.40	45.48	39.81	35.13	31.25	16
17	118.45	107.92	**98.55**	82.73	**76.06**	70.08	**64.71**	59.89	51.64	44.91	39.39	34.82	31.02	17
18	115.01	104.97	**96.02**	80.86	**74.45**	68.70	**63.52**	58.87	50.88	44.34	38.96	34.50	30.77	18
19	111.65	102.08	**93.53**	79.02	**72.86**	67.32	**62.34**	57.84	50.11	43.77	38.53	34.17	30.52	19
20	108.36	99.25	**91.09**	77.20	**71.29**	65.96	**61.16**	56.82	49.35	43.19	38.09	33.84	30.27	20
21	105.14	96.47	**88.68**	75.40	**69.73**	64.61	**59.99**	55.81	48.58	42.61	37.65	33.50	30.01	21
22	101.99	93.74	**86.32**	73.61	**68.18**	63.27	**58.82**	54.79	47.81	42.02	37.20	33.16	29.75	22
23	98.91	91.06	**83.99**	71.85	**66.64**	61.93	**57.65**	53.77	47.03	41.43	36.74	32.81	29.48	23
24	95.89	88.43	**81.70**	70.11	**65.12**	60.60	**56.49**	52.76	46.25	40.83	36.28	32.45	29.20	24
25	92.93	85.84	**79.44**	68.38	**63.61**	59.28	**55.33**	51.74	45.47	40.22	35.81	32.08	28.92	25
26	90.03	83.31	**77.22**	66.68	**62.11**	57.96	**54.18**	50.72	44.68	39.61	35.34	31.71	28.63	26
27	87.19	80.82	**75.03**	64.99	**60.63**	56.65	**53.03**	49.71	43.89	39.00	34.85	31.33	28.33	27
28	84.41	78.37	**72.88**	63.32	**59.16**	55.36	**51.88**	48.70	43.10	38.37	34.37	30.95	28.02	28
29	81.69	75.97	**70.76**	61.67	**57.70**	54.06	**50.74**	47.68	42.30	37.75	33.87	30.56	27.71	29
30	79.03	73.62	**68.68**	60.03	**56.25**	52.78	**49.60**	46.67	41.51	37.12	33.37	30.16	27.39	30
31	76.43	71.32	**66.64**	58.42	**54.82**	51.51	**48.47**	45.67	40.71	36.48	32.86	29.75	27.07	31
32	73.89	69.05	**64.62**	56.83	**53.40**	50.24	**47.34**	44.66	39.90	35.84	32.35	29.34	26.74	32
33	71.40	66.83	**62.65**	55.25	**51.99**	48.99	**46.22**	43.66	39.10	35.19	31.83	28.92	26.40	33
34	68.96	64.66	**60.70**	53.70	**50.60**	47.74	**45.10**	42.65	38.29	34.54	31.30	28.49	26.05	34
35	66.58	62.52	**58.79**	52.16	**49.22**	46.50	**43.99**	41.66	37.49	33.89	30.77	28.06	25.69	35
36	64.24	60.43	**56.91**	50.64	**47.86**	45.28	**42.88**	40.66	36.68	33.23	30.23	27.62	25.33	36
37	61.96	58.38	**55.06**	49.14	**46.51**	44.06	**41.78**	39.66	35.86	32.56	29.69	27.17	24.96	37
38	59.74	56.37	**53.25**	47.66	**45.17**	42.85	**40.69**	38.67	35.05	31.89	29.13	26.72	24.59	38
39	57.56	54.40	**51.46**	46.20	**43.84**	41.65	**39.60**	37.69	34.24	31.22	28.58	26.25	24.20	39
40	55.43	52.47	**49.71**	44.76	**42.53**	40.46	**38.52**	36.70	33.42	30.55	28.02	25.79	23.81	40
41	53.35	50.58	**47.99**	43.34	**41.24**	39.27	**37.44**	35.72	32.61	29.87	27.45	25.31	23.41	41
42	51.31	48.72	**46.30**	41.93	**39.95**	38.10	**36.37**	34.74	31.79	29.18	26.87	24.83	23.01	42
43	49.32	46.90	**44.64**	40.54	**38.68**	36.94	**35.31**	33.77	30.97	28.49	26.29	24.34	22.59	43
44	47.38	45.12	**43.01**	39.17	**37.43**	35.79	**34.25**	32.80	30.15	27.80	25.71	23.84	22.17	44
45	45.48	43.38	**41.41**	37.82	**36.18**	34.65	**33.20**	31.83	29.33	27.10	25.11	23.33	21.74	45
46	43.61	41.67	**39.83**	36.48	**34.95**	33.51	**32.15**	30.87	28.51	26.40	24.51	22.82	21.30	46
47	41.79	39.99	**38.28**	35.16	**33.73**	32.38	**31.11**	29.90	27.68	25.69	23.91	22.30	20.85	47
48	40.01	38.34	**36.76**	33.86	**32.53**	31.26	**30.07**	28.94	26.86	24.98	23.29	21.77	20.39	48
49	38.27	36.73	**35.26**	32.57	**31.33**	30.15	**29.04**	27.98	26.03	24.27	22.67	21.23	19.92	49
50	36.57	35.14	**33.79**	31.30	**30.15**	29.05	**28.01**	27.03	25.20	23.54	22.04	20.68	19.44	50
51	34.90	33.59	**32.35**	30.04	**28.97**	27.96	**26.99**	26.07	24.37	22.82	21.41	20.12	18.95	51
52	33.28	32.07	**30.93**	28.80	**27.81**	26.87	**25.98**	25.12	23.53	22.09	20.77	19.56	18.46	52
53	31.68	30.58	**29.53**	27.57	**26.66**	25.80	**24.97**	24.18	22.70	21.35	20.12	18.99	17.95	53
54	30.13	29.12	**28.16**	26.36	**25.53**	24.73	**23.96**	23.23	21.86	20.61	19.46	18.40	17.43	54
55	28.61	27.69	**26.81**	25.17	**24.41**	23.67	**22.97**	22.29	21.03	19.87	18.80	17.81	16.90	55
56	27.12	26.29	**25.49**	24.00	**23.30**	22.62	**21.98**	21.36	20.20	19.12	18.13	17.22	16.37	56
57	25.68	24.92	**24.20**	22.84	**22.20**	21.59	**21.00**	20.43	19.36	18.38	17.46	16.61	15.82	57
58	24.27	23.59	**22.93**	21.70	**21.12**	20.56	**20.03**	19.51	18.53	17.63	16.78	16.00	15.27	58
59	22.89	22.28	**21.70**	20.58	**20.06**	19.55	**19.07**	18.60	17.71	16.88	16.10	15.38	14.71	59
60	21.55	21.01	**20.48**	19.48	**19.01**	18.55	**18.11**	17.69	16.88	16.13	15.42	14.76	14.14	60
61	20.25	19.76	**19.29**	18.40	**17.98**	17.57	**17.17**	16.79	16.06	15.37	14.73	14.13	13.57	61
62	18.98	18.55	**18.13**	17.33	**16.96**	16.59	**16.24**	15.89	15.24	14.62	14.04	13.50	12.98	62
63	17.74	17.36	**16.99**	16.29	**15.95**	15.62	**15.31**	15.00	14.42	13.87	13.34	12.85	12.39	63
64	16.52	16.19	**15.87**	15.25	**14.96**	14.67	**14.39**	14.12	13.60	13.11	12.64	12.20	11.79	64
65	15.34	15.05	**14.77**	14.23	**13.98**	13.72	**13.48**	13.24	12.78	12.35	11.94	11.54	11.17	65
66	14.19	13.94	**13.70**	13.23	**13.01**	12.79	**12.58**	12.37	11.97	11.59	11.22	10.88	10.55	66
67	13.06	12.85	**12.64**	12.24	**12.05**	11.86	**11.68**	11.50	11.15	10.82	10.51	10.20	9.92	67
68	11.96	11.78	**11.61**	11.27	**11.10**	10.94	**10.79**	10.63	10.34	10.05	9.78	9.52	9.27	68
69	10.89	10.74	**10.59**	10.31	**10.17**	10.03	**9.90**	9.77	9.52	9.28	9.05	8.83	8.61	69

Table 17 Multipliers for loss of earnings to pension age 80 (males) *continued*

Age at date of trial	Multipliers calculated with allowance for projected mortality from the 2018-based population projections and rate of return of:													Age at date of trial
	-2.0%	-1.75%	**-1.5%**	-1.0%	**-0.75%**	-0.5%	**-0.25%**	0.0%	0.5%	1.0%	1.5%	2.0%	2.5%	
70	9.83	9.71	**9.59**	9.36	**9.24**	9.13	**9.02**	8.91	8.71	8.50	8.31	8.12	7.94	70
71	8.80	8.70	**8.60**	8.41	**8.32**	8.23	**8.14**	8.06	7.89	7.72	7.56	7.41	7.26	71
72	7.78	7.71	**7.63**	7.48	**7.41**	7.34	**7.27**	7.20	7.06	6.93	6.80	6.68	6.56	72
73	6.79	6.73	**6.67**	6.56	**6.50**	6.44	**6.39**	6.34	6.23	6.13	6.03	5.93	5.84	73
74	5.80	5.76	**5.72**	5.63	**5.59**	5.55	**5.51**	5.47	5.39	5.32	5.24	5.17	5.10	74
75	4.83	4.80	**4.77**	4.72	**4.69**	4.66	**4.63**	4.60	4.55	4.49	4.44	4.39	4.34	75
76	3.87	3.85	**3.83**	3.80	**3.78**	3.76	**3.74**	3.72	3.69	3.65	3.62	3.58	3.55	76
77	2.92	2.90	**2.89**	2.87	**2.86**	2.85	**2.84**	2.83	2.81	2.79	2.77	2.75	2.73	77
78	1.96	1.95	**1.95**	1.94	**1.93**	1.93	**1.92**	1.92	1.91	1.90	1.89	1.88	1.87	78
79	0.99	0.99	**0.98**	0.98	**0.98**	0.98	**0.98**	0.98	0.97	0.97	0.97	0.97	0.97	79

Table 18 Multipliers for loss of earnings to pension age 80 (females)

Age at date of trial	Multipliers calculated with allowance for projected mortality from the 2018-based population projections and rate of return of:													Age at date of trial
	-2.0%	-1.75%	**-1.5%**	-1.0%	**-0.75%**	-0.5%	**-0.25%**	0.0%	0.5%	1.0%	1.5%	2.0%	2.5%	
16	124.91	113.50	**103.38**	86.36	**79.20**	72.81	**67.09**	61.96	53.22	46.12	40.31	35.53	31.57	16
17	121.37	110.48	**100.79**	84.47	**77.59**	71.43	**65.90**	60.95	52.47	45.56	39.90	35.23	31.34	17
18	117.90	107.51	**98.25**	82.60	**75.98**	70.05	**64.72**	59.93	51.72	45.00	39.49	34.92	31.11	18
19	114.50	104.60	**95.75**	80.75	**74.39**	68.68	**63.54**	58.91	50.96	44.44	39.06	34.60	30.87	19
20	111.17	101.73	**93.28**	78.92	**72.82**	67.32	**62.37**	57.90	50.20	43.87	38.64	34.28	30.63	20
21	107.92	98.92	**90.86**	77.11	**71.25**	65.97	**61.20**	56.89	49.44	43.30	38.20	33.95	30.38	21
22	104.72	96.16	**88.47**	75.32	**69.70**	64.62	**60.03**	55.87	48.67	42.72	37.76	33.62	30.13	22
23	101.59	93.45	**86.12**	73.55	**68.16**	63.28	**58.86**	54.86	47.90	42.13	37.32	33.28	29.86	23
24	98.53	90.79	**83.80**	71.79	**66.63**	61.95	**57.70**	53.84	47.13	41.54	36.86	32.93	29.60	24
25	95.53	88.17	**81.52**	70.05	**65.11**	60.62	**56.54**	52.83	46.35	40.94	36.40	32.57	29.32	25
26	92.59	85.60	**79.27**	68.34	**63.61**	59.31	**55.39**	51.82	45.57	40.34	35.94	32.21	29.04	26
27	89.71	83.08	**77.06**	66.63	**62.11**	57.99	**54.24**	50.80	44.79	39.73	35.46	31.84	28.75	27
28	86.89	80.60	**74.89**	64.95	**60.63**	56.69	**53.09**	49.79	44.00	39.12	34.98	31.46	28.45	28
29	84.13	78.17	**72.75**	63.29	**59.17**	55.40	**51.94**	48.78	43.21	38.50	34.50	31.08	28.15	29
30	81.43	75.79	**70.64**	61.64	**57.71**	54.11	**50.81**	47.77	42.42	37.87	34.00	30.69	27.84	30
31	78.78	73.45	**68.57**	60.02	**56.27**	52.83	**49.67**	46.76	41.62	37.24	33.50	30.29	27.53	31
32	76.19	71.15	**66.53**	58.41	**54.84**	51.56	**48.54**	45.76	40.82	36.61	33.00	29.89	27.20	32
33	73.66	68.90	**64.52**	56.82	**53.42**	50.30	**47.41**	44.75	40.02	35.97	32.49	29.48	26.87	33
34	71.18	66.68	**62.55**	55.25	**52.02**	49.04	**46.29**	43.75	39.22	35.32	31.97	29.06	26.53	34
35	68.75	64.51	**60.61**	53.69	**50.63**	47.79	**45.17**	42.74	38.41	34.67	31.44	28.63	26.19	35
36	66.37	62.38	**58.70**	52.15	**49.25**	46.55	**44.06**	41.74	37.60	34.02	30.91	28.20	25.83	36
37	64.05	60.29	**56.82**	50.63	**47.88**	45.32	**42.95**	40.74	36.79	33.35	30.37	27.76	25.47	37
38	61.77	58.24	**54.97**	49.13	**46.52**	44.10	**41.84**	39.75	35.97	32.69	29.82	27.31	25.10	38
39	59.54	56.23	**53.15**	47.65	**45.18**	42.88	**40.74**	38.75	35.15	32.01	29.26	26.85	24.72	39
40	57.36	54.25	**51.37**	46.18	**43.85**	41.68	**39.65**	37.76	34.33	31.34	28.70	26.38	24.33	40
41	55.22	52.32	**49.61**	44.73	**42.53**	40.48	**38.56**	36.76	33.51	30.65	28.13	25.91	23.94	41
42	53.13	50.42	**47.88**	43.29	**41.22**	39.29	**37.47**	35.77	32.68	29.96	27.56	25.43	23.54	42
43	51.09	48.55	**46.18**	41.88	**39.93**	38.10	**36.39**	34.78	31.86	29.27	26.98	24.94	23.12	43
44	49.09	46.72	**44.50**	40.47	**38.64**	36.93	**35.31**	33.80	31.03	28.57	26.39	24.44	22.70	44
45	47.13	44.93	**42.86**	39.09	**37.37**	35.76	**34.24**	32.81	30.19	27.87	25.79	23.93	22.27	45
46	45.22	43.17	**41.24**	37.72	**36.11**	34.60	**33.17**	31.83	29.36	27.16	25.18	23.42	21.83	46
47	43.34	41.44	**39.65**	36.37	**34.87**	33.45	**32.11**	30.85	28.52	26.44	24.57	22.89	21.38	47
48	41.51	39.75	**38.08**	35.03	**33.63**	32.31	**31.05**	29.87	27.68	25.72	23.95	22.36	20.92	48
49	39.72	38.09	**36.55**	33.71	**32.41**	31.17	**30.00**	28.89	26.84	24.99	23.33	21.82	20.45	49
50	37.97	36.46	**35.04**	32.41	**31.20**	30.05	**28.96**	27.92	26.00	24.26	22.69	21.27	19.97	50
51	36.25	34.87	**33.55**	31.12	**30.00**	28.93	**27.92**	26.95	25.16	23.53	22.05	20.71	19.48	51
52	34.58	33.30	**32.10**	29.85	**28.81**	27.82	**26.88**	25.98	24.31	22.79	21.41	20.14	18.99	52
53	32.94	31.77	**30.66**	28.60	**27.64**	26.73	**25.85**	25.02	23.47	22.05	20.75	19.57	18.48	53
54	31.34	30.27	**29.26**	27.36	**26.48**	25.64	**24.83**	24.06	22.62	21.30	20.09	18.98	17.96	54
55	29.77	28.80	**27.88**	26.14	**25.33**	24.56	**23.81**	23.10	21.77	20.55	19.42	18.39	17.43	55
56	28.25	27.36	**26.52**	24.94	**24.20**	23.49	**22.81**	22.15	20.92	19.79	18.75	17.79	16.89	56
57	26.75	25.96	**25.19**	23.75	**23.07**	22.43	**21.80**	21.20	20.08	19.03	18.07	17.18	16.35	57
58	25.30	24.58	**23.88**	22.58	**21.97**	21.37	**20.81**	20.26	19.23	18.27	17.38	16.56	15.79	58
59	23.87	23.22	**22.60**	21.42	**20.87**	20.33	**19.82**	19.32	18.38	17.50	16.69	15.93	15.22	59
60	22.48	21.90	**21.34**	20.29	**19.79**	19.30	**18.84**	18.39	17.53	16.73	15.99	15.29	14.64	60
61	21.12	20.61	**20.11**	19.16	**18.71**	18.28	**17.86**	17.45	16.68	15.96	15.28	14.65	14.05	61
62	19.80	19.34	**18.90**	18.05	**17.65**	17.27	**16.89**	16.53	15.83	15.18	14.57	13.99	13.45	62
63	18.50	18.10	**17.71**	16.96	**16.61**	16.26	**15.93**	15.60	14.98	14.40	13.85	13.33	12.84	63
64	17.23	16.88	**16.54**	15.88	**15.57**	15.27	**14.97**	14.68	14.13	13.61	13.12	12.66	12.22	64
65	15.99	15.68	**15.39**	14.82	**14.54**	14.28	**14.02**	13.77	13.28	12.82	12.39	11.97	11.58	65
66	14.78	14.52	**14.26**	13.77	**13.53**	13.30	**13.07**	12.85	12.43	12.03	11.65	11.28	10.93	66
67	13.59	13.37	**13.15**	12.73	**12.53**	12.33	**12.13**	11.94	11.58	11.23	10.90	10.58	10.27	67
68	12.44	12.25	**12.06**	11.70	**11.53**	11.36	**11.20**	11.04	10.72	10.42	10.14	9.86	9.60	68
69	11.30	11.15	**10.99**	10.69	**10.55**	10.41	**10.27**	10.13	9.87	9.61	9.37	9.14	8.91	69

Table 18 Multipliers for loss of earnings to pension age 80 (females) *continued*

Age at date of trial	Multipliers calculated with allowance for projected mortality from the 2018-based population projections and rate of return of:													Age at date of trial
	-2.0%	-1.75%	**-1.5%**	-1.0%	**-0.75%**	-0.5%	**-0.25%**	0.0%	0.5%	1.0%	1.5%	2.0%	2.5%	
70	10.19	10.06	**9.94**	9.69	**9.57**	9.46	**9.34**	9.23	9.01	8.80	8.60	8.40	8.21	70
71	9.11	9.00	**8.90**	8.70	**8.61**	8.51	**8.42**	8.33	8.15	7.98	7.81	7.65	7.49	71
72	8.04	7.96	**7.88**	7.72	**7.65**	7.57	**7.50**	7.43	7.28	7.15	7.01	6.88	6.76	72
73	7.00	6.93	**6.87**	6.75	**6.69**	6.64	**6.58**	6.52	6.42	6.31	6.21	6.10	6.01	73
74	5.97	5.92	**5.88**	5.79	**5.75**	5.70	**5.66**	5.62	5.54	5.46	5.38	5.31	5.24	74
75	4.95	4.92	**4.89**	4.83	**4.80**	4.77	**4.74**	4.71	4.66	4.60	4.55	4.49	4.44	75
76	3.96	3.94	**3.92**	3.88	**3.86**	3.84	**3.82**	3.80	3.76	3.73	3.69	3.66	3.62	76
77	2.97	2.95	**2.94**	2.92	**2.91**	2.90	**2.89**	2.88	2.86	2.84	2.82	2.80	2.78	77
78	1.98	1.97	**1.97**	1.96	**1.95**	1.95	**1.95**	1.94	1.93	1.92	1.91	1.90	1.89	78
79	0.99	0.99	**0.99**	0.99	**0.99**	0.99	**0.98**	0.98	0.98	0.98	0.98	0.97	0.97	79

Table 19 Multipliers for loss of pension commencing age 50 (males)

Age at date of trial	Multipliers calculated with allowance for projected mortality from the 2018-based population projections and rate of return of:													Age at date of trial
	-2.0%	-1.75%	**-1.5%**	-1.0%	**-0.75%**	-0.5%	**-0.25%**	0.0%	0.5%	1.0%	1.5%	2.0%	2.5%	
0	169.44	140.02	**115.90**	79.81	**66.39**	55.32	**46.17**	38.59	27.09	19.13	13.59	9.71	6.98	0
1	166.05	137.58	**114.18**	79.05	**65.94**	55.08	**46.09**	38.63	27.26	19.35	13.81	9.92	7.16	1
2	162.19	134.74	**112.13**	78.04	**65.26**	54.67	**45.86**	38.54	27.33	19.50	14.00	10.10	7.33	2
3	158.38	131.93	**110.08**	77.02	**64.58**	54.23	**45.61**	38.43	27.40	19.65	14.18	10.28	7.50	3
4	154.65	129.17	**108.07**	76.02	**63.90**	53.80	**45.38**	38.32	27.47	19.80	14.36	10.47	7.67	4
5	151.00	126.46	**106.09**	75.01	**63.23**	53.38	**45.14**	38.23	27.53	19.96	14.55	10.65	7.85	5
6	147.44	123.81	**104.14**	74.03	**62.56**	52.96	**44.90**	38.12	27.61	20.10	14.73	10.85	8.04	6
7	143.96	121.22	**102.23**	73.06	**61.91**	52.54	**44.66**	38.02	27.67	20.26	14.92	11.05	8.22	7
8	140.56	118.67	**100.34**	72.09	**61.26**	52.12	**44.41**	37.91	27.74	20.41	15.11	11.24	8.40	8
9	137.24	116.17	**98.49**	71.15	**60.60**	51.70	**44.17**	37.81	27.81	20.57	15.30	11.44	8.61	9
10	133.99	113.73	**96.67**	70.20	**59.96**	51.29	**43.94**	37.70	27.87	20.72	15.50	11.65	8.80	10
11	130.80	111.32	**94.89**	69.27	**59.32**	50.88	**43.70**	37.59	27.93	20.88	15.69	11.86	9.00	11
12	127.70	108.97	**93.14**	68.35	**58.68**	50.47	**43.46**	37.49	28.00	21.03	15.89	12.07	9.21	12
13	124.67	106.67	**91.41**	67.44	**58.06**	50.06	**43.22**	37.38	28.06	21.20	16.09	12.28	9.42	13
14	121.71	104.42	**89.72**	66.55	**57.44**	49.66	**42.99**	37.27	28.13	21.35	16.30	12.50	9.64	14
15	118.81	102.20	**88.05**	65.66	**56.83**	49.25	**42.75**	37.16	28.20	21.51	16.50	12.73	9.86	15
16	115.99	100.04	**86.42**	64.78	**56.21**	48.85	**42.52**	37.05	28.26	21.67	16.71	12.95	10.08	16
17	113.23	97.93	**84.82**	63.93	**55.62**	48.46	**42.29**	36.95	28.33	21.84	16.92	13.18	10.31	17
18	110.54	95.87	**83.26**	63.08	**55.03**	48.08	**42.06**	36.85	28.40	22.00	17.14	13.42	10.55	18
19	107.93	93.84	**81.72**	62.25	**54.44**	47.69	**41.83**	36.75	28.46	22.17	17.35	13.66	10.79	19
20	105.37	91.87	**80.21**	61.43	**53.86**	47.31	**41.60**	36.64	28.54	22.34	17.58	13.90	11.04	20
21	102.88	89.94	**78.74**	60.62	**53.30**	46.93	**41.38**	36.54	28.61	22.51	17.80	14.15	11.31	21
22	100.45	88.05	**77.29**	59.82	**52.74**	46.56	**41.17**	36.44	28.68	22.68	18.03	14.41	11.56	22
23	98.07	86.20	**75.87**	59.03	**52.18**	46.20	**40.94**	36.34	28.75	22.86	18.26	14.66	11.84	23
24	95.75	84.39	**74.48**	58.25	**51.63**	45.83	**40.73**	36.24	28.82	23.03	18.50	14.93	12.10	24
25	93.49	82.61	**73.11**	57.50	**51.09**	45.47	**40.51**	36.15	28.89	23.21	18.73	15.20	12.38	25
26	91.29	80.88	**71.76**	56.73	**50.55**	45.10	**40.30**	36.05	28.96	23.39	18.98	15.48	12.67	26
27	89.13	79.18	**70.45**	55.99	**50.02**	44.74	**40.09**	35.95	29.03	23.57	19.23	15.75	12.97	27
28	87.03	77.52	**69.16**	55.26	**49.50**	44.39	**39.88**	35.85	29.11	23.75	19.47	16.04	13.27	28
29	84.98	75.90	**67.89**	54.54	**48.98**	44.05	**39.66**	35.77	29.18	23.94	19.73	16.33	13.57	29
30	82.98	74.32	**66.65**	53.83	**48.47**	43.71	**39.46**	35.67	29.26	24.12	19.98	16.62	13.89	30
31	81.03	72.77	**65.43**	53.13	**47.97**	43.37	**39.26**	35.58	29.34	24.31	20.24	16.93	14.22	31
32	79.13	71.26	**64.25**	52.44	**47.47**	43.03	**39.06**	35.50	29.42	24.51	20.51	17.23	14.55	32
33	77.28	69.77	**63.08**	51.77	**46.99**	42.70	**38.87**	35.41	29.51	24.71	20.78	17.56	14.90	33
34	75.48	68.33	**61.95**	51.11	**46.51**	42.38	**38.67**	35.33	29.59	24.90	21.05	17.88	15.25	34
35	73.73	66.92	**60.82**	50.45	**46.04**	42.06	**38.48**	35.24	29.67	25.10	21.33	18.21	15.60	35
36	72.01	65.55	**59.73**	49.81	**45.58**	41.75	**38.30**	35.16	29.76	25.31	21.62	18.55	15.97	36
37	70.35	64.21	**58.67**	49.18	**45.12**	41.44	**38.11**	35.09	29.86	25.51	21.91	18.90	16.35	37
38	68.73	62.90	**57.64**	48.57	**44.68**	41.14	**37.94**	35.02	29.95	25.74	22.20	19.25	16.75	38
39	67.16	61.62	**56.62**	47.97	**44.24**	40.85	**37.76**	34.95	30.05	25.96	22.52	19.60	17.15	39
40	65.63	60.37	**55.63**	47.38	**43.81**	40.56	**37.60**	34.89	30.15	26.18	22.82	19.99	17.56	40
41	64.14	59.17	**54.65**	46.80	**43.40**	40.28	**37.44**	34.83	30.26	26.40	23.14	20.36	18.00	41
42	62.69	57.99	**53.71**	46.25	**42.99**	40.01	**37.28**	34.77	30.37	26.64	23.47	20.76	18.44	42
43	61.29	56.85	**52.79**	45.69	**42.59**	39.74	**37.13**	34.73	30.49	26.88	23.80	21.16	18.89	43
44	59.92	55.72	**51.89**	45.16	**42.20**	39.48	**36.98**	34.69	30.61	27.12	24.14	21.57	19.35	44
45	58.59	54.63	**51.02**	44.63	**41.82**	39.24	**36.85**	34.65	30.73	27.38	24.49	22.00	19.83	45
46	57.30	53.58	**50.16**	44.12	**41.45**	38.99	**36.71**	34.61	30.86	27.64	24.85	22.43	20.33	46
47	56.05	52.55	**49.32**	43.62	**41.09**	38.75	**36.59**	34.58	30.99	27.91	25.22	22.88	20.84	47
48	54.82	51.54	**48.51**	43.13	**40.74**	38.52	**36.46**	34.56	31.14	28.18	25.59	23.34	21.36	48
49	53.64	50.57	**47.72**	42.66	**40.40**	38.30	**36.35**	34.54	31.28	28.46	25.98	23.81	21.91	49
50	52.50	49.62	**46.95**	42.19	**40.06**	38.08	**36.24**	34.53	31.44	28.74	26.38	24.30	22.47	50

Table 20 Multipliers for loss of pension commencing age 50 (females)

Age at date of trial	Multipliers calculated with allowance for projected mortality from the 2018-based population projections and rate of return of:													Age at date of trial
	-2.0%	-1.75%	**-1.5%**	-1.0%	**-0.75%**	-0.5%	**-0.25%**	0.0%	0.5%	1.0%	1.5%	2.0%	2.5%	
0	183.15	151.02	**124.73**	85.52	**71.00**	59.03	**49.17**	41.02	28.69	20.19	14.30	10.18	7.30	0
1	179.48	148.37	**122.87**	84.70	**70.50**	58.77	**49.08**	41.06	28.86	20.42	14.54	10.40	7.49	1
2	175.40	145.39	**120.72**	83.66	**69.81**	58.35	**48.86**	40.98	28.95	20.59	14.72	10.60	7.67	2
3	171.39	142.44	**118.59**	82.60	**69.12**	57.93	**48.62**	40.88	29.04	20.76	14.93	10.80	7.85	3
4	167.46	139.54	**116.49**	81.58	**68.44**	57.50	**48.40**	40.79	29.13	20.92	15.12	11.00	8.03	4
5	163.61	136.71	**114.42**	80.54	**67.75**	57.08	**48.17**	40.71	29.22	21.10	15.33	11.19	8.23	5
6	159.85	133.92	**112.38**	79.53	**67.08**	56.65	**47.93**	40.62	29.30	21.27	15.52	11.40	8.42	6
7	156.18	131.19	**110.38**	78.53	**66.40**	56.24	**47.71**	40.53	29.38	21.44	15.73	11.61	8.61	7
8	152.58	128.51	**108.42**	77.54	**65.74**	55.82	**47.47**	40.44	29.47	21.62	15.94	11.82	8.82	8
9	149.06	125.89	**106.49**	76.57	**65.07**	55.40	**47.24**	40.34	29.56	21.79	16.15	12.04	9.03	9
10	145.62	123.31	**104.58**	75.60	**64.42**	54.99	**47.01**	40.25	29.64	21.96	16.36	12.26	9.24	10
11	142.27	120.78	**102.71**	74.63	**63.78**	54.58	**46.78**	40.16	29.73	22.13	16.58	12.49	9.45	11
12	138.98	118.31	**100.88**	73.69	**63.13**	54.17	**46.55**	40.07	29.81	22.32	16.79	12.71	9.67	12
13	135.77	115.88	**99.07**	72.76	**62.50**	53.77	**46.33**	39.97	29.90	22.50	17.02	12.94	9.90	13
14	132.63	113.50	**97.30**	71.83	**61.86**	53.36	**46.10**	39.88	29.99	22.67	17.24	13.18	10.13	14
15	129.56	111.18	**95.56**	70.92	**61.24**	52.96	**45.87**	39.79	30.08	22.86	17.47	13.42	10.37	15
16	126.57	108.90	**93.84**	70.02	**60.62**	52.56	**45.64**	39.70	30.16	23.04	17.70	13.67	10.61	16
17	123.64	106.67	**92.17**	69.13	**60.01**	52.17	**45.43**	39.61	30.24	23.22	17.93	13.92	10.86	17
18	120.78	104.48	**90.52**	68.26	**59.41**	51.78	**45.20**	39.52	30.33	23.42	18.17	14.17	11.11	18
19	118.00	102.34	**88.90**	67.39	**58.81**	51.40	**44.98**	39.42	30.41	23.60	18.41	14.44	11.37	19
20	115.27	100.24	**87.31**	66.54	**58.21**	51.01	**44.76**	39.33	30.50	23.79	18.65	14.70	11.64	20
21	112.60	98.19	**85.74**	65.69	**57.63**	50.63	**44.54**	39.25	30.59	23.98	18.89	14.97	11.92	21
22	110.00	96.18	**84.21**	64.86	**57.05**	50.25	**44.33**	39.15	30.68	24.18	19.15	15.24	12.20	22
23	107.46	94.20	**82.70**	64.04	**56.47**	49.87	**44.11**	39.06	30.77	24.37	19.40	15.52	12.49	23
24	104.97	92.27	**81.22**	63.23	**55.90**	49.49	**43.89**	38.98	30.86	24.56	19.65	15.81	12.78	24
25	102.54	90.37	**79.77**	62.42	**55.34**	49.12	**43.67**	38.88	30.95	24.76	19.92	16.10	13.08	25
26	100.17	88.52	**78.34**	61.63	**54.78**	48.76	**43.46**	38.79	31.03	24.96	20.18	16.40	13.38	26
27	97.85	86.70	**76.93**	60.85	**54.22**	48.39	**43.25**	38.71	31.13	25.16	20.44	16.69	13.69	27
28	95.59	84.92	**75.56**	60.07	**53.67**	48.04	**43.04**	38.61	31.22	25.37	20.71	17.00	14.02	28
29	93.38	83.18	**74.21**	59.31	**53.13**	47.67	**42.83**	38.53	31.30	25.57	20.99	17.31	14.35	29
30	91.22	81.48	**72.88**	58.56	**52.60**	47.32	**42.62**	38.44	31.40	25.78	21.27	17.63	14.68	30
31	89.12	79.81	**71.58**	57.82	**52.07**	46.97	**42.41**	38.36	31.49	25.99	21.55	17.95	15.03	31
32	87.07	78.18	**70.31**	57.10	**51.56**	46.62	**42.21**	38.27	31.59	26.20	21.84	18.29	15.39	32
33	85.06	76.59	**69.06**	56.38	**51.05**	46.28	**42.01**	38.19	31.68	26.41	22.13	18.63	15.75	33
34	83.10	75.03	**67.84**	55.67	**50.53**	45.93	**41.82**	38.11	31.77	26.64	22.43	18.98	16.13	34
35	81.20	73.51	**66.63**	54.97	**50.04**	45.61	**41.62**	38.03	31.87	26.86	22.72	19.33	16.50	35
36	79.34	72.01	**65.46**	54.29	**49.55**	45.28	**41.43**	37.95	31.98	27.08	23.04	19.69	16.90	36
37	77.52	70.56	**64.29**	53.62	**49.05**	44.95	**41.23**	37.88	32.08	27.31	23.35	20.05	17.30	37
38	75.75	69.12	**63.16**	52.95	**48.58**	44.62	**41.05**	37.80	32.19	27.53	23.66	20.43	17.72	38
39	74.02	67.73	**62.06**	52.30	**48.11**	44.30	**40.86**	37.73	32.29	27.77	23.99	20.82	18.14	39
40	72.35	66.37	**60.97**	51.66	**47.64**	44.00	**40.68**	37.66	32.40	28.00	24.32	21.20	18.57	40
41	70.70	65.04	**59.91**	51.03	**47.19**	43.69	**40.50**	37.60	32.51	28.24	24.65	21.61	19.03	41
42	69.11	63.74	**58.87**	50.41	**46.73**	43.39	**40.33**	37.53	32.62	28.49	24.99	22.02	19.48	42
43	67.54	62.47	**57.85**	49.80	**46.29**	43.09	**40.16**	37.47	32.74	28.74	25.34	22.44	19.96	43
44	66.03	61.23	**56.85**	49.20	**45.86**	42.80	**39.99**	37.41	32.85	28.99	25.69	22.87	20.44	44
45	64.55	60.02	**55.87**	48.62	**45.43**	42.51	**39.83**	37.36	32.98	29.25	26.06	23.31	20.94	45
46	63.12	58.84	**54.93**	48.04	**45.02**	42.23	**39.67**	37.30	33.10	29.51	26.43	23.76	21.45	46
47	61.71	57.69	**54.00**	47.48	**44.60**	41.95	**39.52**	37.26	33.23	29.78	26.80	24.22	21.97	47
48	60.35	56.57	**53.08**	46.93	**44.21**	41.69	**39.37**	37.21	33.37	30.05	27.19	24.69	22.52	48
49	59.02	55.47	**52.20**	46.40	**43.82**	41.43	**39.22**	37.17	33.50	30.34	27.59	25.18	23.08	49
50	57.74	54.41	**51.33**	45.87	**43.43**	41.18	**39.09**	37.14	33.65	30.63	27.99	25.68	23.66	50

Table 21 Multipliers for loss of pension commencing age 55 (males)

Age at date of trial	Multipliers calculated with allowance for projected mortality from the 2018-based population projections and rate of return of:													Age at date of trial
	-2.0%	-1.75%	**-1.5%**	-1.0%	**-0.75%**	-0.5%	**-0.25%**	0.0%	0.5%	1.0%	1.5%	2.0%	2.5%	
0	155.45	127.78	105.19	71.60	59.20	49.02	40.64	33.75	23.36	16.26	11.37	7.99	5.65	0
1	152.28	125.52	103.60	70.89	58.77	48.79	40.56	33.77	23.50	16.44	11.55	8.16	5.80	1
2	148.70	122.88	101.70	69.96	58.15	48.41	40.35	33.68	23.55	16.56	11.71	8.31	5.93	2
3	145.16	120.29	99.81	69.03	57.53	48.01	40.11	33.58	23.60	16.68	11.85	8.46	6.07	3
4	141.71	117.73	97.95	68.11	56.90	47.61	39.89	33.47	23.65	16.80	12.00	8.61	6.20	4
5	138.32	115.23	96.13	67.18	56.28	47.22	39.67	33.37	23.70	16.93	12.15	8.76	6.35	5
6	135.01	112.77	94.34	66.29	55.67	46.83	39.44	33.26	23.76	17.05	12.30	8.92	6.49	6
7	131.79	110.38	92.57	65.39	55.07	46.44	39.22	33.16	23.80	17.18	12.46	9.07	6.64	7
8	128.64	108.03	90.84	64.50	54.47	46.05	38.99	33.06	23.86	17.30	12.60	9.23	6.79	8
9	125.55	105.71	89.13	63.64	53.87	45.67	38.77	32.96	23.90	17.42	12.76	9.39	6.95	9
10	122.54	103.46	87.46	62.77	53.28	45.29	38.55	32.85	23.95	17.54	12.92	9.56	7.10	10
11	119.59	101.23	85.81	61.91	52.69	44.91	38.32	32.75	23.99	17.67	13.07	9.73	7.26	11
12	116.72	99.06	84.20	61.07	52.11	44.53	38.10	32.64	24.04	17.79	13.23	9.89	7.43	12
13	113.91	96.93	82.61	60.24	51.54	44.15	37.87	32.53	24.09	17.93	13.40	10.06	7.59	13
14	111.16	94.86	81.05	59.42	50.98	43.79	37.66	32.43	24.13	18.05	13.57	10.24	7.77	14
15	108.48	92.81	79.52	58.61	50.41	43.41	37.44	32.32	24.19	18.18	13.73	10.42	7.94	15
16	105.87	90.82	78.02	57.80	49.85	43.04	37.22	32.21	24.23	18.31	13.90	10.60	8.11	16
17	103.32	88.88	76.55	57.02	49.30	42.68	37.00	32.11	24.28	18.44	14.07	10.79	8.30	17
18	100.83	86.97	75.11	56.24	48.76	42.33	36.79	32.01	24.33	18.57	14.24	10.98	8.49	18
19	98.41	85.10	73.70	55.48	48.22	41.97	36.57	31.91	24.37	18.71	14.42	11.16	8.68	19
20	96.05	83.29	72.31	54.72	47.69	41.62	36.36	31.81	24.43	18.84	14.60	11.36	8.87	20
21	93.75	81.51	70.96	53.99	47.17	41.27	36.15	31.71	24.48	18.98	14.77	11.56	9.08	21
22	91.49	79.76	69.62	53.25	46.66	40.92	35.95	31.60	24.53	19.11	14.96	11.76	9.28	22
23	89.30	78.06	68.32	52.53	46.15	40.59	35.74	31.51	24.57	19.25	15.15	11.97	9.50	23
24	87.16	76.39	67.04	51.82	45.64	40.25	35.54	31.41	24.62	19.39	15.34	12.18	9.71	24
25	85.07	74.76	65.78	51.12	45.14	39.92	35.33	31.31	24.68	19.54	15.52	12.39	9.93	25
26	83.03	73.16	64.55	50.43	44.65	39.58	35.13	31.22	24.73	19.68	15.72	12.62	10.16	26
27	81.04	71.60	63.34	49.74	44.17	39.25	34.94	31.12	24.78	19.82	15.92	12.83	10.39	27
28	79.10	70.07	62.16	49.08	43.68	38.93	34.74	31.02	24.83	19.97	16.11	13.06	10.63	28
29	77.20	68.58	60.99	48.42	43.21	38.61	34.54	30.93	24.88	20.11	16.32	13.29	10.87	29
30	75.36	67.13	59.85	47.77	42.74	38.29	34.34	30.83	24.94	20.26	16.52	13.52	11.12	30
31	73.56	65.70	58.74	47.13	42.29	37.98	34.15	30.74	24.99	20.41	16.73	13.77	11.37	31
32	71.81	64.31	57.66	46.50	41.82	37.67	33.97	30.66	25.05	20.56	16.94	14.01	11.64	32
33	70.10	62.94	56.58	45.88	41.38	37.37	33.78	30.57	25.12	20.72	17.16	14.26	11.91	33
34	68.44	61.62	55.54	45.28	40.94	37.06	33.59	30.48	25.17	20.87	17.38	14.52	12.18	34
35	66.83	60.32	54.51	44.68	40.51	36.78	33.42	30.40	25.23	21.03	17.59	14.78	12.46	35
36	65.25	59.06	53.51	44.09	40.09	36.48	33.25	30.31	25.30	21.20	17.82	15.05	12.75	36
37	63.71	57.83	52.54	43.52	39.67	36.20	33.07	30.24	25.37	21.36	18.06	15.33	13.04	37
38	62.22	56.63	51.59	42.96	39.26	35.92	32.90	30.16	25.44	21.53	18.29	15.60	13.35	38
39	60.78	55.45	50.66	42.41	38.86	35.65	32.74	30.09	25.50	21.71	18.54	15.88	13.67	39
40	59.37	54.31	49.75	41.86	38.46	35.38	32.58	30.03	25.58	21.88	18.78	16.19	13.99	40
41	57.99	53.20	48.86	41.33	38.09	35.12	32.42	29.96	25.66	22.06	19.03	16.48	14.33	41
42	56.66	52.12	47.99	40.83	37.71	34.87	32.28	29.90	25.74	22.25	19.29	16.79	14.67	42
43	55.37	51.07	47.15	40.32	37.34	34.62	32.13	29.85	25.83	22.43	19.56	17.11	15.02	43
44	54.11	50.04	46.33	39.83	36.99	34.37	31.99	29.80	25.92	22.63	19.82	17.43	15.38	44
45	52.88	49.04	45.53	39.35	36.64	34.15	31.85	29.75	26.01	22.83	20.10	17.77	15.76	45
46	51.70	48.07	44.74	38.87	36.29	33.91	31.72	29.70	26.10	23.03	20.39	18.11	16.14	46
47	50.55	47.13	43.97	38.41	35.96	33.69	31.60	29.66	26.20	23.24	20.68	18.46	16.54	47
48	49.42	46.20	43.23	37.96	35.64	33.47	31.47	29.62	26.31	23.46	20.98	18.83	16.94	48
49	48.33	45.31	42.51	37.53	35.32	33.27	31.36	29.60	26.42	23.68	21.28	19.19	17.37	49
50	47.28	44.44	41.80	37.10	35.01	33.06	31.25	29.57	26.54	23.90	21.60	19.58	17.80	50
51	46.25	43.59	41.11	36.70	34.71	32.87	31.15	29.55	26.66	24.13	21.92	19.98	18.26	51
52	45.26	42.77	40.45	36.29	34.42	32.68	31.05	29.54	26.79	24.38	22.25	20.38	18.72	52
53	44.31	41.97	39.81	35.91	34.14	32.51	30.96	29.53	26.92	24.63	22.60	20.81	19.21	53
54	43.37	41.20	39.18	35.53	33.88	32.34	30.89	29.53	27.06	24.89	22.96	21.24	19.71	54
55	42.48	40.47	38.58	35.17	33.63	32.18	30.82	29.55	27.22	25.16	23.33	21.69	20.23	55

Table 22 Multipliers for loss of pension commencing age 55 (females)

Age at date of trial	Multipliers calculated with allowance for projected mortality from the 2018-based population projections and rate of return of:													Age at date of trial
	-2.0%	-1.75%	**-1.5%**	-1.0%	**-0.75%**	-0.5%	**-0.25%**	0.0%	0.5%	1.0%	1.5%	2.0%	2.5%	
0	168.99	138.63	**113.89**	77.21	**63.72**	52.66	**43.58**	36.12	24.92	17.28	12.05	8.45	5.96	0
1	165.56	136.17	**112.16**	76.45	**63.26**	52.41	**43.49**	36.14	25.06	17.48	12.25	8.63	6.11	1
2	161.77	133.40	**110.17**	75.49	**62.63**	52.02	**43.28**	36.06	25.13	17.61	12.41	8.79	6.26	2
3	158.02	130.67	**108.21**	74.52	**61.99**	51.63	**43.06**	35.97	25.20	17.76	12.58	8.95	6.40	3
4	154.36	127.97	**106.26**	73.58	**61.36**	51.24	**42.85**	35.88	25.27	17.89	12.73	9.11	6.55	4
5	150.78	125.34	**104.35**	72.63	**60.73**	50.84	**42.63**	35.80	25.34	18.03	12.90	9.27	6.70	5
6	147.28	122.75	**102.47**	71.70	**60.11**	50.45	**42.41**	35.71	25.40	18.18	13.06	9.44	6.86	6
7	143.86	120.22	**100.61**	70.77	**59.49**	50.07	**42.20**	35.62	25.47	18.32	13.23	9.62	7.02	7
8	140.51	117.74	**98.80**	69.86	**58.88**	49.69	**41.98**	35.53	25.54	18.46	13.41	9.79	7.18	8
9	137.23	115.30	**97.01**	68.97	**58.26**	49.30	**41.76**	35.43	25.61	18.60	13.58	9.96	7.35	9
10	134.03	112.91	**95.25**	68.07	**57.66**	48.91	**41.56**	35.34	25.67	18.74	13.75	10.14	7.52	10
11	130.91	110.57	**93.52**	67.19	**57.07**	48.54	**41.33**	35.26	25.74	18.89	13.93	10.33	7.69	11
12	127.86	108.28	**91.83**	66.32	**56.48**	48.16	**41.12**	35.17	25.80	19.04	14.11	10.51	7.87	12
13	124.87	106.03	**90.15**	65.46	**55.89**	47.79	**40.91**	35.07	25.88	19.19	14.29	10.70	8.05	13
14	121.95	103.82	**88.52**	64.61	**55.31**	47.42	**40.70**	34.98	25.94	19.33	14.47	10.89	8.23	14
15	119.10	101.67	**86.91**	63.77	**54.74**	47.04	**40.49**	34.89	26.01	19.48	14.66	11.09	8.42	15
16	116.32	99.56	**85.33**	62.94	**54.17**	46.68	**40.27**	34.80	26.07	19.63	14.85	11.29	8.62	16
17	113.60	97.50	**83.78**	62.13	**53.61**	46.32	**40.07**	34.71	26.14	19.78	15.04	11.49	8.82	17
18	110.94	95.47	**82.26**	61.32	**53.05**	45.95	**39.86**	34.61	26.20	19.94	15.24	11.70	9.02	18
19	108.35	93.48	**80.77**	60.53	**52.50**	45.60	**39.65**	34.52	26.27	20.08	15.43	11.91	9.23	19
20	105.82	91.54	**79.30**	59.74	**51.95**	45.24	**39.45**	34.43	26.33	20.25	15.63	12.13	9.44	20
21	103.34	89.64	**77.85**	58.96	**51.41**	44.89	**39.24**	34.35	26.40	20.39	15.83	12.34	9.66	21
22	100.93	87.78	**76.44**	58.21	**50.89**	44.54	**39.04**	34.25	26.47	20.56	16.03	12.56	9.89	22
23	98.56	85.95	**75.05**	57.45	**50.35**	44.19	**38.83**	34.16	26.54	20.71	16.24	12.79	10.12	23
24	96.25	84.17	**73.68**	56.70	**49.83**	43.84	**38.63**	34.08	26.61	20.87	16.45	13.02	10.35	24
25	94.00	82.41	**72.35**	55.96	**49.31**	43.50	**38.42**	33.99	26.68	21.03	16.66	13.26	10.59	25
26	91.79	80.69	**71.03**	55.23	**48.79**	43.17	**38.23**	33.89	26.74	21.20	16.88	13.50	10.84	26
27	89.65	79.02	**69.73**	54.52	**48.29**	42.82	**38.03**	33.81	26.81	21.36	17.09	13.74	11.08	27
28	87.55	77.37	**68.46**	53.81	**47.78**	42.50	**37.83**	33.71	26.88	21.53	17.31	13.99	11.34	28
29	85.50	75.76	**67.22**	53.10	**47.28**	42.16	**37.63**	33.63	26.94	21.69	17.53	14.24	11.61	29
30	83.50	74.19	**65.99**	52.42	**46.80**	41.83	**37.43**	33.54	27.02	21.86	17.77	14.49	11.87	30
31	81.55	72.65	**64.80**	51.74	**46.31**	41.51	**37.24**	33.46	27.09	22.03	17.99	14.75	12.14	31
32	79.65	71.14	**63.63**	51.07	**45.84**	41.19	**37.05**	33.37	27.16	22.20	18.23	15.03	12.43	32
33	77.79	69.67	**62.48**	50.42	**45.37**	40.87	**36.86**	33.29	27.23	22.37	18.46	15.29	12.72	33
34	75.98	68.23	**61.35**	49.77	**44.90**	40.55	**36.68**	33.20	27.30	22.56	18.70	15.57	13.02	34
35	74.21	66.82	**60.24**	49.12	**44.44**	40.25	**36.49**	33.13	27.38	22.74	18.94	15.86	13.32	35
36	72.49	65.44	**59.16**	48.50	**43.99**	39.94	**36.31**	33.05	27.46	22.91	19.20	16.15	13.63	36
37	70.81	64.10	**58.09**	47.88	**43.54**	39.64	**36.13**	32.97	27.53	23.10	19.45	16.44	13.95	37
38	69.17	62.78	**57.04**	47.27	**43.11**	39.34	**35.96**	32.89	27.62	23.28	19.70	16.74	14.28	38
39	67.57	61.49	**56.03**	46.68	**42.67**	39.05	**35.78**	32.82	27.69	23.47	19.97	17.05	14.61	39
40	66.02	60.24	**55.03**	46.08	**42.24**	38.76	**35.60**	32.75	27.78	23.66	20.23	17.36	14.96	40
41	64.49	59.01	**54.05**	45.50	**41.82**	38.48	**35.44**	32.67	27.87	23.85	20.50	17.69	15.32	41
42	63.02	57.81	**53.09**	44.94	**41.40**	38.20	**35.27**	32.60	27.95	24.05	20.78	18.01	15.68	42
43	61.57	56.64	**52.16**	44.38	**41.00**	37.92	**35.11**	32.54	28.04	24.25	21.06	18.36	16.06	43
44	60.17	55.49	**51.24**	43.83	**40.60**	37.66	**34.95**	32.48	28.12	24.45	21.34	18.70	16.44	44
45	58.80	54.38	**50.34**	43.29	**40.21**	37.39	**34.79**	32.42	28.22	24.67	21.64	19.05	16.84	45
46	57.48	53.29	**49.47**	42.76	**39.83**	37.12	**34.65**	32.36	28.31	24.87	21.94	19.41	17.24	46
47	56.18	52.23	**48.62**	42.25	**39.44**	36.87	**34.50**	32.31	28.41	25.09	22.24	19.78	17.65	47
48	54.92	51.20	**47.78**	41.75	**39.08**	36.62	**34.36**	32.26	28.53	25.31	22.56	20.16	18.08	48
49	53.69	50.19	**46.97**	41.25	**38.72**	36.38	**34.21**	32.21	28.62	25.54	22.87	20.55	18.53	49
50	52.51	49.21	**46.16**	40.77	**38.36**	36.14	**34.09**	32.17	28.74	25.78	23.20	20.94	18.98	50
51	51.35	48.25	**45.40**	40.30	**38.03**	35.92	**33.96**	32.14	28.86	26.02	23.53	21.36	19.45	51
52	50.23	47.33	**44.64**	39.85	**37.70**	35.70	**33.84**	32.10	28.98	26.26	23.88	21.79	19.94	52
53	49.14	46.43	**43.91**	39.39	**37.37**	35.49	**33.72**	32.09	29.12	26.51	24.23	22.22	20.44	53
54	48.09	45.56	**43.20**	38.97	**37.06**	35.28	**33.62**	32.07	29.25	26.78	24.60	22.67	20.96	54
55	47.08	44.72	**42.52**	38.55	**36.76**	35.09	**33.53**	32.06	29.40	27.05	24.98	23.14	21.50	55

Table 23 Multipliers for loss of pension commencing age 60 (males)

Age at date of trial	Multipliers calculated with allowance for projected mortality from the 2018-based population projections and rate of return of:													Age at date of trial
	-2.0%	-1.75%	**-1.5%**	-1.0%	**-0.75%**	-0.5%	**-0.25%**	0.0%	0.5%	1.0%	1.5%	2.0%	2.5%	
0	140.13	114.55	**93.76**	63.06	**51.81**	42.63	**35.11**	28.95	19.76	13.55	9.34	6.46	4.49	0
1	137.23	112.48	**92.31**	62.41	**51.42**	42.41	**35.02**	28.96	19.87	13.70	9.48	6.59	4.61	1
2	133.95	110.08	**90.58**	61.57	**50.85**	42.06	**34.82**	28.87	19.91	13.79	9.60	6.71	4.71	2
3	130.71	107.71	**88.86**	60.72	**50.29**	41.69	**34.61**	28.77	19.94	13.89	9.71	6.83	4.82	3
4	127.55	105.38	**87.17**	59.88	**49.72**	41.33	**34.40**	28.67	19.97	13.98	9.83	6.94	4.92	4
5	124.45	103.10	**85.52**	59.05	**49.16**	40.97	**34.19**	28.57	20.01	14.08	9.96	7.06	5.03	5
6	121.43	100.86	**83.89**	58.24	**48.60**	40.62	**33.98**	28.46	20.04	14.17	10.07	7.19	5.15	6
7	118.48	98.68	**82.28**	57.43	**48.06**	40.27	**33.78**	28.37	20.08	14.28	10.19	7.31	5.26	7
8	115.60	96.54	**80.71**	56.62	**47.52**	39.91	**33.57**	28.26	20.11	14.37	10.31	7.43	5.37	8
9	112.79	94.43	**79.16**	55.84	**46.97**	39.56	**33.36**	28.17	20.14	14.46	10.43	7.56	5.50	9
10	110.04	92.38	**77.64**	55.05	**46.44**	39.21	**33.16**	28.06	20.17	14.56	10.56	7.68	5.62	10
11	107.34	90.35	**76.14**	54.27	**45.90**	38.87	**32.94**	27.96	20.20	14.66	10.68	7.82	5.74	11
12	104.72	88.38	**74.68**	53.51	**45.37**	38.53	**32.74**	27.86	20.23	14.75	10.80	7.95	5.87	12
13	102.16	86.44	**73.24**	52.76	**44.85**	38.18	**32.53**	27.75	20.26	14.85	10.94	8.08	6.00	13
14	99.65	84.56	**71.83**	52.02	**44.34**	37.84	**32.33**	27.65	20.29	14.95	11.07	8.22	6.13	14
15	97.20	82.70	**70.44**	51.28	**43.83**	37.50	**32.12**	27.54	20.32	15.05	11.19	8.36	6.27	15
16	94.82	80.89	**69.08**	50.56	**43.32**	37.16	**31.92**	27.44	20.35	15.15	11.33	8.50	6.40	16
17	92.50	79.12	**67.75**	49.85	**42.83**	36.84	**31.72**	27.34	20.38	15.25	11.46	8.65	6.54	17
18	90.23	77.39	**66.45**	49.15	**42.34**	36.51	**31.52**	27.24	20.41	15.35	11.59	8.79	6.69	18
19	88.03	75.69	**65.16**	48.45	**41.85**	36.19	**31.32**	27.14	20.44	15.46	11.73	8.94	6.83	19
20	85.88	74.04	**63.91**	47.77	**41.37**	35.87	**31.12**	27.04	20.47	15.56	11.87	9.09	6.98	20
21	83.78	72.43	**62.69**	47.11	**40.90**	35.55	**30.93**	26.94	20.50	15.66	12.01	9.24	7.15	21
22	81.73	70.84	**61.47**	46.45	**40.44**	35.23	**30.74**	26.84	20.54	15.76	12.15	9.40	7.30	22
23	79.73	69.30	**60.30**	45.79	**39.97**	34.93	**30.54**	26.74	20.56	15.87	12.30	9.56	7.47	23
24	77.78	67.79	**59.14**	45.15	**39.52**	34.62	**30.36**	26.65	20.59	15.98	12.45	9.73	7.63	24
25	75.88	66.30	**58.00**	44.52	**39.06**	34.32	**30.17**	26.55	20.63	16.09	12.59	9.89	7.80	25
26	74.03	64.86	**56.88**	43.89	**38.61**	34.00	**29.98**	26.46	20.66	16.20	12.74	10.06	7.97	26
27	72.22	63.44	**55.79**	43.28	**38.18**	33.71	**29.80**	26.36	20.69	16.30	12.90	10.23	8.15	27
28	70.46	62.06	**54.72**	42.68	**37.74**	33.41	**29.61**	26.26	20.73	16.42	13.04	10.41	8.33	28
29	68.74	60.71	**53.67**	42.08	**37.31**	33.12	**29.43**	26.17	20.75	16.52	13.21	10.58	8.51	29
30	67.07	59.39	**52.64**	41.49	**36.89**	32.83	**29.24**	26.07	20.79	16.64	13.36	10.76	8.70	30
31	65.43	58.10	**51.63**	40.92	**36.48**	32.55	**29.07**	25.98	20.82	16.75	13.52	10.95	8.89	31
32	63.84	56.84	**50.66**	40.35	**36.06**	32.26	**28.90**	25.90	20.86	16.87	13.68	11.13	9.10	32
33	62.29	55.60	**49.68**	39.79	**35.66**	31.98	**28.72**	25.81	20.90	16.99	13.85	11.33	9.30	33
34	60.78	54.41	**48.75**	39.25	**35.26**	31.71	**28.54**	25.72	20.94	17.10	14.02	11.53	9.51	34
35	59.32	53.23	**47.82**	38.70	**34.87**	31.44	**28.38**	25.64	20.98	17.23	14.19	11.73	9.72	35
36	57.89	52.09	**46.92**	38.18	**34.49**	31.17	**28.22**	25.55	21.02	17.35	14.36	11.94	9.94	36
37	56.50	50.98	**46.04**	37.66	**34.11**	30.92	**28.05**	25.47	21.06	17.47	14.55	12.15	10.17	37
38	55.14	49.89	**45.18**	37.15	**33.74**	30.66	**27.89**	25.39	21.11	17.60	14.72	12.36	10.40	38
39	53.84	48.83	**44.34**	36.66	**33.37**	30.41	**27.74**	25.32	21.15	17.74	14.91	12.57	10.64	39
40	52.56	47.80	**43.52**	36.16	**33.01**	30.16	**27.58**	25.25	21.20	17.86	15.10	12.81	10.88	40
41	51.31	46.80	**42.72**	35.69	**32.67**	29.93	**27.44**	25.17	21.26	18.00	15.29	13.03	11.14	41
42	50.11	45.82	**41.94**	35.23	**32.33**	29.70	**27.30**	25.11	21.31	18.14	15.49	13.27	11.40	42
43	48.94	44.87	**41.18**	34.77	**31.99**	29.46	**27.16**	25.05	21.37	18.28	15.69	13.51	11.67	43
44	47.80	43.94	**40.44**	34.33	**31.67**	29.24	**27.02**	24.99	21.43	18.43	15.90	13.75	11.93	44
45	46.69	43.04	**39.72**	33.89	**31.35**	29.03	**26.89**	24.94	21.49	18.58	16.11	14.01	12.22	45
46	45.62	42.16	**39.00**	33.47	**31.04**	28.81	**26.76**	24.88	21.55	18.73	16.32	14.27	12.51	46
47	44.58	41.31	**38.31**	33.05	**30.73**	28.60	**26.64**	24.83	21.62	18.90	16.55	14.54	12.81	47
48	43.56	40.48	**37.65**	32.64	**30.44**	28.40	**26.52**	24.78	21.70	19.05	16.78	14.82	13.12	48
49	42.57	39.68	**36.99**	32.25	**30.15**	28.21	**26.41**	24.75	21.78	19.22	17.01	15.09	13.44	49
50	41.62	38.89	**36.35**	31.86	**29.86**	28.01	**26.30**	24.71	21.86	19.39	17.25	15.38	13.76	50
51	40.69	38.13	**35.74**	31.49	**29.59**	27.83	**26.19**	24.67	21.94	19.57	17.50	15.69	14.10	51
52	39.80	37.38	**35.14**	31.13	**29.33**	27.66	**26.10**	24.65	22.03	19.75	17.75	16.00	14.45	52
53	38.94	36.66	**34.56**	30.78	**29.07**	27.49	**26.00**	24.62	22.12	19.94	18.01	16.32	14.81	53
54	38.09	35.97	**34.00**	30.43	**28.83**	27.33	**25.93**	24.61	22.23	20.13	18.29	16.65	15.20	54

Table 23 Multipliers for loss of pension commencing age 60 (males) *continued*

Age at date of trial	Multipliers calculated with allowance for projected mortality from the 2018-based population projections and rate of return of:													Age at date of trial
	-2.0%	-1.75%	**-1.5%**	-1.0%	**-0.75%**	-0.5%	**-0.25%**	0.0%	0.5%	1.0%	1.5%	2.0%	2.5%	
55	37.28	35.31	**33.45**	30.11	**28.60**	27.18	**25.85**	24.61	22.34	20.34	18.57	16.99	15.58	55
56	36.51	34.66	**32.93**	29.80	**28.38**	27.04	**25.79**	24.61	22.46	20.55	18.86	17.34	15.99	56
57	35.76	34.05	**32.44**	29.51	**28.17**	26.92	**25.73**	24.63	22.60	20.78	19.16	17.72	16.42	57
58	35.06	33.47	**31.96**	29.23	**27.99**	26.81	**25.70**	24.65	22.74	21.02	19.49	18.11	16.87	58
59	34.38	32.91	**31.52**	28.98	**27.82**	26.72	**25.68**	24.70	22.90	21.28	19.83	18.52	17.34	59
60	33.75	32.39	**31.10**	28.75	**27.67**	26.64	**25.68**	24.76	23.07	21.56	20.19	18.95	17.83	60

Table 24 Multipliers for loss of pension commencing age 60 (females)

Age at date of trial	Multipliers calculated with allowance for projected mortality from the 2018-based population projections and rate of return of:													Age at date of trial
	-2.0%	-1.75%	**-1.5%**	-1.0%	**-0.75%**	-0.5%	**-0.25%**	0.0%	0.5%	1.0%	1.5%	2.0%	2.5%	
0	153.45	125.21	**102.30**	68.54	**56.23**	46.17	**37.97**	31.26	21.26	14.54	9.99	6.89	4.78	0
1	150.29	122.94	**100.71**	67.85	**55.80**	45.94	**37.88**	31.27	21.38	14.70	10.15	7.03	4.90	1
2	146.80	120.41	**98.89**	66.98	**55.22**	45.58	**37.68**	31.19	21.43	14.81	10.27	7.16	5.02	2
3	143.36	117.90	**97.10**	66.09	**54.64**	45.23	**37.47**	31.09	21.48	14.92	10.41	7.29	5.13	3
4	139.99	115.43	**95.32**	65.23	**54.07**	44.86	**37.28**	31.01	21.54	15.03	10.53	7.42	5.24	4
5	136.70	113.03	**93.57**	64.37	**53.49**	44.50	**37.08**	30.93	21.59	15.14	10.67	7.55	5.37	5
6	133.48	110.66	**91.85**	63.52	**52.93**	44.15	**36.87**	30.84	21.63	15.26	10.80	7.68	5.49	6
7	130.35	108.34	**90.16**	62.68	**52.36**	43.79	**36.68**	30.75	21.68	15.37	10.94	7.82	5.62	7
8	127.27	106.07	**88.51**	61.85	**51.81**	43.45	**36.47**	30.66	21.74	15.49	11.08	7.96	5.74	8
9	124.26	103.84	**86.88**	61.04	**51.25**	43.09	**36.27**	30.57	21.78	15.60	11.22	8.10	5.88	9
10	121.33	101.65	**85.27**	60.23	**50.70**	42.74	**36.08**	30.48	21.83	15.71	11.35	8.24	6.01	10
11	118.46	99.51	**83.70**	59.42	**50.17**	42.39	**35.87**	30.39	21.88	15.82	11.50	8.39	6.15	11
12	115.66	97.42	**82.15**	58.64	**49.63**	42.05	**35.67**	30.30	21.93	15.95	11.64	8.54	6.28	12
13	112.92	95.36	**80.63**	57.86	**49.10**	41.71	**35.48**	30.21	21.98	16.06	11.78	8.68	6.43	13
14	110.24	93.35	**79.14**	57.08	**48.56**	41.37	**35.28**	30.12	22.03	16.18	11.93	8.83	6.57	14
15	107.63	91.38	**77.67**	56.32	**48.05**	41.03	**35.08**	30.03	22.08	16.30	12.08	8.99	6.72	15
16	105.08	89.45	**76.23**	55.57	**47.53**	40.70	**34.88**	29.94	22.12	16.41	12.23	9.15	6.88	16
17	102.59	87.57	**74.82**	54.83	**47.02**	40.37	**34.70**	29.85	22.17	16.53	12.39	9.31	7.03	17
18	100.15	85.71	**73.44**	54.10	**46.51**	40.03	**34.50**	29.76	22.22	16.66	12.54	9.47	7.19	18
19	97.78	83.90	**72.08**	53.38	**46.01**	39.71	**34.30**	29.67	22.26	16.77	12.69	9.65	7.35	19
20	95.46	82.13	**70.74**	52.67	**45.52**	39.38	**34.12**	29.58	22.31	16.90	12.85	9.82	7.52	20
21	93.19	80.39	**69.43**	51.96	**45.03**	39.07	**33.92**	29.49	22.36	17.02	13.01	9.99	7.69	21
22	90.98	78.69	**68.14**	51.27	**44.55**	38.74	**33.74**	29.40	22.40	17.15	13.17	10.16	7.87	22
23	88.82	77.03	**66.88**	50.58	**44.06**	38.43	**33.54**	29.31	22.45	17.27	13.34	10.33	8.05	23
24	86.70	75.40	**65.63**	49.91	**43.59**	38.10	**33.35**	29.23	22.51	17.40	13.50	10.52	8.23	24
25	84.65	73.80	**64.42**	49.24	**43.12**	37.79	**33.16**	29.14	22.55	17.52	13.67	10.71	8.42	25
26	82.63	72.23	**63.22**	48.58	**42.65**	37.49	**32.98**	29.04	22.59	17.65	13.84	10.90	8.61	26
27	80.67	70.71	**62.04**	47.93	**42.19**	37.17	**32.79**	28.96	22.65	17.78	14.01	11.08	8.80	27
28	78.75	69.21	**60.89**	47.29	**41.73**	36.88	**32.61**	28.87	22.70	17.91	14.19	11.28	9.00	28
29	76.87	67.74	**59.76**	46.65	**41.28**	36.57	**32.43**	28.78	22.74	18.04	14.36	11.48	9.21	29
30	75.05	66.31	**58.65**	46.03	**40.84**	36.27	**32.24**	28.70	22.79	18.18	14.55	11.67	9.41	30
31	73.27	64.91	**57.56**	45.41	**40.39**	35.98	**32.06**	28.61	22.84	18.31	14.72	11.88	9.62	31
32	71.53	63.53	**56.50**	44.81	**39.96**	35.68	**31.89**	28.52	22.89	18.44	14.91	12.10	9.85	32
33	69.83	62.20	**55.46**	44.21	**39.54**	35.39	**31.71**	28.44	22.94	18.57	15.09	12.31	10.07	33
34	68.18	60.89	**54.43**	43.62	**39.11**	35.10	**31.54**	28.36	22.99	18.72	15.28	12.53	10.30	34
35	66.57	59.61	**53.42**	43.04	**38.70**	34.82	**31.36**	28.28	23.04	18.86	15.47	12.75	10.53	35
36	65.00	58.35	**52.44**	42.48	**38.29**	34.54	**31.20**	28.20	23.10	19.00	15.67	12.98	10.78	36
37	63.46	57.13	**51.47**	41.92	**37.88**	34.26	**31.02**	28.12	23.15	19.14	15.87	13.20	11.02	37
38	61.97	55.93	**50.53**	41.36	**37.49**	33.99	**30.86**	28.03	23.22	19.28	16.07	13.44	11.28	38
39	60.51	54.76	**49.61**	40.83	**37.09**	33.72	**30.69**	27.96	23.26	19.43	16.28	13.69	11.54	39
40	59.10	53.62	**48.70**	40.29	**36.70**	33.46	**30.53**	27.89	23.32	19.58	16.49	13.93	11.80	40
41	57.71	52.50	**47.82**	39.77	**36.32**	33.20	**30.37**	27.81	23.39	19.73	16.70	14.18	12.09	41
42	56.37	51.41	**46.95**	39.25	**35.94**	32.94	**30.22**	27.74	23.45	19.88	16.92	14.43	12.36	42
43	55.05	50.35	**46.10**	38.75	**35.57**	32.68	**30.07**	27.68	23.51	20.04	17.14	14.70	12.65	43
44	53.77	49.31	**45.27**	38.25	**35.21**	32.44	**29.91**	27.61	23.57	20.20	17.36	14.97	12.95	44
45	52.52	48.30	**44.45**	37.77	**34.85**	32.20	**29.76**	27.54	23.64	20.36	17.59	15.24	13.25	45
46	51.32	47.31	**43.67**	37.29	**34.51**	31.96	**29.63**	27.48	23.71	20.52	17.83	15.52	13.56	46
47	50.14	46.35	**42.89**	36.82	**34.16**	31.72	**29.48**	27.42	23.78	20.69	18.06	15.81	13.88	47
48	48.99	45.41	**42.13**	36.37	**33.83**	31.49	**29.35**	27.37	23.86	20.86	18.31	16.10	14.21	48
49	47.87	44.50	**41.40**	35.92	**33.50**	31.27	**29.21**	27.31	23.93	21.04	18.56	16.40	14.55	49
50	46.80	43.61	**40.67**	35.48	**33.17**	31.05	**29.09**	27.26	24.01	21.22	18.81	16.71	14.90	50
51	45.75	42.74	**39.97**	35.05	**32.87**	30.84	**28.96**	27.22	24.10	21.41	19.07	17.04	15.26	51
52	44.73	41.90	**39.29**	34.64	**32.57**	30.64	**28.85**	27.18	24.19	21.60	19.34	17.37	15.64	52
53	43.74	41.09	**38.63**	34.23	**32.27**	30.44	**28.73**	27.15	24.29	21.80	19.62	17.71	16.02	53
54	42.78	40.30	**37.99**	33.84	**31.98**	30.25	**28.63**	27.13	24.39	22.00	19.90	18.05	16.42	54

Table 24 Multipliers for loss of pension commencing age 60 (females) *continued*

Age at date of trial	Multipliers calculated with allowance for projected mortality from the 2018-based population projections and rate of return of:													Age at date of trial
	-2.0%	-1.75%	**-1.5%**	-1.0%	**-0.75%**	-0.5%	**-0.25%**	0.0%	0.5%	1.0%	1.5%	2.0%	2.5%	
55	41.86	39.54	**37.37**	33.47	**31.71**	30.07	**28.54**	27.10	24.50	22.21	20.20	18.42	16.83	55
56	40.96	38.80	**36.77**	33.11	**31.45**	29.90	**28.45**	27.09	24.62	22.44	20.50	18.79	17.26	56
57	40.10	38.08	**36.19**	32.75	**31.20**	29.74	**28.38**	27.09	24.74	22.66	20.82	19.17	17.70	57
58	39.28	37.39	**35.63**	32.42	**30.96**	29.59	**28.30**	27.09	24.88	22.91	21.15	19.58	18.17	58
59	38.48	36.73	**35.09**	32.11	**30.74**	29.46	**28.25**	27.11	25.02	23.16	21.49	19.99	18.65	59
60	37.72	36.10	**34.58**	31.80	**30.53**	29.33	**28.20**	27.14	25.18	23.42	21.85	20.43	19.15	60

Table 25 Multipliers for loss of pension commencing age 65 (males)

Age at date of trial	Multipliers calculated with allowance for projected mortality from the 2018-based population projections and rate of return of:													Age at date of trial
	-2.0%	-1.75%	**-1.5%**	-1.0%	**-0.75%**	-0.5%	**-0.25%**	0.0%	0.5%	1.0%	1.5%	2.0%	2.5%	trial
0	123.47	100.34	**81.64**	54.23	**44.27**	36.18	**29.60**	24.24	16.31	11.02	7.48	5.09	3.48	0
1	120.85	98.48	**80.33**	53.64	**43.91**	35.97	**29.51**	24.24	16.39	11.13	7.59	5.19	3.57	1
2	117.91	96.33	**78.79**	52.89	**43.40**	35.66	**29.33**	24.15	16.42	11.20	7.68	5.29	3.65	2
3	115.00	94.21	**77.26**	52.14	**42.90**	35.33	**29.13**	24.05	16.43	11.27	7.77	5.37	3.73	3
4	112.16	92.12	**75.75**	51.39	**42.39**	35.00	**28.94**	23.95	16.45	11.35	7.86	5.46	3.81	4
5	109.38	90.08	**74.27**	50.64	**41.89**	34.68	**28.75**	23.85	16.47	11.42	7.95	5.55	3.89	5
6	106.67	88.08	**72.82**	49.92	**41.39**	34.36	**28.56**	23.75	16.49	11.49	8.03	5.65	3.98	6
7	104.03	86.13	**71.39**	49.20	**40.91**	34.05	**28.37**	23.66	16.51	11.56	8.13	5.74	4.06	7
8	101.45	84.22	**69.98**	48.48	**40.42**	33.73	**28.17**	23.56	16.53	11.63	8.22	5.83	4.15	8
9	98.92	82.33	**68.60**	47.78	**39.94**	33.41	**27.98**	23.47	16.54	11.70	8.31	5.93	4.24	9
10	96.46	80.50	**67.25**	47.08	**39.46**	33.10	**27.80**	23.36	16.55	11.77	8.41	6.02	4.33	10
11	94.05	78.70	**65.92**	46.39	**38.98**	32.79	**27.60**	23.26	16.56	11.84	8.50	6.12	4.42	11
12	91.70	76.93	**64.61**	45.71	**38.51**	32.48	**27.41**	23.16	16.58	11.91	8.59	6.22	4.52	12
13	89.41	75.21	**63.34**	45.05	**38.05**	32.17	**27.22**	23.06	16.59	11.99	8.69	6.32	4.62	13
14	87.17	73.52	**62.07**	44.39	**37.59**	31.87	**27.04**	22.96	16.61	12.06	8.79	6.42	4.72	14
15	84.98	71.86	**60.84**	43.74	**37.14**	31.56	**26.85**	22.86	16.63	12.13	8.88	6.53	4.82	15
16	82.85	70.25	**59.63**	43.09	**36.68**	31.26	**26.67**	22.76	16.64	12.20	8.98	6.63	4.91	16
17	80.78	68.68	**58.45**	42.46	**36.24**	30.96	**26.48**	22.67	16.65	12.28	9.08	6.75	5.02	17
18	78.75	67.14	**57.29**	41.84	**35.81**	30.67	**26.30**	22.57	16.67	12.35	9.18	6.86	5.13	18
19	76.78	65.62	**56.15**	41.22	**35.37**	30.38	**26.11**	22.47	16.68	12.43	9.28	6.96	5.24	19
20	74.86	64.16	**55.04**	40.62	**34.94**	30.09	**25.93**	22.37	16.70	12.50	9.39	7.08	5.35	20
21	72.99	62.72	**53.95**	40.03	**34.53**	29.81	**25.75**	22.28	16.71	12.58	9.49	7.19	5.47	21
22	71.16	61.31	**52.87**	39.44	**34.11**	29.52	**25.58**	22.18	16.73	12.65	9.60	7.31	5.58	22
23	69.38	59.94	**51.83**	38.86	**33.70**	29.25	**25.40**	22.08	16.74	12.73	9.71	7.43	5.71	23
24	67.64	58.60	**50.81**	38.29	**33.29**	28.97	**25.23**	21.99	16.75	12.80	9.82	7.55	5.82	24
25	65.95	57.28	**49.79**	37.74	**32.89**	28.70	**25.05**	21.90	16.77	12.88	9.92	7.67	5.95	25
26	64.30	55.99	**48.80**	37.18	**32.49**	28.42	**24.88**	21.80	16.78	12.96	10.03	7.80	6.07	26
27	62.69	54.73	**47.84**	36.63	**32.10**	28.15	**24.72**	21.71	16.79	13.04	10.15	7.93	6.21	27
28	61.12	53.51	**46.89**	36.10	**31.71**	27.88	**24.55**	21.61	16.81	13.12	10.26	8.06	6.34	28
29	59.59	52.31	**45.96**	35.57	**31.33**	27.62	**24.37**	21.53	16.82	13.19	10.38	8.19	6.47	29
30	58.10	51.14	**45.04**	35.05	**30.95**	27.36	**24.20**	21.43	16.84	13.27	10.49	8.32	6.62	30
31	56.65	49.99	**44.16**	34.54	**30.59**	27.11	**24.04**	21.34	16.85	13.35	10.61	8.46	6.76	31
32	55.24	48.88	**43.29**	34.04	**30.21**	26.85	**23.88**	21.26	16.87	13.44	10.73	8.59	6.91	32
33	53.86	47.79	**42.43**	33.55	**29.86**	26.60	**23.72**	21.16	16.89	13.53	10.86	8.74	7.06	33
34	52.52	46.73	**41.60**	33.06	**29.50**	26.35	**23.56**	21.08	16.91	13.60	10.98	8.89	7.21	34
35	51.23	45.69	**40.78**	32.58	**29.16**	26.11	**23.41**	20.99	16.93	13.69	11.10	9.03	7.36	35
36	49.95	44.68	**39.98**	32.12	**28.82**	25.87	**23.25**	20.91	16.95	13.78	11.23	9.19	7.53	36
37	48.72	43.69	**39.21**	31.66	**28.48**	25.64	**23.10**	20.83	16.97	13.86	11.37	9.34	7.69	37
38	47.52	42.73	**38.45**	31.21	**28.15**	25.41	**22.95**	20.74	17.00	13.96	11.49	9.50	7.86	38
39	46.36	41.79	**37.71**	30.77	**27.83**	25.18	**22.81**	20.67	17.01	14.05	11.64	9.65	8.04	39
40	45.23	40.88	**36.99**	30.33	**27.50**	24.96	**22.66**	20.60	17.04	14.14	11.77	9.82	8.21	40
41	44.13	40.00	**36.28**	29.91	**27.20**	24.74	**22.53**	20.52	17.08	14.24	11.91	9.99	8.40	41
42	43.06	39.13	**35.59**	29.51	**26.90**	24.53	**22.40**	20.45	17.10	14.34	12.06	10.16	8.59	42
43	42.02	38.29	**34.92**	29.10	**26.59**	24.32	**22.26**	20.39	17.14	14.44	12.20	10.34	8.78	43
44	41.02	37.47	**34.26**	28.71	**26.31**	24.11	**22.13**	20.33	17.17	14.54	12.35	10.52	8.98	44
45	40.03	36.67	**33.63**	28.32	**26.02**	23.92	**22.01**	20.26	17.21	14.65	12.51	10.70	9.18	45
46	39.09	35.90	**33.00**	27.94	**25.74**	23.73	**21.88**	20.20	17.24	14.76	12.66	10.89	9.39	46
47	38.17	35.15	**32.39**	27.57	**25.47**	23.54	**21.77**	20.14	17.28	14.88	12.83	11.09	9.61	47
48	37.26	34.41	**31.80**	27.21	**25.20**	23.35	**21.65**	20.09	17.33	14.99	12.99	11.29	9.83	48
49	36.39	33.71	**31.23**	26.86	**24.94**	23.17	**21.54**	20.04	17.38	15.11	13.16	11.49	10.06	49
50	35.56	33.01	**30.66**	26.52	**24.69**	22.99	**21.43**	20.00	17.43	15.23	13.34	11.70	10.29	50
51	34.73	32.34	**30.12**	26.19	**24.44**	22.83	**21.33**	19.95	17.48	15.35	13.51	11.93	10.54	51
52	33.94	31.68	**29.59**	25.86	**24.20**	22.67	**21.24**	19.91	17.54	15.48	13.69	12.15	10.79	52
53	33.18	31.05	**29.08**	25.55	**23.97**	22.51	**21.14**	19.88	17.59	15.62	13.88	12.38	11.05	53
54	32.43	30.43	**28.58**	25.24	**23.75**	22.36	**21.06**	19.85	17.66	15.76	14.09	12.62	11.33	54

Table 25 Multipliers for loss of pension commencing age 65 (males) *continued*

Age at date of trial	Multipliers calculated with allowance for projected mortality from the 2018-based population projections and rate of return of:													Age at date of trial
	-2.0%	-1.75%	**-1.5%**	-1.0%	**-0.75%**	-0.5%	**-0.25%**	0.0%	0.5%	1.0%	1.5%	2.0%	2.5%	
55	31.72	29.85	**28.10**	24.95	**23.54**	22.22	**20.98**	19.83	17.74	15.90	14.29	12.86	11.61	55
56	31.03	29.28	**27.64**	24.68	**23.34**	22.08	**20.91**	19.81	17.81	16.05	14.50	13.12	11.90	56
57	30.38	28.73	**27.20**	24.42	**23.15**	21.97	**20.85**	19.81	17.91	16.21	14.72	13.40	12.21	57
58	29.76	28.22	**26.78**	24.16	**22.98**	21.86	**20.80**	19.81	18.00	16.39	14.96	13.68	12.53	58
59	29.15	27.73	**26.38**	23.93	**22.82**	21.76	**20.77**	19.83	18.11	16.57	15.20	13.97	12.86	59
60	28.59	27.27	**26.01**	23.72	**22.68**	21.68	**20.75**	19.86	18.23	16.78	15.46	14.28	13.22	60
61	28.05	26.83	**25.66**	23.53	**22.55**	21.62	**20.74**	19.91	18.37	16.98	15.74	14.61	13.59	61
62	27.55	26.41	**25.33**	23.36	**22.44**	21.57	**20.75**	19.97	18.52	17.21	16.04	14.96	13.99	62
63	27.08	26.03	**25.04**	23.20	**22.34**	21.54	**20.77**	20.04	18.69	17.46	16.35	15.33	14.41	63
64	26.65	25.68	**24.76**	23.06	**22.28**	21.53	**20.81**	20.14	18.88	17.73	16.68	15.72	14.85	64
65	26.23	25.35	**24.51**	22.95	**22.23**	21.54	**20.88**	20.25	19.08	18.02	17.04	16.14	15.32	65

Table 26 Multipliers for loss of pension commencing age 65 (females)

Age at date of trial	Multipliers calculated with allowance for projected mortality from the 2018-based population projections and rate of return of:													Age at date of trial
	-2.0%	-1.75%	**-1.5%**	-1.0%	**-0.75%**	-0.5%	**-0.25%**	0.0%	0.5%	1.0%	1.5%	2.0%	2.5%	
0	136.44	110.71	**89.93**	59.53	**48.53**	39.59	**32.35**	26.45	17.74	11.95	8.09	5.49	3.75	0
1	133.58	108.66	**88.50**	58.90	**48.14**	39.38	**32.25**	26.45	17.84	12.08	8.22	5.61	3.84	1
2	130.43	106.38	**86.86**	58.12	**47.62**	39.06	**32.07**	26.37	17.87	12.17	8.31	5.71	3.94	2
3	127.32	104.12	**85.25**	57.33	**47.10**	38.73	**31.88**	26.28	17.90	12.26	8.42	5.81	4.02	3
4	124.29	101.90	**83.65**	56.56	**46.59**	38.41	**31.70**	26.19	17.94	12.33	8.52	5.91	4.11	4
5	121.31	99.74	**82.09**	55.79	**46.07**	38.08	**31.52**	26.11	17.98	12.43	8.63	6.01	4.21	5
6	118.41	97.60	**80.55**	55.03	**45.57**	37.76	**31.33**	26.03	18.00	12.52	8.73	6.11	4.30	6
7	115.58	95.52	**79.03**	54.28	**45.06**	37.44	**31.15**	25.94	18.04	12.60	8.83	6.22	4.39	7
8	112.81	93.48	**77.55**	53.54	**44.56**	37.13	**30.96**	25.85	18.07	12.69	8.94	6.33	4.49	8
9	110.09	91.48	**76.09**	52.81	**44.06**	36.81	**30.77**	25.76	18.10	12.78	9.05	6.43	4.59	9
10	107.45	89.51	**74.64**	52.09	**43.57**	36.49	**30.60**	25.67	18.14	12.86	9.15	6.54	4.69	10
11	104.87	87.59	**73.24**	51.37	**43.09**	36.18	**30.41**	25.59	18.16	12.95	9.26	6.66	4.80	11
12	102.34	85.71	**71.85**	50.67	**42.61**	35.87	**30.22**	25.50	18.20	13.04	9.37	6.77	4.90	12
13	99.87	83.86	**70.49**	49.97	**42.13**	35.56	**30.05**	25.41	18.23	13.13	9.49	6.88	5.01	13
14	97.46	82.05	**69.16**	49.28	**41.65**	35.26	**29.87**	25.32	18.26	13.22	9.60	7.00	5.12	14
15	95.11	80.29	**67.84**	48.59	**41.20**	34.95	**29.68**	25.24	18.29	13.31	9.72	7.12	5.24	15
16	92.82	78.56	**66.56**	47.92	**40.73**	34.65	**29.50**	25.15	18.32	13.39	9.83	7.24	5.36	16
17	90.57	76.87	**65.30**	47.27	**40.27**	34.35	**29.33**	25.06	18.35	13.49	9.95	7.36	5.47	17
18	88.38	75.21	**64.05**	46.61	**39.82**	34.05	**29.14**	24.97	18.38	13.58	10.07	7.49	5.59	18
19	86.25	73.58	**62.84**	45.97	**39.37**	33.76	**28.97**	24.88	18.41	13.67	10.19	7.62	5.71	19
20	84.16	72.00	**61.65**	45.33	**38.93**	33.46	**28.80**	24.79	18.44	13.77	10.31	7.75	5.84	20
21	82.13	70.44	**60.47**	44.70	**38.49**	33.18	**28.61**	24.71	18.47	13.85	10.43	7.88	5.97	21
22	80.14	68.92	**59.33**	44.09	**38.06**	32.89	**28.45**	24.62	18.50	13.96	10.56	8.01	6.11	22
23	78.20	67.43	**58.19**	43.47	**37.62**	32.60	**28.27**	24.53	18.53	14.04	10.68	8.15	6.24	23
24	76.30	65.97	**57.08**	42.87	**37.20**	32.31	**28.09**	24.45	18.56	14.14	10.81	8.29	6.38	24
25	74.46	64.54	**56.00**	42.28	**36.78**	32.03	**27.92**	24.36	18.59	14.23	10.94	8.44	6.52	25
26	72.65	63.14	**54.93**	41.69	**36.36**	31.75	**27.75**	24.27	18.61	14.33	11.07	8.58	6.67	26
27	70.89	61.77	**53.88**	41.11	**35.95**	31.47	**27.58**	24.19	18.65	14.42	11.19	8.72	6.81	27
28	69.17	60.43	**52.85**	40.54	**35.54**	31.20	**27.41**	24.09	18.68	14.52	11.33	8.87	6.96	28
29	67.48	59.13	**51.84**	39.97	**35.14**	30.93	**27.24**	24.01	18.70	14.62	11.46	9.02	7.12	29
30	65.85	57.84	**50.85**	39.41	**34.74**	30.65	**27.07**	23.93	18.74	14.72	11.61	9.17	7.27	30
31	64.26	56.59	**49.89**	38.86	**34.35**	30.39	**26.90**	23.84	18.77	14.82	11.74	9.33	7.43	31
32	62.70	55.36	**48.94**	38.33	**33.96**	30.13	**26.74**	23.75	18.80	14.92	11.88	9.49	7.60	32
33	61.18	54.17	**48.01**	37.80	**33.59**	29.86	**26.58**	23.68	18.83	15.02	12.02	9.65	7.77	33
34	59.70	53.00	**47.10**	37.28	**33.20**	29.60	**26.42**	23.59	18.85	15.13	12.16	9.82	7.94	34
35	58.26	51.86	**46.20**	36.76	**32.84**	29.35	**26.26**	23.51	18.89	15.23	12.31	9.98	8.11	35
36	56.86	50.74	**45.33**	36.26	**32.47**	29.10	**26.10**	23.43	18.92	15.33	12.46	10.16	8.30	36
37	55.48	49.65	**44.46**	35.76	**32.10**	28.85	**25.94**	23.35	18.95	15.44	12.61	10.33	8.48	37
38	54.14	48.58	**43.62**	35.27	**31.75**	28.60	**25.79**	23.27	19.00	15.55	12.76	10.50	8.68	38
39	52.84	47.54	**42.81**	34.79	**31.39**	28.36	**25.63**	23.19	19.02	15.66	12.92	10.69	8.86	39
40	51.58	46.53	**42.00**	34.31	**31.05**	28.12	**25.48**	23.12	19.06	15.76	13.08	10.87	9.06	40
41	50.34	45.53	**41.21**	33.85	**30.71**	27.89	**25.34**	23.04	19.10	15.88	13.23	11.06	9.28	41
42	49.14	44.56	**40.44**	33.39	**30.37**	27.65	**25.19**	22.97	19.14	15.99	13.40	11.25	9.48	42
43	47.96	43.62	**39.69**	32.94	**30.04**	27.42	**25.05**	22.90	19.18	16.11	13.56	11.45	9.70	43
44	46.82	42.69	**38.95**	32.49	**29.71**	27.20	**24.91**	22.83	19.21	16.22	13.73	11.66	9.92	44
45	45.71	41.79	**38.22**	32.07	**29.40**	26.98	**24.77**	22.76	19.26	16.34	13.91	11.86	10.15	45
46	44.64	40.91	**37.53**	31.64	**29.09**	26.76	**24.64**	22.69	19.30	16.46	14.08	12.07	10.38	46
47	43.59	40.05	**36.84**	31.23	**28.78**	26.54	**24.50**	22.63	19.34	16.59	14.26	12.29	10.61	47
48	42.57	39.22	**36.16**	30.82	**28.48**	26.34	**24.38**	22.57	19.40	16.71	14.44	12.50	10.86	48
49	41.57	38.41	**35.51**	30.42	**28.19**	26.13	**24.25**	22.51	19.44	16.84	14.63	12.73	11.11	49
50	40.61	37.62	**34.87**	30.03	**27.89**	25.94	**24.13**	22.46	19.50	16.98	14.82	12.96	11.37	50
51	39.68	36.85	**34.25**	29.65	**27.62**	25.74	**24.01**	22.41	19.56	17.12	15.02	13.20	11.63	51
52	38.77	36.10	**33.64**	29.29	**27.35**	25.56	**23.90**	22.36	19.62	17.26	15.21	13.45	11.91	52
53	37.89	35.38	**33.06**	28.92	**27.08**	25.37	**23.79**	22.32	19.68	17.40	15.43	13.70	12.20	53
54	37.03	34.68	**32.49**	28.57	**26.82**	25.20	**23.69**	22.29	19.76	17.55	15.64	13.96	12.50	54

Table 26 Multipliers for loss of pension commencing age 65 (females) *continued*

Age at date of trial	Multipliers calculated with allowance for projected mortality from the 2018-based population projections and rate of return of:													Age at date of trial
	-2.0%	-1.75%	**-1.5%**	-1.0%	**-0.75%**	-0.5%	**-0.25%**	0.0%	0.5%	1.0%	1.5%	2.0%	2.5%	
55	36.22	34.00	**31.94**	28.23	**26.57**	25.03	**23.60**	22.25	19.83	17.71	15.86	14.23	12.80	55
56	35.42	33.34	**31.40**	27.92	**26.34**	24.87	**23.50**	22.22	19.91	17.88	16.09	14.51	13.11	56
57	34.65	32.70	**30.89**	27.60	**26.12**	24.73	**23.43**	22.21	19.99	18.04	16.33	14.80	13.44	57
58	33.92	32.09	**30.39**	27.30	**25.90**	24.58	**23.35**	22.19	20.09	18.23	16.57	15.10	13.78	58
59	33.21	31.51	**29.91**	27.02	**25.69**	24.46	**23.29**	22.20	20.20	18.41	16.82	15.40	14.14	59
60	32.53	30.94	**29.45**	26.74	**25.50**	24.33	**23.23**	22.21	20.31	18.61	17.09	15.73	14.51	60
61	31.87	30.40	**29.01**	26.48	**25.32**	24.22	**23.19**	22.22	20.42	18.81	17.37	16.07	14.89	61
62	31.24	29.89	**28.60**	26.24	**25.15**	24.13	**23.17**	22.25	20.56	19.03	17.66	16.42	15.30	62
63	30.65	29.40	**28.20**	26.01	**25.01**	24.05	**23.15**	22.28	20.70	19.26	17.97	16.79	15.72	63
64	30.08	28.92	**27.83**	25.81	**24.87**	23.98	**23.14**	22.34	20.86	19.51	18.29	17.18	16.17	64
65	29.55	28.48	**27.48**	25.61	**24.75**	23.93	**23.15**	22.41	21.03	19.77	18.63	17.59	16.64	65

Table 27 Multipliers for loss of pension commencing age 68 (males)

Age at date of trial	Multipliers calculated with allowance for projected mortality from the 2018-based population projections and rate of return of:													Age at date of trial
	-2.0%	-1.75%	**-1.5%**	-1.0%	**-0.75%**	-0.5%	**-0.25%**	0.0%	0.5%	1.0%	1.5%	2.0%	2.5%	
0	112.83	91.37	**74.06**	48.81	**39.69**	32.31	**26.32**	21.47	14.32	9.59	6.45	4.35	2.95	0
1	110.40	89.64	**72.84**	48.27	**39.35**	32.11	**26.23**	21.45	14.39	9.68	6.54	4.43	3.02	1
2	107.67	87.64	**71.42**	47.57	**38.88**	31.82	**26.06**	21.37	14.40	9.74	6.62	4.51	3.08	2
3	104.98	85.68	**70.00**	46.88	**38.42**	31.51	**25.87**	21.27	14.41	9.80	6.69	4.58	3.15	3
4	102.35	83.75	**68.61**	46.19	**37.95**	31.21	**25.69**	21.17	14.42	9.86	6.76	4.65	3.21	4
5	99.77	81.87	**67.25**	45.50	**37.48**	30.91	**25.51**	21.08	14.43	9.92	6.84	4.73	3.28	5
6	97.26	80.02	**65.90**	44.83	**37.02**	30.61	**25.33**	20.98	14.44	9.97	6.91	4.81	3.36	6
7	94.81	78.22	**64.58**	44.16	**36.58**	30.32	**25.16**	20.89	14.45	10.03	6.99	4.89	3.43	7
8	92.43	76.45	**63.29**	43.50	**36.13**	30.02	**24.97**	20.79	14.46	10.08	7.06	4.96	3.49	8
9	90.09	74.71	**62.01**	42.86	**35.68**	29.72	**24.79**	20.70	14.47	10.14	7.14	5.04	3.58	9
10	87.82	73.02	**60.76**	42.21	**35.23**	29.43	**24.62**	20.60	14.47	10.20	7.22	5.12	3.64	10
11	85.58	71.35	**59.54**	41.57	**34.79**	29.15	**24.43**	20.51	14.47	10.25	7.29	5.20	3.72	11
12	83.42	69.72	**58.33**	40.95	**34.36**	28.86	**24.26**	20.41	14.48	10.31	7.37	5.29	3.80	12
13	81.30	68.13	**57.16**	40.34	**33.93**	28.57	**24.08**	20.31	14.49	10.37	7.45	5.37	3.88	13
14	79.22	66.58	**56.00**	39.73	**33.51**	28.29	**23.90**	20.21	14.49	10.43	7.53	5.45	3.97	14
15	77.20	65.05	**54.86**	39.13	**33.09**	28.01	**23.72**	20.12	14.50	10.48	7.61	5.54	4.05	15
16	75.24	63.56	**53.74**	38.53	**32.67**	27.72	**23.55**	20.02	14.50	10.54	7.69	5.62	4.13	16
17	73.32	62.11	**52.66**	37.95	**32.26**	27.45	**23.38**	19.92	14.51	10.60	7.77	5.72	4.21	17
18	71.45	60.69	**51.59**	37.38	**31.86**	27.18	**23.21**	19.83	14.52	10.66	7.85	5.81	4.30	18
19	69.64	59.29	**50.54**	36.81	**31.46**	26.91	**23.03**	19.74	14.52	10.72	7.93	5.90	4.39	19
20	67.87	57.94	**49.52**	36.26	**31.06**	26.64	**22.86**	19.64	14.53	10.78	8.02	5.99	4.48	20
21	66.14	56.62	**48.52**	35.71	**30.68**	26.37	**22.69**	19.55	14.53	10.84	8.10	6.08	4.58	21
22	64.45	55.32	**47.53**	35.17	**30.30**	26.11	**22.53**	19.45	14.54	10.90	8.19	6.18	4.67	22
23	62.81	54.06	**46.57**	34.64	**29.91**	25.86	**22.36**	19.36	14.54	10.96	8.28	6.28	4.78	23
24	61.21	52.82	**45.62**	34.11	**29.54**	25.60	**22.20**	19.27	14.54	11.02	8.37	6.38	4.87	24
25	59.65	51.61	**44.69**	33.60	**29.16**	25.34	**22.03**	19.17	14.55	11.08	8.45	6.47	4.97	25
26	58.13	50.43	**43.78**	33.09	**28.80**	25.08	**21.87**	19.08	14.55	11.14	8.54	6.58	5.07	26
27	56.65	49.27	**42.90**	32.59	**28.44**	24.84	**21.71**	18.99	14.56	11.20	8.64	6.68	5.18	27
28	55.21	48.15	**42.03**	32.10	**28.08**	24.59	**21.55**	18.90	14.57	11.26	8.73	6.79	5.29	28
29	53.80	47.04	**41.17**	31.61	**27.73**	24.35	**21.39**	18.81	14.57	11.32	8.83	6.90	5.40	29
30	52.43	45.97	**40.33**	31.13	**27.38**	24.10	**21.23**	18.71	14.57	11.39	8.92	7.00	5.51	30
31	51.09	44.92	**39.52**	30.67	**27.05**	23.87	**21.08**	18.63	14.58	11.45	9.01	7.11	5.63	31
32	49.80	43.90	**38.73**	30.20	**26.70**	23.63	**20.93**	18.55	14.59	11.51	9.11	7.22	5.75	32
33	48.53	42.89	**37.94**	29.75	**26.37**	23.40	**20.78**	18.45	14.60	11.58	9.21	7.34	5.87	33
34	47.30	41.92	**37.18**	29.31	**26.04**	23.16	**20.62**	18.37	14.61	11.64	9.31	7.46	6.00	34
35	46.11	40.97	**36.42**	28.87	**25.72**	22.94	**20.48**	18.29	14.61	11.71	9.41	7.58	6.12	35
36	44.94	40.04	**35.69**	28.44	**25.41**	22.72	**20.33**	18.20	14.62	11.78	9.51	7.71	6.25	36
37	43.81	39.14	**34.99**	28.02	**25.10**	22.50	**20.18**	18.12	14.63	11.84	9.62	7.83	6.38	37
38	42.71	38.26	**34.29**	27.61	**24.79**	22.29	**20.05**	18.04	14.65	11.92	9.72	7.96	6.52	38
39	41.65	37.39	**33.61**	27.20	**24.50**	22.08	**19.91**	17.97	14.65	12.00	9.84	8.08	6.66	39
40	40.61	36.56	**32.95**	26.80	**24.20**	21.87	**19.77**	17.89	14.67	12.06	9.94	8.22	6.81	40
41	39.59	35.75	**32.30**	26.41	**23.92**	21.67	**19.64**	17.81	14.69	12.14	10.05	8.35	6.96	41
42	38.61	34.95	**31.66**	26.04	**23.64**	21.47	**19.52**	17.74	14.71	12.22	10.17	8.50	7.11	42
43	37.67	34.19	**31.05**	25.67	**23.36**	21.27	**19.39**	17.68	14.73	12.29	10.29	8.64	7.26	43
44	36.75	33.44	**30.45**	25.31	**23.09**	21.08	**19.26**	17.61	14.75	12.38	10.41	8.78	7.42	44
45	35.84	32.70	**29.87**	24.95	**22.83**	20.90	**19.14**	17.55	14.77	12.46	10.53	8.93	7.59	45
46	34.98	32.00	**29.29**	24.60	**22.57**	20.72	**19.02**	17.48	14.79	12.55	10.66	9.08	7.76	46
47	34.13	31.31	**28.74**	24.26	**22.32**	20.54	**18.92**	17.42	14.82	12.64	10.79	9.24	7.93	47
48	33.30	30.63	**28.20**	23.93	**22.07**	20.36	**18.80**	17.37	14.84	12.72	10.92	9.40	8.10	48
49	32.51	29.99	**27.67**	23.61	**21.83**	20.19	**18.69**	17.31	14.88	12.82	11.06	9.56	8.29	49
50	31.74	29.35	**27.15**	23.29	**21.59**	20.03	**18.59**	17.26	14.91	12.91	11.20	9.73	8.48	50
51	30.99	28.74	**26.66**	22.99	**21.36**	19.87	**18.49**	17.21	14.94	13.00	11.34	9.91	8.67	51
52	30.27	28.13	**26.17**	22.69	**21.14**	19.72	**18.39**	17.17	14.99	13.11	11.48	10.09	8.88	52
53	29.57	27.56	**25.70**	22.40	**20.93**	19.57	**18.30**	17.13	15.02	13.21	11.64	10.27	9.08	53
54	28.88	27.00	**25.25**	22.12	**20.72**	19.43	**18.22**	17.09	15.07	13.32	11.80	10.47	9.30	54

Table 27: Multipliers for loss of pension commencing age 68 (males) *continued*

Age at date of trial	Multipliers calculated with allowance for projected mortality from the 2018-based population projections and rate of return of:													Age at date of trial
	-2.0%	-1.75%	**-1.5%**	-1.0%	**-0.75%**	-0.5%	**-0.25%**	0.0%	0.5%	1.0%	1.5%	2.0%	2.5%	
55	28.23	26.46	**24.81**	21.85	**20.52**	19.29	**18.13**	17.07	15.12	13.44	11.96	10.66	9.52	55
56	27.60	25.94	**24.38**	21.60	**20.34**	19.16	**18.07**	17.04	15.18	13.55	12.12	10.87	9.76	56
57	27.00	25.44	**23.98**	21.35	**20.16**	19.05	**17.99**	17.02	15.25	13.68	12.30	11.09	10.01	57
58	26.43	24.97	**23.60**	21.12	**19.99**	18.94	**17.94**	17.01	15.32	13.82	12.49	11.31	10.26	58
59	25.88	24.52	**23.23**	20.90	**19.84**	18.84	**17.90**	17.02	15.40	13.96	12.69	11.55	10.52	59
60	25.37	24.09	**22.89**	20.70	**19.71**	18.75	**17.87**	17.03	15.49	14.13	12.90	11.79	10.81	60
61	24.87	23.69	**22.56**	20.52	**19.58**	18.69	**17.85**	17.06	15.60	14.29	13.12	12.05	11.11	61
62	24.41	23.31	**22.26**	20.36	**19.47**	18.64	**17.85**	17.10	15.72	14.47	13.35	12.33	11.42	62
63	23.98	22.96	**21.99**	20.20	**19.38**	18.60	**17.86**	17.15	15.85	14.67	13.60	12.63	11.75	63
64	23.58	22.63	**21.73**	20.07	**19.31**	18.58	**17.88**	17.22	16.00	14.88	13.87	12.95	12.10	64
65	23.19	22.32	**21.50**	19.96	**19.25**	18.57	**17.92**	17.30	16.15	15.12	14.16	13.28	12.48	65
66	22.85	22.05	**21.29**	19.88	**19.22**	18.59	**17.99**	17.41	16.34	15.36	14.46	13.64	12.88	66
67	22.55	21.82	**21.12**	19.82	**19.21**	18.63	**18.08**	17.55	16.55	15.64	14.80	14.03	13.32	67
68	22.27	21.61	**20.97**	19.79	**19.23**	18.70	**18.19**	17.70	16.79	15.94	15.17	14.45	13.78	68

Table 28 Multipliers for loss of pension commencing age 68 (females)

Age at date of trial	Multipliers calculated with allowance for projected mortality from the 2018-based population projections and rate of return of:													Age at date of trial
	-2.0%	-1.75%	**-1.5%**	-1.0%	**-0.75%**	-0.5%	**-0.25%**	0.0%	0.5%	1.0%	1.5%	2.0%	2.5%	
0	125.52	101.49	**82.14**	53.97	**43.83**	35.62	**28.98**	23.60	15.70	10.48	7.03	4.73	3.20	0
1	122.86	99.58	**80.81**	53.39	**43.46**	35.41	**28.89**	23.59	15.78	10.59	7.14	4.82	3.27	1
2	119.92	97.46	**79.29**	52.66	**42.98**	35.11	**28.72**	23.51	15.80	10.66	7.22	4.91	3.36	2
3	117.03	95.37	**77.80**	51.93	**42.49**	34.81	**28.54**	23.42	15.82	10.74	7.31	5.00	3.43	3
4	114.20	93.30	**76.32**	51.22	**42.02**	34.50	**28.37**	23.34	15.85	10.80	7.39	5.08	3.50	4
5	111.43	91.29	**74.87**	50.50	**41.54**	34.20	**28.19**	23.26	15.88	10.88	7.49	5.16	3.58	5
6	108.74	89.31	**73.44**	49.80	**41.07**	33.90	**28.01**	23.18	15.90	10.95	7.57	5.25	3.66	6
7	106.11	87.38	**72.03**	49.10	**40.60**	33.60	**27.85**	23.09	15.92	11.02	7.66	5.34	3.74	7
8	103.53	85.48	**70.66**	48.42	**40.14**	33.31	**27.66**	23.01	15.95	11.10	7.75	5.43	3.82	8
9	101.00	83.63	**69.31**	47.74	**39.68**	33.01	**27.49**	22.91	15.97	11.17	7.84	5.52	3.91	9
10	98.54	81.80	**67.97**	47.07	**39.22**	32.72	**27.32**	22.83	15.99	11.24	7.93	5.61	3.99	10
11	96.15	80.02	**66.67**	46.40	**38.78**	32.43	**27.14**	22.75	16.01	11.31	8.02	5.71	4.08	11
12	93.80	78.28	**65.39**	45.76	**38.33**	32.14	**26.97**	22.66	16.03	11.39	8.11	5.80	4.17	12
13	91.51	76.57	**64.12**	45.11	**37.89**	31.85	**26.80**	22.57	16.06	11.46	8.21	5.90	4.26	13
14	89.27	74.89	**62.89**	44.47	**37.44**	31.57	**26.63**	22.49	16.08	11.53	8.30	6.00	4.35	14
15	87.09	73.25	**61.67**	43.84	**37.02**	31.28	**26.46**	22.40	16.10	11.61	8.40	6.10	4.44	15
16	84.96	71.65	**60.48**	43.22	**36.58**	31.00	**26.29**	22.32	16.12	11.68	8.50	6.20	4.54	16
17	82.88	70.09	**59.32**	42.61	**36.17**	30.72	**26.12**	22.23	16.14	11.76	8.60	6.30	4.64	17
18	80.85	68.55	**58.17**	42.01	**35.74**	30.44	**25.95**	22.14	16.16	11.84	8.70	6.41	4.74	18
19	78.87	67.04	**57.04**	41.41	**35.33**	30.17	**25.78**	22.06	16.18	11.91	8.79	6.52	4.84	19
20	76.94	65.57	**55.94**	40.83	**34.92**	29.89	**25.62**	21.97	16.20	11.99	8.89	6.63	4.95	20
21	75.05	64.14	**54.85**	40.24	**34.51**	29.63	**25.45**	21.89	16.22	12.06	8.99	6.74	5.05	21
22	73.21	62.73	**53.80**	39.68	**34.12**	29.36	**25.29**	21.80	16.24	12.14	9.10	6.84	5.17	22
23	71.41	61.35	**52.75**	39.11	**33.71**	29.09	**25.12**	21.71	16.26	12.21	9.21	6.96	5.28	23
24	69.65	60.00	**51.72**	38.55	**33.32**	28.82	**24.96**	21.63	16.28	12.29	9.31	7.08	5.39	24
25	67.94	58.68	**50.73**	38.00	**32.93**	28.56	**24.79**	21.54	16.30	12.37	9.42	7.20	5.51	25
26	66.26	57.38	**49.74**	37.46	**32.54**	28.30	**24.63**	21.45	16.31	12.45	9.53	7.32	5.63	26
27	64.64	56.12	**48.76**	36.92	**32.16**	28.04	**24.47**	21.37	16.34	12.52	9.63	7.43	5.75	27
28	63.04	54.88	**47.82**	36.39	**31.78**	27.79	**24.31**	21.28	16.36	12.61	9.74	7.56	5.87	28
29	61.49	53.67	**46.89**	35.87	**31.41**	27.53	**24.15**	21.20	16.37	12.68	9.86	7.68	6.01	29
30	59.97	52.49	**45.97**	35.36	**31.05**	27.28	**23.99**	21.12	16.39	12.77	9.97	7.80	6.13	30
31	58.50	51.33	**45.08**	34.85	**30.68**	27.04	**23.83**	21.03	16.41	12.85	10.08	7.93	6.26	31
32	57.06	50.20	**44.21**	34.36	**30.32**	26.79	**23.68**	20.95	16.44	12.93	10.20	8.07	6.40	32
33	55.65	49.10	**43.35**	33.87	**29.98**	26.54	**23.52**	20.87	16.45	13.01	10.31	8.20	6.54	33
34	54.29	48.02	**42.51**	33.39	**29.62**	26.30	**23.37**	20.78	16.47	13.10	10.43	8.34	6.68	34
35	52.96	46.97	**41.68**	32.91	**29.28**	26.07	**23.22**	20.70	16.49	13.18	10.55	8.48	6.82	35
36	51.66	45.93	**40.88**	32.44	**28.94**	25.83	**23.07**	20.63	16.51	13.26	10.68	8.62	6.98	36
37	50.39	44.93	**40.08**	31.99	**28.60**	25.60	**22.92**	20.54	16.53	13.35	10.80	8.76	7.13	37
38	49.16	43.94	**39.31**	31.53	**28.28**	25.37	**22.78**	20.46	16.56	13.43	10.92	8.91	7.29	38
39	47.95	42.98	**38.56**	31.09	**27.95**	25.14	**22.63**	20.39	16.58	13.52	11.06	9.06	7.44	39
40	46.79	42.05	**37.82**	30.65	**27.62**	24.92	**22.49**	20.32	16.60	13.61	11.19	9.21	7.61	40
41	45.64	41.13	**37.09**	30.22	**27.31**	24.70	**22.35**	20.24	16.63	13.70	11.31	9.37	7.78	41
42	44.54	40.24	**36.38**	29.80	**27.00**	24.48	**22.21**	20.16	16.66	13.79	11.45	9.52	7.95	42
43	43.45	39.37	**35.69**	29.39	**26.69**	24.26	**22.08**	20.10	16.69	13.89	11.59	9.69	8.13	43
44	42.40	38.51	**35.01**	28.98	**26.39**	24.06	**21.94**	20.03	16.71	13.98	11.72	9.86	8.31	44
45	41.38	37.69	**34.34**	28.58	**26.10**	23.85	**21.81**	19.96	16.74	14.08	11.87	10.02	8.49	45
46	40.39	36.88	**33.70**	28.19	**25.81**	23.65	**21.68**	19.89	16.77	14.17	12.01	10.19	8.68	46
47	39.42	36.09	**33.07**	27.81	**25.52**	23.44	**21.55**	19.82	16.79	14.27	12.16	10.38	8.87	47
48	38.48	35.32	**32.44**	27.43	**25.25**	23.25	**21.43**	19.76	16.84	14.37	12.31	10.55	9.08	48
49	37.56	34.57	**31.85**	27.07	**24.98**	23.06	**21.30**	19.70	16.86	14.48	12.46	10.74	9.28	49
50	36.68	33.85	**31.25**	26.71	**24.70**	22.88	**21.19**	19.64	16.90	14.59	12.61	10.93	9.49	50
51	35.82	33.14	**30.68**	26.35	**24.45**	22.70	**21.08**	19.59	16.95	14.70	12.78	11.13	9.71	51
52	34.98	32.45	**30.13**	26.02	**24.20**	22.52	**20.97**	19.53	16.99	14.82	12.94	11.33	9.94	52
53	34.17	31.78	**29.59**	25.68	**23.95**	22.35	**20.86**	19.49	17.04	14.93	13.11	11.54	10.17	53
54	33.39	31.14	**29.06**	25.36	**23.71**	22.18	**20.76**	19.45	17.09	15.05	13.28	11.75	10.41	54

Table 28: Multipliers for loss of pension commencing age 68 (females) *continued*

Age at date of trial	Multipliers calculated with allowance for projected mortality from the 2018-based population projections and rate of return of:													Age at date of trial
	-2.0%	-1.75%	**-1.5%**	-1.0%	**-0.75%**	-0.5%	**-0.25%**	0.0%	0.5%	1.0%	1.5%	2.0%	2.5%	
55	32.63	30.52	**28.56**	25.05	**23.48**	22.02	**20.67**	19.41	17.15	15.18	13.47	11.97	10.66	55
56	31.90	29.91	**28.06**	24.75	**23.26**	21.87	**20.58**	19.38	17.21	15.31	13.65	12.20	10.91	56
57	31.19	29.32	**27.59**	24.45	**23.05**	21.74	**20.51**	19.35	17.27	15.44	13.85	12.43	11.18	57
58	30.51	28.76	**27.13**	24.18	**22.85**	21.59	**20.43**	19.33	17.35	15.59	14.04	12.67	11.46	58
59	29.86	28.22	**26.69**	23.92	**22.65**	21.48	**20.37**	19.32	17.43	15.74	14.25	12.93	11.75	59
60	29.24	27.71	**26.27**	23.66	**22.47**	21.35	**20.30**	19.32	17.51	15.90	14.47	13.19	12.05	60
61	28.63	27.21	**25.86**	23.42	**22.30**	21.25	**20.26**	19.33	17.60	16.07	14.70	13.47	12.36	61
62	28.06	26.73	**25.48**	23.19	**22.14**	21.16	**20.22**	19.33	17.71	16.25	14.94	13.76	12.70	62
63	27.51	26.28	**25.12**	22.98	**22.00**	21.07	**20.19**	19.35	17.83	16.43	15.19	14.06	13.03	63
64	26.98	25.85	**24.77**	22.79	**21.87**	21.00	**20.18**	19.40	17.95	16.63	15.45	14.38	13.39	64
65	26.49	25.44	**24.45**	22.60	**21.75**	20.94	**20.17**	19.44	18.09	16.85	15.73	14.71	13.78	65
66	26.03	25.06	**24.14**	22.44	**21.65**	20.90	**20.18**	19.51	18.24	17.09	16.03	15.07	14.18	66
67	25.58	24.70	**23.86**	22.30	**21.57**	20.88	**20.21**	19.58	18.41	17.33	16.34	15.43	14.61	67
68	25.18	24.37	**23.61**	22.18	**21.51**	20.87	**20.26**	19.68	18.59	17.59	16.68	15.84	15.06	68

Table 29 Multipliers for loss of pension commencing age 70 (males)

Age at date of trial	Multipliers calculated with allowance for projected mortality from the 2018-based population projections and rate of return of:													Age at date of trial
	-2.0%	-1.75%	**-1.5%**	-1.0%	**-0.75%**	-0.5%	**-0.25%**	0.0%	0.5%	1.0%	1.5%	2.0%	2.5%	
0	105.49	85.21	**68.89**	45.17	**36.63**	29.73	**24.16**	19.64	13.03	8.67	5.80	3.88	2.61	0
1	103.19	83.57	**67.74**	44.65	**36.31**	29.54	**24.06**	19.63	13.09	8.75	5.88	3.96	2.68	1
2	100.60	81.69	**66.40**	43.99	**35.86**	29.27	**23.90**	19.54	13.09	8.80	5.95	4.03	2.74	2
3	98.06	79.84	**65.06**	43.34	**35.42**	28.97	**23.72**	19.45	13.10	8.85	6.00	4.09	2.79	3
4	95.58	78.01	**63.74**	42.69	**34.98**	28.68	**23.55**	19.35	13.10	8.90	6.07	4.15	2.85	4
5	93.14	76.24	**62.46**	42.04	**34.54**	28.40	**23.38**	19.26	13.10	8.96	6.14	4.21	2.91	5
6	90.77	74.49	**61.19**	41.41	**34.10**	28.12	**23.20**	19.16	13.11	9.00	6.20	4.29	2.97	6
7	88.46	72.79	**59.95**	40.78	**33.68**	27.84	**23.04**	19.07	13.12	9.05	6.27	4.35	3.03	7
8	86.21	71.12	**58.73**	40.15	**33.26**	27.56	**22.86**	18.98	13.12	9.10	6.33	4.42	3.09	8
9	84.01	69.48	**57.53**	39.55	**32.83**	27.28	**22.69**	18.89	13.12	9.14	6.39	4.49	3.16	9
10	81.86	67.89	**56.35**	38.94	**32.41**	27.00	**22.52**	18.80	13.12	9.19	6.47	4.56	3.22	10
11	79.75	66.32	**55.19**	38.34	**32.00**	26.73	**22.34**	18.70	13.12	9.24	6.53	4.63	3.29	11
12	77.71	64.78	**54.06**	37.75	**31.58**	26.46	**22.17**	18.60	13.12	9.29	6.59	4.70	3.36	12
13	75.71	63.28	**52.96**	37.17	**31.18**	26.18	**22.00**	18.51	13.12	9.34	6.67	4.77	3.43	13
14	73.76	61.82	**51.86**	36.60	**30.79**	25.92	**21.84**	18.41	13.12	9.39	6.74	4.84	3.50	14
15	71.85	60.38	**50.79**	36.03	**30.39**	25.65	**21.67**	18.32	13.13	9.43	6.80	4.93	3.57	15
16	70.00	58.98	**49.74**	35.47	**29.99**	25.38	**21.50**	18.22	13.13	9.48	6.87	4.99	3.64	16
17	68.19	57.62	**48.72**	34.93	**29.61**	25.12	**21.33**	18.13	13.13	9.53	6.94	5.08	3.71	17
18	66.43	56.28	**47.72**	34.39	**29.23**	24.87	**21.17**	18.04	13.13	9.58	7.01	5.16	3.79	18
19	64.72	54.97	**46.73**	33.85	**28.85**	24.61	**21.00**	17.95	13.12	9.63	7.08	5.23	3.87	19
20	63.06	53.70	**45.77**	33.33	**28.47**	24.36	**20.84**	17.85	13.13	9.68	7.16	5.31	3.95	20
21	61.43	52.45	**44.83**	32.82	**28.12**	24.10	**20.68**	17.76	13.13	9.73	7.23	5.39	4.04	21
22	59.84	51.23	**43.90**	32.31	**27.76**	23.85	**20.53**	17.66	13.13	9.78	7.31	5.48	4.11	22
23	58.30	50.04	**42.99**	31.81	**27.39**	23.61	**20.36**	17.57	13.12	9.83	7.38	5.56	4.20	23
24	56.79	48.88	**42.11**	31.31	**27.04**	23.37	**20.21**	17.49	13.12	9.88	7.46	5.65	4.28	24
25	55.32	47.74	**41.24**	30.84	**26.69**	23.13	**20.05**	17.40	13.12	9.93	7.53	5.73	4.37	25
26	53.90	46.64	**40.38**	30.35	**26.34**	22.88	**19.89**	17.31	13.12	9.98	7.61	5.82	4.46	26
27	52.50	45.55	**39.55**	29.88	**26.01**	22.64	**19.74**	17.21	13.12	10.03	7.69	5.91	4.55	27
28	51.15	44.49	**38.73**	29.42	**25.67**	22.41	**19.59**	17.12	13.12	10.08	7.76	6.00	4.65	28
29	49.82	43.45	**37.93**	28.97	**25.34**	22.18	**19.43**	17.04	13.12	10.13	7.85	6.09	4.74	29
30	48.54	42.45	**37.14**	28.51	**25.01**	21.95	**19.28**	16.94	13.12	10.19	7.93	6.18	4.84	30
31	47.28	41.46	**36.38**	28.08	**24.69**	21.73	**19.13**	16.86	13.12	10.24	8.01	6.28	4.94	31
32	46.07	40.50	**35.63**	27.64	**24.37**	21.50	**18.99**	16.78	13.12	10.29	8.09	6.38	5.04	32
33	44.88	39.56	**34.89**	27.22	**24.06**	21.28	**18.84**	16.69	13.13	10.35	8.18	6.48	5.15	33
34	43.72	38.65	**34.18**	26.80	**23.75**	21.06	**18.69**	16.61	13.12	10.39	8.26	6.58	5.25	34
35	42.61	37.75	**33.48**	26.38	**23.45**	20.85	**18.56**	16.52	13.12	10.46	8.34	6.68	5.36	35
36	41.51	36.88	**32.79**	25.98	**23.15**	20.64	**18.42**	16.44	13.13	10.51	8.43	6.79	5.47	36
37	40.44	36.04	**32.13**	25.58	**22.86**	20.43	**18.27**	16.36	13.13	10.56	8.53	6.90	5.58	37
38	39.41	35.21	**31.48**	25.20	**22.57**	20.23	**18.14**	16.28	13.14	10.63	8.61	7.00	5.70	38
39	38.42	34.40	**30.84**	24.82	**22.29**	20.03	**18.01**	16.20	13.14	10.69	8.71	7.11	5.82	39
40	37.44	33.62	**30.22**	24.44	**22.01**	19.83	**17.88**	16.13	13.15	10.75	8.80	7.23	5.94	40
41	36.49	32.86	**29.61**	24.08	**21.75**	19.64	**17.75**	16.05	13.16	10.81	8.89	7.34	6.08	41
42	35.57	32.12	**29.01**	23.73	**21.48**	19.46	**17.63**	15.98	13.17	10.87	9.00	7.46	6.21	42
43	34.69	31.40	**28.45**	23.38	**21.21**	19.26	**17.51**	15.92	13.18	10.93	9.10	7.58	6.34	43
44	33.83	30.70	**27.88**	23.04	**20.97**	19.08	**17.39**	15.85	13.19	11.00	9.19	7.70	6.47	44
45	32.98	30.01	**27.34**	22.71	**20.72**	18.91	**17.27**	15.79	13.20	11.07	9.30	7.83	6.61	45
46	32.17	29.35	**26.80**	22.38	**20.47**	18.74	**17.15**	15.72	13.22	11.14	9.41	7.96	6.76	46
47	31.38	28.71	**26.28**	22.06	**20.23**	18.56	**17.05**	15.66	13.23	11.22	9.52	8.09	6.90	47
48	30.60	28.07	**25.77**	21.75	**20.00**	18.39	**16.93**	15.60	13.25	11.29	9.63	8.24	7.05	48
49	29.86	27.47	**25.28**	21.45	**19.77**	18.24	**16.83**	15.55	13.28	11.37	9.74	8.37	7.21	49
50	29.14	26.87	**24.79**	21.15	**19.55**	18.08	**16.73**	15.49	13.30	11.44	9.86	8.51	7.37	50
51	28.44	26.30	**24.33**	20.87	**19.33**	17.93	**16.63**	15.44	13.32	11.52	9.98	8.67	7.54	51
52	27.76	25.73	**23.87**	20.58	**19.12**	17.78	**16.54**	15.39	13.35	11.61	10.10	8.82	7.71	52
53	27.11	25.19	**23.44**	20.31	**18.92**	17.64	**16.44**	15.34	13.38	11.69	10.23	8.98	7.88	53
54	26.47	24.67	**23.01**	20.04	**18.72**	17.50	**16.36**	15.31	13.42	11.78	10.37	9.14	8.07	54

Table 29 Multipliers for loss of pension commencing age 70 (males) *continued*

Age at date of trial	Multipliers calculated with allowance for projected mortality from the 2018-based population projections and rate of return of:													Age at date of trial
	-2.0%	-1.75%	**-1.5%**	-1.0%	**-0.75%**	-0.5%	**-0.25%**	0.0%	0.5%	1.0%	1.5%	2.0%	2.5%	
55	25.86	24.17	**22.59**	19.79	**18.54**	17.37	**16.28**	15.28	13.46	11.88	10.51	9.30	8.26	55
56	25.27	23.68	**22.20**	19.55	**18.36**	17.24	**16.21**	15.24	13.50	11.97	10.64	9.48	8.45	56
57	24.71	23.21	**21.82**	19.32	**18.18**	17.13	**16.14**	15.22	13.55	12.08	10.79	9.67	8.67	57
58	24.18	22.77	**21.46**	19.10	**18.03**	17.03	**16.08**	15.20	13.61	12.20	10.96	9.86	8.88	58
59	23.66	22.35	**21.12**	18.89	**17.88**	16.93	**16.04**	15.20	13.67	12.32	11.12	10.06	9.10	59
60	23.18	21.95	**20.80**	18.70	**17.75**	16.84	**16.00**	15.20	13.74	12.45	11.30	10.26	9.34	60
61	22.71	21.57	**20.49**	18.53	**17.63**	16.78	**15.98**	15.22	13.83	12.59	11.49	10.48	9.60	61
62	22.28	21.21	**20.21**	18.37	**17.52**	16.72	**15.97**	15.25	13.93	12.74	11.68	10.72	9.86	62
63	21.87	20.88	**19.95**	18.22	**17.42**	16.67	**15.96**	15.28	14.04	12.91	11.90	10.97	10.14	63
64	21.49	20.57	**19.70**	18.09	**17.35**	16.65	**15.97**	15.34	14.16	13.09	12.12	11.24	10.44	64
65	21.13	20.28	**19.48**	17.98	**17.29**	16.63	**16.00**	15.40	14.29	13.29	12.37	11.52	10.76	65
66	20.81	20.02	**19.29**	17.90	**17.26**	16.64	**16.05**	15.49	14.45	13.50	12.63	11.83	11.10	66
67	20.52	19.80	**19.12**	17.84	**17.24**	16.67	**16.12**	15.60	14.62	13.74	12.92	12.16	11.47	67
68	20.26	19.60	**18.97**	17.80	**17.24**	16.72	**16.21**	15.73	14.83	13.99	13.23	12.52	11.86	68
69	20.04	19.44	**18.86**	17.78	**17.28**	16.80	**16.34**	15.89	15.05	14.27	13.57	12.90	12.29	69
70	19.84	19.30	**18.78**	17.80	**17.34**	16.90	**16.48**	16.07	15.30	14.59	13.93	13.32	12.75	70

Table 30 Multipliers for loss of pension commencing age 70 (females)

Age at date of trial	Multipliers calculated with allowance for projected mortality from the 2018-based population projections and rate of return of:													Age at date of trial
	-2.0%	-1.75%	**-1.5%**	-1.0%	**-0.75%**	-0.5%	**-0.25%**	0.0%	0.5%	1.0%	1.5%	2.0%	2.5%	
0	117.94	95.13	**76.81**	50.21	**40.67**	32.96	**26.75**	21.72	14.37	9.54	6.36	4.25	2.86	0
1	115.41	93.32	**75.54**	49.65	**40.32**	32.76	**26.66**	21.71	14.43	9.63	6.46	4.33	2.92	1
2	112.63	91.31	**74.11**	48.97	**39.86**	32.48	**26.49**	21.63	14.45	9.70	6.53	4.41	3.00	2
3	109.89	89.33	**72.70**	48.27	**39.40**	32.19	**26.32**	21.54	14.47	9.76	6.61	4.49	3.06	3
4	107.21	87.38	**71.29**	47.60	**38.95**	31.90	**26.15**	21.46	14.49	9.82	6.68	4.56	3.12	4
5	104.58	85.48	**69.92**	46.92	**38.50**	31.61	**25.98**	21.38	14.51	9.89	6.76	4.63	3.19	5
6	102.03	83.60	**68.57**	46.26	**38.05**	31.32	**25.82**	21.30	14.53	9.95	6.83	4.71	3.26	6
7	99.54	81.77	**67.24**	45.60	**37.61**	31.04	**25.65**	21.22	14.54	10.01	6.91	4.79	3.33	7
8	97.10	79.98	**65.94**	44.95	**37.17**	30.77	**25.48**	21.13	14.56	10.08	6.99	4.87	3.40	8
9	94.70	78.22	**64.66**	44.32	**36.73**	30.48	**25.31**	21.04	14.58	10.14	7.07	4.95	3.48	9
10	92.38	76.49	**63.40**	43.68	**36.30**	30.20	**25.15**	20.96	14.60	10.20	7.15	5.03	3.55	10
11	90.11	74.81	**62.17**	43.05	**35.88**	29.92	**24.98**	20.88	14.61	10.26	7.23	5.12	3.63	11
12	87.88	73.16	**60.96**	42.44	**35.45**	29.65	**24.81**	20.79	14.63	10.33	7.31	5.20	3.71	12
13	85.72	71.54	**59.76**	41.83	**35.04**	29.38	**24.65**	20.70	14.65	10.39	7.40	5.28	3.79	13
14	83.60	69.96	**58.60**	41.22	**34.62**	29.11	**24.49**	20.62	14.66	10.45	7.48	5.37	3.87	14
15	81.53	68.41	**57.45**	40.63	**34.22**	28.83	**24.33**	20.54	14.68	10.52	7.56	5.46	3.95	15
16	79.52	66.90	**56.33**	40.04	**33.81**	28.57	**24.16**	20.45	14.69	10.58	7.65	5.55	4.04	16
17	77.55	65.42	**55.23**	39.47	**33.41**	28.31	**24.00**	20.37	14.70	10.65	7.74	5.63	4.12	17
18	75.63	63.96	**54.14**	38.90	**33.01**	28.04	**23.84**	20.28	14.72	10.72	7.83	5.73	4.21	18
19	73.76	62.54	**53.08**	38.34	**32.62**	27.78	**23.67**	20.19	14.73	10.77	7.91	5.83	4.30	19
20	71.93	61.16	**52.04**	37.78	**32.23**	27.52	**23.52**	20.11	14.74	10.85	8.00	5.92	4.39	20
21	70.15	59.80	**51.02**	37.23	**31.85**	27.27	**23.35**	20.03	14.76	10.91	8.09	6.02	4.49	21
22	68.41	58.47	**50.02**	36.70	**31.47**	27.01	**23.20**	19.94	14.77	10.98	8.18	6.11	4.59	22
23	66.71	57.17	**49.03**	36.16	**31.09**	26.76	**23.04**	19.86	14.78	11.04	8.27	6.21	4.69	23
24	65.05	55.90	**48.06**	35.64	**30.72**	26.50	**22.88**	19.78	14.80	11.11	8.36	6.32	4.78	24
25	63.43	54.65	**47.12**	35.12	**30.35**	26.25	**22.72**	19.69	14.81	11.17	8.46	6.42	4.89	25
26	61.85	53.43	**46.19**	34.60	**29.99**	26.01	**22.57**	19.60	14.82	11.24	8.55	6.53	4.99	26
27	60.32	52.24	**45.27**	34.10	**29.63**	25.76	**22.42**	19.52	14.84	11.31	8.64	6.63	5.09	27
28	58.81	51.07	**44.38**	33.60	**29.27**	25.52	**22.27**	19.43	14.85	11.38	8.74	6.74	5.20	28
29	57.34	49.93	**43.50**	33.11	**28.91**	25.28	**22.11**	19.35	14.86	11.44	8.84	6.84	5.32	29
30	55.91	48.82	**42.65**	32.63	**28.57**	25.03	**21.95**	19.27	14.87	11.52	8.94	6.95	5.42	30
31	54.53	47.72	**41.81**	32.15	**28.22**	24.80	**21.80**	19.19	14.89	11.59	9.03	7.06	5.54	31
32	53.16	46.66	**40.98**	31.68	**27.89**	24.57	**21.66**	19.10	14.90	11.65	9.14	7.19	5.66	32
33	51.84	45.62	**40.18**	31.22	**27.56**	24.33	**21.51**	19.03	14.91	11.72	9.24	7.30	5.78	33
34	50.55	44.60	**39.38**	30.77	**27.22**	24.10	**21.36**	18.94	14.92	11.80	9.34	7.42	5.91	34
35	49.30	43.61	**38.61**	30.32	**26.90**	23.88	**21.22**	18.86	14.94	11.87	9.44	7.54	6.03	35
36	48.08	42.63	**37.85**	29.88	**26.58**	23.66	**21.08**	18.78	14.95	11.94	9.55	7.67	6.16	36
37	46.88	41.69	**37.10**	29.45	**26.26**	23.44	**20.93**	18.70	14.96	12.01	9.66	7.78	6.29	37
38	45.72	40.76	**36.37**	29.02	**25.95**	23.22	**20.79**	18.62	14.99	12.08	9.77	7.91	6.43	38
39	44.58	39.86	**35.67**	28.61	**25.64**	23.00	**20.65**	18.55	14.99	12.16	9.88	8.05	6.57	39
40	43.49	38.98	**34.97**	28.19	**25.34**	22.80	**20.51**	18.48	15.01	12.23	9.99	8.17	6.71	40
41	42.41	38.11	**34.28**	27.79	**25.04**	22.58	**20.38**	18.40	15.04	12.31	10.10	8.31	6.86	41
42	41.37	37.28	**33.61**	27.39	**24.75**	22.38	**20.24**	18.33	15.05	12.38	10.22	8.45	7.01	42
43	40.35	36.46	**32.96**	27.00	**24.46**	22.17	**20.12**	18.26	15.07	12.47	10.34	8.59	7.16	43
44	39.36	35.65	**32.33**	26.61	**24.17**	21.98	**19.98**	18.19	15.08	12.54	10.46	8.74	7.32	44
45	38.39	34.88	**31.70**	26.24	**23.90**	21.78	**19.86**	18.12	15.11	12.63	10.58	8.88	7.48	45
46	37.46	34.12	**31.10**	25.87	**23.63**	21.58	**19.73**	18.05	15.13	12.71	10.71	9.03	7.64	46
47	36.55	33.37	**30.50**	25.51	**23.35**	21.39	**19.61**	17.98	15.15	12.80	10.83	9.19	7.80	47
48	35.67	32.66	**29.91**	25.16	**23.09**	21.21	**19.49**	17.92	15.18	12.88	10.96	9.34	7.98	48
49	34.80	31.95	**29.35**	24.81	**22.83**	21.02	**19.37**	17.85	15.20	12.97	11.09	9.50	8.16	49
50	33.97	31.27	**28.79**	24.48	**22.58**	20.85	**19.26**	17.80	15.23	13.06	11.22	9.66	8.34	50
51	33.16	30.60	**28.26**	24.14	**22.34**	20.68	**19.15**	17.75	15.26	13.16	11.36	9.84	8.53	51
52	32.37	29.96	**27.74**	23.83	**22.10**	20.51	**19.04**	17.69	15.29	13.26	11.50	10.01	8.72	52
53	31.61	29.33	**27.23**	23.51	**21.86**	20.34	**18.93**	17.64	15.33	13.35	11.65	10.19	8.93	53
54	30.88	28.73	**26.74**	23.20	**21.63**	20.18	**18.84**	17.60	15.37	13.45	11.80	10.37	9.13	54

Table 30 Multipliers for loss of pension commencing age 70 (females) *continued*

Age at date of trial	Multipliers calculated with allowance for projected mortality from the 2018-based population projections and rate of return of:													Age at date of trial
	-2.0%	-1.75%	**-1.5%**	-1.0%	**-0.75%**	-0.5%	**-0.25%**	0.0%	0.5%	1.0%	1.5%	2.0%	2.5%	
55	30.17	28.14	**26.26**	22.91	**21.41**	20.03	**18.75**	17.55	15.42	13.56	11.96	10.56	9.35	55
56	29.48	27.57	**25.80**	22.63	**21.21**	19.89	**18.66**	17.52	15.46	13.68	12.12	10.76	9.56	56
57	28.82	27.02	**25.35**	22.35	**21.01**	19.75	**18.58**	17.49	15.51	13.79	12.29	10.96	9.79	57
58	28.18	26.49	**24.92**	22.09	**20.81**	19.62	**18.50**	17.46	15.57	13.92	12.46	11.17	10.03	58
59	27.57	25.99	**24.51**	21.84	**20.63**	19.50	**18.44**	17.45	15.64	14.04	12.64	11.39	10.29	59
60	26.98	25.50	**24.11**	21.60	**20.46**	19.38	**18.38**	17.44	15.71	14.18	12.83	11.62	10.54	60
61	26.41	25.03	**23.73**	21.37	**20.30**	19.28	**18.33**	17.44	15.79	14.32	13.02	11.85	10.81	61
62	25.87	24.58	**23.37**	21.16	**20.14**	19.19	**18.29**	17.43	15.88	14.47	13.23	12.10	11.10	62
63	25.35	24.16	**23.02**	20.95	**20.00**	19.10	**18.26**	17.44	15.97	14.63	13.44	12.36	11.39	63
64	24.86	23.75	**22.70**	20.77	**19.87**	19.03	**18.23**	17.48	16.07	14.81	13.67	12.64	11.70	64
65	24.40	23.36	**22.39**	20.59	**19.76**	18.97	**18.22**	17.51	16.19	14.99	13.91	12.92	12.03	65
66	23.96	23.01	**22.10**	20.43	**19.66**	18.92	**18.22**	17.56	16.32	15.20	14.16	13.23	12.38	66
67	23.54	22.66	**21.83**	20.30	**19.58**	18.90	**18.24**	17.62	16.46	15.41	14.44	13.55	12.74	67
68	23.16	22.35	**21.60**	20.18	**19.52**	18.88	**18.27**	17.70	16.62	15.63	14.73	13.90	13.13	68
69	22.81	22.08	**21.38**	20.08	**19.47**	18.89	**18.33**	17.81	16.80	15.88	15.04	14.27	13.54	69
70	22.48	21.82	**21.19**	20.00	**19.45**	18.92	**18.41**	17.92	17.00	16.16	15.38	14.65	13.98	70

Table 31 Multipliers for loss of pension commencing age 75 (males)

Age at date of trial	Multipliers calculated with allowance for projected mortality from the 2018-based population projections and rate of return of:													Age at date of trial
	-2.0%	-1.75%	**-1.5%**	-1.0%	**-0.75%**	-0.5%	**-0.25%**	0.0%	0.5%	1.0%	1.5%	2.0%	2.5%	
0	86.33	69.28	**55.64**	35.99	**28.99**	23.36	**18.85**	15.22	9.94	6.52	4.29	2.83	1.87	0
1	84.37	67.89	**54.66**	35.55	**28.70**	23.19	**18.76**	15.19	9.98	6.57	4.34	2.88	1.92	1
2	82.18	66.30	**53.53**	34.99	**28.32**	22.95	**18.61**	15.11	9.97	6.60	4.39	2.93	1.96	2
3	80.03	64.74	**52.40**	34.44	**27.95**	22.70	**18.45**	15.02	9.97	6.63	4.43	2.97	2.00	3
4	77.94	63.20	**51.30**	33.89	**27.57**	22.45	**18.30**	14.93	9.96	6.66	4.47	3.01	2.03	4
5	75.88	61.70	**50.21**	33.34	**27.20**	22.21	**18.15**	14.85	9.95	6.70	4.52	3.05	2.07	5
6	73.88	60.23	**49.15**	32.81	**26.83**	21.97	**18.00**	14.75	9.95	6.72	4.56	3.10	2.12	6
7	71.93	58.80	**48.10**	32.28	**26.47**	21.73	**17.85**	14.67	9.94	6.76	4.61	3.15	2.16	7
8	70.03	57.40	**47.08**	31.75	**26.11**	21.48	**17.69**	14.58	9.94	6.78	4.65	3.19	2.20	8
9	68.18	56.02	**46.07**	31.24	**25.75**	21.24	**17.54**	14.50	9.93	6.81	4.69	3.24	2.25	9
10	66.37	54.68	**45.08**	30.73	**25.40**	21.01	**17.40**	14.41	9.91	6.84	4.74	3.29	2.29	10
11	64.60	53.36	**44.11**	30.22	**25.05**	20.77	**17.24**	14.33	9.90	6.87	4.78	3.34	2.33	11
12	62.88	52.08	**43.17**	29.73	**24.70**	20.54	**17.09**	14.24	9.89	6.89	4.82	3.38	2.38	12
13	61.20	50.82	**42.24**	29.25	**24.36**	20.31	**16.94**	14.15	9.88	6.93	4.87	3.43	2.42	13
14	59.56	49.59	**41.32**	28.76	**24.03**	20.08	**16.80**	14.06	9.87	6.95	4.91	3.48	2.47	14
15	57.96	48.39	**40.43**	28.29	**23.69**	19.85	**16.65**	13.97	9.86	6.98	4.95	3.53	2.52	15
16	56.41	47.22	**39.55**	27.82	**23.35**	19.62	**16.50**	13.88	9.85	7.01	5.00	3.57	2.56	16
17	54.90	46.07	**38.70**	27.36	**23.03**	19.40	**16.36**	13.80	9.84	7.04	5.04	3.63	2.61	17
18	53.42	44.96	**37.86**	26.91	**22.71**	19.18	**16.21**	13.71	9.83	7.06	5.09	3.68	2.66	18
19	51.99	43.86	**37.04**	26.46	**22.39**	18.96	**16.06**	13.63	9.81	7.10	5.13	3.73	2.71	19
20	50.60	42.80	**36.23**	26.02	**22.07**	18.75	**15.92**	13.54	9.81	7.12	5.18	3.79	2.77	20
21	49.24	41.76	**35.45**	25.60	**21.77**	18.53	**15.78**	13.46	9.80	7.15	5.23	3.84	2.83	21
22	47.91	40.75	**34.67**	25.17	**21.47**	18.31	**15.65**	13.36	9.79	7.17	5.28	3.89	2.87	22
23	46.63	39.76	**33.92**	24.75	**21.16**	18.11	**15.50**	13.28	9.77	7.21	5.32	3.95	2.94	23
24	45.37	38.79	**33.19**	24.34	**20.87**	17.90	**15.37**	13.20	9.76	7.23	5.38	4.01	2.99	24
25	44.15	37.84	**32.46**	23.94	**20.57**	17.70	**15.23**	13.11	9.75	7.26	5.42	4.06	3.05	25
26	42.96	36.92	**31.75**	23.53	**20.28**	17.48	**15.09**	13.03	9.73	7.29	5.47	4.12	3.10	26
27	41.80	36.02	**31.06**	23.14	**20.00**	17.28	**14.96**	12.95	9.72	7.32	5.52	4.17	3.16	27
28	40.67	35.14	**30.38**	22.76	**19.71**	17.08	**14.82**	12.86	9.71	7.35	5.56	4.24	3.22	28
29	39.57	34.28	**29.72**	22.38	**19.43**	16.89	**14.68**	12.78	9.69	7.37	5.62	4.29	3.28	29
30	38.51	33.45	**29.06**	22.00	**19.15**	16.69	**14.55**	12.69	9.68	7.40	5.67	4.35	3.35	30
31	37.47	32.63	**28.43**	21.64	**18.89**	16.50	**14.42**	12.61	9.67	7.43	5.72	4.41	3.41	31
32	36.46	31.84	**27.82**	21.27	**18.62**	16.31	**14.30**	12.54	9.66	7.46	5.77	4.47	3.48	32
33	35.47	31.05	**27.20**	20.92	**18.36**	16.12	**14.17**	12.45	9.65	7.49	5.82	4.54	3.55	33
34	34.52	30.30	**26.62**	20.57	**18.10**	15.93	**14.04**	12.38	9.63	7.51	5.88	4.61	3.62	34
35	33.60	29.56	**26.03**	20.23	**17.85**	15.76	**13.92**	12.30	9.62	7.55	5.92	4.67	3.68	35
36	32.69	28.85	**25.47**	19.89	**17.60**	15.57	**13.80**	12.22	9.61	7.58	5.98	4.74	3.75	36
37	31.81	28.15	**24.92**	19.56	**17.35**	15.40	**13.67**	12.14	9.60	7.60	6.04	4.81	3.82	37
38	30.96	27.47	**24.38**	19.24	**17.11**	15.22	**13.55**	12.06	9.59	7.64	6.09	4.87	3.90	38
39	30.14	26.80	**23.86**	18.93	**16.88**	15.05	**13.43**	12.00	9.58	7.67	6.15	4.94	3.98	39
40	29.34	26.15	**23.34**	18.61	**16.64**	14.88	**13.32**	11.92	9.57	7.70	6.20	5.02	4.06	40
41	28.55	25.53	**22.84**	18.31	**16.42**	14.72	**13.20**	11.85	9.57	7.73	6.26	5.09	4.14	41
42	27.79	24.92	**22.35**	18.02	**16.19**	14.56	**13.10**	11.78	9.56	7.77	6.33	5.16	4.22	42
43	27.07	24.33	**21.89**	17.73	**15.97**	14.39	**12.98**	11.72	9.56	7.80	6.39	5.24	4.31	43
44	26.36	23.75	**21.42**	17.45	**15.76**	14.24	**12.88**	11.65	9.55	7.84	6.44	5.31	4.39	44
45	25.66	23.19	**20.97**	17.17	**15.55**	14.09	**12.77**	11.59	9.54	7.88	6.51	5.39	4.48	45
46	25.00	22.64	**20.53**	16.90	**15.34**	13.94	**12.66**	11.52	9.54	7.91	6.57	5.48	4.57	46
47	24.35	22.12	**20.10**	16.63	**15.14**	13.79	**12.57**	11.46	9.53	7.96	6.64	5.56	4.66	47
48	23.71	21.60	**19.69**	16.37	**14.95**	13.64	**12.46**	11.39	9.53	7.99	6.71	5.65	4.75	48
49	23.10	21.11	**19.28**	16.12	**14.76**	13.51	**12.37**	11.34	9.53	8.04	6.78	5.73	4.85	49
50	22.51	20.61	**18.88**	15.87	**14.56**	13.37	**12.28**	11.28	9.54	8.07	6.85	5.82	4.95	50
51	21.94	20.15	**18.50**	15.64	**14.38**	13.24	**12.19**	11.23	9.54	8.12	6.92	5.91	5.05	51
52	21.38	19.68	**18.13**	15.40	**14.20**	13.11	**12.10**	11.17	9.54	8.17	6.99	6.00	5.16	52
53	20.85	19.24	**17.77**	15.18	**14.03**	12.99	**12.01**	11.12	9.55	8.21	7.07	6.10	5.27	53
54	20.32	18.81	**17.42**	14.95	**13.86**	12.86	**11.93**	11.08	9.56	8.26	7.16	6.20	5.39	54

Table 31 Multipliers for loss of pension commencing age 75 (males) *continued*

Age at date of trial	Multipliers calculated with allowance for projected mortality from the 2018-based population projections and rate of return of:													Age at date of trial
	-2.0%	-1.75%	**-1.5%**	-1.0%	**-0.75%**	-0.5%	**-0.25%**	0.0%	0.5%	1.0%	1.5%	2.0%	2.5%	
55	19.83	18.40	**17.08**	14.74	**13.70**	12.74	**11.85**	11.04	9.57	8.32	7.24	6.30	5.50	55
56	19.34	18.00	**16.75**	14.54	**13.55**	12.63	**11.79**	11.00	9.59	8.37	7.32	6.41	5.62	56
57	18.88	17.62	**16.44**	14.34	**13.40**	12.53	**11.71**	10.96	9.61	8.43	7.41	6.53	5.76	57
58	18.45	17.26	**16.14**	14.15	**13.26**	12.43	**11.65**	10.93	9.63	8.49	7.51	6.64	5.89	58
59	18.02	16.91	**15.86**	13.98	**13.14**	12.34	**11.60**	10.91	9.66	8.56	7.61	6.77	6.02	59
60	17.63	16.58	**15.59**	13.82	**13.02**	12.25	**11.56**	10.89	9.69	8.65	7.72	6.89	6.17	60
61	17.25	16.26	**15.33**	13.66	**12.90**	12.19	**11.52**	10.89	9.74	8.72	7.83	7.03	6.33	61
62	16.89	15.96	**15.10**	13.52	**12.80**	12.12	**11.49**	10.89	9.79	8.81	7.95	7.17	6.49	62
63	16.55	15.69	**14.88**	13.39	**12.71**	12.07	**11.47**	10.89	9.85	8.91	8.08	7.33	6.66	63
64	16.24	15.43	**14.67**	13.27	**12.64**	12.03	**11.45**	10.91	9.92	9.02	8.22	7.50	6.84	64
65	15.94	15.19	**14.48**	13.17	**12.57**	12.00	**11.45**	10.94	9.99	9.14	8.37	7.67	7.04	65
66	15.67	14.97	**14.31**	13.08	**12.52**	11.98	**11.47**	10.98	10.08	9.27	8.53	7.86	7.25	66
67	15.43	14.78	**14.16**	13.02	**12.49**	11.98	**11.50**	11.04	10.18	9.41	8.71	8.06	7.48	67
68	15.20	14.60	**14.03**	12.97	**12.47**	12.00	**11.54**	11.11	10.31	9.57	8.90	8.29	7.71	68
69	15.01	14.46	**13.92**	12.93	**12.47**	12.03	**11.61**	11.20	10.44	9.74	9.11	8.52	7.98	69
70	14.84	14.33	**13.84**	12.92	**12.49**	12.08	**11.69**	11.31	10.60	9.94	9.34	8.78	8.27	70
71	14.70	14.23	**13.78**	12.94	**12.54**	12.16	**11.79**	11.44	10.77	10.16	9.60	9.07	8.58	71
72	14.59	14.16	**13.75**	12.98	**12.61**	12.26	**11.92**	11.59	10.98	10.40	9.87	9.38	8.91	72
73	14.52	14.12	**13.75**	13.05	**12.71**	12.39	**12.07**	11.78	11.21	10.68	10.19	9.73	9.30	73
74	14.47	14.12	**13.79**	13.15	**12.85**	12.55	**12.27**	11.99	11.48	10.99	10.54	10.11	9.71	74
75	14.48	14.17	**13.87**	13.29	**13.02**	12.76	**12.50**	12.25	11.78	11.34	10.93	10.54	10.17	75

Table 32 Multipliers for loss of pension commencing age 75 (females)

Age at date of trial	Multipliers calculated with allowance for projected mortality from the 2018-based population projections and rate of return of:													Age at date of trial
	-2.0%	-1.75%	**-1.5%**	-1.0%	**-0.75%**	-0.5%	**-0.25%**	0.0%	0.5%	1.0%	1.5%	2.0%	2.5%	
0	97.99	78.54	**63.01**	40.65	**32.71**	26.33	**21.22**	17.11	11.15	7.30	4.79	3.15	2.09	0
1	95.82	76.99	**61.93**	40.17	**32.40**	26.15	**21.13**	17.09	11.20	7.37	4.86	3.21	2.13	1
2	93.44	75.28	**60.71**	39.59	**32.01**	25.90	**20.98**	17.01	11.20	7.41	4.91	3.27	2.18	2
3	91.10	73.60	**59.51**	39.00	**31.62**	25.65	**20.83**	16.93	11.21	7.45	4.97	3.32	2.23	3
4	88.81	71.93	**58.32**	38.43	**31.23**	25.40	**20.68**	16.85	11.22	7.49	5.01	3.38	2.27	4
5	86.58	70.31	**57.15**	37.85	**30.85**	25.15	**20.53**	16.78	11.22	7.53	5.08	3.42	2.32	5
6	84.39	68.72	**56.00**	37.28	**30.47**	24.90	**20.38**	16.70	11.22	7.58	5.12	3.48	2.37	6
7	82.27	67.16	**54.87**	36.72	**30.08**	24.66	**20.24**	16.62	11.23	7.62	5.18	3.54	2.42	7
8	80.19	65.64	**53.77**	36.17	**29.71**	24.42	**20.08**	16.54	11.23	7.66	5.23	3.59	2.47	8
9	78.16	64.15	**52.69**	35.63	**29.33**	24.18	**19.93**	16.45	11.24	7.70	5.29	3.64	2.52	9
10	76.18	62.68	**51.62**	35.10	**28.97**	23.93	**19.79**	16.38	11.24	7.74	5.34	3.70	2.57	10
11	74.25	61.25	**50.57**	34.56	**28.61**	23.69	**19.64**	16.30	11.24	7.78	5.40	3.76	2.63	11
12	72.36	59.85	**49.55**	34.04	**28.24**	23.46	**19.49**	16.22	11.24	7.82	5.45	3.82	2.68	12
13	70.52	58.48	**48.54**	33.53	**27.89**	23.22	**19.35**	16.13	11.25	7.87	5.51	3.87	2.74	13
14	68.72	57.14	**47.55**	33.01	**27.53**	22.99	**19.21**	16.06	11.25	7.90	5.57	3.93	2.79	14
15	66.97	55.83	**46.58**	32.50	**27.19**	22.75	**19.06**	15.98	11.25	7.95	5.63	4.00	2.85	15
16	65.26	54.55	**45.63**	32.01	**26.84**	22.52	**18.91**	15.90	11.25	7.98	5.68	4.06	2.91	16
17	63.59	53.30	**44.70**	31.52	**26.50**	22.30	**18.78**	15.82	11.25	8.03	5.75	4.12	2.97	17
18	61.96	52.07	**43.79**	31.04	**26.16**	22.07	**18.63**	15.74	11.25	8.07	5.81	4.18	3.02	18
19	60.38	50.87	**42.89**	30.57	**25.83**	21.84	**18.48**	15.65	11.25	8.11	5.86	4.25	3.08	19
20	58.83	49.70	**42.01**	30.10	**25.50**	21.62	**18.35**	15.57	11.25	8.16	5.92	4.32	3.15	20
21	57.32	48.55	**41.15**	29.63	**25.17**	21.40	**18.20**	15.50	11.25	8.19	5.98	4.38	3.21	21
22	55.85	47.43	**40.31**	29.18	**24.85**	21.18	**18.07**	15.42	11.25	8.24	6.04	4.44	3.28	22
23	54.42	46.33	**39.48**	28.73	**24.52**	20.96	**17.92**	15.33	11.25	8.28	6.11	4.51	3.35	23
24	53.01	45.26	**38.66**	28.28	**24.21**	20.74	**17.78**	15.26	11.25	8.32	6.16	4.59	3.42	24
25	51.65	44.21	**37.87**	27.85	**23.90**	20.53	**17.64**	15.18	11.25	8.36	6.23	4.66	3.49	25
26	50.31	43.18	**37.09**	27.41	**23.59**	20.32	**17.51**	15.09	11.24	8.40	6.29	4.73	3.56	26
27	49.02	42.18	**36.32**	26.99	**23.28**	20.10	**17.37**	15.02	11.25	8.44	6.35	4.80	3.62	27
28	47.76	41.20	**35.57**	26.57	**22.98**	19.90	**17.24**	14.93	11.25	8.49	6.42	4.87	3.70	28
29	46.52	40.24	**34.83**	26.15	**22.68**	19.69	**17.10**	14.86	11.24	8.53	6.48	4.94	3.78	29
30	45.31	39.31	**34.11**	25.74	**22.39**	19.48	**16.96**	14.78	11.24	8.57	6.55	5.01	3.85	30
31	44.15	38.39	**33.41**	25.34	**22.09**	19.28	**16.83**	14.70	11.24	8.62	6.61	5.09	3.93	31
32	43.01	37.49	**32.71**	24.95	**21.81**	19.08	**16.70**	14.62	11.24	8.65	6.69	5.18	4.01	32
33	41.89	36.63	**32.04**	24.56	**21.53**	18.88	**16.56**	14.55	11.23	8.70	6.75	5.25	4.09	33
34	40.81	35.77	**31.38**	24.18	**21.24**	18.68	**16.44**	14.47	11.23	8.74	6.82	5.33	4.18	34
35	39.76	34.94	**30.73**	23.80	**20.97**	18.49	**16.31**	14.39	11.23	8.79	6.88	5.41	4.26	35
36	38.74	34.12	**30.10**	23.43	**20.70**	18.30	**16.18**	14.32	11.23	8.83	6.96	5.50	4.34	36
37	37.74	33.34	**29.46**	23.07	**20.43**	18.10	**16.05**	14.24	11.22	8.87	7.03	5.57	4.43	37
38	36.76	32.56	**28.86**	22.71	**20.17**	17.91	**15.93**	14.16	11.23	8.92	7.09	5.66	4.53	38
39	35.81	31.80	**28.27**	22.37	**19.90**	17.73	**15.80**	14.09	11.22	8.96	7.17	5.75	4.61	39
40	34.90	31.07	**27.69**	22.01	**19.65**	17.55	**15.68**	14.02	11.22	9.01	7.24	5.83	4.71	40
41	33.99	30.35	**27.11**	21.68	**19.40**	17.37	**15.56**	13.95	11.23	9.05	7.31	5.92	4.81	41
42	33.13	29.65	**26.56**	21.34	**19.15**	17.19	**15.44**	13.87	11.23	9.10	7.39	6.01	4.91	42
43	32.27	28.97	**26.01**	21.01	**18.90**	17.01	**15.32**	13.81	11.23	9.15	7.47	6.11	5.01	43
44	31.44	28.30	**25.48**	20.69	**18.66**	16.85	**15.21**	13.74	11.22	9.19	7.54	6.21	5.11	44
45	30.64	27.65	**24.96**	20.38	**18.43**	16.67	**15.09**	13.67	11.23	9.24	7.63	6.30	5.22	45
46	29.87	27.02	**24.46**	20.07	**18.20**	16.50	**14.98**	13.60	11.23	9.29	7.71	6.39	5.32	46
47	29.11	26.40	**23.96**	19.77	**17.96**	16.34	**14.87**	13.54	11.23	9.34	7.79	6.50	5.43	47
48	28.37	25.80	**23.47**	19.47	**17.75**	16.18	**14.76**	13.47	11.24	9.39	7.87	6.60	5.55	48
49	27.65	25.22	**23.01**	19.18	**17.53**	16.02	**14.65**	13.41	11.24	9.45	7.96	6.70	5.67	49
50	26.96	24.65	**22.54**	18.90	**17.31**	15.87	**14.55**	13.35	11.25	9.51	8.04	6.81	5.78	50
51	26.29	24.09	**22.10**	18.62	**17.10**	15.72	**14.45**	13.29	11.26	9.56	8.13	6.92	5.90	51
52	25.63	23.56	**21.66**	18.35	**16.90**	15.57	**14.35**	13.23	11.27	9.62	8.22	7.04	6.04	52
53	25.00	23.04	**21.24**	18.08	**16.70**	15.43	**14.25**	13.18	11.28	9.68	8.31	7.16	6.17	53
54	24.39	22.54	**20.83**	17.83	**16.50**	15.28	**14.16**	13.13	11.30	9.74	8.41	7.27	6.30	54

Table 32 Multipliers for loss of pension commencing age 75 (females) *continued*

Age at date of trial	Multipliers calculated with allowance for projected mortality from the 2018-based population projections and rate of return of:													Age at date of trial
	-2.0%	-1.75%	**-1.5%**	-1.0%	**-0.75%**	-0.5%	**-0.25%**	0.0%	0.5%	1.0%	1.5%	2.0%	2.5%	
55	23.80	22.05	**20.44**	17.58	**16.31**	15.15	**14.08**	13.08	11.32	9.80	8.51	7.40	6.44	55
56	23.23	21.58	**20.05**	17.34	**16.14**	15.02	**13.99**	13.04	11.34	9.87	8.61	7.53	6.58	56
57	22.68	21.12	**19.68**	17.11	**15.97**	14.90	**13.92**	13.00	11.36	9.94	8.72	7.65	6.73	57
58	22.15	20.68	**19.32**	16.88	**15.80**	14.78	**13.84**	12.96	11.39	10.02	8.83	7.79	6.88	58
59	21.64	20.26	**18.98**	16.68	**15.64**	14.68	**13.78**	12.94	11.42	10.10	8.94	7.93	7.05	59
60	21.15	19.86	**18.65**	16.47	**15.48**	14.56	**13.71**	12.91	11.46	10.18	9.07	8.08	7.21	60
61	20.68	19.47	**18.33**	16.27	**15.34**	14.47	**13.65**	12.89	11.50	10.27	9.19	8.23	7.38	61
62	20.23	19.09	**18.02**	16.09	**15.20**	14.38	**13.60**	12.87	11.55	10.36	9.32	8.39	7.57	62
63	19.80	18.74	**17.73**	15.91	**15.08**	14.30	**13.56**	12.86	11.60	10.46	9.46	8.56	7.76	63
64	19.39	18.40	**17.46**	15.75	**14.96**	14.22	**13.53**	12.87	11.66	10.57	9.61	8.74	7.96	64
65	19.01	18.07	**17.20**	15.59	**14.86**	14.16	**13.50**	12.88	11.73	10.69	9.76	8.93	8.17	65
66	18.64	17.78	**16.95**	15.45	**14.76**	14.10	**13.48**	12.89	11.80	10.82	9.93	9.12	8.40	66
67	18.29	17.48	**16.73**	15.33	**14.68**	14.07	**13.48**	12.92	11.89	10.95	10.10	9.33	8.63	67
68	17.97	17.22	**16.53**	15.22	**14.61**	14.03	**13.48**	12.96	11.98	11.10	10.29	9.56	8.88	68
69	17.67	16.99	**16.33**	15.13	**14.56**	14.02	**13.51**	13.02	12.10	11.26	10.50	9.80	9.14	69
70	17.40	16.77	**16.17**	15.04	**14.52**	14.02	**13.55**	13.09	12.22	11.44	10.72	10.04	9.43	70
71	17.14	16.58	**16.03**	15.00	**14.51**	14.05	**13.59**	13.17	12.37	11.63	10.96	10.32	9.74	71
72	16.93	16.41	**15.90**	14.96	**14.52**	14.09	**13.68**	13.28	12.54	11.85	11.21	10.62	10.07	72
73	16.75	16.28	**15.81**	14.95	**14.55**	14.15	**13.78**	13.41	12.73	12.09	11.50	10.95	10.44	73
74	16.60	16.17	**15.76**	14.97	**14.61**	14.26	**13.91**	13.58	12.95	12.36	11.82	11.31	10.83	74
75	16.49	16.11	**15.74**	15.04	**14.70**	14.38	**14.07**	13.77	13.20	12.67	12.17	11.71	11.27	75

Table 33 Multipliers for loss of pension commencing age 80 (males)

Age at date of trial	Multipliers calculated with allowance for projected mortality from the 2018-based population projections and rate of return of:													Age at date of trial
	-2.0%	-1.75%	**-1.5%**	-1.0%	**-0.75%**	-0.5%	**-0.25%**	0.0%	0.5%	1.0%	1.5%	2.0%	2.5%	
0	66.35	52.88	**42.17**	26.89	**21.50**	17.21	**13.78**	11.04	7.10	4.59	2.97	1.93	1.26	0
1	64.76	51.75	**41.38**	26.53	**21.27**	17.05	**13.69**	11.01	7.12	4.62	3.00	1.96	1.29	1
2	63.00	50.47	**40.47**	26.08	**20.96**	16.86	**13.57**	10.93	7.11	4.63	3.04	1.99	1.31	2
3	61.27	49.22	**39.56**	25.63	**20.66**	16.65	**13.43**	10.86	7.09	4.65	3.06	2.02	1.33	3
4	59.59	47.99	**38.68**	25.19	**20.34**	16.45	**13.31**	10.77	7.08	4.66	3.08	2.04	1.35	4
5	57.94	46.79	**37.81**	24.74	**20.04**	16.24	**13.18**	10.70	7.06	4.68	3.11	2.07	1.38	5
6	56.34	45.61	**36.96**	24.32	**19.74**	16.05	**13.05**	10.62	7.05	4.69	3.13	2.10	1.41	6
7	54.78	44.47	**36.12**	23.89	**19.46**	15.85	**12.93**	10.54	7.03	4.71	3.16	2.13	1.43	7
8	53.26	43.35	**35.30**	23.47	**19.16**	15.65	**12.79**	10.46	7.02	4.72	3.18	2.15	1.45	8
9	51.78	42.25	**34.50**	23.06	**18.87**	15.45	**12.66**	10.39	7.00	4.73	3.21	2.18	1.49	9
10	50.34	41.18	**33.71**	22.65	**18.59**	15.26	**12.54**	10.31	6.98	4.74	3.24	2.21	1.51	10
11	48.92	40.13	**32.94**	22.24	**18.30**	15.07	**12.41**	10.23	6.96	4.76	3.25	2.24	1.54	11
12	47.56	39.11	**32.19**	21.85	**18.02**	14.88	**12.29**	10.16	6.95	4.77	3.28	2.27	1.57	12
13	46.22	38.11	**31.45**	21.46	**17.74**	14.68	**12.16**	10.08	6.93	4.78	3.31	2.29	1.59	13
14	44.92	37.14	**30.72**	21.08	**17.48**	14.50	**12.04**	10.00	6.91	4.79	3.33	2.32	1.63	14
15	43.65	36.18	**30.01**	20.70	**17.21**	14.31	**11.91**	9.92	6.90	4.80	3.35	2.36	1.65	15
16	42.42	35.25	**29.32**	20.32	**16.93**	14.12	**11.79**	9.84	6.88	4.81	3.38	2.38	1.68	16
17	41.22	34.35	**28.64**	19.96	**16.67**	13.94	**11.67**	9.77	6.86	4.83	3.40	2.41	1.70	17
18	40.05	33.47	**27.98**	19.60	**16.42**	13.76	**11.55**	9.69	6.84	4.84	3.43	2.44	1.74	18
19	38.92	32.60	**27.33**	19.24	**16.16**	13.59	**11.42**	9.62	6.82	4.85	3.45	2.47	1.77	19
20	37.82	31.76	**26.69**	18.89	**15.90**	13.41	**11.30**	9.54	6.80	4.86	3.48	2.50	1.80	20
21	36.75	30.94	**26.08**	18.55	**15.66**	13.23	**11.18**	9.46	6.78	4.87	3.50	2.53	1.84	21
22	35.70	30.14	**25.46**	18.22	**15.42**	13.05	**11.07**	9.38	6.76	4.88	3.53	2.56	1.86	22
23	34.68	29.36	**24.87**	17.88	**15.18**	12.89	**10.95**	9.31	6.74	4.89	3.56	2.59	1.90	23
24	33.69	28.60	**24.29**	17.55	**14.94**	12.72	**10.84**	9.23	6.72	4.90	3.59	2.63	1.93	24
25	32.73	27.86	**23.72**	17.24	**14.70**	12.55	**10.72**	9.16	6.70	4.92	3.61	2.66	1.96	25
26	31.80	27.13	**23.16**	16.91	**14.47**	12.38	**10.60**	9.09	6.68	4.93	3.63	2.70	1.99	26
27	30.89	26.42	**22.62**	16.60	**14.24**	12.22	**10.49**	9.01	6.66	4.93	3.67	2.73	2.03	27
28	30.01	25.74	**22.09**	16.30	**14.01**	12.05	**10.38**	8.93	6.64	4.95	3.68	2.76	2.07	28
29	29.15	25.07	**21.57**	16.00	**13.79**	11.90	**10.26**	8.87	6.62	4.95	3.72	2.79	2.10	29
30	28.32	24.42	**21.06**	15.71	**13.57**	11.74	**10.15**	8.79	6.59	4.96	3.74	2.82	2.14	30
31	27.50	23.77	**20.56**	15.42	**13.36**	11.58	**10.04**	8.71	6.57	4.97	3.77	2.86	2.17	31
32	26.71	23.16	**20.09**	15.13	**13.14**	11.43	**9.94**	8.65	6.56	4.98	3.79	2.89	2.21	32
33	25.94	22.55	**19.60**	14.86	**12.94**	11.27	**9.83**	8.57	6.54	5.00	3.82	2.93	2.25	33
34	25.20	21.96	**19.15**	14.58	**12.73**	11.12	**9.72**	8.51	6.52	5.00	3.85	2.97	2.29	34
35	24.48	21.39	**18.69**	14.31	**12.53**	10.98	**9.62**	8.43	6.49	5.01	3.87	3.00	2.33	35
36	23.78	20.83	**18.25**	14.05	**12.33**	10.82	**9.52**	8.36	6.47	5.02	3.90	3.04	2.37	36
37	23.10	20.29	**17.83**	13.79	**12.13**	10.68	**9.41**	8.30	6.46	5.03	3.93	3.08	2.41	37
38	22.43	19.76	**17.41**	13.54	**11.94**	10.54	**9.31**	8.23	6.44	5.05	3.96	3.11	2.45	38
39	21.80	19.24	**17.01**	13.29	**11.76**	10.40	**9.21**	8.16	6.41	5.06	3.99	3.15	2.50	39
40	21.18	18.74	**16.61**	13.04	**11.57**	10.26	**9.11**	8.10	6.40	5.06	4.01	3.19	2.54	40
41	20.57	18.26	**16.22**	12.80	**11.39**	10.14	**9.02**	8.03	6.38	5.07	4.04	3.23	2.59	41
42	19.99	17.79	**15.84**	12.58	**11.22**	10.01	**8.93**	7.97	6.36	5.09	4.08	3.27	2.63	42
43	19.43	17.34	**15.48**	12.35	**11.04**	9.87	**8.83**	7.91	6.35	5.10	4.11	3.31	2.68	43
44	18.88	16.89	**15.12**	12.13	**10.87**	9.74	**8.74**	7.85	6.33	5.11	4.13	3.35	2.72	44
45	18.34	16.45	**14.77**	11.91	**10.71**	9.62	**8.65**	7.79	6.31	5.13	4.17	3.40	2.77	45
46	17.84	16.03	**14.43**	11.70	**10.54**	9.50	**8.56**	7.72	6.29	5.14	4.20	3.44	2.82	46
47	17.34	15.63	**14.10**	11.49	**10.38**	9.38	**8.48**	7.67	6.28	5.16	4.23	3.48	2.87	47
48	16.85	15.23	**13.78**	11.28	**10.22**	9.26	**8.39**	7.61	6.26	5.17	4.27	3.53	2.92	48
49	16.38	14.85	**13.47**	11.09	**10.07**	9.15	**8.31**	7.56	6.25	5.18	4.30	3.57	2.98	49
50	15.93	14.48	**13.16**	10.89	**9.91**	9.03	**8.23**	7.50	6.24	5.20	4.34	3.62	3.03	50
51	15.49	14.12	**12.86**	10.71	**9.77**	8.92	**8.15**	7.45	6.22	5.21	4.37	3.68	3.09	51
52	15.06	13.76	**12.57**	10.52	**9.63**	8.82	**8.07**	7.40	6.22	5.23	4.40	3.72	3.14	52
53	14.66	13.42	**12.30**	10.35	**9.49**	8.71	**7.99**	7.34	6.20	5.25	4.44	3.77	3.20	53
54	14.25	13.09	**12.03**	10.17	**9.35**	8.61	**7.93**	7.30	6.20	5.27	4.49	3.83	3.27	54

Table 33 Multipliers for loss of pension commencing age 80 (males) *continued*

Age at date of trial	Multipliers calculated with allowance for projected mortality from the 2018-based population projections and rate of return of:													Age at date of trial
	-2.0%	-1.75%	**-1.5%**	-1.0%	**-0.75%**	-0.5%	**-0.25%**	0.0%	0.5%	1.0%	1.5%	2.0%	2.5%	
55	13.87	12.78	**11.77**	10.00	**9.22**	8.51	**7.85**	7.26	6.19	5.29	4.53	3.88	3.33	55
56	13.51	12.47	**11.52**	9.84	**9.10**	8.42	**7.79**	7.21	6.18	5.31	4.57	3.93	3.39	56
57	13.15	12.18	**11.28**	9.69	**8.98**	8.33	**7.72**	7.17	6.19	5.33	4.61	4.00	3.47	57
58	12.82	11.90	**11.05**	9.54	**8.87**	8.25	**7.66**	7.13	6.19	5.36	4.67	4.06	3.54	58
59	12.50	11.64	**10.82**	9.40	**8.76**	8.17	**7.61**	7.10	6.18	5.39	4.72	4.13	3.61	59
60	12.20	11.38	**10.62**	9.27	**8.66**	8.09	**7.57**	7.07	6.19	5.43	4.77	4.19	3.69	60
61	11.90	11.14	**10.42**	9.14	**8.56**	8.02	**7.52**	7.05	6.20	5.47	4.83	4.26	3.77	61
62	11.62	10.90	**10.23**	9.03	**8.47**	7.96	**7.48**	7.04	6.22	5.51	4.89	4.33	3.86	62
63	11.36	10.69	**10.06**	8.91	**8.39**	7.91	**7.45**	7.02	6.24	5.55	4.96	4.42	3.95	63
64	11.13	10.49	**9.89**	8.81	**8.32**	7.86	**7.42**	7.01	6.27	5.61	5.03	4.51	4.04	64
65	10.89	10.30	**9.74**	8.72	**8.25**	7.82	**7.40**	7.01	6.30	5.67	5.10	4.60	4.15	65
66	10.68	10.12	**9.60**	8.64	**8.20**	7.78	**7.39**	7.02	6.34	5.73	5.19	4.70	4.26	66
67	10.49	9.97	**9.48**	8.58	**8.16**	7.77	**7.39**	7.04	6.39	5.81	5.28	4.81	4.38	67
68	10.31	9.83	**9.36**	8.52	**8.13**	7.76	**7.40**	7.07	6.45	5.89	5.39	4.93	4.51	68
69	10.15	9.70	**9.27**	8.47	**8.11**	7.76	**7.43**	7.11	6.52	5.98	5.50	5.05	4.66	69
70	10.01	9.59	**9.19**	8.44	**8.10**	7.77	**7.46**	7.16	6.59	6.09	5.62	5.20	4.81	70
71	9.89	9.50	**9.13**	8.44	**8.11**	7.80	**7.50**	7.21	6.68	6.20	5.76	5.35	4.97	71
72	9.80	9.43	**9.09**	8.44	**8.13**	7.84	**7.56**	7.29	6.80	6.33	5.91	5.52	5.15	72
73	9.72	9.38	**9.06**	8.46	**8.18**	7.91	**7.64**	7.39	6.92	6.48	6.08	5.71	5.36	73
74	9.67	9.36	**9.06**	8.51	**8.25**	7.99	**7.75**	7.51	7.07	6.65	6.28	5.92	5.58	74
75	9.65	9.37	**9.10**	8.57	**8.33**	8.10	**7.87**	7.65	7.23	6.85	6.49	6.15	5.83	75
76	9.66	9.40	**9.15**	8.67	**8.45**	8.23	**8.03**	7.82	7.43	7.08	6.73	6.42	6.12	76
77	9.70	9.47	**9.25**	8.81	**8.61**	8.41	**8.21**	8.02	7.67	7.33	7.02	6.72	6.44	77
78	9.79	9.58	**9.37**	8.98	**8.80**	8.61	**8.44**	8.27	7.94	7.63	7.34	7.07	6.81	78
79	9.93	9.74	**9.57**	9.21	**9.04**	8.88	**8.72**	8.56	8.27	7.99	7.72	7.47	7.22	79
80	10.14	9.97	**9.81**	9.50	**9.35**	9.20	**9.06**	8.92	8.66	8.40	8.16	7.94	7.72	80

Table 34 Multipliers for loss of pension commencing age 80 (females)

Age at date of trial	Multipliers calculated with allowance for projected mortality from the 2018-based population projections and rate of return of:													Age at date of trial
	-2.0%	-1.75%	**-1.5%**	-1.0%	**-0.75%**	-0.5%	**-0.25%**	0.0%	0.5%	1.0%	1.5%	2.0%	2.5%	
0	76.82	61.17	**48.74**	31.02	**24.78**	19.80	**15.85**	12.68	8.15	5.25	3.39	2.20	1.44	0
1	75.04	59.90	**47.85**	30.62	**24.52**	19.65	**15.76**	12.66	8.17	5.30	3.44	2.24	1.46	1
2	73.10	58.50	**46.86**	30.14	**24.20**	19.44	**15.64**	12.58	8.16	5.32	3.47	2.27	1.50	2
3	71.19	57.13	**45.88**	29.66	**23.88**	19.24	**15.50**	12.51	8.16	5.35	3.51	2.31	1.53	3
4	69.33	55.78	**44.92**	29.19	**23.56**	19.02	**15.38**	12.43	8.16	5.36	3.54	2.35	1.55	4
5	67.51	54.47	**43.97**	28.72	**23.24**	18.82	**15.25**	12.37	8.15	5.39	3.58	2.37	1.59	5
6	65.74	53.17	**43.04**	28.26	**22.93**	18.61	**15.12**	12.30	8.14	5.42	3.60	2.41	1.62	6
7	64.02	51.91	**42.12**	27.80	**22.62**	18.41	**15.00**	12.23	8.14	5.44	3.64	2.45	1.65	7
8	62.33	50.68	**41.23**	27.35	**22.31**	18.21	**14.86**	12.15	8.13	5.46	3.67	2.48	1.68	8
9	60.68	49.47	**40.36**	26.92	**22.00**	18.00	**14.74**	12.07	8.12	5.48	3.71	2.51	1.71	9
10	59.08	48.28	**39.49**	26.48	**21.70**	17.80	**14.62**	12.00	8.12	5.50	3.74	2.55	1.75	10
11	57.52	47.13	**38.65**	26.04	**21.40**	17.60	**14.48**	11.93	8.11	5.52	3.78	2.59	1.78	11
12	55.99	46.00	**37.82**	25.62	**21.11**	17.40	**14.36**	11.86	8.10	5.55	3.81	2.63	1.81	12
13	54.50	44.89	**37.00**	25.21	**20.82**	17.21	**14.24**	11.78	8.10	5.58	3.84	2.66	1.85	13
14	53.05	43.81	**36.21**	24.79	**20.52**	17.02	**14.12**	11.71	8.09	5.59	3.88	2.70	1.88	14
15	51.63	42.76	**35.43**	24.38	**20.25**	16.82	**13.99**	11.64	8.08	5.62	3.92	2.74	1.92	15
16	50.26	41.73	**34.66**	23.97	**19.96**	16.63	**13.86**	11.57	8.06	5.63	3.95	2.78	1.96	16
17	48.91	40.72	**33.92**	23.58	**19.68**	16.44	**13.75**	11.49	8.05	5.66	3.99	2.81	2.00	17
18	47.60	39.73	**33.18**	23.19	**19.41**	16.25	**13.62**	11.42	8.04	5.69	4.02	2.85	2.03	18
19	46.33	38.76	**32.46**	22.81	**19.14**	16.07	**13.50**	11.35	8.03	5.70	4.06	2.90	2.07	19
20	45.09	37.83	**31.76**	22.43	**18.86**	15.88	**13.38**	11.27	8.02	5.73	4.09	2.94	2.11	20
21	43.87	36.91	**31.06**	22.05	**18.60**	15.70	**13.25**	11.20	8.01	5.74	4.13	2.98	2.15	21
22	42.70	36.01	**30.39**	21.69	**18.34**	15.52	**13.14**	11.13	8.00	5.77	4.17	3.01	2.19	22
23	41.55	35.13	**29.72**	21.32	**18.07**	15.34	**13.02**	11.05	7.99	5.79	4.20	3.05	2.24	23
24	40.42	34.27	**29.07**	20.97	**17.82**	15.15	**12.90**	10.99	7.98	5.81	4.24	3.10	2.27	24
25	39.33	33.43	**28.44**	20.62	**17.57**	14.98	**12.78**	10.91	7.97	5.83	4.28	3.15	2.32	25
26	38.26	32.61	**27.82**	20.26	**17.31**	14.80	**12.66**	10.83	7.95	5.85	4.31	3.19	2.36	26
27	37.23	31.81	**27.20**	19.93	**17.07**	14.63	**12.54**	10.77	7.94	5.87	4.35	3.23	2.40	27
28	36.22	31.03	**26.60**	19.59	**16.82**	14.46	**12.43**	10.69	7.93	5.89	4.39	3.28	2.45	28
29	35.23	30.27	**26.01**	19.25	**16.57**	14.28	**12.32**	10.62	7.91	5.91	4.42	3.32	2.50	29
30	34.27	29.52	**25.44**	18.93	**16.34**	14.11	**12.19**	10.55	7.90	5.94	4.47	3.36	2.54	30
31	33.35	28.79	**24.88**	18.60	**16.10**	13.95	**12.08**	10.48	7.89	5.96	4.50	3.41	2.58	31
32	32.44	28.08	**24.33**	18.29	**15.87**	13.78	**11.97**	10.40	7.88	5.97	4.54	3.46	2.64	32
33	31.55	27.39	**23.80**	17.98	**15.65**	13.61	**11.86**	10.34	7.86	5.99	4.57	3.50	2.69	33
34	30.69	26.72	**23.27**	17.67	**15.41**	13.45	**11.75**	10.26	7.84	6.02	4.61	3.55	2.74	34
35	29.86	26.06	**22.75**	17.37	**15.19**	13.30	**11.64**	10.20	7.83	6.04	4.65	3.60	2.78	35
36	29.05	25.41	**22.25**	17.08	**14.97**	13.14	**11.53**	10.13	7.82	6.05	4.69	3.65	2.84	36
37	28.25	24.79	**21.75**	16.79	**14.75**	12.98	**11.42**	10.06	7.80	6.08	4.73	3.69	2.89	37
38	27.48	24.17	**21.27**	16.50	**14.55**	12.82	**11.32**	9.98	7.80	6.09	4.77	3.74	2.95	38
39	26.73	23.57	**20.81**	16.22	**14.33**	12.67	**11.21**	9.92	7.78	6.12	4.82	3.80	3.00	39
40	26.01	23.00	**20.34**	15.94	**14.12**	12.52	**11.10**	9.85	7.77	6.13	4.86	3.85	3.06	40
41	25.30	22.42	**19.89**	15.67	**13.92**	12.37	**11.00**	9.79	7.76	6.16	4.90	3.90	3.12	41
42	24.62	21.87	**19.45**	15.41	**13.72**	12.22	**10.90**	9.72	7.75	6.18	4.94	3.95	3.17	42
43	23.94	21.34	**19.02**	15.14	**13.52**	12.08	**10.80**	9.66	7.73	6.20	4.98	4.01	3.24	43
44	23.29	20.81	**18.61**	14.89	**13.33**	11.94	**10.70**	9.59	7.71	6.22	5.02	4.07	3.30	44
45	22.66	20.30	**18.19**	14.64	**13.14**	11.80	**10.60**	9.53	7.71	6.24	5.07	4.12	3.36	45
46	22.05	19.80	**17.80**	14.39	**12.96**	11.66	**10.51**	9.46	7.69	6.26	5.12	4.17	3.42	46
47	21.46	19.32	**17.41**	14.15	**12.76**	11.52	**10.41**	9.40	7.68	6.29	5.16	4.24	3.48	47
48	20.88	18.85	**17.03**	13.92	**12.59**	11.39	**10.32**	9.34	7.68	6.31	5.21	4.29	3.55	48
49	20.31	18.39	**16.66**	13.69	**12.41**	11.26	**10.22**	9.28	7.66	6.34	5.25	4.35	3.62	49
50	19.77	17.95	**16.29**	13.46	**12.23**	11.13	**10.13**	9.22	7.65	6.37	5.30	4.41	3.69	50
51	19.25	17.51	**15.95**	13.24	**12.07**	11.01	**10.04**	9.17	7.64	6.39	5.35	4.48	3.76	51
52	18.73	17.10	**15.60**	13.03	**11.91**	10.89	**9.96**	9.11	7.64	6.42	5.39	4.55	3.83	52
53	18.24	16.69	**15.28**	12.81	**11.74**	10.76	**9.87**	9.06	7.63	6.44	5.45	4.61	3.91	53
54	17.76	16.30	**14.95**	12.61	**11.58**	10.64	**9.79**	9.01	7.63	6.47	5.50	4.68	3.99	54

Table 34 Multipliers for loss of pension commencing age 80 (females) *continued*

Age at date of trial	Multipliers calculated with allowance for projected mortality from the 2018-based population projections and rate of return of:													Age at date of trial
	-2.0%	-1.75%	**-1.5%**	-1.0%	**-0.75%**	-0.5%	**-0.25%**	0.0%	0.5%	1.0%	1.5%	2.0%	2.5%	
55	17.31	15.92	**14.64**	12.41	**11.43**	10.53	**9.72**	8.96	7.63	6.50	5.56	4.75	4.07	55
56	16.85	15.55	**14.34**	12.22	**11.28**	10.42	**9.63**	8.91	7.63	6.54	5.61	4.82	4.15	56
57	16.43	15.18	**14.05**	12.03	**11.15**	10.32	**9.57**	8.87	7.62	6.57	5.67	4.89	4.23	57
58	16.01	14.84	**13.77**	11.85	**11.00**	10.22	**9.49**	8.82	7.63	6.61	5.73	4.97	4.32	58
59	15.62	14.52	**13.50**	11.69	**10.87**	10.13	**9.43**	8.79	7.64	6.65	5.79	5.05	4.42	59
60	15.24	14.20	**13.24**	11.51	**10.74**	10.03	**9.36**	8.75	7.65	6.69	5.86	5.14	4.51	60
61	14.87	13.89	**12.98**	11.36	**10.63**	9.94	**9.31**	8.73	7.66	6.73	5.93	5.22	4.61	61
62	14.51	13.60	**12.74**	11.21	**10.51**	9.86	**9.26**	8.69	7.68	6.78	6.00	5.32	4.72	62
63	14.18	13.32	**12.51**	11.06	**10.40**	9.79	**9.21**	8.67	7.70	6.83	6.08	5.41	4.82	63
64	13.86	13.05	**12.29**	10.93	**10.30**	9.71	**9.17**	8.66	7.72	6.89	6.16	5.51	4.93	64
65	13.56	12.80	**12.09**	10.79	**10.21**	9.65	**9.13**	8.64	7.75	6.95	6.24	5.62	5.06	65
66	13.27	12.56	**11.89**	10.67	**10.12**	9.59	**9.10**	8.64	7.78	7.02	6.33	5.73	5.19	66
67	13.00	12.33	**11.71**	10.57	**10.04**	9.55	**9.08**	8.64	7.82	7.09	6.43	5.84	5.32	67
68	12.74	12.12	**11.55**	10.48	**9.98**	9.51	**9.06**	8.64	7.87	7.17	6.54	5.98	5.46	68
69	12.51	11.93	**11.39**	10.39	**9.92**	9.48	**9.06**	8.67	7.92	7.26	6.66	6.11	5.61	69
70	12.29	11.76	**11.25**	10.31	**9.88**	9.46	**9.07**	8.69	7.99	7.36	6.78	6.25	5.77	70
71	12.08	11.60	**11.13**	10.26	**9.84**	9.46	**9.08**	8.73	8.07	7.46	6.92	6.41	5.95	71
72	11.91	11.46	**11.02**	10.21	**9.83**	9.47	**9.12**	8.78	8.17	7.59	7.07	6.59	6.14	72
73	11.76	11.35	**10.94**	10.19	**9.84**	9.49	**9.17**	8.86	8.27	7.73	7.23	6.78	6.35	73
74	11.63	11.25	**10.88**	10.18	**9.85**	9.55	**9.24**	8.95	8.40	7.89	7.42	6.98	6.57	74
75	11.54	11.19	**10.85**	10.21	**9.90**	9.61	**9.33**	9.06	8.54	8.07	7.62	7.22	6.83	75
76	11.47	11.15	**10.84**	10.25	**9.97**	9.70	**9.45**	9.20	8.72	8.27	7.86	7.47	7.11	76
77	11.44	11.15	**10.87**	10.33	**10.08**	9.83	**9.59**	9.36	8.92	8.51	8.12	7.76	7.42	77
78	11.45	11.19	**10.93**	10.44	**10.22**	9.99	**9.77**	9.56	9.16	8.78	8.43	8.10	7.78	78
79	11.50	11.26	**11.04**	10.60	**10.39**	10.19	**10.00**	9.81	9.44	9.10	8.77	8.47	8.18	79
80	11.60	11.39	**11.19**	10.80	**10.62**	10.44	**10.27**	10.10	9.77	9.46	9.17	8.90	8.63	80

Table 35 Discounting factors for term certain

Term	Factor to discount value of multiplier for a period of deferment													Term
	-2.0%	-1.75%	**-1.5%**	-1.0%	**-0.75%**	-0.5%	**-0.25%**	0.0%	0.5%	1.0%	1.5%	2.0%	2.5%	
1	1.0204	1.0178	**1.0152**	1.0101	**1.0076**	1.0050	**1.0025**	1.0000	0.9950	0.9901	0.9852	0.9804	0.9756	1
2	1.0412	1.0359	**1.0307**	1.0203	**1.0152**	1.0101	**1.0050**	1.0000	0.9901	0.9803	0.9707	0.9612	0.9518	2
3	1.0625	1.0544	**1.0464**	1.0306	**1.0228**	1.0152	**1.0075**	1.0000	0.9851	0.9706	0.9563	0.9423	0.9286	3
4	1.0842	1.0732	**1.0623**	1.0410	**1.0306**	1.0203	**1.0101**	1.0000	0.9802	0.9610	0.9422	0.9238	0.9060	4
5	1.1063	1.0923	**1.0785**	1.0515	**1.0384**	1.0254	**1.0126**	1.0000	0.9754	0.9515	0.9283	0.9057	0.8839	5
6	1.1289	1.1117	**1.0949**	1.0622	**1.0462**	1.0305	**1.0151**	1.0000	0.9705	0.9420	0.9145	0.8880	0.8623	6
7	1.1519	1.1315	**1.1116**	1.0729	**1.0541**	1.0357	**1.0177**	1.0000	0.9657	0.9327	0.9010	0.8706	0.8413	7
8	1.1754	1.1517	**1.1285**	1.0837	**1.0621**	1.0409	**1.0202**	1.0000	0.9609	0.9235	0.8877	0.8535	0.8207	8
9	1.1994	1.1722	**1.1457**	1.0947	**1.0701**	1.0461	**1.0228**	1.0000	0.9561	0.9143	0.8746	0.8368	0.8007	9
10	1.2239	1.1931	**1.1632**	1.1057	**1.0782**	1.0514	**1.0253**	1.0000	0.9513	0.9053	0.8617	0.8203	0.7812	10
11	1.2489	1.2143	**1.1809**	1.1169	**1.0863**	1.0567	**1.0279**	1.0000	0.9466	0.8963	0.8489	0.8043	0.7621	11
12	1.2743	1.2360	**1.1989**	1.1282	**1.0945**	1.0620	**1.0305**	1.0000	0.9419	0.8874	0.8364	0.7885	0.7436	12
13	1.3004	1.2580	**1.2171**	1.1396	**1.1028**	1.0673	**1.0331**	1.0000	0.9372	0.8787	0.8240	0.7730	0.7254	13
14	1.3269	1.2804	**1.2356**	1.1511	**1.1112**	1.0727	**1.0357**	1.0000	0.9326	0.8700	0.8118	0.7579	0.7077	14
15	1.3540	1.3032	**1.2545**	1.1627	**1.1195**	1.0781	**1.0383**	1.0000	0.9279	0.8613	0.7999	0.7430	0.6905	15
16	1.3816	1.3264	**1.2736**	1.1745	**1.1280**	1.0835	**1.0409**	1.0000	0.9233	0.8528	0.7880	0.7284	0.6736	16
17	1.4098	1.3500	**1.2930**	1.1863	**1.1365**	1.0889	**1.0435**	1.0000	0.9187	0.8444	0.7764	0.7142	0.6572	17
18	1.4386	1.3741	**1.3126**	1.1983	**1.1451**	1.0944	**1.0461**	1.0000	0.9141	0.8360	0.7649	0.7002	0.6412	18
19	1.4679	1.3986	**1.3326**	1.2104	**1.1538**	1.0999	**1.0487**	1.0000	0.9096	0.8277	0.7536	0.6864	0.6255	19
20	1.4979	1.4235	**1.3529**	1.2226	**1.1625**	1.1054	**1.0513**	1.0000	0.9051	0.8195	0.7425	0.6730	0.6103	20
21	1.5285	1.4488	**1.3735**	1.2350	**1.1713**	1.1110	**1.0540**	1.0000	0.9006	0.8114	0.7315	0.6598	0.5954	21
22	1.5596	1.4746	**1.3944**	1.2475	**1.1801**	1.1166	**1.0566**	1.0000	0.8961	0.8034	0.7207	0.6468	0.5809	22
23	1.5915	1.5009	**1.4157**	1.2601	**1.1890**	1.1222	**1.0593**	1.0000	0.8916	0.7954	0.7100	0.6342	0.5667	23
24	1.6240	1.5276	**1.4372**	1.2728	**1.1980**	1.1278	**1.0619**	1.0000	0.8872	0.7876	0.6995	0.6217	0.5529	24
25	1.6571	1.5548	**1.4591**	1.2856	**1.2071**	1.1335	**1.0646**	1.0000	0.8828	0.7798	0.6892	0.6095	0.5394	25
26	1.6909	1.5825	**1.4814**	1.2986	**1.2162**	1.1392	**1.0672**	1.0000	0.8784	0.7720	0.6790	0.5976	0.5262	26
27	1.7254	1.6107	**1.5039**	1.3117	**1.2254**	1.1449	**1.0699**	1.0000	0.8740	0.7644	0.6690	0.5859	0.5134	27
28	1.7606	1.6394	**1.5268**	1.3250	**1.2347**	1.1507	**1.0726**	1.0000	0.8697	0.7568	0.6591	0.5744	0.5009	28
29	1.7966	1.6686	**1.5501**	1.3384	**1.2440**	1.1565	**1.0753**	1.0000	0.8653	0.7493	0.6494	0.5631	0.4887	29
30	1.8332	1.6983	**1.5737**	1.3519	**1.2534**	1.1623	**1.0780**	1.0000	0.8610	0.7419	0.6398	0.5521	0.4767	30
31	1.8706	1.7286	**1.5976**	1.3656	**1.2629**	1.1681	**1.0807**	1.0000	0.8567	0.7346	0.6303	0.5412	0.4651	31
32	1.9088	1.7594	**1.6220**	1.3793	**1.2724**	1.1740	**1.0834**	1.0000	0.8525	0.7273	0.6210	0.5306	0.4538	32
33	1.9478	1.7907	**1.6467**	1.3933	**1.2820**	1.1799	**1.0861**	1.0000	0.8482	0.7201	0.6118	0.5202	0.4427	33
34	1.9875	1.8226	**1.6717**	1.4074	**1.2917**	1.1858	**1.0888**	1.0000	0.8440	0.7130	0.6028	0.5100	0.4319	34
35	2.0281	1.8551	**1.6972**	1.4216	**1.3015**	1.1918	**1.0916**	1.0000	0.8398	0.7059	0.5939	0.5000	0.4214	35
36	2.0695	1.8881	**1.7230**	1.4359	**1.3113**	1.1978	**1.0943**	1.0000	0.8356	0.6989	0.5851	0.4902	0.4111	36
37	2.1117	1.9217	**1.7493**	1.4504	**1.3212**	1.2038	**1.0970**	1.0000	0.8315	0.6920	0.5764	0.4806	0.4011	37
38	2.1548	1.9560	**1.7759**	1.4651	**1.3312**	1.2098	**1.0998**	1.0000	0.8274	0.6852	0.5679	0.4712	0.3913	38
39	2.1988	1.9908	**1.8030**	1.4799	**1.3413**	1.2159	**1.1025**	1.0000	0.8232	0.6784	0.5595	0.4619	0.3817	39
40	2.2437	2.0263	**1.8304**	1.4948	**1.3514**	1.2220	**1.1053**	1.0000	0.8191	0.6717	0.5513	0.4529	0.3724	40
41	2.2894	2.0624	**1.8583**	1.5099	**1.3616**	1.2282	**1.1081**	1.0000	0.8151	0.6650	0.5431	0.4440	0.3633	41
42	2.3362	2.0991	**1.8866**	1.5252	**1.3719**	1.2343	**1.1109**	1.0000	0.8110	0.6584	0.5351	0.4353	0.3545	42
43	2.3838	2.1365	**1.9153**	1.5406	**1.3823**	1.2405	**1.1136**	1.0000	0.8070	0.6519	0.5272	0.4268	0.3458	43
44	2.4325	2.1745	**1.9445**	1.5561	**1.3927**	1.2468	**1.1164**	1.0000	0.8030	0.6454	0.5194	0.4184	0.3374	44
45	2.4821	2.2133	**1.9741**	1.5719	**1.4032**	1.2530	**1.1192**	1.0000	0.7990	0.6391	0.5117	0.4102	0.3292	45
46	2.5328	2.2527	**2.0042**	1.5877	**1.4138**	1.2593	**1.1220**	1.0000	0.7950	0.6327	0.5042	0.4022	0.3211	46
47	2.5845	2.2928	**2.0347**	1.6038	**1.4245**	1.2657	**1.1248**	1.0000	0.7910	0.6265	0.4967	0.3943	0.3133	47
48	2.6372	2.3337	**2.0657**	1.6200	**1.4353**	1.2720	**1.1277**	1.0000	0.7871	0.6203	0.4894	0.3865	0.3057	48
49	2.6911	2.3752	**2.0971**	1.6363	**1.4461**	1.2784	**1.1305**	1.0000	0.7832	0.6141	0.4821	0.3790	0.2982	49
50	2.7460	2.4175	**2.1291**	1.6529	**1.4570**	1.2848	**1.1333**	1.0000	0.7793	0.6080	0.4750	0.3715	0.2909	50
51	2.8020	2.4606	**2.1615**	1.6696	**1.4681**	1.2913	**1.1362**	1.0000	0.7754	0.6020	0.4680	0.3642	0.2838	51
52	2.8592	2.5044	**2.1944**	1.6864	**1.4792**	1.2978	**1.1390**	1.0000	0.7716	0.5961	0.4611	0.3571	0.2769	52
53	2.9175	2.5490	**2.2278**	1.7035	**1.4903**	1.3043	**1.1419**	1.0000	0.7677	0.5902	0.4543	0.3501	0.2702	53
54	2.9771	2.5944	**2.2617**	1.7207	**1.5016**	1.3109	**1.1447**	1.0000	0.7639	0.5843	0.4475	0.3432	0.2636	54
55	3.0378	2.6406	**2.2962**	1.7381	**1.5129**	1.3174	**1.1476**	1.0000	0.7601	0.5785	0.4409	0.3365	0.2572	55

Table 35 Discounting factors for term certain *continued*

Term	Factor to discount value of multiplier for a period of deferment													Term
	-2.0%	-1.75%	**-1.5%**	-1.0%	**-0.75%**	-0.5%	**-0.25%**	0.0%	0.5%	1.0%	1.5%	2.0%	2.5%	
56	3.0998	2.6877	**2.3312**	1.7556	**1.5244**	1.3241	**1.1505**	1.0000	0.7563	0.5728	0.4344	0.3299	0.2509	56
57	3.1631	2.7355	**2.3667**	1.7733	**1.5359**	1.3307	**1.1534**	1.0000	0.7525	0.5671	0.4280	0.3234	0.2448	57
58	3.2277	2.7843	**2.4027**	1.7913	**1.5475**	1.3374	**1.1562**	1.0000	0.7488	0.5615	0.4217	0.3171	0.2388	58
59	3.2935	2.8339	**2.4393**	1.8094	**1.5592**	1.3441	**1.1591**	1.0000	0.7451	0.5560	0.4154	0.3109	0.2330	59
60	3.3607	2.8843	**2.4764**	1.8276	**1.5710**	1.3509	**1.1621**	1.0000	0.7414	0.5504	0.4093	0.3048	0.2273	60
61	3.4293	2.9357	**2.5141**	1.8461	**1.5828**	1.3577	**1.1650**	1.0000	0.7377	0.5450	0.4032	0.2988	0.2217	61
62	3.4993	2.9880	**2.5524**	1.8647	**1.5948**	1.3645	**1.1679**	1.0000	0.7340	0.5396	0.3973	0.2929	0.2163	62
63	3.5707	3.0412	**2.5913**	1.8836	**1.6069**	1.3713	**1.1708**	1.0000	0.7304	0.5343	0.3914	0.2872	0.2111	63
64	3.6436	3.0954	**2.6308**	1.9026	**1.6190**	1.3782	**1.1737**	1.0000	0.7267	0.5290	0.3856	0.2816	0.2059	64
65	3.7180	3.1505	**2.6708**	1.9218	**1.6312**	1.3852	**1.1767**	1.0000	0.7231	0.5237	0.3799	0.2761	0.2009	65
66	3.7938	3.2066	**2.7115**	1.9412	**1.6436**	1.3921	**1.1796**	1.0000	0.7195	0.5185	0.3743	0.2706	0.1960	66
67	3.8713	3.2638	**2.7528**	1.9608	**1.6560**	1.3991	**1.1826**	1.0000	0.7159	0.5134	0.3688	0.2653	0.1912	67
68	3.9503	3.3219	**2.7947**	1.9806	**1.6685**	1.4061	**1.1856**	1.0000	0.7124	0.5083	0.3633	0.2601	0.1865	68
69	4.0309	3.3811	**2.8373**	2.0007	**1.6811**	1.4132	**1.1885**	1.0000	0.7088	0.5033	0.3580	0.2550	0.1820	69
70	4.1132	3.4413	**2.8805**	2.0209	**1.6938**	1.4203	**1.1915**	1.0000	0.7053	0.4983	0.3527	0.2500	0.1776	70
71	4.1971	3.5026	**2.9243**	2.0413	**1.7066**	1.4275	**1.1945**	1.0000	0.7018	0.4934	0.3475	0.2451	0.1732	71
72	4.2827	3.5650	**2.9689**	2.0619	**1.7195**	1.4346	**1.1975**	1.0000	0.6983	0.4885	0.3423	0.2403	0.1690	72
73	4.3702	3.6285	**3.0141**	2.0827	**1.7325**	1.4418	**1.2005**	1.0000	0.6948	0.4837	0.3373	0.2356	0.1649	73
74	4.4593	3.6931	**3.0600**	2.1038	**1.7456**	1.4491	**1.2035**	1.0000	0.6914	0.4789	0.3323	0.2310	0.1609	74
75	4.5503	3.7589	**3.1066**	2.1250	**1.7588**	1.4564	**1.2065**	1.0000	0.6879	0.4741	0.3274	0.2265	0.1569	75
76	4.6432	3.8258	**3.1539**	2.1465	**1.7721**	1.4637	**1.2095**	1.0000	0.6845	0.4694	0.3225	0.2220	0.1531	76
77	4.7380	3.8940	**3.2019**	2.1682	**1.7855**	1.4710	**1.2126**	1.0000	0.6811	0.4648	0.3178	0.2177	0.1494	77
78	4.8347	3.9633	**3.2507**	2.1901	**1.7990**	1.4784	**1.2156**	1.0000	0.6777	0.4602	0.3131	0.2134	0.1457	78
79	4.9333	4.0339	**3.3002**	2.2122	**1.8125**	1.4859	**1.2187**	1.0000	0.6743	0.4556	0.3084	0.2092	0.1422	79
80	5.0340	4.1058	**3.3504**	2.2345	**1.8262**	1.4933	**1.2217**	1.0000	0.6710	0.4511	0.3039	0.2051	0.1387	80

Table 36 Multipliers for pecuniary loss for term certain

Term	Multipliers for regular frequent payments for a term certain at rate of return of:													Term
	-2.0%	-1.75%	**-1.5%**	-1.0%	**-0.75%**	-0.5%	**-0.25%**	0.0%	0.5%	1.0%	1.5%	2.0%	2.5%	
1	1.01	1.01	**1.01**	1.01	**1.00**	1.00	**1.00**	1.00	1.00	1.00	0.99	0.99	0.99	1
2	2.04	2.04	**2.03**	2.02	**2.02**	2.01	**2.01**	2.00	1.99	1.98	1.97	1.96	1.95	2
3	3.09	3.08	**3.07**	3.05	**3.03**	3.02	**3.01**	3.00	2.98	2.96	2.93	2.91	2.89	3
4	4.17	4.14	**4.12**	4.08	**4.06**	4.04	**4.02**	4.00	3.96	3.92	3.88	3.85	3.81	4
5	5.26	5.23	**5.19**	5.13	**5.10**	5.06	**5.03**	5.00	4.94	4.88	4.82	4.76	4.70	5
6	6.38	6.33	**6.28**	6.18	**6.14**	6.09	**6.05**	6.00	5.91	5.82	5.74	5.66	5.58	6
7	7.52	7.45	**7.38**	7.25	**7.19**	7.12	**7.06**	7.00	6.88	6.76	6.65	6.54	6.43	7
8	8.68	8.59	**8.50**	8.33	**8.25**	8.16	**8.08**	8.00	7.84	7.69	7.54	7.40	7.26	8
9	9.87	9.75	**9.64**	9.42	**9.31**	9.21	**9.10**	9.00	8.80	8.61	8.42	8.24	8.07	9
10	11.08	10.94	**10.80**	10.52	**10.39**	10.25	**10.13**	10.00	9.75	9.52	9.29	9.07	8.86	10
11	12.32	12.14	**11.97**	11.63	**11.47**	11.31	**11.15**	11.00	10.70	10.42	10.15	9.88	9.63	11
12	13.58	13.37	**13.16**	12.75	**12.56**	12.37	**12.18**	12.00	11.65	11.31	10.99	10.68	10.39	12
13	14.87	14.61	**14.37**	13.89	**13.66**	13.43	**13.21**	13.00	12.59	12.19	11.82	11.46	11.12	13
14	16.18	15.88	**15.59**	15.03	**14.76**	14.50	**14.25**	14.00	13.52	13.07	12.64	12.23	11.84	14
15	17.52	17.17	**16.84**	16.19	**15.88**	15.58	**15.29**	15.00	14.45	13.93	13.44	12.98	12.54	15
16	18.89	18.49	**18.10**	17.36	**17.00**	16.66	**16.32**	16.00	15.38	14.79	14.24	13.71	13.22	16
17	20.28	19.83	**19.38**	18.54	**18.14**	17.75	**17.37**	17.00	16.30	15.64	15.02	14.43	13.88	17
18	21.71	21.19	**20.69**	19.73	**19.28**	18.84	**18.41**	18.00	17.22	16.48	15.79	15.14	14.53	18
19	23.16	22.58	**22.01**	20.94	**20.43**	19.93	**19.46**	19.00	18.13	17.31	16.55	15.83	15.17	19
20	24.64	23.99	**23.35**	22.15	**21.58**	21.04	**20.51**	20.00	19.03	18.14	17.30	16.51	15.78	20
21	26.16	25.42	**24.71**	23.38	**22.75**	22.15	**21.56**	21.00	19.94	18.95	18.03	17.18	16.39	21
22	27.70	26.88	**26.10**	24.62	**23.93**	23.26	**22.62**	22.00	20.84	19.76	18.76	17.83	16.97	22
23	29.28	28.37	**27.50**	25.88	**25.11**	24.38	**23.67**	23.00	21.73	20.56	19.48	18.47	17.55	23
24	30.88	29.89	**28.93**	27.14	**26.30**	25.50	**24.74**	24.00	22.62	21.35	20.18	19.10	18.11	24
25	32.53	31.43	**30.38**	28.42	**27.51**	26.63	**25.80**	25.00	23.50	22.13	20.87	19.72	18.65	25
26	34.20	33.00	**31.85**	29.71	**28.72**	27.77	**26.86**	26.00	24.38	22.91	21.56	20.32	19.19	26
27	35.91	34.59	**33.34**	31.02	**29.94**	28.91	**27.93**	27.00	25.26	23.68	22.23	20.91	19.71	27
28	37.65	36.22	**34.86**	32.34	**31.17**	30.06	**29.00**	28.00	26.13	24.44	22.90	21.49	20.21	28
29	39.43	37.87	**36.40**	33.67	**32.41**	31.21	**30.08**	29.00	27.00	25.19	23.55	22.06	20.71	29
30	41.24	39.55	**37.96**	35.01	**33.66**	32.37	**31.16**	30.00	27.86	25.94	24.20	22.62	21.19	30
31	43.10	41.27	**39.54**	36.37	**34.92**	33.54	**32.23**	31.00	28.72	26.67	24.83	23.17	21.66	31
32	44.99	43.01	**41.15**	37.74	**36.18**	34.71	**33.32**	32.00	29.58	27.41	25.46	23.70	22.12	32
33	46.91	44.79	**42.79**	39.13	**37.46**	35.89	**34.40**	33.00	30.43	28.13	26.07	24.23	22.57	33
34	48.88	46.59	**44.45**	40.53	**38.75**	37.07	**35.49**	34.00	31.27	28.85	26.68	24.74	23.01	34
35	50.89	48.43	**46.13**	41.95	**40.04**	38.26	**36.58**	35.00	32.12	29.56	27.28	25.25	23.43	35
36	52.94	50.30	**47.84**	43.37	**41.35**	39.45	**37.67**	36.00	32.95	30.26	27.87	25.74	23.85	36
37	55.03	52.21	**49.58**	44.82	**42.67**	40.65	**38.77**	37.00	33.79	30.95	28.45	26.23	24.26	37
38	57.16	54.15	**51.34**	46.28	**43.99**	41.86	**39.87**	38.00	34.62	31.64	29.02	26.70	24.65	38
39	59.34	56.12	**53.13**	47.75	**45.33**	43.07	**40.97**	39.00	35.44	32.32	29.58	27.17	25.04	39
40	61.56	58.13	**54.95**	49.24	**46.68**	44.29	**42.07**	40.00	36.26	33.00	30.14	27.63	25.42	40
41	63.83	60.17	**56.79**	50.74	**48.03**	45.52	**43.18**	41.00	37.08	33.67	30.69	28.08	25.78	41
42	66.14	62.25	**58.66**	52.26	**49.40**	46.75	**44.29**	42.00	37.89	34.33	31.23	28.52	26.14	42
43	68.50	64.37	**60.56**	53.79	**50.78**	47.99	**45.40**	43.00	38.70	34.98	31.76	28.95	26.49	43
44	70.91	66.53	**62.49**	55.34	**52.16**	49.23	**46.51**	44.00	39.51	35.63	32.28	29.37	26.83	44
45	73.36	68.72	**64.45**	56.90	**53.56**	50.48	**47.63**	45.00	40.31	36.27	32.80	29.78	27.17	45
46	75.87	70.95	**66.44**	58.48	**54.97**	51.74	**48.75**	46.00	41.10	36.91	33.30	30.19	27.49	46
47	78.43	73.23	**68.46**	60.08	**56.39**	53.00	**49.88**	47.00	41.90	37.54	33.80	30.59	27.81	47
48	81.04	75.54	**70.51**	61.69	**57.82**	54.27	**51.00**	48.00	42.69	38.16	34.30	30.98	28.12	48
49	83.70	77.89	**72.59**	63.32	**59.26**	55.54	**52.13**	49.00	43.47	38.78	34.78	31.36	28.42	49
50	86.42	80.29	**74.70**	64.96	**60.71**	56.82	**53.26**	50.00	44.25	39.39	35.26	31.74	28.72	50
51	89.20	82.73	**76.85**	66.62	**62.17**	58.11	**54.40**	51.00	45.03	40.00	35.73	32.10	29.00	51
52	92.03	85.21	**79.03**	68.30	**63.65**	59.41	**55.54**	52.00	45.80	40.60	36.20	32.47	29.28	52
53	94.92	87.74	**81.24**	69.99	**65.13**	60.71	**56.68**	53.00	46.57	41.19	36.66	32.82	29.56	53
54	97.86	90.31	**83.48**	71.71	**66.63**	62.01	**57.82**	54.00	47.34	41.78	37.11	33.17	29.82	54
55	100.87	92.93	**85.76**	73.44	**68.14**	63.33	**58.97**	55.00	48.10	42.36	37.55	33.51	30.08	55

Table 36 Multipliers for pecuniary loss for term certain *continued*

Term	Multipliers for regular frequent payments for a term certain at rate of return of:													Term
	-2.0%	-1.75%	**-1.5%**	-1.0%	**-0.75%**	-0.5%	**-0.25%**	0.0%	0.5%	1.0%	1.5%	2.0%	2.5%	
56	103.94	95.59	**88.08**	75.18	**69.65**	64.65	**60.11**	56.00	48.86	42.93	37.99	33.84	30.34	56
57	107.07	98.30	**90.43**	76.95	**71.18**	65.98	**61.27**	57.00	49.61	43.50	38.42	34.17	30.59	57
58	110.27	101.06	**92.81**	78.73	**72.73**	67.31	**62.42**	58.00	50.36	44.07	38.84	34.49	30.83	58
59	113.53	103.87	**95.23**	80.53	**74.28**	68.65	**63.58**	59.00	51.11	44.63	39.26	34.80	31.06	59
60	116.85	106.73	**97.69**	82.35	**75.84**	70.00	**64.74**	60.00	51.85	45.18	39.67	35.11	31.29	60
61	120.25	109.64	**100.18**	84.19	**77.42**	71.35	**65.90**	61.00	52.59	45.73	40.08	35.41	31.52	61
62	123.71	112.60	**102.72**	86.04	**79.01**	72.71	**67.07**	62.00	53.33	46.27	40.48	35.70	31.74	62
63	127.25	115.62	**105.29**	87.91	**80.61**	74.08	**68.24**	63.00	54.06	46.81	40.88	36.00	31.95	63
64	130.85	118.69	**107.90**	89.81	**82.22**	75.46	**69.41**	64.00	54.79	47.34	41.26	36.28	32.16	64
65	134.53	121.81	**110.55**	91.72	**83.85**	76.84	**70.59**	65.00	55.52	47.86	41.65	36.56	32.36	65
66	138.29	124.99	**113.24**	93.65	**85.49**	78.23	**71.76**	66.00	56.24	48.39	42.02	36.83	32.56	66
67	142.12	128.22	**115.97**	95.60	**87.14**	79.62	**72.95**	67.00	56.95	48.90	42.40	37.10	32.75	67
68	146.03	131.52	**118.75**	97.57	**88.80**	81.03	**74.13**	68.00	57.67	49.41	42.76	37.36	32.94	68
69	150.02	134.87	**121.56**	99.56	**90.47**	82.44	**75.32**	69.00	58.38	49.92	43.12	37.62	33.13	69
70	154.10	138.28	**124.42**	101.57	**92.16**	83.85	**76.51**	70.00	59.09	50.42	43.48	37.87	33.31	70
71	158.25	141.75	**127.32**	103.61	**93.86**	85.28	**77.70**	71.00	59.79	50.91	43.83	38.12	33.48	71
72	162.49	145.28	**130.27**	105.66	**95.57**	86.71	**78.90**	72.00	60.49	51.41	44.17	38.36	33.65	72
73	166.82	148.88	**133.26**	107.73	**97.30**	88.15	**80.10**	73.00	61.19	51.89	44.51	38.60	33.82	73
74	171.23	152.54	**136.30**	109.82	**99.04**	89.59	**81.30**	74.00	61.88	52.37	44.85	38.83	33.98	74
75	175.74	156.27	**139.38**	111.94	**100.79**	91.04	**82.50**	75.00	62.57	52.85	45.18	39.06	34.14	75
76	180.33	160.06	**142.51**	114.07	**102.56**	92.50	**83.71**	76.00	63.26	53.32	45.50	39.29	34.30	76
77	185.02	163.92	**145.69**	116.23	**104.33**	93.97	**84.92**	77.00	63.94	53.79	45.82	39.51	34.45	77
78	189.81	167.85	**148.92**	118.41	**106.13**	95.45	**86.14**	78.00	64.62	54.25	46.14	39.72	34.60	78
79	194.69	171.85	**152.19**	120.61	**107.93**	96.93	**87.35**	79.00	65.29	54.71	46.45	39.93	34.74	79
80	199.68	175.92	**155.52**	122.83	**109.75**	98.42	**88.57**	80.00	65.97	55.16	46.75	40.14	34.88	80

ACTUARIAL FORMULAE AND BASIS

The functions tabulated are:

Tables 1 and 2	$\bar{a}_x$
Tables 3 and 4	$\bar{a}_{x:\overline{50-x}\rceil}$
Tables 5 and 6	$\bar{a}_{x:\overline{55-x}\rceil}$
Tables 7 and 8	$\bar{a}_{x:\overline{60-x}\rceil}$
Tables 9 and 10	$\bar{a}_{x:\overline{65-x}\rceil}$
Tables 11 and 12	$\bar{a}_{x:\overline{68-x}\rceil}$
Tables 13 and 14	$\bar{a}_{x:\overline{70-x}\rceil}$
Tables 15 and 16	$\bar{a}_{x:\overline{75-x}\rceil}$
Tables 17 and 18	$\bar{a}_{x:\overline{80-x}\rceil}$
Tables 19 and 20	$_{(50-x)\mid}\bar{a}_x$
Tables 21 and 22	$_{(55-x)\mid}\bar{a}_x$
Tables 23 and 24	$_{(60-x)\mid}\bar{a}_x$
Tables 25 and 26	$_{(65-x)\mid}\bar{a}_x$
Tables 27 and 28	$_{(68-x)\mid}\bar{a}_x$
Tables 29 and 30	$_{(70-x)\mid}\bar{a}_x$
Tables 31 and 32	$_{(75-x)\mid}\bar{a}_x$
Tables 33 and 34	$_{(80-x)\mid}\bar{a}_x$
Table 35	$1 / (1 + i)^n$
Table 36	$\bar{a}_{\overline{n}\rceil}$

- Mortality assumptions for 2018–based official population projections for the United Kingdom.
- Loadings: None.
- Rate of return: As stated in the tables.

A9: Personal Injury Discount Rate – Outcome of Review

Statement placed by the Rt Hon David Gauke MP, Lord Chancellor, in the libraries of the Houses of Parliament on 15 July 2019

1. As Lord Chancellor, I have power under Section A1 of the Damages Act 1996 from time to time to prescribe the rate of return that the Court must take into account when determining the rate of investment return to be expected from the investment of damages awarded as a lump sum in respect of future pecuniary loss in personal injury cases. The Civil Liability Act 2018 amended the Damages Act 1996 by introducing a new methodology to be used by me in setting the rate, and by setting a timetable for this first review conducted under the new methodology, which I have observed in full.

2. In the course of my review, I have considered all the material provided to me, including the advice of the Government Actuary and the Treasury; responses to a Call for Evidence which the Ministry of Justice convened to inform this review; and the Equalities Statement published alongside this Statement. However, at all times I have remained cognisant of my duties under the Damages Act 1996 and have been careful only to take account of those matters that are relevant to my determination of the rate. The process of review has been thorough, reflecting the complexity and importance of the subject matter.

3. This statement sets out the decision I have reached as a result of this exercise and a summary of my reasons for that decision.

Decision

4. I have concluded that a discount rate of minus 0.25% is the appropriate rate.

Reasons

5. I emphasise at the outset that, while the reforms enacted last year have provided a clearer legislative framework for this process, the procedure for setting the discount rate remains a complex and technical one. It involves making a series of assumptions and judgements in considering the evidence and economic variables that apply. Some of these judgements are finely balanced and involve making predictions about the future which are inherently uncertain.

6. The rate should be the rate that, in my opinion, a recipient of relevant damages could reasonably expect to receive if they invested their damages award for the purpose of securing that—

   (a) the relevant damages would meet the losses and costs for which they are awarded;

   (b) the relevant damages would meet those losses and costs at the time or times when they fall to be met by the relevant damages; and

   (c) the relevant damages would be exhausted at the end of the period for which they are awarded.

   Together these factors may be said to be the codification of the guiding principle for the award of damages, as set out by the House of Lords in *Wells v Wells* [1999] 1 AC 34 per Lord Hope of Craighead:

" . . . the object of the award of damages for future expenditure is to place the injured party as nearly as possible in the same financial position he or she would have been in but for the accident. The aim is to award such a sum of money as will amount to no more, and at the same time no less, than the net loss". . . . "

7. In determining the rate on this basis, the 1996 Act, as amended, requires me to make certain assumptions and to have regard to certain factors, as detailed in paragraph 4 of Schedule A1 to the 1996 Act.

8. I must assume that the relevant damages are payable in a lump sum (rather than under an order for periodical payments), I must assume that the recipient of the relevant damages is properly advised on the investment of those damages, and that they invest in a diversified portfolio of investments. I must also assume that the sums are invested using an approach which involves more risk than very low risk, but less risk than would ordinarily be accepted by a prudent and properly advised individual investor who has different financial aims.

9. I must also have regard to actual returns available to investors, and actual investments made by investors of relevant damages. I must also make such allowances for taxation, inflation and investment management costs as I think appropriate.

10. In arriving at my conclusion, I have had close regard to the expert advice of the Government Actuary. He has set out in his report the full detail of the analytical approach taken, and the evidence from which it was drawn. I highlight certain aspects of the Government Actuary's advice below, but, for the avoidance of doubt, I have considered the entirety of that advice.

11. I consider the Government Actuary's baseline assumption of a representative claimant investing over a period of 43 years to be a reasonable one. It is supported by responses to the Ministry's Call for Evidence, suggesting the average duration for serious personal injury cases was between 40 and 45 years.

12. I consider reasonable the Government Actuary's approach in selecting a representative portfolio (within a range of low risk portfolios), resulting (on his calculations) in a median rate of return of around CPI[1] plus 2% per annum. In adopting this representative portfolio, I consider the suggested division between 42.5% allocation to growth assets (generating higher returns over the longer term): and a 57.5% allocation to matching assets (generating lower returns but offering greater certainty) to be an appropriate one.

13. The advice also addresses how to assess and quantify the effect of tax and expenses for each claimant. I note the caution of the Government Actuary on how this can vary depending on individual circumstances, but nevertheless consider that I must arrive at a reasonable combined figure. I accept the expert advice from the Government Actuary that the expense assumption should correspond with the basis of the investment returns modelled for a representative claimant. This aspect must be taken in the round, and I consider that the Government Actuary's conclusion that a figure of plus 0.75% for tax and expenses is a reasonable one.

14. So far as the effect of inflation on investment returns is concerned, again, I note that the position will vary from claimant to claimant across a spectrum, and the Call for Evidence did not offer a consensus on the impact of damage inflation. I have accepted the expert conclusion of the Government Actuary that a claimant's damages should be assumed (on average, and in general) as inflating by CPI plus 1% per annum.

[1] CPI–Consumer Price Index

15. On the baseline assumptions adopted in the Government Actuary's advice (which I consider to be reasonable), the analysis suggests that for a representative claimant the combined expected net return could be reasonably be expected to be plus 0.25%. On the Government Actuary's advice, setting the rate at this level would result in an even (50:50) risk of claimants being under or over-compensated.

16. However, I have regarded that conclusion as a starting point for my determination rather than an end point for the reasons set out below. In doing so I have drawn on the advice from the Government Actuary on projected claimant outcomes and the sensitivity analysis he has undertaken in relation to the data.

17. I consider that a rate of plus 0.25% would run too high a risk of under-compensating claimants. At this level, the representative claimant as modelled by the Government 1 CPI – Consumer Price Index Actuary has only an approximately 50% chance of being fully compensated and approximately only a 65% chance of receiving 90% compensation. I consider this to give rise to too great a risk that the representative claimant will be undercompensated, or under-compensated by more than 10%.

18. If I were to set a rate of 0%, the representative claimant as modelled by the Government Actuary would have approximately a 60% chance of receiving full compensation and approximately a 72% chance of receiving at least 90% compensation.

19. However, those are the percentages yielded by the baseline assumptions, and I bear in mind that the Government Actuary's report includes an analysis of the sensitivity of the rate to those assumptions. I consider it reasonable to build in further prudence, when setting the rate, in order to recognise that in any individual case one or more of those baseline assumptions may not apply (either resulting in additional over-compensation or under-compensation), and in particular with regard to the Government Actuary's analysis of the rate as applied to shorter term awards.

20. I note that, on the baseline assumptions, at a rate of minus 0.25%, the representative claimant as modelled by the Government Actuary has approximately a two-thirds chance of receiving full compensation and a 78% chance of receiving at least 90% compensation. Such a claimant is approximately twice as likely to be overcompensated as under-compensated and is approximately four times as likely to receive at least 90% compensation as they are to be under-compensated by more than 10%. I consider that this leaves a reasonable additional margin of prudence which reflects the sensitivities of the rate to the baseline assumptions.

21. In making my determination I have also (as required) considered the projected levels of over-compensation, bearing in mind that the claimant should also have a reasonable expectation that the award will be exhausted at the end of the term of the award. If the rate were set at minus 0.5% then the representative claimant as modelled by the Government Actuary would have approximately a 70% chance of the award not being exhausted at the end of the term and approximately a 20% chance of having more than 10% of the award remaining at the end of the term of the award, and the median expectation is of over compensation of almost 20%. I consider that this gives rise to too great a risk that the award will not be exhausted at the term of the award, or that there may be more than 10% of the award remaining at that time.

22. **For all of these reasons, I have decided that the discount rate should be minus 0.25%.**

23. The Government Actuary has also provided an analysis and developed a working model for me to consider prescribing dual rates. This would involve a lower short term rate, a switchover period after a set number of years (15 is suggested) and then moving to a higher long term rate. I found the case for a dual rate an interesting one, with some promising indications, particularly in relation to addressing the position of short term claimants.

24. However, I do not consider that it would be appropriate to adopt a dual rate for this review, as at present we lack the quantity and depth of evidence required to conclude that the proposed model would be more appropriate than a single rate. For example, it may be appropriate to assume a different portfolio of investments and a different allowance for tax and expenses for claimants with shorter and longer term awards.

25. I consider that the potential of the dual rate, and its potential consequences (positive and negative) should be explored in more detail, and I have asked my officials to set in train a consultation in due course to examine this in greater depth, and to inform the next discount review and the work of the expert panel who will be advising me.

26. I have considered and noted the possible impact that the prescribing of a single rate may have on protected groups under the Equality Act 2010, but consider any such impact reasonable and justified in the light of all the matters set out above.

The Rt Hon David Gauke MP
Lord Chancellor
15 July 2019

Group B

Damages

B

B1: General damages table following *Heil v Rankin* and *Simmons v Castle*

General introduction

1. These tables are for updating awards of general damages in the light of *Heil v Rankin*[1] and *Simmons v Castle*[2]. At Tables E1 and E2 there are a Retail Prices Index and an inflation table.

2. While the Court of Appeal in *Heil* said that it did not intend to lay down a mathematical formula, a graph which is a shallow curve was annexed to the judgment. That curve approximately represents an uplift on an original award of £A of

$$£A\text{-}10{,}000/420{,}000 \times £A$$

3. In *Simmons v Castle* the Court of Appeal increased awards for general damages by 10 per cent, unless the claimant fell within s.44(6) of the Legal Aid, Sentencing and Punishment of Offenders Act 2012.[3]

4. For example:

   a. The claimant in *Chan v Chan* was awarded £75,000 in January 1988.

   b. Update £75,000 to 23 March 2000 in line with the Retail Prices Index, giving £122,250.

   c. Subtract £10,000 (giving £112,250), and divide by £420,000 (giving an uplift factor of 0.27).

   d. Apply this to the original award giving [0.27 × £122,250] = 33,008.

   e. The original award was therefore worth [122,250 + 33,008] = £155,258 on 23.3.2000.

   f. Update from 23.3.2000 to the present and, unless s.44(6) applies, increase by 10 per cent. That is, multiply by [present RPI × 1.10 / RPI on 23.3.2000].

5. Note that because the degree of uplift varies with the size of the original award, it is inaccurate to apply the *Heil* uplift to a figure already adjusted for inflation to a date later than 23 March 2000.

TO UPDATE A PRE-*HEIL v RANKIN* AWARD

The table which follows shows the factor to allow for inflation from an earlier date to 23 March 2000. The second table shows, at £1,000 intervals, the figure uplifted following *Heil*. Update award as follows:

Damages awarded, say, January 1990 x inflation increase to 23 March 2000 (from first table). Award uplifted under *Heil* (from second table).

Uplift for inflation from 23 March 2000 to date of trial; and add 10 per cent (unless s.44(6) applies).

[1] [2000] 2 W.L.R. 1173.

[2] [2012] EWCA Civ 1039 and [2012] EWCA Civ 1288.

[3] In *Summers v Bundy* [2016] EWCA Civ 126, the Court held that cases within s.44(6) are the only exception and the judge has no discretion to dispense with the uplift in other cases.

TABLE TO UPDATE FOR INFLATION TO MARCH 2000

	J	F	M	A	M	J	J	A	S	O	N	D	
1980	2.708	2.670	2.634	2.547	2.524	2.500	2.480	2.474	2.459	2.443	2.424	2.411	1980
1981	2.396	2.374	2.339	2.274	2.259	2.246	2.236	2.220	2.207	2.187	2.165	2.151	1981
1982	2.139	2.138	2.120	2.078	2.063	2.057	2.057	2.056	2.057	2.047	2.037	2.041	1982
1983	2.038	2.030	2.026	1.998	1.990	1.985	1.974	1.965	1.957	1.950	1.943	1.938	1983
1984	1.939	1.931	1.925	1.900	1.893	1.888	1.890	1.872	1.869	1.857	1.852	1.853	1984
1985	1.846	1.832	1.815	1.777	1.769	1.765	1.768	1.764	1.765	1.762	1.756	1.753	1985
1986	1.750	1.743	1.741	1.724	1.721	1.722	1.727	1.722	1.713	1.710	1.696	1.690	1986
1987	1.684	1.677	1.674	1.654	1.653	1.653	1.654	1.649	1.645	1.637	1.629	1.630	1987
1988	1.630	1.624	1.618	1.592	1.586	1.580	1.578	1.561	1.554	1.538	1.531	1.527	1988
1989	1.517	1.506	1.500	1.473	1.464	1.459	1.458	1.454	1.444	1.433	1.421	1.418	1989
1990	1.409	1.401	1.387	1.346	1.334	1.329	1.328	1.315	1.302	1.292	1.295	1.296	1990
1991	1.293	1.286	1.282	1.265	1.261	1.256	1.259	1.256	1.251	1.246	1.242	1.241	1991
1992	1.242	1.236	1.232	1.213	1.209	1.209	1.213	1.212	1.208	1.204	1.205	1.210	1992
1993	1.221	1.213	1.209	1.198	1.193	1.194	1.197	1.192	1.187	1.188	1.189	1.187	1993
1994	1.192	1.185	1.182	1.168	1.164	1.164	1.169	1.164	1.161	1.160	1.159	1.153	1994
1995	1.153	1.146	1.142	1.130	1.126	1.124	1.129	1.123	1.118	1.124	1.124	1.117	1995
1996	1.121	1.116	1.112	1.104	1.101	1.101	1.105	1.100	1.095	1.095	1.094	1.091	1996
1997	1.091	1.086	1.084	1.077	1.073	1.069	1.069	1.062	1.057	1.056	1.055	1.053	1997
1998	1.056	1.051	1.047	1.036	1.030	1.031	1.033	1.029	1.024	1.024	1.024	1.024	1998
1999	1.031	1.029	1.026	1.019	1.017	1.017	1.020	1.018	1.013	1.011	1.010	1.007	1999
2000	1.011	1.005											2000
	J	F	M	A	M	J	J	A	S	O	N	D	

TABLE OF UPLIFTS FOLLOWING *HEIL v RANKIN*

Old	New	Old	New	Old	New	Old	New
0–10,000	No change	45,000	48,750	80,000	93,333	115,000	143,750
11,000	11,026	46,000	49,942	81,000	94,693	116,000	142,276
12,000	12,057	47,000	51,140	82,000	96,057	117,000	146,807
13,000	13,092	48,000	52,342	83,000	97,426	118,000	148,343
14,000	14,133	49,000	53,549	84,000	98,800	119,000	149,883
15,000	15,178	50,000	54,761	85,000	100,179	120,000	151,428
16,000	16,228	51,000	55,978	86,000	101,562	121,000	152,979
17,000	17,283	52,000	57,200	87,000	102,945	122,000	154,533
18,000	18,342	53,000	58,426	88,000	104,343	123,000	156,093
19,000	19,407	54,000	59,657	89,000	105,740	124,000	157,657
20,000	20,476	55,000	60,892	90,000	107,142	125,000	159,226
21,000	21,549	56,000	62,133	91,000	108,549	126,000	160,800
22,000	22,628	57,000	63,378	92,000	109,961	127,000	162,379
23,000	23,711	58,000	64,628	93,000	111,378	128,000	163,962
24,000	24,799	59,000	65,883	94,000	112,800	129,000	165,549
25,000	25,892	60,000	67,142	95,000	114,226	130,000	167,143
26,000	26,990	61,000	68,407	96,000	115,657	131,000	168,740
27,000	28,092	62,000	69,676	97,000	117,092	132,000	170,343
28,000	29,199	63,000	70,949	98,000	118,533	133,000	171,950
29,000	30,311	64,000	72,228	99,000	119,978	134,000	173,562
30,000	31,428	65,000	73,511	100,000	121,428	135,000	175,179
31,000	32,550	66,000	74,799	101,000	122,883	136,000	176,800
32,000	33,676	67,000	76,092	102,000	124,342	137,000	178,426
33,000	34,807	68,000	77,390	103,000	125,807	138,000	180,057

TABLE OF UPLIFTS FOLLOWING *HEIL v RANKIN continued*

Old	New	Old	New	Old	New	Old	New
34,000	35,942	69,000	78,692	104,000	127,276	139,000	181,692
35,000	37,083	70,000	79,999	105,000	128,745	140,000	183,333
36,000	38,228	71,000	81,311	106,000	130,229	141,000	184,978
37,000	39,378	72,000	82,628	107,000	131,712	142,000	186,628
38,000	40,533	73,000	83,950	108,000	133,200	143,000	188,283
39,000	41,692	74,000	85,276	109,000	134,693	144,000	189,942
40,000	42,857	75,000	86,607	110,000	136,190	145,000	191,607
41,000	44,026	76,000	87,942	111,000	137,693	146,000	193,276
42,000	45,199	77,000	89,283	112,000	139,200	147,000	194,949
43,000	46,378	78,000	90,629	113,000	140,712	148,000	196,628
44,000	47,561	79,000	91,979	114,000	142,229	149,000	198,311
						150,000	200,000

UPLIFT FOR INFLATION, AND *SIMMONS v CASTLE,* FROM MARCH 2000 TO TRIAL

The Retail Prices Index on 23 March 2000 was 168.4. 168.4 ÷ 110% = 153.1. In June 2024 the RPI was 387.3.
The uplift for inflation from March 2000 is calculated as follows:

£award × (RPI at date of trial) / 153.1. (Note that using the figure of 153.1 already takes account of the *Simmons v Castle* 10 per cent uplift.)

For an award that was worth £5,000 in March 2000, this would give at June 2024:
£5,000 × 387.3 / 153.1 = £12,649.

TO UPDATE A POST-*HEIL v RANKIN,* BUT PRE-*SIMMONS v CASTLE,* AWARD

Awards since *Heil* but before the *Simmons* uplift should be updated in this way:

£award × 1.1 × (RPI at date of trial)/(RPI at date of award).

For an award that was worth £5,000 in June 2008, this gives at June 2024 (unless s.44(6) applies):
£5,000 × 1.1 × 387.3 / 216.8 = £9,825.

TO UPDATE A POST-*SIMMONS v CASTLE* AWARD

Awards which already include the *Simmons v Castle* uplift (generally awards since 1 March 2013 unless s.44(6) applied to them), should be updated in this way:

£award x (RPI at date of trial)/(RPI at date of award).

For an award that was worth £5,000 in June 2013, this would give at June 2024:
£5,000 × 387.3 / 249.7 = £7,755.

B2: Bereavement damages

1. Damages for bereavement are awarded under s.1A of the Fatal Accidents Act 1976. This is a fixed sum, set by statute as amended (see below).

2. The claim for bereavement damages can only be brought by:

   (i) a bereaved spouse or civil partner; or

   (ii) where the deceased was a minor (under the age of 18) who never married, by:

   (a) either of the parents if the deceased was legitimate; or
   (b) the mother if the deceased was illegitimate.

3. Where there is a claim for damages for bereavement for the benefit of the parents of the deceased, s.1A(4) of the Fatal Accidents Act 1976 provides that:

   "The sum awarded shall be divided equally between them (subject to any deduction falling to be made in respect of costs not recovered from the defendant)."

   Where the parents are divorced or separated and only one parent makes the claim, that parent will hold half of the bereavement damages on trust for the other parent.

4. The Administration of Justice Act 1982 contains a provision (at s.1A(5)) for the Lord Chancellor to vary the statutory sum. Pursuant to the Fatal Accidents Act 1976 (Remedial Order) 2020 which was enacted on 15 September 2020 and came into force on 6 October 2020, bereavement damages may be claimed by a co-habiting partner who was living with the deceased in the same household immediately before the date of death and had been living with the deceased in the same household for at least two years before the date of death. The co-habiting partner must have been living during the whole of that period as the wife, husband or civil partner of the deceased:

– if the death was before 1 January 1983, the award is	**nil**
– if the death was between 1 January 1983 and 31 March 1991, the award is	**£3,500**
– if the death was between 1 April 1991 and 31 March 2002, the award is	**£7,500**
– if the death was between 1 April 2002 and 31 December 2007, the award is	**£10,000**
– if the death was between 1 January 2008 and 31 March 2013, the award is	**£11,800**
– if the death was between 1 April 2013 and 30 April 2020 the award is	**£12,980**
– if the death was on or after 1 May 2020, the award is	**£15,120**

5. The claimant is entitled to interest on bereavement damages from the date of death to the date of trial or settlement of the action—see *Prior v Hastie.*[1] The appropriate rate is the full investment account rate: *Khan v Duncan.*

   The Remedial Order 2020 as above also amends s.1A (4) of the Fatal Accidents Act to provide that, where more than one person is entitled to an award of bereavement damages, the award must be

[1] [1987] C.L.Y. 1219.

shared equally between them. Previously, this provision applied only where both parents were entitled to an award but as a result of the amendments made following *Smith v Lancashire*, it is possible that an award might be payable to more than one person under subs.(2) (a) and (2) (aa).

6. Section 1(1A) of the Law Reform (Miscellaneous Provisions) Act 1934 provides that: "The right of a person to claim under section 1A of the Fatal Accidents Act 1976 (bereavement) shall not survive for the benefit of his estate on his death."

B3: Accommodation claims

1. An injured claimant may require special accommodation because of an acquired disability. Common examples are amputees and wheelchair users.

2. In many cases, the claimant will be advised to buy and adapt a house. Insofar as the costs of adaptation do not increase the value of the property, they can be claimed as "costs thrown away" and recovered in full.

3. The claimant can also recover in full the costs of a move that would not otherwise have occurred (stamp duty, legal costs, solicitors' fees etc.) and any additional annual running costs which arise because of the need to live in bigger or adapted premises.

4. The courts have also considered how to deal with the problem of compensating claimants who need to spend substantial capital sums to house themselves suitably. The difficulty is that there are two conflicting principles: the accommodation requirement versus the probability that the claimant (or the estate of the claimant) will enjoy a "windfall" benefit which is not compensation for the injuries sustained.

5. On Friday 9 October 2020, the Court of Appeal delivered judgment in *Swift v Carpenter.*[2] The Court of Appeal unanimously dismissed the defendant's appeal and gave long-awaited guidance on the assessment of accommodation claims. In summary, per the judgment of Irwin LJ at paragraphs 202 to 211, it was held that:

   (i) The Court was not bound to follow the formula for additional capital costs which was given by the Court of Appeal in *Roberts v Johnstone* [1989] QB 878. That was because *Roberts* dealt not with a point of legal principle but with guidance as to the calculation of loss (*Knauer v Ministry of Justice* [2016] UKSC 9 distinguished).
   (ii) There were two principles of law at issue. First, that the claimant should receive fair and reasonable (but not excessive) compensation. Secondly, that the award of damages should seek to avoid a "windfall" to the claimant or her estate.
   (iii) Insofar as these principles conflicted, the principle of fair compensation should take precedence. To do otherwise and deprive the claimant of damages for fear of a windfall would be " ... *to put the cart before the horse...* " (per Irwin LJ, para.146).
   (iv) Having heard extensive evidence from various experts, the Court concluded that the claimant should be awarded the additional costs of capital purchase less its reversionary value.
   (v) The reversionary value was calculated using a discount rate of 5% applied to the claimant's life expectancy. In this case, this meant that the claimant would receive £900,000 less £98,087 (life expectancy of 45.43 years) giving a total damages award of £801,913.

6. Irwin LJ noted that the current market for reversionary interests is small. At para.201 of his judgment, he observed that:

   "It is entirely possible following this decision... that an expanded market in the sale of such reversionary interests will develop. Claimants who have sustained a significant limitation of their damages by reference to the 'windfall' may seek to recoup that shortfall by selling the reversion. That is perhaps more likely to arise in cases of shorter life expectancy, where the valuation of the reversion will, by definition, be larger and the reduction in damages greater."

[2] [2020] EWCA Civ 1295. A table for the calculation of reversionary interest values was provided by the Court of Appeal as part of their judgment. The table is reproduced at section B4 overleaf.

7. There has been no appeal to the Supreme Court and therefore *Swift v Carpenter* can be treated as settled law which is unlikely to change for some time. Underhill LJ emphasised in para.222 of his judgment that the *Swift* guidance will only be revisited in response to really significant changes of economic circumstances and rarely (if ever) by a first-instance court.

However, it was also recognised that the guidance was intended for claimants with relatively long lives (the court noting from the Government Actuary that the average span of a personal injury claim is around 43 years of future life) and the position may be different for claimants with short life expectancies (see further per Irwin LJ at paras.171 and 210, and per Underhill LJ at para.228).

Simplified Worked Example

The claimant has a 40-year life expectancy. She needs to move to a suitable house which will cost £300,000 more than her present accommodation. The costs of the move are £30,000. She would not have moved but for the injuries which disclose the claim. The adaptation work will cost £350,000 and the value of the property will rise by £50,000 because of the adaptations. The additional annual costs of running the new home (heating, repairs, insurance, council tax etc) will be £5,000 p.a.

The claim is therefore as follows:

Costs "Thrown Away"	
Moving Costs	£30,000
Adaptations which do not add to the capital value	£300,000
Increased annual costs (£5,000 x 42.07[3])	£210,350
TOTAL	£540,350[4]
Capital Claim applying the principles of *Swift v Carpenter*	
Additional capital costs of buying the house	£300,000
Increase in value because of adaptation	£50,000[4]
TOTAL additional capital commitment	£350,000
Less value of the reversionary interest assuming a 40-year life expectancy:–	
£350,000 × 0.14205 (see table in Section B4)	(£49,718)
TOTAL	£300,282

Readers are strongly recommended to obtain expert evidence from an architect to support or refute these claims. As is clear from the calculations above, accommodation will be a substantial element of the schedules advanced by many badly injured claimants.

8. Inflationary Increases

Readers will be aware that there has been significant inflation which has affected building costs in the last three years. In the calendar year 2022 building costs peaked at 26% (see *https://bcis.co.uk*).

[3] Ogden Table 36, 40-year term certain, -0.25% Discount Rate.

[4] Betterment was not dealt with by the Court of Appeal. However, it should probably be included in the calculation as above.

Additionally, utility costs will rise and fall depending on national and international factors such as the Russian invasion of Ukraine and Government subsidies. The latest information is available on this Government website *energyprices.stats@beis.gov.uk.*

House prices may also rise and fall as a result of interest rate changes and other economic fluctuations. *Facts and Figures* includes statistics about property costs and the websites which can be used for recent updates.

It is important to ensure that prior to settlement discussions or trial, expert reports are appropriately updated.

The expert must consider any change in building costs, additional utility bills and house prices since the reports were written and served.

B4: Value of reversionary and life interests

Value of reversionary interest and life interest of 1 at 5% as per judgment in *Swift v Carpenter*

Life expectancy in years	Value of reversion	Value of life interest	Life expectancy in years	Value of reversion	Value of life interest	Life expectancy in years	Value of reversion	Value of life interest
1	0.95238	0.04762	36	0.17266	0.82734	71	0.03130	0.96870
2	0.90703	0.09297	37	0.16444	0.83556	72	0.02981	0.97019
3	0.86384	0.13616	38	0.15661	0.84339	73	0.02839	0.97161
4	0.82270	0.17730	39	0.14915	0.85085	74	0.02704	0.97296
5	0.78353	0.21647	40	0.14205	0.85795	75	0.02575	0.97425
6	0.74622	0.25378	41	0.13528	0.86472	76	0.02453	0.97547
7	0.71068	0.28932	42	0.12884	0.87116	77	0.02336	0.97664
8	0.67684	0.32316	43	0.12270	0.87730	78	0.02225	0.97775
9	0.64461	0.35539	44	0.11686	0.88314	79	0.02119	0.97881
10	0.61391	0.38609	45	0.11130	0.88870	80	0.02018	0.97982
11	0.58468	0.41532	46	0.10600	0.89400	81	0.01922	0.98078
12	0.55684	0.44316	47	0.10095	0.89905	82	0.01830	0.98170
13	0.53032	0.46968	48	0.09614	0.90386	83	0.01743	0.98257
14	0.50507	0.49493	49	0.09156	0.90844	84	0.01660	0.98340
15	0.48102	0.51898	50	0.08720	0.91280	85	0.01581	0.98419
16	0.45811	0.54189	51	0.08305	0.91695	86	0.01506	0.98494
17	0.43630	0.56370	52	0.07910	0.92090	87	0.01434	0.98566
18	0.41552	0.58448	53	0.07533	0.92467	88	0.01366	0.98634
19	0.39573	0.60427	54	0.07174	0.92826	89	0.01301	0.98699
20	0.37689	0.62311	55	0.06833	0.93167	90	0.01239	0.98761
21	0.35894	0.64106	56	0.06507	0.93493	91	0.01180	0.98820
22	0.34185	0.65815	57	0.06197	0.93803	92	0.01124	0.98876
23	0.32557	0.67443	58	0.05902	0.94098	93	0.01070	0.98930
24	0.31007	0.68993	59	0.05621	0.94379	94	0.01019	0.98981
25	0.29530	0.70470	60	0.05354	0.94646	95	0.00971	0.99029
26	0.28124	0.71876	61	0.05099	0.94901	96	0.00924	0.99076
27	0.26785	0.73215	62	0.04856	0.95144	97	0.00880	0.99120
28	0.25509	0.74491	63	0.04625	0.95375	98	0.00838	0.99162
29	0.24295	0.75705	64	0.04404	0.95596	99	0.00798	0.99202
30	0.23138	0.76862	65	0.04195	0.95805	100	0.00760	0.99240
31	0.22036	0.77964	66	0.03995	0.96005	101	0.00724	0.99276
32	0.20987	0.79013	67	0.03805	0.96195	102	0.00690	0.99310
33	0.19987	0.80013	68	0.03623	0.96377	103	0.00657	0.99343
34	0.19035	0.80965	69	0.03451	0.96549	104	0.00626	0.99374
35	0.18129	0.81871	70	0.03287	0.96713	105	0.00596	0.99404

B5: Periodical payments

The circumstances in which a periodical payment should be made

The Damages Act 1996 as amended now empowers the Court to order Periodical Payments for future losses. Provisions dealing with the making of a periodical payments order are contained in CPR rr.41.4 to 41.10 and the attendant Practice Directions. Rule 41.7 provides that:

> "When considering–
>
> (a) its indication as to whether periodical payments or a lump sum is likely to be the more appropriate form for all or part of an award of damages under rule 41.6; or
>
> (b) whether to make an order under section 2(1)(a) of the 1996 Act,
>
> the court shall have regard to all the circumstances of the case and in particular the form of award which best meets the claimant's needs, having regard to the factors set out in Practice Direction 41B."

The factors involved are derived from the Practice Direction supplementing Pt.41 which provides that:

> "The factors which the court shall have regard to under rule 41.7 include–
>
> (1) the scale of the annual payments taking into account any deduction for contributory negligence;
>
> (2) the form of award preferred by the claimant including–
>
> (a) the reasons for the claimant's preference; and
>
> (b) the nature of any financial advice received by the claimant when considering the form of award; and
>
> (3) the form of award preferred by the defendant including the reasons for the defendant's preference."

Practitioners representing claimants may wish to obtain financial advice in order to decide whether or not to ask the Court to make an award for Periodical Payments. Such advice will be particularly useful in difficult cases such as those involving incomplete recovery (contributory negligence or agreed reduction of damages for litigation risk in a clinical negligence claim).

Circumstances in which periodical payments are not available

Section 2(3) of the 1996 Act provides that:

> "(3) A court may not make an order for periodical payments unless satisfied that the continuity of payment under the order is reasonably secure."

Continuity of payment will only be secure in three situations, each dignified by its own sub-clause in subs.2(4):

> "(4) For the purposes of subsection (3) the continuity of payment under an order is reasonably secure if–

(a) it is protected by a guarantee given under section 6 of or the Schedule to this Act,

(b) it is protected by a scheme under section 213 of the Financial Services and Markets Act 2000 (compensation) (whether or not as modified by section 4 of this Act), or

(c) the source of payment is a government or health service body."

The effect of this is that Periodical Payments will not be available unless the defendant is either a government body (such as the NHSLA) or a UK insurer within one of the two statutory schemes. Hence practitioners must ascertain whether or not the defendant is within those schemes well before the matter comes to trial or settlement meeting.

The indexation of periodical payments

Section 2(8) of the Damages Act 1996 (as amended) provides that orders for periodical payments are to be treated as providing for the amount of the payment ordered to vary with the Retail Prices Index ("RPI"). However, s.2(9) of the Damages Act 1996 then stipulates that an order for periodical payments may include provision disapplying s.2(8) or modifying its effect.

In *Thompstone v Tameside and Glossop NHS Trust*,[1] the Court of Appeal held that the appropriate means of indexation of future costs of care and case management would be by reference to ASHE 6115 (see next section of *Facts & Figures*) which was the most reliable way of "tracking" changes to these costs.

Consequently, the ASHE 6115 indexation will apply to periodical payments in respect of future care and case management. The Retail Prices Index will be used for future losses which are goods-based (such as future equipment and assistive technology). In *Sarwar v Ali and Motor Insurers Bureau*,[2] Lloyd Jones J awarded a periodical payment for future losses of earnings and index-linked the loss by reference to the ASHE aggregated earnings data for male full-time employees. Theoretically, it would be possible for a party to contend for another means of indexation, although to our knowledge this has not been successfully attempted in a reported case.

Although it is theoretically possible to compensate future losses of earnings via periodical payments, this creates formidable difficulties of indexation, especially if there are residual earnings. Readers are referred to paras 167 to 177 of the Introduction to the 8th Edition of the Ogden Tables which deals with these points in greater detail.

"Model Order" for periodical payments

The leading case is now *RH v University Hospitals Bristol NHS Foundation Trust*.[3] Swift J held that since there had been a change in statistical methodology used to generate the ASHE 6115 indexation, there was a need to adapt the previous model order made by Sir Christopher Holland on 2 December 2008.[4] The model order approved in *RH* may be used for periodical payments and it deals with the complex issues of indexation and changes to payments caused by that indexation. The NHSLA continues to uprate indexed payments on 15 December each year although other defendants and

[1] [2008] AER 72.
[2] [2007] LS Law Med 375.
[3] [2013] EWHC 229.
[4] [2009] P.I.Q.R. P153.

insurers may have different preferences. Clearly, the starting date must be set at sufficient distance to allow its satisfactory introduction; this is likely to be more protracted if the claimant has a deputy.

Is the claimant still alive?

In *Long v Norwich Union*,[5] Mackay J held that a claimant was not entitled to recover the costs of proving that he was still alive at the date of periodical payment. The court held that this cost would be covered by the award for the costs of deputyship; alternatively, it might be said that the modest costs of this type borne by the claimant would be covered by the interest generated on the advance payments to be made under the order.

[5] [2009] EWHC 715 QB.

B6: Step-by-Step Guide to Finding the Annual Estimates for Hourly Pay for ASHE (6115) SOC 2000

The data collection point for the Annual Survey of Hours and Earnings (ASHE) is in April each year. The data are collected over the summer and the first release of estimates takes place in October/November/December of that year. These are provisional estimates which are revised and published as revised (final) estimates the following October/November/December. The following estimates reported in the table below were published for ASHE SOC 2000 (6115) on 12 December 2013, 19 November 2014, 18 November 2015, 26 October 2016, 26 October 2017, 25 October 2018, 29 October 2019, 3 November 2020, 26 October 2021, 26 October 2022 and 1 November 2023. In this edition, estimates for 2023 are provisional and will be replaced by revised estimates in October/November/December 2024.

ASHE estimates are available online. They can be found on the website of the Office for National Statistics (ONS). Step-by-step instructions to locate estimates for ASHE SOC 2000 6115 are provided here. You need not follow all these instructions each time you consult the tables as you can either download the tables as an Excel file or you can save the web link. ONS has introduced an alternative method to access ASHE but has retained the method described here. Ignore the 15 January 2024 release and the new method.

Reclassification of occupational categories occurs every ten years. There are two reclassifications in the table: between 2010 and 2011 and between 2020 and 2021. The first is a change from SOC 2000 to SOC 2010 and the second a change from SOC 2010 to 2020.

The classification for carers changed in SOC 2010 to include two separate categories, ASHE 6145 care workers and home carers and ASHE 6146 senior care workers. The codes changed in SOC 2020 to 6135 and 6136 but the definitions remain unchanged.

For the purposes of the indexation of future care, separate classifications for carers should be ignored and the classification based on SOC 2000 6115 used instead. The occupational earnings tables for SOC 2000 6115 can be found at Table 26. The title for this table is Care Workers (SOC20 6135 & 6136 (Equiv. to SOC10 6145 & 6146, SOC 2000 6115)).

1. Find the home page of the Office for National Statistics (ONS) at: *www.ONS.gov.uk*.

2. Type in ASHE 2023 Table 26 in the search box at the top of this page and click Search.

3. Refine the search using the menu on the left-hand side by checking the boxes for Data and then Datasets.

4. The title for this table is Earnings and hours worked, care workers: ASHE Table 26. Select the data set released on 1 November 2023 and not the data set released on 15 January 2024.

5. Clicking on the table title opens a list of zip files for care workers from 2023–2011.

6. Opening each zip file will produce a contents list of Excel files each of which contain a different set of earnings estimates for carers.

7. Hourly pay for carers is in Care Workers 2020 SOC 6135 & 6136 (equiv. to SOC 2010 6145 & 6146 and equiv. to SOC 2000 6115) Table 26.5a Hourly Pay-Gross. A double click on the table title will take you to a worksheet in an Excel file. If you are sure that you have located the file that you want, save it using file save in Excel.

8. Once in the Excel file, check the bottom tab. "All" refers to all employees (male and female, part and full-time).

9. Read across the centile estimates. Shading indicates the reliability of the estimate. Where the estimate of the error is less than 5 per cent (indicates reliability), there is no shading. ASHE 6115 estimates are normally reliable due to a large sample size. The key to the shading can be found at the bottom and at the right-hand side of the table.

10. If you have not already saved this file at step 7 above, this table can be saved now, either in part or in full. If the file is saved before the revised release in October/November/December 2024, make a note that the 2023 estimates are provisional.

ASHE SOC 2000 6115 (SOC 2020 6135 & 6136) 2011–2023
Centile estimates for hourly earnings (£) for UK employees and annual growth rate (%)

From 2011 onwards ASHE 6115 was reclassified and split into two categories, namely ASHE 6145 and 6146 for care workers and home carers, and senior care workers, respectively. These codes changed under SOC 2020 to 6135 and 6136. The following table summarises earnings estimates at the percentiles of ASHE (6115) from 2011 to 2023 and shows the annual percentage increase (except in the years of reclassification).

Year	10th	20th	25th	30th	40th	50th	60th	70th	75th	80th	90th
2011	£6.05	£6.44	£6.65	£6.87	£7.28	£7.83	£8.45	£9.17	£9.67	£10.22	£11.92
2012	£6.21	£6.57	£6.80	£7.00	£7.44	£7.92	£8.51	£9.21	£9.69	£10.25	£11.97
Increase 2011–2012	2.64%	2.02%	2.26%	1.89%	2.20%	1.15%	0.71%	0.44%	0.21%	0.29%	0.42%
2013	£6.30	£6.61	£6.80	£7.00	£7.40	£7.91	£8.50	£9.22	£9.73	£10.29	£12.02
Increase 2012–2013	1.45%	0.61%	0.00%	0.00%	0.54%	0.13%	0.12%	0.11%	0.41%	0.39%	0.42%
2014	£6.41	£6.74	£6.94	£7.12	£7.53	£8.00	£8.55	£9.23	£9.72	£10.21	£11.95
Increase 2013–2014	1.75%	1.97%	2.06%	1.71%	1.76%	1.14%	0.59%	0.11%	0.10%	0.78%	0.58%
2015	£6.63	£6.98	£7.10	£7.29	£7.72	£8.18	£8.73	£9.44	£9.88	£10.38	£12.21
Increase 2014–2015	3.43%	3.56%	2.31%	2.39%	2.52%	2.25%	2.11%	2.28%	3.04%	1.67%	2.18%
2016	£7.20	£7.36	£7.50	£7.70	£8.08	£8.50	£9.02	£9.76	£10.18	£10.75	£12.50
Increase 2015–2016	8.60%	5.44%	5.63%	5.62%	4.66%	3.91%	3.32%	3.39%	3.04%	3.56%	2.38%
2017	£7.50	£7.75	£7.92	£8.06	£8.42	£8.84	£9.36	£10.04	£10.50	£11.02	£12.87
Increase 2016–2017	4.17%	5.30%	5.60%	4.68%	4.21%	4.00%	3.77%	2.87%	3.14%	2.51%	2.96%
2018	£7.83	£8.02	£8.20	£8.37	£8.72	£9.15	£9.70	£10.37	£10.81	£11.46	£13.35
Increase 2017–2018	4.40%	3.48%	3.54%	3.85%	3.56%	3.51%	3.63%	3.29%	2.95%	3.99%	3.73%
2019	£8.21	£8.45	£8.59	£8.75	£9.07	£9.50	£10.03	£10.81	£11.25	£11.87	£13.83
Increase 2018–2019	4.85%	5.36%	4.76%	4.54%	4.01%	3.83%	3.40%	4.24%	4.07%	3.58%	3.60%
2020	£8.72	£8.98	£9.08	£9.25	£9.60	£10.02	£10.66	£11.34	£11.87	£12.50	£14.26
Increase 2019–2020	6.21%	6.27%	5.70%	5.71%	5.84%	5.47%	6.28%	4.90%	5.51%	5.31%	3.11%
2021	£8.97	£9.21	£9.34	£9.50	£9.85	£10.24	£10.81	£11.53	£12.03	£12.66	£14.56
2022	£9.60	£9.98	£10.05	£10.22	£10.55	£11.01	£11.58	£12.39	£12.87	£13.49	£15.57
Increase 2021–2022	7.02%	8.36%	7.60%	7.58%	7.11%	7.52%	7.12%	7.46%	6.98%	6.56%	6.94%
2023 (first release)	10.47	10.83	10.94	11.05	11.43	11.89	12.45	13.17	13.71	14.43	16.59
Increase 2022–2023	9.06%	8.52%	8.86%	8.12%	8.34%	7.99%	7.51%	6.30%	6.53%	6.97%	6.55%

Source: ONS, ASHE (https://www.ons.gov.uk) ASHE Table 26.5a SOC2020 6135 & 6136 (equivalent to SOC10 6145 & 6146, SOC 2000 6115).

Notes: Estimates for 2023 are first release and will be revised in October/November 2024.

For reasons of consistency and predictability, several larger defendants and insurers, such as the NHSLA, prefer to uprate annual periodical payments for care and case management by reference to the same percentile, usually the 80th percentile, across all their cases even if another percentile might be more appropriate on the facts of a particular case.

Group C

Interest Rates

C

C1: Interest base rates

Introductory note

1. The data for this table are obtained from retail banks Barclays, Lloyds TSB, HSBC and National Westminster. Since 3 August 2006, these retail banks' base rates have been identical to the Bank of England's Official Bank Rate.

Date	New rate (%)
1989	
25 May	13.75
31 August	13.84
4 September	13.88
8 September	13.75
6 October	14.88
8 October	13.88
1990	
8 October	13.88
1991	
13 February	13.38
27 February	12.88
22 March	12.38
12 April	11.88
24 May	11.38
12 July	10.88
4 September	10.38
1992	
5 May	9.88
22 September	8.88
17 September	10.00
22 September	9.00
16 October	8.00
13 November	7.00
1993	
26 January	6.00
23 November	5.50
1994	
8 February	5.25
12 September	5.75
7 December	6.25
1995	
2 February	6.75
13 December	6.50
1996	
18 January	6.25
8 March	6.00
6 June	5.75
30 October	6.00
1997	
7 May	6.25
9 June	6.50
11 July	6.75
8 August	7.00
7 November	7.25
1998	
5 June	7.50
9 October	7.25
6 November	6.75
11 December	6.25
1999	
8 January	6.00
5 February	5.50
8 April	5.25
10 June	5.00
8 September	5.25
4 November	5.50
2000	
13 January	5.75
10 February	6.00
2001	
8 February	5.75
5 April	5.50
10 May	5.25
2 August	5.00
18 September	4.75
4 October	4.50
8 November	4.00
2003	
7 February	3.75
10 July	3.50
6 November	3.75
2004	
5 February	4.00
6 May	4.25
10 June	4.50
5 August	4.75
2005	
4 August	4.50
2006	
3 August	4.75
9 November	5.00
2007	
11 January	5.25
10 May	5.50
5 July	5.75
6 December	5.50
2008	
7 February	5.25
10 April	5.00
8 October	4.50
6 November	3.00
4 December	2.00
2009	
8 January	1.50
5 February	1.00
5 March	0.50
2016	
4 August	0.25
2017	
2 November	0.50
2018	
2 August	0.75
2020	
11 March	0.25
19 March	0.10
2021	
6 May	0.10
15 December	0.25
2022	
3 February	0.50
17 March	0.75
5 May	1.00
16 June	1.25
4 August	1.75
22 September	2.25
3 November	3.00
15 December	3.50
2023	
2 February	4.00
23 March	4.25
11 May	4.50
22 June	5.00
3 August	5.25
2024	
1 August	5.00

C2: Real and nominal interest rates and price inflation

Introductory notes

1. Price inflation is calculated as the rate of change of the Retail Prices Index.
2. The nominal interest rate is based on the rate on 20-year British Government Securities.
3. No account has been taken of tax in these figures.

	Price Inflation %	**Nominal Interest Rate** %	**Real Interest Rate** %
1980	18.03	13.78	(4.25)
1981	11.88	14.74	2.86
1982	8.70	12.88	4.18
1983	4.44	10.80	6.36
1984	5.01	10.69	5.68
1985	6.04	10.62	4.58
1986	3.40	9.87	6.47
1987	4.16	9.47	5.31
1988	4.92	9.36	4.44
1989	7.79	9.58	1.79
1990	9.44	11.08	1.64
1991	5.91	9.92	4.01
1992	3.73	9.12	5.39
1993	1.57	7.87	6.30
1994	2.48	8.05	5.57
1995	3.41	8.26	4.85
1996	2.44	8.10	5.66
1997	3.12	7.09	3.97
1998	3.42	5.45	2.03
1999	1.56	4.70	3.14
2000	2.93	4.70	1.77
2001	1.84	4.78	2.94
2002	1.62	4.83	3.21
2003	2.91	4.64	1.73
2004	2.96	4.78	1.82
2005	2.84	4.39	1.55
2006	3.20	4.29	1.09
2007	4.26	4.73	0.47
2008	4.00	4.68	0.68
2009	(0.53)	4.25	4.78
2010	4.61	4.24	(0.37)
2011	5.21	3.83	(1.38)
2012	3.22	2.86	(0.36)
2013	3.05	3.19	0.14
2014	2.38	3.10	0.72
2015	0.98	2.41	1.43
2016	1.74	1.91	0.17
2017	3.58	1.82	(1.76)
2018	3.35	1.84	(1.51)
2019	2.55	1.31	(1.24)
2020	1.50	0.74	(0.76)
2021	4.04	1.14	(2.90)
2022	11.53	2.63	(8.90)
2023	9.81	4.20	(5.61)
Averages:			
1980–89	7.44	11.18	3.74
1990–99	3.71	7.96	4.25
2000–09	2.60	4.61	2.01
2010–19	3.07	2.65	(0.42)
2020–23	6.72	2.18	(4.54)

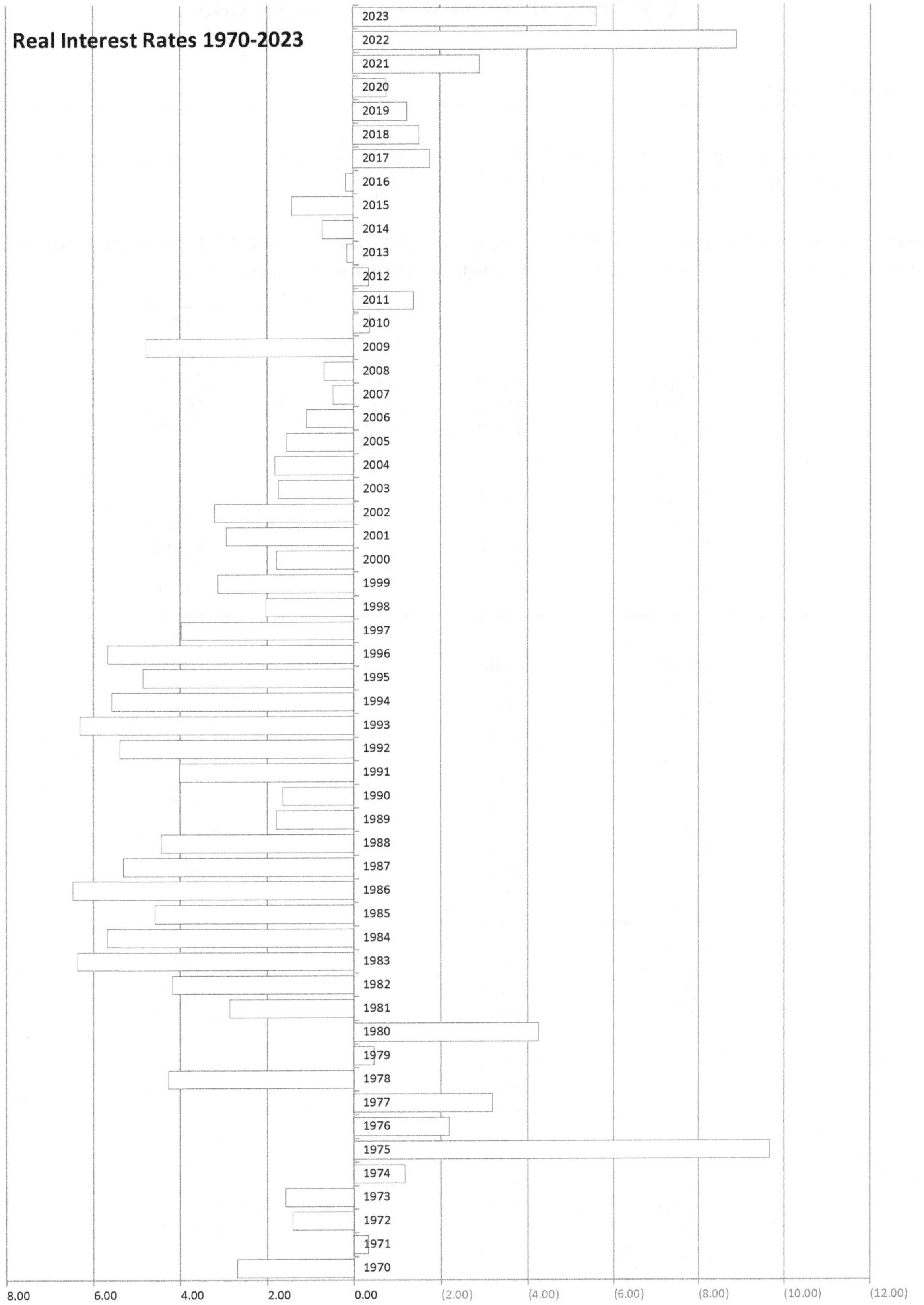
Real Interest Rates 1970-2023
2023
2022
2021
2020
2019
2018
2017
2016
2015
2014
2013
2012
2011
2010
2009
2008
2007
2006
2005
2004
2003
2002
2001
2000
1999
1998
1997
1996
1995
1994
1993
1992
1991
1990
1989
1988
1987
1986
1985
1984
1983
1982
1981
1980
1979
1978
1977
1976
1975
1974
1973
1972
1971
1970
8.00
6.00
4.00
2.00
0.00
(2.00)
(4.00)
(6.00)
(8.00)
(10.00)
(12.00)

C3: Special investment account rates

Introductory notes

This is a composite table including both the Short-term Investment Account rate and the succeeding High Court Special Investment Account rate.

The manner of crediting interest is set out in Court Fund Rules 1987 r.27. Interest accruing to a special investment account is credited without the deduction of income tax.

From:		%
1 October	1965	5.000%
1 September	1966	5.500%
1 March	1968	6.000%
1 March	1969	6.500%
1 March	1970	7.000%
1 March	1971	7.500%
1 March	1973	8.000%
1 March	1974	9.000%
1 February	1977	10.000%
1 March	1979	12.500%
1 January	1980	15.000%
1 January	1981	12.500%
1 December	1981	15.000%
1 March	1982	14.000%
1 July	1982	13.000%
1 April	1983	12.500%
1 April	1984	12.000%
1 August	1986	11.500%
1 January	1987	12.250%
1 April	1987	11.750%
1 November	1987	11.250%
1 December	1987	11.000%
1 May	1988	9.500%
1 August	1988	11.000%
1 November	1988	12.250%
1 January	1989	13.000%
1 November	1989	14.250%
1 April	1991	12.000%
1 October	1991	10.250%
1 February	1993	8.000%
1 August	1999	7.000%
1 February	2002	6.000%
1 February	2009	3.000%
1 June	2009	1.500%
1 July	2009	0.500%
1 June	2020	0.100%
29 April	2022	0.645%
5 July	2022	1.250%
2 September	2022	1.750%
25 October	2022	2.250%
18 November	2022	3.000%
16 January	2023	3.500%
13 February	2023	4.000%
21 April	2023	4.250%
13 June	2023	4.500%
23 August	2023	6.000%
12 June	2024	5.250%

C4: Special and general damages interest

Introductory notes

Special damages

The appropriate rate of interest for special damages is the rate, over the period for which the interest is awarded, which is payable on the court special account. This rate was reduced to 5.25% on 12 June 2024. Interest since June 1987 has been paid daily on a 1/365th basis, even in a leap year such as 2020.

In cases of continuing special damages, half the appropriate rate from the date of injury to the date of trial is awarded. In cases where the special damages have ceased and are thus limited to a finite period, there are conflicting Court of Appeal decisions as to whether the award should be half the appropriate rate from injury to trial (*Dexter v Courtaulds*[1]) or the full special account rate from a date within the period to which the special damages are limited (*Prokop v DHSS*[2]).

The relevant rates since 1965 are set out in Table C3.

The table on the next page records the total of these rates from January 1981. In the left-hand column is shown the month from the first day of which interest is assumed to run. The right-hand column shows the percentage interest accumulated from the first day of each month to 31 July 2024 (including both of those days).

Continued use may be made of this table by adding to the figures in it 1/365th of the special account rate for each day from 1 August 2024 onwards, using Table C6, which records the number of days between two dates in a two-year period.

Suppose that interest runs from 1 January 2011 to 15 October 2024. The total to 31 July 2024 is 14.16% (see Table C4). The period from 1 August 2024 to 15 October 2024 is a period of 76 days. If the rate remains at 5.25% pa, the appropriate addition will be 5.25% × 107 days ÷ 365 days, which is 1.09%. Thus, the grand total from 1 January 2011 to 15 October 2024 will be 14.16% + 1.09% = 15.25%.

General damages

In personal injury cases, the normal rate of interest on general damages for pain, suffering and loss of amenity was by convention two per cent per annum. In *Lawrence v Chief Constable of Staffordshire*[3] the Court of Appeal held that in spite of *Wells v Wells*,[4] the rate should remain at two per cent. Interest runs from the date of service of proceedings.

Scotland and Northern Ireland

The notes above and the tables on the next page apply in England and Wales. For interest on damages in Scotland or Northern Ireland please refer to tables **C9** and **C10**.

[1] [1984] 1 W.L.R. 372; [1984] 1 All E.R. 70.
[2] [1985] C.L.Y. 1037.
[3] CA, transcript 29 June 2000.
[4] [1999] 1 A.C. 345; [1998] 3 W.L.R. 329.

Table of cumulative interest at the special account rate from the first day of each month to 31 July 2024

	1991	1992	1993	1994	1995	1996	1997	1998	1999	2000
Jan	150.85	138.74	128.46	120.27	112.27	104.27	96.25	88.25	80.25	72.66
Feb	149.64	137.87	127.59	119.59	111.59	103.59	95.57	87.57	79.57	72.07
Mar	148.55	137.05	126.97	118.97	110.97	102.95	94.95	86.95	78.95	71.51
Apr	147.34	136.18	126.29	118.29	110.29	102.27	94.27	86.27	78.27	70.92
May	146.35	135.34	125.64	117.64	109.64	101.62	93.62	85.62	77.62	70.34
Jun	145.33	134.47	124.96	116.96	108.96	100.94	92.94	84.94	76.94	69.75
Jul	144.34	133.63	124.30	116.30	108.30	100.28	92.28	84.28	76.28	69.17
Aug	143.33	132.76	123.62	115.62	107.62	99.60	91.60	83.60	75.60	68.58
Sep	142.31	131.88	122.94	114.94	106.94	98.92	90.92	82.92	75.00	67.99
Oct	141.32	131.04	122.28	114.28	106.28	98.26	90.26	82.26	74.43	67.41
Nov	140.45	130.17	121.60	113.60	105.60	97.58	89.58	81.58	73.83	66.82
Dec	139.61	129.33	120.95	112.95	104.95	96.93	88.93	80.93	73.26	66.24

	2001	2002	2003	2004	2005	2006	2007	2008	2009	2010
Jan	65.65	58.65	52.56	46.56	40.54	34.54	28.54	22.54	16.53	14.66
Feb	65.05	58.05	52.05	46.05	40.03	34.03	28.03	22.03	16.02	14.61
Mar	64.51	57.59	51.59	45.57	39.57	33.57	27.57	21.56	15.79	14.58
Apr	63.92	57.08	51.08	45.06	39.06	33.06	27.06	21.05	15.53	14.53
May	63.34	56.59	50.59	44.57	38.57	32.57	26.57	20.56	15.29	14.49
Jun	62.75	56.08	50.08	44.06	38.06	32.06	26.06	20.05	15.03	14.45
Jul	62.17	55.59	49.59	43.57	37.57	31.57	25.57	19.55	14.91	14.41
Aug	61.58	55.08	49.08	43.06	37.06	31.06	25.06	19.04	14.87	14.37
Sep	60.99	54.57	48.57	42.55	36.55	30.55	24.55	18.53	14.82	14.32
Oct	60.41	54.07	48.07	42.06	36.06	30.06	24.06	18.04	14.78	14.28
Nov	59.82	53.56	47.56	41.55	35.55	29.55	23.55	17.53	14.74	14.24
Dec	59.24	53.07	47.07	41.05	35.05	29.05	23.05	17.04	14.70	14.20

	2011	2012	2013	2014	2015	2016	2017	2018	2019	2020
Jan	14.16	13.66	13.16	12.66	12.16	11.66	11.15	10.65	10.15	9.65
Feb	14.11	13.61	13.11	12.61	12.11	11.61	11.11	10.61	10.11	9.61
Mar	14.08	13.57	13.07	12.57	12.07	11.57	11.07	10.57	10.07	9.57
Apr	14.03	13.53	13.03	12.53	12.03	11.53	11.03	10.53	10.03	9.53
May	13.99	13.49	12.99	12.49	11.99	11.49	10.99	10.49	9.99	9.49
Jun	13.95	13.45	12.95	12.45	11.95	11.45	10.95	10.45	9.95	9.45
Jul	13.91	13.41	12.91	12.41	11.91	11.41	10.91	10.41	9.91	9.44
Aug	13.87	13.36	12.86	12.36	11.86	11.36	10.86	10.36	9.86	9.43
Sep	13.82	13.32	12.82	12.32	11.82	11.32	10.82	10.32	9.82	9.42
Oct	13.78	13.28	12.78	12.28	11.78	11.28	10.78	10.28	9.78	9.41
Nov	13.74	13.24	12.74	12.24	11.74	11.24	10.74	10.24	9.74	9.40
Dec	13.70	13.20	12.70	12.20	11.70	11.20	10.70	10.20	9.70	9.40

	2021	2022	2023	2024
Jan	9.39	9.29	8.17	3.40
Feb	9.38	9.28	7.89	2.89
Mar	9.37	9.27	7.60	2.41
Apr	9.36	9.26	7.26	1.90
May	9.35	9.25	6.93	1.41
Jun	9.35	9.20	6.57	0.90
Jul	9.34	9.14	6.21	0.45
Aug	9.33	9.04	5.82	
Sep	9.32	8.94	5.40	
Oct	9.31	8.80	4.91	
Nov	9.30	8.64	4.40	
Dec	9.30	8.43	3.91	

If the rate remains at 5.25%, interest to the last day of successive later months can be found to a date after 31 July 2024 by adding the figure from the following table:

	2024	**2025**
Jan		2.65
Feb		3.05
Mar		3.50
Apr		3.93
May		4.37
Jun		4.80
Jul		5.25
Aug	0.45	
Sep	0.88	
Oct	1.32	
Nov	1.75	
Dec	2.20	

Section C5: Base rate + 10 per cent

Introductory notes

1. Under the Civil Procedure Rules 1998 r.36.17, where the judgment is more advantageous to the claimant than the proposals in a claimant's Part 36 offer, the court may order interest on the sums awarded and on the costs, for some or all of the period starting with the latest date on which the defendant could have accepted the Part 36 offer without needing the permission of the court, at a rate not exceeding 10 per cent above base rate. Where the rule applies, the court will make those orders unless it considers it unjust to do so.

2. Since January 2009 base rates plus 10 per cent have been as follows. For base rates from 1997–2008 see the 2016/17 edition of *Facts and Figures.*

		Rate + 10%			Rate + 10%			Rate + 10%
2009	8 January	11.50%	**2022**	3 February	10.50%	**2023**	2 February	14.00%
	5 February	11.00%		17 March	10.75%		23 March	14.25%
	5 March	10.50%		5 May	11.00%		11 May	14.50%
2016	4 August	10.25%		16 June	11.25%		22 June	15.00%
2017	2 November	10.50%		4 August	11.75%		3 August	15.25%
2018	2 August	10.75%		22 September	12.25%	**2024**	1 August	15.00%
2020	11 March	10.25%		3 November	13.00%			
	19 March	10.10%		15 December	13.50%			
2021	16 December	10.25%						

The following table shows cumulative interest at 10 per cent above base rate from the first day of each month until 30 June 2024 (including both dates). Interest for parts of a month can be found by following the method in the notes to Table C4.

	2014	2015	2016	2017	2018	2019	2020	2021	2022	2023	2024
January	117.16	106.66	96.16	85.74	75.45	64.84	54.09	43.84	33.73	22.26	7.60
February	116.27	105.77	95.27	84.87	74.55	63.93	53.18	42.98	32.86	21.12	6.31
March	115.47	104.97	94.44	84.08	73.75	63.10	52.33	42.20	32.06	20.05	5.10
April	114.57	104.07	93.55	83.21	72.86	62.19	51.45	41.35	31.15	18.85	3.80
May	113.71	103.21	92.68	82.37	71.99	61.31	50.62	40.52	30.27	17.68	2.55
June	112.82	102.32	91.79	81.50	71.10	60.40	49.76	39.66	29.34	16.45	1.25
July	111.96	101.46	90.93	80.65	70.24	59.51	48.93	38.83	28.42	15.25	
August	111.06	100.56	90.04	79.78	69.35	58.60	48.07	37.97	27.47	14.00	
September	110.17	99.67	89.16	78.91	68.44	57.69	47.21	37.11	26.47	12.70	
October	109.31	98.81	88.32	78.07	67.55	56.80	46.38	36.28	25.50	11.45	
November	108.42	97.92	87.45	77.20	66.64	55.89	45.52	35.42	24.46	10.15	
December	107.56	97.06	86.61	76.34	65.76	55.01	44.69	34.59	23.39	8.90	

Interest to the last day of successive later months can be found to a date after 30 June 2024 by adding the figure from the following table:

July 2024	1.30	November 2024	6.31	March 2025	11.28
August 2024	2.57	December 2024	7.58	April 2025	12.51
September 2024	3.80	January 2025	8.86	May 2025	13.79
October 2024	5.08	February 2025	10.01	June 2025	15.02

C6: Number of days between two dates

Introductory notes

Deduct the number of the opening date from the number of the closing date (where necessary adding a day for 29 February).
Example: 14 October–19 March (where the February is not a leap year) is 443 – 287 = 156 days.
Note that the calculation produces the *interval* between the two dates; so that it includes the first date and excludes the last date. For example, 1 January to 31 January is calculated as 31 – 1 = 30 days, not 31. If the last date is to be included then add "1" to the number of days.

Day of month	Day numbers																								Day of month
	Jan	Feb	Mar	Apr	May	Jun	Jul	Aug	Sep	Oct	Nov	Dec	Jan	Feb	Mar	Apr	May	Jun	Jul	Aug	Sep	Oct	Nov	Dec	
1	1	32	60	91	121	152	182	213	244	274	305	335	366	397	425	456	486	517	547	578	609	639	670	700	**1**
2	2	33	61	92	122	153	183	214	245	275	306	336	367	398	426	457	487	518	548	579	610	640	671	701	**2**
3	3	34	62	93	123	154	184	215	246	276	307	337	368	399	427	458	488	519	549	580	611	641	672	702	**3**
4	4	35	63	94	124	155	185	216	247	277	308	338	369	400	428	459	489	520	550	581	612	642	673	703	**4**
5	5	36	64	95	125	156	186	217	248	278	309	339	370	401	429	460	490	521	551	582	613	643	674	704	**5**
6	6	37	65	96	126	157	187	218	249	279	310	340	371	402	430	461	491	522	552	583	614	644	675	705	**6**
7	7	38	66	97	127	158	188	219	250	280	311	341	372	403	431	462	492	523	553	584	615	645	676	706	**7**
8	8	39	67	98	128	159	189	220	251	281	312	342	373	404	432	463	493	524	554	585	616	646	677	707	**8**
9	9	40	68	99	129	160	190	221	252	282	313	343	374	405	433	464	494	525	555	586	617	647	678	708	**9**
10	10	41	69	100	130	161	191	222	253	283	314	344	375	406	434	465	495	526	556	587	618	648	679	709	**10**
11	11	42	70	101	131	162	192	223	254	284	315	345	376	407	435	466	496	527	557	588	619	649	680	710	**11**
12	12	43	71	102	132	163	193	224	255	285	316	346	377	408	436	467	497	528	558	589	620	650	681	711	**12**
13	13	44	72	103	133	164	194	225	256	286	317	347	378	409	437	468	498	529	559	590	621	651	682	712	**13**
14	14	45	73	104	134	165	195	226	257	287	318	348	379	410	438	469	499	530	560	591	622	652	683	713	**14**
15	15	46	74	105	135	166	196	227	258	288	319	349	380	411	439	470	500	531	561	592	623	653	684	714	**15**
16	16	47	75	106	136	167	197	228	259	289	320	350	381	412	440	471	501	532	562	593	624	654	685	715	**16**
17	17	48	76	107	137	168	198	229	260	290	321	351	382	413	441	472	502	533	563	594	625	655	686	716	**17**
18	18	49	77	108	138	169	199	230	261	291	322	352	383	414	442	473	503	534	564	595	626	656	687	717	**18**
19	19	50	78	109	139	170	200	231	262	292	323	353	384	415	443	474	504	535	565	596	627	657	688	718	**19**
20	20	51	79	110	140	171	201	232	263	293	324	354	385	416	444	475	505	536	566	597	628	658	689	719	**20**
21	21	52	80	111	141	172	202	233	264	294	325	355	386	417	445	476	506	537	567	598	629	659	690	720	**21**
22	22	53	81	112	142	173	203	234	265	295	326	356	387	418	446	477	507	538	568	599	630	660	691	721	**22**
23	23	54	82	113	143	174	204	235	266	296	327	357	388	419	447	478	508	539	569	600	631	661	692	722	**23**
24	24	55	83	114	144	175	205	236	267	297	328	358	389	420	448	479	509	540	570	601	632	662	693	723	**24**
25	25	56	84	115	145	176	206	237	268	298	329	359	390	421	449	480	510	541	571	602	633	663	694	724	**25**
26	26	57	85	116	146	177	207	238	269	299	330	360	391	422	450	481	511	542	572	603	634	664	695	725	**26**
27	27	58	86	117	147	178	208	239	270	300	331	361	392	423	451	482	512	543	573	604	635	665	696	726	**27**
28	28	59	87	118	148	179	209	240	271	301	332	362	393	424	452	483	513	544	574	605	636	666	697	727	**28**
29	29		88	119	149	180	210	241	272	302	333	363	394		453	484	514	545	575	606	637	667	698	728	**29**
30	30		89	120	150	181	211	242	273	303	334	364	395		454	485	515	546	576	607	638	668	699	729	**30**
31	31		90		151		212	243		304		365	396		455		516		577	608		669		730	**31**

C7: Decimal years

An alternative way of calculating interest is with a table expressing intervals as decimals of a year. It is in some respects simpler than using Table C6 (Number of Days) as it avoids the need to divide by 365.

The first table below gives days, weeks and months as decimals of a year.

The second table gives the period between corresponding days of two months, with the earlier month down the left-hand side and the later month across the top. Thus, from the two figures in bold one sees that from 1 April–1 June is 0.167 years; from 1 June to the next 1 April is 0.833 years. The calculation again produces the interval between the dates: 1 January–1 February is 31 days (not 32).

Days, weeks and months expressed as decimals of a year

Days

1	0.003	2	0.005	3	0.008	4	0.011	5	0.014	6	0.016	7	0.019	8	0.022	9	0.025	10	0.027
11	0.030	12	0.033	13	0.036	14	0.038	15	0.041	16	0.044	17	0.047	18	0.049	19	0.052	20	0.055
21	0.058	22	0.060	23	0.063	24	0.066	25	0.068	26	0.071	27	0.074	28	0.077	29	0.079	30	0.082

Weeks

1	0.019	2	0.038	3	0.058	4	0.077	5	0.096	6	0.115	7	0.134	8	0.153	9	0.173	10	0.192

Months

28 days	0.077	29 days	0.079	30 days	0.082	31 days	.085

Intervals between corresponding days of months as decimals of a year

Earlier month	Later month: Jan	Feb	Mar	Apr	May	Jun
Jan	1.000	0.085	0.162	0.247	0.329	0.414
Feb	0.915	1.000	0.077	0.162	0.244	0.329
Mar	0.838	0.923	1.000	0.085	0.167	0.252
Apr	0.753	0.838	0.915	1.000	0.082	0.167
May	0.671	0.756	0.833	0.918	1.000	0.085
Jun	0.586	0.671	0.748	0.833	0.915	1.000
Jul	0.504	0.589	0.666	0.751	0.833	0.918
Aug	0.419	0.504	0.581	0.666	0.748	0.833
Sept	0.334	0.419	0.496	0.581	0.663	0.748
Oct	0.252	0.337	0.414	0.499	0.581	0.666
Nov	0.167	0.252	0.329	0.414	0.496	0.581
Dec	0.085	0.170	0.247	0.332	0.414	0.499

Earlier month	Jul	Aug	Sept	Oct	Nov	Dec
Jan	0.496	0.581	0.666	0.748	0.833	0.915
Feb	0.411	0.496	0.581	0.663	0.748	0.830
Mar	0.334	0.419	0.504	0.586	0.671	0.753
Apr	0.249	0.334	0.419	0.501	0.586	0.668
May	0.167	0.252	0.337	0.419	0.504	0.586
Jun	0.082	0.167	0.252	0.334	0.419	0.501
Jul	1.000	0.085	0.170	0.252	0.337	0.419
Aug	0.915	1.000	0.085	0.167	0.252	0.334
Sept	0.830	0.915	1.000	0.082	0.167	0.249
Oct	0.748	0.833	0.918	1.000	0.085	0.167
Nov	0.663	0.748	0.833	0.915	1.000	0.082
Dec	0.581	0.666	0.751	0.833	0.918	1.000

Example: to calculate interest at eight per cent from 3 June 2024 to 15 April 2025

3 June to 15 June	=	12 days	=	0.033 years		
15 June to 15 April the following year			=	0.833		
Total 3.6.24 to 15.4.25			=	0.866 years		
Interest at 8% from 3.6.24 to 15.4.25			=	0.866 × 8	=	6.928%

C8: Judgment debt interest rates (England and Wales)

Introductory notes

Under the Administration of Justice Act 1970 s.44, interest rates under the Judgments Act 1838 s.17 on High Court judgments are determined by Judgment Debts (Rate of Interest) Orders. Under the County Courts (Interest on Judgment Debts) Order 1991, the general rule is that every judgment debt of not less than £5,000 carries interest from the date on which it was given, at the same rate as on High Court judgments.

From	At%	From	At%	From	At%	From	At%
20 April 1971	7.5	3 December 1979	12.5	8 June 1982	14	16 April 1985	15
1 March 1977	10	9 June 1980	15	10 November 1982	12	1 April 1993 to date	8

C9: Judicial rates of interest (Scotland)

From	At%	From	At%	From	At%
4 May 1965	5	7 January 1975	11	16 August 1985	15
6 January 1970	7	5 April 1983	12	1 April 1993 to date	8

The courts have, and exercise, a discretion to adopt a different rate in any particular case—*Farstad Supply AS v Enviroco Ltd.*[1] The Scottish Law Commission—Report on Interest on Debt and Damages (Scot Law Com No 203)—was of the view that there was uncertainty as to when interest started to run on particular heads of damage, and that the current 8% judicial rate of interest was uncommercial and not truly compensatory. It recommended reform but its proposals were not implemented.

The judge may (as in England and Wales) award interest at half the judicial rate on accumulating past losses: see the discussion in para.52 of *Sheridan v News Group Ltd.*[2]

C10: Interest on damages and judgments (Northern Ireland)

From	At%
19 April 1993	8

Under the Judgments Enforcement (NI) Order 1981 art.127, interest on judgments is at a rate prescribed by Rules of Court. The relevant rule is Rules of the Court of Judicature 1980 Order 42 r.9(2).

On pre-judgment damages the power to award simple interest is in the Judicature (Northern Ireland) Act 1978 s.33A and the County Courts (Northern Ireland) Order 1980 art.45A, "at such rate as the court thinks fit or as rules of court may provide".

The courts generally award interest at 2% on general damages from the date of the writ—*Wilson v Gilroy and MIB.*[3] On special damages interest runs generally from the date of the loss, at rates ranging from 4%—*Re Hutton (a minor)*[4] and *Stewart v Martin*[5]—to as low as 2%—*BA Kitchens Components Ltd v Jowat (UK) Ltd.*[6]

[1] [2013] CSIH 9.
[2] [2018] CSIH 76.
[3] [2008] NICA 23.
[4] [2019] NIQB 6 (here the rate ran from the date of issue of the writ.)
[5] [2019] NIQB 7.
[6] [2021] NIQB 3.

Group D

Investment

D

D1:	Share price index (FTSE 100)
D2:	Graph of share price index
D3:	Index-linked stock

D1: Share price index (FTSE 100)

FTSE®100 (on last day of month)

	1993	1994	1995	1996	1997	1998	1999	2000
Jan	2807.2	3491.8	2991.6	3759.3	4275.8	5458.5	5896.0	6268.5
Feb	2868.0	3328.1	3009.3	3727.6	4308.3	5767.3	6175.1	6232.6
Mar	2878.7	3086.4	3137.9	3699.7	4312.9	5932.2	6295.3	6540.2
Apr	2813.1	3125.3	3216.7	3817.9	4436.0	5928.4	6552.2	6327.4
May	2840.7	2970.5	3319.4	3747.8	4621.3	5870.7	6226.2	6359.4
Jun	2900.0	2919.2	3314.6	3711.0	4604.6	5832.6	6318.5	6312.7
Jul	2926.5	3082.6	3463.3	3703.2	4907.5	5837.1	6231.9	6365.3
Aug	3100.0	3251.3	3477.8	3867.6	4817.5	5249.4	6246.4	6672.7
Sep	3037.5	3026.3	3508.2	3953.7	5244.2	5064.4	6029.8	6294.2
Oct	3171.0	3097.4	3529.1	3979.1	4842.3	5438.4	6255.7	6438.4
Nov	3166.9	3081.4	3664.3	4058.0	4831.8	5743.9	6597.2	6142.2
Dec	3418.4	3065.5	3689.3	4118.5	5135.5	5882.6	6930.2	6222.5
	2001	**2002**	**2003**	**2004**	**2005**	**2006**	**2007**	**2008**
Jan	6297.5	5164.8	3567.4	4390.7	4852.3	5760.3	6203.1	5879.8
Feb	5917.9	5101.0	3655.6	4492.2	4968.5	5791.5	6171.5	5884.3
Mar	5633.7	5271.8	3613.3	4385.7	4894.4	5964.6	6308.0	5702.1
Apr	5967.0	5165.6	3926.0	4489.7	4801.7	6023.1	6449.2	6087.3
May	5796.2	5085.1	4048.1	4430.7	4964.0	5723.8	6621.5	6053.5
Jun	5642.5	4656.4	4031.2	4464.1	5113.2	5833.4	6607.9	5625.9
Jul	5529.1	4246.2	4157.0	4413.1	5282.3	5928.3	6360.1	5411.9
Aug	5345.0	4227.3	4161.1	4459.3	5296.9	5906.1	6303.3	5636.6
Sep	4903.4	3721.8	4091.3	4570.8	5477.7	5960.8	6466.8	4902.5
Oct	5039.7	4039.7	4287.6	4624.2	5317.3	6129.2	6721.6	4377.3
Nov	5203.6	4169.4	4342.6	4703.2	5423.2	6048.9	6432.5	4288.0
Dec	5217.4	3940.4	4476.9	4814.3	5618.8	6220.8	6456.9	4434.2
	2009	**2010**	**2011**	**2012**	**2013**	**2014**	**2015**	**2016**
Jan	4149.6	5188.5	5862.9	5681.6	6276.9	6510.4	6749.4	6083.8
Feb	3830.1	5354.5	5994.0	5871.5	6360.8	6809.7	6946.7	6097.1
Mar	3926.1	5679.6	5908.8	5768.5	6411.7	6598.4	6773.0	6174.9
Apr	4243.7	5553.3	6069.9	5737.8	6430.1	6780.0	6960.6	6241.9
May	4417.9	5188.4	5990.0	5320.9	6583.1	6844.5	6984.4	6230.8
Jun	4249.2	4916.9	5945.7	5571.2	6215.5	6743.9	6521.0	6504.3
Jul	4608.4	5258.0	5815.2	5635.3	6621.1	6730.1	6696.3	6724.4
Aug	4908.9	5225.2	5394.5	5711.5	6412.9	6819.8	6247.9	6781.5
Sep	5133.9	5548.6	5128.5	5742.1	6462.2	6622.7	6061.6	6899.3
Oct	5044.6	5675.2	5544.2	5782.7	6731.4	6546.5	6361.1	6954.2
Nov	5190.7	5528.3	5505.4	5866.8	6650.6	6722.6	6356.1	6783.8
Dec	5412.9	5899.9	5572.3	5897.8	6749.1	6566.1	6242.3	7142.8
	2017	**2018**	**2019**	**2020**	**2021**	**2022**	**2023**	**2024**
Jan	7099.2	7533.6	6968.3	7286.0	6407.5	7464.4	7771.7	7630.6
Feb	7263.4	7231.9	7074.7	6580.3	6483.4	7458.3	7876.3	7630.0
Mar	7322.9	7056.6	7279.2	5672.0	6713.6	7515.7	7631.7	7952.6
Apr	7203.9	7509.3	7418.2	5901.2	6969.8	7544.6	7870.6	7836.2
May	7520.0	7678.2	7161.7	6076.6	7022.6	7607.7	7446.1	
Jun	7312.7	7636.9	7425.6	6169.7	7037.5	7169.3	7531.5	
Jul	7372.0	7748.8	7586.8	5897.8	7032.3	7423.4	7699.4	
Aug	7430.6	7432.4	7207.2	5963.6	7119.7	7284.2	7439.1	
Sep	7372.8	7510.2	7408.2	5866.1	7086.4	6893.8	7608.1	
Oct	7493.7	7128.1	7248.4	5577.3	7237.6	7094.5	7321.7	
Nov	7326.7	6980.2	7346.5	6266.2	7059.5	7573.1	7453.8	
Dec	7687.8	6728.1	7542.4	6460.5	7384.5	7451.7	7733.2	

D2: Graph of share price index

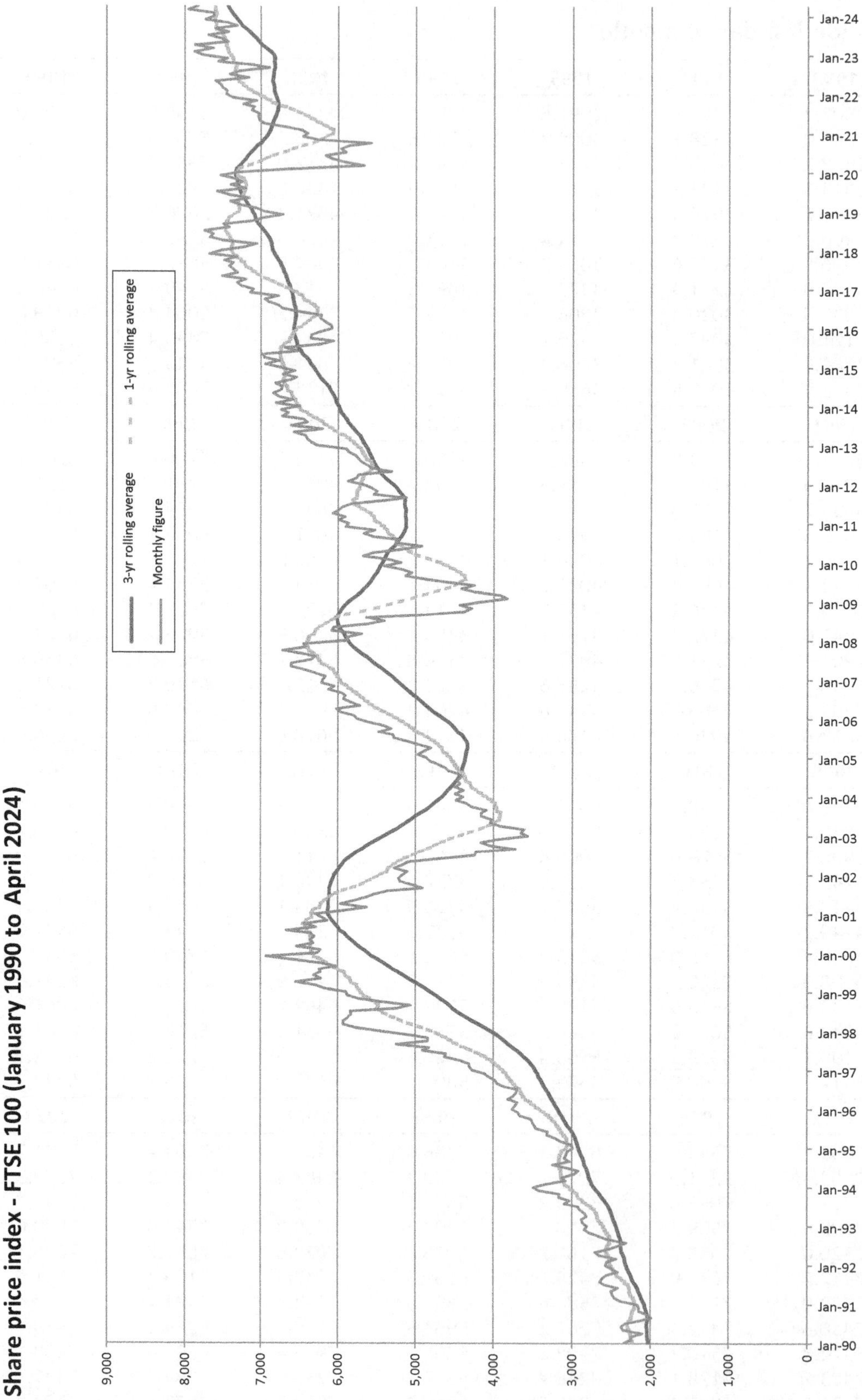

D3: Index-linked stock

Return on index-linked Government securities

	2010		2011		2012		2013		2014	
	Gross	Net	Gross	Net	Gross	Net	Gross	Net	Gross	Net
January	0.54%	0.39%	0.50%	0.35%	-0.47%	-0.62%	-0.50%	-0.65%	-0.24%	-0.39%
February	0.55%	0.40%	0.42%	0.27%	-0.43%	-0.58%	-0.53%	-0.68%	-0.23%	-0.38%
March	0.40%	0.25%	0.44%	0.29%	-0.44%	-0.59%	-0.76%	-0.91%	-0.32%	-0.47%
April	0.40%	0.25%	0.33%	0.18%	-0.36%	-0.51%	-0.71%	-0.86%	-0.33%	-0.48%
May	0.46%	0.31%	0.31%	0.16%	-0.54%	-0.69%	-0.53%	-0.68%	-0.38%	-0.53%
June	0.43%	0.28%	0.30%	0.15%	-0.36%	-0.51%	-0.19%	-0.34%	-0.28%	-0.43%
July	0.54%	0.39%	0.05%	-0.10%	-0.40%	-0.55%	-0.23%	-0.38%	-0.33%	-0.48%
August	0.21%	0.06%	0.06%	0.09%	0.19%	0.64%	0.26%	-0.41%	-0.58%	-0.73%
September	0.20%	0.05%	-0.14%	-0.29%	-0.26%	-0.41%	-0.28%	-0.43%	-0.52%	-0.67%
October	0.23%	0.08%	-0.08%	-0.23%	-0.24%	-0.39%	-0.34%	-0.49%	-0.58%	-0.73%
November	0.26%	0.11%	-0.31%	-0.46%	-0.40%	-0.55%	-0.27%	-0.42%	-0.81%	-0.96%
December	0.14%	-0.01%	-0.47%	-0.62%	-0.42%	-0.57%	-0.14%	-0.29%	-0.87%	-1.02%

	2015		2016		2017		2018		2019	
	Gross	Net	Gross	Net	Gross	Net	Gross	Net	Gross	Net
January	-1.02%	-1.17%	-0.91%	-1.06%	-1.88%	-2.03%	-1.62%	-1.77%	-1.77%	-1.92%
February	-0.85%	-1.00%	-0.92%	-1.07%	-1.92%	-2.07%	-1.61%	-1.76%	-1.75%	-1.90%
March	-1.03%	-1.18%	-1.00%	-1.15%	-2.03%	-2.18%	-1.74%	-1.89%	-2.13%	-2.28%
April	-0.98%	-1.13%	-0.89%	-1.04%	-2.04%	-2.19%	-1.63%	-1.78%	-2.00%	-2.15%
May	-0.97%	-1.12%	-0.96%	-1.11%	-1.97%	-2.12%	-1.75%	-1.90%	-2.19%	-2.34%
June	-0.84%	-0.99%	-1.43%	-1.58%	-1.80%	-1.95%	-1.69%	-1.84%	-2.09%	-2.24%
July	-0.91%	-1.06%	-1.59%	-1.74%	-1.75%	-1.90%	-1.68%	-1.83%	-2.31%	-2.46%
August	-0.87%	-1.02%	-1.96%	-2.11%	-1.96%	-2.11%	-1.68%	-1.83%	-2.48%	-2.63%
September	-0.90%	-1.05%	-1.92%	-2.07%	-1.81%	-1.96%	-1.64%	-1.79%	-2.53%	-2.68%
October	-0.85%	-1.00%	-1.91%	-2.06%	-1.67%	-1.82%	-1.72%	-1.87%	-1.98%	-2.13%
November	-0.92%	-1.07%	-1.68%	-1.83%	-1.69%	-1.84%	-1.66%	-1.81%	-2.09%	-2.24%
December	-0.66%	-0.81%	-1.86%	-2.01%	-1.78%	-1.93%	-1.75%	-1.90%	-2.02%	-2.17%

	2020		2021		2022		2023		2024	
	Gross	Net	Gross	Net	Gross	Net	Gross	Net	Gross	Net
January	-2.20%	-2.35%	-2.50%	-2.65%	-2.61%	-2.76%	0.23%	0.08%	0.94%	0.79%
February	-2.27%	-2.42%	-2.23%	-2.38%	-2.70%	-2.85%	0.51%	0.36%	1.17%	1.02%
March	-2.15%	-2.30%	-2.35%	-2.50%	-2.63%	-2.78%	0.14%	-0.01%	0.76%	0.61%
April	-2.27%	-2.42%	-2.34%	-2.49%	-2.36%	-2.51%	0.49%	0.34%	0.99%	0.84%
May	-2.51%	-2.66%	-2.48%	-2.63%	-1.93%	-2.08%	0.95%	0.80%		
June	-2.52%	-2.67%	-2.40%	-2.55%	-1.29%	-1.44%	0.98%	0.83%		
July	-2.60%	-2.75%	-2.68%	-2.83%	-1.56%	-1.71%	1.05%	0.90%		
August	-2.47%	-2.62%	-2.69%	-2.84%	-1.16%	-1.31%	1.09%	0.94%		
September	-2.51%	-2.66%	-2.59%	-2.74%	-0.27%	-0.42%	1.13%	0.98%		
October	-2.55%	-2.70%	-2.75%	-2.90%	-0.26%	-0.41%	1.29%	1.14%		
November	-2.53%	-2.68%	-3.07%	-3.22%	-0.25%	-0.40%	1.14%	0.99%		
December	-2.57%	-2.72%	-2.72%	-2.87%	0.27%	0.12%	0.73%	0.58%		

1. The above table shows the month end gross redemption yields of British Government index-linked stocks with over five years to maturity.

2. The net percentage yield shown above up to and including 2004 is stated after deducting tax at 15% (this was the assumption used in Wells v Wells and by the Lord Chancellor when he set the discount rate in 2001).

3. From 2005 to 2008 (inclusive) a fixed deduction of 0.25% has been allowed for tax instead of a percentage. This is because, in spite of reducing yields in this period, taxable interest remained high in this period so that applying a percentage to the combined gross yield would understate the deduction for tax. The actual average tax rate will vary depending on the size of the award.

4. From 2009 a fixed deduction of 0.15% has been allowed for tax. The average Income Tax deduction on taxable interest has been calculated by expert accountants as ranging from 0% to 0.30% depending on the size of the award, so 0.15% is adopted as the midpoint of the range.

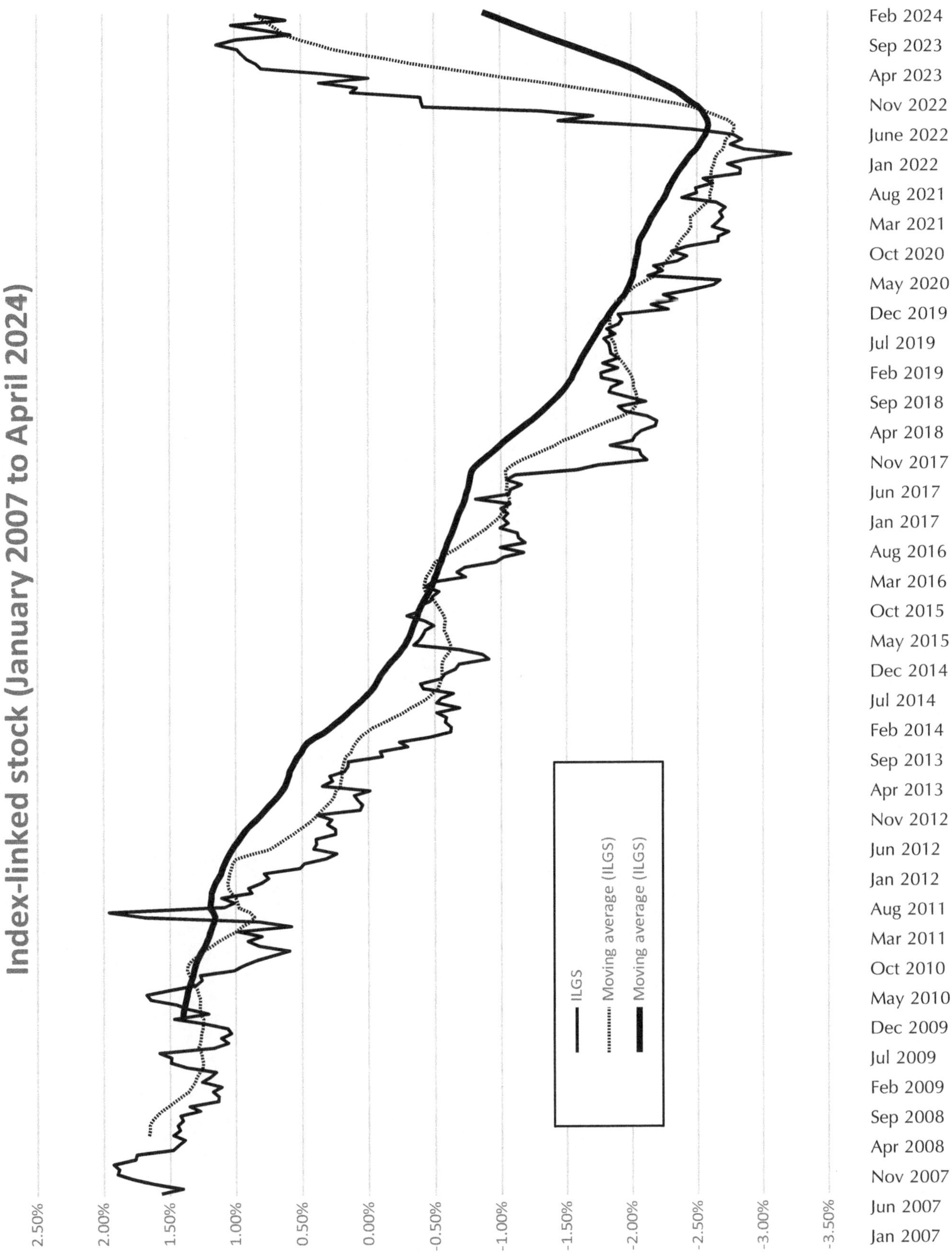
Index-linked stock (January 2007 to April 2024)
ILGS
Moving average (ILGS)
Moving average (ILGS)
2.50%
2.00%
1.50%
1.00%
0.50%
0.00%
-0.50%
-1.00%
-1.50%
-2.00%
-2.50%
-3.00%
-3.50%
Jan 2007
Jun 2007
Nov 2007
Apr 2008
Sep 2008
Feb 2009
Jul 2009
Dec 2009
May 2010
Oct 2010
Mar 2011
Aug 2011
Jan 2012
Jun 2012
Nov 2012
Apr 2013
Sep 2013
Feb 2014
Jul 2014
Dec 2014
May 2015
Oct 2015
Mar 2016
Aug 2016
Jan 2017
Jun 2017
Nov 2017
Apr 2018
Sep 2018
Feb 2019
Jul 2019
Dec 2019
May 2020
Oct 2020
Mar 2021
Aug 2021
Jan 2022
June 2022
Nov 2022
Apr 2023
Sep 2023
Feb 2024

Group E

Prices

E

E1: Retail Prices Index

	Jan	Feb	Mar	Apr	May	June	July	Aug	Sept	Oct	Nov	Dec	
2024	378.0	381.0	383.0	385.0	386.4	387.3	387.5						**2024**
2023	360.3	364.5	367.2	372.8	375.3	376.4	374.2	376.6	378.4	377.8	377.3	379.0	**2023**
2022	317.7	320.2	323.5	334.6	337.1	340.0	343.2	345.2	347.6	356.2	358.3	360.4	**2022**
2021	294.6	296.0	296.9	301.1	301.9	304.0	305.5	307.4	308.6	312.0	314.3	317.7	**2021**
2020	290.6	292.0	292.6	292.6	292.2	292.7	294.2	293.3	294.3	294.3	293.5	295.4	**2020**
2019	283.0	285.0	285.1	288.2	289.2	289.6	289.5	291.7	291.0	290.4	291.0	291.9	**2019**
2018	276.0	278.1	278.3	279.7	280.7	281.5	281.7	284.2	284.1	284.5	284.6	285.6	**2018**
2017	265.5	268.4	269.3	270.6	271.7	272.3	272.9	274.7	275.1	275.3	275.8	278.1	**2017**
2016	258.8	260.0	261.1	261.4	262.1	263.1	263.4	264.4	264.9	264.8	265.5	267.1	**2016**
2015	255.4	256.7	257.1	258.0	258.5	258.9	258.6	259.8	259.6	259.5	259.8	260.6	**2015**
2014	252.6	254.2	254.8	255.7	255.9	256.3	256.0	257.0	257.6	257.7	257.1	257.5	**2014**
2013	245.8	247.6	248.7	249.5	250.0	249.7	249.7	251.0	251.9	251.9	252.1	253.4	**2013**
2012	238.0	239.9	240.8	242.5	242.4	241.8	242.1	243.0	244.2	245.6	245.6	246.8	**2012**
2011	229.0	231.3	232.5	234.4	235.2	235.2	234.7	236.1	237.9	238.0	238.5	239.4	**2011**
2010	217.9	219.2	220.7	222.8	223.6	224.1	223.6	224.5	225.3	225.8	226.8	228.4	**2010**
2009	210.1	211.4	211.3	211.5	212.8	213.4	213.4	214.4	215.3	216.0	216.6	218.0	**2009**
2008	**209.8**	211.4	212.1	214.0	215.1	216.8	216.5	217.2	218.4	217.7	216.0	212.9	**2008**
2007	**201.6**	**203.1**	**204.4**	**205.4**	**206.2**	**207.3**	**206.1**	**207.3**	**208.0**	**208.9**	**209.7**	210.9	**2007**
2006	193.4	194.2	195.0	196.5	197.7	198.5	198.5	199.2	**200.1**	**200.4**	**201.1**	**202.7**	**2006**
2005	188.9	189.6	190.5	191.6	192.0	192.2	192.2	192.6	193.1	193.3	193.6	194.1	**2005**
2004	183.1	183.8	184.6	185.7	186.5	186.8	186.8	187.4	188.1	188.6	189.0	189.9	**2004**
2003	178.4	179.3	179.9	181.2	181.5	181.3	181.3	181.6	182.5	182.6	182.7	183.5	**2003**
2002	173.3	173.8	174.5	175.7	176.2	176.2	175.9	176.4	177.6	177.9	178.2	178.5	**2002**
2001	171.1	172.0	172.2	173.1	174.2	174.4	173.3	174.0	174.6	174.3	173.6	173.4	**2001**
2000	166.6	167.5	168.4	170.1	170.7	171.1	170.5	170.5	171.7	171.6	172.1	172.2	**2000**
1999	163.4	163.7	164.1	165.2	165.6	165.6	165.1	165.5	166.2	166.5	166.7	167.3	**1999**
1998	159.5	160.3	160.8	162.6	163.5	163.4	163.0	163.7	164.4	164.5	164.4	164.4	**1998**
1997	154.4	155.0	155.4	156.3	156.9	157.5	157.5	158.5	159.3	159.5	159.6	160.0	**1997**
1996	150.2	150.9	151.5	152.6	152.9	153.0	152.4	153.1	153.8	153.8	153.9	154.4	**1996**
1995	146.0	146.9	147.5	149.0	149.6	149.8	149.1	149.9	150.6	149.8	149.8	150.7	**1995**
1994	141.3	142.1	142.5	144.2	144.7	144.7	144.0	144.7	145.0	145.2	145.3	146.0	**1994**
1993	137.9	138.8	139.3	140.6	141.1	141.0	140.7	141.3	141.9	141.8	141.6	141.9	**1993**
1992	135.6	136.3	136.7	138.8	139.3	139.3	138.8	138.9	139.4	139.9	139.7	139.2	**1992**
1991	130.2	130.9	131.4	133.1	133.5	134.1	133.8	134.1	134.6	135.1	135.6	135.7	**1991**
1990	119.5	120.2	121.4	125.1	126.2	126.7	126.8	128.1	129.3	130.3	130.0	129.9	**1990**
1989	111.0	111.8	112.3	114.3	115.0	115.4	115.5	115.8	116.6	117.5	118.5	118.8	**1989**
1988	103.3	103.7	104.1	105.8	106.2	106.6	106.7	107.9	108.4	109.5	110.0	110.3	**1988**
1987	100.0	100.4	100.6	101.8	101.9	101.9	101.8	102.1	102.4	102.9	103.4	103.3	**1987**
	Jan	**Feb**	**Mar**	**Apr**	**May**	**June**	**July**	**Aug**	**Sept**	**Oct**	**Nov**	**Dec**	

Source: Office for National Statistics licensed under the Open Government Licence V.I.O.

Note:

To calculate the equivalent value of a lump sum, divide by the RPI at the time and multiply the result by the current RPI. Thus, £460 in June 1990 would be calculated as: 460 × (current RPI/126.7), to show the relative value of that amount in "today's money". For RPI figures between 1947 and 1987 refer to Facts and Figures 2019/2020 or earlier editions.

E2: Inflation table

Introductory notes

The table shows the value for each January in earlier years of £1 then, in terms of the value of the £ in January 2024.

Price inflation is measured by reference to the Retail Prices Index.

Year	Multiplier	Year	Multiplier	Year	Multiplier
1948	49.48	1983	4.58	2018	1.37
1949	47.31	1984	4.35	2019	1.34
1950	45.65	1985	4.14	2020	1.30
1951	43.95	1986	3.93	2021	1.28
1952	38.93	1987	3.78	2022	1.19
1953	37.28	1988	3.66	2023	1.05
1954	36.77	1989	3.41	2024	1.00
1955	35.33	1990	3.16		
1956	33.60	1991	2.90		
1957	32.20	1992	2.79		
1958	31.09	1993	2.74		
1959	30.43	1994	2.68		
1960	30.58	1995	2.59		
1961	29.93	1996	2.52		
1962	28.59	1997	2.45		
1963	27.86	1998	2.37		
1964	27.31	1999	2.31		
1965	26.12	2000	2.27		
1966	25.02	2001	2.21		
1967	24.14	2002	2.18		
1968	23.52	2003	2.12		
1969	22.16	2004	2.06		
1970	21.11	2005	2.00		
1971	19.45	2006	1.95		
1972	17.99	2007	1.88		
1973	16.70	2008	1.80		
1974	14.91	2009	1.80		
1975	12.44	2010	1.73		
1976	10.08	2011	1.65		
1977	8.65	2012	1.59		
1978	7.87	2013	1.54		
1979	7.20	2014	1.50		
1980	6.08	2015	1.48		
1981	5.38	2016	1.46		
1982	4.80	2017	1.42		

E3: House price indices

Introductory notes

1. The Office for Statistics Regulation designated the UK HPI as a National Statistic in September 2018. The new single official house price index is available at: *https://landregistry.data.gov.uk/app/ukhpi*. The main sources of price paid data used in the UK HPI are HM Land Registry for England and Wales, Registers of Scotland and Land and Property Services Northern Ireland. The index is published monthly, with Northern Ireland figures updated quarterly on behalf of the Office for National Statistics, Registers of Scotland and Land and Property Services Northern Ireland.

2. The UK HPI has wide coverage of both cash and mortgage transactions and a large data source (land registrations such as that maintained by HM Land Registry) allowing data to be published down to a local authority level with further breakdowns available by property type, buyer status, funding status and property status. The search tool permits data over a defined period of time dating back to January 1995 to be identified and downloaded according to the numerous subset categories.

3. The index applies a statistical method, called a hedonic regression model, to the various sources of data on property price and attributes to produce estimates of the change in house prices each period. Historic data within the tables is derived. Under the UK HPI, data is available from 1995 for England and Wales, 2004 for Scotland and 2005 for Northern Ireland. A longer back-series has been derived by using the historic path of the Office for National Statistics HPI to construct a series back to 1968.

4. There are two notes of specific caution when applying the tables on a national and regional level respectively:

    i. The UK HPI, introduced in June 2016, includes all residential properties purchased for market value in the UK. However, as sales only appear in the UK HPI once the purchases have been registered, there can be a delay before transactions feed into the index. As such, caution is advised when interpreting price changes in the most recent periods as they can be revised.

    ii. It is advised that low number of sales transactions in some local authorities can lead to volatility in the estimates at these levels. Geographies with low number of sales transactions should be analysed in the context of their longer-term trends rather than focusing on monthly movements.

5. Given the event of the data search tool provided by the UK HPI from national house price data, down to local authority breakdowns, the annual regional indices are not reproduced in this edition. Standard Report Data (simple mean averages) can be generated from national level down to type of property and postcodes through the following link: *http://landregistry.data.gov.uk/app/standard-reports*.

6. There remain many other price indices that are publicly available. These include the Halifax (HHPI), Nationwide, the Financial Times, the Royal Institute of Chartered Surveyors, Hometrack, Rightmove and Zoopla to name but a few.

7. The editors of *Facts & Figures* have used the Halifax data in editions prior to 2021. The Index Year for the Halifax data previously used was 1983. The UK HPI index year is 2015, which seems an appropriate index year when taking into account demographics and the evolution of demand in the residential housing market since 1983. Furthermore, the UK HPI now appears to include the most comprehensive data sources. In certain circumstances, the data offered by other indices may remain useful, particularly if earlier indexation is desired.

Period	Sales volume	House price index: All property types	Average price: All property types	Percentage change (yearly): All property types
1993-01		28.05	£53,484	-5.34
1994-01		28.65	£54,623	2.13
1995-01		29.08	£55,437	1.49
1996-01		29.67	£56,576	2.05
1997-01		31.84	£60,698	7.29
1998-01		34.74	£66,231	9.12
1999-01		38.24	£72,903	10.07
2000-01		44.38	£84,620	16.07
2001-01		48.85	£93,136	10.06
2002-01		51.2	£97,623	4.82
2003-01		65.47	£124,836	27.88
2004-01		71.84	£136,976	9.72
2005-01	65834	79	£150,633	9.97
2006-01	88382	83.9	£159,970	6.2
2007-01	101538	92.71	£176,758	10.49
2008-01	67660	97.44	£185,782	5.11
2009-01	31422	82.47	£157,234	-15.37
2010-01	41085	87.83	£167,469	6.51
2011-01	42399	87.75	£167,300	-0.1
2012-01	49493	87.02	£165,908	-0.83
2013-01	49129	87.96	£167,716	1.09
2014-01	75540	93.45	£178,182	6.24
2015-01	66819	100	£190,665	7.01
2016-01	70959	107.76	£205,464	7.76
2017-01	68663	112.89	£215,243	4.76
2018-01	68243	117.77	£224,544	4.32
2019-01	65597	119.75	£228,314	1.68
2020-01	68585	121.65	£231,940	1.59
2021-01	78287	130.96	£249,690	7.65
2022-01	63840	144.38	£275,282	10.25
2023-01	61062	152.3	£290,381	6.5

E4: How prices have changed over 17 years

Item	2005	2020	March 2024	Average annual change from 2005 to 2024	Source
Milk (pint)	£0.35	£0.43	£0.65	4.5%	ONS
White sliced loaf 800 gm	£0.65	£1.05	£1.39	5.99%	ONS
RPI Average Price-Eggs per dozen[1]	£1.55	£2.25	£3.18	5.53%	ONS
Ave price Sugar: Granulated (kilo)	£0.75	£0.73	£1.15	2.8%	ONS
Draught lager (pint)	£2.36	£3.75	£4.71	5.24%	ONS
20 king-size cigarettes	£4.39	£11.12	£15.66	13.51%	ONS
Unleaded petrol (litre)	£0.81	£1.05	£1.45	4.16%	ONS
House price (all UK):	150,633	£231,185	£285,000[1]	4.95%	ONS
Weekly state pension	£82.05	£175.20	£221.20	8.9%	DWP
Gold (per oz)	£230	£1,440	£1,616[2]	33.48%	ONS CG:AS: Level: Monetary Gold
Heating oil, per 1000 litres	NA	£412.05	£691.31	NA	ONS
McDonald's Big Mac	£2.38	£3.19	£4.59	4.89%	MacDonalds

Note: The ONS statistics are averages taken over a wide range of sources.

[1] Estimated data for UK house prices is only available to November 2023, so the figure is for November 2023 and the average inflation is calculated over 18 years.
[2] Figure for 2023 Q4.

Group F

Earnings

F1: Earnings losses in personal injury and fatal accident cases

1. **Purpose of note**

The purpose of this note is to provide some basic guidance on what information to request from a claimant in order to make an initial assessment as to whether an earnings loss is likely to arise.

2. **Nature of occupation**

Identify at an early stage into which category of occupation the claimant falls:

Employment
— Employee without ownership rights.
— Director/shareholder (of private company).

Self-employment
— Sole trader.
— Partner.

3. **Relevant dates**

For the purposes of proposing the periods for which information should be requested, relevant dates will be identified as follows:

For an individual in employment
(References here are to tax years ending on 5 April although the tax for many salaried employees will often effectively run from 1 April to 31 March.)

D1 6 April three years before D2.
D2 5 April immediately preceding D3.
D3 Incident date.
D4 5 April immediately preceding D5.
D5 Present time.

For business accounts
D6 Date of beginning of accounting period three years before D7.
D7 Date of end of accounting period immediately preceding D3.
D8 Date of end of accounting period immediately preceding D5.

A full three years' pre-accident financial information should often be sufficient (having regard to the need for proportionality), although documentation for a longer period may be appropriate if it emerges that business results have been volatile.

For an individual in employment

D1		D2	D3 Incident		D4	D5
06-April 05-April	06-April 05-April	06-April 05-April	06-April 05-April	06-April 05-April	06-April 05-April	05-April Present time
Tax year −3	Tax year −2	Tax year −1	Tax year 0	Tax year +1	Current tax year −1	Current tax year

D6		D7	D3 Incident		D8	D5
Beginning End Accounts year −3	Beginning End Accounts year −2	Beginning End Accounts year −1	Beginning End Accounts year 0	Beginning End Accounts year +1	Beginning End Current accounts year −1	Beginning Present time Current accounts year

4. **Employment: Employee without ownership rights**

This is the likely category for most employees—but excluding in particular those who are directors and/or shareholders with a degree of control over private companies.

In the absence of detailed representations from the employer, or from an employment expert, the earnings history may be the only useful guide to potential earnings but for the incident giving rise to the claim.

The most useful documentation will usually be a comprehensive set of pay advices (monthly, sometimes four-weekly, or weekly) because these may be expected to show:

- basic pay level (and dates/amounts of periodic increases),
- overtime (if paid) and any other regular or periodic enhancements,
- bonuses (and dates/amounts paid),
- sick pay (and dates), and
- employee pension contributions.

Request:

- **Pay advices (whether from employment or subsequent pension) from D1 to D5.**
- **Details of benefits other than pay for each tax year between D1 and D2 and for each tax year since D2.**

5. **Employment: Director/shareholders**

This category relates mainly to those individuals who have a degree of ownership or control, probably in a private company, and whose remuneration as such may not be a fair reflection of the personal reward available from the business.

For instance:

- profits may have been drawn by way of dividend for reasons of tax efficiency; or
- profits (which the claimant could have drawn) have been re-invested in the business.

It may well be appropriate to assess loss along the lines that would be adopted in relation to a sole trader or partner, that is:

- first to identify whether a business loss has occurred that is attributable to the claim incident; and
- if so, go on to identify the share of the business loss suffered personally by the claimant.

In such a case, it will often be appropriate to review not only the remuneration history of the individual but also the dividend history. Benefits history may also be important.

Request:

Regarding the business

- **full accounts (including detailed profit and loss accounts) from D6 to D8,**

  and consider requesting

- **figures for monthly (preferably) or quarterly sales from D6 to D5.**

  (Important if the claimant's role is likely to have influenced sales levels; the figures should show trends and seasonality, etc.)

Regarding the claimant

- **pay advices (whether from employment or pension) from D1 to D5, and**
- **tax returns from D1 to D4.**

  (Mainly to check remuneration and dividends received in each tax year, but also benefits and any personal pension contributions, etc.)

6. **Self-employment: Sole trader**

   Request:

   - **full accounts from D6 to D8,**
   - **figures for monthly or quarterly sales from D6 to D5, and**
   - **tax returns from D1 to D4.**

     (Mainly to check private usage deductions from business expenses, capital allowances, personal pension contributions, etc.)

7. **Self-employment: Partner**

   Approach will be:

   - first to identify whether a business loss has occurred that is attributable to the claim incident, and
   - if so, go on to identify the share of the business loss suffered personally by the claimant.

   Request:

   Regarding the business

   - **full partnership accounts from D6 to D8, and**
   - **figures for monthly (preferably) or quarterly sales from D6 to D5.**

   Regarding the claimant

   - **personal tax returns from D1 to D4.**

     (Mainly to check personal pension contributions, etc.)

8. **Benefits other than pay (employees)**

   In the first instance, it is probably sufficient simply to ask, in relation to any employee (including a company director), for:

   - **details of any non-pecuniary benefits in employment, and any pension benefits.**

9. **Other points**

- **Company searches**

Searches of small UK limited companies seldom yield helpful results as regards accounts because the contents of the accounts to be filed are invariably in abbreviated form, sometimes only a balance sheet.

In cases where there are doubts about full disclosure, a search may be useful in identifying whether a claimant has more directorships than advised, or possibly a history of connections with insolvent companies.

- **Permanent Health Insurance income**

Where a claimant receives insurance money through his employer, this will usually be evident from review of the pay advices.

As to whether credit needs to be given by the claimant for such insurance money for claim purposes will probably depend on the nature of the underlying policy. See *Gaca v Pirelli General Plc.*[1]

- **Ill-health pension**

Where a claimant receives an ill-health pension following an incident, this should again be evident from review of the pay advices.

Generally, no credit is to be given for actual pension in a loss of earnings claim: *Parry v Cleaver.*[2]

- **Partnerships**

There may be cases where the profit-sharing arrangements do not reflect the realistic commercial input of the respective partners. This issue may arise particularly where spouses are business partners. The court may be prepared to put aside the historic arrangements in assessing loss: *Ward v Newalls Insulation Co Ltd.*[3]

[1] [2004] 1 W.L.R. 2683.
[2] [1970] A.C. 1.
[3] [1998] 1 W.L.R. 1722.

F2: Lost years

Introduction

1. Where a living adult[1] claimant's life expectancy has been reduced by reason of the defendant's tort, the claimant may suffer financial losses during his or her "lost years", i.e. the years after his or her death but before the date he or she was expected to have passed away in the absence of the injury.[2] Take, for example, a claimant who had a normal life expectancy before developing mesothelioma due to the defendant's negligence. If the claimant's life expectancy is now reduced to age 50 years, he will have "lost years" claims for loss of earnings from age 50 to his normal retirement age and for loss of pension from his retirement age until the date he would have died (calculated by reference to normal life expectancy in the absence of any pre-existing condition).[3]

Approach to Assessment

2. A detailed analysis of types of lost years claim that can be made and the applicable principles for assessing damages for lost years is beyond the scope of this book.[4]

3. Where the reduction in life expectancy is modest, instead of making a detailed calculation, the judge may simply decide to make a small upwards adjustment to the loss of earnings multiplier.[5]

4. However, where the court decides to adopt an accurate multiplier and multiplicand method for assessing lost years the approach is as follows:

   - Calculate the net annual multiplicand (whether loss of earnings, loss of pension etc.).
   - Apply the applicable percentage deduction for living expenses.[6]
   - Calculate the multiplier for the lost years.
   - Apply any applicable discount for contingencies other than mortality.
   - Multiply the adjusted annual loss by the adjusted multiplier.

[1] Claims for lost years cannot be made on behalf of young children: *Croke v Wiseman* [1982] 1 W.L.R. 71. However, note that this decision is inconsistent with two previous House of Lords authorities. It seems illogical and discriminatory that there is a pecuniary head of loss which cannot be claimed by some claimants merely because of their age: see further *Iqbal v Whipps Cross University NHS Trust* [2007] EWCA Civ 1190; and *Totham v King's College Hospitals NHS Foundation Trust* [2015] EWHC 97 (QB).

[2] In *Pickett v BRE* [1980] AC 136 the House of Lords held that an adult claimant is entitled to recover damages for loss of financial expectations during the lost years. Such losses are deemed to be the claimant's own pecuniary losses. Importantly, it is not necessary for the claimant to have dependants before being able to claim such losses.

[3] For calculating normal life expectancy based upon projected life expectancy data from the ONS, please see the tables at A3 or use the 0% column of Table 1 for men or Table 2 for women.

[4] See further *McGregor on Damages* (20th edition, Sweet & Maxwell, 2017), *Kemp & Kemp on Damages* (looseleaf, Sweet and Maxwell); and *Schedules of Loss: Calculating Damages* (4th edition, Bloomsbury Publishing, 2018).

[5] For example, in *Hunt v Severs* [1993] QB 815 the Court of Appeal upheld the trial judge's calculation of lost years reached by adding 0.5 to the claimant multiplier for loss of earnings. A similar approach was adopted in *Sarwar (1) Ali (2) MIB [2007] EWHC 1225 (Admin)* to reflect loss of pension during the lost years.

[6] Different deductions for living expenses are made depending upon the circumstances of the claimant. Unfortunately, there is limited judicial guidance regarding the meaning or calculation of living expenses. However, percentage discounts for living expenses in the region of 50% might be expected for married claimants with no dependants (*Phipps v Brooks Dry Cleaning Services Ltd* [1996] P.I.Q.R. Q100); 25–50% for married claimants with children; and 50–75% for unmarried claimants.

A Worked Example

5. The claimant, who pursues her claim in England, is married with no dependants. She is aged 50 at trial. She obtained a degree at university and has a job earning £30,000 net p.a. But for her injury, the claimant would have worked to a normal retirement age of 68. Thereafter, at present day values, she would have had a private pension of £7,500 p.a. and a full state pension of £203.85 per week or £10,636.60 p.a. By reason of the defendant's negligence she is expected to live to 55. Applying a discount rate of -0.25% the calculation for lost years is as follows:

   Loss of Earnings During the Lost Years

   Annual net earnings multiplicand is £30,000 p.a.

   The discount for living expenses is 50%.

   The adjusted multiplicand is £30,000 × 50% = £15,000.

   The multiplier from age 55 to 68 is 12.86 (Table 12).

   A discount for contingencies of 0.85 is applied Table C, Level 3.

   The adjusted multiplier is 12.86 × 0.85 = 10.93.

   The discount factor for five years accelerated receipt (Table 35) is 1.0126.

   Subtotal loss of earnings during the lost years is therefore £15,000 × 10.93 × 1.0126 = £166,015.77.

   Loss of Pension During the Lost Years

   Annual pension multiplicand is £7,500, plus £10,636.60 = £18,136.60. Income tax is payable at 20% beyond £12,570. This reduces the net multiplicand to £17,023.28.

   The discount for living expenses is 50%.

   The adjusted multiplicand is £17,023.28 × 50% = £8,511.64.

   The multiplier from age 68 for life is 21.19 (Table 28, at age 50).

   A discount for contingencies of 0.85 is applied (Table C).[7]

   The adjusted multiplier is 21.19 × 0.85 = 18.01.

   Subtotal loss of pension during the lost years is therefore £8,511.64 × 18.01 = £153,294.64.

6. Therefore the total claim for lost years is £166,015.77 + £153,294.64 = £319,310.41.

[7] In the absence of specific discount factors for contingencies other than mortality in respect of pension loss claims, many practitioners apply the same discount for contingencies suggested for loss of earnings claims as set out in Tables A–D of the Ogden Guidance notes. However, arguably a different (lower) discount factor may be appropriate, especially if the claimant has an entitlement to an ill-health retirement pension.

F3: Payroll documents

SPECIMEN PAY ADVICE

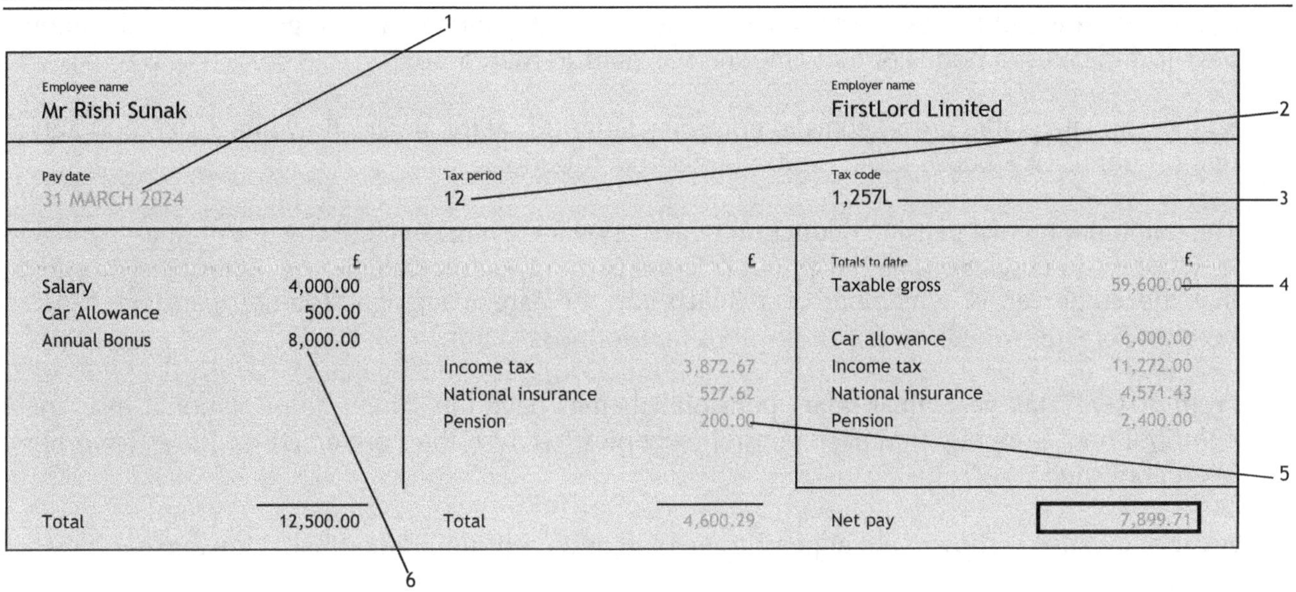

Employee name Mr Rishi Sunak				Employer name FirstLord Limited	
Pay date 31 MARCH 2024		Tax period 12		Tax code 1,257L	
	£		£	Totals to date	£
Salary	4,000.00			Taxable gross	59,600.00
Car Allowance	500.00				
Annual Bonus	8,000.00			Car allowance	6,000.00
		Income tax	3,872.67	Income tax	11,272.00
		National insurance	527.62	National insurance	4,571.43
		Pension	200.00	Pension	2,400.00
Total	12,500.00	Total	4,600.29	Net pay	7,899.71

Points to note

1. As good a starting point as any is usually a pay advice at the end of the **last full tax year**, but try also to obtain all subsequent pay advices whether to date of trial in a personal injury case or to date of death if a fatal accident.

2. It is worth bearing in mind that some employers pay every four weeks, and on rare occasions every two weeks, rather than necessarily monthly or weekly. The tax period should help to identify payment frequency.

3. The tax code, **1257L**, represents the basic tax allowance of £12,570. This indicates that the tax inspector has no reason to make any adjustment to the standard code to collect additional tax due in the year.

   This in turn implies that the employee has no non-cash taxable benefits from the employer.

   The most common taxable benefits are probably health insurance cover and those related to private use of motor vehicles.

   By way of example, were the employee enjoying taxable benefits to a value of £1,000 p.a, the code could be expected to be 1,157L. Application of this code would result in the tax due on the benefit being collected under PAYE over the course of the tax year.

4. In the illustration shown above, the **gross taxable income** figure requires some reconciliation to other figures.

   The year-end figures suggest that salary has probably been running consistently at £4,000 per month (i.e. £48,000 per annum), with a £200 per month pension contribution. That would produce a taxable total of £45,600 in the year, suggesting that there has been additional pay of £14,000 in arriving at the taxable gross figure of £59,600.

Assuming the car allowance of £500 was paid every month in the tax year, gives an annual total of £6,000. This still leaves £8,000 unaccounted for in the annual taxable gross, but as the above payslip indicates, a bonus of that amount was paid in March 2025.

So the annual taxable gross seems to comprise £48,000 salary, a car allowance of £6,000 and a one-off bonus of £8,000, less £2,400 pension contributions.

5. The combination of a **pension deduction** which appears to represent exactly 5% of salary, and the fact that those deductions are taken out of gross earnings before calculating income tax, suggests that the employee is a member of a final salary or career average revalued earnings (CARE) pension scheme, which may give rise to a pension loss claim.

   From 2016/17 tax year, final salary pension schemes have the same rate of National Insurance contributions as money purchase pension schemes because the contracted-out rates have now been abolished.

6. A **car allowance** is shown, but appears to be paid as a cash sum, rather than a taxable car benefit.

SPECIMEN P60

1 2

P60 End of Year Certificate

Tax year to 5 April 2024

To the employee:

Please keep this certificate in a safe place as **you will need it if you have to fill in a tax return. You also need it to make a claim for tax credits or to renew your claim.**

It also helps you check that your employer is using the correct National Insurance number and deducting the right rate of National Insurance contributions.

By law you are required to tell HM Revenue & Customs about any income that is not fully taxed, even if you are not sent a tax return.

HM Revenue & Customs

*The figures marked * should be used for your tax return, if you get one.*

Employee's details

Surname	RISHI
Forenames or initials	SUNAK
National insurance number	NH 01 02 03 C
Works/payroll number	12345

Pay and Income Tax details

3

	Pay	Tax Deducted
In previous employment(s)	0.00	0.00
In this employment	* 57600.00	10472.00
Total for year	57600.00	10472.00
Final tax code		1257L

4

National Insurance contributions in this employment

NIC table letter	Earnings at the Lower Earnings Limited (LEL) where earnings are equal to or exceeding the LEL £	Earnings above the LEL, up to and including the Primary Threshold (PT) £	Earnings above the PT, up to and including the Upper Earnings Limit (UEL) £	Employee's contributions due on all earnings above the PT £
A	123	12447	37700	4530.10

Statutory payments

Included in the pay 'in this employment' figure above

	£
Statutory Maternity Pay	0.00
Statutory Paternity Pay	0.00
Statutory Shared Parental	0.00
Statutory Adoption Pay	0.00

5

Other details

Student Loan deductions in this employment *(whole £s only)* £ 0

To employee

RISHI SUNAK
10 DOWNING STREET
LONDON
SW1A 2AA

Your employer's full name and address (including postcode)

FIRST LORD LIMITED
123 HIGH STREET
LONDON
SW1B 2BB

Employer PAYE reference 365 / C01984

Certificate by Employer/Paying Office:

This form shows your total pay for Income Tax purposes in this employment for the year.

Any overtime, bonus, commission etc, Statutory Sick Pay, Statutory Maternity Pay, Statutory Paternity Pay, Statutory Shared Parental Pay or Statuary Adoption Pay is included.

P60 (2023-2024) *Do not destroy*

Points to note

1 The top third of the P60 contains basic details, including the tax year to which the P60 relates, the full name of the employee and the total 'taxable' earnings for the relevant year.

2 The employee's name, National Insurance number and payroll number are set out in the top right of the P60. The National Insurance number is required to ensure that the employee receives the correct National Insurance credits on their HMRC record, whereas the payroll number is the employer's unique reference relating to this particular employee.

3 The pay and income tax section of the P60 details the total 'taxable' earnings for the employee in the tax year (which will be net of pension contributions), as well as the total amount of income tax deducted at source by the employer.

4 The middle third of the P60 concerns National Insurance and breaks down the employee's gross earnings into bands; [a] earnings up to the Lower Earnings Limit (LEL), [b] earnings between the LEL and Primary Threshold (PT), [c] earnings between the PT and the Upper Earnings Limit (UEL). Note that in this example, the total earnings in all three NI bands adds up to £50,270, which is less than the 'taxable' earnings of £57,600. This is because the taxable earnings exceed the UEL and any earnings in excess of £50,270 are subject to the National Insurance surcharge of 2.00%, rather than the full composite rate of 11.50% (based on rates for 2023/24).

In addition, there is sufficient information in the above P60 to determine that the Claimant is probably making pension contributions. For example, note that National Insurance is payable at 11.50% on £37,700, which is £4,335.50. The total National Insurance paid was actually £4,530.10. The difference of £194.60 is the National Insurance payable at 2.00% on earnings above the UEL of £50,270. Hence the earnings above the UEL is £194.60 divided by 2.00%, which is £9,730. The total of the earnings up to the UEL of £50,270 and the calculated earnings above the UEL of £9,730, is £60,000. This is more than the taxable earnings of £57,600 specified at the top of the P60. The difference of £2,400 is exactly 4% of the total gross earnings of £60,000, which is the standard pension contribution under the current workplace pension rules.

5 The bottom third of the P60 contains the names and addresses of the employee and employer, as well as the employer's payroll reference.

F4: National Minimum Wage and National Living Wage

Introductory notes

1. The National Minimum Wage became law on April 1, 1999 and the National Living Wage became law on April 1, 2016.

2. The National Minimum Wage and National Living Wage are the minimum amount of pay to which workers over a specified age are entitled. Up to 30 September 2004, the minimum age for the National Minimum Wage was 18. Since October 1, 2004 a new rate of National Minimum Wage has been available to workers under 18 who are no longer of compulsory school age. The National Living Wage was introduced on 1 April 2016 for workers aged 25 and older. The National Minimum Wage still applies for workers aged under 25.

3. Most adult workers who are resident in the UK, who have a written, oral or implied contract and who are not genuinely self-employed, are entitled to the National Minimum Wage or National Living Wage.

4. The National Minimum Wage and National Living Wage are enforced by HM Revenue and Customs.

5. There are currently four levels of National Minimum Wage: a development rate for those aged between 18 and 20; a main rate for workers aged between 21 and 24; from 1 October 2004, a rate for workers under 18 who are no longer of compulsory school age; and, from 1 October 2010, an apprentice minimum wage (see note 8 below).

6. The main rate was extended to workers aged 21 or over from October 2010. Prior to that the qualifying age for the main rate was 22. Correspondingly the development rate has been available to those aged between 18 and 20 from October 2010. Prior to that it was available to those aged between 18 and 21.

7. A development rate is available, subject to various conditions, to workers aged 22 or over who started a new job with a new employer and did accredited training, being a course approved by the UK government to obtain a vocational qualification, was abolished for pay reference periods starting on or after 1 October 2006. When applicable, the accredited training rate could only be paid for the first six months of the new job, after which the National Minimum Wage main rate applied.

8. A new apprentice minimum wage was introduced with effect from 1 October 2010, available to apprentices aged under 19, or apprentices aged 19 or over but in the first year of their apprenticeship. From 1 April 2022 the apprentice rate has been set equal to the rate for under 18s.

9. The government has announced that they will align the National Minimum Wage and National Living Wage cycles so that both rates are amended in April each year. This took place with effect from April 2017.

National Minimum Wage

Pay reference periods starting on or after	1st October							1st April						
	2011 £/hr	2012 £/hr	2013 £/hr	2014 £/hr	2015 £/hr	2016 £/hr	2017 £/hr	2018 £/hr	2019 £/hr	2020 £/hr	2021 £/hr	2022 £/hr	2023 £/hr	2024 £/hr
Rate for apprentices aged under 19, or 19 or over but in the first year of their apprenticeship (note 8)	2.60	2.65	2.68	2.73	3.30	3.40	3.50	3.70	3.90	4.15	4.30	4.81	5.28	6.40
Workers under 18 who are no longer of compulsory school age (notes 2 and 5)	3.68	3.68	3.72	3.79	3.87	4.00	4.05	4.20	4.35	4.55	4.62	4.81	5.28	6.40
Development rate for workers aged 18 to 20 years (from October 2010) (notes 5 and 6)	4.98	4.98	5.03	5.13	5.30	5.55	5.60	5.90	6.15	6.45	6.56	6.83	7.49	8.60
Main rate for workers aged 21 or over from October 2010 and for workers aged 21 to 24 years from April 2016 (notes 2, 5, and 9)	6.08	6.19	6.31	6.50	6.70	6.95	7.05	7.38	7.70	8.20	8.36	9.18	10.18	11.44

National Living Wage:

	Pay reference periods starting on or after 1 April													
	2011 £/hr	2012 £/hr	2013 £/hr	2014 £/hr	2015 £/hr	2016 £/hr	2017 £/hr	2018 £/hr	2019 £/hr	2020 £/hr	2021 £/hr	2022 £/hr	2023 £/hr	2024 £/hr
For workers aged 25 or over from April 2016 (see note 2)	n/a	n/a	n/a	n/a	n/a	7.20	7.50	7.83	8.21	8.72	8.91	9.50	10.42	11.44

F5: Regional unemployment statistics

In previous years, tables showing the average duration of claims for Jobseeker's Allowance have been drawn from the Office of National Statistics Economic and Labour Market Review. This is no longer being produced.

The tables below have been based on data available on the Nomis website for March 2024.

North East
Median duration (weeks)

Age	Male	Female	All
Under 17	0.0	0.0	0.0
17	0.0	0.0	0.0
18	2.0	1.0	2.0
19	6.0	8.0	8.0
20–24	8.3	6.0	7.7
25–29	11.9	9.6	11.2
30–34	22.3	16.1	19.7
35–39	45.5	130.0	78.0
40–44	45.5	23.6	32.5
45–49	56.3	22.4	26.0
50–54	35.8	78.0	45.5
55–59	#	43.3	229.7
60+	#	#	#

North West
Median duration (weeks)

Age	Male	Female	All
Under 17	0.0	0.0	0.0
17	0.0	0.0	0.0
18	6.0	1.0	5.0
19	3.0	8.0	6.0
20–24	6.8	5.7	6.2
25–29	10.2	7.9	9.3
30–34	12.1	11.6	11.9
35–39	16.1	14.4	15.4
40–44	17.0	12.7	15.5
45–49	17.3	14.8	16.3
50–54	21.2	16.1	19.3
55–59	22.2	18.9	20.8
60+	58.5	22.6	26.0

Yorkshire and the Humber
Median duration (weeks)

Age	Male	Female	All
Under 17	0.0	0.0	0.0
17	0.0	0.0	0.0
18	4.0	1.0	4.0
19	6.0	4.0	5.0
20–24	8.5	6.9	8.0
25–29	12.0	10.2	11.2
30–34	16.4	12.2	14.5
35–39	21.2	19.0	20.3
40–44	19.6	19.2	19.5
45–49	22.0	18.7	20.7
50–54	25.3	17.5	22.6
55–59	24.2	17.2	21.5
60+	113.5	17.6	24.3

East Midlands
Median duration (weeks)

Age	Male	Female	All
Under 17	0.0	0.0	0.0
17	0.0	0.0	0.0
18	3.3	2.0	3.3
19	6.0	8.0	8.0
20–24	8.9	7.0	8.1
25–29	10.1	9.4	9.9
30–34	13.7	12.0	12.7
35–39	14.6	13.5	14.3
40–44	13.9	16.7	14.9
45–49	15.8	16.1	15.9
50–54	16.1	12.6	14.8
55–59	18.6	16.0	17.4
60+	19.1	17.0	18.1

West Midlands
Median duration (weeks)

Age	Male	Female	All
Under 17	0.0	0.0	0.0
17	0.0	0.0	0.0
18	2.7	0.7	2.7
19	3.0	1.0	2.8
20–24	7.9	8.6	8.2
25–29	10.6	9.4	10.1
30–34	16.2	14.5	15.5
35–39	23.5	18.2	21.3
40–44	24.9	23.8	24.5
45–49	133.7	21.4	27.8
50–54	254.2	25.7	85.1
55–59	#	25.1	152.3
60+	#	34.7	182.0

East
Median duration (weeks)

Age	Male	Female	All
Under 17	0.0	0.0	0.0
17	0.0	0.0	0.0
18	1.0	1.5	2.0
19	4.0	6.0	4.7
20–24	7.2	6.2	6.7
25–29	8.8	7.9	8.5
30–34	12.0	10.5	11.2
35–39	11.4	11.3	11.4
40–44	12.5	11.9	12.2
45–49	13.4	13.5	13.4
50–54	14.3	11.3	12.7
55–59	17.5	12.9	15.6
60+	19.8	15.3	18.0

London
Median duration (weeks)

Age	Male	Female	All
Under 17	0.0	0.0	0.0
17	0.0	0.0	0.0
18	8.8	6.0	8.7
19	7.0	6.0	6.8
20–24	7.6	6.7	7.2
25–29	9.8	8.4	9.0
30–34	11.1	9.9	10.5
35–39	14.4	12.6	13.5
40–44	15.1	13.9	14.6
45–49	19.2	19.2	19.2
50–54	23.5	20.8	22.4
55–59	#	25.5	196.0
60+	#	#	#

South East
Median duration (weeks)

Age	Male	Female	All
Under 17	0.0	0.0	0.0
17	0.0	0.0	0.0
18	2.0	0.8	1.2
19	6.0	4.0	4.5
20–24	7.6	6.9	7.3
25–29	9.6	8.5	9.1
30–34	11.0	9.7	10.4
35–39	10.7	11.8	11.3
40–44	11.8	11.3	11.6
45–49	11.7	11.0	11.4
50–54	12.9	11.2	12.2
55–59	15.7	12.1	13.9
60+	19.1	16.8	18.1

South West
Median duration (weeks)

Age	Male	Female	All
Under 17	0.0	0.0	0.0
17	0.0	0.0	0.0
18	3.0	4.0	4.0
19	2.0	3.3	3.5
20–24	7.3	6.8	7.0
25–29	8.8	7.2	8.0
30–34	11.2	9.4	10.4
35–39	9.7	10.8	10.2
40–44	10.8	10.7	10.8
45–49	12.6	10.8	11.8
50–54	11.9	11.8	11.9
55–59	11.8	11.2	11.5
60+	14.2	13.5	13.9

England
Median duration (weeks)

Age	Male	Female	All
Under 17	10.5	0.0	13.0
17	0.0	0.0	2.0
18	3.7	1.8	3.2
19	4.9	5.8	5.4
20–24	7.7	6.7	7.3
25–29	10.1	8.6	9.4
30–34	12.5	10.9	11.8
35–39	15.0	13.3	14.3
40–44	15.6	14.2	15.1
45–49	17.8	15.2	16.8
50–54	19.6	15.8	18.2
55–59	23.0	17.6	20.7
60+	33.0	21.5	24.7

Wales
Median duration
(weeks)

Age	Male	Female	All
Under 17	0.0	0.0	0.0
17	0.0	0.0	0.0
18	1.5	0.0	1.5
19	13.0	3.0	5.0
20–24	6.1	6.2	6.2
25–29	9.8	9.8	9.8
30–34	15.5	11.7	13.5
35–39	13.4	13.5	13.6
40–44	15.6	10.7	13.9
45–49	22.1	14.7	19.1
50–54	18.2	15.8	17.3
55–59	21.4	18.6	20.3
60+	24.5	19.5	22.1

Scotland
Median duration
(weeks)

Age	Male	Female	All
Under 17	0.0	0.0	0.0
17	0.0	0.0	0.0
18	2.0	4.0	2.7
19	7.0	9.0	8.0
20–24	7.9	5.2	6.6
25–29	9.7	10.0	9.8
30–34	13.9	19.0	16.2
35–39	20.3	15.0	17.9
40–44	23.8	21.4	22.8
45–49	24.3	19.0	22.5
50–54	169.0	18.7	25.5
55–59	247.0	20.0	25.6
60+	#	29.2	178.6

Northern Ireland
Median duration
(weeks)

Age	Male	Female	All
Under 17	0.0	0.0	0.0
17	0.0	0.0	0.0
18	0.7	0.0	0.7
19	1.0	0.0	1.0
20–24	8.0	7.0	7.8
25–29	#	#	#
30–34	#	#	#
35–39	#	#	#
40–44	#	#	#
45–49	#	#	#
50–54	#	#	#
55–59	#	#	#
60+	#	#	#

United Kingdom
Median duration
(weeks)

Age	Male	Female	Al
Under 17	10.5	0.0	13.0
17	0.0	0.0	2.0
18	3.2	2.3	3.0
19	5.2	6.1	5.8
20–24	7.6	6.6	7.2
25–29	10.5	8.9	9.8
30–34	13.4	11.6	12.5
35–39	16.8	14.2	15.6
40–44	17.4	15.5	16.6
45–49	19.8	16.4	18.5
50–54	21.7	17.1	19.9
55–59	25.2	18.8	22.4
60+	127.0	22.9	31.2

These figures are suppressed by the ONS as they are classified as statistically unreliable.

Labour force survey - national and regional - headline indicators (seasonally adjusted)

ONS Crown Copyright Reserved [from Nomis on 10 May 2024]

date	Dec 2023-Feb 2024
sex	Male
value type	Level
rate	Rates

Area	All persons - aged 16 and over		All persons - aged 16 to 64		Total economically active - aged 16 to 64		Total in employment-aged 16 to 64		Total unemployed - aged 16 to 64	
	number	rate	number	rate	number	rate	number	rate	number	rate
England	22,528,307	-	17,625,800	-	14,392,082	81.7	13,744,792	78.0	647,290	4.5
Northern Ireland	737,802	-	581,659	-	448,935	77.2	437,435	75.2	11,500	2.6
Scotland	2,179,539	-	1,682,191	-	1,357,067	80.7	1,281,154	76.2	75,913	5.6
United Kingdom	26,698,175	-	20,828,675	-	16,905,459	81.2	16,144,240	77.5	761,219	4.5
Wales	1,252,527	-	939,025	-	707,374	75.3	680,858	72.5	26,516	3.7
East	2,522,640	-	1,934,627	-	1,598,142	82.6	1,528,061	79.0	70,080	4.4
East Midlands	1,969,527	-	1,514,545	-	1,259,032	83.1	1,180,125	77.9	78,906	6.3
London	3,442,421	-	2,959,974	-	2,409,708	81.4	2,312,232	78.1	97,476	4.0
North East	1,070,180	-	814,507	-	609,841	74.9	587,271	72.1	22,570	3.7
North West	2,971,702	-	2,318,658	-	1,857,179	80.1	1,761,897	76.0	95,283	5.1
South East	3,675,257	-	2,830,329	-	2,393,966	84.6	2,284,080	80.7	109,886	4.6
South West	2,311,506	-	1,708,584	-	1,418,593	83.0	1,373,889	80.4	44,704	3.2
West Midlands	2,370,688	-	1,842,684	-	1,512,926	82.1	1,433,130	77.8	79,797	5.3
Yorkshire and The Humber	2,194,386	-	1,701,892	-	1,332,696	78.3	1,284,107	75.5	48,589	3.6

- These figures are missing.

The employment rate is the number of people in employment divided by the population of the same age group. The unemployment rate is the number of unemployed people divided by the economically active population of the same age group. The inactivity rate is the number of inactive people divided by the population of the same age group.

Labour force survey - national and regional - headline indicators (seasonally adjusted)

ONS Crown Copyright Reserved [from Nomis on 10 May 2024]

date	Dec 2023-Feb 2024
sex	Female
value type	Level
rate	Rates

Area	All persons - aged 16 and over		All persons - aged 16 to 64		Total economically active - aged 16 to 64		Total in employment- aged 16 to 64		Total unemployed - aged 16 to 64	
	number	rate	number	rate	number	rate	number	rate	number	rate
England	23,858,224	-	18,219,282	-	13,675,380	75.1	13,101,435	71.9	573,945	4.2
Northern Ireland	772,742	-	596,678	-	415,299	69.6	407,395	68.3	7,904	1.9
Scotland	2,357,336	-	1,751,235	-	1,299,247	74.2	1,265,491	72.3	33,757	2.6
United Kingdom	28,311,867	-	21,535,639	-	16,054,929	74.6	15,412,042	71.6	642,887	4.0
Wales	1,323,565	-	968,444	-	665,003	68.7	637,722	65.9	27,281	4.1
East	2,666,140	-	1,990,719	-	1,509,726	75.8	1,463,453	73.5	46,273	3.1
East Midlands	2,058,451	-	1,548,989	-	1,130,345	73.0	1,067,548	68.9	62,797	5.6
London	3,731,170	-	3,144,892	-	2,387,974	75.9	2,285,655	72.7	102,318	4.3
North East	1,134,174	-	842,935	-	601,171	71.3	580,293	68.8	20,879	3.5
North West	3,123,035	-	2,379,524	-	1,720,875	72.3	1,625,729	68.3	95,146	5.5
South East	3,908,882	-	2,927,351	-	2,304,751	78.7	2,223,342	76.0	81,409	3.5
South West	2,449,713	-	1,762,133	-	1,360,273	77.2	1,311,423	74.4	48,851	3.6
West Midlands	2,478,508	-	1,875,411	-	1,374,823	73.3	1,309,160	69.8	65,663	4.8
Yorkshire and The Humber	2,308,151	-	1,747,328	-	1,285,442	73.6	1,234,832	70.7	50,610	3.9

- These figures are missing.

The employment rate is the number of people in employment divided by the population of the same age group. The unemployment rate is the number of unemployed people divided by the economically active population of the same age group. The inactivity rate is the number of inactive people divided by the population of the same age group.

Labour force survey - national and regional - headline indicators (seasonally adjusted)

date	Dec 2023-Feb 2024
sex	Female
value type	Level
rate	Rates

Area	All persons - aged 16 and over		All persons - aged 16 to 64		Total economically active - aged 16 to 64		Total in employment- aged 16 to 64		Total unemployed - aged 16 to 64	
	number	rate	number	rate	number	rate	number	rate	number	rate
England	46,386,531	-	35,845,082	-	28,067,462	78.3	26,846,227	74.9	1,221,235	4.4
Northern Ireland	1,510,544	-	1,178,337	-	864,234	73.3	844,830	71.7	19,404	2.2
Scotland	4,536,875	-	3,433,426	-	2,656,315	77.4	2,546,645	74.2	109,670	4.1
United Kingdom	55,010,042	-	42,364,314	-	32,960,388	77.8	31,556,283	74.5	1,404,106	4.3
Wales	2,576,092	-	1,907,469	-	1,372,377	71.9	1,318,580	69.1	53,797	3.9
East	5,188,780	-	3,925,346	-	3,107,868	79.2	2,991,515	76.2	116,353	3.7
East Midlands	4,027,978	-	3,063,534	-	2,389,377	78.0	2,247,674	73.4	141,703	5.9
London	7,173,591	-	6,104,866	-	4,797,681	78.6	4,597,887	75.3	199,794	4.2
North East	2,204,354	-	1,657,442	-	1,211,012	73.1	1,167,564	70.4	43,448	3.6
North West	6,094,737	-	4,698,182	-	3,578,054	76.2	3,387,626	72.1	190,429	5.3
South East	7,584,139	-	5,757,680	-	4,698,717	81.6	4,507,422	78.3	191,295	4.1
South West	4,761,219	-	3,470,717	-	2,778,866	80.1	2,685,312	77.4	93,555	3.4
West Midlands	4,849,196	-	3,718,095	-	2,887,749	77.7	2,742,290	73.8	145,459	5.0
Yorkshire and The Humber	4,502,537	-	3,449,220	-	2,618,138	75.9	2,518,939	73.0	99,199	3.8

- These figures are missing.

The employment rate is the number of people in employment divided by the population of the same age group. The unemployment rate is the number of unemployed people divided by the economically active population of the same age group. The inactivity rate is the number of inactive people divided by the population of the same age group.

Labour Force Survey

The tables report headline labour market indicators for the UK and its constituent regions and nations. These are reported for the working age population (16–64 years) and include the number economically active in the working age population, the number in employment or self-employment (or government employment scheme) and the number unemployed. The statistics are derived from the Labour Force Survey (LFS) for December 2023 to February 2024. Updated statistics are available on NOMIS (*www.nomisweb.co.uk*). The UK statistics are reported in Table A02 and the regional statistics are reported in Tables HI01–HI11.

Unemployment is defined using the ILO definition and includes those who were without work during the reference week but who are currently available for work and who were either actively seeking work in the past four weeks or who had already found a job to start within the next three months. This definition of unemployment is independent of whether or not the individual is eligible to claim benefit.

Those who are either employed or unemployed (and looking for work) are defined as economically active. The economically inactive are calculated by the difference between the estimate in col.1, the working age population and the estimate in col.2, the economically active working age population. Many people who are disabled will be inactive rather than unemployed.

Non-employment includes unemployment and inactivity. It is the difference between col.1 and col.5.

Claimant Count v ILO Unemployment

Along with a large number of other countries, the United Kingdom publishes two defined measures of unemployment that complement each other.

One comes from a monthly count of those claiming unemployment-related benefits. This administrative measure is known as the "Claimant Count".

The other comes from a quarterly survey of households, the Labour Force Survey (LFS). This survey measure is accepted as an international standard because it is based on methods recommended by the International Labour Organisation (ILO). It is known as the *p* and is used by the European Union (EU) and the Organisation for Economic Co-operation and Development (OECD).

Both measures have their advantages and disadvantages.

The advantage of the Claimant Count is that it is available quickly and monthly and because it is a 100 per cent count, it also provides precise information on very small areas.

The ILO measure on the other hand, as well as being internationally standard, springs from a data source (the Labour Force Survey) which allows unemployment to be analysed in the context of other labour market information and a variety of demographic characteristics.

A disadvantage of the Claimant Count is that it can be affected if there are changes to the benefit system from which it is derived.

Although changes in the benefit system may also affect the labour market behaviour of respondents to the LFS, the ILO definition itself is entirely independent of the benefit system. Comparatively the LFS results, based on the ILO measure, are not reliable for areas smaller than counties or the larger local authority districts, because of sample size restrictions. Estimates of less than 10,000 persons unemployed (after grossing up) are not shown in published tables because they are subject to unacceptably high sampling error and are, therefore, unreliable.

This said, government statistics apply recognised statistical procedures in order to minimise these disadvantages and maintain the relevance of both measures as accurate labour market indicators.

Claimant Count Rates (as of March 2024)

Area	2010	2011	2012	2013	2014	2015	2016	2017	2018	2019	2020	2021	2022	2023	2024
North East	6.7	4.7	5.4	5.4	4.2	4.0	3.9	3.3	3.9	4.3	7.6	7.2	4.7	4.2	3.9
North West	5.2	4.0	4.4	4.2	3.2	2.2	2.7	2.5	3.1	3.3	7.7	7.0	4.7	4.2	4.2
Yorkshire and the Humber	5.6	4.2	4.7	4.7	3.8	3.2	2.6	2.3	2.7	3.0	6.9	6.6	4.4	4.0	4.2
East Midlands	4.6	3.4	3.7	3.6	2.7	2.2	1.7	1.6	1.9	2.3	5.8	5.5	3.6	3.3	3.4
West Midlands	5.9	4.6	4.7	4.5	3.6	3.0	2.8	2.4	3.0	3.4	7.6	7.4	5.2	4.8	4.9
East	3.8	2.9	3.0	3.0	2.2	1.6	1.4	1.4	1.7	2.0	5.8	5.5	3.4	2.8	3.1
London	4.5	4.0	4.1	3.9	2.9	2.1	1.9	2.1	2.4	2.7	8.2	8.5	5.3	4.7	5.1
South East	3.1	2.5	2.5	2.4	1.8	1.3	1.2	1.2	1.5	1.8	5.8	5.3	3.2	2.8	2.9
South West	3.1	2.5	2.6	2.5	1.9	1.3	1.3	1.4	1.8	2.0	5.9	5.0	3.0	2.4	2.6
England	4.5	3.7	3.9	3.7	2.9	2.1	2.0	1.9	2.3	2.6	6.8	6.5	4.2	3.7	3.9
Wales	5.2	3.8	4.0	4.0	3.4	3.2	2.6	2.0	2.5	2.8	6.3	4.9	3.7	3.3	3.2
Scotland	4.9	4.0	4.2	4.0	3.2	2.9	2.7	2.3	2.9	3.0	6.2	6.1	3.6	3.1	3.0
Northern Ireland	6.4	6.1	5.3	5.5	4.9	5.1	3.5	2.5	2.4	2.5	5.5	6.4	3.2	3.0	3.1
United Kingdom	**4.6**	**3.7**	**3.9**	**3.7**	**2.9**	**2.3**	**2.1**	**2.0**	**2.4**	**2.7**	**6.7**	**5.8**	**4.1**	**3.6**	**3.8**

Percentages, seasonally adjusted annual averages

ILO Unemployment Rates (Dec 2023-Feb 2024 - 16+)

Area	2010	2011	2012	2013	2014	2015	2016	2017	2018	2019	2020	2021	2022	2023	2024
North East	10.2	9.8	10.8	10.0	9.7	7.7	6.8	5.4	4.6	5.7	5.2	5.7	5.4	4.2	3.6
North West	7.7	8.5	9.5	8.2	8.3	6.2	4.9	4.2	4.1	3.7	4.1	5.3	4.3	3.8	5.1
Yorkshire and the Humber	9.3	8.7	9.7	9.3	8.8	6.0	5.3	5.1	4.4	4.9	3.9	4.9	4.2	3.5	3.6
East Midlands	8.0	7.9	8.3	8.0	7.2	5.0	4.3	4.1	4.0	4.3	3.7	5.1	2.8	3.5	5.9
West Midlands	9.9	8.7	8.5	9.5	8.4	6.5	5.6	5.9	5.1	5.0	4.8	5.5	5.1	4.6	4.9
East	6.2	6.7	6.6	6.9	5.9	5.1	4.4	4.1	3.6	3.0	3.6	3.8	3.2	4.0	3.6
London	9.4	9.4	8.9	8.7	8.2	6.2	5.6	6	5.2	4.3	4.6	7.2	4.6	4.7	4.4
South East	6.3	5.7	6.3	6.8	5.3	4.5	3.5	3.5	3.4	3.0	3.0	3.4	3.4	3.9	4.0
South West	6.3	5.7	5.9	6.4	6.0	4.5	3.6	3.4	3.3	2.7	3.0	4.1	2.9	2.3	3.2
England	7.9	7.8	8.1	8.0	7.3	5.6	4.7	4.6	4.2	3.9	3.9	5.0	4.0	3.9	4.3
Wales	8.7	7.9	9.0	8.3	6.9	6.2	4.4	4.8	4.4	4.4	3.0	4.8	3.0	3.5	3.7
Scotland	8.1	7.7	7.9	7.5	7.1	5.9	4.7	4	4.3	3.3	4.6	4.4	3.5	3.0	4.0
Northern Ireland	8.0	7.1	6.9	8.3	7.7	6.0	5.7	5.4	3.3	3.1	2.3	3.7	2.5	2.4	2.2
United Kingdom	**8.0**	**7.8**	**8.1**	**8.0**	**7.3**	**5.6**	**4.7**	**4.6**	**4.2**	**3.8**	**3.9**	**4.9**	**3.8**	**3.8**	**4.2**

Percentages, Spring each year, seasonally adjusted

F6: Average weekly earnings index

Average weekly earnings index

Whole economy, excluding bonuses and arrears of pay, and seasonally adjusted.

These figures show the level estimates for the whole economy, seasonally adjusted, and expressed as an index, based to 2000 = 100. This index is used to measure wages growth.

AWE is published as a level of earnings, in pounds per employee per week. To meet user demand, main AWE series are also published as indices, based to 2000 = 100. These indices are calculated by dividing AWE for the current month by the average of the months in 2000 and multiplying by 100.

	2003	2004	2005	2006	2007	2008	2009
January	110.8	114.6	119.3	124.2	128.9	134.2	138.0
February	111.1	114.7	119.5	124.6	129.4	134.8	138.3
March	111.3	115.1	120.2	124.8	130.0	135.3	138.2
April	111.7	115.6	120.6	125.0	130.1	136.3	138.7
May	112.0	116.0	120.8	125.7	131.0	135.9	138.9
June	112.2	116.3	121.2	126.3	131.6	136.3	139.0
July	112.5	116.7	121.9	126.3	132.1	136.7	138.6
August	112.9	117.2	122.4	126.5	132.7	137.0	138.8
September	113.3	117.4	122.8	127.1	132.9	137.3	139.1
October	113.6	118.0	123.0	127.9	132.9	137.8	139.2
November	114.0	118.3	123.3	128.2	133.6	137.9	139.3
December	114.5	119.1	123.6	128.7	133.8	138.0	139.8
Yearly Average	112.5	116.6	121.6	126.3	131.6	136.5	138.8

	2010	2011	2012	2013	2014	2015	2016
January	140.5	143.6	145.0	146.6	149.2	151.5	155.0
February	140.4	143.3	145.8	146.8	148.6	152.1	155.6
March	141.1	143.4	146.2	147.0	148.5	152.7	155.4
April	140.7	143.6	146.0	148.0	148.7	152.9	156.7
May	140.6	143.8	146.3	147.9	148.9	153.1	156.2
June	141.0	143.8	146.6	147.9	149.2	153.4	156.7
July	141.6	144.0	146.6	148.1	149.3	153.6	156.9
August	141.9	144.1	147.2	148.1	149.7	153.6	157.2
September	142.2	144.6	146.8	148.0	150.7	153.5	157.7
October	142.3	144.9	146.8	148.3	151.2	153.7	157.8
November	142.6	145.2	147.3	148.3	150.9	154.2	158.4
December	142.5	145.2	147.0	148.9	151.3	154.5	158.1
Yearly Average	141.5	144.1	146.5	147.8	149.7	153.2	156.8

	2017	2018	2019	2020	2021	2022	2023
January	158.1	162.0	167.9	172.4	179.7	187.5	199.9
February	158.3	162.4	167.7	172.5	180.3	187.8	201.4
March	158.6	163.0	168.0	172.0	180.6	188.5	202.4
April	159.2	163.0	169.7	169.6	182.2	189.5	203.9
May	159.7	163.6	170.0	169.7	182.3	191.3	206.1
June	159.9	164.0	170.6	170.4	182.4	191.7	207.2
July	160.2	164.8	171.0	172.7	182.8	192.9	208.0
August	160.8	165.5	171.3	174.8	183.5	194.1	209.0
September	161.1	165.7	171.6	176.7	184.0	195.2	209.8
October	161.5	166.6	171.8	178.0	184.8	196.8	208.7
November	161.8	166.9	172.1	179.2	185.5	198.0	210.3
December	162.3	167.2	172.4	179.9	186.4	198.6	211.1
Yearly Average	162.3	164.5	170.3	174.0	182.9	192.7	206.5

F6: Average weekly earnings index

	2024
January	211.8
February	213.4
March	214.9
April	215.8
May	216.8
June	217.6
July	
August	
September	
October	
November	
December	
Yearly Average	

ONS index reference: K54L – whole economy

F7: Average weekly earnings

These figures are the average (mean and median) gross weekly earnings of full-time employees on adult rates whose pay was not affected by absence. They are collected and published by the Office for National Statistics (ONS) in the Annual Survey of Hours and Earnings (ASHE).

	Mean		Median	
	Men	Women	Men	Women
	£	£	£	£
1997	408.7	297.2	349.7	260.5
1998	427.1	309.6	362.8	270.0
1999	442.4	326.5	374.3	284.0
2000	453.3	337.6	389.7	296.7
2001	490.3	366.9	407.3	313.2
2002	513.8	383.2	421.2	327.1
2003	525.0	396.0	431.9	338.6
2004	556.8	420.2	463.0	360.8
2005	569.0	435.2	471.0	435.6
2006	589.8	450.0	487.1	453.0
2007	605.0	463.8	498.3	394.8
2008	634.0	484.4	522.0	412.4
2009	643.0	501.2	531.0	425.8
2010	653.3	513.1	538.2	439.0
2011	658.4	515.5	538.2	440.0
2012	660.7	525.1	546.0	448.9
2013	677.0	533.0	556.2	458.9
2014	674.0	539.3	558.6	461.5
2015	680.3	546.2	567.2	470.2
2016	699.3	562.3	577.5	480.5
2017	715.9	577.7	590.9	493.2
2018	742.8	598.1	608.2	509.0
2019	760.0	620.2	629.2	527.9
2020	754.6	640.1	617.5	543.5
2021	780.5	649.2	650.7	558.5
2022	811.3	681.4	683.2	587.7
2023 (p)	857.9	728.0	725.0	628.9

The above ASHE figures are taken from Table 14.1a (revised) other than the latest year which is provisional (p).

F8: Average earnings statistics

Introductory notes

1. It will usually be possible to obtain agreement, or a direction, that the earnings shown in the Annual Survey of Hours and Earnings (ASHE) may be adduced in evidence without formal proof but occasionally it may be necessary to adduce formal proof. This is done by calling a witness from the Office for National Statistics (ONS).

2. ASHE provides information about the levels, distribution and make-up of earnings and hours of paid work for employees. The data are collected and published by the ONS. ASHE replaced the New Earnings Survey (NES) in 2004.

3. ASHE is based upon a one per cent sample of employees taken from HM Revenue and Customs PAYE records. ASHE does not cover the self-employed nor employees not paid in the reference period.

4. ASHE is collected in April of each year and is published as a first release the following Oct/Nov/Dec. A second and final release is published in Oct/Nov/Dec a year later and includes any revisions to the estimates which may be required. The revisions are usually small.

5. The Tables reproduced here relate to a sample restricted to full-time employees on adult rates of pay whose pay was not affected by absence for weekly pay and, for annual pay, who have been employed in the same job for more than a year. The estimates are disaggregated by sex and by a four-digit occupational classification. They are provisional first release estimates for 2023. They were published by the ONS on 1 November 2023.

6. The earnings information relates to weekly and annual gross pay before tax, national insurance or other deductions and excludes payments in kind. Earnings are reported for full-time employees who are defined as those who work more than 30 paid hours per week.

7. Two measures of typical earnings are reported, the mean and median. The median is ONS's preferred measure of average earnings as it is less affected by the relatively small number of very high earners which skews the distribution of earnings. The median provides a better indication of typical earnings than does the mean.

8. Earnings are reported by occupational codes. It is helpful to understand the Standard Occupational Classification (SOC) as an ordered taxonomy of jobs in which narrowly defined jobs at the four-digit level (unit groups) are included within a wider definition at the three-digit level which in turn are included within a wider category at the two-digit level and a still wider category at the one-digit level. The hierarchy is based upon the type of job and on the level of skill. The tables reported here use SOC 2020. There are 412 four-digit occupational unit groups in SOC 2020 which cluster to form 104 minor groups, 26 sub-major groups and nine major groups. As an example, Rail Travel Assistants, 6215, are included within the three-digit group Leisure and Travel Services (621) and at the two-digit level, within Leisure, Travel and Related Personal Service Occupations (62), and, at the one-digit level, within Caring, Leisure and other Personal Service Occupations (6). n.e.c. stands for "not elsewhere classified".

9. Reclassification of occupational categories occurs every ten years and occurred as an additional release between the first release ASHE 2021 and the final release ASHE 2021. ASHE first release estimates for 2023 are published according to SOC 2020.

10. Statistics derived from samples are called "estimates" because they estimate the population parameters that we are interested in. All sample estimates are subject to a degree of unreliability due to sampling variation. This is measured by ONS in the form of the coefficient of variation (CV) and is published in the series of Tables b which accompany the sample estimates in the series of Tables a. The CV is the ratio of the standard error of the estimate to the estimate itself. The smaller is the CV, the higher the precision (or quality) of the estimate. The ONS defines four standards of reliability in relation to the size of the CV: less than five per cent, 5–10 per cent, 10 to 20 per cent and greater than 20 per cent. An estimate with a CV of less than five per cent is the most reliable. Estimates with CVs of greater than 20 per cent are considered insufficiently reliable and are not published. Those in-between are shaded in the ONS publication, though not in the reproduction here.

11. Tables of ASHE estimates are published online where alternative breakdowns can be found, for example by region, age group, industrial sector etc. and at 10 points across the earnings distribution. In Oct/Nov/Dec 2024, the estimates published online for 2023 will be the revised final release ones. A further advantage of the online source is the shading according to the levels of reliability referred to in para.10 above. The tables can be found on the website of the ONS. Step-by-step instructions to find the estimates produced here are provided below. You need not follow these step-by-step instructions each time you consult the tables as you can either download the tables as an Excel file or you can save the web link.

12. Find the home page of the ONS at: *https://www.ONS.gov.uk.*

13. Type ASHE 2023 Table 14 in the search box at the top of this page and click Search.

14. Refine the search using the menu on the left-hand side by checking the boxes for Data and then Datasets.

15. From the list of tables select the table title Earnings and hours worked, occupation by four-digit SOC:ASHE Table14 released on 1 November 2023. Clicking on the table title will open a list of zip files by year.

16. Opening the zip file will produce a contents list of Excel files each of which contains different tables of earnings estimates.

17. Weekly pay by occupational group is in Occupation SOC20 (4) Table 14.1a Weekly pay—Gross 2023. A double click on the table title will take you to a worksheet in an Excel file. If you are sure that you have located the file that you want, save it using file save in Excel. Weekly pay is measured for the reference week in April 2023.

18. Annual pay by occupational group is in Table 14.7a Annual Pay—Gross 2023. A double click on the table title will take you to a worksheet in an Excel file. Annual estimates are provided for the tax year that ended in April 2023.

19. Once in the Excel file, check the bottom tabs. Choose "Male Full-time" or "Female Full-time" to view the tables reproduced here. The median is reported in column 3 and the mean in column 5.

20. Note that all files marked with a file extension "b" report the coefficient of variation on the estimate (see 10. above).

21. The shading indicates the reliability of the estimate. Where the estimate of the sampling error is less than five per cent, there is no shading. The key to the shading can be found at the bottom and at the right-hand side of the table. The shading is not reproduced here.

22. If you have not already saved this file at step 17 above, this table can be saved now either in part or in full. If the file is saved prior to the revised release, make a note that the 2023 estimates are provisional. They will be replaced in the revised release in Oct/Nov/Dec 2024.

Gross pay for full-time male employees in the UK on adult rates where pay was not affected by absence 2023

n.e.c. = not elsewhere classified
X = not reported cv <20%
.. = disclosive
: not applicable

Occupation SOC 2020	Code	Gross Weekly Pay in April 2023			Gross Annual Pay April 2022-2023		
		Number of jobs (thousand)	Median £	Mean £	Number of jobs (thousand)	Median £	Mean £
All employees		11,832	725.0	857.9	9,976	37,382	45,612
Managers, directors and senior officials	1	1,646	1,015.7	1,238.9	1,460	52,184	70,972
Corporate managers and directors	11	1,319	1,143.1	1,342.3	1,170	58,730	77,545
Chief Executives and Senior Officials	111	68	1,602.5	1,950.0	61	89,135	131,161
Chief executives and senior officials	1111	65	1,626.5	2,003.0	57	90,524	136,417
Elected officers and representatives	1112	x	x	x	x	x	x
Production Managers and Directors	112	490	1,041.4	1,207.1	438	52,961	65,258
Production managers and directors in manufacturing	1121	384	1,054.1	1,243.5	347	53,525	67,407
Production managers and directors in construction	1122	98	996.6	1,053.8	83	51,431	55,258
Production managers and directors in mining and energy	1123	9	974.5	1,319.9	x	52,407	x
Functional Managers and Directors	113	527	1,437.4	1,589.9	465	76,269	94,907
Financial managers and directors	1131	222	1,533.2	1,717.0	196	81,509	102,749
Marketing, sales and advertising directors	1132	140	1,589.6	1,631.0	122	87,918	97,137
Public relations and communications directors	1133	x	1,509.9	1,868.8	x	87,736	x
Purchasing managers and directors	1134	34	1,039.5	1,106.5	x	x	60,289
Charitable organisation managers and directors	1135	x	x	819.1	x	x	42,859
Human resource managers and directors	1136	46	1,046.3	1,184.9	x	x	64,577
Information technology directors	1137	35	1,544.0	1,610.1	31	79,676	92,262
Functional managers and directors n.e.c.	1139	43	1,417.3	1,581.5	38	73,431	91,739
Directors in Logistics, Warehousing and Transport	114	8	1,371.4	1,650.5	x	x	x
Directors in logistics, warehousing and transport	1140	8	1,371.4	1,650.5	x	x	x
Managers and Directors in Retail and Wholesale	115	213	697.8	837.2	189	35,835	45,350
Managers and directors in retail and wholesale	1150	213	697.8	837.2	189	35,835	45,350
Senior Officers in Protective Services	116	10	1,173.6	1,284.5	9	61,444	66,935
Officers in armed forces	1161	:			:		
Senior police officers	1162	x	1,183.6	1,311.6	x	61,220	67,457
Senior officers in fire, ambulance, prison and related services	1163	x	1,146.8	1,250.0	x	x	66,290
Health and Social Services Managers and Directors	117	x	x	1,293.4	x	x	x
Health services and public health managers and directors	1171	x	x	1,351.9	x	x	x
Social services managers and directors	1172	x	x	x	x	x	x
Other managers and proprietors	12	327	723.7	821.5	290	37,796	44,459
Managers and Proprietors in Agriculture Related Services	121	18	689.9	740.8	17	36,003	37,483
Managers and proprietors in agriculture and horticulture	1211	13	696.9	768.2	13	36,339	38,603
Managers and proprietors in forestry, fishing and related services	1212	x	631.1	673.5	x	32,663	34,593
Managers and Proprietors in Hospitality and Leisure Services	122	54	637.8	708.7	44	33,801	38,247
Hotel and accommodation managers and proprietors	1221	8	633.9	x	x	32,427	x
Restaurant and catering establishment managers and proprietors	1222	21	629.1	636.4	17	33,868	32,313
Publicans and managers of licensed premises	1223	8	603.5	643.1	x	32,271	33,075
Leisure and sports managers	1224	17	666.8	732.6	14	34,897	38,423
Travel agency managers and proprietors	1225	..			x	x	37,695
Managers and Proprietors in Health and Care Services	123	14	820.9	1,068.2	12	43,132	x
Health care practice managers	1231	x	x	x	x	x	x
Residential, day and domiciliary care managers and proprietors	1232	12	820.9	993.6	10	42,485	x

Gross pay for full-time male employees in the UK on adult rates where pay was not affected by absence 2023

n.e.c. = not elsewhere classified
X = not reported cv <20%
.. = disclosive
: not applicable

Occupation SOC 2020	Code	Gross Weekly Pay in April 2023 Number of jobs (thousand)	Median £	Mean £	Gross Annual Pay April 2022-2023 Number of jobs (thousand)	Median £	Mean £
Early education and childcare services proprietors	1233	:			:		
Managers in Logistics, Warehousing and Transport	124	142	709.8	776.8	128	36,956	40,658
Managers in transport and distribution	1241	51	802.7	862.4	47	41,598	45,038
Managers in storage and warehousing	1242	74	651.6	682.0	67	33,680	35,892
Managers in logistics	1243	17	824.1	934.0	15	41,654	48,433
Managers and Proprietors in Other Services	125	99	795.0	927.6	89	42,307	50,482
Property, housing and estate managers	1251	62	782.6	881.4	56	42,190	47,891
Garage managers and proprietors	1252	x	757.8	971.9	x	x	x
Hairdressing and beauty salon managers and proprietors	1253	x	x	768.3	x	x	x
Waste disposal and environmental services managers	1254	x	905.6	932.8	x	x	49,751
Managers and directors in the creative industries	1255	x	842.4	941.6	x	x	50,577
Betting shop and gambling establishment managers	1256	..			..		
Hire services managers and proprietors	1257	x	580.5	688.0	x	x	40,321
Directors in consultancy services	1258	x	x	x	x	x	x
Managers and proprietors in other services n.e.c.	1259	13	790.4	1,064.6	12	40,142	x
Professional occupations	2	3,696	907.4	996.2	3,088	46,164	51,937
Science, research, engineering and technology professionals	21	1,481	922.1	989.6	1,239	47,505	51,592
Natural and Social Science Professionals	211	74	800.7	847.7	56	44,005	50,131
Chemical scientists	2111	14	618.2	692.9	x	39,852	42,064
Biological scientists	2112	x	623.9	793.5	x	x	44,633
Biochemists and biomedical scientists	2113	15	851.2	977.1	12	47,458	x
Physical scientists	2114	x	959.3	983.0	x	51,816	52,157
Social and humanities scientists	2115	x	613.2	660.7	x	35,606	34,692
Natural and social science professionals n.e.c.	2119	22	855.8	893.1	17	43,237	50,580
Engineering Professionals	212	434	911.2	946.2	370	46,886	49,030
Civil engineers	2121	71	872.8	925.9	58	45,642	48,657
Mechanical engineers	2122	39	852.8	889.0	33	42,290	45,300
Electrical engineers	2123	45	1,064.4	1,112.3	40	54,001	58,384
Electronics engineers	2124	12	959.5	988.8	x	50,026	51,532
Production and process engineers	2125	51	860.9	895.8	43	44,725	46,394
Aerospace engineers	2126	11	975.8	962.7	x	46,309	48,832
Engineering project managers and project engineers	2127	77	957.6	993.9	67	49,145	52,342
Engineering professionals n.e.c.	2129	128	855.2	902.3	106	43,714	45,593
Information Technology Professionals	213	837	976.1	1,045.1	698	50,000	54,030
IT project managers	2131	22	1,087.0	1,091.1	18	55,547	55,833
IT managers	2132	182	1,030.4	1,086.3	162	52,009	56,772
IT business analysts, architects and systems designers	2133	140	1,046.0	1,100.4	117	53,071	57,576
Programmers and software development professionals	2134	353	978.4	1,047.8	277	50,024	53,543
Cyber security professionals	2135	22	852.7	923.5	16	45,787	50,632
IT quality and testing professionals	2136	12	780.1	780.4	x	39,072	39,705
IT network professionals	2137	41	826.4	877.3	38	42,906	45,485
Information technology professionals n.e.c.	2139	64	880.0	975.6	59	45,041	50,114
Web and Multimedia Design Professionals	214	45	594.7	672.7	x	x	36,954
Web design professionals	2141	x	858.3	909.0	x	x	x
Graphic and multimedia designers	2142	36	574.9	618.6	x	x	32,480
Conservation and Environment Professionals	215	39	728.3	774.4	34	37,851	40,159
Conservation professionals	2151	10	730.2	770.2	x	38,317	41,092
Environment professionals	2152	29	720.3	775.8	27	37,734	39,886

Gross pay for full-time male employees in the UK on adult rates where pay was not affected by absence 2023

n.e.c. = not elsewhere classified X = not reported cv <20% .. = disclosive : not applicable **Occupation SOC 2020**	**Code**	**Gross Weekly Pay in April 2023** **Number of jobs (thousand)**	**Median £**	**Mean £**	**Gross Annual Pay April 2022-2023** **Number of jobs (thousand)**	**Median £**	**Mean £**
Research and Development (R&D) and Other Research Professionals	216	53	1,032.4	1,090.9	45	50,336	57,081
Research and development (R&D) managers	2161	46	1,063.4	1,117.7	39	54,293	58,859
Other researchers, unspecified discipline	2162	x	844.9	915.9	x	41,568	44,265
Health professionals	22	422	913.6	1,043.7	328	45,747	53,468
Medical Practitioners	221	128	1,225.6	1,454.3	93	64,907	78,983
Generalist medical practitioners	2211	29	873.6	932.8	19	41,888	45,067
Specialist medical practitioners	2212	99	1,346.5	1,604.3	74	71,888	87,844
Therapy Professionals	222	39	783.7	800.1	29	40,871	41,289
Physiotherapists	2221	21	798.4	828.4	17	40,683	41,822
Occupational therapists	2222	x	722.5	756.6	x	x	38,628
Speech and language therapists	2223	..			..		
Psychotherapists and cognitive behaviour therapists	2224	x	x	697.3	x	x	37,981
Clinical psychologists	2225	x	x	883.9	..		
Other psychologists	2226	x	x	850.4	x	x	44,154
Therapy professionals n.e.c.	2229	x	647.7	721.1	x	x	38,648
Nursing Professionals	223	169	793.0	843.7	135	39,877	40,756
Midwifery nurses	2231	x	x	808.8	x	x	40,048
Community nurses	2232	x	786.9	821.1	x	37,753	38,184
Specialist nurses	2233	9	852.5	873.3	x	40,881	43,244
Nurse practitioners	2234	18	808.6	859.2	14	42,261	43,623
Mental health nurses	2235	x	x	874.4	x	x	42,263
Children's nurses	2236	..			:		
Other nursing professionals	2237	128	777.9	841.1	103	38,861	40,296
Veterinarians	224	x	978.9	1,070.6	x	x	51,694
Veterinarians	2240	x	978.9	1,070.6	x	x	51,694
Other Health Professionals	225	81	916.5	929.0	66	48,357	49,088
Pharmacists	2251	16	950.5	1,021.7	12	49,892	53,337
Optometrists	2252	x	x	861.4	x	x	50,085
Dental practitioners	2253	x	x	x	..		
Medical radiographers	2254	12	866.8	907.3	x	45,310	47,433
Paramedics	2255	27	971.9	967.2	24	50,793	50,271
Podiatrists	2256	x	x	827.6	x	x	40,441
Other health professionals n.e.c.	2259	22	814.1	842.3	17	43,656	45,744
Teaching and other educational professionals	23	513	908.1	964.4	482	44,456	47,411
Teaching Professionals	231	459	897.6	932.7	431	43,862	45,769
Higher education teaching professionals	2311	112	1,012.7	1,065.6	99	50,242	53,402
Further education teaching professionals	2312	34	769.0	815.6	32	40,957	41,521
Secondary education teaching professionals	2313	189	911.6	925.6	184	44,862	45,525
Primary education teaching professionals	2314	98	843.2	891.9	92	41,373	42,130
Nursery education teaching professionals	2315	x	858.4	892.0	x	x	40,591
Special needs education teaching professionals	2316	x	710.5	745.9	x	x	35,114
Teachers of English as a foreign language	2317	x	x	725.4	x	x	38,376
Teaching professionals n.e.c.	2319	13	597.2	640.7	x	32,615	33,099
Other Educational Professionals	232	53	1,057.1	1,237.0	51	53,300	61,293
Head teachers and principals	2321	22	1,423.6	1,646.0	21	71,691	80,862
Education managers	2322	16	944.4	1,026.4	15	42,485	50,576
Education advisers and school inspectors	2323	x	788.2	813.5	x	x	40,113
Early education and childcare services managers	2324	x	x	649.2	x	x	31,544
Other educational professionals n.e.c	2329	x	881.8	989.8	x	44,555	51,688
Business, media and public service professionals	24	1,280	884.9	1,000.8	1,039	45,594	53,967
Legal Professionals	241	76	958.2	1,264.1	64	x	71,982
Barristers and judges	2411	x	1,100.0	1,116.3	x	x	58,616
Solicitors and lawyers	2412	50	1,050.9	1,440.0	x	x	x
Legal professionals n.e.c.	2419	20	531.2	865.6	15	26,729	x
Finance Professionals	242	200	852.8	1,000.6	158	44,647	57,509
Chartered and certified accountants	2421	58	933.1	980.1	49	48,139	53,716
Finance and investment analysts and advisers	2422	126	808.6	1,005.7	96	42,323	59,890

Gross pay for full-time male employees in the UK on adult rates where pay was not affected by absence 2023

n.e.c. = not elsewhere classified
X = not reported cv <20%
.. = disclosive
: not applicable

Occupation SOC 2020	Code	Gross Weekly Pay in April 2023 – Number of jobs (thousand)	Gross Weekly Pay in April 2023 – Median £	Gross Weekly Pay in April 2023 – Mean £	Gross Annual Pay April 2022-2023 – Number of jobs (thousand)	Gross Annual Pay April 2022-2023 – Median £	Gross Annual Pay April 2022-2023 – Mean £
Taxation experts	2423	16	1,026.0	1,034.8	13	52,405	54,267
Business, Research and Administrative Professionals	243	363	914.7	1,014.3	284	48,022	55,604
Management consultants and business analysts	2431	180	955.0	1,059.6	140	50,244	58,386
Marketing and commercial managers	2432	57	958.2	1,035.9	48	47,666	55,058
Actuaries, economists and statisticians	2433	25	865.0	1,001.6	17	47,816	57,131
Business and related research professionals	2434	52	756.9	818.2	40	36,983	47,371
Professional/Chartered company secretaries	2435	..			..		
Business, research and administrative professionals n.e.c.	2439	49	1,048.0	1,029.6	40	53,623	53,902
Business and Financial Project Management Professionals	244	212	1,103.2	1,160.8	172	55,802	60,136
Business and financial project management professionals	2440	212	1,103.2	1,160.8	172	55,802	60,136
Architects, Chartered Architectural Technologists, Planning Officers, Surveyors and Construction Professionals	245	186	836.0	902.9	155	42,767	47,000
Architects	2451	25	886.5	953.5	22	46,082	49,138
Chartered architectural technologists, planning officers and consultants	2452	12	729.9	773.1	x	39,573	41,308
Quantity surveyors	2453	39	955.9	1,043.5	33	46,728	51,644
Chartered surveyors	2454	74	785.2	841.5	59	41,122	44,845
Construction project managers and related professionals	2455	36	824.3	884.9	31	40,627	46,488
Welfare Professionals	246	58	630.6	671.8	49	32,002	34,402
Social workers	2461	23	780.0	794.2	18	41,274	41,234
Probation officers	2462	x	x	620.0	..		
Clergy	2463	29	529.3	571.8	26	28,027	29,272
Youth work professionals	2464	x	x	812.2	x	x	40,556
Welfare professionals n.e.c.	2469	x	694.7	686.6	x	x	35,787
Librarians and Related Professionals	247	x	639.2	734.8	x	33,263	37,802
Librarians	2471	x	x	824.4	x	x	43,165
Archivists and curators	2472	x	x	653.8	x	x	33,325
Quality and Regulatory Professionals	248	122	826.4	911.3	99	41,987	47,857
Quality control and planning engineers	2481	45	787.0	828.3	38	40,629	41,996
Quality assurance and regulatory professionals	2482	70	864.4	979.3	57	42,948	52,349
Environmental health professionals	2483	x	770.4	767.2	x	x	41,500
Media Professionals	249	56	815.9	849.9	50	x	44,479
Newspaper and periodical editors	2491	13	820.2	812.0	x	42,284	43,167
Newspaper and periodical journalists and reporters	2492	12	779.9	789.4	x	42,154	41,627
Public relations professionals	2493	14	724.3	779.6	x	38,373	40,714
Advertising accounts managers and creative directors	2494	18	891.8	975.3	x	x	49,980
Associate professional occupations	3	2,042	706.3	821.8	1,705	37,499	44,562
Science, engineering and technology associate professionals	31	592	650.6	693.6	505	33,320	35,778
Science, Engineering and Production Technicians	311	341	666.4	705.0	300	34,112	36,048
Laboratory technicians	3111	24	487.4	558.9	18	25,354	29,645
Electrical and electronics technicians	3112	11	705.2	789.6	x	34,417	39,861
Engineering technicians	3113	69	794.5	821.6	60	40,042	41,917
Building and civil engineering technicians	3114	x	599.7	672.5	x	x	34,259
Quality assurance technicians	3115	19	591.7	644.1	18	29,649	30,993
Planning, process and production technicians	3116	39	670.3	718.4	34	34,517	37,150
Science, engineering and production technicians n.e.c.	3119	174	650.2	679.0	156	33,105	34,704
CAD, Drawing and Architectural Technicians	312	37	637.0	690.2	31	32,058	35,629

Gross pay for full-time male employees in the UK on adult rates where pay was not affected by absence 2023

n.e.c. = not elsewhere classified X = not reported cv <20% .. = disclosive : not applicable		Gross Weekly Pay in April 2023			Gross Annual Pay April 2022-2023		
Occupation SOC 2020	**Code**	**Number of jobs (thousand)**	**Median £**	**Mean £**	**Number of jobs (thousand)**	**Median £**	**Mean £**
CAD, drawing and architectural technicians	3120	37	637.0	690.2	31	32,058	35,629
Information Technology Technicians	313	214	623.9	676.0	174	32,701	35,339
IT operations technicians	3131	65	622.3	684.0	56	31,221	35,706
IT user support technicians	3132	135	629.1	672.6	106	32,983	35,227
Database administrators and web content technicians	3133	14	612.6	671.3	12	31,117	34,648
Health and social care associate professionals	32	93	549.6	573.8	73	27,516	28,743
Health Associate Professionals	321	12	523.6	581.0	x	26,779	29,665
Dispensing opticians	3211	..			x	x	26,035
Pharmaceutical technicians	3212	x	x	554.8	x	x	29,779
Medical and dental technicians	3213	8	528.9	604.4	x	27,616	30,717
Complementary health associate professionals	3214	..			..		
Health associate professionals n.e.c.	3219	..			..		
Welfare and Housing Associate Professionals	322	75	554.2	578.1	57	28,670	28,965
Youth and community workers	3221	24	575.5	595.2	19	29,015	30,474
Child and early years officers	3222	x	524.8	555.8	x	25,698	27,762
Housing officers	3223	14	615.4	636.0	x	31,898	30,923
Counsellors	3224	x	x	579.5	x	x	31,440
Welfare and housing associate professionals n.e.c.	3229	27	524.3	540.2	20	25,265	26,658
Teaching and Childcare Associate Professionals	323	x	477.2	502.3	x	x	23,852
Higher level teaching assistants	3231	x	x	497.8	x	x	23,773
Early education and childcare practitioners	3232	x	x	508.5	x	x	23,990
Veterinary nurses	324	x	x	518.4	..		
Veterinary nurses	3240	x	x	518.4	..		
Protective service occupations	33	230	835.8	843.5	210	44,642	44,039
Protective Service Occupations	331	230	835.8	843.5	210	44,642	44,039
Non-commissioned officers and other ranks	3311	:			:		
Police officers (sergeant and below)	3312	163	867.5	866.3	148	46,050	45,201
Fire service officers (watch manager and below)	3313	46	753.6	789.7	44	39,306	41,170
Prison service officers (below principal officer)	3314	x	666.8	709.7	x	33,260	37,520
Protective service associate professionals n.e.c.	3319	16	745.0	815.9	14	39,447	43,159
Culture, media and sports occupations	34	77	614.7	x	62	32,915	x
Artistic, Literary and Media Occupations	341	36	632.4	726.1	30	33,532	38,960
Artists	3411	x	x	691.1	x	x	38,480
Authors, writers and translators	3412	x	664.8	734.3	x	36,203	38,370
Actors, entertainers and presenters	3413	..			..		
Dancers and choreographers	3414	:			:		
Musicians	3415	x	x	931.4	x	x	44,748
Arts officers, producers and directors	3416	12	753.0	866.1	x	34,948	46,025
Photographers, audio-visual and broadcasting equipment operators	3417	12	550.8	586.4	x	29,512	31,139
Design Occupations	342	22	697.1	796.3	x	x	43,683
Interior designers	3421	10	652.0	788.5	x	x	45,123
Clothing, fashion and accessories designers	3422	x	x	788.0	x	x	49,276
Design occupations n.e.c.	3429	9	706.4	807.7	x	x	41,029
Sports and Fitness Occupations	343	20	504.6	x	15	24,390	x
Sports players	3431	x	x	x	x	x	x
Sports coaches, instructors and officials	3432	13	478.4	573.4	x	23,057	27,973
Fitness and wellbeing instructors	3433	x	x	421.1	x	x	21,446
Business and public service associate professionals	35	1,050	750.1	893.8	856	40,871	49,750
Transport Associate Professionals	351	10	1,463.3	1,560.3	x	68,727	76,679
Aircraft pilots and air traffic controllers	3511	x	1,491.1	1,653.3	x	72,867	80,839
Ship and hovercraft officers	3512	x	x	1,303.0	x	x	66,213
Legal Associate Professionals	352	15	622.3	770.5	11	33,189	44,634
Legal associate professionals	3520	15	622.3	770.5	11	33,189	44,634
Finance Associate Professionals	353	86	849.8	1,066.2	76	45,199	66,913
Brokers	3531	x	x	x	x	x	x

Gross pay for full-time male employees in the UK on adult rates where pay was not affected by absence 2023

n.e.c. = not elsewhere classified
X = not reported cv <20%
.. = disclosive
: not applicable

Occupation SOC 2020	Code	Gross Weekly Pay in April 2023 Number of jobs (thousand)	Median £	Mean £	Gross Annual Pay April 2022-2023 Number of jobs (thousand)	Median £	Mean £
Insurance underwriters	3532	12	658.9	1,209.0	x	x	x
Financial and accounting technicians	3533	16	930.8	996.7	13	47,919	54,489
Financial accounts managers	3534	51	861.1	993.1	46	44,948	54,554
Business Associate Professionals	354	131	641.7	715.0	108	33,360	39,635
Estimators, valuers and assessors	3541	30	678.1	739.8	27	35,359	38,690
Importers and exporters	3542	x	x	748.6	x	x	42,113
Project support officers	3543	25	619.0	668.3	20	33,034	34,637
Data analysts	3544	38	658.1	708.8	32	33,701	36,870
Business associate professionals n.e.c.	3549	36	584.8	732.0	27	29,919	x
Sales, Marketing and Related Associate Professionals	355	612	833.7	953.9	502	45,458	52,219
Buyers and procurement officers	3551	30	648.3	700.1	24	35,216	37,030
Business sales executives	3552	129	632.4	741.3	100	37,054	42,521
Merchandisers	3553	x	528.4	638.4	x	x	33,279
Marketing associate professionals	3554	62	608.9	688.1	48	32,259	37,715
Estate agents and auctioneers	3555	13	555.6	603.6	12	29,607	35,761
Sales accounts and business development managers	3556	364	1,013.7	1,121.3	307	55,000	60,222
Events managers and organisers	3557	11	555.8	591.2	x	31,237	32,213
Public Services Associate Professionals	356	49	731.2	727.8	38	38,726	38,363
Public services associate professionals	3560	49	731.2	727.8	38	38,726	38,363
HR, Training and Other Vocational Associate Guidance Professionals	357	98	597.8	658.5	71	31,730	36,683
Human resources and industrial relations officers	3571	46	558.5	638.7	32	30,391	38,259
Careers advisers and vocational guidance specialists	3572	x	x	555.5	x	x	30,388
Information technology trainers	3573	..			..		
Other vocational and industrial trainers	3574	48	635.0	684.0	37	33,048	35,618
Regulatory Associate Professionals	358	50	790.4	855.0	43	40,188	44,011
Inspectors of standards and regulations	3581	11	656.9	732.2	x	35,168	37,855
Health and safety managers and officers	3582	39	843.3	888.4	33	41,824	45,912
Administrative and secretarial occupations	4	638	552.9	621.8	528	28,649	31,789
Administrative occupations	41	607	555.8	625.5	503	28,827	31,976
Administrative Occupations: Government and Related Organisations	411	82	541.7	590.8	72	28,714	30,219
National government administrative occupations	4111	71	541.2	590.3	63	28,622	30,003
Local government administrative occupations	4112	10	542.7	604.3	8	29,179	32,487
Officers of non-governmental organisations	4113	x	x	516.6	x	x	x
Administrative Occupations: Finance	412	142	541.1	609.9	114	27,367	31,160
Credit controllers	4121	7	506.2	580.3	x	25,210	31,165
Book-keepers, payroll managers and wages clerks	4122	71	594.2	662.2	58	29,471	33,656
Bank and post office clerks	4123	31	504.9	566.7	27	25,386	28,698
Finance officers	4124	6	557.8	569.5	x	29,712	29,424
Financial administrative occupations n.e.c.	4129	27	489.8	539.0	x	x	27,509
Administrative Occupations: Records	413	118	532.8	580.4	101	27,456	30,097
Records clerks and assistants	4131	30	515.2	564.6	24	26,255	29,259
Pensions and insurance clerks and assistants	4132	10	515.7	545.4	9	26,627	28,181
Stock control clerks and assistants	4133	45	536.6	589.3	41	27,874	30,452
Transport and distribution clerks and assistants	4134	30	564.6	607.1	24	29,035	31,833
Library clerks and assistants	4135	x	x	481.0	x	x	23,995
Human resources administrative occupations	4136	x	x	496.3	x	x	24,474
Administrative Occupations: Office Managers and Supervisors	414	85	691.4	782.4	74	36,019	40,967
Office managers	4141	48	769.2	831.4	41	x	43,525
Office supervisors	4142	17	610.2	660.7	x	x	33,429
Customer service managers	4143	20	675.9	771.3	18	35,099	41,408
Other Administrative Occupations	415	180	536.1	608.7	142	27,638	30,212

Gross pay for full-time male employees in the UK on adult rates where pay was not affected by absence 2023

n.e.c. = not elsewhere classified
X = not reported cv <20%
.. = disclosive
: not applicable

Occupation SOC 2020	Code	Gross Weekly Pay in April 2023: Number of jobs (thousand)	Gross Weekly Pay in April 2023: Median £	Gross Weekly Pay in April 2023: Mean £	Gross Annual Pay April 2022-2023: Number of jobs (thousand)	Gross Annual Pay April 2022-2023: Median £	Gross Annual Pay April 2022-2023: Mean £
Sales administrators	4151	12	498.0	520.7	10	25,740	25,986
Data entry administrators	4152	5	482.6	532.5	x	23,754	27,556
Other administrative occupations n.e.c.	4159	162	540.8	617.8	128	27,990	30,646
Secretarial and related occupations	42	32	509.3	552.1	25	24,994	27,971
Secretarial and Related Occupations	421	32	509.3	552.1	25	24,994	27,971
Medical secretaries	4211	x	x	447.8	x	x	23,333
Legal secretaries	4212	x	x	456.6	x	x	23,750
School secretaries	4213	x	x	589.7	x	x	32,172
Company secretaries and administrators	4214	..			..		
Personal assistants and other secretaries	4215	10	581.5	623.9	8	30,010	30,829
Receptionists	4216	18	484.0	511.1	14	23,870	25,641
Typists and related keyboard occupations	4217	..			..		
Skilled trades occupations	5	1,341	630.1	673.9	1,160	32,347	34,016
Skilled agricultural and related trades	51	81	487.3	523.0	69	24,440	26,002
Agricultural and Related Trades	511	81	487.3	523.0	69	24,440	26,002
Farmers	5111	x	600.6	632.6	x	29,835	29,442
Horticultural trades	5112	x	x	512.5	x	x	23,675
Gardeners and landscape gardeners	5113	28	497.6	520.0	x	x	26,576
Groundsmen and greenkeepers	5114	33	461.4	489.5	x	x	x
Agricultural and fishing trades n.e.c.	5119	12	517.1	577.8	11	24,273	28,160
Skilled metal, electrical and electronic trades	52	814	682.5	725.8	723	34,770	36,512
Metal Forming, Welding and Related Trades	521	55	615.4	647.0	51	31,262	32,059
Sheet metal workers	5211	9	553.1	588.3	9	26,017	28,832
Metal plate workers, smiths, moulders and related occupations	5212	x	584.8	630.8	x	31,294	33,678
Welding trades	5213	38	620.3	653.1	36	31,695	32,320
Pipe fitters	5214	x	x	828.1	x	x	38,550
Metal Machining, Fitting and Instrument Making Trades	522	360	704.1	753.4	326	35,312	37,309
Metal machining setters and setter-operators	5221	52	618.2	650.4	49	32,505	33,385
Tool makers, tool fitters and markers-out	5222	7	703.9	757.0	x	36,512	38,535
Metal working production and maintenance fitters	5223	288	726.2	773.0	259	36,359	38,093
Precision instrument makers and repairers	5224	8	589.3	614.9	x	29,977	32,136
Air-conditioning and refrigeration installers and repairers	5225	x	790.4	876.2	x	39,818	40,613
Vehicle Trades	523	137	627.3	658.9	121	32,627	33,639
Vehicle technicians, mechanics and electricians	5231	96	619.0	645.1	86	32,234	32,314
Vehicle body builders and repairers	5232	20	599.3	606.6	x	x	31,851
Vehicle paint technicians	5233	7	603.6	625.6	x	31,029	32,851
Aircraft maintenance and related trades	5234	7	782.7	892.5	x	44,735	49,395
Boat and ship builders and repairers	5235	x	629.1	709.2	x	x	x
Rail and rolling stock builders and repairers	5236	x	x	873.5	x	x	47,575
Electrical and Electronic Trades	524	221	696.0	729.0	187	35,847	37,500
Electricians and electrical fitters	5241	98	698.5	717.5	87	35,548	36,260
Telecoms and related network installers and repairers	5242	23	635.9	696.7	16	34,130	39,065
TV, video and audio servicers and repairers	5243	x	x	516.8	x	x	26,587
Computer system and equipment installers and servicers	5244	11	627.5	662.0	9	30,981	33,416
Security system installers and repairers	5245	8	659.6	686.0	x	35,796	34,466
Electrical service and maintenance mechanics and repairers	5246	58	714.3	752.2	49	36,178	38,591
Electrical and electronic trades n.e.c.	5249	20	762.1	833.4	18	40,108	43,223
Skilled Metal, Electrical and Electronic Trades Supervisors	525	41	767.1	794.2	39	38,674	39,869
Skilled metal, electrical and electronic trades supervisors	5250	41	767.1	794.2	39	38,674	39,869

Gross pay for full-time male employees in the UK on adult rates where pay was not affected by absence 2023

n.e.c. = not elsewhere classified
X = not reported cv <20%
.. = disclosive
: not applicable

Occupation SOC 2020	Code	Gross Weekly Pay in April 2023 Number of jobs (thousand)	Median £	Mean £	Gross Annual Pay April 2022-2023 Number of jobs (thousand)	Median £	Mean £
Skilled construction and building trades	53	240	625.0	652.6	216	31,951	32,753
Construction and Building Trades	531	174	606.7	628.0	157	30,998	31,341
Steel erectors	5311	x	602.6	696.0	x	x	34,873
Stonemasons and related trades	5312	x	x	646.4	x	x	34,551
Bricklayers	5313	7	598.0	584.7	x	30,940	30,718
Roofers, roof tilers and slaters	5314	10	560.0	560.0	x	x	x
Plumbers & heating and ventilating installers and repairers	5315	54	678.7	684.5	47	35,175	34,949
Carpenters and joiners	5316	57	593.2	606.7	51	29,734	29,914
Glaziers, window fabricators and fitters	5317	17	574.0	590.4	18	26,584	27,382
Construction and building trades n.e.c.	5319	22	576.2	605.4	18	29,106	30,604
Building Finishing Trades	532	28	590.3	609.4	25	30,097	31,146
Plasterers	5321	x	639.0	621.0	x	32,375	32,334
Floorers and wall tilers	5322	8	617.6	639.9	x	32,557	32,415
Painters and decorators	5323	16	560.4	590.9	13	28,734	30,076
Construction and Building Trades Supervisors	533	38	783.8	797.3	34	39,305	40,348
Construction and building trades supervisors	5330	38	783.8	797.3	34	39,305	40,348
Textiles, printing and other skilled trades	54	206	527.2	553.1	152	26,385	27,574
Textiles and Garments Trades	541	13	488.1	525.4	12	25,023	26,269
Upholsterers	5411	x	502.4	516.3	x	23,380	25,157
Footwear and leather working trades	5412	x	x	526.7	x	x	27,017
Tailors and dressmakers	5413	x	x	507.0	x	x	25,351
Textiles, garments and related trades n.e.c.	5419	x	504.2	551.3	x	25,814	27,693
Printing Trades	542	13	529.5	579.7	13	27,016	29,102
Pre-press technicians	5421	x	x	644.2	x	x	x
Printers	5422	7	591.2	603.2	x	28,844	30,128
Print finishing and binding workers	5423	x	x	513.0	x	25,700	26,079
Food Preparation and Hospitality Trades	543	161	526.8	548.4	111	26,153	27,032
Butchers	5431	23	510.6	552.2	20	26,081	27,069
Bakers and flour confectioners	5432	6	452.6	496.9	x	21,868	24,570
Fishmongers and poultry dressers	5433	x	x	506.8	x	x	24,300
Chefs	5434	111	536.6	551.6	69	26,692	27,016
Cooks	5435	x	456.7	455.6	x	x	23,341
Catering and bar managers	5436	16	536.6	567.2	13	27,472	29,202
Other Skilled Trades	544	19	564.7	593.6	17	30,073	30,901
Glass and ceramics makers, decorators and finishers	5441	x	x	533.3	x	x	24,499
Furniture makers and other craft woodworkers	5442	9	551.9	584.8	9	28,466	29,734
Florists	5443	:			:		
Other skilled trades n.e.c.	5449	9	576.2	609.2	x	31,813	33,206
Caring, leisure and other service occupations	6	330	506.0	543.7	251	25,442	26,362
Caring personal service occupations	61	233	503.3	537.5	169	24,876	25,477
Teaching and Childcare Support Occupations	611	25	424.5	445.1	18	20,639	21,255
Early education and childcare assistants	6111	x	x	521.9	x	x	23,620
Teaching assistants	6112	14	415.7	430.3	9	19,483	19,997
Educational support assistants	6113	8	421.4	439.7	x	21,337	21,951
Childminders	6114	..			..		
Nannies and au pairs	6116	:			:		
Playworkers	6117	:			:		
Animal Care and Control Services	612	11	483.1	498.2	8	23,879	24,508
Pest control officers	6121	x	549.4	579.1	x	x	28,334
Animal care services occupations n.e.c.	6129	8	478.7	465.8	x	22,377	22,525
Caring Personal Services	613	197	516.6	551.4	143	25,525	26,053
Nursing auxiliaries and assistants	6131	84	516.5	560.6	62	25,198	25,884
Ambulance staff (excluding paramedics)	6132	11	555.2	584.4	8	29,031	30,048
Dental nurses	6133	x	x	400.2	..		
Houseparents and residential wardens	6134	x	x	648.7	x	x	29,099
Care workers and home carers	6135	72	501.8	533.4	50	24,379	24,739

Gross pay for full-time male employees in the UK on adult rates where pay was not affected by absence 2023

n.e.c. = not elsewhere classified X = not reported cv <20% .. = disclosive : not applicable Occupation SOC 2020	Code	Gross Weekly Pay in April 2023 Number of jobs (thousand)	Median £	Mean £	Gross Annual Pay April 2022-2023 Number of jobs (thousand)	Median £	Mean £
Senior care workers	6136	19	531.2	557.2	x	x	28,015
Care escorts	6137	x	x	513.8	x	x	26,560
Undertakers, mortuary and crematorium assistants	6138	8	563.6	561.1	7	28,789	27,980
Leisure, travel and related personal service occupations	62	88	518.3	560.9	75	26,575	28,356
Leisure and Travel Services	621	35	575.9	620.8	30	29,690	31,192
Sports and leisure assistants	6211	11	463.1	488.4	x	22,310	23,410
Travel agents	6212	x	574.0	580.1	x	30,422	31,889
Air travel assistants	6213	x	560.4	587.0	x	29,925	31,341
Rail travel assistants	6214	14	740.3	769.3	13	36,792	37,736
Leisure and travel service occupations n.e.c.	6219	x	x	505.9	x	x	25,068
Hairdressers and Related Services	622	x	458.1	457.6	x	20,481	21,442
Hairdressers and barbers	6221	x	466.2	475.8	x	x	22,985
Beauticians and related occupations	6222	x	x	439.2	x	x	18,124
Housekeeping and Related Services	623	39	499.9	520.2	34	25,341	26,362
Housekeepers and related occupations	6231	x	479.5	495.0	x	25,003	24,770
Caretakers	6232	36	499.9	522.6	31	25,335	26,518
Cleaning and Housekeeping Managers and Supervisors	624	9	530.3	560.2	8	26,688	29,028
Cleaning and housekeeping managers and supervisors	6240	9	530.3	560.2	8	26,688	29,028
Bed and Breakfast and Guest House Owners and Proprietors	625	:			:		
Bed and breakfast and guest house owners and proprietors	6250	:			:		
Community and civil enforcement occupations	63	9	528.7	536.0	8	27,428	26,294
Community and Civil Enforcement Occupations	631	9	528.7	536.0	8	27,428	26,294
Police community support officers	6311	x	577.6	586.1	x	x	29,153
Parking and civil enforcement occupations	6312	7	498.6	518.6	x	24,302	25,389
Sales and customer service occupations	7	298	492.4	535.0	254	24,496	26,577
Sales occupations	71	199	483.8	523.2	172	23,739	25,705
Sales Assistants and Retail Cashiers	711	160	472.6	519.3	140	23,125	25,261
Sales and retail assistants	7111	143	470.0	518.4	126	22,994	25,269
Retail cashiers and check-out operators	7112	x	405.5	429.7	x	x	19,436
Telephone salespersons	7113	x	447.2	479.1	x	x	24,231
Pharmacy and optical dispensing assistants	7114	x	427.1	437.4	x	20,857	20,098
Vehicle and parts salespersons and advisers	7115	10	540.4	585.7	8	26,695	28,442
Sales Related Occupations	712	13	518.5	531.1	10	26,529	27,829
Collector salespersons and credit agents	7121	..			..		
Debt, rent and other cash collectors	7122	3	470.7	489.5	x	24,476	25,088
Roundspersons and van salespersons	7123	x	502.1	520.3	x	26,413	26,398
Market and street traders and assistants	7124	:			..		
Visual merchandisers and related occupations	7125	x	x	480.3	x	x	x
Sales related occupations n.e.c.	7129	7	536.6	558.8	5	30,336	30,799
Shopkeepers and Sales Supervisors	713	26	523.1	543.4	21	25,583	27,619
Shopkeepers and owners - retail and wholesale	7131	x	x	682.6	x	x	35,609
Sales supervisors - retail and wholesale	7132	25	516.6	537.2	20	25,251	27,240
Customer service occupations	72	99	509.7	558.7	82	26,003	28,396
Customer Service Occupations	721	91	497.2	548.4	75	25,165	27,673
Call and contact centre occupations	7211	8	457.6	489.7	7	23,798	25,201
Telephonists	7212	x	x	581.0	x	x	28,935
Communication operators	7213	x	575.0	615.5	x	x	31,972
Market research interviewers	7214	x	x	499.8	x	x	25,814
Customer service occupations n.e.c.	7219	79	498.3	551.8	65	25,289	27,820
Customer Service Supervisors	722	8	598.8	673.1	7	33,327	35,796
Customer service supervisors	7220	8	598.8	673.1	7	33,327	35,796

Gross pay for full-time male employees in the UK on adult rates where pay was not affected by absence 2023

n.e.c. = not elsewhere classified
X = not reported cv <20%
.. = disclosive
: not applicable

Occupation SOC 2020	Code	Gross Weekly Pay in April 2023			Gross Annual Pay April 2022-2023		
		Number of jobs (thousand)	Median £	Mean £	Number of jobs (thousand)	Median £	Mean £
Process, plant and machine operatives	8	943	617.5	667.5	811	30,719	32,710
Process, plant and machine operatives	81	420	574.6	615.9	366	28,758	30,539
Process Operatives	811	141	536.9	575.4	123	27,194	28,629
Food, drink and tobacco process operatives	8111	85	521.6	555.4	75	26,598	27,374
Textile process operatives	8112	7	574.4	579.2	6	28,242	28,475
Chemical and related process operatives	8113	11	589.1	644.7	11	31,360	33,551
Plastics process operatives	8114	11	521.1	559.9	9	26,131	27,737
Metal making and treating process operatives	8115	12	590.0	644.5	11	30,571	32,822
Process operatives n.e.c.	8119	14	546.3	588.6	11	27,821	28,821
Metal Working Machine Operatives	812	9	584.5	632.7	8	31,829	32,414
Metal working machine operatives	8120	9	584.5	632.7	8	31,829	32,414
Plant and Machine Operatives	813	40	583.7	618.7	34	29,086	30,080
Paper and wood machine operatives	8131	9	542.1	598.8	9	28,559	29,410
Mining and quarry workers and related operatives	8132	x	641.7	632.1	x	x	29,832
Energy plant operatives	8133	x	697.9	743.8	x	x	34,629
Water and sewerage plant operatives	8134	9	638.9	661.5	7	33,077	32,966
Printing machine assistants	8135	8	525.9	583.0	7	26,265	28,443
Plant and machine operatives n.e.c.	8139	8	552.8	582.5	7	25,535	27,897
Assemblers and Routine Operatives	814	124	586.6	619.1	110	28,982	30,684
Assemblers (electrical and electronic products)	8141	12	521.2	556.5	11	25,364	26,749
Assemblers (vehicles and metal goods)	8142	35	704.8	708.9	30	35,492	34,258
Routine inspectors and testers	8143	20	627.7	664.2	18	32,383	34,552
Weighers, graders and sorters	8144	x	589.5	625.0	x	x	31,813
Tyre, exhaust and windscreen fitters	8145	10	512.1	549.9	7	29,295	30,198
Sewing machinists	8146	x	470.1	508.7	x	x	24,350
Assemblers and routine operatives n.e.c.	8149	43	530.0	564.9	40	26,499	27,777
Construction Operatives	815	94	600.0	655.7	78	30,406	32,339
Scaffolders, stagers and riggers	8151	9	679.8	784.4	9	35,563	37,797
Road construction operatives	8152	15	678.0	708.0	12	33,342	35,149
Rail construction and maintenance operatives	8153	7	915.6	919.3	5	38,920	40,668
Construction operatives n.e.c.	8159	64	552.2	597.6	52	27,917	29,948
Production, Factory and Assembly Supervisors	816	13	684.4	715.4	x	x	37,013
Production, factory and assembly supervisors	8160	13	684.4	715.4	x	x	37,013
Transport and mobile machine drivers and operatives	82	522	661.2	709.1	446	32,711	34,491
Road Transport Drivers	821	417	658.1	688.5	356	32,342	33,184
Large goods vehicle drivers	8211	203	748.1	775.6	172	37,275	37,329
Bus and coach drivers	8212	57	646.4	669.9	47	31,471	32,893
Taxi and cab drivers and chauffeurs	8213	x	x	507.0	x	x	26,460
Delivery drivers and couriers	8214	60	526.9	545.9	50	25,294	25,976
Driving instructors	8215	x	x	659.4	x	x	34,487
Road transport drivers n.e.c.	8219	93	559.8	608.1	84	27,456	29,246
Mobile Machine Drivers and Operatives	822	68	600.0	645.1	56	29,895	31,860
Crane drivers	8221	5	875.3	906.8	x	42,997	42,776
Fork-lift truck drivers	8222	21	524.0	560.0	x	27,235	27,898
Mobile machine drivers and operatives n.e.c.	8229	42	618.1	657.0	34	31,242	32,638
Other Drivers and Transport Operatives	823	38	1,047.4	1,053.4	34	52,709	52,295
Train and tram drivers	8231	19	1,231.4	1,233.4	19	63,484	61,789
Marine and waterways transport operatives	8232	x	676.9	701.4	x	x	35,633
Air transport operatives	8233	6	551.9	576.1	x	27,642	27,918
Rail transport operatives	8234	8	998.3	1,188.4	7	49,359	51,153
Other drivers and transport operatives n.e.c.	8239	x	x	663.6	x	x	30,340
Elementary occupations	9	898	500.4	538.4	718	25,387	26,291
Elementary trades and related occupations	91	164	495.5	531.0	127	25,372	26,569
Elementary Agricultural Occupations	911	30	494.4	528.4	24	25,955	26,595
Farm workers	9111	19	500.2	529.2	16	26,120	26,742
Forestry and related workers	9112	x	498.2	542.6	x	x	26,964

Gross pay for full-time male employees in the UK on adult rates where pay was not affected by absence 2023

n.e.c. = not elsewhere classified
X = not reported cv <20%
.. = disclosive
: not applicable

Occupation SOC 2020	Code	Gross Weekly Pay in April 2023 Number of jobs (thousand)	Median £	Mean £	Gross Annual Pay April 2022-2023 Number of jobs (thousand)	Median £	Mean £
Fishing and other elementary agriculture occupations n.e.c.	9119	8	469.8	522.2	x	24,056	26,037
Elementary Construction Occupations	912	53	512.9	561.1	38	26,213	28,071
Groundworkers	9121	12	682.2	693.3	10	35,330	35,973
Elementary construction occupations n.e.c.	9129	41	488.4	523.5	28	24,339	25,163
Elementary Process Plant Occupations	913	82	486.8	512.6	65	24,641	25,676
Industrial cleaning process occupations	9131	9	463.2	488.4	6	22,924	24,763
Packers, bottlers, canners and fillers	9132	42	480.4	501.7	32	24,000	25,124
Elementary process plant occupations n.e.c.	9139	31	510.7	534.6	26	25,896	26,576
Elementary administration and service occupations	92	734	502.3	540.1	591	25,391	26,231
Elementary Administration Occupations	921	87	575.2	621.1	81	28,308	29,289
Postal workers, mail sorters and messengers	9211	75	608.4	647.1	74	28,945	29,957
Elementary administration occupations n.e.c.	9219	12	440.7	457.6	8	22,353	22,684
Elementary Cleaning Occupations	922	86	450.3	468.2	69	23,040	23,282
Window cleaners	9221	x	x	467.3	x	x	21,195
Street cleaners	9222	4	469.7	489.9	x	24,044	25,165
Cleaners and domestics	9223	47	444.6	467.8	37	21,979	22,826
Launderers, dry cleaners and pressers	9224	x	402.8	411.6	x	20,222	20,942
Refuse and salvage occupations	9225	19	459.6	478.5	16	23,890	24,678
Vehicle valeters and cleaners	9226	11	450.4	461.8	8	22,636	22,371
Elementary cleaning occupations n.e.c.	9229	x	x	464.1	x	x	24,094
Elementary Security Occupations	923	76	567.7	579.8	59	28,195	28,562
Security guards and related occupations	9231	76	567.1	579.3	59	28,182	28,523
School midday and crossing patrol occupations	9232	:			:		
Exam invigilators	9233	..			..		
Elementary Sales Occupations	924	x	x	451.9	x	x	22,872
Shelf fillers	9241	x	x	435.3	x	x	22,061
Elementary sales occupations n.e.c.	9249	..			..		
Elementary Storage Occupations	925	392	510.0	554.9	328	25,531	26,621
Elementary storage supervisors	9251	22	548.4	585.5	21	27,736	29,267
Warehouse operatives	9252	356	508.4	554.7	297	25,330	26,476
Delivery operatives	9253	10	448.1	472.6	7	22,131	22,901
Elementary storage occupations n.e.c.	9259	5	612.0	592.5	x	29,214	30,435
Other Elementary Services Occupations	926	92	426.1	436.3	52	20,235	20,329
Bar and catering supervisors	9261	7	467.7	488.5	x	20,138	21,818
Hospital porters	9262	x	x	455.9	x	x	24,502
Kitchen and catering assistants	9263	51	424.2	431.9	28	20,627	19,950
Waiters and waitresses	9264	14	410.7	404.0	7	17,613	18,454
Bar staff	9265	11	420.0	438.6	6	20,065	20,020
Coffee shop workers	9266	x	x	427.8	x	x	21,530
Leisure and theme park attendants	9267	x	x	449.1	x	x	18,637
Other elementary services occupations n.e.c.	9269	x	457.6	489.4	x	22,251	24,748

Figures for Number of Jobs are for indicative purposes only and should not be considered an accurate estimate of employee job counts.

Source: *Annual Survey of Hours and Earnings, Office for National Statistics,* Tables 14.1a and 14.7a.

Gross pay for full-time female employees in the UK on adult rates where pay was not affected by absence 2023

n.e.c. = not elsewhere classified
X = not reported cv <20%
.. = disclosive
: not applicable

Occupation SOC 2020	Code	Gross Weekly Pay in April 2023 Number of jobs (thousand)	Median £	Mean £	Gross Annual Pay April 2022-2023 Number of jobs (thousand)	Median £	Mean £
All employees		8,235	628.9	728.0	6,837	31,672	37,247
Managers, directors and senior officials	1	937	872.0	1,055.0	820	43,654	58,635
Corporate managers and directors	11	729	958.2	1,147.3	642	47,936	64,523
Chief Executives and Senior Officials	111	38	1,483.5	1,598.9	35	77,396	91,181
Chief executives and senior officials	1111	36	1,483.6	1,624.7	33	77,070	92,573
Elected officers and representatives	1112	x	x	1,152.3	x	x	x
Production Managers and Directors	112	142	931.7	1,095.9	122	45,076	53,729
Production managers and directors in manufacturing	1121	133	943.6	1,111.7	115	45,339	54,308
Production managers and directors in construction	1122	8	701.6	811.9	x	x	x
Production managers and directors in mining and energy	1123	x	x	1,133.5	x	x	x
Functional Managers and Directors	113	400	1,091.7	1,283.4	352	55,511	76,427
Financial managers and directors	1131	160	1,121.5	1,379.2	145	56,243	91,447
Marketing, sales and advertising directors	1132	71	1,424.1	1,505.9	61	72,039	84,365
Public relations and communications directors	1133	7	1,492.1	1,465.2	x	74,910	75,915
Purchasing managers and directors	1134	21	905.0	939.5	20	47,279	49,151
Charitable organisation managers and directors	1135	x	859.4	887.3	x	x	43,837
Human resource managers and directors	1136	98	958.2	1,018.1	83	47,808	53,730
Information technology directors	1137	9	1,458.2	1,643.6	x	76,293	91,429
Functional managers and directors n.e.c.	1139	31	1,084.2	1,255.5	26	57,948	66,820
Directors in Logistics, Warehousing and Transport	114	x	x	1,303.0	x	x	67,752
Directors in logistics, warehousing and transport	1140	x	x	1,303.0	x	x	67,752
Managers and Directors in Retail and Wholesale	115	133	592.5	681.3	118	29,436	34,051
Managers and directors in retail and wholesale	1150	133	592.5	681.3	118	29,436	34,051
Senior Officers in Protective Services	116	x	x	1,073.5	x	x	52,366
Officers in armed forces	1161	:			:		
Senior police officers	1162	x	x	1,077.5	x	x	52,366
Senior officers in fire, ambulance, prison and related services	1163	..			:		
Health and Social Services Managers and Directors	117	11	887.2	906.7	10	42,081	46,407
Health services and public health managers and directors	1171	x	x	1,270.5	x	x	65,492
Social services managers and directors	1172	9	831.9	824.4	x	40,859	42,124
Other managers and proprietors	12	208	670.8	731.9	178	33,694	37,419
Managers and Proprietors in Agriculture Related Services	121	x	569.5	611.6	x	28,971	29,801
Managers and proprietors in agriculture and horticulture	1211	x	x	675.6	x	x	32,510
Managers and proprietors in forestry, fishing and related services	1212	x	x	509.2	x	x	24,715
Managers and Proprietors in Hospitality and Leisure Services	122	38	607.4	647.4	31	30,821	33,307
Hotel and accommodation managers and proprietors	1221	x	615.8	723.4	x	32,974	39,285
Restaurant and catering establishment managers and proprietors	1222	14	594.2	604.5	11	28,997	29,430
Publicans and managers of licensed premises	1223	7	652.9	691.5	x	35,703	35,848
Leisure and sports managers	1224	11	595.4	634.2	x	29,944	32,201
Travel agency managers and proprietors	1225	..			..		
Managers and Proprietors in Health and Care Services	123	52	765.6	810.9	x	x	41,242
Health care practice managers	1231	13	761.3	831.9	13	41,101	42,942
Residential, day and domiciliary care managers and proprietors	1232	38	767.2	808.2	x	x	x

Gross pay for full-time female employees in the UK on adult rates where pay was not affected by absence 2023

n.e.c. = not elsewhere classified
X = not reported cv <20%
.. = disclosive
: not applicable

Occupation SOC 2020	Code	Gross Weekly Pay in April 2023 Number of jobs (thousand)	Median £	Mean £	Gross Annual Pay April 2022-2023 Number of jobs (thousand)	Median £	Mean £
Early education and childcare services proprietors	1233	x	x	571.5	..		
Managers in Logistics, Warehousing and Transport	124	45	633.8	718.1	41	31,008	36,313
Managers in transport and distribution	1241	12	753.9	880.4	11	39,991	44,212
Managers in storage and warehousing	1242	27	564.9	628.0	25	28,460	31,126
Managers in logistics	1243	x	794.8	786.6	x	44,477	43,750
Managers and Proprietors in Other Services	125	67	670.7	736.8	56	33,770	38,047
Property, housing and estate managers	1251	40	678.8	745.1	33	34,696	38,477
Garage managers and proprietors	1252	x	x	x	x	x	x
Hairdressing and beauty salon managers and proprietors	1253	x	x	594.0	x	x	30,179
Waste disposal and environmental services managers	1254	x	x	837.0	x	x	42,501
Managers and directors in the creative industries	1255	x	643.3	756.9	x	x	37,907
Betting shop and gambling establishment managers	1256	..			..		
Hire services managers and proprietors	1257	x	x	649.8	x	x	34,538
Directors in consultancy services	1258	x	x	1,112.3	..		
Managers and proprietors in other services n.e.c.	1259	12	575.4	649.9	x	29,810	32,937
Professional occupations	2	2,746	803.6	861.2	2,320	40,489	43,053
Science, research, engineering and technology professionals	21	363	811.8	878.9	298	41,496	45,105
Natural and Social Science Professionals	211	56	751.5	795.8	44	38,620	41,107
Chemical scientists	2111	x	613.3	638.1	x	32,134	31,472
Biological scientists	2112	x	761.8	829.9	x	x	43,979
Biochemists and biomedical scientists	2113	18	787.9	880.3	15	42,135	44,207
Physical scientists	2114	x	x	854.4	x	x	45,145
Social and humanities scientists	2115	x	743.6	726.9	x	35,966	36,784
Natural and social science professionals n.e.c.	2119	18	728.3	764.3	14	36,809	41,047
Engineering Professionals	212	56	827.7	862.3	46	42,004	43,971
Civil engineers	2121	9	800.9	918.5	x	43,339	47,541
Mechanical engineers	2122	x	838.4	843.7	x	x	49,986
Electrical engineers	2123	x	937.2	933.0	x	x	44,256
Electronics engineers	2124	x	x	835.4	x	x	48,306
Production and process engineers	2125	7	677.1	767.3	x	35,299	38,298
Aerospace engineers	2126	x	x	902.8	x	x	44,403
Engineering project managers and project engineers	2127	11	884.6	917.6	x	44,904	45,353
Engineering professionals n.e.c.	2129	20	768.6	830.9	17	38,851	42,609
Information Technology Professionals	213	176	882.8	958.3	152	43,689	48,516
IT project managers	2131	10	972.6	1,011.0	x	48,303	49,584
IT managers	2132	51	930.8	1,029.0	46	47,286	51,935
IT business analysts, architects and systems designers	2133	24	880.8	934.0	20	43,126	47,652
Programmers and software development professionals	2134	53	862.2	939.9	x	x	45,715
Cyber security professionals	2135	x	x	851.1	x	x	41,945
IT quality and testing professionals	2136	x	823.1	857.4	x	40,349	45,974
IT network professionals	2137	x	772.2	755.4	x	x	39,697
Information technology professionals n.e.c.	2139	23	832.6	926.8	21	42,572	50,393
Web and Multimedia Design Professionals	214	24	551.8	599.7	17	29,856	31,682
Web design professionals	2141	x	675.1	699.2	x	x	39,245
Graphic and multimedia designers	2142	20	537.2	578.9	14	27,887	30,178
Conservation and Environment Professionals	215	19	669.5	687.6	13	34,029	35,667
Conservation professionals	2151	x	682.9	653.2	x	x	34,330
Environment professionals	2152	15	668.5	697.8	10	34,124	36,081

Gross pay for full-time female employees in the UK on adult rates where pay was not affected by absence 2023

n.e.c. = not elsewhere classified
X = not reported cv <20%
.. = disclosive
: not applicable

Occupation SOC 2020	Code	Gross Weekly Pay in April 2023 Number of jobs (thousand)	Median £	Mean £	Gross Annual Pay April 2022-2023 Number of jobs (thousand)	Median £	Mean £
Research and Development (R&D) and Other Research Professionals	216	32	854.5	941.1	x	x	x
Research and development (R&D) managers	2161	25	874.8	979.6	x	x	x
Other researchers, unspecified discipline	2162	6	723.1	786.5	x	39,799	39,986
Health professionals	22	878	798.4	848.7	705	39,859	42,022
Medical Practitioners	221	85	1,080.9	1,214.3	62	54,426	73,239
Generalist medical practitioners	2211	25	840.3	867.3	16	38,614	x
Specialist medical practitioners	2212	60	1,217.3	1,356.6	46	58,104	68,727
Therapy Professionals	222	85	766.8	770.9	63	37,341	38,543
Physiotherapists	2221	25	815.4	826.9	18	41,569	40,641
Occupational therapists	2222	21	771.7	759.5	17	36,770	37,341
Speech and language therapists	2223	8	777.9	814.4	x	36,260	38,772
Psychotherapists and cognitive behaviour therapists	2224	x	x	800.7	x	x	39,862
Clinical psychologists	2225	8	681.7	786.6	x	35,354	40,817
Other psychologists	2226	11	577.7	696.3	x	x	37,495
Therapy professionals n.e.c.	2229	9	621.4	671.6	x	32,044	34,448
Nursing Professionals	223	595	777.9	807.2	491	38,645	38,471
Midwifery nurses	2231	26	821.2	845.8	20	41,552	41,076
Community nurses	2232	38	777.9	767.9	31	38,074	37,595
Specialist nurses	2233	34	857.3	870.9	31	42,764	42,474
Nurse practitioners	2234	50	798.4	800.0	42	41,036	40,766
Mental health nurses	2235	x	829.5	865.3	x	41,041	42,664
Children's nurses	2236	9	753.6	770.2	x	34,024	35,930
Other nursing professionals	2237	431	762.6	804.2	355	37,788	37,773
Veterinarians	224	9	940.6	934.0	x	47,921	49,375
Veterinarians	2240	9	940.6	934.0	x	47,921	49,375
Other Health Professionals	225	105	828.4	843.1	83	41,823	41,848
Pharmacists	2251	24	894.2	882.6	18	43,806	42,642
Optometrists	2252	x	922.8	882.1	x	x	44,991
Dental practitioners	2253	x	x	1,008.2	x	x	55,218
Medical radiographers	2254	20	858.0	875.0	17	42,646	42,814
Paramedics	2255	15	883.0	908.6	14	46,563	45,875
Podiatrists	2256	x	x	862.2	x	x	38,570
Other health professionals n.e.c.	2259	39	727.3	759.7	29	36,766	38,014
Teaching and other educational professionals	23	678	818.9	851.2	656	39,986	40,501
Teaching Professionals	231	594	821.8	845.4	578	39,998	40,046
Higher education teaching professionals	2311	74	901.7	948.5	67	44,734	46,098
Further education teaching professionals	2312	22	768.6	794.0	21	39,395	39,994
Secondary education teaching professionals	2313	197	835.4	856.8	196	40,742	40,585
Primary education teaching professionals	2314	251	811.4	840.2	249	39,581	39,146
Nursery education teaching professionals	2315	13	626.2	627.1	11	30,424	31,322
Special needs education teaching professionals	2316	22	788.1	762.1	19	36,224	35,868
Teachers of English as a foreign language	2317	x	686.9	719.2	x	x	35,944
Teaching professionals n.e.c.	2319	11	610.3	645.2	11	28,411	30,953
Other Educational Professionals	232	84	804.3	891.7	78	39,412	43,861
Head teachers and principals	2321	21	1,276.8	1,352.5	20	62,818	65,613
Education managers	2322	26	798.9	812.1	24	39,070	40,314
Education advisers and school inspectors	2323	9	695.8	772.0	x	37,132	40,441
Early education and childcare services managers	2324	17	526.0	543.6	17	25,219	25,677
Other educational professionals n.e.c	2329	11	765.8	830.5	10	38,957	42,090
Business, media and public service professionals	24	827	800.9	874.9	660	41,204	45,762
Legal Professionals	241	106	766.6	914.1	82	39,991	50,496
Barristers and judges	2411	x	x	778.1	x	x	40,950
Solicitors and lawyers	2412	63	930.0	1,064.8	50	47,631	58,155
Legal professionals n.e.c.	2419	38	547.0	684.3	27	30,506	38,530
Finance Professionals	242	134	813.9	867.0	107	40,626	45,439
Chartered and certified accountants	2421	43	903.8	914.5	38	44,178	46,720
Finance and investment analysts and advisers	2422	79	760.3	827.0	61	38,013	43,597

Gross pay for full-time female employees in the UK on adult rates where pay was not affected by absence 2023

n.e.c. = not elsewhere classified
X = not reported cv <20%
.. = disclosive
: not applicable

Occupation SOC 2020	Code	Gross Weekly Pay in April 2023			Gross Annual Pay April 2022-2023		
		Number of jobs (thousand)	Median £	Mean £	Number of jobs (thousand)	Median £	Mean £
Taxation experts	2423	12	814.4	964.3	x	42,193	53,304
Business, Research and Administrative Professionals	243	222	832.9	906.8	170	42,768	47,632
Management consultants and business analysts	2431	87	849.8	926.7	66	43,718	48,193
Marketing and commercial managers	2432	48	875.5	923.4	39	44,683	48,849
Actuaries, economists and statisticians	2433	11	855.1	1,009.0	x	46,599	51,171
Business and related research professionals	2434	41	712.7	733.1	32	36,141	38,351
Professional/Chartered company secretaries	2435	x	x	1,070.0	x	x	x
Business, research and administrative professionals n.e.c.	2439	33	984.3	1,003.7	24	49,652	54,381
Business and Financial Project Management Professionals	244	107	939.5	1,015.5	89	47,458	51,354
Business and financial project management professionals	2440	107	939.5	1,015.5	89	47,458	51,354
Architects, Chartered Architectural Technologists, Planning Officers, Surveyors and Construction Professionals	245	44	788.8	805.9	35	41,848	42,088
Architects	2451	12	812.3	824.3	x	42,436	44,233
Chartered architectural technologists, planning officers and consultants	2452	x	689.3	731.3	x	x	36,759
Quantity surveyors	2453	10	790.0	816.3	x	39,283	40,412
Chartered surveyors	2454	13	819.5	806.3	9	43,782	43,710
Construction project managers and related professionals	2455	x	728.8	850.6	x	x	45,313
Welfare Professionals	246	86	773.6	761.1	74	39,467	38,570
Social workers	2461	70	786.2	787.8	61	40,491	39,834
Probation officers	2462	x	x	725.3	..		
Clergy	2463	7	516.1	553.6	x	26,928	29,168
Youth work professionals	2464	x	x	757.5	x	x	37,034
Welfare professionals n.e.c.	2469	7	665.6	706.7	x	31,137	35,184
Librarians and Related Professionals	247	11	614.3	653.4	9	31,755	33,159
Librarians	2471	7	511.6	625.4	x	x	31,951
Archivists and curators	2472	x	683.6	697.6	x	34,757	34,775
Quality and Regulatory Professionals	248	68	798.4	839.4	58	39,853	42,848
Quality control and planning engineers	2481	17	766.6	809.1	15	37,873	39,381
Quality assurance and regulatory professionals	2482	46	803.4	859.2	38	41,772	44,968
Environmental health professionals	2483	x	702.4	756.3	x	34,597	36,415
Media Professionals	249	50	687.2	725.4	36	36,442	39,396
Newspaper and periodical editors	2491	10	690.4	745.6	x	37,802	39,276
Newspaper and periodical journalists and reporters	2492	x	636.5	681.5	x	34,155	36,793
Public relations professionals	2493	20	650.1	676.9	12	33,401	34,899
Advertising accounts managers and creative directors	2494	15	766.3	796.9	10	38,958	45,969
Associate professional occupations	3	1,554	598.8	675.8	1,244	31,000	35,059
Science, engineering and technology associate professionals	31	197	563.1	614.9	162	28,614	31,378
Science, Engineering and Production Technicians	311	102	537.0	577.1	84	27,300	29,635
Laboratory technicians	3111	31	480.0	508.9	24	24,354	26,242
Electrical and electronics technicians	3112	x	x	578.2	..		
Engineering technicians	3113	12	757.0	715.5	12	35,991	36,307
Building and civil engineering technicians	3114	x	x	559.4	x	x	29,777
Quality assurance technicians	3115	12	546.4	565.1	10	25,687	27,335
Planning, process and production technicians	3116	13	569.8	672.6	11	30,967	35,938
Science, engineering and production technicians n.e.c.	3119	30	523.4	557.8	25	26,458	27,971
CAD, Drawing and Architectural Technicians	312	11	555.8	581.0	x	27,271	29,275

Gross pay for full-time female employees in the UK on adult rates where pay was not affected by absence 2023

n.e.c. = not elsewhere classified X = not reported cv <20% .. = disclosive : not applicable		Gross Weekly Pay in April 2023			Gross Annual Pay April 2022-2023		
Occupation SOC 2020	**Code**	**Number of jobs (thousand)**	**Median £**	**Mean £**	**Number of jobs (thousand)**	**Median £**	**Mean £**
CAD, drawing and architectural technicians	3120	11	555.8	581.0	x	27,271	29,275
Information Technology Technicians	313	83	610.6	665.8	70	31,163	33,685
IT operations technicians	3131	21	592.8	629.6	19	29,510	32,414
IT user support technicians	3132	44	622.5	665.8	39	31,019	33,187
Database administrators and web content technicians	3133	18	597.4	708.3	13	31,500	36,914
Health and social care associate professionals	32	302	516.3	542.6	254	25,963	27,018
Health Associate Professionals	321	31	503.8	535.3	27	25,918	27,898
Dispensing opticians	3211	x	x	525.0	x	x	26,895
Pharmaceutical technicians	3212	13	533.2	558.7	11	26,727	29,193
Medical and dental technicians	3213	11	484.4	521.3	x	24,832	27,489
Complementary health associate professionals	3214	..			..		
Health associate professionals n.e.c.	3219	x	462.6	507.6	x	x	25,838
Welfare and Housing Associate Professionals	322	199	553.1	573.2	158	28,235	29,227
Youth and community workers	3221	54	567.9	585.1	43	28,999	30,285
Child and early years officers	3222	35	555.4	577.2	28	28,452	29,352
Housing officers	3223	29	613.5	616.0	23	30,916	30,746
Counsellors	3224	x	508.8	582.6	x	26,957	31,188
Welfare and housing associate professionals n.e.c.	3229	76	535.6	546.4	60	26,793	27,672
Teaching and Childcare Associate Professionals	323	63	438.6	451.5	60	21,060	20,993
Higher level teaching assistants	3231	17	460.0	469.8	17	22,083	22,643
Early education and childcare practitioners	3232	46	424.8	444.8	43	20,316	20,356
Veterinary nurses	324	10	521.1	527.8	x	24,370	25,678
Veterinary nurses	3240	10	521.1	527.8	x	24,370	25,678
Protective service occupations	33	99	746.6	774.6	86	40,243	39,889
Protective Service Occupations	331	99	746.6	774.6	86	40,243	39,889
Non-commissioned officers and other ranks	3311	:			:		
Police officers (sergeant and below)	3312	75	763.8	781.6	64	40,893	40,261
Fire service officers (watch manager and below)	3313	7	760.8	758.5	x	40,158	39,529
Prison service officers (below principal officer)	3314	x	x	623.3	x	x	25,248
Protective service associate professionals n.e.c.	3319	14	700.8	772.5	13	38,310	40,802
Culture, media and sports occupations	34	57	574.9	636.8	45	30,511	34,203
Artistic, Literary and Media Occupations	341	24	606.7	691.0	17	32,378	37,984
Artists	3411	x	x	594.3	x	x	28,574
Authors, writers and translators	3412	x	605.6	624.2	x	x	31,831
Actors, entertainers and presenters	3413	x	x	571.8	..		
Dancers and choreographers	3414	..			..		
Musicians	3415	:			:		
Arts officers, producers and directors	3416	9	700.4	857.4	x	37,574	x
Photographers, audio-visual and broadcasting equipment operators	3417	x	522.1	548.6	x	x	29,474
Design Occupations	342	20	590.4	651.8	19	32,091	34,950
Interior designers	3421	10	582.3	643.1	x	31,183	34,255
Clothing, fashion and accessories designers	3422	x	x	750.4	x	x	40,998
Design occupations n.e.c.	3429	x	551.9	594.1	x	30,612	31,304
Sports and Fitness Occupations	343	13	475.9	512.2	x	22,484	26,212
Sports players	3431	x	x	x	..		
Sports coaches, instructors and officials	3432	9	486.2	512.3	x	23,472	26,178
Fitness and wellbeing instructors	3433	x	x	449.1	x	x	20,602
Business and public service associate professionals	35	899	638.1	725.5	698	33,580	38,300
Transport Associate Professionals	351	x	x	995.1	..		
Aircraft pilots and air traffic controllers	3511	..			..		
Ship and hovercraft officers	3512	..			..		
Legal Associate Professionals	352	23	560.1	624.7	18	28,461	33,064
Legal associate professionals	3520	23	560.1	624.7	18	28,461	33,064
Finance Associate Professionals	353	96	737.9	814.1	83	39,091	43,382
Brokers	3531	x	x	860.4	x	x	x

Gross pay for full-time female employees in the UK on adult rates where pay was not affected by absence 2023

n.e.c. = not elsewhere classified
X = not reported cv <20%
.. = disclosive
: not applicable

Occupation SOC 2020	Code	Gross Weekly Pay in April 2023 Number of jobs (thousand)	Median £	Mean £	Gross Annual Pay April 2022-2023 Number of jobs (thousand)	Median £	Mean £
Insurance underwriters	3532	11	632.4	706.4	x	30,585	39,083
Financial and accounting technicians	3533	15	856.3	913.5	13	43,196	47,637
Financial accounts managers	3534	68	743.4	808.0	59	39,252	42,355
Business Associate Professionals	354	123	571.2	612.9	92	29,388	31,948
Estimators, valuers and assessors	3541	13	613.8	720.8	11	33,042	39,852
Importers and exporters	3542	x	x	591.0	x	x	30,144
Project support officers	3543	37	580.7	613.6	25	30,571	31,656
Data analysts	3544	19	641.0	641.2	13	32,499	33,069
Business associate professionals n.e.c.	3549	51	526.9	576.5	39	26,899	29,718
Sales, Marketing and Related Associate Professionals	355	427	665.1	781.2	322	35,480	41,631
Buyers and procurement officers	3551	27	619.4	645.7	24	31,641	32,835
Business sales executives	3552	69	574.7	625.0	52	30,792	33,993
Merchandisers	3553	11	481.2	525.1	x	26,457	26,937
Marketing associate professionals	3554	89	555.8	603.3	60	30,000	32,807
Estate agents and auctioneers	3555	10	462.6	523.6	x	26,727	28,652
Sales accounts and business development managers	3556	193	907.0	996.9	152	47,733	51,932
Events managers and organisers	3557	27	532.1	559.3	18	27,827	30,364
Public Services Associate Professionals	356	51	720.5	702.9	40	36,833	36,006
Public services associate professionals	3560	51	720.5	702.9	40	36,833	36,006
HR, Training and Other Vocational Associate Guidance Professionals	357	157	574.9	620.8	122	29,803	32,256
Human resources and industrial relations officers	3571	100	574.9	611.8	78	29,180	31,819
Careers advisers and vocational guidance specialists	3572	x	525.2	547.5	x	26,934	27,878
Information technology trainers	3573	x	x	731.2	x	x	36,134
Other vocational and industrial trainers	3574	48	597.9	645.5	38	31,324	33,569
Regulatory Associate Professionals	358	23	755.2	779.6	20	37,182	39,090
Inspectors of standards and regulations	3581	x	692.8	669.6	x	x	34,823
Health and safety managers and officers	3582	19	766.4	805.1	16	39,107	40,121
Administrative and secretarial occupations	4	1,288	516.5	564.3	1,080	26,200	28,166
Administrative occupations	41	1,057	521.6	569.7	884	26,400	28,352
Administrative Occupations: Government and Related Organisations	411	104	537.6	553.1	91	27,811	28,270
National government administrative occupations	4111	82	538.9	559.2	73	27,965	28,356
Local government administrative occupations	4112	19	492.8	529.8	15	26,286	27,889
Officers of non-governmental organisations	4113	x	526.0	535.0	x	x	28,121
Administrative Occupations: Finance	412	250	524.5	571.8	211	26,442	28,372
Credit controllers	4121	15	528.2	553.9	x	x	28,102
Book-keepers, payroll managers and wages clerks	4122	143	540.9	600.8	120	27,308	29,880
Bank and post office clerks	4123	37	487.1	523.2	34	24,007	25,019
Finance officers	4124	13	545.2	578.6	11	27,819	29,303
Financial administrative occupations n.e.c.	4129	42	495.2	520.8	34	25,311	26,193
Administrative Occupations: Records	413	142	493.6	518.6	113	25,000	26,083
Records clerks and assistants	4131	71	490.0	516.6	56	24,830	25,884
Pensions and insurance clerks and assistants	4132	16	483.7	500.9	13	24,606	24,847
Stock control clerks and assistants	4133	24	498.8	526.2	20	25,584	26,767
Transport and distribution clerks and assistants	4134	18	536.6	554.6	14	27,210	28,602
Library clerks and assistants	4135	4	462.6	486.2	x	22,517	23,580
Human resources administrative occupations	4136	9	479.1	486.8	x	23,117	24,308
Administrative Occupations: Office Managers and Supervisors	414	149	632.4	683.0	129	32,134	34,295
Office managers	4141	108	661.8	700.3	92	33,299	34,889
Office supervisors	4142	20	550.9	579.0	17	28,652	29,613
Customer service managers	4143	22	624.3	692.8	21	31,694	35,446
Other Administrative Occupations	415	411	497.3	549.1	341	25,000	26,863

Gross pay for full-time female employees in the UK on adult rates where pay was not affected by absence 2023

n.e.c. = not elsewhere classified X = not reported cv <20% .. = disclosive : not applicable		Gross Weekly Pay in April 2023			Gross Annual Pay April 2022-2023		
Occupation SOC 2020	**Code**	**Number of jobs (thousand)**	**Median £**	**Mean £**	**Number of jobs (thousand)**	**Median £**	**Mean £**
Sales administrators	4151	28	498.3	511.4	24	25,384	25,667
Data entry administrators	4152	6	440.8	501.9	x	21,413	26,976
Other administrative occupations n.e.c.	4159	377	498.0	552.6	313	24,995	26,953
Secretarial and related occupations	42	231	494.4	540.0	196	24,644	27,329
Secretarial and Related Occupations	421	231	494.4	540.0	196	24,644	27,329
Medical secretaries	4211	21	473.2	471.8	18	24,796	24,356
Legal secretaries	4212	14	469.7	504.0	13	23,700	25,935
School secretaries	4213	10	447.0	480.8	8	22,442	24,021
Company secretaries and administrators	4214	x	x	589.0	x	x	x
Personal assistants and other secretaries	4215	96	599.5	642.0	83	30,435	32,941
Receptionists	4216	86	433.9	455.5	71	21,426	22,037
Typists and related keyboard occupations	4217	x	x	444.2	x	x	23,132
Skilled trades occupations	5	142	503.0	544.1	113	25,175	27,142
Skilled agricultural and related trades	51	8	511.5	526.6	x	25,950	25,857
Agricultural and Related Trades	511	8	511.5	526.6	x	25,950	25,857
Farmers	5111	x	x	547.7	x	x	x
Horticultural trades	5112	x	x	488.7	x	x	25,039
Gardeners and landscape gardeners	5113	x	x	525.5	x	x	24,466
Groundsmen and greenkeepers	5114	..			..		
Agricultural and fishing trades n.e.c.	5119	x	x	562.8	x	x	29,711
Skilled metal, electrical and electronic trades	52	32	606.9	668.8	26	31,230	34,803
Metal Forming, Welding and Related Trades	521	..			..		
Sheet metal workers	5211	:			:		
Metal plate workers, smiths, moulders and related occupations	5212	..			..		
Welding trades	5213	..			:		
Pipe fitters	5214	:			:		
Metal Machining, Fitting and Instrument Making Trades	522	13	607.4	703.8	11	33,235	36,143
Metal machining setters and setter-operators	5221	x	x	x	x	x	36,842
Tool makers, tool fitters and markers-out	5222	..			..		
Metal working production and maintenance fitters	5223	11	660.8	725.1	x	34,319	36,827
Precision instrument makers and repairers	5224	x	x	541.0	x	x	26,163
Air-conditioning and refrigeration installers and repairers	5225	:			:		
Vehicle Trades	523	x	479.8	544.9	x	22,731	26,136
Vehicle technicians, mechanics and electricians	5231	x	x	526.6	x	x	24,701
Vehicle body builders and repairers	5232	..			..		
Vehicle paint technicians	5233	..			..		
Aircraft maintenance and related trades	5234	x	x	544.7	x	x	x
Boat and ship builders and repairers	5235	:			:		
Rail and rolling stock builders and repairers	5236	..			..		
Electrical and Electronic Trades	524	9	576.5	637.9	x	29,484	34,828
Electricians and electrical fitters	5241	x	x	545.4	x	x	26,047
Telecoms and related network installers and repairers	5242	x	x	667.1	x	x	43,515
TV, video and audio servicers and repairers	5243	..			:		
Computer system and equipment installers and servicers	5244	..			..		
Security system installers and repairers	5245	:			:		
Electrical service and maintenance mechanics and repairers	5246	x	574.1	624.5	x	x	30,594
Electrical and electronic trades n.e.c.	5249	..			..		
Skilled Metal, Electrical and Electronic Trades Supervisors	525	x	718.2	750.2	x	36,215	39,093
Skilled metal, electrical and electronic trades supervisors	5250	x	718.2	750.2	x	36,215	39,093

Gross pay for full-time female employees in the UK on adult rates where pay was not affected by absence 2023

n.e.c. = not elsewhere classified
X = not reported cv <20%
.. = disclosive
: not applicable

Occupation SOC 2020	Code	Gross Weekly Pay in April 2023 Number of jobs (thousand)	Median £	Mean £	Gross Annual Pay April 2022-2023 Number of jobs (thousand)	Median £	Mean £
Skilled construction and building trades	53	12	536.2	566.6	x	28,670	30,354
Construction and Building Trades	531	x	504.3	524.2	x	x	30,448
Steel erectors	5311	:			..		
Stonemasons and related trades	5312	..			..		
Bricklayers	5313	:			:		
Roofers, roof tilers and slaters	5314	..			..		
Plumbers & heating and ventilating installers and repairers	5315	x	x	542.7	x	x	36,817
Carpenters and joiners	5316	x	x	535.3	..		
Glaziers, window fabricators and fitters	5317	:			:		
Construction and building trades n.e.c.	5319	x	x	489.6	x	x	25,903
Building Finishing Trades	532	x	x	512.6	x	x	25,868
Plasterers	5321	:			:		
Floorers and wall tilers	5322	:			:		
Painters and decorators	5323	x	x	512.6	x	x	25,868
Construction and Building Trades Supervisors	533	x	592.4	632.2	x	29,365	31,571
Construction and building trades supervisors	5330	x	592.4	632.2	x	29,365	31,571
Textiles, printing and other skilled trades	54	91	479.1	499.0	72	23,474	24,145
Textiles and Garments Trades	541	x	445.9	476.6	x	20,465	22,156
Upholsterers	5411	:			:		
Footwear and leather working trades	5412	x	x	488.1	x	x	22,763
Tailors and dressmakers	5413	x	x	507.6	x	x	25,888
Textiles, garments and related trades n.e.c.	5419	x	x	433.4	x	x	20,092
Printing Trades	542	x	512.8	523.2	x	x	26,139
Pre-press technicians	5421	x	x	500.2	x	x	26,494
Printers	5422	x	x	535.3	x	x	27,173
Print finishing and binding workers	5423	x	x	519.9	x	x	24,496
Food Preparation and Hospitality Trades	543	78	479.9	499.3	60	23,495	24,325
Butchers	5431	x	x	546.4	x	x	26,118
Bakers and flour confectioners	5432	x	438.2	460.8	x	x	22,512
Fishmongers and poultry dressers	5433	..			..		
Chefs	5434	41	485.2	511.9	x	x	25,090
Cooks	5435	12	429.8	430.5	11	21,364	21,050
Catering and bar managers	5436	19	520.3	525.6	16	25,225	25,469
Other Skilled Trades	544	x	449.1	495.3	x	x	x
Glass and ceramics makers, decorators and finishers	5441	x	x	582.1	x	x	27,335
Furniture makers and other craft woodworkers	5442	..			..		
Florists	5443	x	x	453.6	x	x	20,826
Other skilled trades n.e.c.	5449	x	x	484.2	x	x	24,772
Caring, leisure and other service occupations	6	782	471.0	509.7	621	22,940	23,581
Caring personal service occupations	61	692	470.5	510.8	547	22,844	23,462
Teaching and Childcare Support Occupations	611	172	422.5	439.4	145	19,596	20,056
Early education and childcare assistants	6111	38	442.0	455.8	37	20,935	21,378
Teaching assistants	6112	88	413.9	425.5	73	18,877	19,067
Educational support assistants	6113	38	413.6	431.3	29	18,507	19,509
Childminders	6114	x	x	419.6	x	x	20,497
Nannies and au pairs	6116	5	555.7	612.1	x	x	31,560
Playworkers	6117	x	x	509.4	x	x	22,468
Animal Care and Control Services	612	12	445.9	465.5	10	21,539	23,310
Pest control officers	6121	:			:		
Animal care services occupations n.e.c.	6129	12	445.9	465.5	10	21,539	23,310
Caring Personal Services	613	508	495.6	536.2	392	24,300	24,725
Nursing auxiliaries and assistants	6131	211	503.2	552.0	159	25,115	25,344
Ambulance staff (excluding paramedics)	6132	7	555.4	580.0	6	26,957	28,928
Dental nurses	6133	23	442.8	462.3	21	21,751	22,033
Houseparents and residential wardens	6134	x	593.0	615.8	x	31,408	30,624
Care workers and home carers	6135	212	486.5	525.8	160	23,172	23,932

Gross pay for full-time female employees in the UK on adult rates where pay was not affected by absence 2023

n.e.c. = not elsewhere classified
X = not reported cv <20%
.. = disclosive
: not applicable

Occupation SOC 2020	Code	Gross Weekly Pay in April 2023 Number of jobs (thousand)	Median £	Mean £	Gross Annual Pay April 2022-2023 Number of jobs (thousand)	Median £	Mean £
Senior care workers	6136	48	512.5	535.4	40	24,785	25,698
Care escorts	6137	x	x	487.1	x	x	x
Undertakers, mortuary and crematorium assistants	6138	x	535.6	552.8	x	25,479	26,023
Leisure, travel and related personal service occupations	62	86	468.5	496.7	71	23,381	24,297
Leisure and Travel Services	621	28	522.5	546.2	20	27,112	27,971
Sports and leisure assistants	6211	8	466.2	490.9	6	21,836	22,985
Travel agents	6212	10	522.5	553.0	7	28,892	29,705
Air travel assistants	6213	5	513.2	516.0	x	28,050	27,195
Rail travel assistants	6214	x	680.2	719.7	x	34,199	34,780
Leisure and travel service occupations n.e.c.	6219	x	x	575.2	x	x	28,971
Hairdressers and Related Services	622	20	417.8	431.4	17	19,220	19,943
Hairdressers and barbers	6221	12	418.9	439.4	12	19,304	20,088
Beauticians and related occupations	6222	7	407.2	417.9	x	19,030	19,617
Housekeeping and Related Services	623	18	443.3	474.9	15	22,947	24,028
Housekeepers and related occupations	6231	12	443.1	459.1	10	22,590	22,835
Caretakers	6232	6	441.0	506.1	x	23,714	26,305
Cleaning and Housekeeping Managers and Supervisors	624	20	484.2	511.5	18	23,851	24,487
Cleaning and housekeeping managers and supervisors	6240	20	484.2	511.5	18	23,851	24,487
Bed and Breakfast and Guest House Owners and Proprietors	625	..			..		
Bed and breakfast and guest house owners and proprietors	6250	..			..		
Community and civil enforcement occupations	63	4	595.7	597.4	x	27,596	27,524
Community and Civil Enforcement Occupations	631	4	595.7	597.4	x	27,596	27,524
Police community support officers	6311	x	608.6	621.3	x	x	30,145
Parking and civil enforcement occupations	6312	x	x	563.4	x	x	23,989
Sales and customer service occupations	7	326	466.4	503.3	281	22,511	23,833
Sales occupations	71	185	444.0	474.8	163	20,879	22,039
Sales Assistants and Retail Cashiers	711	152	431.7	465.7	135	20,186	21,424
Sales and retail assistants	7111	130	434.9	472.0	116	20,051	21,488
Retail cashiers and check-out operators	7112	x	357.2	376.9	x	17,609	18,614
Telephone salespersons	7113	x	442.2	466.0	x	x	24,063
Pharmacy and optical dispensing assistants	7114	16	425.5	425.4	14	20,846	20,900
Vehicle and parts salespersons and advisers	7115	x	x	548.7	x	x	24,694
Sales Related Occupations	712	11	475.8	496.8	8	24,128	24,696
Collector salespersons and credit agents	7121	..			..		
Debt, rent and other cash collectors	7122	5	451.1	490.5	x	24,137	24,460
Roundspersons and van salespersons	7123	..			..		
Market and street traders and assistants	7124	x	x	551.5	..		
Visual merchandisers and related occupations	7125	x	x	466.6	x	x	22,529
Sales related occupations n.e.c.	7129	4	513.4	511.8	x	24,699	25,305
Shopkeepers and Sales Supervisors	713	23	498.3	524.8	20	24,357	25,150
Shopkeepers and owners - retail and wholesale	7131	x	x	666.7	x	x	x
Sales supervisors - retail and wholesale	7132	22	496.6	520.9	19	24,130	24,999
Customer service occupations	72	141	500.4	540.7	118	25,067	26,322
Customer Service Occupations	721	133	495.3	535.3	110	24,590	25,956
Call and contact centre occupations	7211	12	471.7	487.7	10	23,476	23,917
Telephonists	7212	x	x	586.2	x	x	29,632
Communication operators	7213	4	581.4	590.1	x	29,697	29,707
Market research interviewers	7214	:			:		
Customer service occupations n.e.c.	7219	115	495.0	537.4	95	24,614	25,985
Customer Service Supervisors	722	8	608.9	630.2	8	31,143	31,551
Customer service supervisors	7220	8	608.9	630.2	8	31,143	31,551

Gross pay for full-time female employees in the UK on adult rates where pay was not affected by absence 2023

n.e.c. = not elsewhere classified
X = not reported cv <20%
.. = disclosive
: not applicable

Occupation SOC 2020	Code	Gross Weekly Pay in April 2023			Gross Annual Pay April 2022-2023		
		Number of jobs (thousand)	Median £	Mean £	Number of jobs (thousand)	Median £	Mean £
Process, plant and machine operatives	8	108	491.7	529.5	91	23,479	25,602
Process, plant and machine operatives	81	88	479.4	506.0	75	23,297	24,295
Process Operatives	811	39	463.2	498.6	32	22,939	23,844
Food, drink and tobacco process operatives	8111	31	462.2	494.1	27	22,930	23,704
Textile process operatives	8112	x	x	440.6	x	x	20,860
Chemical and related process operatives	8113	x	x	552.5	x	x	27,360
Plastics process operatives	8114	x	498.2	519.1	x	x	23,039
Metal making and treating process operatives	8115	..			..		
Process operatives n.e.c.	8119	x	x	553.5	x	x	25,949
Metal Working Machine Operatives	812	x	x	482.7	x	x	27,560
Metal working machine operatives	8120	x	x	482.7	x	x	27,560
Plant and Machine Operatives	813	x	520.6	568.2	x	x	25,147
Paper and wood machine operatives	8131	x	x	485.3	x	x	x
Mining and quarry workers and related operatives	8132	:			:		
Energy plant operatives	8133	x	x	813.2	x	x	40,550
Water and sewerage plant operatives	8134	x	x	551.8	x	x	25,768
Printing machine assistants	8135	x	x	495.5	x	x	21,768
Plant and machine operatives n.e.c.	8139	x	x	548.8	..		
Assemblers and Routine Operatives	814	37	471.5	495.3	32	x	24,122
Assemblers (electrical and electronic products)	8141	x	490.4	511.2	x	x	23,312
Assemblers (vehicles and metal goods)	8142	4	510.2	523.0	x	23,754	25,025
Routine inspectors and testers	8143	6	536.0	550.2	6	27,656	27,389
Weighers, graders and sorters	8144	x	x	519.9	x	x	25,020
Tyre, exhaust and windscreen fitters	8145	..			..		
Sewing machinists	8146	6	419.5	434.3	5	20,835	21,644
Assemblers and routine operatives n.e.c.	8149	15	468.6	484.2	x	x	23,326
Construction Operatives	815	5	533.8	543.8	x	25,899	25,239
Scaffolders, stagers and riggers	8151	:			:		
Road construction operatives	8152	x	x	509.6	x	x	24,984
Rail construction and maintenance operatives	8153	x	x	846.2	x	x	36,612
Construction operatives n.e.c.	8159	4	506.3	512.8	x	25,326	23,994
Production, Factory and Assembly Supervisors	816	4	554.9	592.5	x	25,789	27,795
Production, factory and assembly supervisors	8160	4	554.9	592.5	x	25,789	27,795
Transport and mobile machine drivers and operatives	82	21	551.0	629.8	x	x	31,556
Road Transport Drivers	821	13	548.2	598.7	x	x	x
Large goods vehicle drivers	8211	x	695.6	716.6	x	x	x
Bus and coach drivers	8212	4	551.3	614.0	x	28,283	28,074
Taxi and cab drivers and chauffeurs	8213	:			:		
Delivery drivers and couriers	8214	x	425.9	465.8	x	21,383	21,486
Driving instructors	8215	..			:		
Road transport drivers n.e.c.	8219	x	479.3	557.0	x	21,719	25,905
Mobile Machine Drivers and Operatives	822	5	461.1	498.4	x	22,276	24,215
Crane drivers	8221	..			..		
Fork-lift truck drivers	8222	x	x	595.8	x	x	x
Mobile machine drivers and operatives n.e.c.	8229	4	459.1	482.4	x	22,276	23,264
Other Drivers and Transport Operatives	823	3	956.7	959.4	x	54,684	55,763
Train and tram drivers	8231	x	1,224.8	1,196.3	x	x	67,627
Marine and waterways transport operatives	8232	:			:		
Air transport operatives	8233	x	x	523.8	..		
Rail transport operatives	8234	x	x	825.5	x	x	37,017
Other drivers and transport operatives n.e.c.	8239	x	x	758.4	x	x	38,450
Elementary occupations	9	350	446.5	475.9	268	21,800	22,231
Elementary trades and related occupations	91	52	457.6	477.6	40	22,019	22,243
Elementary Agricultural Occupations	911	8	473.1	505.4	x	22,053	22,606
Farm workers	9111	x	473.3	503.9	x	x	26,895

Gross pay for full-time female employees in the UK on adult rates where pay was not affected by absence 2023

n.e.c. = not elsewhere classified
X = not reported cv <20%
.. = disclosive
: not applicable

Occupation SOC 2020	Code	Gross Weekly Pay in April 2023			Gross Annual Pay April 2022-2023		
		Number of jobs (thousand)	Median £	Mean £	Number of jobs (thousand)	Median £	Mean £
Forestry and related workers	9112	..			..		
Fishing and other elementary agriculture occupations n.e.c.	9119	x	470.6	508.5	x	20,080	20,857
Elementary Construction Occupations	912	x	x	505.9	x	x	25,107
Groundworkers	9121	..			..		
Elementary construction occupations n.e.c.	9129	x	x	483.3	x	x	24,129
Elementary Process Plant Occupations	913	42	453.7	471.3	34	21,946	22,098
Industrial cleaning process occupations	9131	x	433.5	448.8	x	20,431	21,844
Packers, bottlers, canners and fillers	9132	31	458.3	475.8	26	21,968	22,079
Elementary process plant occupations n.e.c.	9139	7	440.3	463.7	x	22,066	22,334
Elementary administration and service occupations	92	299	443.5	475.6	227	21,778	22,229
Elementary Administration Occupations	921	24	521.5	551.9	21	26,181	26,726
Postal workers, mail sorters and messengers	9211	18	553.3	592.1	16	27,511	28,207
Elementary administration occupations n.e.c.	9219	6	412.6	424.1	x	21,227	21,092
Elementary Cleaning Occupations	922	66	420.9	445.3	55	20,307	20,596
Window cleaners	9221	:			:		
Street cleaners	9222	..			..		
Cleaners and domestics	9223	60	422.2	447.3	49	20,363	20,607
Launderers, dry cleaners and pressers	9224	5	412.9	419.2	x	19,536	19,918
Refuse and salvage occupations	9225	..			..		
Vehicle valeters and cleaners	9226	x	x	461.0	..		
Elementary cleaning occupations n.e.c.	9229	..			..		
Elementary Security Occupations	923	14	539.4	553.3	11	27,047	26,298
Security guards and related occupations	9231	13	550.9	558.8	10	28,711	26,991
School midday and crossing patrol occupations	9232	x	x	478.1	x	x	21,328
Exam invigilators	9233	..			..		
Elementary Sales Occupations	924	x	x	438.3	x	x	22,253
Shelf fillers	9241	x	x	438.3	x	x	22,253
Elementary sales occupations n.e.c.	9249	:			:		
Elementary Storage Occupations	925	94	479.6	525.8	73	23,489	24,375
Elementary storage supervisors	9251	5	531.0	531.0	x	27,085	26,129
Warehouse operatives	9252	87	475.8	526.3	68	23,423	24,298
Delivery operatives	9253	x	x	446.9	x	x	x
Elementary storage occupations n.e.c.	9259	x	x	540.7	x	x	25,337
Other Elementary Services Occupations	926	99	411.8	419.7	67	19,643	19,186
Bar and catering supervisors	9261	12	444.8	450.6	9	21,943	21,968
Hospital porters	9262	..			..		
Kitchen and catering assistants	9263	51	409.4	422.6	34	19,548	19,608
Waiters and waitresses	9264	17	403.5	403.7	11	18,873	17,753
Bar staff	9265	10	387.5	404.2	7	15,919	16,346
Coffee shop workers	9266	5	414.6	408.2	x	x	18,981
Leisure and theme park attendants	9267	x	403.5	398.1	x	x	17,456
Other elementary services occupations n.e.c.	9269	x	x	430.8	x	x	18,129

Figures for Number of Jobs are for indicative purposes only and should not be considered an accurate estimate of employee job counts.

Source: *Annual Survey of Hours and Earnings, Office for National Statistics,* Tables 14.1a and 14.7a.

F9: Public sector comparable earnings

In the table below we show gross salary ranges and compare with equivalent gross salaries in the public sector

Gross salary range	Comparable public sector salaries
£15,000 to £30,000	Soldier (new entrant) £18,687; National Minimum Wage (37.5 hours pw) £22,308; National Living Wage (37.5 hours pw) £22,308; Healthcare Assistant (B) £22,383; Healthcare Assistant (T) £22,383; Clinical Support Workers (B) £22,816; Army Private (B) £23,496; Clinical Support Workers (T) £24,336; Dental Nurse (B) £25,147; Dental Nurse (T) £27,596; Staff Nurse (B) £28,407; Teacher (Main Scale) (B) £30,000
£30,001 to £40,000	Lieutenant (B) £31,305; Junior Doctor (Foundation) (B) £32,398; Church of England (Residentiary Canons) £33,012; Staff Nurse (T) £34,581; Senior Staff Nurse (B) £35,392; Corporal (B) £35,718; Army Private (T) £35,870; Junior Doctor (Foundation) (T) £37,303; Church of England (Dean) £39,953
£40,001 to £50,000	Sergeant (B) £40,058; Lieutenant (T) £41,262; Teacher (Main Scale) (T) £41,333; Corporal (T) £42,260; Senior Staff Nurse (T) £42,618; Teacher (Upper Scale) (B) £43,266; Ward Sister (B) £43,742; Junior Doctor (Core Training) (B) £43,923; Junior Doctor (Speciality Training) (B) £43,923; Staff Sergeant (B) £44,956; Teacher (Upper Scale) (T) £46,525; Teacher (Leadership Group) (B) £47,185; Captain (B) £47,680; Church of England (Diocesan Bishop) £48,972; Sergeant (T) £49,330
£50,001 to £60,000	Ward Sister (T) £50,056; Speciality Matron (B) £50,952; Junior Doctor (Core Training) (T) £55,329; Warrant Officer (Class 1) (B) £56,383; Captain (T) £56,512; Staff Sergeant (T) £56,858; Speciality Matron (T) £57,349; Senior Matron (B) £58,972; Major (B) £59,799
£60,001 to £90,000	Warrant Officer (Class 1) (T) £60,111; Junior Doctor (Speciality Training) (T) £63,152; Senior Matron (T) £68,525; Consultant Paramedic (B) £70,417; Church of England (Bishop of London) £70,865; Church of England (Archbishop of York) £77,312; Major (T) £78,749; Consultant Paramedic (T) £81,138; Lt Colonel (B) £83,524; Consultant Psychologist (B) £83,571; Member of Parliament £86,584
£90,001 to £120,000	Church of England (Archbishop of Canterbury) £90,216; Hospital Consultant (B) £93,666; Consultant Psychologist (T) £96,376; Lt Colonel (T) £96,556; Chief Nurse (B) £99,891; Colonel (B) £100,979; Select Committee Chairs £103,938; Colonel (T) £110,905; Chief Nurse (T) £114,949
£120,001 to £150,000	Brigadier (B) £120,143; Chief Secretary to the Treasury £121,326; Brigadier (T) £124,964; Hospital Consultant (T) £126,281; District Judges £126,514; Teacher (Leadership Group) (T) £131,056; Department of Transport: Chief Executive £150,000; Ministry of Defence: Director General £150,000; Home Office: Permanent Secretary £150,000; National Crime Agency: Director General £150,000
£150,001 to £200,000	Her Majesty's Treasury: Chief Executive £155,000; Circuit Judges £157,705; Chancellor of the Exchequer £159,038; Senior Masters and Registrars £164,015; Prime Minister £166,574; Senior Circuit Judges £170,304; Home Office: Permanent Secretary £184,999; National Crime Agency: Director General £184,999; Attorney General £187,403
£200,001 and over	Puisne Judge of the High Court £212,351; Her Majesty's Treasury: Chief Executive £224,999; Ministry of Defence: Director General £234,999; Lord Justice of Appeal £241,796; Chancellor of the High Court £254,274; Master of the Rolls £263,256; Lord Chief Justice £294,821; Department of Transport: Chief Executive £644,999

Notes: All categories are subject to varying terms and conditions. (B) and (T) indicate bottom and top of range or seniority for post or rank.

Group G

Tax and National Insurance

G1: Net equivalents to a range of gross annual income figures

	2012/2013 Net equivalent income		2013/2014 Net equivalent income		2014/2015 Net equivalent income	
	Employed	Self-Employed	Employed	Self-Employed	Employed	Self-employed
Gross income £pa	£pa	£pa	£pa	£pa	£pa	£pa
1,000	1,000	1,000	1,000	1,000	1,000	1,000
2,000	2,000	2,000	2,000	2,000	2,000	2,000
3,000	3,000	3,000	3,000	3,000	3,000	3,000
4,000	4,000	4,000	4,000	4,000	4,000	4,000
5,000	5,000	5,000	5,000	5,000	5,000	5,000
6,000	6,000	5,862	6,000	5,860	6,000	5,857
7,000	7,000	6,862	7,000	6,860	7,000	6,857
8,000	7,951	7,827	7,970	7,838	7,995	7,853
9,000	8,652	8,558	8,850	8,748	8,875	8,763
10,000	9,332	9,268	9,618	9,546	9,755	9,673
11,000	10,012	9,978	10,298	10,256	10,435	10,383
12,000	10,692	10,688	10,978	10,966	11,115	11,093
13,000	11,372	11,398	11,658	11,676	11,795	11,803
14,000	12,052	12,108	12,338	12,386	12,475	12,513
15,000	12,732	12,818	13,018	13,096	13,155	13,223
16,000	13,412	13,528	13,698	13,806	13,835	13,933
17,000	14,092	14,238	14,378	14,516	14,515	14,643
18,000	14,772	14,948	15,058	15,226	15,195	15,353
19,000	15,452	15,658	15,738	15,936	15,875	16,063
20,000	16,132	16,368	16,418	16,646	16,555	16,773
21,000	16,812	17,078	17,098	17,356	17,235	17,483
22,000	17,492	17,788	17,778	18,066	17,915	18,193
23,000	18,172	18,498	18,458	18,776	18,595	18,903
24,000	18,852	19,208	19,138	19,486	19,275	19,613
25,000	19,532	19,918	19,818	20,196	19,955	20,323
26,000	20,212	20,628	20,498	20,906	20,635	21,033
27,000	20,892	21,338	21,178	21,616	21,315	21,743
28,000	21,572	22,048	21,858	22,326	21,995	22,453
29,000	22,252	22,758	22,538	23,036	22,675	23,163
30,000	22,932	23,468	23,218	23,746	23,355	23,873
31,000	23,612	24,178	23,898	24,456	24,035	24,583
32,000	24,292	24,888	24,578	25,166	24,715	25,293
33,000	24,972	25,598	25,258	25,876	25,395	26,003
34,000	25,652	26,308	25,938	26,586	26,075	26,713
35,000	26,332	27,018	26,618	27,296	26,755	27,423
40,000	29,732	30,568	30,018	30,846	30,155	30,973
45,000	32,879	33,789	33,063	33,934	33,242	34,115
50,000	35,779	36,689	35,963	36,834	36,142	37,015
55,000	38,679	39,589	38,863	39,734	39,042	39,915
60,000	41,579	42,489	41,763	42,634	41,942	42,815
65,000	44,479	45,389	44,663	45,534	44,842	45,715
70,000	47,379	48,289	47,563	48,434	47,742	48,615
75,000	50,279	51,189	50,463	51,334	50,642	51,515
80,000	53,179	54,089	53,363	54,234	53,542	54,415
85,000	56,079	56,989	56,263	57,134	56,442	57,315
90,000	58,979	59,889	59,163	60,034	59,342	60,215
95,000	61,879	62,789	62,063	62,934	62,242	63,115
100,000	64,779	65,689	64,963	65,834	65,142	66,015
150,000	90,537	91,447	90,187	91,058	90,142	91,015
200,000	114,537	115,447	116,687	117,558	116,642	117,515
250,000	138,537	139,447	143,187	144,058	143,142	144,015
300,000	162,537	163,447	169,687	170,558	169,642	170,515

G1: Net equivalents to a range of gross annual income figures

	2015/16				2015/16		
	Employed				Self-employed		
	Net equivalent income	Net per £100 extra	Reason		Net equivalent income	Net per £100 extra	Reason
Gross income £pa	£pa	£pa		Gross income £pa	£pa	£pa	
1,000	1,000	100		1,000	1,000	100	
2,000	2,000	100		2,000	2,000	100	
3,000	3,000	100		3,000	3,000	100	
4,000	4,000	100		4,000	4,000	100	
5,000	5,000	100		*5,965*	*5,965*	*	← *£146 NIC Class 2*
6,000	6,000	100		6,000	5,854	*	*payable*
7,000	7,000	100		7,000	6,854	*	
8,000	8,000	100		8,000	7,854	*	
8,060	*8,060*	*88*	← *12% NIC Class 1 payable*	*8,060*	*7,914*	*91*	← *9% NIC Class 4 payable*
9,000	8,887	*88*		9,000	8,769	91	
10,000	*9,767*	*68*	← *20% tax payable*	10,000	9,679	91	
10,600	10,295	68		*10,600*	*10,225*	*71*	← *20% tax payable*
11,000	10,567	68		11,000	10,509	71	** £2.80 x 52 weeks = £146*
12,000	11,247	68		12,000	11,219	71	*pa fixed for any level of*
13,000	11,927	68		13,000	11,929	71	*income in excess*
14,000	12,607	68		14,000	12,639	71	*of £5,965 pa. So net*
15,000	13,287	68		15,000	13,349	71	*equivalent of £6,100*
16,000	13,967	68		16,000	14,059	71	*gross is £5,954.*
17,000	14,647	68		17,000	14,769	71	
18,000	15,327	68		18,000	15,479	71	
19,000	16,007	68		19,000	16,189	71	
20,000	16,687	68		20,000	16,899	71	
21,000	17,367	68		21,000	17,609	71	
22,000	18,047	68		22,000	18,319	71	
23,000	18,727	68		23,000	19,029	71	
24,000	19,407	68		24,000	19,739	71	
25,000	20,087	68		25,000	20,449	71	
26,000	20,767	68		26,000	21,159	71	
27,000	21,447	68		27,000	21,869	71	
28,000	22,127	68		28,000	22,579	71	
29,000	22,807	68		29,000	23,289	71	
30,000	23,487	68		30,000	23,999	71	
31,000	24,167	68		31,000	24,709	71	
32,000	24,847	68		32,000	25,419	71	
33,000	25,527	68		33,000	26,129	71	
34,000	26,207	68		34,000	26,839	71	
35,000	26,887	68		35,000	27,549	71	
37,500	28,587	68		37,500	29,324	71	
40,000	30,287	68		40,000	31,099	71	
42,385	*31,909*	*58*	← *NIC Class 1 reduced*	*42,385*	*32,793*	*58*	← *NIC Class 4 reduced to*
45,000	33,426	58	*to 2% and 40% tax*	45,000	34,310	58	*2% and 40% tax payable*
50,000	36,326	58	*payable*	50,000	37,210	58	
55,000	39,226	58		55,000	40,110	58	
60,000	42,126	58		60,000	43,010	58	
65,000	45,026	58		65,000	45,910	58	
70,000	47,926	58		70,000	48,810	58	
75,000	50,826	58		75,000	51,710	58	
80,000	53,726	58		80,000	54,610	58	
85,000	56,626	58		85,000	57,510	58	
90,000	59,526	58		90,000	60,410	58	
95,000	62,426	58		95,000	63,310	58	
100,000	*65,326*	*38*	← *PA reduces here*	*100,000*	*66,210*	*38*	← *PA reduces here*
121,200	*73,382*	*53*	← *PA reduced to zero*	*121,200*	*74,266*	*58*	← *PA reduced to zero*
150,000	90,086	53	← *45% tax payable*	150,000	90,970	53	← *45% tax payable*
200,000	116,586	53		200,000	117,470	53	
250,000	143,086	53		250,000	143,970	53	
300,000	169,586	53		300,000	170,470	53	

	2016/17		
	Employed		
	Net equivalent income	Net per £100 extra	Reason
Gross income £pa	£pa	£pa	
1,000	1,000	100	
2,000	2,000	100	
3,000	3,000	100	
4,000	4,000	100	
5,000	5,000	100	
6,000	6,000	100	
7,000	7,000	100	
8,000	8,000	100	
8,060	*8,060*	*88*	← *12% NIC Class 1 payable*
9,000	8,887	*88*	
10,000	9,767	88	
11,000	*10,647*	*68*	← *20% tax payable*
12,000	11,327	68	
13,000	12,007	68	
14,000	12,687	68	
15,000	13,367	68	
16,000	14,047	68	
17,000	14,727	68	
18,000	15,407	68	
19,000	16,087	68	
20,000	16,767	68	
21,000	17,447	68	
22,000	18,127	68	
23,000	18,807	68	
24,000	19,487	68	
25,000	20,167	68	
26,000	20,847	68	
27,000	21,527	68	
28,000	22,207	68	
29,000	22,887	68	
30,000	23,567	68	
31,000	24,247	68	
32,000	24,927	68	
33,000	25,607	68	
34,000	26,287	68	
35,000	26,967	68	
37,500	28,667	68	
40,000	30,367	68	
43,000	*32,407*	*58*	← *NIC Class 1 reduced to 2% and 40% tax payable*
45,000	33,567	58	
50,000	36,467	58	
55,000	39,367	58	
60,000	42,267	58	
65,000	45,167	58	
70,000	48,067	58	
75,000	50,967	58	
80,000	53,867	58	
85,000	56,767	58	
90,000	59,667	58	
95,000	62,567	58	
100,000	*65,467*	*38*	← *PA reduces here*
122,000	*73,827*	*58*	← *PA reduced to zero*
150,000	*90,067*	*53*	← *45% tax payable*
200,000	116,567	53	
250,000	143,067	53	
300,000	169,567	53	

	2016/17		
	Self-employed		
	Net equivalent income	Net per £100 extra	Reason
Gross income £pa	£pa	£pa	
1,000	1,000	100	
2,000	2,000	100	
3,000	3,000	100	
4,000	4,000	100	
5,965	*5,965*	*	← *£146 NIC Class 2 payable*
6,000	5,854	*	
7,000	6,854	*	
8,000	7,854	*	
8,060	*7,914*	*91*	← *9% NIC Class 4 payable*
9,000	8,769	91	
10,000	9,679	91	
11,000	*10,589*	*71*	← *20% tax payable*
12,000	11,299	71	**£2.80 x 52 weeks = £146 pa fixed for any level of income in excess of £5,965 pa. So net equivalent of £6,100 gross is £5,954.*
13,000	12,009	71	
14,000	12,719	71	
15,000	13,429	71	
16,000	14,139	71	
17,000	14,849	71	
18,000	15,559	71	
19,000	16,269	71	
20,000	16,979	71	
21,000	17,689	71	
22,000	18,399	71	
23,000	19,109	71	
24,000	19,819	71	
25,000	20,529	71	
26,000	21,239	71	
27,000	21,949	71	
28,000	22,659	71	
29,000	23,369	71	
30,000	24,079	71	
31,000	24,789	71	
32,000	25,499	71	
33,000	26,209	71	
34,000	26,919	71	
35,000	27,629	71	
37,500	29,404	71	
40,000	31,179	71	
43,000	*33,309*	*58*	← *NIC Class 4 reduced to 2% and 40% tax payable*
45,000	34,469	58	
50,000	37,369	58	
55,000	40,269	58	
60,000	43,169	58	
65,000	46,069	58	
70,000	48,969	58	
75,000	51,869	58	
80,000	54,769	58	
85,000	57,669	58	
90,000	60,569	58	
95,000	63,469	58	
100,000	*66,369*	*38*	← *PA reduces here*
122,000	*74,729*	*58*	← *PA reduced to zero*
150,000	*90,969*	*53*	← *45% tax payable*
200,000	117,469	53	
250,000	143,969	53	
300,000	170,469	53	

G1: Net equivalents to a range of gross annual income figures

2017/18 Employed			
Gross income £pa	Net equivalent income £pa	Net per £100 extra £pa	Reason
1,000	1,000	100	
2,000	2,000	100	
3,000	3,000	100	
4,000	4,000	100	
5,000	5,000	100	
6,000	6,000	100	
7,000	7,000	100	
8,000	8,000	100	
8,164	*8,164*	*88*	← *Class 1 NI payable at 12%*
9,000	8,900	88	
10,000	9,780	88	
11,000	10,660	78	
11,500	*11,100*	*68*	← *Income tax payable at 20%*
12,000	11,440	68	
13,000	12,120	68	
14,000	12,800	68	
15,000	13,480	68	
16,000	14,160	68	
17,000	14,840	68	
18,000	15,520	68	
19,000	16,200	68	
20,000	16,880	68	
21,000	17,560	68	
22,000	18,240	68	
23,000	18,920	68	
24,000	19,600	68	
25,000	20,280	68	
26,000	20,960	68	
27,000	21,640	68	
28,000	22,320	68	
29,000	23,000	68	
30,000	23,680	68	
31,000	24,360	68	
32,000	25,040	68	
33,000	25,720	68	
34,000	26,400	68	
35,000	27,080	68	
37,500	28,780	68	
40,000	30,480	68	
42,500	32,180	68	
45,000	*33,880*	*	← *Income tax payable at 40%*
45,032	*33,895*	58	*and NI payable at 2%*
50,000	36,776	58	
55,000	39,676	58	
60,000	42,576	58	
65,000	45,476	58	
70,000	48,376	58	
75,000	51,276	58	
80,000	54,176	58	
85,000	57,076	58	
90,000	59,976	58	
95,000	62,876	58	
100,000	*65,776*	*38*	← *PA reduces here*
123,000	*74,516*	*58*	← *PA reduced to zero*
150,000	*90,176*	*53*	← *Income tax payable at 45%*
200,000	116,676	53	
250,000	143,176	53	
300,000	169,676	53	

2017/18 Self-employed			
Gross income £pa	Net equivalent income £pa	Net per £100 extra £pa	Reason
1,000	1,000	100	
2,000	2,000	100	
3,000	3,000	100	
4,000	4,000	100	
5,000	5,000	*	
6,025	*5,877*	*	← *Class 2 NI payable at £2.85 a week*
7,000	6,852	100	
8,000	7,852	100	
8,164	*8,016*	*91*	← *Class 4 NI payable at 9%*
9,000	8,777	91	
10,000	9,687	91	
11,000	10,597	81	
11,500	*11,052*	*71*	← *Income tax payable at 20%*
12,000	11,407	71	
13,000	12,117	71	
14,000	12,827	71	
15,000	13,537	71	
16,000	14,247	71	
17,000	14,957	71	
18,000	15,667	71	
19,000	16,377	71	
20,000	17,087	71	
21,000	17,797	71	
22,000	18,507	71	
23,000	19,217	71	
24,000	19,927	71	
25,000	20,637	71	
26,000	21,347	71	
27,000	22,057	71	
28,000	22,767	71	
29,000	23,477	71	
30,000	24,187	71	
31,000	24,897	71	
32,000	25,607	71	
33,000	26,317	71	
34,000	27,027	71	
35,000	27,737	71	
37,500	29,512	71	
40,000	31,287	71	
42,500	33,062	71	
45,000	*34,837*	*58*	← *Income tax payable at 40%*
47,500	36,287	58	*and NI payable at 2%*
50,000	37,737	58	
55,000	40,637	58	
60,000	43,537	58	
65,000	46,437	58	
70,000	49,337	58	
75,000	52,237	58	
80,000	55,137	58	
85,000	58,037	58	
90,000	60,937	58	
95,000	63,837	58	
100,000	*66,737*	*38*	← *PA reduces here*
123,000	*75,477*	*58*	← *PA reduced to zero*
150,000	*91,137*	*53*	← *Income tax payable at 45%*
200,000	117,637	53	
250,000	144,137	53	
300,000	170,637	53	

	2018/19		
	Employed		
	Net equivalent income	Net per £100 extra	Reason
Gross income £pa	£pa	£pa	
1,000	1,000	100	
2,000	2,000	100	
3,000	3,000	100	
4,000	4,000	100	
5,000	5,000	100	
6,000	6,000	100	
7,000	7,000	100	
8,000	8,000	100	
8,424	*8,424*	*88*	*← Class 1 NI payable at 12%*
9,000	8,931	88	
10,000	9,811	88	
11,000	10,691	88	
11,850	*11,439*	*68*	*← Income tax payable at 20%*
12,000	11,541	68	
13,000	12,221	68	
14,000	12,901	68	
15,000	13,581	68	
16,000	14,261	68	
17,000	14,941	68	
18,000	15,621	68	
19,000	16,301	68	
20,000	16,981	68	
21,000	17,661	68	
22,000	18,341	68	
23,000	19,021	68	
24,000	19,701	68	
25,000	20,381	68	
26,000	21,061	68	
27,000	21,741	68	
28,000	22,421	68	
29,000	23,101	68	
30,000	23,781	68	
31,000	24,461	68	
32,000	25,141	68	
33,000	25,821	68	
34,000	26,501	68	
35,000	27,181	68	
37,500	28,881	68	
40,000	30,581	68	
42,500	32,281	68	
45,000	33,981	68	
46,350	*34,899*	*	*← Income tax payable at 40%*
46,384	*34,915*	*58*	*and NI payable at 2%*
50,000	37,012	58	
55,000	39,912	58	
60,000	42,812	58	
65,000	45,712	58	
70,000	48,612	58	
75,000	51,512	58	
80,000	54,412	58	
85,000	57,312	58	
90,000	60,212	58	
95,000	63,112	58	
100,000	*66,012*	*38*	*← PA reduces here*
123,700	*75,018*	*58*	*← PA reduced to zero*
150,000	*90,272*	*53*	*← Income tax payable at 45%*
200,000	116,772	53	
250,000	143,272	53	
300,000	169,772	53	

	2018/19		
	Self-employed		
	Net equivalent income	Net per £100 extra	Reason
Gross income £pa	£pa	£pa	
1,000	1,000	100	
2,000	2,000	100	
3,000	3,000	100	
4,000	4,000	100	
5,000	5,000	*	
6,205	*6,052*	*100*	*← Class 2 NI payable at*
7,000	6,852	100	*£2.95 a week*
8,000	7,847	100	
8,424	*8,271*	*91*	*← Class 4 NI payable at 9%*
9,000	8,795	91	
10,000	9,705	91	
11,000	10,615	91	
11,850	*11,388*	*71*	*← Income tax payable at 20%*
12,000	11,495	71	
13,000	12,205	71	
14,000	12,915	71	
15,000	13,625	71	
16,000	14,335	71	
17,000	15,045	71	
18,000	15,755	71	
19,000	16,465	71	
20,000	17,175	71	
21,000	17,885	71	
22,000	18,595	71	
23,000	19,305	71	
24,000	20,015	71	
25,000	20,725	71	
26,000	21,435	71	
27,000	22,145	71	
28,000	22,855	71	
29,000	23,565	71	
30,000	24,275	71	
31,000	24,985	71	
32,000	25,695	71	
33,000	26,405	71	
34,000	27,115	71	
35,000	27,825	71	
37,500	29,600	71	
40,000	31,375	71	
42,500	33,150	71	
45,000	34,925	71	
46,350	*35,883*	*58*	*← Income tax payable at 40%*
47,500	*36,550*	*58*	*and NI payable at 2%*
50,000	38,000	58	
55,000	40,900	58	
60,000	43,800	58	
65,000	46,700	58	
70,000	49,600	58	
75,000	52,500	58	
80,000	55,400	58	
85,000	58,300	58	
90,000	61,200	58	
95,000	64,100	58	
100,000	*67,000*	*38*	*← PA reduces here*
123,700	*76,006*	*58*	*← PA reduced to zero*
150,000	*91,260*	*53*	*← Income tax payable at 45%*
200,000	117,760	53	
250,000	144,260	53	
300,000	170,760	53	

G1: Net equivalents to a range of gross annual income figures

	2019/20		
	Employed		
	Net equivalent income	Net per £100 extra	Reason
Gross income £pa	£pa	£pa	
1,000	1,000	100	
2,000	2,000	100	
3,000	3,000	100	
4,000	4,000	100	
5,000	5,000	100	
6,000	6,000	100	
7,000	7,000	100	
8,000	8,000	100	
8,632	*8,632*	*88*	← Class 1 NI payable at 12%
9,000	8,956	88	
10,000	9,836	88	
11,000	10,716	88	
12,000	11,596	*88*	
12,500	*12,036*	*68*	← Income tax payable at 20%
13,000	12,376	68	
14,000	13,056	68	
15,000	13,736	68	
16,000	14,416	68	
17,000	15,096	68	
18,000	15,776	68	
19,000	16,456	68	
20,000	17,136	68	
21,000	17,816	68	
22,000	18,496	68	
23,000	19,176	68	
24,000	19,856	68	
25,000	20,536	68	
26,000	21,216	68	
27,000	21,896	68	
28,000	22,576	68	
29,000	23,256	68	
30,000	23,936	68	
31,000	24,616	68	
32,000	25,296	68	
33,000	25,976	68	
34,000	26,656	68	
35,000	27,336	68	
40,000	30,736	68	
45,000	34,136	68	
50,000	*37,536*	*48*	← Income tax payable at 40%
50,024	*37,547*	*58*	← NI Payable at 2%
55,000	40,433	58	
60,000	43,333	*58*	
65,000	46,233	58	
70,000	49,133	58	
75,000	52,033	58	
80,000	54,933	58	
85,000	57,833	58	
90,000	60,733	58	
95,000	63,633	58	
100,000	*66,533*	*38*	← PA reduces here
125,000	*76,033*	*58*	← PA reduced to zero
150,000	*90,533*	*53*	← Income tax payable at 45%
200,000	117,033	53	
250,000	143,533	53	
300,000	170,033	53	

	2019/20		
	Self–employed		
	Net equivalent income	Net per £100 extra	Reason
Gross income £pa	£pa	£pa	
1,000	1,000	100	
2,000	2,000	100	
3,000	3,000	100	
4,000	4,000	100	
5,000	5,000	*	
6,365	*6,209*	*100*	← Class 2 NI payable at £3.00 a week
7,000	6,844	100	
8,000	7,844	100	
8,632	*8,476*	*91*	← Class 4 NI payable at 9%
9,000	8,811	91	
10,000	9,721	91	
11,000	10,631	91	
12,000	11,541	91	
12,500	*11,996*	*71*	← Income tax payable at 20%
13,000	12,351	71	
14,000	13,061	71	
15,000	13,771	71	
16,000	14,481	71	
17,000	15,191	71	
18,000	15,901	71	
19,000	16,611	71	
20,000	17,321	71	
21,000	18,031	71	
22,000	18,741	71	
23,000	19,451	71	
24,000	20,161	71	
25,000	20,871	71	
26,000	21,581	71	
27,000	22,291	71	
28,000	23,001	71	
29,000	23,711	71	
30,000	24,421	71	
31,000	25,131	71	
32,000	25,841	71	
33,000	26,551	71	
34,000	27,261	71	
35,000	27,971	71	
40,000	31,521	71	
45,000	35,071	71	
← 50,000	*38,621*	*77*	Income tax payable at 40% and NI Payable at 2%
55,000	41,521	58	
60,000	44,421	58	
65,000	47,321	58	
70,000	50,221	58	
75,000	53,121	58	
80,000	56,021	58	
85,000	58,921	58	
90,000	61,821	58	
95,000	64,721	58	
100,000	*67,621*	*38*	← PA reduces here
125,000	*77,121*	*58*	← PA reduced to zero
150,000	91,621	53	← Income tax payable at 45%
200,000	118,121	53	
250,000	144,621	53	
300,000	171,121	53	

2020/21 — Employed

Gross income £pa	Net equivalent income £pa	Net per £100 extra £pa	Reason
1,000	1,000	100	
2,000	2,000	100	
3,000	3,000	100	
4,000	4,000	100	
5,000	5,000	100	
6,000	6,000	100	
7,000	7,000	100	
8,000	8,000	100	
9,000	9,000	100	
9,500	9,500	88	← Class 1 NI payable at 12%
10,000	9,940	88	
11,000	10,820	88	
12,000	11,700	88	
12,500	12,140	68	← Income tax payable at 20%
13,000	12,480	68	
14,000	13,160	68	
15,000	13,840	68	
16,000	14,520	68	
17,000	15,200	68	
18,000	15,880	68	
19,000	16,560	68	
20,000	17,240	68	
21,000	17,920	68	
22,000	18,600	68	
23,000	19,280	68	
24,000	19,960	68	
25,000	20,640	68	
26,000	21,320	68	
27,000	22,000	68	
28,000	22,680	68	
29,000	23,360	68	
30,000	24,040	68	
31,000	24,720	68	
32,000	25,400	68	
33,000	26,080	68	
34,000	26,760	68	
35,000	27,440	68	
40,000	30,840	68	
45,000	34,240	68	
50,000	37,640	48	← Income tax payable at 40%
50,024	37,652	58	← NI Payable at 2%
55,000	40,538	58	
60,000	43,438	58	
65,000	46,338	58	
70,000	49,238	58	
75,000	52,138	58	
80,000	55,038	58	
85,000	57,938	58	
90,000	60,838	58	
95,000	63,738	58	
100,000	66,638	38	← PA reduces here
125,000	76,138	58	← PA reduced to zero
150,000	90,638	53	← Income tax payable at 45%
200,000	117,138	53	
250,000	143,638	53	
300,000	170,138	53	

2020/21 — Self-employed

Gross income £pa	Net equivalent income £pa	Net per £100 extra £pa	Reason
1,000	1,000	100	
2,000	2,000	100	
3,000	3,000	100	
4,000	4,000	100	
5,000	5,000	*	
6,475	6,316	100	← Class 2 NI payable at £3.05 a week
7,000	6,841	100	
8,000	7,841	100	
9,000	8,841	100	
9,500	9,341	91	← Class 4 NI payable at 9%
10,000	9,796	91	
11,000	10,706	91	
12,000	11,616	91	
12,500	12,071	71	← Income tax payable at 20%
13,000	12,426	71	
14,000	13,136	71	
15,000	13,846	71	
16,000	14,556	71	
17,000	15,266	71	
18,000	15,976	71	
19,000	16,686	71	
20,000	17,396	71	
21,000	18,106	71	
22,000	18,816	71	
23,000	19,526	71	
24,000	20,236	71	
25,000	20,946	71	
26,000	21,656	71	
27,000	22,366	71	
28,000	23,076	71	
29,000	23,786	71	
30,000	24,496	71	
31,000	25,206	71	
32,000	25,916	71	
33,000	26,626	71	
34,000	27,336	71	
35,000	28,046	71	
40,000	31,596	71	
45,000	35,146	71	
50,000	38,696	77	← Income tax payable at 40% and NI Payable at 2%
55,000	41,596	58	
60,000	44,496	58	
65,000	47,396	58	
70,000	50,296	58	
75,000	53,196	58	
80,000	56,096	58	
85,000	58,996	58	
90,000	61,896	58	
95,000	64,796	58	
100,000	67,696	38	← PA reduces here
125,000	77,196	58	← PA reduced to zero
150,000	91,696	53	← Income tax payable at 45%
200,000	118,196	53	
250,000	144,696	53	
300,000	171,196	53	

G1: Net equivalents to a range of gross annual income figures

	2021/22		
	Employed		
	Net equivalent income	Net per £100 extra	Reason
Gross income £pa	£pa	£pa	
1,000	1,000	100	
2,000	2,000	100	
3,000	3,000	100	
4,000	4,000	100	
5,000	5,000	100	
6,000	6,000	100	
7,000	7,000	100	
8,000	8,000	100	
9,000	9,000	100	
9,568	*9,568*	*88*	← Class 1 NI payable at 12%
10,000	9,948	88	
11,000	10,828	88	
12,000	11,708	88	
12,570	*12,210*	*68*	← Income tax payable at 20%
13,000	12,502	68	
14,000	13,182	68	
15,000	13,862	68	
16,000	14,542	68	
17,000	15,222	68	
18,000	15,902	68	
19,000	16,582	68	
20,000	17,262	68	
21,000	17,942	68	
22,000	18,622	68	
23,000	19,302	68	
24,000	19,982	68	
25,000	20,662	68	
26,000	21,342	68	
27,000	22,022	68	
28,000	22,702	68	
29,000	23,382	68	
30,000	24,062	68	
31,000	24,742	68	
32,000	25,422	68	
33,000	26,102	68	
34,000	26,782	68	
35,000	27,462	68	
40,000	30,862	68	
45,000	34,262	68	
50,000	37,662	68	
50,270	*37,846*	*48*	← Income tax payable at 40%
50,284	*37,852*	*58*	← NI Payable at 2%
55,270	40,744	58	
60,270	43,644	58	
65,270	46,544	58	
70,270	49,444	58	
75,270	52,344	58	
80,270	55,244	58	
85,270	58,144	58	
90,270	61,044	58	
95,270	63,944	58	
100,000	*66,688*	*38*	← PA starts reducing here
125,140	*76,241*	*58*	← PA reduced to zero
150,000	*90,660*	*53*	← Income tax payable at 45%
200,000	117,160	53	
250,000	143,660	57	
300,000	170,160	53	

	2021/22		
	Self-employed		
	Net equivalent income	Net per £100 extra	Reason
Gross income £pa	£pa	£pa	
1,000	1,000	100	
2,000	2,000	100	
3,000	3,000	100	
4,000	4,000	100	
5,000	5,000	100	
6,000	6,000	*	
6,515	*6,356*	*100*	← Class 2 NI payable at £3.05 a week
7,000	6,841	100	
8,000	7,841	100	
9,000	8,841	100	
9,568	*9,409*	*91*	← Class 4 NI payable at 9%
10,000	9,803	91	
11,000	10,713	91	
12,000	11,623	91	
12,570	*12,141*	*71*	← Income tax payable at 20%
13,000	12,447	71	
14,000	13,157	71	
15,000	13,867	71	
16,000	14,577	71	
17,000	15,287	71	
18,000	15,997	71	
19,000	16,707	71	
20,000	17,417	71	
21,000	18,127	71	
22,000	18,837	71	
23,000	19,547	71	
24,000	20,257	71	
25,000	20,967	71	
26,000	21,677	71	
27,000	22,387	71	
28,000	23,097	71	
29,000	23,807	71	
30,000	24,517	71	
31,000	25,227	71	
32,000	25,937	71	
33,000	26,647	71	
34,000	27,357	71	
35,000	28,067	71	
40,000	31,617	71	
45,000	35,167	71	
50,000	38,717	71	
50,270	*38,908*	*58*	← Income tax payable at 40% and NI Payable at 2%
55,270	41,808	58	
60,270	44,708	58	
65,270	47,608	58	
70,270	50,508	58	
75,270	53,408	58	
80,270	56,308	58	
85,270	59,208	58	
90,270	62,108	58	
95,270	65,008	58	
100,000	*67,752*	*38*	← PA starts reducing here
125,140	*77,305*	*58*	← PA reduced to zero
150,000	*91,724*	*53*	← Income tax payable at 45%
200,000	118,224	53	
250,000	144,724	53	
300,000	171,224	57	

	2022/23		
	Employed		
Gross income £pa	Net equivalent income £pa	Net per £100 extra £pa	Reason
1,000	1,000	100	
2,000	2,000	100	
3,000	3,000	100	
4,000	4,000	100	
5,000	5,000	100	
6,000	6,000	100	
7,000	7,000	100	
8,000	8,000	100	
9,000	9,000	100	
10,000	10,000	100	
11,000	11,000	100	
11,908	11,908	87	*←Class 1 NI payable*
12,000	11,988	87	*at 12.73%*
12,570	12,486	67	*←Incometaxpayableat20%*
13,000	12,775	67	
14,000	13,448	67	
15,000	14,120	67	
16,000	14,793	67	
17,000	15,466	67	
18,000	16,138	67	
19,000	16,811	67	
20,000	17,484	67	
21,000	18,157	67	
22,000	18,829	67	
23,000	19,502	67	
24,000	20,175	67	
25,000	20,847	67	
26,000	21,520	67	
27,000	22,193	67	
28,000	22,865	67	
29,000	23,538	67	
30,000	24,211	67	
31,000	24,884	67	
32,000	25,556	67	
33,000	26,229	67	
34,000	26,902	67	
35,000	27,574	67	
40,000	30,938	67	
45,000	34,301	67	
50,000	37,665	67	
50,270	37,847	57	*←Incometaxpayableat40%*
55,270	40,709	57	*& NI Payable at 2.73%*
60,270	43,572	57	
65,270	46,436	57	
70,270	49,299	57	
75,270	52,163	57	
80,270	55,026	57	
85,270	57,890	57	
90,270	60,753	57	
95,270	63,617	57	
100,000	66,325	37	*← PA starts reducing here*
125,140	75,695	57	*← PA reduced to zero*
150,000	89,932	52	*←Incometaxpayableat45%*
200,000	116,067	52	
250,000	142,202	52	
300,000	168,337	52	

	2022/23		
	Self-employed		
Gross income £pa	Net equivalent income £pa	Net per £100 extra £pa	Reason
1,000	1,000	100	
2,000	2,000	100	
3,000	3,000	100	
4,000	4,000	100	
5,000	5,000	100	
6,000	6,000	100	
7,000	7,000	100	*← Class 2 NI payable at*
8,000	8,000	100	*£3.05 a week*
9,000	9,000	100	
10,000	10,000	100	
11,000	11,000	100	*←Class 4 NI payable at*
11,908	11,908		*10.75% and Class 2 NI*
12,000	11,827	90	*payable at £3.15*
12,570	12,342	70	*←Incometaxpayableat20%*
13,000	12,644	70	
14,000	13,347	70	
15,000	14,049	70	
16,000	14,752	70	
17,000	15,455	70	
18,000	16,157	70	
19,000	16,860	70	
20,000	17,563	70	
21,000	18,266	70	
22,000	18,968	70	
23,000	19,671	70	
24,000	20,374	70	
25,000	21,076	70	
26,000	21,779	70	
27,000	22,482	70	
28,000	23,184	70	
29,000	23,887	70	
30,000	24,590	70	
31,000	25,293	70	
32,000	25,995	70	
33,000	26,698	70	
34,000	27,401	70	
35,000	28,103	70	
40,000	31,617	70	
45,000	35,130	70	
50,000	38,644	70	
50,270	38,834	57	*←Incometaxpayableat40%*
55,270	41,697	57	*and NI Payable at 2.73%*
60,270	44,561	57	
65,270	47,424	57	
70,270	50,288	57	
75,270	53,151	57	
80,270	56,015	57	
85,270	58,878	57	
90,270	61,742	57	
95,270	64,605	57	
100,000	67,314	37	*← PA starts reducing here*
125,140	76,684	57	*← PA reduced to zero*
150,000	90,921	52	*←Incometaxpayableat45%*
200,000	117,056	52	
250,000	143,191	52	
300,000	169,326	56	

G1: Net equivalents to a range of gross annual income figures

	2023/24		
	Employed		
	Net equivalent income	Net per £100 extra	Reason
Gross income £pa	£pa	£pa	
1,000	1,000	100	
2,000	2,000	100	
3,000	3,000	100	
4,000	4,000	100	
5,000	5,000	100	
6,000	6,000	100	
7,000	7,000	100	
8,000	8,000	100	
9,000	9,000	100	
10,000	10,000	100	
11,000	11,000	100	
12,000	12,000	100	
12,570	12,570	68	← *Income tax payable at 20% & Class 1 NI payable at 11.50%*
13,000	12,865	69	
14,000	13,550	69	
15,000	14,235	69	
16,000	14,920	69	
17,000	15,605	69	
18,000	16,290	69	
19,000	16,975	69	
20,000	17,660	69	
21,000	18,345	69	
22,000	19,030	69	
23,000	19,715	69	
24,000	20,400	69	
25,000	21,085	69	
26,000	21,770	69	
27,000	22,455	69	
28,000	23,140	69	
29,000	23,825	69	
30,000	24,510	69	
31,000	25,195	69	
32,000	25,880	69	
33,000	26,565	69	
34,000	27,250	69	
35,000	27,935	69	
40,000	31,360	69	
45,000	34,785	69	
50,000	38,210	68	
50,270	38,395	58	← *Income tax payable at 40% & Class 1 NI payable at 2.00%*
55,000	41,137	58	
60,000	44,037	58	
65,000	46,937	58	
70,000	49,837	58	
75,000	52,737	58	
80,000	55,637	58	
85,000	58,537	58	
90,000	61,437	58	
95,000	64,337	58	
100,000	67,237	38	← *PA starts reducing here*
125,140	76,790	53	← *PA reduced to zero & Income tax payable at 45%*
175,000	103,216	53	
225,000	129,716	53	
275,000	156,216	53	

	2023/24		
	Self-employed		
	Net equivalent income	Net per £100 extra	Reason
Gross income £pa	£pa	£pa	
1,000	1,000	100	
2,000	2,000	100	
3,000	3,000	100	
4,000	4,000	100	
5,000	5,000	100	
6,000	6,000	100	
7,000	7,000	100	
8,000	8,000	100	
9,000	9,000	100	
10,000	10,000	100	
11,000	11,000	100	
12,000	12,000	69	
12,570	12,391	71	← *Income tax payable at 20% & Class 4 NI payable at 9% & Class 2 NI payable at £3.45 pw*
13,000	12,696	71	
14,000	13,406	71	
15,000	14,116	71	
16,000	14,826	71	
17,000	15,536	71	
18,000	16,246	71	
19,000	16,956	71	
20,000	17,666	71	
21,000	18,376	71	
22,000	19,086	71	
23,000	19,796	71	
24,000	20,506	71	
25,000	21,216	71	
26,000	21,926	71	
27,000	22,636	71	
28,000	23,346	71	
29,000	24,056	71	
30,000	24,766	71	
31,000	25,476	71	
32,000	26,186	71	
33,000	26,896	71	
34,000	27,606	71	
35,000	28,316	71	
40,000	31,866	71	
45,000	35,416	71	
50,000	38,966	71	
50,270	39,158	58	← *Income tax payable at 40% & Class 4 NI Payable at 2.00%*
55,000	41,901	58	
60,000	44,801	58	
65,000	47,701	58	
70,000	50,601	58	
75,000	53,501	58	
80,000	56,401	58	
85,000	59,301	58	
90,000	62,201	58	
95,000	65,101	58	
100,000	68,001	38	← *PA starts reducing here*
125,140	77,554	53	← *PA reduced to zero & Income tax payable at 45%*
175,000	103,980	53	
225,000	130,480	53	
275,000	156,980	53	

	2024/25 Employed		
Gross income £pa	Net equivalent income £pa	Net per £100 extra £pa	Reason
1,000	1,000	100	
2,000	2,000	100	
3,000	3,000	100	
4,000	4,000	100	
5,000	5,000	100	
6,000	6,000	100	
7,000	7,000	100	
8,000	8,000	100	
9,000	9,000	100	
10,000	10,000	100	
11,000	11,000	100	
12,000	12,000	100	
12,570	12,570	72	← *Income tax payable at 20% & Class 1 NI payable at 8%*
13,000	12,880	72	
14,000	13,600	72	
15,000	14,320	72	
16,000	15,040	72	
17,000	15,760	72	
18,000	16,480	72	
19,000	17,200	72	
20,000	17,920	72	
21,000	18,640	72	
22,000	19,360	72	
23,000	20,080	72	
24,000	20,800	72	
25,000	21,520	72	
26,000	22,240	72	
27,000	22,960	72	
28,000	23,680	72	
29,000	24,400	72	
30,000	25,120	72	
31,000	25,840	72	
32,000	26,560	72	
33,000	27,280	72	
34,000	28,000	72	
35,000	28,720	72	
40,000	32,320	72	
45,000	35,920	72	
50,000	39,520	72	
50,270	39,714	58	← *Income tax payable at 40% & Class 1 NI payable at 2.00%*
55,000	42,457	58	
60,000	45,357	58	
65,000	48,257	58	
70,000	51,157	58	
75,000	54,057	58	
80,000	56,957	58	
85,000	59,857	58	
90,000	62,757	58	
95,000	65,657	58	
100,000	68,557	38	← *PA starts reducing here*
125,140	78,110	53	← *PA reduced to zero & Income tax payable at 45%*
175,000	104,536	53	
225,000	131,036	53	
275,000	157,536	53	

	2024/25 Self-employed		
Gross income £pa	Net equivalent income £pa	Net per £100 extra £pa	Reason
1,000	1,000	100	
2,000	2,000	100	
3,000	3,000	100	
4,000	4,000	100	
5,000	5,000	100	
6,000	6,000	100	
7,000	7,000	100	
8,000	8,000	100	
9,000	9,000	100	
10,000	10,000	100	
11,000	11,000	100	
12,000	12,000	100	
12,570	12,570	74	← *Income tax payable at 20% & Class 4 NI payable at 6% & Class 2 NI is now voluntary and so is not included here*
13,000	12,888	74	
14,000	13,628	74	
15,000	14,368	74	
16,000	15,108	74	
17,000	15,848	74	
18,000	16,588	74	
19,000	17,328	74	
20,000	18,068	74	
21,000	18,808	74	
22,000	19,548	74	
23,000	20,288	74	
24,000	21,028	74	
25,000	21,768	74	
26,000	22,508	74	
27,000	23,248	74	
28,000	23,988	74	
29,000	24,728	74	
30,000	25,468	74	
31,000	26,208	74	
32,000	26,948	74	
33,000	27,688	74	
34,000	28,428	74	
35,000	29,168	74	
40,000	32,868	74	
45,000	36,568	74	
50,000	40,268	74	
50,270	40,468	58	← *Income tax payable at 40% & Class 4 NI Payable at 2.00%*
55,000	43,211	58	
60,000	46,111	58	
65,000	49,011	58	
70,000	51,911	58	
75,000	54,811	58	
80,000	57,711	58	
85,000	60,611	58	
90,000	63,511	58	
95,000	66,411	58	
100,000	69,311	38	← *PA starts reducing here*
125,140	78,865	53	← *PA reduced to zero & Income tax payable at 45%*
175,000	105,290	53	
225,000	131,790	53	
275,000	158,290	53	

G2: Illustrative net earnings calculations

Individual below state retirement age at 2024/25 tax rates

		Employed person					Self-employed person				
		£pa	£pa	£pa	£pa	£pa	£pa	£pa	£pa	£pa	£pa
Gross income	[a]	15,000	35,000	50,000	110,000	160,000	15,000	35,000	50,000	110,000	160,000
Income tax											
Gross		15,000	35,000	50,000	110,000	160,000	15,000	35,000	50,000	110,000	160,000
Personal allowance *		(12,570)	(12,570)	(12,570)	(7,570)		(12,570)	(12,570)	(12,570)	(7,570)	
Taxable		2,430	22,430	37,430	102,430	160,000	2,430	22,430	37,430	102,430	160,000
Tax payable											
- At 20%		486	4,486	7,486	7,540	7,540	486	4,486	7,486	7,540	7,540
- At 40%					25,892	44,920				25,892	34,976
- At 45%						4,500					15,687
	[b]	486	4,486	7,486	33,432	56,960	486	4,486	7,486	33,432	58,203
National Insurance											
Class 1											
- At 8.00%		193	1,793	2,993	3,016	3,016					
- At 2.00%		0	0	0	1,194	2,194					
Class 2											
- At £3.45 a week **							0	0	0	0	0
Class 4											
- At 6.00%							146	1,346	2,246	2,262	2,262
- At 2.00%							0	0	0	1,195	2,195
	[c]	193	1,793	2,993	4,210	5,210	146	1,346	2,246	3,457	4,457
Net income	[a-b-c]	14,321	28,721	39,521	72,358	97,830	14,368	29,168	40,268	73,111	97,340
Note 1: personal allowance											
Personal allowance		12,570	12,570	12,570	12,570	12,570	12,570	12,570	12,570	12,570	12,570
Restriction for excess of income over limit*					(5,000)	(12,570)				(5,000)	(12,570)
Net allowance		12,570	12,570	12,570	7,570	0	12,570	12,570	12,570	7,570	0

*If gross income does not exceed £100,000, no restriction.
If gross income does exceed £100,000, restriction is the lower of:
(a) (gross pay - £100,000)/2, and
(b) £12,570
** From tax year 2024/2025 Class 2 National Insurance is now voluntary although the rate officially remains at £3.45 a week.

G3: Income tax reliefs and rates

Introductory notes

Personal allowance

Every taxpayer resident in the UK (as well as certain non-UK residents) is entitled to a personal allowance.

From 2010/11, the personal allowance has been subject to an income limit of £100,000. Where total income exceeds this limit, the personal allowance is reduced by 50 per cent of the excess. Accordingly, no personal allowance is available on incomes in excess of £125,140 since 2021/22.

Age-related personal allowance

The age-related personal allowance has been frozen from 2012/13 onwards and from 2016/17 onwards all individuals are entitled to the same personal allowance, regardless of the individuals' date of birth.

Age-related married couple's allowance

Where a couple was married before 5 December 2005, live together and at least one spouse was born before 6 April 1935, the husband can claim married couple's allowance.

Where a couple married or entered into a civil partnership on or after 5 December 2005, live together and at least one spouse or partner was born before 6 April 1935, the person with the higher income can claim married couple's allowance.

For 2024/25 the married couple's allowance is £11,080 and the rate of tax relief is 10%, subject to an income limit of £37,700.

Where the claimant's income exceeds the income limit, the married couple's allowance is reduced by 50% of the excess less any reduction of the personal allowance (as above), until the allowance is equal to the following amounts:

Tax year 2010/11	Minimum allowance £2,670	Tax relief £267
Tax year 2011/12	Minimum allowance £2,800	Tax relief £280
Tax year 2012/13	Minimum allowance £2,960	Tax relief £296
Tax year 2013/14	Minimum allowance £3,040	Tax relief £304
Tax year 2014/15	Minimum allowance £3,140	Tax relief £314
Tax year 2015/16	Minimum allowance £3,220	Tax relief £322
Tax year 2016/17	Minimum allowance £3,220	Tax relief £322
Tax year 2017/18	Minimum allowance £3,260	Tax relief £326
Tax year 2018/19	Minimum allowance £3,360	Tax relief £336
Tax year 2019/20	Minimum allowance £3,450	Tax relief £345
Tax year 2020/21	Minimum allowance £3,510	Tax relief £351
Tax year 2021/22	Minimum allowance £3,530	Tax relief £353
Tax year 2022/23	Minimum allowance £3,640	Tax relief £364
Tax year 2023/24	Minimum allowance £4,010	Tax relief £401
Tax year 2024/25	Minimum allowance £4,010	Tax relief £401

Universal Credit

The Universal Credit payment is made up of a Standard Allowance and any extra amounts that may apply, for example:

- if the claimant has children;
- if the claimant has a disability or health condition that prevents them from working;
- if the claimant needs help paying rent.

How much Universal Credit is received depends on the Claimant's level of earnings.

Standard Allowance	Monthly Allowance
• Single and under age 25	£311.68
• Single and age 25 or over	£393.45
• In a couple and both under age 25	£489.23
• In a couple and one or both are age 25 or over	£617.60

Children	Monthly Allowance
• For the first child (born before 6 April 2017)	£333.33
• For the first child (born on or after 6 April 2017)	£287.92
• For the second child	£287.92 (per child)
• For a severely disabled child	£487.58
• Help with childcare costs (85% of costs up to a maximum of)	£1,014.63 (one child) £1,739.37 (2 or more)

Disability or Health Condition	Monthly Allowance
• Limited capacity for work	£156.11
• Limited capacity for work or work-related activity	£416.19

There are other allowances available depending on individual circumstances including allowances for those who care for the severely disabled and those who need assistance with housing costs.

Taxation of Dividends

Savings income is subdivided into dividends and other savings income, with dividends treated as the top slice of savings income.

Prior to 2016/17 dividends were "grossed up" by the Dividend Tax Credit and tax was payable on dividend income (prior to deducting the Dividend Tax Credit) at the dividend ordinary rate of 10% up to the basic rate limit, and at the dividend upper rate of 32.5% (increased to 33.75% from 2022/23) thereafter up to the higher rate limit. From 2010/11 in addition to these rates, tax is payable on dividend income falling into the additional rate band at the dividend additional rate, as follows:

From tax year 2010/11	42.50%
From tax year 2013/14	37.50%
From tax year 2016/17	38.10%
From tax year 2022/23	39.35%

From 2016/17 that whole methodology of taxing dividends has been changed. The Dividend Tax Credit has been replaced by a tax-free Dividend Allowance. There is no tax payable on the Dividend Allowance, no matter what non-dividend income is received. The Dividend Allowance is as follows:

From tax year 2016/17	£5,000
From tax year 2018/19	£2,000
Tax Year 2023/24	£1,000
Current tax year 2024/25	£500

Tax is payable on any dividend income in excess of the Dividend Allowance at the following rates:

	From 2016/17	From 2022/23
On dividend income within the basic rate band	7.50%	8.75%
On dividend income within the higher rate band	32.50%	33.75%
On dividend income within the additional rate band	38.10%	39.35%

Taxation of Savings

Tax is payable on other savings income at 10% on income in the starting rate band, at 20% on income in the basic rate band, and at 40% thereafter up to the higher rate limit. From 2010/11, in addition to these rates, tax is payable on other savings income falling into the additional rate band at the following rates:

From tax year 2010/11	50%
From tax year 2013/14	45%

Between 2008/09 and 2014/15 there was a 10% starting rate for savings income only. From 2015/16 there is a 0% starting rate for savings only, so the following rates and limits apply:

	Rate	Limit
Tax year 2012/13	10%	£2,710
Tax year 2013/14	10%	£2,790
Tax year 2014/15	10%	£2,880
From tax year 2015/16	0%	£5,000

If the taxpayer's non-savings income exceeds the personal tax allowance of £12,570 (tax year 2024/25) then the starting rate allowance of £5,000 is reduced by the amount by which non-savings income exceed the personal tax allowance. Hence once non-savings income reaches £17,570 the starting rate for savings no longer applies.

From 2016/17 a new Personal Savings Allowance was introduced which means that basic rate taxpayers will not have to pay tax on the first £1,000 of savings income they receive and higher rate taxpayers will not have to pay tax on their first £500 of savings income.

2015/16 to 2024/25

Fiscal year:	2015/16	2016/17	2017/18	2018/19	2019/20	2020/21	2021/22	2022/23	2023/24	2024/25
	£	£	£	£	£	£	£	£	£	£
Income tax reliefs										
Personal allowance	10,600	11,000	11,500	11,850	12,500	12,500	12,570	12,570	12,570	12,570
Income tax rates										
Basic rate band – Payable at 20%	31,785	32,000	33,500	34,500	37,500	37,500	37,700	37,700	37,700	37,700
Higher rate band – Payable at 40%	118,215	118,000	116,500	115,500	112,500	112,500	112,300	112,300	87,440	87,440
Additional rate band – Payable at 45%	Balance	Balance	Balance	Balance	Balance	Balance	Balance	Balance	Balance	Balance

G4: National Insurance contributions

Introductory notes

1. Until April 1977, married women could choose to pay a reduced rate of National Insurance (sometimes called the 'small stamp').

   The reduced rate if you're employed is 1.85% of your weekly earnings between £242 and £967 for the period from 6 April 2024 to 5 April 2025.

   This is instead of the standard rate of National Insurance.

2. Class 1 employee contributions and Class 2 contributions cease to be payable when an individual reaches State pension age.

3. Class 4 contributions are not payable in respect of any fiscal year that starts after State pension age has been reached.

4. Class 3 contributions are voluntary at a flat weekly rate (£17.45 in 2024/25).

5. From 6 April 2009 an Upper Accrual Point (UAP) was introduced at a frozen rate of £770.00 per week for the calculation of the State Second Pension (S2P) and Class 1 National Insurance rebates under contracted-out schemes. From the same date the Upper Earnings Limit (UEL) previously used for these purposes was aligned with the higher rate threshold for income tax.

6. Employment allowance will reduce employers' Class 1 National Insurance each time the payroll is run until the £5,000 allowance (2024/25 rates) has been fully utilised or the tax year ends (whichever is sooner). Claims are only against employers' Class 1 National Insurance paid, up to a maximum of £5,000 each tax year. The employment allowance was £2,000 in 2014/15, £3,000 from 2016/17, £4,000 since 2020/21, and now £5,000 with effect from 2022/23.

   Employment Allowance can be claimed by businesses or charities (including community amateur sports clubs) paying employers' Class 1 National Insurance. Claims can also be made by individuals that employ a care or support worker.

   Claims can not be made if:

   - you are the director and only paid employee in your company;
   - you employ someone for personal, household or domestic work (e.g. a nanny or gardener)—unless they are a care or support worker;
   - you are a public body or business doing more than half your work in the public sector (e.g. local councils and NHS services)—unless you are a charity;
   - you are a service company with only deemed payments of employment income under "IR35 rules".

7. On 6 April 2016 the current basic State pension and S2P were abolished and replaced by a single-tier State pension. The abolition of S2P also meant the end of contracting-out. The measures that

implemented the single-tier State pension and abolition of contracting-out are contained in the Pensions Act 2014.

8. For those retiring on or after 6 April 2016, a New State Pension was introduced. The weekly maximum amount of the New State Pension is as follows:

	Monthly	Annual
Tax year 2016/17	£155.65	£8,094
Tax year 2017/18	£159.55	£8,297
Tax year 2018/19	£164.35	£8,546
Tax year 2019/20	£168.60	£8,767
Tax year 2020/21	£175.20	£9,110
Tax year 2021/22	£179.60	£9,339
Tax year 2022/23	£185.15	£9,628
Tax year 2023/24	£203.85	£10,600
Tax year 2024/25	£221.20	£11,502

2014/15 to 2024/25

Fiscal year:	2016/17 £	2017/18 £	2018/19 £	2019/20 £	2020/21 £	2021/22 £	2022/23 £	2023/24 £	2024/25 £
Class 1 contributions (Employees)									
Lower earnings limit (LEL) (pa)	5,824	5,876	6,032	6,136	6,240	6,240	6,396	6,396	6,396
Primary threshold (PT) (pa)	8,060	8,164	8,424	8,632	9,500	9,568	11,908	* 12,570	12,570
Upper earnings limit (UEL) (pa)	43,000	45,032	46,384	50,024	50,024	50,270	50,270	50,270	50,270
Standard rate									
If earnings below LEL:	Nil	Nil	Nil	Nil	Nil	Nil	Nil	Nil	Nil
If earnings at or above LEL:									
– Contribution rate on earnings up to PT	Nil	Nil	Nil	Nil	Nil	Nil	Nil	Nil	Nil
– Contribution rate on earnings between PT and UEL	12.00%	12.00%	12.00%	12.00%	12.00%	12.00%	12.73%	* 11.50%	* 8.00%
– Contribution rate on earnings above UEL	2.00%	2.00%	2.00%	2.00%	2.00%	2.00%	2.73%	* 2.00%	2.00%
Maximum contribution (pa)	4,193 +2.00% of excess over UEL	4,424 +2.00% of excess over UEL	4,555 +2.00% of excess over UEL	4,967 +2.00% of excess over UEL	4,863 +2.00% of excess over UEL	4,884 +2.00% of excess over UEL	4,603 +2.73% of excess over UEL	4,524 * +2.00% of excess over UEL	4,524 +2.00% of excess over UEL
Class 2 contributions (Self-employed)									
Small earnings exception limit									
Small profits threshold	5,965	6,025	6,205	6,365	6,475	6,515	11,908	* 12,570	12,570
Fixed weekly contributions (pw)	2.80	2.85	2.95	3.00	3.05	3.05	3.15	3.45	Nil
Class 4 contributions (Self-employed)									
Lower profits limit (LPL) (pa)	8,060	8,164	8,424	8,632	9,500	9,568	11,908	* 12,570	12,570
Upper profits limit (UPL) (pa)	43,000	45,000	46,350	50,000	50,000	50,270	50,270	50,270	50,270
Contribution rate on profits between LPL and UPL	9.0%	9.0%	9.0%	9.0%	9.0%	9.0%	9.73%	* 9.00%	6.00%
Contribution rate on profits above UPL	2.0%	2.0%	2.0%	2.0%	2.0%	2.0%	2.73%	* 2.00%	2.00%
Maximum contribution (pa)	3,145 +2.00% of excess over UPL	3,315 +2.00% of excess over UPL	3,413 +2.00% of excess over UPL	3,723 +2.00% of excess over UPL	3,645 +2.00% of excess over UPL	3,663 +2.00% of excess over UPL	3,453 +2.73% of excess over UPL	3,393 +2.00% of excess over UPL	3,393 +2.00% of excess over UPL

Note regarding NI in tax year 2022/23

Note that during the tax year ended 5 April 2023 there were changes to the National Insurance rates and thresholds at different stages throughout the year as follows:

From 6 April 2022 to 5 July 2022	13.25% on earnings between £9,880 and £50,270 a year 3.25% on earnings over £50,270 a year
From 6 July to 5 November 2022	13.25% on earnings between £12,570 and £50,270 a year 3.25% on earnings over £50,270 a year
From 6 November 2022 to 5 April 2023	12.00% on earnings between £12,570 and £50,270 a year 2.00% on earnings over £50,270 a year

For simplicity the above rates and thresholds can be pro-rated to establish weighted annual rates and thresholds as follows:

From 6 April 2022 to 5 April 2023	12.73% on earnings between £11,908 and £50,270 a year 2.73% on earnings over £50,270 a year

A similar weighting exercise has been applied to the self-employed rates for 2022/23 as well.

Note regarding NI in tax year 2023/24

Note that during the tax year ended 5 April 2024 there were changes to the rate of National Insurance part way through the year as follows:

From 6 April 2023 to 5 January 2024	12.00% on earnings between £12,570 and £50,270 a year 2.00% on earnings over £50,270 a year
From 6 January 2024 to 5 April 2024	10.00% on earnings between £12,570 and £50,270 a year 2.00% on earnings over £50,270 a year

For simplicity the above rates and thresholds can be pro-rated to establish weighted annual rates and thresholds as follows

From 6 April 2023 to 5 April 2024	11.50% on earnings between £11,908 and £50,270 a year 2.00% on earnings over £50,270 a year

There was no mid year change to the self-employed national insurance rates in 2023/24

G5: VAT registration thresholds and rates

Registration is required when a person's turnover (taxable supplies from all the person's businesses) exceeds prescribed limits.

Past and future turnover limits apply (looking one year back and one year forward).

Registration is also required if a turnover limit is to be exceeded in a period of 30 days.

The registration levels are:

	Past turnover		Future turnover
	1 year	Unless turnover for next year will not exceed	30 days
	£	£	£
1 April 2004 to 31 March 2005	58,000	56,000	58,000
1 April 2005 to 31 March 2006	60,000	58,000	60,000
1 April 2006 to 31 March 2007	61,000	59,000	61,000
1 April 2007 to 31 March 2008	64,000	62,000	64,000
1 April 2008 to 31 March 2009	67,000	65,000	67,000
1 April 2009 to 31 March 2010	68,000	66,000	68,000
1 April 2010 to 31 March 2011	70,000	68,000	70,000
1 April 2011 to 31 March 2012	73,000	71,000	73,000
1 April 2012 to 31 March 2013	77,000	75,000	77,000
1 April 2013 to 31 March 2014	79,000	77,000	79,000
1 April 2014 to 31 March 2015	81,000	79,000	81,000
1 April 2015 to 31 March 2016	82,000	80,000	82,000
1 April 2016 to 31 March 2017	83,000	81,000	83,000
1 April 2017 to 31 March 2024	85,000	83,000	85,000
From 1 April 2024	90,000	88,000	90,000

De-registration depends on satisfying HM Revenue & Customs that the future annual limit (being the same as the "unless turnover for next year will not exceed" in the table above, e.g. £83,000 since 1 April 2017) will not be exceeded.

Note:

These registration and de-registration limits can be of particular relevance in considering likely turnover levels for businesses such as taxis and driving schools, where VAT registration may render charges uncompetitive (because most such businesses operate below the registration limits).

VAT Rates

Date	VAT Rate
1 April 1991 to 30 November 2008	17.5%
1 December 2008 to 31 December 2009	15.0%
1 January 2010 to 3 January 2011	17.5%
From 4 January 2011 to date	20.0%

Group H

Pension

H1: Notes on pension losses

1. Introduction

The law surrounding pension loss calculation remains unchanged in recent years but pensions themselves, life expectancy and discount rates are vastly different.

- As the prescribed rate has fallen and life expectancy has lengthened, pension loss multipliers for use with defined benefit schemes have rocketed, making even small annual losses into significant claims. Moreover, instead of adjusting theoretical calculations drawn at normal retirement age, based on limited information and not really knowing the difference with earlier retirement (the so-called *Auty* discount), we now have internet access to comprehensive materials in relevant occupations, including the tables of factors used to reduce pension if drawn early. Employee pension scheme portals provide all the evidence one could wish for in an individual case.
- There are markedly fewer defined benefit schemes i.e. those defining income for life in retirement by reference to a formula based on past pay and the number of years of work. Where they still exist, largely in the public sector, they mostly use average earnings over the whole career (revalued for inflation, hence called career average revalued earnings [CARE] schemes). Those valued by reference to the level of pay at retirement, so-called final salary schemes, have mostly been closed to new members. The new CARE schemes continue to give rise to proper claims for pension loss under *Parry v Cleaver*.[2]
- There has been a sharp increase in the use of *money purchase* schemes i.e. those in which earnings are invested, to be realised in all sorts of ways in later life or left to the next generation. There is no formula to apply and the value of the fund depends on the performance of the investments. Auto enrolment workplace schemes are money purchase schemes. There is no loss of pension (only irrecoverable loss of investment opportunity) but the value of an employer's contributions can be claimed as a benefit in kind within the claim for loss of earnings, in which a claimant's contributions need to be retained and their tax efficiency carried through.

2. Wider Principles

The aim, with personal injury damages, is the award of reasonable compensation bearing in mind a fair balancing of the chances and contingencies relevant to any issue. Depending on the shape of the case, there may be different ways of formulating the assumptions from which the main calculations proceed and then fine tuning them to reach a balanced result. The same applies to the calculation of pension loss, which is governed by the modern conventional approach and:

- still assesses damages for personal injuries net of tax;[3]

[1] This section, by James Rowley KC and Matthew White, is a heavily cut down version of the *PIBA Guide to Pension Loss Calculation 2020* [the PIBA Guide], Rowley KC and White, with contributions from Richard Whitehall, Jason Wells, Kane Simons and Hannah Saxena, available to purchase at *www.piba.org.uk*. We will not repeat here at every turn that readers, who want to know more or enjoy a less steep learning curve than space currently permits, should read the PIBA Guide. The arguments are there more developed; the methodology of calculation is laid out in smaller chunks and with repetition; the major pension schemes are summarised, and web links provided to the actuarial tables and other important source materials.

[2] [1970] A.C. 1 H.L. – *"Parry"*

[3] *British Transport Commission v Gourley* [1956] A.C. 185, H.L.

- still takes no account of future inflation (other than through the fixing of the correct discount rate), setting the multiplicand in the value of money at date of trial and ignoring the particular avenues of investment open to an individual claimant;[4]
- presently adopts a rate of discount, set under the Civil Liability Act 2018, at -0.25%;[5]
- no longer makes pre-*Wells* arbitrary judicial discounts, instead using the Ogden Tables as the starting point rather than a check, being slow to depart from the relevant actuarial multiplier on impressionistic grounds or because of previously decided multipliers;[6]
- refuses to make pseudo-findings of future or hypothetical fact on the balance of probabilities but reflects the chances by assessing the damages based upon assumptions which aim at doing justice in monetary terms balancing the favourable and adverse contingencies;[7]
- sometimes explicitly frames assumptions in order to balance all the contingencies completely. (There is then no logical ground for further tinkering. Any sense of unease should lead to re-consideration of the drawing of the assumption, not an arbitrary adjustment;)
- sometimes frames an assumption around a convenient point to facilitate the calculation but leaves out certain elements for later consideration and fine tuning. (When required on account of contingencies not yet factored in, this reasoned adjustment is not at all judicial discounting in a pejorative sense;)
- involves doing one's best[8], making the best use of such tools to assist the process as are available[9], and taking, now that detailed calculations and tables founded on a reasonably reliable basis are available, full advantage of them.[10]

3. The nature of claims for loss of defined benefit pension

Older practitioners cut their teeth on the public service and heavy industry pensions of the 1970s and 1980s and the articles in JPIL in 1995.[11] The leading cases from 1970-2000 show the legal landscape.

3.1 Parry v Cleaver

In *Parry v Cleaver,*[12] loss of pension under the defined benefit Police Pension Scheme was considered and, by a majority of 3:2, the House of Lords established that receipt of ill health pension prior to normal retirement is not to be deducted from a claim for loss of earnings. Since each in the Majority

[4] *Mallett v McMonagle* [1970] A.C. 166 H.L.(N.I.) 175B-176D; *Lim Poh Choo v Camden and Islington Area Health Authority* [1980] A.C. 174 H.L. 193B-194B; upheld on this point in *Wells* – per Lord Lloyd 334A, Lord Steyn 353C and Lord Clyde 361E.

[5] In England and Wales. It is currently -0.75% in Scotland and -1.5% in Northern Ireland.

[6] Wells [1999] 1 A.C. 345 – per Lord Lloyd 347D-E.

[7] There are numerous re-statements of the principle but *loci classici* are at *Mallett v McMonagle* at 173F, 174D and 176E-F; *Wells* – per Lord Hope 356F-357A. Deciding the fair balance in assessing damages for what would have been the rest of the career, hence when and at what level pension would have been paid, is a paradigm situation in which this principle applies. The leading case applying the principles of *loss of chance* in the sphere of pension claims is *Brown v MoD* [2006] P.I.Q.R. Q9.

[8] Wells above – per Lord Lloyd 332H-333A and Lord Clyde 361A.

[9] *Wells* above – per Lord Hope 357E.

[10] Wells above – per Lord Clyde 364C.

[11] A Guide to Pension Loss Calculation [1995] JPIL 107; An Updated Guide to Pension Loss Calculation [1995] JPIL 212.

[12] Above.

expressed himself slightly differently, it is useful to see the reasoning as distilled into the headnote of the Official Law Reports:[13]

> "Per Lord Reid: Moneys received under a contract of insurance are not to be taken into account in assessing damages, since it would be unjust that money spent by an injured man on premiums should enure to the benefit of a tortfeasor, and a contributory pension is a form of insurance. The products of a contributory pension scheme are in fact delayed remuneration for current work (post, pp. 14D-E, 16A, C-D).
>
> Per Lord Pearce: The character of the plaintiff's pension rights brought them within the general principle that private insurance by a plaintiff is not to be taken into account and there is no adequate equitable reason for excluding that principle (post, p. 38A-B).
>
> Per Lord Wilberforce: The police pension should not be considered in computing damages recoverable from a third person for proved loss of earning capacity because (a) that pension was payable in any event and was not dependent on loss of earning capacity and (b) it was the reward of pre-injury services and therefore not relevant to the loss of post-injury wages (post, p. 42G-H).
>
> Per Lord Reid: As regards the plaintiff's police pension, his loss, after reaching police retiring age, was the difference between the full pension he would have received after serving his full time and his ill-health pension. The latter must be brought into account at this point, but not in the earlier period, because in that period one was not comparing like with like (but lost wages with something of a different kind, a pension, gained) whereas in the later period one was comparing like with like (post, p. 20G-21A)."

The Majority view stood the test of time and survived challenge in five cases following on – four from the mining industry and one from the fire brigade – *Auty v NCB,*[14] *Dews v NCB,*[1]5 *Smoker v London Fire and Civil Defence Authority & Wood v British Coal Corporation,*[16] *Longden v British Coal.*[17]

All these cases, apart from *Auty,* reached the House of Lords where resolution usually involved quotation and adoption of the reasoning of Lord Reid in *Parry.* We can safely found our current analysis on the principle that the essence of a defined benefit pension is that it amounts to delayed remuneration for years of earlier work. Two of the three Law Lords in the Majority, including the highly influential Lord Reid, saw those contributions as equivalent to the premiums paid under an insurance policy.

4. Issues of deductibility of additional pension

4.1 The deductibility of additional pension income

- Additional receipts of defined benefit pension, such as when taking early or ill-health retirement following an accident, are not to be deducted under any circumstances from other heads of damage, such as loss of earnings.[18]
- There is no loss of defined benefit pension to the extent that any pension payments are to be made *following* the date when a claimant would have retired. Whether labelled as retirement

[13] Reproduced with the kind permission of the ICLR.
[14] [1985] 1 W.L.R. 784, C.A. – "*Auty*".
[15] [1988] A.C. 1 H.L.
[16] Heard together in the House of Lords [1991] 2 A.C. 502.
[17] [1998] A.C. 653 H.L. – "*Longden*".
[18] *Parry,* per Lord Reid at 20G-21A.

pension or re-labelled following an accident as incapacity/injury pension, they are of one and the same kind and the pension actually payable has to be brought into account in calculating any loss in retirement.[19]

- Defined benefit pension payments prior to the date of assumed retirement are not to be offset against the pension loss claimed in retirement. They are paid in a different accounting period – during the loss of earnings claim, not the claim for loss of pension – and are not to be brought into account against pension loss in the later period.[20]

4.2 The deductibility of *commuted* lump sum payments - *Longden*

- *Commutation* is the technical word applied when, on retirement, the option is exercised to convert up to 25% of the value of the underlying pension fund into a tax-free lump sum.[21] The logic of the above propositions was extended in *Longden*: where an early lump sum is paid as a commutation of lifetime pension payments, giving up part of the regular pension income in exchange for the lump sum, the element of the lump sum derived from the accounting period after normal retirement should be brought into account; that prior to normal retirement should not.[22]

- The proportion to be offset compares multipliers at the current prescribed rate over the periods pre- and post- retirement. Strictly, the proportion should be worked out using multipliers at the date when the commutation was actually made, but usually the multipliers used at trial are close enough:

$$\text{Proportion for offset} = \frac{\text{Pension multiplier}}{\text{Life Multiplier}}$$

5 An introduction to subsidiary propositions

There are a number of other building blocks based on first principles, often conceded in the leading cases and adopted into practice ever since.

- Where a claimant's entitlement in a defined benefit scheme includes a pension for a surviving partner or other beneficiary, usually expressed as a proportion or percentage of the pre-commutation main annual entitlement, it is a loss to be calculated from first principles and recovered.

- Where a claimant is able to obtain alternative work carrying a defined benefit pension, the value of the new pension is to be brought into account to reduce the loss in the retirement period. The loss of pension claim will be lower but the claim for loss of earnings higher, since the credit for residual earnings will be calculated after deduction of pension contributions.[23]

- Where a claimant is able to obtain alternative work carrying a money purchase pension, its handling may be said to be controversial.[24]

[19] Loc. cit.
[20] *Longden* – per Lord Hope at 669G-670A.
[21] This is not the same as giving up precisely 25% of what would be the uncommuted gross annual pension payment.
[22] See Lord Hope at 672D-F.
[23] Lord Hope in *Longden* at 667H made plain that it made no difference to his opinion whether the incapacity pension was or was not derived from the same scheme as the retirement pension which the claimant claims to have lost. By parity of reasoning, it makes no difference if the pension comes from one scheme or a different scheme under another employer. It can only be brought into account to reduce the loss during the period during which the pension loss claim is being made – like for like.
[24] Readers are specifically referred to the discussion in the PIBA Guide at §8.3, which there is no room to include here.

- Other benefits delivered via a pension scheme, such as a lump sum payment on death in service (or shortly after the end of service) can be claimed if lost. The benefit in this example amounts to term life assurance and it is best valued, not by attempting to guess the chances of death during the term as against the insured sum, but by reference to the likely cost of an annual premium to generate the term life cover (amounting to a current year benefit in kind within the claim for future loss of earnings). Some evidence of the likely cost will be required.

- Where life expectancy is impaired, there will be a claim for lost years pension. It must, however, be based on a valid claim for pension loss i.e. not on a money purchase, investment scheme.[25]

- Entitlement to State Pension has been derived – in more or less complicated ways over the years – from the amount of National Insurance contributions made out of earnings. If the ability to earn and the number of years of contributions is curtailed, so might be the amount of future State Pension. It is, in its nature, a defined benefit scheme. Since it is elementary that loss of earnings is calculated deducting NI contributions as well as income tax, it is important to make sure that the entitlement to State Pension is made up so there is no loss.

6 Pensions in the modern era

We can divide modern pensions into two mutually exclusive but comprehensive sets:

- personal pensions;

- workplace pensions.

6.1 Personal pensions in practice

The self-employed barrister is the obvious customer.

- The money you get back from a personal pension usually depends on [1] how much you have paid in, [2] how the investments have performed, and [3] how you decide to take your money.

- When you decide to start to use the personal pension pot, you can take up to 25% of the fund built up as a tax-free lump sum.

- Of what is not taken as a lump sum, you might or might not decide to use some, or all of it, to buy a lifetime income. It is no longer compulsory for any part of the built-up fund to be used to purchase annuities.

- You might, however, decide to reinvest the pot into a flexi-access drawdown fund. The new pot remains under investment and you can make withdrawals and/or buy short-term annuities with it to give a regular income over shorter periods up to five years.

- Moreover, you do not actually have to re-invest in a drawdown fund and can just keep the original pot invested and make withdrawals as and when (subject to some rules).

- If not earning, you can even continue to pay into the investment pot or the drawdown fund. Payments up to £3,600 p.a gross (£2,880 net) attract tax relief if not earning, such that £2,880 paid in is topped up to £3,600 by the Government at the current tax rates.

[25] Where life expectancy is so shortened that it impinges on the loss of earnings claim, the handling of the money purchase pension summarised in Part 8 below will increase the claim for *lost years* earnings.

- In fact, you might never take your money out of the pension pot. It can remain fully invested throughout your entire life. If you die before the age of 75, you can pass on the investment tax-free to your beneficiaries; after 75, they pay tax at their marginal rate.

6.2 Personal pensions compared with *Parry*

The above description of personal pension investments does not fit remotely with *Parry*.

- Payments into the fund are fundamentally investments from remuneration already received and nothing like premiums for an insurance in later life to generate delayed remuneration.

- There is no calculable defined benefit in today's monetary terms, only uncertainty over how the fund will be invested and how it might do against inflation.

- There is no regular stream of payments from retirement to an uncertain date of death (or survivor's death) with payments then extinguished; rather, an investment fund enduring to be handled in all sorts of ways, including being passed down a generation or more.

The barrister looking to put money aside for later life might decide to invest in the very same stocks and shares but using an ISA wrapper carrying a rear-end tax break[26], or invest in a larger home or extension to provide extra capital to live on when downsizing in retirement, or any number of other investments or ventures. No one would suggest that a court should speculate on the potential return of invested earnings in such circumstances; there is no difference in essence with investment in a personal pension plan in the modern world.

So, the lawyer must be fully alive to the difference between claims for true loss of pension, as understood in *Parry*, and claims for loss of investment opportunity of earnings already received: loss of investment opportunity remains irrecoverable as too remote in law even if a court could be persuaded the investment would have been profitable. We can forget personal money purchase schemes entirely in terms of calculating loss of future pension.

7 Workplace pensions

These are arranged by an employer, not by the employee. There are, again, two mutually exclusive but comprehensive sub-sets:

- the defined benefit scheme;

- the money purchase scheme.[27]

Where there is a loss of pension under a defined benefit scheme it is obviously recoverable in law. It is the paradigm situation for pension loss.

[26] While a pension carries front-end tax relief on the contributions, an ISA, into which we can currently invest £20,000 p.a., is not subject to capital gains tax on sale of the investment at the end and is not counted as income for taxation at that time.

[27] In the context of workplace schemes, these are sometimes called defined contribution schemes as distinct from defined benefit schemes. The label is not as good for our purposes, since contributions are defined under both types of workplace scheme. The legally relevant and useful distinction is between the schemes leading to defined benefits (the traditional *Parry* scheme, with formulae for calculating the delayed remuneration from past work) and those involving money purchase (investment of remuneration already received). The term defined contribution is best avoided in the context of pension loss.

The question then arises in respect of money purchase schemes: should the conclusion be the same with those arranged via the workplace as was obvious in the personal sphere? There are some points of difference.

- Whereas under a *personal* money purchase scheme the individual has a complete freedom to decide how much and when to pay in, whether a regular amount or not, under a workplace money purchase scheme with an administrative burden across an entire workforce, there is a certain amount of red tape. Regular contributions into the fund are made with each instalment of remuneration. There is usually, however, a mechanism for the individual to set the percentage or level of the regular amount to be invested, to increase or lower it, and to make additional voluntary contributions [AVCs].
- In the case of a personal money purchase scheme, there is obviously no relevant employer in the picture. In a workplace money purchase scheme, there is, and the employer makes a contribution into the investment fund, often pegged to and in sync with the contribution of the employee.
- The exercise of personal choice in the investments held within the fund is likely to be more circumscribed in a workplace money purchase scheme.

7.1 Workplace and personal money purchase schemes – legally indistinguishable

Are these distinctions sufficient to mark out workplace money purchase schemes as legally different from personal money purchase schemes?

- Workplace money purchase schemes are self-evidently so far removed from defined benefit schemes and the rationale derived from *Parry* that, if there is to be a claim, it will have to be because of a new development.
- The essence of both personal and workplace money purchase schemes lies in their money purchase investment nature: they are essentially the same and loss of investment opportunity remains irrecoverable.
- The only real point of difference lies in one having an employer's contribution to add to the workers' investment, while the other does not.
- The value of the employer's contribution can easily be added to the worker's investment as a current year benefit in kind within the loss of earnings multiplicand.
- There is no need to make an artificial distinction between workplace and personal money purchase claims: there is no recoverable head of loss of pension.

7.2 Auto enrolment schemes are workplace money purchase schemes

Auto enrolment pension schemes[28], the largest of which by far is currently run by the National Employment Savings Trust [NEST], are all workplace money purchase schemes so that, again, there is no claim for loss of pension. As before, the employer's contribution can be added into the loss of earnings multiplicand.[29]

[28] We will not repeat here the basics that are clearly set out in the Explanatory Notes to the 8th edition Ogden Tables at paras.117-118, printed earlier in this work.

[29] As the Ogden choice of multipliers illustrates in the example at para.122—they are from the loss of earnings calculations—the claim is properly conceptualised and presented under loss of earnings not pension.

8 Money purchase scheme summary

- There is no loss of future pension to calculate under either a personal or workplace money purchase scheme.
- Make sure the claimant's contributions are not deducted, as they would be in a *Parry* style scheme, when calculating loss of earnings.
- Make sure any employer contributions are added to the earnings multiplicand as an additional current year monetary benefit.
- Make sure that the proper tax relief is claimed when netting down the earnings multiplicand.

9 Defined benefit schemes in the modern world

- In a defined benefit scheme, the benefits can be defined in a number of ways without altering the fundamental nature of the pension i.e. the losses remain recoverable in law irrespective of the fine tuning of the definitions.
- Definitions continue to apply a formula: a proportion, of pensionable pay, accrued over length of service, paid from retirement age.
- Definitions of pensionable pay have shifted in recent years.
- To enable employers better to control cost, many final salary schemes, in which a member was paid a proportion of final salary for each year worked, have been closed to new members. Workers close to retirement (within 10 years or so) have often been allowed to stay in the existing final salary scheme. New workers have obviously joined the new schemes. Existing workers, not near retirement, have stopped accruing pension under the old final salary schemes, and have been transferred on to the new schemes to build up a new pension on top of the old one.[30]
- Instead of taking the final salary as pensionable earnings to be applied to the formula, the new schemes use a career average revalued earnings [CARE] approach.

[30] The younger judiciary and firefighters successfully challenged this inferior treatment on the grounds of age discrimination in *McCloud v Lord Chancellor and Secretary of State for Justice* and *Sargeant v London Fire and Emergency Planning Authority* [2020] 1 All ER 304 (*McCloud*). The Government accepted the need to address the discriminatory effect of allowing older members to remain in legacy schemes, and legislated to do so in the Public Service Pensions and Judicial Offices Act 2022, which required amendments to pension schemes to remove the discrimination. In simple terms:

(1) From 1 April 2022 all those who continue in service do so as members of the reformed schemes, regardless of age; and

(2) At the point benefits are paid, e.g. at retirement, eligible members will be able to choose to receive legacy pension scheme benefits or benefits equivalent to those available under the reformed pension scheme for service between 1/4/2015 and 31/3/2022. Not all members are better off in the legacy schemes, so it is important that individual members can choose which scheme benefits they want to receive.

A little evidence/analysis will be required from a claimant as to the scheme more likely to have been chosen—the one more beneficial in terms of income on retirement at the preferred age. This will involve consideration with a claimant of (1) when (s)he is likely to have retired—the earlier the age at retirement the more attractive a legacy scheme, since there would have been less dramatic actuarial adjustment with an earlier normal pension age; and (2) the likelihood of career progression—the higher the likely final salary, again the more attractive the legacy scheme is likely to have been. A mathematical purist would take into account any underpayment, or more likely overpayment, of pension contributions in the *McCloud* remedy period if the legacy scheme is likely to be the one chosen on retirement, but this is likely to be a modest sum, and some might therefore consider it ignorable.

9.1 CARE pensions[31]

- Under this way of defining the benefits, pensionable earnings reflect the actual earnings in the individual years throughout a career rather than the earnings at the end, a method that became unaffordable because it gave the benefit of both promotions and wages inflation to the employee.

- Under a CARE defined scheme, the pension is grown incrementally, a year at a time, rather than calculated in one go at the end of a career based on the then known number of years. The relevant proportion of actual earnings in any given year is earmarked; in the next year, the proportion of actual earnings is also earmarked and added to the previous element but only after it has been uprated for a measure of inflation over the previous 12 months; the combined two years' figures are then uprated again for the ensuing year before being added to the proportion of actual earnings for the third year. And so on. The annually revalued pension grows incrementally.

- The resulting CARE pension is still defined, still payable for life on being drawn, still with the old entitlement to commute up to 25% of the overall scheme value on retirement to a tax-free lump sum. It is certainly not an investment fund to be handled liberally, as with a modern money purchase scheme. There is nothing legally relevant to distinguish a CARE pension scheme from *Parry*.

- Many of the older final salary schemes had normal retirement ages of 60; some were altered to age 65 after the millennium. Most of the CARE schemes use State Pension age or 65, whichever is the later, as the Normal Pension Age [NPA].

- As the State Pension age [SPA] is now above 65 for the majority, pension without some abatement for drawing on it early will be difficult or uncongenial for many to attain.

- Levels of contribution vary between CARE schemes and, within schemes, often between workers in different bands of pay. Lower paid workers are generally allowed to contribute a lower proportion of earnings, at the expense of better paid workers who have to contribute a higher percentage. The annual wage brackets, against which the different percentages of contribution are applied, are usually varied on 1 April each year by reference to the rate of the Consumer Prices Index [CPI] the previous September. The loss of earnings multiplicand will have to give credit for the contributions that would have been paid, as before.

- There are usually generous (if awarded) provisions for early ill-health retirement, with distinctions often drawn between those who are rendered unfit for all work (who do much better financially and there may be no loss of pension) compared with those who are not so disabled and can be expected to find alternative employment.

- Modern CARE schemes retain many of the old frills of term life cover leading to a lump sum for dependents on early demise and pension provisions for surviving dependants.

10 The effect of early retirement illustrated

The point illustrated in this part – of the monetary effect of early retirement – is an important one because it makes a very substantial difference.

[31] Here is only a short summary of the generic points. Readers are referred to the *PIBA Guide* where there is an extensive discussion and there are summaries of all the major CARE schemes with web references to the materials.

Let us imagine a male teacher, with his 50th birthday on 1 August 2024, whose future loss of earnings multiplicand is to be approached on the basis of £60,000 p.a. gross, as an average at current rates of pay, until he retires from teaching. Let us say that his online pension benefits statement shows that his period of just over nine years in the scheme since April 2015 has led to a £7,500 p.a. gross CARE annual pension entitlement so far, assuming no commutation.

Since he is now 50, State Pension age, hence NPA for him, is on his 67th birthday. He would have continued to accrue 1/57 for every year he worked as a teacher, based on an average of £60,000 p.a., in line with the balanced assumption from the loss of earnings claim. The figure does not require re-valuation because future losses are calculated by reference to the value of money now, ignoring future inflation.

If he were to have stopped work before age 67, he would, of course, have accrued fewer years to build his entitlement compared with a calculation assuming that he would have made it to the full NPA.

If he were to have drawn his pension early, not only would he have built a smaller entitlement, he would be drawing on it for a correspondingly longer period over his lifetime. The terms of the Teachers' Pension Scheme tell us to apply a linear reduction factor of 3% p.a. for early retirement from NPA back to 65. If he were to leave active service and draw his pension on his 66th birthday, he would be entitled to 97% of his then (at 66) accrued pension; on his 65th, 94% of his then (at 65) accrued pension.

With the drawing of pension before 65, there is an actuarial table to apply to provide the appropriate additional factor for the earlier age. This is applied to the previous factor as at the 65th birthday to reach an overall factor to be applied to whatever has accrued as the entitlement when leaving active service.

The following table sets out the arithmetic for drawing on pension with actuarial reduction, if he were to leave active service and take the pension, on key birthdays from 55 to 67. The earlier the leaving of active service the lower the total accrual of pension; the earlier the drawing, the more severe the overall reduction. The only upside with early drawing is that, for every year the pension would have been taken early, the pension loss multiplier moves up by about 1.

Since he already has a final salary pension entitlement to take up his personal tax allowance (and will be entitled to State Pension at 67 as well), the potential lost pension is netted down for the top slice of tax by 20% to make the calculation all the more realistic. The table speaks for itself. We no longer need to guess at what difference early retirement makes; it is a very big difference.

Calculation of CARE pension for lost career with different assumptions for age at retirement compared with NPA of 67[1]

Retirement age	Past accrual	Future yrs.	Future accrual	Total accrual	Overall factor	Annual pension	Net pension (-20%)	Pension multiplier	Overall net total
55	7,500	5	5,263	12,763	0.5875	7,498	5,999	31.25	187,459
60	7,500	10	10,526	18,026	0.73226	13,200	10,560	26.3	277,727
63	7,500	13	13,684	21,184	0.84788	17,962	14,369	23.36	335,668
65	7,500	15	15,789	23,289	0.94	21,892	17,514	21.43	375,318
66	7,500	16	16,842	24,342	0.97	23,612	18,889	20.48	386,856
67	7,500	17	17,895	25,395	1	25,395	20,316	19.53	396,767

[1] The calculation has been done on a spreadsheet which uses more decimal places than are visible in the table, leading to modest apparent, but not actual, rounding errors.

10.1 Proof of motivation to continue to work

In cases where the evidence for a long-term career is well established, the key determinant is motivation to continue working on towards the full CARE NPA, likely to be at age 67 or 68. For some claimants who have lived the majority of their careers planning around a retirement age of 60, that would mean working on well beyond the NPA for their final salary pension. Do they really want to or need to? Standard Ogden factors, derived many years ago across all sorts of industries and careers, have little attraction when the main moving part in the calculation is a claimant's individual motivation. A qualified and experienced teacher or college lecturer, nurse or doctor, and personnel in the civil service, local government, police, or fire service should, if motivated to work, have little difficulty in continuing in it if remaining medically fit. Re-location and re-deployment in such occupations are often relatively easy options, again if motivated. How could a fit and qualified nurse, motivated to work, not find a position? Some are completely devoted to their work; and yet many, apparently, drop away or retire close to the final salary NPA, rather than the CARE NPA.

10.2 Relevance of the Ogden 8 factor Tables A-D to pension claims

The 8th edition of the Ogden tables is improved in many ways, and there is now more commentary relevant to pension claims, including two example calculations.

At Para. 119 of the Explanatory Notes, the Working Party make plain its support for internal consistency in claims for loss of earnings and pension, particularly in using the same choice of retirement age and level of pay in both calculations. This is clearly very good advice.

In the example CARE calculation at Para. 123 of the Notes, the Working Party uses a man aged 50 with NPA at 67, coincidentally the same as in our example, but utilising the Local Government Pension Scheme rather than the Teachers' Pension Scheme. As one would expect given the context, the Ogden commentary on the calculation has to be terse. It has deliberately chosen a straightforward example to calculate, without survivor pension or further promotion or improvement in pay. It is said to lead to an approximate pension loss.

There is no clash in underlying principle between Ogden and the more developed example calculation we will shortly give. We have no issue with the Ogden method if there is a truly broad brush approach to approximate loss of earnings and pension, using the Ogden factors consistently across the heads of damage. Our conviction, however, is that the Ogden factors are a poor substitute for evaluating the motivation of a claimant, in a specific occupation with a CARE pension (and often also with a substantial final salary pension entitlement at a lower age), to work on well into their 60s in that same career. This applies all the more where women are concerned as the data from which the Ogden factors were derived concerned their retirement at the age of 60.

While the Ogden Working Party could not possibly provide access to the actuarial reduction tables for each occupation, the PIBA Guide does[32] and they are easy to apply. If a balanced finding is made as to the fair assumption for age at retirement, a bespoke calculation can be done that balances the main financial contingencies automatically.

11 Development of adjustment to reach a fully balanced result

There will be comparatively little room for adjustment if the main assumptions for wage and retirement age are carefully and tightly drawn for an apparently well-motivated claimant, established in an occupation carrying a defined benefit pension.

[32] Indeed, we cannot provide access to all the materials here or detailed advice on evidence gathering. See footnote 1 and the PIBA Guide as a source of materials.

As the possibilities widen and the drawing of balanced assumptions becomes more difficult, if the assumptions are drawn around a merely mathematically convenient, as against truly balanced, starting point, there will be much more room to articulate reasons on the evidence to moderate or enhance the resulting figure. But adjusting at the end, without knowing the effects on the figures of leaving active service and drawing pension early, is to be avoided where possible in favour of drawing the primary assumptions more closely to the evidence and using the actuarial tables in the first place.

If there is no convenient starting point, only competing staging posts for calculations that are merely illustrative of a wide range of uncertainties, consideration of the resulting figures against the flavour of the evidence will lead to a reasoned, but necessarily broad brush, award, somewhere along the potential spectrum. The amount of reasoning offered may be limited but that will be fine as long as it is commensurate with the quality of the evidence.

11.1 Formal demise of the *Auty* discount

The downward adjustment in *Auty* from the initially calculated figure was no more than an exercise in the conventional approach to reach a balanced award for a future loss. Since the initial calculation was not based on a balanced assumption at all but taken at full NPA, there had to be a significant reduction. We deliberately do not reveal the amount of the discount in *Auty*; nothing at all is to be gained by looking at the size of adjustment in reported cases, always fact-sensitive, particularly elderly cases.[33] There can never be any rule of thumb, whether on the basis of a discount supposedly being between 10% and 20% or some other mantra. It all depends on where you start from and the effort made in drawing the assumptions more finely in the first place.

12 General tips in calculation

12.1 Netting down the pension loss – simplified

The personal allowance (2024/25) is £12,570 and basic rate tax is payable at 20% on the next £37,700 i.e. up to £50,270 p.a. This makes netting down pension loss very simple in the overwhelming majority of cases. Unless a government brings back complicated marginal rates of tax, with the Basic State Pension using up the majority of the tax free allowance on annual pension income, all the *lost* pension is likely to lie within the 20% tax bracket. We agree with the Ogden Working Party that almost all pension loss calculations can now be simplified to reducing the multiplicand by 20% for tax.

12.2 Survivor's pension loss

Most defined benefit pension schemes provide for a scheme member to nominate a financially dependent relative to receive a smaller pension if the member predeceases them – the modern take on the idea of widow's pension. It is expressed as a percentage of the gross annual pension of the member. This percentage is taken after any actuarial reduction for early retirement or enhancement for ill-health retirement i.e. it is the relevant percentage of the member's actual pension entitlement. Commutation of the member's entitlement, however, usually comes only after the survivor's proportion has been fixed: a member usually commutes his/her own entitlement and not that of the potential survivor. If we work out the fair assumption for the member's lost career pension, the relevant proportion under any scheme will give us the fair assumption for the lost survivor's pension.

If there will be entitlement anyway to a survivor's pension, it is to be brought into account to reduce the loss, but only during any period where a claim for loss of survivor's pension is being made.

[33] Every case is fact-specific and a moment's thought shows how foolish it is to look at discounts made when NPAs were at 60, life expectancy was much shorter, judicial discounts were rife, and courts almost certainly did not have in front of them the actuarial tables of the day governing early retirement that are now easily available.

The period of survivor loss runs from the end of the scheme member's mean expectation of life to the end of the nominated survivor's mean expectation of life.[34]

Survivor's life multiplier – member's life multiplier = survivor pension multiplier

Calculation is straightforward, if approached within the structured example we have set out below.

12.3 Commutation

Anecdotally, commutation is said to be common[35] but whether those retiring in fact take the maximum commutation is unknown. There is no doubt that it is advantageous to commute from a tax point of view. For if the lump sum is not extracted on retirement, when up to 25% of the value of the pension fund[36] can be taken tax-free, the whole of the pension will be taxed as current year income when paid later. Coming as an additional top slice of income each year, it will typically attract basic rate tax at 20%.[37]

Apart from the tax break, however, commutation is not meant to penalise or to enhance the pension – the formula for calculation is designed to keep a balance. We should not be surprised if calculations, with or without commuting to a lump sum, come out similarly, except for the 20% tax break on 25% of the fund valuation at date of retirement, so within about 5% of each other. Since, however, pension funds are not valued using multipliers and multiplicands with a -0.25% discount rate, the result is not arithmetically quite the same as enhancing or reducing an overall pension loss calculation by 5%.

Where we are dealing with claims for loss of pension that are difficult to quantify because the assumptions can only be drawn with imprecision even if doing one's best – someone who is young or the pattern of career has yet to be become clear – it is unnecessary to complicate the main calculation further for the chance of whether a claimant would have commuted or not and, if so, how much. If there is a fog of uncertainty this is one of the situations in which it is preferable to draw the calculation around a simpler assumption without commutation and then to fine tune the result slightly – here enhancing it – for the contingency so far left out of account.

Where career and contingencies are clearer, and especially where a claimant has retired before trial and actually commuted, it will be the order of the day to do the arithmetic taking into account commutation and comparing lump sums under *Longden* – see above. We work out the balanced assumption for the loss of lump sum and then subtract the proportion of the lump sum (commuted over the remaining lifetime) actually paid that corresponds with the period of loss of pension. The example below will illustrate the method.

[34] This is the way it is conventionally done and is the method used in the worked example below. An actuary, however, might well maintain that the survivor pension multiplier should be written as the difference between the survivor's life multiplier and the multiplier for *joint life of the claimant and the survivor.*

[35] Informal actuarial advice agrees commutation is common but not universal and taken up in about 75% to 80% of cases. The smaller the pension, the lower the take up; with larger pensions, the proportion approaches 100%. It partly depends on how generous the commutation factors are and whether the pension payments are inflation-proofed.

[36] There are two limits on the amount which may be commuted. It is the lesser of (a) 25% of the full pension fund value (note, not 25% of the annual pension, although many make that mistake), or (b) 25% of the member's available Lifetime Allowance. Where there is sufficient Lifetime Allowance remaining for commutation, it is necessary to consider what 25% of the full pension fund value is. This is reached by using the scheme commutation factor. In a scheme where £1 annual pension given up gives £12 lump sum, the maximum lump sum is 30/7 of annual pre-commutation pension (sometimes expressed as 12/2.8), and the maximum commutation is 20/56 of annual pension (sometimes expressed as 35.7%).

[37] Some high-flyers, with good pensions or outside income, might well find themselves having to pay tax at 40% and it will be all the more important for them to extract the maximum lump sum and find a relatively tax-efficient way to handle it thereafter. The option of leaving the money in place, as with money purchase schemes, and using it as a tax-efficient way of leaving money to the next generation, is not open to those in defined benefit schemes.

12.4 Loss of State Pension

- The State Pension scheme is a universal, defined benefit pension scheme and any losses are legally recoverable following *Parry*.
- The new State Pension [nSP] scheme was introduced on 6 April 2016 and is much simpler than previous versions.
- It is payable from State Pension age [SPA] for life and taxable as income in the year in which it is received.
- Workers and their employers contribute to it through National Insurance contributions [NICs] out of earnings but the State also contributes/subsidises.
- The size of the pension, as a proportion of the full State Pension (£221.20 per week from April 2024 × 52.179 weeks p.a. as an average = £11,542 p.a.), depends on the number of years of NICs or National Insurance credits accrued as at the date of SPA – the current formula is that 1/35 of the full State Pension accrues for each qualifying year of contributions or credits, with a threshold of 10 years before there is any entitlement.
- State Pension forecasts can be obtained at *https://www.gov.uk/check-state-pension* or by post using the address given at that link. They reveal the number of qualifying years achieved and remaining for any claimant.
- NIC credits come automatically with certain disability-related State benefits, including Employment and Support Allowance [ESA], which are very often paid to claimants in the long term after more serious accidents. In such a case there is no loss of qualifying years to the extent that credits make up for the lost NICs.
- Even when ESA is not being claimed, if a claimant satisfies the same statutory test of being unfit for work (s)he can apply for the equivalent NI credits without drawing the benefit. If the claim is proceeding on the basis of a total loss of earnings, a court can hardly apply a clashing assumption when it comes to whether there is a loss of qualifying years.
- Even where NI credits do not accrue automatically and cannot be claimed (for instance where there is some residual earning capacity), they can be made up through voluntary Class 3 NICs (current cost £17.45 a week). The loss is therefore of qualifying years (not future State Pension) and is valued at £911 p.a. because a claimant, if furnished with such a sum, can buy credits to make up the lost years of contributions [£17.45/week x average 52.179 weeks p.a.].

13 Detailed calculation of a modern claim

In earlier discussions we used the illustration of a teacher aged 50 with NPA of 67. We introduced the idea that he[38] might have retired at different ages and of the imperative to evaluate the motivation of a claimant to continue in work to anywhere near full SPA, especially if they have a significant final salary pension due to be paid at 60. Our teacher had current earnings at £60,000 p.a.

Let us now add in the idea that the teacher had a chance of a £10,000 pa promotion in roughly three years' time. He already had 9.33 years of accrual under the new CARE scheme (April 2015 – August

[38] We would like to have drawn this example around a female teacher but, since female life expectancy continues to outstrip male, it would have destroyed the survivor pension loss illustration for a couple of roughly similar age retiring at the same time.

2024) and 17 years under the final salary scheme. The CARE accrual to date is £7,500 p.a. and we can prove it through the latest pension statement via the Teachers' My Pension portal. The court hears evidence as to motivation to continue in work and as to the chance of the promotion and finds the chance of the promotion was 25%. Given the final salary pension payable at 60 and his partner's similar pension due a year later (she is a year younger than him, currently aged 49), the court finds that the fair assumption for the claimant's age at retirement is 61, coinciding with his partner being 60. (Note: this is not a bogus future finding of fact on the balance of probabilities. He may have retired earlier or later but 61 represents the closest balanced assumption, from which the calculation can best flow.) There is a finding that he is overwhelmingly likely to have commuted his maximum entitlement, derived – see fn.36 – by applying the formula 30/7 to the gross annual pension, at a cost to that pension of £1 for every £12 taken.[39]

For simplicity we will assume that our teacher was likely to treat the pension benefits accrued over the seven years from 1/4/15 to 31/3/22 – the *McCloud* remedy period – as having accrued under the CARE scheme.

Experimentation with tables calculating all elements in one go show them to be over-cumbersome. Rather, calculations are better attempted in smaller segments with the key ingredients identified in bold, ready to be carried down into a collection table where the gross figures are netted down for tax and the relevant multipliers are applied. Complicating elements and short explanations are removed into footnotes so that the calculation can flow.

Calculation for CARE retirement pension income, involving commutation				
Pension components on the balanced assumptions for lost career				
Already accrued pension[40]:	7,500			
Lost accrual between now and retirement at a balanced assumption of age 61:				
Baseline assumption: 11 years × 1/57 × £60,000	11,579			
Chance assumption with promotion in 3 years' time: 8 years × 1/57 × extra £10,000 × 25% chance	351			
Total pension accrued at 61:		19,430		
Early actuarial retirement before NPA (67):				
Reduction in period NPA to 65: 2 years at 3%		× 0.94		
		18,264		
Actuarial factor for assumed retirement age before 65[41]		× 0.817		
Pre-commutation gross pension			14,922	
Survivor's pension at 37.5% of the above gross figure:	**5,596**			
Commutation of claimant's pension				
Less assumption for **commuted lump sum**[42]		**63,951**		
at a cost of (from the annual gross pension)		÷ 12		
			–5,329	
Total gross annual pension for lost career (bold figures carried down)				**9,593**

[39] The various formulae under different schemes are found in the PIBA Guide.

[40] Under tier 2 ill-health retirement provisions, this pension of £7,500 can be taken immediately without actuarial reduction; the survivor's pension will be 37.5% of it = £2,813.

[41] This factor is taken from Table ER7 in *Teachers' Pension Scheme: Early retirement in normal health – Factors and Guidance* 24 June 2019 available at *https://www.teacherspensions.co.uk/members/resources/factors.aspx*. Guidance in finding factors for all relevant occupations is found in §23 of the PIBA Guide.

[42] The claimant would almost certainly have commuted his maximum entitlement, derived from £14,922 x 30/7.

Loss of commuted lump sum			
Lump sum on the fair assumption for lost career (brought down)		63,951	
Lump sum received[43]	32,143		
Deductible proportion after normal retirement: – pension multiplier / life multiplier[44]	× 25.32/36.24		
		– 22,458	
Loss on assumed retirement at 61			**41,493**

We cannot just ignore the potential for a loss under the capped final salary scheme entirely, even though accrual of qualifying years ended in 2015. While the number of years is capped, the level of final pensionable pay is not. Where there will be a lost future promotion (including a chance of one) or a rise up the pay scales though length of service has been cut short, there will be a slice of damage since final pensionable pay would have been higher.

Furthermore, in a case where a claimant would have worked past NPA to a later age (here to 61 instead of 60), there is also a lost component of actuarial uplift (for late retirement) on the baseline pension. In the example below the factor to apply for drawing pension a year later is 1.048. Thus, our teacher has lost a 4.8% uplift to his baseline final salary pension of £12,750 p.a.

Both elements are relatively small in this example because the chance of promotion was only 25%, and the pension deferral was only by one year, but they nevertheless add up to £29,120 within the collection table below, which is far too much to forget.

Final Salary [NPA60] components on the assumptions for lost career			
Loss of chance accrual (brought down):			
Lost income:			
£10,000 × 25% = £2,500 × 17 years × 1/80	531		
Factor for uplift for deferring from 60 to 61[45]	× 1.048		
		556	
Lost uplifted element on pension for deferred drawing at 61:			
£60,000 × 1/80 × 17 years =	12,750		
[Factor -1]	× 0.048		
		612	
Lost annual final salary pension		**1,168**	
Lost automatic lump sum:			
3 × annual pension		× 3	
			3,504
Lost survivor pension:			
1/160 rather than 1/80, so ½ of 1,168		**584**	

[43] A matter of factual proof via the claimant's online portal but, say, the maximum with tier 2 ill-health retirement based on the prior accrual of £7,500 x 30/7.

[44] Adopt the multipliers that will be used below in the calculation of the claim unless it is stale and the lump sum was paid a long time ago, when the relevant multipliers will have to be worked out appropriate for that date.

[45] As with taking pension early leading to an actuarial reduction, so deferring the taking of pension beyond NPA (here 60) to 61 leads to the opposite, a small enhancement, under the Teachers' Pension Scheme. Tables will be found in the links we provide in §23 of the PIBA Guide. It is not so in all schemes: in the NHS 1995 Scheme, for example, carrying on working beyond 60 leads to no uplift in pension when it is drawn – pension not drawn at 60 is effectively lost. Of course, while logically correct this line of the calculation highlights a tactical problem for a claimant if advancing a case for retirement substantially beyond the point of NPA for a pretty decent, final salary pension with CARE pension top up (albeit that part being actuarially reduced). How likely is a claimant in this position to have worked on for long beyond the NPA for the final salary scheme?

We can now collect the elements of the calculation together, net them down for tax where necessary, and apply the split multipliers.

Collection	To make up lost State Pension[46]	Tax-free at age 61[47]	Claimant: pension for life[48]	Survivor: pension for life[49]	
Annual cost of NICs	911				
Lost lump sum under CARE scheme		41,493			
Lost lump sum under Final Salary scheme		3,504			
Gross CARE pension based on lost career			9,593	5,596	
Gross CARE pension now payable			–7,500	–2,813	
Gross Final Salary lost income			1,168	584	
Gross losses			3,261	3,367	
less basic rate tax at 20%			× 0.80	× 0.80	
Totals	911	44,997	2,609	2,694	
Multipliers / early recovery factor	× 10.13	× 1.0279	× 25.32	× 3.98	
Totals	9,228	46,252	66,060	10,721	**132,261**

14 Claims early and/or in a speculative career

Apart from clearing the decks of irrecoverable money purchase pensions, most of this section so far has concerned the valuation of defined benefit pension claims where the claimant is properly established in a career and the broad assumption for long service is not seriously in doubt. Statistics show, however, that some careers have a significant early fall-out rate and many lose the chance of a career early on or even before it has started.

In cases where a claimant is early on in a career, assistance can be obtained from available statistical information as to average career length/ progression. There is an abundance of such data held by the Ministry of Defence for use in claims involving service personnel, but many occupations carrying defined benefit pensions are run by Departments of State and there are statistics available online if you search for relevant reports.

[46] The multiplier for purchasing NICs to make up State Pension entitlement equates with the earnings multiplier but capped at that which will make up the lifetime credits to reach 35 years for the full pension. Since he had been accruing qualifying years through NICs for 17 years under the NPA60 scheme and 8.33 years under the CARE scheme = 25.33 years, we are assuming for this example that he needs another ten years' worth (part years do not count) to make things up – a multiplier of 10.13. Do check a claimant's online State Pension forecast for an accurate number of years required to make things up. The way that older State Pension contributions are counted is complicated, but it is easy to check accrued entitlement online.

[47] The loss of lump sum is adjusted over 11 years from 61 back to 50 using Ogden Table 35. An actuary might well adjust again for the chance of death between 50 and 61 but it is not commonly done by others in practice.

[48] Since the claimant would have retired straight on to his pensions, the multiplier in the period of pension loss is the balance of the life multiplier from 61, using the Ogden Additional Tables at age 50.

[49] This conventional multiplier (but see above at footnote 34) is the difference between the surviving partner's life multiplier and the claimant's life multiplier, both derived from Ogden Tables 1 or 2 (or the final columns of the new Additional Tables).

Use of statistics can inform the fair approach to calculating likely pension loss, remembering that the objective is to reach a balanced assumption that is fair to both sides. The statistics alone do not give the answer. Rather, it is necessary for the court to consider the particular claimant compared with the statistics. Proof of motivation to follow a career is relevant, but it is easy for a claimant to assert that (s)he was motivated. In many careers with CARE pensions, length of service is intimately linked to the objective ability. Not all will continue in a hierarchical profession when they have reached their limits and are being overtaken in the promotion stakes by younger people, still less will they continue in work they find essentially too difficult. The task is to compare how well a claimant is doing so far compared with expected career paths and to see what inferences can properly be drawn. Since the assessment is one of *loss of chance*, there will be a flattening out of awards towards the average: a court will very rarely be able to forecast, definitively and fairly, a truly long or short, brilliant or hopeless, career.[50]

15 Pension and the *lost years*

Let us stick with our example of an injured teacher, aged 50, and the fair, balanced assumption still set for retirement at age 61, rather than NPA at 67. This time, the injury is severe and mean expectation of life is reduced and only to age 67.

There will be a claim for lost CARE pension between 61 and 67 but it is small in comparison with the claim for *lost years* pension. The teacher has bought that pension through years of contributions and work (and will do so between age 50 and 61 through having loss of earnings calculated net of NICs and large pension contributions). There are 3 elements to the claim and, if he had lived, he would have enjoyed, payable for an unimpaired expectation of life:

- the gross NPA 60 final salary pension;[51]
- the CARE pension, calculated above;
- State Pension of £11,542 (2024–25 rates).

Lost years income			
Gross multiplicands:			
NPA 60 pension (including loss of chance of promotion)	13,918		
CARE pension	9,593		
State Pension	11,542		
	35,053		
To net (no NICs in retirement)		30,558	
Lost years proportion – say		× 50%	
		15,279	
Full life multiplier from 67		× 19.53	
			298,399

[50] As usual, the discussion is more detailed in the PIBA Guide and we have had to keep things very general here.
[51] 17 years x 1/80 x £60,000 = £12,750 + the £531 loss of chance element calculated above = £13,281, uplifted for deferred drawing from age 60 to 61 (x 1.048).

H2: Net equivalents to a range of gross annual pension figures

Introductory notes

1. The following table sets out the net equivalents to a range of annual pension figures in 2024/25, distinguishing between a single person and a married person.

2. The table is followed by illustrative net pension calculations for each marital status and age category, at income levels of £15,000, £20,000, £30,000, £50,000, £110,000 and £160,000 per annum.

3. Since pensions are not subject to National Insurance contributions, the net equivalent figures represent the gross pension less income tax. Given that liability to primary Class 1 National Insurance contributions falls away when the earner has reached State Pension age [note 2 of G4], it follows that the net equivalent figures for those of State Pension age or over apply equally to earnings from employment and pensions.

4. Similarly, given that Class 4 contributions are not payable in respect of any fiscal year that starts after State Pension age has been reached [note 3 of G4], it follows that the net equivalent figures for those of State Pension age or over apply also to earnings from self-employment where State Pension age has been reached in a prior fiscal year.

	2024/25 Net equivalent pension				
	Single, or married where neither spouse was born before 6.4.35		**Married, where either spouse was born before 6.4.35**		**Reason**
Gross pension £pa	**£pa**	**Net per £100 extra**	**£pa**	**Net per £100 extra**	
1,000	1,000	100	1,000	100	
2,000	2,000	100	2,000	100	
3,000	3,000	100	3,000	100	
4,000	4,000	100	4,000	100	
5,000	5,000	100	5,000	100	
6,000	6,000	100	6,000	100	
7,000	7,000	100	7,000	100	
8,000	8,000	100	8,000	100	
9,000	9,000	100	9,000	100	
10,000	10,000	100	10,000	100	
11,502	*11,502*	*100*	*11,502*	*100*	*< State pension amount*
12,000	12,000	100	12,000	100	
12,570	*12,570*	*100*	*12,570*	*80*	*< Income tax payable at 20%*
13,000	13,000	100	12,914	80	
14,000	14,000	100	13,714	80	
15,000	15,000	100	14,514	80	
16,000	16,000	100	15,314	80	
17,000	17,000	100	16,114	80	
18,000	18,000	82	16,914	80	
19,000	18,822	80	17,714	80	
20,000	19,622	80	18,514	80	
21,000	20,422	80	19,314	80	
22,000	21,222	80	20,114	80	
23,000	22,022	80	20,914	80	
23,650	*22,542*	*80*	*21,434*	*80*	*< State pension + married couple's allowance*
24,000	22,822	80	21,714	80	
25,000	23,622	80	22,514	80	
26,000	24,422	80	23,314	80	
27,000	25,222	80	24,114	80	
28,000	26,022	80	24,914	80	
29,000	26,822	80	25,714	80	
30,000	27,622	80	26,514	80	
31,000	28,422	80	27,314	80	
32,000	29,222	80	28,114	80	
33,000	30,022	80	28,914	80	
34,000	30,822	80	29,714	80	
35,000	31,622	80	30,514	80	
36,000	32,422	80	31,314	80	
37,700	33,782	75	32,674	80	
39,000	34,757	75	33,714	80	
42,000	37,007	75	36,114	80	
45,000	39,257	75	38,514	80	
48,000	41,507	75	40,914	80	
50,270	*43,210*	*59*	*42,730*	*60*	*< Income tax payable at 40%*
55,000	45,995	60	45,568	60	
60,000	48,995	60	48,568	60	
65,000	51,995	60	51,568	60	
70,000	54,995	60	54,568	60	
75,000	57,995	60	57,568	60	
80,000	60,995	60	60,568	60	
85,000	63,995	60	63,568	60	
90,000	66,995	60	66,568	60	
95,000	69,995	60	69,568	60	
100,000	*72,995*	*40*	*72,568*	*40*	*< PTA starts to reduce here*
125,140	*83,051*	*55*	*82,624*	*55*	*< PTA reduced to zero here*
150,000	96,724	55	96,297	55	*& Income tax payable at 45%*
200,000	124,224	55	123,797	55	
250,000	151,724	55	151,297	55	
300,000	179,224	55	178,797	55	

H3: Illustrative net pension calculations

Single person* at 2024/25 rates

		£pa	£pa	£pa	£pa	£pa	£pa
Gross pension	[a]	15,000	20,000	30,000	50,000	110,000	160,000
Income tax							
Gross		15,000	20,000	30,000	50,000	110,000	160,000
Personal allowance (see note 1 below)		(12,570)	(12,570)	(12,570)	(12,570)	(7,570)	–
Taxable		2,430	7,430	17,430	37,430	102,430	160,000
Tax payable							
– At 20%		486	1,486	3,486	7,486	7,500	7,500
– At 40%		–	–	–	–	25,892	34,976
– At 45%		–	–	–	–	–	15,687
	[b]	486	1,486	3,486	7,486	33,392	58,163
Net income	[a-b]	14,514	18,514	26,514	42,514	76,608	101,837
Net % of gross		96.8%	92.6%	88.4%	85.0%	69.6%	63.6%
Note 1: personal allowance							
Personal allowance		12,570	12,570	12,570	12,570	12,570	12,570
Restriction for excess of income over limit#		–	–	–	–	(5,000)	(12,570)
Net allowance		12,570	12,570	12,570	12,570	7,570	–

If gross pay does not exceed £100,000, no restriction.
If gross pay does exceed £100,000, restriction is the lower of:
(a) (gross pay–£100,000)/2, and
(b) £12,570

* = and married persons that do not meet the criteria shown in the married persons' calculations on the next page.

Married person at 2024/25 rates

(But only applies if at least one spouse born before 6 April 1935 and full married couple's allowance allocated to pensioner in this calculation) *

		£pa	£pa	£pa	£pa	£pa	£pa
Gross pension	[a]	15,000	20,000	30,000	50,000	110,000	160,000
Income tax							
Gross		15,000	20,000	30,000	50,000	110,000	160,000
Personal allowance (see note 1 below)		(12,570)	(12,570)	(12,570)	(12,570)	(7,570)	–
Taxable		2,430	7,430	17,430	37,430	102,430	160,000
Tax payable							
– At 20%		486	1,486	3,486	7,486	7,540	7,540
– At 40%		–	–	–	–	25,892	34,976
– At 45%		–	–	–	–	–	15,687
		486	1,486	3,486	7,486	33,432	58,203
Relief for married couple's allowance (note 2)		(1,108)	(1,108)	(1,108)	(493)	(427)	(427)
	[b]	–	378	2,378	6,993	33,005	57,776
Net income	[a-b]	15,000	19,622	27,622	43,007	76,995	102,224
Net % of gross		100.0%	98.1%	92.1%	86.0%	70.0%	63.9%

Note 1: personal allowance

Personal allowance	12,570	12,570	12,570	12,570	12,570	12,570
Restriction for excess of income over limit#	–	–	–	–	(5,000)	(12,570)
Net allowance	12,570	12,570	12,570	12,570	7,570	–

If gross pay does not exceed £100,000, no restriction.
If gross pay does exceed £100,000, restriction is the lower of:
(a) (gross pay–£100,000)/2, and
(b) £12,570

Note 2: married couple's allowance

Married couple's allowance	11,080	11,080	11,080	11,080	11,080	11,080
Restriction for excess of income over limit ^	–	–	–	(6,150)	(6,810)	(6,810)
Net allowance	11,080	11,080	11,080	4,930	4,270	4,270
Relief at 10%	1,108	1,108	1,108	493	427	427

^ If gross pension does not exceed £37,700, no restriction.
If gross pension does exceed £37,700, restriction is the lower of:
(a) [(gross pension–£37,700)/2] less restriction of personal allowance, and
(b) £11,080 - £4,270 = £6,810

* If these criteria are not met, use Single Person calculator shown above

H4: State pension age timetables

Introductory notes

The following tables show how the legislated increases in State pension age will be phased in. A State pension age calculator is provided on the Gov.uk website: *www.gov.uk/state-pension-age*. This calculator tells people when they will reach their State pension age, under current legislation, based on their gender and date of birth.

The Pensions Act 2014 provides for a regular review of the State pension age, at least once every five years. The Government is not planning to revise the existing timetables for the equalisation of State pension age to 65 or the rise in the State pension age to 66 or 67. However, the timetable for the increase in the State pension age from 67 to 68 is expected to change from the current legislated position. The Government announced on 19 July 2017 that the increase in the State pension age from 67 to 68 would be phased in between 2037 and 2039 (instead of between 2044 and 2046). Those born in the 1980s may expect to have a State pension age of 69 and those born in the 1990s a State pension age of 70. Before any future changes could become law Parliament would need to approve the plans.

Changes under the Pensions Act 2011

Under the Pensions Act 2011, women's State pension age will increase more quickly to 65 between April 2016 and November 2018. From March 2019 the State pension age for both men and women will start to increase to reach 66 by October 2020.

Women's State pension age under the Pensions Act 2011

Date of birth	Date State pension age reached
6 April 1953 – 5 May 1953	6 July 2016
6 May 1953 – 5 June 1953	6 November 2016
6 June 1953 – 5 July 1953	6 March 2017
6 July 1953 – 5 August 1953	6 July 2017
6 August 1953 – 5 September 1953	6 November 2017
6 September 1953 – 5 October 1953	6 March 2018
6 October 1953 – 5 November 1953	6 July 2018
6 November 1953 – 5 December 1953	6 November 2018

Increase in State pension age from 65 to 66, men and women

Date of birth	Date State pension age reached
6 December 1953 – 5 January 1954	6 March 2019
6 January 1954 – 5 February 1954	6 May 2019
6 February 1954 – 5 March 1954	6 July 2019
6 March 1954 – 5 April 1954	6 September 2019
6 April 1954 – 5 May 1954	6 November 2019
6 May 1954 – 5 June 1954	6 January 2020
6 June 1954 – 5 July 1954	6 March 2020
6 July 1954 – 5 August 1954	6 May 2020
6 August 1954 – 5 September 1954	6 July 2020
6 September 1954 – 5 October 1954	6 September 2020
6 October 1954 – 5 April 1960	66th birthday

Increase in State pension age from 66 to 67 under the Pensions Act 2014

The Pensions Act 2014 brought the increase in the State pension age from 66 to 67 forward by eight years. The State pension age for men and women will now increase to 67 between 2026 and 2028. The Government also changed the way in which the increase in State pension age is phased so that rather than reaching State pension age on a specific date, people born between 6 April 1960 and 5 March 1961 will reach their State pension age at 66 years and the specified number of months.

Increase in State pension age from 66 to 67, men and women

Date of birth	Date State pension age reached
6 April 1960 – 5 May 1960	66 years and 1 month
6 May 1960 – 5 June 1960	66 years and 2 months
6 June 1960 – 5 July 1960	66 years and 3 months
6 July 1960 – 5 August 1960	66 years and 4 months*
6 August 1960 – 5 September 1960	66 years and 5 months
6 September 1960 – 5 October 1960	66 years and 6 months
6 October 1960 – 5 November 1960	66 years and 7 months
6 November 1960 – 5 December 1960	66 years and 8 months
6 December 1960 – 5 January 1961	66 years and 9 months#
6 January 1961 – 5 February 1961	66 years and 10 months^
6 February 1961 – 5 March 1961	66 years and 11 months
6 March 1961 – 5 April 1977~	67 years

* = A person born on 31 July 1960 is considered to reach the age of 66 years and 4 months on 30 November 2026.
# = A person born on 31 December 1960 is considered to reach the age of 66 years and 9 months on 30 September 2027.
^ = A person born on 31 January 1961 is considered to reach the age of 66 years and 10 months on 30 November 2027.
~ = For people born after 5 April 1969 but before 6 April 1977, under the Pensions Act 2007, State pension age was already 67.

Increase in State pension age from 67 to 68

Under the Pensions Act 2007 the State pension age for men and women is planned to increase from 67 to 68 between 2044 and 2046.

In the Autumn Statement on 5 December 2013, the Chancellor announced that the Government believed that future generations should spend up to a third of their adult life in retirement. This principle implied that State pension age should rise to 68 by the 2030s, and 69 by the 2040s.

The Pensions Act 2014 provided for a regular review of the State pension age, at least once every five years. The reviews would be based around the idea that people should be able to spend a certain proportion of their adult life drawing a State pension. As well as life expectancy, they would take into account a range of factors relevant to setting the pension age. The first review was completed in July 2017, following a report from the Government Actuary[1] and an independent review by Sir John Cridland[2], both published in March 2017. The Government announced on 19 July 2017[3] that the increase in the State pension age from 67 to 68 would be phased in between 2037 and 2039 (instead of between 2044 and 2046). However, this proposal still requires primary legislation.

[1] Periodic review of rules about State Pension Age: Report by the Government Actuary.
[2] Independent Review of the State Pension Age: Smoothing the Transition. Sir John Cridland.
[3] State pension age review. July 2017.

A further Review of the State Pension Age was published on 30 January 2023, with a report from the Government Actuary[4] and a report on an independent review carried out by Baroness Lucy Neville-Rolfe.[5] The government published the conclusions of this second review on 30 January 2023 and stated as follows:

> "We plan to have a further review within two years of the next Parliament to consider age 68. This will ensure that the government is able to consider the latest information which was not available to the independent reviewer at the time. This includes 2021 Census data, the current economic position, the impact on the labour market of our package of measures to tackle inactivity and any other relevant factors. The current rules for the rise from 67 to 68 therefore remain appropriate and the government does not intend to change the existing legislation prior to the conclusion of the next review. All options for the rise to the State Pension age from 67 to 68 that meet the 10 years notice period will be in scope at the next review."

The information in the table below is based on the current law (Pensions Act 2007).

Increase in State pension age from 67 to 68, men and women

Date of birth	Date State pension age reached
6 April 1977 – 5 May 1977	6 May 2044
6 May 1977 – 5 June 1977	6 July 2044
6 June 1977 – 5 July 1977	6 September 2044
6 July 1977 – 5 August 1977	6 November 2044
6 August 1977 – 5 September 1977	6 January 2045
6 September 1977 – 5 October 1977	6 March 2045
6 October 1977 – 5 November 1977	6 May 2045
6 November 1977 – 5 December 1977	6 July 2045
6 December 1977 – 5 January 1978	6 September 2045
6 January 1978 – 5 February 1978	6 November 2045
6 February 1978 – 5 March 1978	6 January 2046
6 March 1978 – 5 April 1978	6 March 2046
6 April 1978 onwards	68th birthday

If a similar phasing were adopted for the proposed increase in State pension age from 67 to 68 between 2037 and 2039, the impact of the change in retirement age would be as follows:

Date of birth	Date State pension age reached
6 April 1970 – 5 May 1970	6 May 2037
6 May 1970 – 5 June 1970	6 July 2037
6 June 1970 – 5 July 1970	6 September 2037
6 July 1970 – 5 August 1970	6 November 2037
6 August 1970 – 5 September 1970	6 January 2038
6 September 1970 – 5 October 1970	6 March 2038
6 October 1970 – 5 November 1970	6 May 2038
6 November 1970 – 5 December 1970	6 July 2038
6 December 1977 – 5 January 1971	6 September 2038
6 January 1971 – 5 February 1971	6 November 2038
6 February 1971 – 5 March 1971	6 January 2039
6 March 1971 – 5 April 1971	6 March 2039
6 April 1971 onwards	68th birthday

[4] Periodic review of rules about State Pension age: Report by the Government Actuary. March 2023.
[5] Independent Review of the State Pension Age 2022. Final Report. March 2023.

Group I

Benefits, Allowances, Charges

I1: Social security benefits (non-means-tested)

How they work

Generally, all of these benefits may be claimed independently of each other. Some benefits can lead to entitlement or increases in others, known as 'passporting'. However, there are also over-lapping benefit rules which prevent more than one income replacement benefit being payable. If the claimant is entitled to more than one income replacement benefit, then the amount of the highest will be payable. Many benefits are contributory, entitlement being dependent on satisfying conditions as to amount of national insurance contributions paid or, in some cases, credited. Entitlement to some non-means-tested benefits is affected if claimants are in hospital or in full-time care. Claims for all benefits must normally be made in writing although some can be claimed on-line or by telephone. Claims can be backdated only to a limited extent (varying according to the type of benefit). Most benefits are affected by the claimant's immigration status and/or length of residence in UK. Seek advice from Citizens Advice if this is an issue—*https://www.citizensadvice.org.uk/*.

A. Income replacement

1. Retirement

Retirement Pension (if reached pension age before 6 April 2016)

	2024/25
Claimant (Category A or B)	£169.50
(Category B—lower basic pension)	£101.55

A person may qualify in their own right (Category A) or on death of spouse/civil partner (Category B) or as a spouse or civil partner who is a dependent of a category A recipient (Category B—lower).

Special rules apply for parents, carers, divorced people, widows and widowers. As from April 2010, there have been no new claims for the extra payment added to the Retirement Pension if someone has an adult dependent. This 'adult dependency increase' stopped altogether in April 2020, meaning some pensioners saw a reduction in pension of around £70 but they may be able to claim pension credit to compensate for this loss. Women who reached state pension age before 6 April 2016 and are covered by the old state pension system may have missed out, however.

Married women could claim an enhanced rate of state pension when their husband reached age 65 in cases where they only had a small individual state pension entitlement themselves. At current rates, the amount claimed could be as much as £101.55 per week, equivalent to 60 per cent of the full basic state pension rate of £169.50. To see the full range of people who may have missed out on extra pension that they are entitled to, possibly going back many years: *https://www.moneysavingexpert.com/reclaim/married-women/missingstate-pension-boost/*.

Women in their 60s or 70s who stayed at home to care for children before 2010 may also be missing out on £1,000s in state pension payments due to errors in their national insurance record. This is because they missed out on Home Responsibilities Protection (HRP). This reduced the number of qualifying years you needed to get the full basic State Pension by up to 22 years. To claim Home Responsibilities Protection (HRP) for past periods, you can apply online or by post. It was replaced in 2010 by National Insurance Credits. *https://www.tax.service.gov.uk/guidance/Check-if-you-are-eligible-to-apply-for-Home-Responsibilities-Protection/start/about-this-guidance*

State pension age increased for men and women to 66 in October 2020—check the precise pension age on: https://www.gov.uk/state-pensionage. There is a test case due to be heard in summer of 2024 which may mean backdated pension for some or all the of the women who lost out when the pension age was raised.

New State Pension (reaching pension age after 6 April 2016) £221.20

No additions for dependents or transfer of pension rights in cases of bereavement. Both old-style and new-style pensions can be highly variable according to contribution history as well as any additional pensions earned e.g. State Earnings Related Pension or if receipt is deferred beyond pension age. Contributory and taxable. For information see *https://www.gov.uk/government/publications/application-for-a-state-pension-statement and https://www.gov.uk/government/publications/application-for-a-state-pension-forecast-on-divorce-or-dissolution-br20. Also see https://www.gov.uk/guidance/request-information-about-underpaid-state-pension-for-someone-who-has-died if winding-up an estate.*

2. Ill Health

i. Statutory Sick Pay 2024–2025

Standard rate	£116.75

Paid by the employer for up to 168 days (28 six-day weeks), to employees earning not less than £123 gross p.w. Taxable.

ii. Employment and Support Allowance (ESA) 2024–2025
– weekly amounts but paid fortnightly

Single person under 25 or lone parent age 16 or 17:	£71.70
Single person 25 or over or lone parent 18 or over:	£90.50
Couple (both under 18) with a child—assessment rate £101.50 and main rate	£142.25
Couple (both under 18) – assessment rate £67.20 and main rate	£90.50
Couple 18+ assessment rate and main rate	£142.25
(may be less if one partner is aged 16-17)	
Single people with no component (assessment rate in first 13 weeks)—age 25 or over:	£90.50
Work-related activity component (awarded before 1 April 2017)	£35.95
Work-related activity component (awarded after 1 April 2017)	£0.00
Single people with the support group component:	£47.70
Enhanced disability (single)	£20.85
Enhanced disability (couple)	£29.75
Severe disability (single)	£81.50
Severe disability (couple—one qualifies)	£81.50
Severe disability (couple—both qualify)	£163.00
Carers	£45.60

ESA includes both a contributory and "income-related" (means-tested) benefit. Contributory ESA is now referred to for new claims as new-style ESA. Both versions of ESA are based on either limited capability for work (placed in "work-related activity group") or limited capability for work-related activity (not required to look for work or undertake work-related activity and placed in "support group"). Anyone making new claim for ESA after 1 April 2017 will only get basic rate of £90.50 (single) or £142.25 (couple) if placed in work-related activity group, unless on income-related ESA and getting the enhanced or severe disability elements. Lower rates for under 25s during assessment period are shown above.

Contributory (C-ESA)—also now referred to by DWP as "new-style" ESA: time-limited to one year for those in work-related activity group but unlimited whilst in support group; also, no spouse's additions, and no housing costs allowances. Entitlement to contributory benefits depends on payment of appropriate National Insurance Contributions. First £85 p.w. of works, private or occupational pension are ignored for new-style or C-ESA, then benefit reduced by 50p for each additional £1.

Income related ESA (IRESA): assessment, housing costs and capital rules modelled on IS (Table 29). Child maintenance disregarded for IRESA. Earnings of up to £184.00 p.w. (so long as less than 16 hours a week are worked) are allowed indefinitely on "new-style" or C-ESA and IRESA as "permitted work" without affecting benefit payment. Occupational pension counts in full against IRESA. Passport to other benefits including full HB and CTB (HB & CTB: Table 29) and prescriptions if on IRESA. May be due similar help if on "new-style" C-ESA depending on other or partners income. "New-style" contributory ESA taxable: IRESA not. IRESA being phased out and replaced by universal credit (2016–2025).
ESA paid at main rate plus support group for anyone with proof of terminal illness (death could reasonably be expected within 12 months).

iii. Carer's Allowance **2024–2025**
Claimant £81.90

Paid to people 16 or over (no upper age limit) who spend at least 35 hours p.w. caring for recipient of higher or middle rates Care Component of Disability Living Allowance, either rate of Attendance Allowance or Personal Independence Payment (daily living element), or Constant Attendance Allowance or Scottish equivalents. Claimant can earn no more than £151 p.w. net and must not be in full-time education. If earnings exceed the limit in any one week, the whole carer's allowance is not due for that week. However, claimants are entitled to offset against earnings up to half any sums paid to someone else (not close relative) to care for either recipient of allowances or carer's children under 16. Not dependent on national insurance but can't be paid in addition to any other N.I. benefit, including state pensions. May still be worth claiming however, in order to get an "underlying entitlement" to it, as this can lead to increase in most means-tested benefits such as universal credit, housing benefit and council tax support or pension credit. Carer's Allowance is taxable.
Benefit rates for Carer's Allowance back to 2000 are in App.1.
Carer's Allowance Supplement is paid in Scotland to people getting carer's allowance. For 2024/25, the first payment will be £288.60 in June and the second payment in December will be £288.60. There is also a Scottish Young Carers Grant, paid once a year for 16-18 year-olds who can't get carer's allowance because they are in education. It is currently £383.75. In Scotland, Carer's Allowance is being phased out and replaced by a Carers Support Payment (£81.90 per week) during 2024/25.

3. Unemployment—Jobseeker's Allowance (JSA)

i. Contributory JSA (C-JSA)		**2024–2025**
Claimant	18–24	£71.70
	25 and over	£90.50

ii. Income-based JSA (IBJSA) **2024–2025**

Claimant	16–24	£71.70
	25 and over	£90.50
Couple	Both 18 or over	£142.25

(lower amounts if one or both are under 18).

Premiums: as for IS (Table 29).
IBJSA is being phased out, and has been replaced by Universal Credit for new claims.
Contributory JSA (now referred to by DWP as "new-style" JSA) is flat-rate payment; without dependant allowances: paid for up to 26 weeks.
IBJSA is now only paid for long-standing claims where entitlement to C-JSA has stopped. It has IS-style rules for income, capital, premiums and mortgage interest (i.e. now paid only as a loan). Child maintenance is disregarded. Claimants will be migrated on to Universal Credit by the end of 2024.
Claimants of either form of JSA must be under 66, available for and actively seeking work, and have a current Claimant Commitment (agreement with Job Centre regarding finding work): IBJSA is a passport to other benefits including full HB & CTB. Not available for those under 18 or those working 16+ hours p.w. Only main rates shown—premiums can be added according to disability/ill-health as per ESA. New-style JSA is taxable.

4. Maternity/paternity/adoption

i. Statutory Maternity Pay (SMP) **2024–2025**
Payable to employees earning on average at least £123 a week. Higher rate (first 6 weeks) 90 per cent of average weekly wage. Lower rate (for up to next 33 weeks) £184.03 Paid by employer for a maximum of 39 weeks. Taxable.

ii. Statutory Paternity Pay (SPP) **2024–2025**

Rate	£184.03[1]

Payable for up to two weeks. Additional SPP at same rate if upon mother's return to work, baby 20 weeks old and she would otherwise still be entitled to SMP, SAP or MA. Not payable beyond mother's 39-week maternity period. Taxable.

iii. Maternity Allowance **2024–2025**

Average earnings threshold	£30.00[2]
Standard rate	£184.03

Paid to claimants not entitled to SMP but employed or self-employed for at least 26 weeks in 66 weeks before due date, and average pay when working is over earnings threshold. Maximum 39 weeks (during which may work up to 10 days). Non-taxable.
Qualifying conditions based on length of service and average earnings. (2) Or (if less) 90 per cent of the parent's weekly average earnings.

[1] Qualifying conditions based on length of service and average earnings.
[2] Or (if less) 90 per cent of the parent's weekly average earnings.

iv. Statutory Adoption Pay **2024–2025**
Payable to employees earning on average at least £123 a week

Standard rate	£184.03

Paid by employer for a maximum of 39 weeks.
Taxable.

v. Surestart Maternity Grant **2024–2025**

Standard one-off payment	£500.00

Subject to complex conditions, related to receipt of "qualifying benefit". Available only for first child.
In Scotland, there is a one-off Best Start Grant of £754.65 instead for your first child and £377.35 for subsequent children.
In Scotland, there are also Early Learning Payments, Pregnancy and Baby Payments, School Age Payments and a Best Start Foods prepaid purchase card. See *https://www.gov.scot/policies/social-security* for details and *https://www.socialsecurity.gov.scot/news-events/news/social-security-payment-rates-increased-for-2024* for rates.

5. Bereavement

Bereavement benefit, bereavement allowance, bereavement support payment and widowed parent's allowance are all contributory i.e. based on the deceased person's national insurance record (unless death caused by industrial injury or disease).

i. Bereavement Benefit (if bereaved before 6 April 2017) – no longer payable
Eligible age 16-65.

ii. Bereavement Allowance – no longer payable

iii. Widowed Parent's Allowance (WPA)—if bereaved before 6/4/2017 £149.40

Available to bereaved spouses/civil partners who are under State pension age and in receipt of child benefit who do not remarry or cohabit. Can be paid in addition to wages and not affected by any occupational pension that is received. Counts as income when means-tested benefits are calculated.

iv. Bereavement Support Payment for deaths occurring on or after 6 April 2017

Standard Rate (bereaved without children) lump sum £2500. Standard Rate (spouse or civil partner) monthly payment £100 for maximum of 18 months. Higher Rate (bereaved with children) lump sum £3500 and Higher Rate monthly payment £350 for maximum of 18 months. Unlike widowed parents allowance, it is still paid if spouse/civil partner/cohabitee remarries or cohabits. Does not count as income when means-tested benefits are calculated. Can be claimed from age 16 to 65. A change in the law in February 2023 extended BSP to bereaved cohabitees if they have children. The change was retrospective and applied to any cohabiting parent who was bereaved since April 2017. However, benefit could only be backdated if a claim was made by February 2024, although new claims can be made by a bereaved parent who was co-habiting at the time of their partners death.

B. Special needs

All of the below allowances are based on need and a medical assessment, but there are no restrictions on how they are used. All are non-contributory, not means-tested, non-taxable and are ignored as income for means-tested benefits. There are complicated rules in place if people are in residential or nursing care or hospital and are not fully self-funding—notify DWP if this occurs. Anyone who is terminally-ill (death being reasonably expected within 12 months) automatically get the highest rate of attendance allowance, PIP daily living and DLA Care without the need for the assessment that would otherwise be necessary.

1. Personal Independence Payment (PIP) 2024–2025

PIP is replacing DLA for all new claims for people aged 16-65, and as DLA claims come up for renewal (unless claimant born before April 1948).

Care Component	Enhanced	£108.55
	Standard	£72.65
Mobility Component	Enhanced	£75.75
	Standard	£28.70

The claimant must qualify before reaching 66 (if older, see Attendance Allowance) but can continue in payment beyond pension age if awarded beforehand. Not available to under-16s (see Disability Living Allowance). In Scotland, the equivalent benefit is called Adult Disability Payment.

2. Attendance Allowance

	2024–2025
Higher rate (day and night care)	£108.55
Lower rate (day or night care)	£72.65

Paid for care needs of those who make a first claim after pension age. Based solely on care and support needs, not mobility.

3. Disability Living Allowance

	2024–2025
Care—higher rate	£108.55
Care—middle rate	£72.65
Care—lower rate	£28.70
Mobility—higher rate	£75.75
Mobility—lower rate	£28.70

DLA replaced in Scotland by a Disabled Child Payment, paid at an equivalent rate but up to 18th birthday, not 16th as in the rest of the UK.

C. Children

1. Child Benefit (CB)

	2024–2025
Only/elder/eldest child	£25.60
Each subsequent child	£16.95

A child must be under 16, or under 20 and in full time secondary education. There is a tax liability of 5% of the benefit per £1000 of excess income if either the claimant or their partner earns over £60,000 a year, which reaches 100% of the benefit at £80,000. Otherwise non-taxable. Non-contributory. Administered by HMRC. Not affected by 'two-child' limit that applies to means-tested benefits. Generally disregarded in means-tested benefits except if claimant caught by 'benefit cap'.

There is a Scottish child payment is £26.70 a week per eligible child, payable every four weeks, for families on Universal Credit or any other means-tested benefit (except housing/council tax benefit). There is no limit on how many children within a family can get Scottish child payment, so it will still be paid for a child affected by the two-child limit in universal credit or child tax credit.

2. Guardian's allowance — 2024–2025: £21.75

Payable with child benefit to those raising the child or children where at least one of the child's parents has died and the other is either also deceased, or is in prison, unknown or not traceable. Not to be confused with Special Guardianship in child care law.

Appendix 1

These are the rates of Carer's Allowance going back to 2000. For a list back to 1976, see Institute for Fiscal Studies *https://ifs.org.uk/sites/default/files/2022-10/carer_2022.xlsx*

10/04/2000	40.40
09/04/2001	41.75
11/09/2002	42.45
07/04/2003	43.15
05/04/2004	44.35
11/04/2005	45.70
10/04/2006	46.95
09/04/2007	48.65
08/04/2008	50.55
06/04/2009	53.10
12/04/2010	53.90
11/04/2011	55.55
09/04/2012	58.45
08/04/2013	59.75
07/04/2014	61.35

06/04/2015	62.10
11/04/2016	62.10
10/04/2017	62.70
09/04/2018	64.60
08/04/2019	66.15
06/04/2020	67.25
12/04/2021	67.60
11/04/2022	69.70
10/04/2023	76.75
08/04/2023	81.90

12: Social security benefits and tax credits (means-tested)

Universal Credit (UC)

Administered solely by DWP. Means-tested. Not taxable. Paid to people of working age only (including couples where only one person is below pension age) as a replacement for six "legacy" benefits – income support, child and working tax credits, housing benefit (but not council tax support) and the income-related versions of ESA and JSA (see below). A small number of people over pension age who are getting tax credits (e.g. caring for children or still in lower-paid employment) will be given the option of claiming pension credit or universal credit when tax credits end.

Universal Credit has now been introduced for almost all relevant new claims. Between May 2022 and December 2025, the DWP will manage the migration of almost all existing customers of legacy benefits to UC. If people move across to UC before then due to a change of circumstances ("natural migration") or move voluntarily, they may get less benefit. If they move as part of "managed migration", their total benefit income is protected (although frozen at the transferred level).

Although UC shares many characteristics of other means-tested benefits (capital limit of £16,000; requirement to look for work or be covered by a medical certificate or be a carer etc; private rents met only up to certain levels; benefit cap/two-child policy/bedroom tax all still applying; no help with mortgages except as a loan), it also has its own rules. Some of the amounts are substantially different especially for people with disabilities or a disabled child.

UC is also paid monthly in arrears, and the rent element is normally paid to the claimant to pass to the landlord (except in cases of arrears or vulnerability). See *www.universalcreditinfo.net* for more information. The perceived advantage of UC is that a person would be entitled to the maximum whilst out of work and will remain on UC, but at a tapered rate, as they move into work. It is supposed to be more flexible and adaptable than having to stop claiming JSA/income support/ESA and start claiming in-work benefits.

Universal Credit

Standard Allowances (2024/25)	**Monthly**
Single: Aged 25 years and over	£393.45
Single: Aged under 25	£311.68
Couple: One/both aged 25 or over	£617.60
Couple: Both aged under 25	£489.23
Additional Elements	
First child (born before 6.4.2017)	£333.33
Other first or all subsequent children	£287.92
Higher: Disabled child	£487.58
Lower: Disabled child	£156.11
Limited Capability for Work (awarded prior to 3 April 2017)	£156.11
Limited Capability for Work-Related Activity	£416.19
Carer	£198.31
Childcare Maximum	
One child (85% of eligible cost up to maximum of ...)	£1014.63
Two or more children (85% of eligible cost up to a maximum of ...)	£1739.37

Non-dependant Deduction	
Rented Housing (per non-dep aged 21 or over unless exempt)	£91.47
Owner Occupier Housing Costs (except eligible service charges and a loan towards mortgage interest)	£0
Work Allowance for parents and disabled workers	
(amount that can be earned before UC reduced)	
Higher: claimants without housing costs met by Universal Credit	£673
Lower: claimants with housing costs met by Universal Credit	£404
Taper (rate at which UC is reduced for each £1 earned above £0 or above work allowance if applied)	55%
Capital	
Lower Limit	£6,000
Higher Limit	£16,000
Tariff Income: £4.35 per £250 between £6,000 and £16,000	

Housing Benefit (HB) and Council Tax Support (CTS)

No new claims for people of working age except in limited circumstances i.e people in certain types of supported or temporary accommodation. Replaced by an element within universal credit (UC). Still available to people aged 66 or over. HB meets rent costs up to a certain level. It can be paid whether the person is in or out of work, with the amount of help given towards the rent being based on a comparison of their actual income with what they would get if they were out of work. The higher the income, the more the tenant is expected to pay (generally 65p for every £1 earned above the out-of-work level of income).

Neither UC nor HB may meet the full cost of the rent in some circumstances e.g. if a private rent is deemed to be too high for the area; if there are nominally spare bedrooms in the property; if a non-dependent who isn't exempt from the charge lives with the claimant; if the total benefit income is above a benefit cap figure; if the rent includes costs such as food, fuel, supervision (see below).

HB is administered by local councils. The main difference between HB and UC is that the default position for UC is that the rental element is paid to the claimant for them to pass to their landlord. However, claimants on UC and landlords can request an alternative payment arrangement (APA). This is known as MPTL (managed payment to landlord).

HB is assessed using income support figures as the baseline—see below. HB for people over pension age, which is not being replaced by universal credit, is based on slightly higher rates for those who turned pension age before 1 April 2021.

Council Tax Support (CTS) is also known as Council Tax Reduction or Relief, was formerly known as council tax benefit. This is means-tested support for tenants and owner-occupiers who have a council tax bill. Although the national framework of CTS is fairly standard, local councils can make variations for those of a working age. It is generally, but not totally, based on the same figures used in the HB calculation.

CTS is not incorporated into universal credit and people getting UC need to make a separate claim for it.

CTS is separate to the system of discounts, exemptions and reductions that are available on a non-means-tested basis e.g. for a single person, students, some carers, or in cases of severe mental impairment, or for an empty property. See *https://www.gov.uk/council-tax.*

Income Support (IS) 2024–2025

Now largely phased out and paid to a small number of those under 66, on low income, who are not working or working less than 16 hrs per week e.g. carers and foster carers. Not for the unemployed (see Universal Credit above or JSA: Table 28) or claimants who are sick/disabled (see Universal Credit above or ESA: Table 28) or most childless people under 18. Being phased out by April 2025 in favour of universal credit. For example, entitlement for lone parents ceased once youngest child reached five, unless they also had responsibilities as a carer for a disabled person. At that point, the lone parent would have switched to universal credit.

Main rates only are shown.

IS brings automatic entitlement on income grounds to other benefits including maximum HB and CTS and health costs such as prescriptions. A need level is established from the allowances and premiums shown below. Mortgage interest has not been included since 1 April 2018, except as an interest-bearing loan repayable to the DWP on death or resale. These loans are also limited to mortgages of up to £200,000 and only after a three-month waiting period. IS brings a person's other income up to the need level. There are detailed rules on the application of premiums and disregarded income. Spousal maintenance counts as income but all child maintenance is disregarded. No disregard for childcare costs (but see tax credits and universal credit below).

Capital up to £6,000 is disregarded (£10,000 for those in residential/nursing homes; £3,000 for child). Capital between £6,000 and £16,000 is deemed to produce tariff income of £1 for each £250 (or part) over £6,000. There is no entitlement to IS if capital exceeds £16,000, disregarding value of home, unless capital arises from personal injury (in which case it is ignored for 12 months and then indefinitely if placed in a trust). "Notional capital" rules penalise deliberate deprivation of capital to obtain IS. It is non-contributory.

Income support (and income-related versions of JSA/ESA)

Personal allowances	**Weekly**
Single Under 25	£71.70
25 or over	£90.50
Lone parent Under 18	£71.70
18 or over	£90.50
Couple – both 18 or over	£142.25
(Couple where one or both are under 18 have lower rates)	
Premium	
Carer	£45.60
Disability (not paid on ESA) Single	£42.50
Couple	£60.60
Enhanced disability: Single person	£20.85
Couple	£29.75
Severe disability	
(single person or couple where one qualifies)	£81.50
(couple – both qualify)	£163.00

Pension Credit (PC) 2024–2025

PC comprises two elements: Guarantee Credit (GC) for those of pension age whose income is below the "standard minimum guarantee"; and Savings Credit for those pension age and over with modest savings or income. Either or both are claimable.

Age at which GC available rose in line with increases in State pension age, which is now 66; this is key age for other benefits and working-age or retirement age-related provisions:

See *https://www.gov.uk/state-pension-age.*

Means-tested, some income disregarded. No upper capital limit. £10,000 disregarded; thereafter tariff income is £1 for every £500 (or part).

State pension is taken into account as income. Administered by the DWP's Pension Service. Child maintenance disregarded; no provision for childcare costs. Housing costs as for IS, including mortgage interest being paid only as a loan from April 2018 (but without the waiting period that applies to those below pension age). Guarantee Credit is a passport to maximum HB and CTS. Since February 2019, pension credit includes an element for children (instead of receiving child tax credit), unless child tax credit was already in payment by that date.

Both members of a couple making a claim for pension credit after May 2019 have to be over pension age. Prior to that, only one member needed to be. These "mixed-age" couples are directed towards universal credit instead, where the amounts paid are generally less, the savings rule is less generous and there is an expectation that the younger partner should look for work.

Non-contributory. Not taxable. From November 2024, only people getting pension credit will get the £200/£300 winter fuel payment, previously paid to all people of pension age.

Pension credit (weekly)

Minimum guarantee	
Single	£218.15
Couple	£332.95
Severe disability (single or one qualifies)	£81.50
Severe disability (couple)	£163.00
Carer	£45.60
Children Only/eldest child	£76.79
Other children	£66.29
Disabled child Lower rate	£35.93
Higher rate	£112.21
Savings credit	
Threshold Single	£189.80
Couple	£301.22
Maximum Single	£17.01
Couple	£19.04

No new savings credit claims being accepted, except from people who reached pension age before 1 April 2016.

Tax Credits 2024–2025

No new claims unless already getting one element already. To be replaced by universal credit. This includes a number of people of pension age and above who are still employed or have dependent children, who have been getting child or working tax credit. They will be offered the option of claiming universal credit or pension credit and will need advice about which is their best option.

	Annual
Working tax credit	
Basic element	£2435
Couple /lone parent	£2500
30 hours or more per week	£1015
Disability	£3935
Severe disability	£1705
Childcare 70% of up to 175.00 a week (one child) and up to 300.00 for two or more children	
Child tax credit	
Family	£545
Child	£3,455
Disability or Disabled child	£4,170
Severely disabled child	£1,680
Thresholds	
Working tax credit	£7,955
Child tax credit only	£19,995

Working Tax Credit (WTC) 2024–2025

No new claims can be made, as WTC is replaced by universal credit, unless the person is already getting child tax credit. Existing claimants remain entitled until migrated over to UC by a relevant change of circumstances or voluntarily or at request of DWP (by March 2025). There will then be no new claims for WTC or CTC at all.

Based on gross annual income: in-work support for families with child/children where lone parent works at least 16 hours p.w., or couple's combined work hours total 24 hours p.w., with one parent working at least 16 hours p.w. Extra payment for working at least 30 hours p.w. Also available for some households without child, including those aged 25 and over working at least 30 hours p.w., and those aged 66 and over or with disability, working at least 16 hours p.w. Up to first threshold, claimants receive the maximum. Credit then tapers by 41p per £1 of income as income rises above first threshold. Claimant loses main element of WTC first, then childcare element, then child element of any CTC.

WTC includes help with child care costs but these were not increased in 2023 or again in 2024 when the help available under Universal Credit was increased substantially, so some parents may find it beneficial to switch.

Elements are cumulative. Complex assessment rules. Maintenance and student finance ignored. Assessed on previous year's annual income; joint incomes for couples (disregarding £300 of certain types of unearned income).

Awards provisional until end of year notice identifies under/overpayments. Disregard of £2,500 before in-year falls or rises in income affect entitlement; Administered by HMRC.

Child Tax Credit (CTC) 2024–2025

Based on gross annual income. First the per-child element then the family element tapered by 41p per £1 of income once income above £19,995 (WTC abated first).

One family element per family. Paid to nominated main carer. No new claims can be made as CTC is replaced by universal credit (unless already receiving working tax credit), but existing claimants remain entitled until migrated over to UC by a relevant change of circumstances or voluntarily or at request of DWP (by March 2025) Administered by HMRC.

NB: Since 6 April 2017, no new basic child elements will be added for children born after that date where the claimant already has two child elements in place except in specific circumstances (conceived due to rape or due to a controlling or coercive relationship, or certain multiple births or adoption/special guardianship). See *https://www.gov.uk/guidance/claiming-benefits-for-2-or-more-children.*

NB: There is also an additional benefit cap in place, which limits an individual claim for couples and people with children to a maximum of £22,020 a year outside London and £25,323 inside London (£16,967 and £14,753 respectively for single childless claimants). It includes universal credit, housing benefit, child benefit and all means-tested or N.I. based benefits including tax credits. It generally affects people with children and/or high rents. Families that include a disabled person or a carer or where a parent is working above a certain amount (16 hours per week at National Living Wage—currently £793.00 a month) are exempt from being capped. See *https://www.gov.uk/benefit-cap.*

13: Recoupment and offsetting of social security benefits

The Social Security (Recovery of Benefits) Act 1997

The Social Security (Recovery of Benefits) Act 1997 makes provision for the Compensation Recovery Unit ('CRU') of the Department for Work and Pensions ('DWP') to recoup from a defendant certain social security benefits which have been paid to a claimant which are linked to the injuries or disease from which the claimant suffered.

Before making any payment for compensation, a defendant is under a duty to apply for a certificate of recoverable benefits (commonly referred to as a 'CRU certificate'). The certificate specifies the benefits which the defendant is liable to repay and remains in force for a period specified on the certificate itself.

Under the 1997 Act, only certain benefits – those identified as 'listed benefits' – can be recouped from a defendant. The listed benefits are set out in column 2 of Schedule 2 of the Act, which is reproduced below. Further, the provisions of the Act only apply to benefits which have been paid during a defined period: the 'relevant period' as defined in section 3 of the Act. The relevant period begins on:

- the day following an accident or injury, or
- in a disease case, on the date that a listed benefit is first claimed in consequence of the disease.

The relevant period ends on:

- the date a compensation payment is made in final discharge of a claim, or
- the date an agreement is made between the defendant and claimant under which an earlier compensation payment is treated as having been made in final discharge of any claim, or
- the date 5 years after the relevant period begins, whichever comes first.

The defendant may offset its expenditure against the claimant's damages award but only to the extent that the claimant is being compensated for the same sort of losses which the benefits in question are supposed to alleviate. As such, a defendant is only permitted to make deductions from heads of loss specified in column 1 of Schedule 2 of the Act. The amount of the deduction will comprise the total sum of the benefits listed in column 2 which are on the CRU certificate.

Schedule 2 of the Social Security (Recovery of Benefits) Act 1997 provides as follows:

(1)	(2)
Head of compensation	***Benefit***
1. Compensation for earnings lost during the relevant period	Universal Credit Disablement pension payable under section 103 of the 1992 Act[1] Employment and support allowance Incapacity benefit Income support Invalidity pension and allowance Jobseeker's allowance Reduced earnings allowance Severe disablement allowance Sickness benefit Statutory sick pay Unemployability supplement Unemployment benefit
2. Compensation for cost of care incurred during the relevant period	Attendance allowance Daily living component of personal independence payment Care component of disability living allowance Disablement pension increase payable under section 104 or 105 of the 1992 Act[2]
3. Compensation for loss of mobility during the relevant period	Mobility allowance Mobility component of personal independence payment Mobility component of disability living allowance

As to offsetting, the full amount of each recoverable benefit is deducted from the relevant head of loss. Where the amount of compensation in respect of a particular head of loss is less than the amount of a listed benefit to be recovered, the defendant is liable to pay the difference. No account is taken of contributory negligence[3]. Each of the heads of loss listed under column 1 of Schedule 2 refer to losses 'during the relevant period'. Accordingly, there can be no offsetting against any future losses.

By way of example of the application of offsetting[4]:

[1] Social Security Contributions and Benefits Act 1992.
[2] Social Security Contributions and Benefits Act 1992.
[3] This can cause difficulties drafting and interpreting Part 36 offers and extra care should be taken where there is likely to be a significant discount for contributory negligence. See: *Williams v Devon County Council* [2003] EWCA Civ 365; *Hilton International Hotels (UK) Ltd v Smith* [2001] P.I.Q.R. P14; and *Bruce v Genesis Fast Food Ltd* [2003] EWHC 788 (QB), [2004] P.I.Q.R. P9.
[4] The example is drawn from the DWP's Recovery of benefits and lump sum payments and NHS charges: technical guidance but has been updated by the authors of this section to reflect benefits which would currently be in payment. The DWP's guidance is accessible here: *https://www.gov.uk/government/publications/recovery-of-benefits-and-or-lump-sum-payments-and-nhs-charges-technical-guidance/recovery-of-benefits-and-lump-sum-payments-and-nhs-charges-technical-guidance.*

Suppose compensation totalling £100,000 is agreed and is broken down as follows: £40,000 in respect of general damages, £30,000 in respect of loss of earnings and £30,000 in respect of loss of mobility.

A CRU Certificate lists Employment and Support Allowance totalling £5,000, Universal Credit totalling £10,000 and Personal Independence Payment (mobility component) totalling £10,000.

A defendant may not offset anything against the general damages element of the award. Employment and Support Allowance and Universal Credit can be offset against the loss of earnings head of compensation. Therefore a total of £15,000 can be deducted from the loss of earnings sum, leaving £15,000 to be paid to the claimant.

Similarly, the defendant may offset the £10,000 paid by way of Personal Independence Payment (mobility component) against the loss of mobility head of compensation, leaving £20,000 to be paid to the claimant.

The claimant settled their claim for £100,000. Following offsetting, they receive £75,000 from the defendant in addition to the £25,000 they have already received from the state benefits system.

Challenging a CRU certificate

It should be noted that there exists the right to challenge a CRU certificate via review, mandatory reconsideration and ultimately by appeal. Not infrequently, CRU certificates are incorrect and may be nil when benefits have been paid or suggest a high level of recoupment when the claimant was already in receipt of benefits and there is no link between the receipt of the benefits and the index injury.

A defendant, the injured person, or either party's representative may ask CRU to review any aspect of a certificate at any time. Following a review, CRU will either confirm in writing that the certificate is correct or issue a new certificate.

Once a claim has settled, a party wishing to challenge a CRU certificate will need to apply to CRU for mandatory reconsideration of the certificate. If, following mandatory reconsideration, a party believes that a certificate is still wrong, it is open to the party to appeal. The right of appeal cannot be exercised until the claim for damages has been finally disposed of and CRU has been paid the amount on the certificate. An appeal may be made by a compensator or by an injured person where there has been some offset of the recoverable benefits against the damages award.[5]

Where a certificate is changed on appeal or review, CRU must repay any overpayment to the compensator.[6] If the amount payable is increased, the compensator must foot the additional bill.[7]

Benefits falling outside the 1997 Act

As detailed above, the statutory scheme for recoupment only applies to listed benefits. By definition, any benefit not contained within Schedule 2 is not covered by the scheme. In the UK, this includes:

- Bereavement allowance

[5] More precisely, by an injured person whose compensation payment has been reduced in accordance with s.8 or 8A of the 1997 Act or reg.12 or 12A of the Social Security (Recovery of Benefits) (Lump Sum Payments) Regulations (SI 2008/1596).

[6] Section 14(2) of the 1997 Act and reg.11(1) of the Social Security (Recovery of Benefits) Regulations (SI 1997/2205).

[7] Section 14(3) of the 1997 Act and reg.11(2) of the Social Security (Recovery of Benefits) Regulations (SI 1997/2205).

- Bereavement benefit
- Bereavement support payment
- Carer's allowance[8]
- Child benefit
- Child tax credit
- Council tax support[9]
- Guardian's allowance
- Housing benefit[10]
- Maternity allowance
- Statutory adoption pay
- Statutory maternity pay
- Statutory paternity pay
- Sure start maternity grant
- Widowed parent's allowance
- Working tax credit

Where a claimant moves to and resides in a foreign jurisdiction, he or she may well be entitled to similar statutory benefits. Such benefits will have different names and inevitably fall outside of the listed benefits in Sch.2.

A detailed treatment of the principles governing offsetting of state benefits outside the statutory scheme is beyond the scope of this chapter. The principles are governed by the common law.[11] In broad terms, however, a claimant is required to offset benefits they have received as a result of a tort provided that the claimant's claim for damages contains a head of loss which is intended to provide for the same need as the benefit in question.

It should be noted that damages payable under the Fatal Accidents Act 1976 are exempted from the operation of the statutory scheme created by the 1997 Act.[12] As regards benefits falling outside the statutory scheme, consideration should be given to s.4 Fatal Accidents Act 1976 which provides that in assessing damages in respect of a person's death, benefits which have accrued or may accrue as a result of the death shall be disregarded.

[8] See *Massey v Tameside & Glossop Acute Services NHS Trust* [2007] EWHC 317 (Admin).

[9] See *Smith v Rod Jenkins* [2003] EWHC 1356 (QB). *Smith* concerned Council tax benefit, the predecessor to Council tax support, but the same principles will apply.

[10] See *Clenshaw v Tanner* [2002] EWCA Civ 1848.

[11] See *Hodgson v Trapp* [1989] A.C. 807.

[12] See Sch.1, para.8 of the 1997 Act and reg.2(2)(a) of the Social Security (Recovery of Benefits) Regulations (SI 1997/2205).

14: Personal injury trusts

Introduction

Following a serious personal injury a client may receive substantial sums of money, be they from a claim for damages, personal accident insurance payouts, charitable gifts, or other sources.

Such clients often have to live for many years, if not the rest of their lives, with the personal, social and financial repercussions that arise because of their injury. They may be left unable to work, their family members may give up jobs to provide care, and they may have expensive ongoing costs to pay for, such as the costs of private care, case management, specialist aids and equipment. They will also continue to have their regular living costs to meet, including the maintenance of any children or dependant relatives.

Therefore, it is important to ensure that each client is provided with proper and complete advice, and practical support where required, to ensure that:

- they get the best possible award from their personal injury claim;
- they are able to claim all of the state benefits they are entitled to and statutory care and support they need, both now and in years to come; and
- they have a suitable structure in place to properly manage and invest their award in the future.

It is, of course, important for any legal advisor to ensure that they have given each and every client the proper advice with regard to each of these matters. To fail to do so has in the past led to a number of personal injury lawyers being found to have been negligent because they have not provided their clients with proper advice about the possible use of personal injury trusts.

What is a personal injury trust?

A personal injury trust is a formal structure in which to hold and manage any funds which the client has received as a consequence of their personal injury.

A formal trust deed should be put in place, which sets out the rules for the management of the funds. It is important that it is the right kind of trust, that best suits the client's requirements in their particular circumstances.

The trust deed should specify the trustees—two or more people, or a trust corporation, who are then in charge of the trust. The trustees should together make decisions about the management of the trust funds, including any payments made out of those funds, and are under an obligation to exercise their powers for the benefit of those named as beneficiaries. In most cases there will only be one beneficiary, the injured person.

The benefits of a personal injury trust

There are several benefits of having a personal injury trust in place, which include the following (albeit not an exhaustive list):

- If held in a personal injury trust, capital derived from a payment made in consequence of any personal injury to the claimant or the claimant's partner is disregarded for the purpose of many means-tested state benefits and services.

  Therefore, a client (and their partner if they claim benefits together) can continue to receive these benefits, despite having funds within the trust which, if held by them personally, would have left them with too much capital to remain entitled.

  These means-tested state benefits include Income Support, Income Related Employment and Support Allowance, Income Based Job Seekers Allowance, Universal Credit, Housing Benefit and Council Tax Support. If a person is claiming a disabled facilities grant, having their funds in a personal injury trust will mean that they will still be able to claim their passport benefit which should mean they do not have to make a financial contribution.
- The trust structure can help to protect the interests of young, older, disabled or otherwise vulnerable clients.

  Because of the requirement to have trustees in place who must each authorise all transactions within the trust, a client can be protected if their trustees are vigilant to any inappropriate proposals for the use of the funds.

  A steadfast trustee, be they a solicitor, interested family friend or parent, can exercise their effective veto against the use of trust funds to ensure that the funds are only applied in the client's best interests. The balance of power will depend on the type of trust chosen, and clients who fear that they may need extra safeguards should be advised carefully about this.
- A client can benefit from the knowledge, experience and wisdom of their trustees.

  Having appropriate trustees appointed can provide a client with important advice and support when making big decisions. Particularly when dealing with a large lump sum, this can be invaluable to ensure that decisions are appropriate to protect and ensure the long-term interests of the client.

  Some clients prefer to have an appropriately experienced solicitor appointed as one of their trustees, so that they can give advice on matters such as investment decisions, budgeting, and large items of capital expenditure. The solicitor trustee should be experienced in dealing with these matters and have come across the issues many times. As this is the injured person's first time and only chance, a professional trustee can be invaluable.
- The personal injury trust helps to define and "ring fence" the funds that arise as a consequence of the client's personal injury, keeping them separate from other assets that may belong to the client.

  This can be of help if the client's circumstances change in the future and they suddenly find that they may be eligible for means-tested benefits or care funding; for example, if they have to go in to a care home, or if they separate from a working partner.

  The personal injury trust "wrapper" can also help to define what funds were awarded for their future needs. This can help to differentiate the funds if the client goes through a divorce or any other process where their personal finances are taken into consideration.

The basic rules for entitlement to means-tested benefits

The rules for assessing a client's entitlement to means-tested benefits are detailed and complex.

However, when considering how personal injury funds may affect a client's entitlement to means-tested benefits, the key principles for Income Support, Income Related Employment and Support Allowance, Income Based Job Seeker's Allowance, Universal Credit, Housing Benefit and Council Tax Support are, broadly speaking, as follows:

- When considering a client's capital, it is important to consider both the personal injury funds that they are due to receive, as well as any savings or investments that they already hold.

- The first payment of any money derived from a personal injury will be ignored for 52 weeks from the date of receipt. An interim payment, or indeed any other payment received as a consequence of the injury, will qualify as the first payment. The rules under the Universal Credit Regulations are more generous and exempt each payment for 52 weeks. The intention of this disregard is that the claimant will have an appropriate period to seek advice and set up the trust.
- If a client has capital below £6,000, then their capital will not affect their entitlement. This lower threshold is £10,000 for those living in a care home or independent hospital.
- If a client has capital between £6,000 and £16,000, then their entitlement will be reduced. For capital between those two thresholds they will be treated as having income of £1 for every £250 or part thereof above £6,000. For Universal Credit, the tariff income is £4.35 per month per excess £250 (or part thereof).
- If a client has capital over £16,000 they will be excluded from entitlement altogether.
- A client and their partner (with whom they live) will share a capital allowance, so it is important to look at their capital together. They should ideally have less than £6,000 between them both, if they are to maintain full entitlement.
- Certain assets, such as the value of the home a client lives in and their personal possessions, are disregarded when calculating capital.
- Any income received by the client, including that received by their partner, is deducted from the amount of benefits payable, albeit subject to some personal disregards and allowances.

The basic rules for entitlement to means-tested benefits for elderly clients

Pension Credit is available to people reaching state pension age. This varies depending on when somebody was born but for example, for somebody born between 5 April 1961 and 5 April 1977 this would be 67; but for somebody born on 5 April 1978 this would be 67, 11 months and one day. The lower capital threshold is £10,000, and above that amount tariff income from a client's capital is assumed at a rate of £1 for every £500, or part thereof. There is no upper capital threshold. Income derived from a personal injury settlement is ignored, whether paid from a trust or otherwise. Actual capital is ignored, except to the extent that it creates assumed tariff income.

If a person receives Pension Credit Guarantee Credit then personal injury monies are ignored completely, whether in a trust or not, both in respect of capital and income. In addition, in order to access the disregard for residential care funding a trust will be required and so it is best to advise clients to consider a trust even if it appears their damages will be disregarded at the moment.

Before Universal Credit was introduced, a couple could qualify for Pension Credit based on the age of the oldest member of that couple. New rules introduced in May 2019, operate to make the youngest person's age relevant instead. Therefore, a couple with one member over state pension age and one member under state pension age would find themselves in the less generous Universal Credit regime rather than the Pension Credit regime. That can make a difference to requirements to seek work etc.

Welfare reform

Since the implementation of the Welfare Reform Act 2012 in March 2013, Council Tax Benefit was abolished from 31 March 2013 and replaced by a discretionary scheme designed by local authorities. Each local authority has its own scheme although there is a national precedent scheme which local authorities can adopt. Ten per cent less money is available to reduce people's Council Tax than was previously available under the Council Tax Benefit scheme. Local authorities have to protect the position of pensioners. The net result is that in many local authority areas, people of working age are having to pay a proportion of their Council Tax even if they would previously have been entitled to full Council Tax Benefit. A number of people have been caught out by this in the belief that they are entitled to full Council Tax Support and so have not paid a great deal of attention to the Council Tax statement which comes once a year until they receive a summons for non-payment.

April 2013 also saw the introduction of the benefit cap with the stated policy aim of encouraging more people into work, by imposing reductions on the total amount households receive by way of benefits.

The Government currently expects all households claiming legacy benefits and tax credits to have moved to Universal Credit by the end of 2024/25. The benefits position of people in different areas are likely to be different for some time until the full roll out has been achieved.

Care funding

Adult funding in England

The Care Act 2014 was implemented on 1 April 2015. It applies in England only. It has applied to all cases since 1 April 2016, regardless of whether they have been reassessed under the Act.

There are some significant differences to the treatment of domiciliary care and in particular the treatment of periodical payments to which disregards now apply in some circumstances. The Care and Support (Charging and Assessment of Resources) Regulations 2014 (CSCAR) apply to the means testing of all residential and domiciliary care under the Act.

Capital placed in a personal injury trust is disregarded for means assessment purposes, both for home and residential care. The arguments raised by local authorities pre-Care Act that they had discretion to take account of the care element of such assets in domiciliary care cases have no arguable basis under the CSCAR.

For the year 2024–2025 there is an upper capital limit for assessable capital of £23,250. There is a lower capital limit of £14,250 for 2024–25. These limits have been in place since April 2010. Between these two limits, the adult is treated as having tariff income of £1 for every £250 or part of £250. Amendments to the upper capital limit will appear in reg.12 of the charging regulations and to the lower limit in reg.25.

Investment income paid to a deputy or trustee of a PI trust is disregarded.

Periodical payments paid into a personal injury trust are also disregarded as income. Claimants lacking capacity whose advisers are considering periodical payments which in consequence will be paid to a deputy should seek specialist advice. Our view is that these payments are disregarded.

The question of whether periodical payments made to the claimant in person for meeting care needs are disregarded is subject to some debate. The position taken here is that periodical payments to the claimant from the trust by the trustees (or otherwise direct to the claimant) are disregarded up to £20.

If periodical payments to the claimant in person are unused after the relevant period and accumulate as capital in the hands of the claimant to a sum exceeding the lower capital limit, they will be taken into account under the general capital limits.

Payments made by trustees directly to a domiciliary care provider are disregarded. It is possible that regular payments made by trustees to a residential care provider may be treated as the income of the resident.

Means testing reform

Section 15 of the Care Act provides that the cost to an adult of their care and support other than for daily living costs may be capped.

Government proposals issued on 7 September 2021 for a cap on the amount anyone in England will need to spend on their personal care over their lifetime have now been placed on indefinite hold. If introduced, the cap will be £86,000. At that point the upper capital limit will rise from £23,250 to £100,000. The lower capital limit will increase to £20,000 from £14,250. The precise mechanics are yet to be formulated and will be subject to Parliamentary approval.

Importantly, the cap will not cover the daily living costs for people in care homes. These costs will be set at a notional national figure set out in regulations. The purpose of separately identifying daily living costs reflects the fact that if a person was not in residential care they would have to pay bills such as food and utility costs and possibly rent. The cap will be implemented for adults of all ages. Between the lower capital limit of £20,000 and the upper capital limit of £100,000 you will be treated as having £1 per week for every £250 of capital above the lower capital limit in the same way as now.

Care funding for minors in England

The provision of care support for minors in England continues to be provided under ss.17 & 18 of the Children Act 1989 and under s.2 of the Chronically Sick and Disabled Persons Act 1970.

Section 29 sets out that a local authority may charge for these services except where they are for advice, guidance or counselling. There are no regulations made under this section.

The section also states that where the child is under 16, the person to be charged is the "parent". Where the child is over 16, it is the child.

The means testing position is complicated by the fact that s.17(8) states that:

> "Before giving any assistance or imposing any conditions, a local authority shall have regard to the means of the child concerned and of each of his parents."

There is no case law deciding how this relates to s.29. It is submitted that if the two provisions are to work together in a sensible manner, s.29 should qualify the generality of s.17(8).

The Social Services and Well-Being (Wales) Act 2014

This Act was implemented on 5 April 2016. A major difference between this Act and the Care Act in England, is that the Welsh Act incorporates care and support provision for minors and so replaces the Children Act 1989 and the Chronically Sick & Disabled Persons Act 1970.

Part 5 of the Act deals with charging and financial assessment. Section 59 permits a local authority to make a charge for providing the service. Section 60 states that a charge for a service provided to a child may be imposed upon an adult with parental responsibility for that child.

The Care and Support (Financial Assessment) (Wales) Regulations 2015 and the Care and Support (Charging) (Wales) Regulations 2015 provide a unified scheme for the means testing of domiciliary and residential support. This scheme of charging does not apply to looked after and accommodated children under Pt.6.

There is a capital limit which for the year 2024–2025 is £50,000 for residential care means assessment and £24,000 for domiciliary care assessment. Revised limits are specified from time to time in reg.11 of the Care and Support (Charging) (Wales) Regulations 2015. There is no tariff income scheme in Wales and so there is no lower limit for capital below which tariff income does not apply.

The disregards for personal injury trust capital and the first capital payment to the claimant in person in consequence of a personal injury, are the same as those now applying in England under the Care Act 2014.

Investment income paid to a trustee of a PI trust is disregarded.

As in England, periodical payments are defined as income (para.16(6) 2015 financial assessment regulations). Otherwise, periodical payments are treated differently in Wales. In practice they are disregarded because contributions from income to the cost of domiciliary support are in any event limited to £100 per week (2024–2025) and this cap also applies to income in the form of periodical payments. Revised income cap limits are specified from time to time in reg.7 of the Care and Support (Charging) (Wales) Regulations 2015.

Paragraph 14 of Sch.1 of the 2015 financial assessment regulations suggests that income type payments made out of a trust by the trustees to the claimant or periodical payments made to the claimant direct from the insurer are disregarded unless they are to pay for care. Periodical payments made direct to the claimant should be disregarded if they are awarded for care which the council accepts is a genuine need but does not fit within the new statutory eligibility criteria. There is a further condition that they are actually used for that purpose. The aim is to allow such payments to be used for topping up care. However even if all these conditions are met, they are then subject to a cap of £20. The complexity of this regulation seems unnecessary having regard to the overall income cap.

Where it is proposed that periodical payments are paid into a personal injury trust, they should be disregarded in full.

If periodical payments to the claimant in person are unused and accumulate as capital in the hands of the claimant to a sum exceeding the capital limit, they will be taken into account under the general capital limits.

Payments made by trustees directly to a domiciliary care provider are disregarded. It is possible that regular payments made by trustees to a residential care provider may be treated as the income of the resident.

There are no proposals for care capping contained in the Welsh Care Act.

National Care Service for Wales

On 10 November 2022 the Welsh Government published a report by an Expert Group commissioned to investigate the establishment of a national care service for Wales, free at the point of need.

On 18 April 2024, the Welsh Government announced the launch of the new National Office for Care and Support. Through its 10 year programme, the National Office is tasked with bringing into effect the establishment of a national care service for Wales.

What funds can go into a personal injury trust?

The benefits regulations for most benefits take a wide definition, allowing any sums of capital to be disregarded if they are "derived from a payment made in consequence of any personal injury to the claimant or the claimant's partner". However, the Universal Credit regulations refer to "compensation" in the title to the disregard section and "a sum awarded" in the disregard itself. The effect of that may be to narrow the types of funds which can be protected in a personal injury trust for injured people who are claiming Universal Credit. Some clients may find that they are in a dual system where certain funds within a trust might be disregarded for care purposes for example but not for Universal Credit. For most benefits however the wider definition means that the use of personal injury trusts is not just limited to awards of damages, and can include:

- A personal injury award, including interim payments received during the course of a claim.
- A Criminal Injuries Compensation Authority award.
- A Motor Insurers' Bureau award.
- Payments from the Armed Forces Compensation Scheme, and similar schemes.
- Payments from various "no fault" schemes, sometimes set up by government bodies both here and abroad, such as payments from the Irish Residential Institutions Redress Board. It has been noted that the Social Security (Income and Capital Disregards) (Amendment) Regulations (SI 2021/1405) created new disregards for various schemes including those compensated for child abuse. These cover the Historical Institutional Abuse Northern Ireland Act 2019, Redress for Survivors (Historical Child Abuse in Care) (Scotland) Act 2021, Lambeth Children's Homes Redress Scheme and the London Borough of Islington's proposed supported payment scheme. A more recent update to the regulations (SI 2023/640) expanded the existing disregard to include Grenfell Tower payments and Post Office compensation payments. Those will not affect means tested benefits where they are in a Personal Injury Trust. The authors are not aware of an equivalent scheme for care at present.
- Funds received from a Periodical Payment or Structured Settlement.
- Charitable or public donations following an accident.
- Funds received from accident or travel insurance.
- Funds received from a professional negligence claim paid to compensate for an undervalued or negligently pursued personal injury claim.

It is vitally important to remember that, although the capital disregard is quite wide, the income disregard is rather more restricted. Where a person receives income from, for example, a personal accident policy or an occupational ill health pension, it is unlikely that those funds would be able to be disregarded, even if they are placed into a personal injury trust.

When to set up a personal injury trust

It is important that, if at all possible, a personal injury trust is set up before a client receives their funds.

Lawyers should be aware that any client funds held on their Client Account may be treated as the client's money by the benefits agency and local authority. Therefore, any funds held on Client Account can jeopardise a client's benefit entitlement and consideration should be given to the suitability of a personal injury trust straight away.

Lawyers also run the risk that if funds remain on their client account, and they are aware that the client has not notified the benefits agency, they could find their firm obliged to report the client's non-disclosure as defrauding the benefits agency. Furthermore, they run the risk that they may be construed as aiding and abetting the client in a possible benefits fraud.

While it is usually best advice that a personal injury trust should be set up sooner rather than later, it is possible to set up a trust after the funds have been received and held personally by the client for some time. There is no restriction upon when personal injury funds must be placed into a trust, so funds can be held for months, or years, before a client arranges to place them in a trust. This does not allow the client to claim retrospectively for any benefits that they have missed out on prior to the trust being set up.

However, a client will have to demonstrate to the satisfaction of the benefits agency, or local authority, that the funds placed into the trust are purely those arising from their personal injury. There is a risk that the funds may over time have been mixed up with, or diluted by, other income or capital belonging to the client. For example, if personal injury money and personal injury money only has been used to purchase a house, that would be much more straightforward to add to the trust than money that has been put in the client's own bank account and used for all sorts of things. Therefore, clients may find that they have some difficulty persuading the authorities that all of the funds should be disregarded.

Setting up a personal injury trust

It will be necessary to appoint appropriate trustees. There should be at least two trustees or a trust corporation, and no more than four. They must be over 18 years of age and mentally capable of acting as a trustee. It is usually best to avoid trustees whose health and age might make them incapable of fulfilling their obligations in the foreseeable future.

The choice of trustees is an important one, as they will for all intents and purposes have full control over the personal injury trust and the assets held within it. It is important to consider whether they will be able to work well together and continue to act in the best interests of the beneficiaries. For this reason, some caution should be exercised before appointing partners, spouses, or other family members as trustees, if there is a risk of the relationship breaking down in the future. Often partners or spouses will shy away from wanting to be involved in a personal injury trust, particularly if they have appeared on the scene after the injury and are concerned that people might question their motives.

Some clients may prefer to have an appropriately experienced solicitor appointed as one of their trustees. This allows an impartial and professional person to assist in the trustees' deliberations and decision making. It can help to ensure that the trustees are making decisions together which are appropriate to the needs of the beneficiaries, as well as providing the professional expertise and experience that can be invaluable when making difficult decisions.

It is also important that a client receives the correct advice about the right kind of trust to put in place. Consideration needs to be given to the client's particular circumstances, their potential liability to tax and the provision that they may wish to make for their family in the future. This will in turn affect whether the client is named as the sole beneficiary of the trust, or whether other beneficiaries are named and, if so, whether the trustees have any discretion in how they apply funds for their benefit.

For the vast majority of clients, a bare trust will be the most appropriate. The person setting up the trust retains control over appointing trustees and can break the trust if they want to. For that reason, though, this type of trust may not be appropriate for people who are concerned that they might use that power in a way that does not benefit them. That might be because somebody knows they have had addiction issues in the past or are vulnerable to pressure from family members or hangers on wanting to separate them from their funds. For clients in that position, the usual solution will be a form of trust within s.89 of the Inheritance Tax Act. There are certain qualifying conditions for such a trust, mainly related to the type of benefits a client receives. Unfortunately for some clients, they do not meet the qualifying conditions but do have a vulnerability that would make such a trust advisable. They can face a difficult choice between protection and tax.

The client being advised about Personal Injury Trusts should be advised about wills at the same time.

Once the advice is given, and the necessary decisions are made, the trust deed will need to be prepared by the instructed lawyer, before being signed in the presence of witnesses, and dated. The personal injury trust will usually have a suitable title, such as the "John Smith Personal Injury Trust."

Once a personal injury trust is set up

Once a personal injury trust is set up, the trustees' first act will usually be to open a bank or building society account to hold the trust funds. The account should be suitably named, such as the "Josephine Anne Bloggs Personal Injury Trust". The account should usually require that each and every one of the trustees is required to sign to authorise all transactions on account, including all cheques. Some financial institutions such as those managing investments happy to operate a single signature system provided all of the trustees have given their instructions and that can be helpful when trustees are geographically dispersed.

Once the trustees have set up the trust bank account, the personal injury lawyer can confidently arrange for a cheque to be issued for the personal injury funds, ensuring that the cheque is made payable to the trust, i.e. payable to the "Josephine Anne Bloggs Personal Injury Trust", and not to the client personally.

The trustees will need to keep to certain rules in order to be able to use funds from the trust without affecting the client's benefit entitlement, namely:

- Any income arising from the funds in the trust, such as interest or dividends, should be paid into a trust account, and not paid to the client personally
- The trustees can transfer funds into the client's own personal account, but should take care to ensure that the client's capital (including the capital held by their partner if they are claiming benefits as a couple) stays below £6,000 at all times, which is the lower capital threshold for most means-tested benefits.
- Possibly the simplest way to use funds from the trust is to make direct payments from the trust to third parties. This way the funds go directly from the trust account, to the third party and do not go through the client's hands in any way.
- Any further assets set up to be held by the trustees, be they bank accounts, investments or property, should be set up with the same restrictions as the original trust bank account, namely:
  - in the name of the trust, or trustees; and
  - with the restriction that each and every one of the trustees is required to sign all transactions with regard to that asset unless an alternative system has been agreed for convenience but the consent of all the trustees will always be needed.

Is a client likely to benefit from a personal injury trust in the future?

For many clients it is easy to determine that they are entitled to means-tested benefits, or care funding, at the time that they receive their funds, and so it makes sense to protect their entitlement straight away by setting up a personal injury trust.

However, some clients may at the time have no entitlement to means-tested benefits, and so a personal injury trust may not seem immediately relevant. In such cases careful consideration should be given to the client's potential to claim means-tested benefits in the future.

A client may become entitled to means-tested benefits in the future if their relevant circumstances change, which may include:

- If they need to move to live in a residential care home.
- If they move out of the family home to live on their own.
- If they leave full or part-time education.
- If they are discharged from hospital or residential care.
- If they and their spouse divorce or separate.
- When they reach a significant age for benefits purposes, such as 16, 18 or 60 years of age or state pension age, which is 66 for people retiring at the moment and rises to 67. There is a helpful online calculator at *gov.uk*
- If they or their partner lose their job, retire or are medically unable to continue to work.
- If they, or their partner, lose their entitlement to another benefit or source of income.
- If they, or their partner, find their health deteriorates and they become entitled to higher rates of disability benefits, which in turn have a knock-on effect for some means-tested benefits.
- If they, or their partner, find that they have used up their pre-existing savings (those which have not arisen from the personal injury claim and which have previously prevented them claiming means-tested benefits) and so find that they would become entitled to means-tested benefits if their personal injury funds were disregarded as capital.

In such cases clients should be advised to use up their pre-existing savings with some caution. The benefits agency or local authority can ask to look at a person's history of expenditure, and any gifts made, to see if the client has in the opinion of the authority, deliberately depleted their estate in order to gain entitlement to means-tested benefits or services. If the authority feels that a client has deliberately depleted their estate in such a manner, they can decide to treat the spent funds as "notional capital", essentially treating the client as if they still have the funds and leaving them with no entitlement to the means-tested benefit or service which they have applied for. Therefore, it is important that clients keep a careful record of their expenditure to demonstrate that their use of funds has been reasonable and not a deliberate attempt to deplete their estate.

The 52-week rule

Payments received as a consequence of a personal injury are disregarded for the purpose of assessing entitlement to means tested benefits for the first 52 weeks after they are received.

However, that disregard applies only to the first payment received as a consequence of that personal injury, which may often be the client's first interim payment. It is also important to check to see a client has received other earlier payments, which may count as their "first payment", such as payments from an accident insurance policy or even a capital payment from a charity.

Any later payments, including further interim payments, are not protected by this disregard after the expiry of the original 52-week period.

Under the Universal Credit regulations there is a disregard of 52 weeks for every payment. That may be helpful for some clients who receive smaller awards but if they decide not to set up a trust they will need to be extremely careful in monitoring the various 52 week disregard periods. Establishing which funds form part of which interim and when the disregard therefore runs out could be quite tricky and the client would be caught out.

Therefore, when receiving a first payment as a consequence of a personal injury, a client may choose not to set up a trust if they anticipate spending enough of that sum to bring their capital below the relevant threshold by the end of the 52-week period. However, they should be advised to hold that payment in a bank account separate from any other funds. That way, if towards the end of period they find that they unexpectedly have funds remaining, they can still arrange to place them into a personal injury trust safe in the knowledge that the funds have not become mixed up with other capital in any way. Clients do need to be advised that the deprivation rules will still apply. If they deliberately use their capital in ways which are designed to mean that they keep their benefits then the benefits authorities could still treat them as owning it.

However, in many cases it will be appropriate to set up a personal injury trust as soon as any funds are received, regardless of the 52-week rule. Where the amount of funds due to the client overall are almost certainly going to last longer than that period, there is little if no benefit in delaying the setting up of a personal injury trust which is likely to remain in place to manage the client's funds for many years to come.

There is a common misconception that a person in receipt of personal injury compensation only has 52 weeks to set up a trust. That is not correct. If they wish to have continuous access to means-tested benefits then they should set up the trust within 52 weeks of the first payment received in consequence of a personal injury. However, some clients choose to set a trust up much later. As mentioned above, it is very important that injury related funds are held separately so it is clear what money can be placed into a personal injury trust at a later date. A person can only claim benefits from the date on which they put the money into a personal injury trust. For example, if Bob receives his first and only payment for personal injury on 3 January 2020, that payment would be disregarded for 52 weeks. Bob decided not to put his payment into a personal injury trust. He then decided on 3 January 2023 that a trust was a good idea and put the money in on that date. He will be able to claim means-tested benefits from 3 January 2023 going forward but cannot go back two years and claim the benefits between the 52 week disregard running out and the date he sets the trust up.

Personal injury trusts for children and protected parties

In most cases the decision as to whether or not to set up a personal injury trust is one for the client to make for themselves, albeit with the benefit of good advice from a lawyer. The matter does not require court approval in any way.

However, if a client is unable to make their own decision it will be necessary to obtain approval from the appropriate court with authority to make a decision on behalf of the client (CPR r.21.11 and supplementary Practice Direction), namely:

- The High Court will need to approve the establishment of a personal injury trust to manage an infant's funds until the infant reaches 18 years of age.
- In cases involving mentally incapable people, including infants who are expected to lack capacity to manage their financial affairs when they reach the age of 18, the Court of Protection will need to approve the establishment of a personal injury trust, in preference to the appointment of a Deputy for Property and Affairs. Following the case of *Re HM*,[1] the court is likely to approve the establishment of trusts in limited circumstances only. The case of *OH v Craven* has said that there is not a preference for deputyship as such, as was widely thought to be the case after *HM*. The Court is still highly likely to prefer a deputyship to a trust in most cases and this has been the case in practice.

[1] (2011) C.O.P. 11875043 11 April 2011.

15: Claims for loss of earnings and maintenance at public expense

Section 5 of the Administration of Justice Act 1982 provides:

> **Maintenance at public expense to be taken into account in assessment of damages.**
>
> In an action under the law of England and Wales or the law of Northern Ireland for damages for personal injuries (including any such action arising out of a contract) any saving to the injured person which is attributable to his maintenance wholly or partly at public expense in a hospital, nursing home or other institution shall be set off against any income lost by him as a result of his injuries.

It is worth noting that the maintenance to be considered is at public expense but does not necessarily have to be provided by a public institution. Furthermore, the savings must relate to money the claimant would have spent on maintenance and this amount would be deducted from the loss of earnings claimed. It is open to argument whether maintenance includes expenses other than food.[1]

This deduction is comparable to (but not the same as) the common law principle that where a claimant is in a private hospital or home (in respect of which damages are claimed from the defendant), credit must be given for the domestic expenses thereby saved. This is the "domestic element" which was discussed in *Fairhurst v St Helens and Knowsley Health Authority*.[2] The principle is clear, but there is a dearth of authority on how to value such maintenance.

Caution should be taken not to confuse this with the long-established principle that where a third party has gratuitously come to the injured person's financial rescue by payment of medical or living expenses, or continued payment of wages, or by way of a general sum not in relation to a particular head of loss, the benefits so conferred upon the injured person do not go in mitigation of their damages.

It is worth looking at the House of Lords' decision in *O'Brien v Independent Assessor*,[3] in which it held (in the context of statutory compensation for miscarriages of justice), that living expenses are deductible from the claim of a wrongly-convicted defendant for loss of the earnings that he would have received had he not been wrongfully imprisoned. The Assessor had awarded the three appellants:

- O'Brien: £143,497 for past loss of earnings, less £37,158 saved living expenses.
- Michael and Vincent Hickey: "A substantial figure for loss of earnings" less 25 per cent saved living expenses

In upholding these deductions, the House of Lords did not give any guidance on how to assess them, but said:

> 30 . . . the appropriate deduction is a highly judgmental matter . . .
>
> 35 . . . I agree with my noble and learned friend, Lord Brown of Eaton-under-Heywood, that wrongful imprisonment cannot sensibly be characterised in any way as conferring a benefit (para 92 of his opinion). The justification for the deduction is, to my mind, that compensation is intended, so far as lost earnings are concerned, to provide the claimant with the sum that, had he been at liberty he would have had at his disposal to expend or save as he chose. Expenditure on the bare necessities of life is an essential, not a choice. So the deduction is necessary to achieve the object of the lost earnings element of a compensation award.

[1] Collaterally, The Law Reform (Personal Injuries) Act 1948 s.2(4), lays down that the possibility of avoiding expenses or part of them by making use of the facilities of the National Health Service is to be disregarded.

[2] [1994] 8 WLUK 25.

[3] [2007] UKHL 10, [2007] 2 A.C. 312. Not to be confused with the more saintly protagonist of *O'Brien v Ministry of Justice [2017]* UKSC 46.

16: Foster care allowances

Introductory notes:

All foster parents receive a foster care allowance to help cover the cost of caring for a child. Additional payments may be available, depending on:

- Any specific needs that the child might have.
- The number of children fostered.
- The skills and experience of the foster parents.
- The services provided by the fostering parents.

The Department for Education publishes National Minimum Allowances (NMAs) for foster carers in England, with the expectation that all fostering services meet these amounts. These are available from *https://www.gov.uk/support-for-foster-parents/help-with-the-cost-of-fostering.* In order to ascertain the actual amount that each foster service will provide, it is necessary to contact the relevant fostering service.

The following are the NMA's for the tax year commencing 6 April 2024 to 5 April 2025, they are updated every April; Amount paid per week by age band:

	Age 0 to 2	Age 3 to 4	Age 5 to 10	Age 11 to 14	Age 16 to 17
London	191	195	217	248	289
South East	183	189	208	238	278
Rest of England	165	170	187	213	249

In *Spittle v Bunney*[1] it was said that the cost of fostering services is not an appropriate measure for the value of the loss of a (deceased) mother's services, but the case is not uncontroversial.

Children stop being in care when they reach 18, even if they are still living with foster carers. There is no minimum allowance when the child is old enough to leave foster care (18).

[1] [1988] 1 W.L.R. 847.

Group J

Court of Protection

J

J1: Note on the Court of Protection

1. Introduction:

The last few years have been a time of what feels like unprecedented change in the legal sector and the role of the professional deputy has not been immune to this period of adjustment. There have been a number of developments which have impacted directly on professional deputies. Some have been implemented under the Office of the Public Guardian (OPG)'s new model of supervision, including the closer monitoring of deputyship fees. The key changes can be summarised as follows:

- The introduction of the OPG Professional Deputy Standards 2015, updated in 2023.
- The introduction of the Good Practice Guidance from the OPG and the Senior Court Costs Office (SCCO) in relation to professional deputy costs.
- The implementation of the revised Court of Protection Rules 2017.
- Changes to the annual reporting requirements of the OPG.
- The requirement to provide annual fee estimates to the OPG.
- The transition of clients who were receiving Disability Living Allowance to Personal Independence Payments.
- A sharp rise in the number of deputyship clients being reassessed as no longer eligible for certain welfare benefits, with an increased need for Professional Deputies to commission and oversee welfare benefits reviews and appeals.
- New OPG guidance for the calculation of family care payments.
- The introduction of the Care Act 2014 with significant implications for clients in receipt of Local Authority funded care, including clients who have received personal injury awards.
- The introduction of a revised National framework for NHS continuing healthcare and NHS funded nursing care with significant implications for clients who are eligible for non means-tested funding.
- A sharp fall in the availability and level of statutory care funding leading to a significant rise in the number of complaints and appeals made, requiring oversight by professional deputies.
- Revised National Institute for Health Care and Excellence ("NICE") Guidelines for decision making and mental capacity.
- Increased globalisation involving more deputyship clients who have assets abroad and an increased number of foreign nationals who have fallen within the jurisdiction of our Court of Protection.
- The General Data Protection Regulations (GDPR) which impact on how professional deputies can gather, store, release and use data relating to clients and their wider networks.
- A plethora of Court of Protection case law regarding capacity, best interests decision making, trusts, statutory wills and various other deputyship related issues.
- Changes to the court guideline rates and the setting up of a working party to look at how these will be reviewed in the future.

An abundance of developments for those professional deputies who directly employ support workers including:

- Health and Social Care Act 2008 (Regulated Activities) Regulations 2014 which ensure that Deputies must comply with the Care Quality Commission when employing support workers who carry out "regulated activities" in relation to care.
- Pension auto-enrolment.
- A large number of relevant employment law cases dealing specifically with the employment of carers.
- And then came Covid-19 and furlough.

It is difficult to ascertain the precise impact of each of these developments on professional deputyship costs, some changes will have had zero or minimal impact and a number will have been absorbed as practice "overheads". However, when viewed as a whole it is clear that the role of the professional deputy has gradually but undoubtedly become more complex and time-consuming and this does have a cost consequence whether it be for the deputy's practice or their client.

Whilst Court Guideline Hourly Rates (GHR's) have been reviewed with a suggestion that ongoing reviews will be more frequent than the previous decade, the impact of this has not fully filtered through to most cases subject to the assessment process, in part due to the significant and possibly unprecedented delays in the assessment process at the COP division of the SCCO, but in some cases there has been a gradual increase in deputyship costs as a result of the additional responsibilities placed upon the deputy, the complexity of their client's lives or a combination of both. It is therefore imperative that careful consideration is given to the likely deputyship costs that may accrue during a clients lifetime.

2. The Mental Capacity Act 2005

The Mental Capacity Act 2005 ("the Act") came into force on 1 October 2007. At the time of its inception, the Act was considered a fundamental change in the law. It is intended to empower incapacitated adults and provide a framework for those who work with and for, them.

The Act as amended and its accompanying Code of Practice ("the Code") govern all dealings with those who lack capacity to make decisions about some or all aspects of their property and affairs or their health and welfare.

Capacity is time and function-specific—in other words, is someone capable of making a decision or carrying out an action at the time that the decision or action is needed? A person may be capable of making many decisions or very few and that may change over time or with circumstances.

It is important to remember that there is no general level below which a claimant lacks capacity and above which they do not. The statement that a person "lacks capacity" in itself is meaningless but still frequently seen even amongst the reports of professionals. Clearly some claimants will lack the capacity needed to deal with all aspects of their financial affairs, but others will have various and varying levels of retained capacity which may allow them to deal with certain issues.

In order to determine whether someone has capacity to make a decision the principles set out in s.1 of the Act must be adhered to:

(1) A person must be assumed to have capacity unless it is established that he lacks capacity.

(2) A person is not to be treated as unable to make that decision unless all practicable steps to help him to do so have been taken without success.

(3) A person is not to be treated as unable to make a decision merely because he makes an unwise decision.

(4) An act done, or decision made, under the Act for or on behalf of a person who lacks capacity must be done, or made, in his best interests.

(5) Before the act is done, or the decision is made, regard must be had to whether the purpose for which it is needed can be as effectively achieved in a way that is less restrictive of the person's rights and freedom of action.

The Act says that a person lacks capacity in relation to a matter if at the material time he is unable to make a decision for himself because of an impairment of, or a disturbance in the functioning of, the mind. It goes on to say that it doesn't matter whether the impairment or disturbance is permanent or temporary and that a lack of capacity should not be established by mere reference to a person's age or appearance or an aspect of his behaviour which might lead to unjustified assumptions about his capacity.

The test for establishing whether someone lacks capacity is based upon the balance of probabilities and not beyond all reasonable doubt.

The Act says that a person is unable to make a decision for himself if he is unable:

(1) To understand the information relevant to the decision.

A person must not be regarded as unable to understand the relevant information if he can understand an explanation of it given in a way which is appropriate to his circumstances; this may involve the explanation being delivered using simple language, visual aids or other means including a translator. Information relevant to the decision includes information about the reasonably foreseeable consequences of deciding one way or another or failing to make the decision at all.

(2) To retain that information.

The fact that someone can only retain relevant information for a short period of time doesn't mean that they should be regarded as unable to make the decision.

(3) To use or weigh up that information as part of the process of making the decision.

(4) To communicate their decision by whatever means.

Failing to meet any one of the first three tests will establish a lack of capacity to make a specific decision. However, someone who passes the first three tests but is unable to communicate their decision will be deemed to lack capacity, even though medically they may have full capacity. It is therefore vitally important to ensure that everything possible is done to maximise a claimant's capacity including their ability to communicate, before concluding that capacity is lacking.

A deputy is required to use appropriate ways to communicate with the claimant and the use of the client's preferred language is cited as an example, this may involve the commissioning of translation services or it may involve liaising with a speech and language therapist to ensure that communication is maximised and this may give rise to additional quantum issues. Seeing the claimant in an environment where they are most comfortable such as their own home and allowing them appropriate amounts of time to process information may also help to maximise their capacity and communication potential.

3. The scope and authority of the Court of Protection

If a claimant lacks capacity to make a decision, the Court of Protection is there to help. The Act established a new court (albeit with the same name). This new court is a superior court of record with authority equivalent to that of the High Court. Its powers extend to health and welfare issues, and financial matters.

Those empowered to act on the orders or declarations of the court are known as deputies, and claimants who fall within the court's jurisdiction are referred to as "P". The OPG supervises deputies. The court now publishes its judgments which is of assistance to practitioners, as are the Practice Notes issued by the OPG and the Court. Professional deputies must also adhere to a set of published professional deputyship standards. The Act has greatly changed the role of the deputy and this has become an increasingly specialist field of practice.

4. The appointment of a property and affairs deputy

The court will confer on a deputy powers which should be as limited in scope and duration as is reasonably practicable in the circumstances. For a claimant with a head injury, the court is more likely to make an order which gives the deputy wide powers given the number of decisions that will need to be made on P's behalf. However, despite these wide powers, there is an ongoing duty on the deputy to make only the decisions that P is unable to make. This goes to the heart of the Act and its underlying aim, which is to empower, rather than limit, the decision-making capabilities of a person living with a mental impairment. Despite these wide powers the deputy may still need to return to the court for further authority or satisfy the court on certain issues. There is also an ongoing need to satisfy the Public Guardian who monitors the conduct of all deputies.

5. When to make an application

Whilst a deputy may not be needed until such time as funds become available that the claimant is unable to manage, it can take up to nine months for a deputy to be appointed, sometimes longer. The introduction of an online portal has helped but this does not extend to all applications. It will therefore be prudent to make an application in good time.

Rule 14.5 of the Solicitors' Accounts Rules provides that a solicitor must not provide banking facilities through a client account. The management of an interim payment through a client account may give rise to a breach of this rule.

6. Invoking the court's jurisdiction

The court must have evidence to show that a person has a mental impairment that brings them within the scope of the Act and that they are unable to make or take decisions and actions which are needed. This is addressed in the form COP3 (an Assessment of Capacity).

The practitioner giving instructions for the capacity assessment will set out in Part A of the COP3 form:

- the matters that the court is being asked to decide;
- the order sought;
- the reasons why the claimant will benefit from the order; and
- any other relevant information.

The capacity assessor will then use this information to inform their assessment.

Where there is conflicting medical evidence as to the claimant's capacity, within ongoing personal injury litigation there has been an important change in the Court of Protection's approach to the appointment of a deputy. In *Loughlin v Singh [2013] EWHC 1641 (QB)* Kenneth Parker J made it clear that when an application is made for the appointment of a deputy the Court of Protection must be given "all the material which, on proper reflection, is necessary for a just and accurate decision", this being a direct reference to material relating to P's mental capacity.

Historically, where there has been conflicting evidence in relation to the claimant's capacity to manage aspects of their finances, the Court of Protection has often appointed a deputy, albeit that the order may have been time limited and required further directions to be sought on conclusion of the litigation. This approach was taken against a background of the deputy being bound by the Mental Capacity Act 2005 and empowered only to make decisions that P is unable to make and the ongoing duty placed upon the deputy to keep capacity under review.

The Court of Protection has changed its approach to cases where there is ongoing personal injury litigation coupled with conflicting evidence on the issue of mental capacity. In such cases it will no longer appoint a deputy until the issue of capacity has been addressed by the Court having conduct of that litigation. At the time of publication this is not incorporated within a Practice Direction or judgment but is the Court's stated practice.

7. Surety bonds for deputies

For the deputy to act, the court requires that a surety be put in place to safeguard P's assets. The level of security is set by the court, and can be based on a number of factors, including the size of the claimant's estate and the extent to which the deputy will have access to it. The bond safeguards the claimant's assets from any financial loss suffered as a result of the deputy failing to perform their duties. The surety bond is required even though a professional deputy has professional indemnity insurance.

Although Judge Hazel Marshall laid down in the case of *Re H [2009] EWHC 1331 (COP)* clear guidelines to be followed when calculating a suitable level of surety, the level of surety remains in the discretion of the judiciary and this can see a range of bond levels within cases of apparent similarity.

The fee for the bond will depend upon the level of surety that the court sets. Sureties can be obtained from a provider of the deputy's choice, but the court and OPG have from time to time identified preferred providers, following completion of a tendering process. With effect from 1 April 2023 there are 3 preferred providers, Howdens, Marsh and Insynch Insurance Solutions Ltd. At the time of publishing Howdens and Marsh have said that with the exception of very low-level bonds, which are unlikely to apply in a damages award except on an interim basis, the premiums will be due on an annual basis for life and based on a per cent of the bond value. Insynch have yet to publish their terms. These new arrangements will not affect the arrangements in place for existing bonds but they may impact upon bond reviews, including post settlement increases, so care should be taken to anticipate this given the significant departure from the previous fee structure. Other bond providers are available to use, provided the terms of the bond are acceptable to the Public Guardian. Other providers may have different charging structures.

Sureties are typically set at £150,000 – £350,000 for solicitors acting as professional deputies in high value personal injury and clinical negligence claims but on occasions they can be significantly higher.

It is now usual practice for the order appointing the deputy to require a review of the bond level on the release of a significant interim payment and on settlement of a personal injury litigation claim. In addition, the deputy is under an ongoing duty to keep the value of assets they manage under review and ask the court to reconsider the bond level if there is any other substantial change in the value of P's assets. Applications of this nature are usually dealt with on the papers.

It is not certain whether the new charging structure will now be the future model but it does mirror that which was in place for many years prior to the previous review. The April 2023 change sees a substantial increase and this may now be a disbursement with ongoing volatility.

8. Professional or lay deputy?

There is no prescribed limit above or below which a professional deputy appointment is deemed appropriate. In cases involving large awards (exceeding, say, £500,000), a professional is often preferred by the court and it can remove the sort of tensions that can arise when a family member is appointed. In high value, complex cases (such as multi-million-pound cerebral palsy cases), the court is unlikely to allow a lay deputy to be appointed as a sole deputy but may consider a joint appointment with a professional. A joint appointment is likely to increase deputyship costs because of the need to consult and it will almost certainly increase the level of the bond.

9. Decision-making by deputies

When a deputy makes a decision on behalf of a person, it must be one which is in their best interests. The Act does not define "best interests" but in s.4 it sets out some guidelines. The overriding rule is that the deputy or any other decision-maker must consider all relevant circumstances and "so far as is reasonably practicable" also permit and encourage the claimant to be involved, as far as possible, in the decision-making process. If it is practicable and appropriate the deputy should also consult with others before making a decision on the claimant's behalf, e.g. family and other persons who are involved in the claimant's life, which may include other professionals such as those within a therapeutic multidisciplinary team.

The deputy must also consider whether the claimant might have capacity in the future; if so, decisions may have to be deferred.

10. The role of the financial deputy

With high-value awards, deputyship can be likened to running a small business. There are also some legal and technical elements of deputyship work, which sometimes require the input of other professionals. These can include:

- Instructing solicitors to deal with employment issues, especially regarding directly employed support workers.
- Instructing a property finder to locate a suitable property for rent/purchase (or a plot on which a suitable property can be built) and negotiate the rent or purchase price.
- Instructing surveyors and appointing a solicitor to act in the purchase.
- Instructing a construction lawyer to advise on a building/adaptation contract.
- Commissioning architects, structural engineers and quantity surveyors.
- Instructing and approving the budget of an education lawyer in the case of a young person under the age of 25 if there are likely to be challenges to their Education Health and Care Plan.

Routine, day-to-day management tasks for deputies include:

- Applications to the Court of Protection and liaising with the OPG and the court visitor where necessary.
- Preparation of annual accounts and a report to the OPG, including the provision of a cost budget.
- Arranging and funding the deputyship bond.
- Completion of tax returns and making payments to HMRC.
- Dealing with requests for capital expenditure.
- Setting budgets.
- Considering and approving investment proposals.
- Liaising with case managers and their assistants.

- Paying household bills.
- Arranging payroll services and ensuring that funds are available in order to pay wages, national insurance, pension contributions etc.
- Arranging workplace pensions and dealing with the associated administration.
- Meeting the cost of staff training.
- Contracting with treating therapists.
- Liaising with the claimant and, wherever possible, taking all practical steps to enable them to make their own decisions.
- Ensuring that P receives the correct state funding, tax exemptions, etc.
- Buying aids and equipment.
- Buying vehicles and arranging for their adaptation, maintenance and licensing etc.
- Contributing to the arrangements for holidays and funding them.
- Arranging and paying for household support, cleaning and gardening.
- Appointing, monitoring and liaising with a financial advisor regarding the investment of P's funds.
- Approving an activity budget for P.
- Arranging all necessary maintenance contracts and insurance policies including employer's liability insurance, employer's protection insurance, equipment insurance, house and contents insurance, vehicle insurance and breakdown cover. Obtaining insurance disclosure declarations from employees where relevant.
- Agreeing the value of gratuitous care payments to family members where appropriate and in line with OPG guidance.

11. Visiting the Client

The deputy (or an appropriately qualified person acting on their behalf) must visit the claimant at least once a year. There may be other ways to stay in touch, such as video conferencing, but a visit to a client's home can be extremely informative and an annual visit should be undertaken whenever possible in order to meet the OPG deputy standards. It should also be noted that the Deputyship Standards require the deputy to conduct visits to the client at least once a year and that at such times the condition of their property should be checked so as to ensure that it is adequately maintained.

It may be necessary to make more frequent visits in the early years, particularly after settlement, or during a house adaptation. A time of crisis may also generate the need for more direct contact.

12. Other assets.

In some cases, a claimant may have assets other than those secured by their damages award and if they lack the capacity to manage those assets it will fall to the deputy to manage them. Care should be taken to enquire about the extent of those assets and whether they bring an added layer of complexity or activity which may impact upon the length of time that the deputy may need to spend in their general administration work. This could for example involve dealing with overseas assets and the need to engage with the capacity law applicable to other jurisdictions or the winding up of a business that the claimant is no longer able to run. This may involve liaison with other professionals such as overseas lawyers or accountants.

13. Approval of damages awards by the Court of Protection

The Court of Protection is no longer required to approve a personal injury settlement: Civil Procedure (Amendment) Rules 2007. However, if the court appoints a deputy while litigation is ongoing it is highly likely that the order appointing them will require the deputy to return to the court of protection to seek further directions on the making of an interim payment or at the time of a final settlement. These applications usually require the deputy to seek a review of the bond level and to submit a post settlement budget for the following three years and this will usually involve close liaison with the appointed financial advisor.

14. Welfare deputies and deprivation of liberty

Historically very few welfare deputies have been appointed. If court assistance is needed with such issues, matters have often been dealt with by way of one-off declarations. Welfare deputyships were only for the most severely disabled, whose circumstances called for frequent and regular welfare decisions to be made for them. This was in line with the guidance given in the Code of Practice which says that such appointments should only be made "in the most difficult cases". The Court of Protection considered this issue in the case of *Re Lawson, Mottram and Hopton [2019] EWCOP 22*. In his judgment, Hayden J said that the most likely conclusion in most cases may be that it is not in the best interests of the protected person for a personal welfare deputy to be appointed but he also said, "*It requires to be emphasised, unambiguously, that this is not a presumption, nor should it even be regarded as the starting point.*" He said that the Code of Practice "*requires to be revisited*".

Whilst the Code remains in its current form any application for the appointment of a personal welfare deputy will need to demonstrate why the decision-making structure set out in the MCA 2005 is inadequate and not permitting a decision which is in the claimant's best interests. If the claimant's circumstances are such that health and welfare applications may be needed, additional provision may be required and specialist advice should be sought from a health and welfare deputyship expert.

In circumstances where a claimant's liberty is said to be deprived within the deprivation of liberty regime, the responsibility for securing a deprivation of liberty order rests with the Local Authority. However, in the matter of *ACC [2020] EWCOP 9* HHJ Hilder said:

> *"the requirement on the Deputy is to bring the need for welfare proceedings to the attention of the Court. So if, having been properly alerted by the property and affairs Deputy, the appropriate body or institution drags its heels in referring a non-property-and-affairs issue to court, the Deputy may—without specific authority to do so—appropriately make an application to draw this to the attention of the court and seek further directions. Moreover, the Deputy should do so".*

In the event that a body or institution does fail to act and it is necessary for the property and affairs deputy to apply to the court and seek further directions they will ordinarily seek an order for costs against the failing body or institution, that may or may not be successful and there may be a shortfall between their costs and the costs which they recover, all of which will need to be met from a costs contingency.

15. Remuneration of the deputy and the deputy's staff

The professional deputy is entitled to be paid. Deputyship orders will usually give the deputy the option of taking fixed costs or having costs assessed on the basis of the hourly rates set by the SCCO. However, care should be taken when the deputy is administering small interim payments as the ability to claim annual general management fees even at the level of fixed costs is severely restricted unless explicit permission is given by the court.

16. Fixed costs in the Court of Protection

In low-cost cases, fixed costs provide an alternative to an assessment but they are unlikely to be appropriate in high value claims where the deputy will be administering significant sums. An updated Practice Direction 19B on this subject was issued on 1 April 2024 and it sets out the latest fixed fees, reference should be made to the Practice Direction for the dates on which the fees will come into effect and some of the exceptions. Previous Practice Directions cover earlier periods. The most popular fixed costs for the most straightforward of cases are set out below.

There is no obligation to take fixed costs and the costs associated with this work can still be submitted for assessment in the usual way.

NB Different rates apply to public authority deputies.

Costs on appointment of a property and affairs deputy

For work up to and including the date upon which the court makes an order appointing the deputy, an amount not exceeding £1,204 + VAT can be claimed.

Annual general management costs for a professional property and affairs deputy

The following will be payable on the anniversary of the court order:

- For the first year, an amount not exceeding £2,116 + VAT.
- For the second and subsequent years, an amount not exceeding £1,672+ VAT.
- If P's net assets are below £20,300, the professional deputy is not permitted to apply for assessed costs, instead they may take an annual management fee not exceeding 4.5 per cent of P's net assets on the anniversary of the court order appointing them + VAT.

Applications to the court under practice direction 9D - £633 + VAT.

The deputy's annual report or account

For work undertaken in the preparation and lodgement of a report or an account with the Public Guardian: an amount not exceeding £336 + VAT.

Tax returns made on or after 1 April 2024

For the preparation of a basic HMRC income tax return (bank or NS&I interest and taxable benefits, discretionary trust or estate income): an amount not exceeding £317.00 + VAT.

Hybrid costs

Tax returns

The deputy is allowed to use P's funds to pay for the completion of a complex tax return as a specialist service that P would normally be expected to pay for if P retained capacity. Where the deputy wishes to instruct their own practice, in accordance with the judgment of Senior Judge Hilder in *Re ACC* [2020] EWCOP 9; [2020] C.O.P.L.R. 406 they should obtain three quotes (including from their own practice) and decide which quote to accept as being in P's best interests. This decision should be included in the deputy's report to the OPG. If the deputy wishes to accept their own practice's quote which is over £2,000 (plus VAT and disbursements), the deputy should seek the court's specific authority before completing the tax return work.

Conveyancing costs

The deputy is allowed to use P's funds to pay for the conveyancing costs of selling or buying a property as a specialist service that P would normally be expected to pay for if P retained capacity. Where the deputy is selling or purchasing a property on behalf of P and wishes to instruct their own practice, they should apply the practice set out in the preceding paragraph and again if the deputy wishes to accept their own practice's quote which is over £2,000 (plus VAT), the deputy must seek the court's specific authority before undertaking the conveyancing work.

17. Assessed costs in the Court of Protection

In large value damages claims it is rarely appropriate to take fixed costs, and in most cases the deputy's costs will need to be assessed using the guideline hourly rates (GHR) applicable to the geographical location of the deputy.

Up until the judgement of Master Whalan in the matter of *PLK & Ors* [2020] EWHC B28 *(Costs)* on 30 September 2020, there had been no change in the GHR for over 10 years. Master Whalan recognised that whilst he had no power to review or amend the GHR:

> *"... in 2020 the GHR cannot be applied reasonably or equitably without some form of monetary uplift that recognises the erosive effect of inflation and, no doubt, other commercial pressures since the last formal review in 2010".*

Within his judgement Master Whalan recognised the importance of both consistency and certainty in relation to the assessment of COP costs saying that:

> *"The importance of judicial consistency is, of course, axiomatic, but it assumes a particular relevance in the COP, where the protected party's assets very often derive from an award of damages. If COP costs are not predictable accurately, then a protected party's legal representatives will be unable to plead or assess quantum accurately in any substantive inter parties litigation".*

Master Whalan went on to direct that Costs Officers conducting COP assessments should exercise some broad, pragmatic flexibility when applying the 2010 GHR's to the time claimed within COP bills and that if the rates claimed fell within approximately 120 per cent of the 2010 GHR's, then they should be regarded as being prima facie reasonable. Rates claimed above this level being correspondingly unreasonable. Master Whalan was keen to stress that he did not purport to revise the GHR as he had no power to do so; but his direction was a practical attempt to assist Costs Officers. Master Whalan went on to say that this approach could be adopted immediately and would be applicable to all outstanding COP bills regardless of whether the time within them related to work undertaken in 2018/19/20 or subsequently. A subsequent practice direction issued by the SSCO:*https://www.judiciary.uk/wp-content/uploads/2020/10/Practice-Note-COP-1.pdf* provided some clarity as to the date from which these revised rates could apply, but broadly speaking, as a result of this judgement the hourly rates that professional deputies were permitted to recover increased, with effect from 1 October 2020 provided the deputy could demonstrate that there had been no breach of the indemnity principle.

However, Master Whalan made it very clear that the outcome of the GHR review which was then being undertaken by the Hourly Rates Working Group under the direction of Mr Justice Stewart would, in due course, prevail.

In April 2021 the Civil Justice Council published the outcome of that review and a further review in 2022 and with effect from 1 October 2021 and then 1 January 2024 new GHR's were introduced. The figures provided in the narrative and the tables in J2 are based on the most recent published GHR as set out below. It is understood that the rates will be reviewed on an annual basis in line with the Services Producer prices Index but a further working party has been set up to examine the methodology which should underpin the GHR's.

Guideline rates 20.10.2020 – 30.09.2021					
Fee earner grade	**GHR London 1**	**GHR London 2**	**GHR London 3**	**National 1**	**National 2**
A	409	317	229 – 267	217	201
B	296	242	172 – 229	192	177
C	226	196	192	161	146
D	138	126	177	118	111

Guideline rates 01.10.2021 – 31.12.2023					
Fee earner grade	**GHR London 1**	**GHR London 2**	**GHR London 3**	**National 1**	**National 2**
A	512	373	282	261	255
B	348	289	232	218	218
C	270	244	185	178	177
D	186	139	129	126	126

Guideline rates 01.01.2024 Ongoing					
Fee earner grade	**GHR London 1**	**GHR London 2**	**GHR London 3**	**National 1**	**National 2**
A	546	398	301	278	272
B	371	308	247	233	233
C	288	260	197	190	189
D	198	148	138	134	134

Here a detailed costs assessment is to be undertaken, a professional deputy can, where the period covered by the remuneration ends on or after 1 April 2017, raise quarterly interim bills for a sum not exceeding 75 per cent of their estimated fees for that deputyship year; before that date the sum was 60 per cent. A bill is then sent to the SCCO for assessment at the end of the deputyship year. If the quarterly "on account" bills exceed that which is subsequently allowed on assessment, the claimant must be credited with the overpayment. This provision relates to general management costs but the rules committee have indicated that the COP will consider requests for a similar provision to apply to work undertaken up the making of a first order and other one off applications such as a statutory will application.

As can been seen from the tables above, work within a deputyship team will be undertaken by various fee earners falling within the categories set out below:

- Grade A—solicitor or fellow of the Institute of Legal Executives (Chartered Legal Executive or CILEX) with over eight years' post-qualification experience – the deputy is usually a Grade A Fee earner.
- Grade B—solicitors and Chartered Legal Executives with over four years' post-qualifications experience.
- Grade C—other solicitors, Chartered Legal Executives and other fee earners of equivalent experience with less than four years' post-qualifications experience.
- Grade D—trainee solicitors, paralegals and fee earners.

If work is undertaken at an inappropriate grade, the higher-grade fee earner will only recover the lower grade hourly rate. The SCCO will also look carefully at the allocation of work within the classes of fee earners and proportionality of charges. The OPG and the SCCO have issued joint "Good Practice Guidance" on deputyship costs which can be found at: *https://www.gov.uk/government/publications/professional-deputy-costs/professional-deputy-costs-web-version.*

Charges for the appointment of professional deputies and general management undertaken by them

It is important to carefully cost for future deputyship costs and disbursements as they can be a significant head of loss. An independent expert's statement or report is usually preferable over an "in-house" report in order to establish objectivity, but a witness statement from the appointed deputy is often of assistance to the expert.

Whilst historically the deputy expert may have prepared their report on a "desktop" basis being guided by the evidence of others, there may be some cases where the deputyship expert will gain a greater insight into the deputy's role by meeting with the claimant, or if appropriate, relevant family members and consideration should be given to this on a case-by-case basis.

The introduction of the Act and the Code has undoubtedly led to an increase in the time, and therefore the costs, incurred by deputies. The ongoing need to assess capacity in all areas of financial decision-making, and the need to consult with the claimant or others before best interest decisions are made, all add to the time spent.

The initial application

This and most other applications will generally be dealt with on the papers and without a hearing, but nonetheless the initial application may take at least nine months, from the time it is submitted to the court as may an application for the appointment of a new deputy.

Further applications and dealing with conflicts of interest

A deputy will need to make further applications to the court from time to time, this may be because their appointment is time limited, a conflict of interest situation arises, there is a breakdown in their relationship with the claimant or the actions they need to take fall outside of the "general authority" in the Order that appoints them.

In the matter of *ACC [2020] EWCOP 9* the Senior Judge of the Court of Protection HHJ Hilder, considered what might amounts to a reasonable interpretation of "general authority" within the context of the general authority given to a deputy at the time of their appointment and then attempted to define this.

It was felt that the "general authority" encompasses authority to make a decision / do an act in respect of P's property and affairs in relation to ordinary non-contentious legal tasks, including obtaining legal advice, as are ancillary to giving effect to that authority. In particular:

- an authority to purchase or sell property – including conveyancing;
- an authority to let property – including dealing with leases or tenancy agreements;
- an authority to conduct P's business – including dealing with employment contracts of that business;
- the preparation of an annual tax return – including obtaining advice as to the completion of the return;
- discharging P's financial responsibilities under a tenancy – including obtaining advice as to liabilities under the tenancy;
- applying P's funds so as to ensure that the costs of his care arrangements are met – including dealing with employment contracts of directly employed carers;
- making an application to the Court of Protection for further directions /specific authority in respect of welfare issues but not the seeking of advice or other steps preliminary to litigation in respect of welfare issues;
- specific authority is required to conduct litigation on behalf of P except where the contemplated litigation is in the Court of Protection in respect of a property and affairs issue, or it is to seek directions in respect of a welfare issue.

Steps can be taken in contemplation of contentious litigation up to receiving the Letter of Response and in particular:

- an authority to let property encompasses taking steps to form a view as to whether there are grounds to evict a tenant of the property;
- taking steps to form a view about whether a debt said to have been incurred by P is properly payable pursuant to s.7 of the Mental Capacity Act 2005;
- steps up to but not including the delivery of a letter of appeal in respect of a decision that P is not eligible for continuing healthcare funding.

Steps in contemplation of contentious litigation can include obtaining Counsel's opinion but no further and will not encompass steps in contemplation of an appeal against the decision of an Education, Health and Care Plan. Specific authority is also required to use the claimant's funds to pay a third party's legal costs, even if those costs related to litigation for the benefit of the claimant.

In addition, where a deputy wishes to instruct their own firm to carry out legal tasks, special measures are required to address the conflict of interest and:

- the deputy *may* seek prior authority from the Court of Protection;
- the deputy is *required* to seek—in a manner which is proportionate to the magnitude of the costs involved and the importance of the issue to P—three quotations from appropriate providers (including one from his own firm), and determine where to give instructions in the best interests of P;
- the deputy *must* seek prior authority from the Court if the anticipated costs exceed £2,000 + VAT;
- the deputy *must* clearly set out any legal fees incurred in their account to the Public Guardian and append the notes of the decision-making process to their return.

The Official Solicitor will act as P's litigation friend without charge in any of the existing classes of cases in which they act where P lacks capacity to litigate, if there is no other person willing to act without charging, and there is a source of funding to cover the costs of solicitors and counsel.

The judgement in *Re ACC [2020] EWCOP 9*, whilst providing varying levels of clarification in a number of areas makes it clear that a deputy's "general authority" will not empower them to take all of the decisions that may need to be taken throughout a claimant's lifetime and there will be a need for them to return to the Court for further authority on various occasions, and in accordance with the Court Rules this will need to be done by way of a formal application. There may for example also be limitations on the deputy's powers in the initial order due to the claimant's prognosis in relation to capacity or because the claimant is a child approaching adulthood. Some orders contain restrictions on property sales and acquisitions. Sometimes orders are time-limited because they are made before a claim has settled or when a large interim payment has been made. Such events can trigger a need to seek further orders. Where action needs to be taken urgently and there is no power to act the deputy will need to make a retrospective application for specific authority and will need to explain why the matter was so urgent that authority could not have been sought before proceeding.

Ramifications of "the ACC judgement" continue to have implications on practice and procedure with issues coming back before the judiciary for consideration, further commentary on its impact is anticipated and any expert should be asked to address this issue in their reports.

Applications under the Trustee Act

If the claimant has preowned assets such as a family home which is in joint ownership and that property needs to be disposed of, a separate application to the court will be needed. This is because when two or more people own real property, they will be trustees of that property and if the claimant is a trustee of property by virtue of their joint ownership and they are incapable of managing their property and affairs they will not be able to sign any legally binding documents in relation to that property. Section 20(3)(c) of the Mental Capacity Act 2005 restricts deputies from carrying out trustee functions so a separate application to the Court of Protection for the appointment of a new trustee will be needed.

Applications for the appointment of a new trustee for real property can be divided into two main categories. Those where there is an existing and capable co-owner ("the continuing trustee"), and those where the incapable person is the only surviving trustee because e.g. the other joint owner has died. Where there is a continuing trustee, or trustees, an application needs to be made under s.36(9) of the Trustee Act 1925 seeking permission for the continuing trustee to appoint a new trustee in place of the incapable person. Where the incapable person is the only remaining trustee, an application needs to be made to the court under s.54 of the Trustee Act 1925 for an order appointing at least two trustees in their place.

Wills and statutory wills

No one under the age of 18 can make a will.

Criteria laid down in *Banks v Goodfellow (1870) L.R. 5 QB* provides that in order to give instructions for a will a person over the age of 18 must be able to understand:

- what they are doing when they make a will and the effect of that;
- the extent of their property and estate;
- the nature of the claims of those they propose to benefit or exclude from the will; and

- they must be suffering from no disorder of the mind or insane delusion that would result in an unwanted distribution of their estate.

Clients with testamentary capacity

If the deputy obtains a capacity report which confirms the claimant has testamentary capacity, the claimant can give instructions for and execute a will.

In calculating the likely costs associated with the making of a will, regard should be given to any factor which may add to the time that will be taken, whether that be in preparation or in meetings. Additional time may be needed to take account of cognitive issues such as slowness of processing or communication issues which require the use of specialist equipment or translation services. It may also be necessary to work in conjunction with other members of the claimant's multi-disciplinary team such as a speech and language therapist and/or a psychologist who will assist the deputy to maximise the claimant's capacity. This may involve producing explanatory documents in a form that the claimant can understand and a number of preparatory meetings. It is important that this process is thorough in order to avoid any post death challenges to the claimant's will and the work should be carefully costed for within this task or it will erode other heads of deputyship time.

Clients who lack testamentary capacity

If it is established that the claimant lacks testamentary capacity, an application can be made to the court for a statutory will to be approved on their behalf.

Practice Direction 9E, which supplements the Court of Protection Rules 2017, sets out the detailed procedure to be followed. Consideration must be given to what the claimant would do if they were able to make a will for themselves, their beliefs and personal values, how they have acted and made decisions for themselves in the past, and the content of any wills made prior to their incapacity. If the claimant is able to participate in the process and contribute to the content of the proposed will, they should be supported to do so. Again, this may take extra time and involve additional cost.

The cost of an application to make a statutory will can be significant. The procedure requires the involvement of the Official Solicitor, who will be invited to represent the claimant. Others who are adversely or materially affected by the application, e.g. those who might lose their entitlement under the intestacy rules if there is no existing will, or whose entitlement may be changed by the making of a new will, may be represented and usually at the cost of the claimant.

A capacity assessment in the court's form COP3 will be needed. GP's are increasingly unwilling to undertake these assessments except in the most straightforward of cases and input from a specialist practitioner may be needed. The fee could be between £700 to £1,000 or more if the litigation is not ongoing or it would be inappropriate for the litigation expert to assist. The assessor will need to read the claimant's medical history and may need to visit them on more than one occasion.

A court fee of £408.00 is payable on making the application, and a further £494 for an attended hearing. Hearings are usually only required if there is a serious dispute over the proposed will. In the simplest cases, costs can amount to a few thousand pounds; in the most difficult of cases they can be tens of thousands of pounds. The usual rule is that all parties' costs are paid out of the claimant's estate, but the court can make an order for costs against any party who it believes has acted unreasonably. Regard should be had to the particular circumstances of the claimant including communication and cultural issues, the claimant's family, and the possibility of future relationships and children and the breakdown of those relationships. It is not unreasonable to make provision for two or three wills over the lifetime of a young person with a normal life expectancy, perhaps more if they have sufficient capacity to form relationships and have children.

Contingency for the unexpected or times of crisis

It can be very difficult to accurately weigh up how head-injured claimants will behave in the long term. It is prudent to include a contingency fund for unexpected events. Sometimes there is talk of cases "settling down" after the early post-settlement years, but some claimants will never fall within this description, due to the nature of their brain injury or premorbid personality. These cases frequently result in high general management costs in which case, such additional costs may be better reflected in the annual provision, rather than within a large contingency sum.

The financial consequences of relationship breakdown

In the case of claimants who are likely to form relationships it may be prudent to ensure that steps are taken to protect their funds in the event of relationship breakdown, that protection may be afforded by prenuptial or cohabitation agreements. If the claimant lacks capacity to enter into these agreements, court approval may be needed. The advice of a family lawyer may also be needed.

18. Fees of the Court, the OPG and the SCCO

The current fees are:

- For the appointment of a deputy: £408.
- For an attended hearing (in addition to the application fee): £494.
- On the appointment of a deputy: £100.
- Supervision fee: £320 p.a. unless (which is unlikely) there is minimal supervision (when the fee is £35 per annum).
- The fee on the submission of a bill of costs for assessment is £96 per bill.

Fee remissions and exemptions

These are available for both Court of Protection and OPG fees and are based on the claimant's financial circumstances. Further details can be found at: *https://www.gov.uk/government/publications/deputy-fees-remission-or-exemption.*

19. Keeping up to date

Information about the OPG can be found on the DIRECTGOV site; information about the Court of Protection is on the HMCS website.

SOME IMPORTANT INFORMATION ABOUT BENEFITS RELEVANT TO DEPUTIES

1. Income Support Regulations 1987 (as amended)

52-week disregard

There is a period of 52 weeks running from the day of receipt of the first payment (no matter how small) in consequence of a personal injury claim, during which the capital received will be disregarded. However, you do not receive a separate 52-week period on the occasion of future payments. For example:

- £10,000 interim payment received on 1 January 2018.
- £100,000 final compensation received 1 July 2018.
- The 52-week period of disregard starts on the date of the first payment; so that the disregard for the £100,000 expired on 1 January 2019.

In most cases, interim payments are received over a much longer period; this may mean that the disregard will run out well before the interim payment is exhausted. As a result, the funds received have to be disclosed. However, if the funds are held by the deputy under a deputyship order, they are disregarded regardless of the 52-week period.

2. Funds held in a trust or subject to the order or direction of the Court of Protection

Under the Regulations, funds received as a consequence of a personal injury are disregarded entirely if they are either held in trust or are under the control of the Court of Protection.

J2: The incidence of deputyship costs over a claimant's life

1. The appointment of a deputy is likely to arise during a personal injury or clinical negligence claim, when a claimant lacks capacity to manage their financial affairs.

2. Deputyship costs are a recoverable head of loss:

   a. if the incapacity preceded the index injury;
   b. but it is only in consequence of that injury that the claimant has financial affairs and property of sufficient size and complexity to warrant the appointment of a deputy; and
   c. where the incapacity is a direct consequence of the injury.

3. The Court of Protection will appoint a deputy for infants where the damages are significant, and the probability is that the infant will not acquire legal capacity on attaining his or her majority.

4. On an admission of liability or judgment, an application should be made without delay so that the deputyship can be put in place as soon as possible, and interim funds can be applied for the claimant's benefit. The Court of Protection must, however, be satisfied that there are going to be funds to manage and there is no dispute about capacity.

5. The order appointing a deputy will provide authority for the professional deputy to be paid for the work undertaken.

6. On appointment the court will require the deputy to enter into a surety bond. At the time of publishing the preferred providers for sureties have changed from 1 to 3 and some tariffs and structures have not been published. Reference should be made to the information in J2 and to the bond providers websites. The surety is usually arranged by way of a bond, which is now subject to an annual premium.

7. A one-off fee will be payable to the OPG on the appointment of a deputy and thereafter an annual supervision fee. Some cases are deemed to require no supervision, but that will not be the case for claimants with a damages award.

8. The management of the claimant's affairs will proceed in annual stages, known as deputyship years. In many cases the earlier years of a deputyship will see higher costs than in later years but for some claimants costs can remain high for some time. Costs are given in the accompanying breakdown for the first 1 – 4 deputyship years, within which it is contemplated that significant structural issues will be addressed including:

   - acquisition and/or adaptation of accommodation,
   - the major/initial investment decisions, and
   - the establishment, through case managers or otherwise, of care and other support regimes.

   These could be post-settlement or on receipt of a significant interim payment.

9. The impact of continuing litigation should be factored in. Litigation will inevitably increase costs because:

   - long-term/annual budgeting will not generally be possible while the deputyship is in its infancy and the claimant is dependent upon interim payments;

- liaison with the litigation team will be needed, to consider the claimant's requirements for interim funding and the adequacy of offers;
- stresses will occur to the claimant and the claimant's family. These can be expected to extend beyond the conclusion of the litigation. The first two or three years after litigation are likely to be unsettled.

10. **Caution**: i the cost of work undertaken by the deputy or the deputy's team which could properly be claimed within the context of ongoing litigation (e.g. providing information to support applications for interim payments on account of damages, or providing information for the purpose of conducting the litigation) will be disallowed by the SCCO as deputyship general management costs and it is important that the litigation team obtain cost estimates for this work from the deputy and include these costs in their cost budget. These costs can be significant in long-running complex cases.

    Caution: ii Large interim payments may mean that houses are purchased and adapted pre settlement and the need to implement a full support team and MDT may mean that a move to rental accommodation is needed. There will always need to be flexibility which allows the claimants needs to be paramount and the deputyship expert should tailor their evidence to reflect this.

    Caution: iii The costs associated with a need to move to a rental property as a temporary measure should not be underestimated. This may require the deputy to commission adaptations and then reinstatement works and that will also involve negotiations with the landlord. This will be in addition to all the usual costs associated with a move.

11. The general management costs identified for "the first two deputyship years" are for a case of medium level complexity. Such costs will vary from case to case. General management costs might amount to £14,500.00–£48,000.00 or more and it is not uncommon for them to be significantly more in high-value cases where property issues can be complex, particularly in the case of a young person. The estimated costs assume that in the first year a property is found and adaptation works are begun, and that in the second year the adaptation works are all but completed and the care and treatment regimens are put in place. The third (and possibly the fourth) year allow for things to settle down. It is not uncommon however for claimants undergoing community rehabilitation to reside in a rental property either to assess how they cope with community living and/or to put in place a support team which cannot be accommodated with their existing home which is often too small. In these circumstances the deputy will find themselves dealing with landlords or their agents, many of whom may not fully understand the concept of deputyship and why a claimant tenant cannot fulfil the usual requirements to produce evidence of wages and a personal deposit. Adaptations may also be needed followed by a restoration of the property on vacation. The cost of the deputy undertaking this additional work will need to be factored into those early years.

12. Matters may settle down to a general routine after that period. In a typical case of catastrophic injury, general management costs of £14,500.00–£24,000.00 as an average are not uncommon. In some cases, they will be higher and may remain at a high or higher level for some time, particularly in those cases which involve young people or adults with an element of retained capacity as they can pose substantial challenges to the running of the deputyship. Whilst a reduction in costs may be anticipated in later years that will not always be the case particularly if there are complex family issues to address, including relationship breakdowns or greater care and accommodation needs all of which will require greater deputyship input.

13. In addition to the annual visit, claimants will often need face-to-face meetings, so that the deputy can provide appropriate explanations for their decisions. The cost for these meetings should be

included in the claim. If the claimant has special communication needs (e.g. the use of assistive technology or the need for an interpreter) additional provision should be made for the time spent in preparing for and conducting such meetings. If the claimant cannot be consulted, time will be spent in consulting with others.

14. Some claimants have behavioural problems which can be difficult to overcome and which require greater than usual time to manage. Additional costs should be included to allow for this where appropriate. It is not unusual in such cases to see annual costs well in excess of £36,000 + VAT and disbursements. The case of *Robshaw v United Lincolnshire Hospitals NHS Trust [2015] EWHC 923 (QB)* (a case heard at the time of the 2001 GHR's) acknowledges that there is no "one cap fits all" approach to deputyship costs. The annual cost will principally depend upon how active the deputy has been, which in turn will depend upon a large number of factors. These include the size and complexity of the deputyship; the number of carers, treating clinicians and therapists; the claimant's behaviour; and the family dynamics. The Covid–19 pandemic raised significant issues for deputies to address many in relation to directly employed support teams, including the need for lay-offs and the availability of the furlough scheme and against a backdrop of volatile investment markets.

15. Issues will arise periodically during the claimant's lifetimes which are impossible to foresee in terms of frequency or the levels of input that might be needed; this may include changes in family circumstances, such as the death of a close family member, the birth of a child or the breakdown in a relationship. The claimant may also get in trouble with the police or there might be an unexpected significant event which occurs with one of the claimant's carers. A contingency sum should be claimed to reflect the additional deputyship costs which are likely to arise in dealing with such issues. There are two main methods of calculating the contingency lump sum. The first is to claim an estimated one-off lump sum for all contingencies over the claimant's lifetime, often between £30,000–£80,000 including VAT or more depending upon the extent of the claimant's life expectancy, the complexity of the deputyship and the scope for crisis situations to develop. The second is to claim an estimated amount per crisis and to estimate how frequently such crisis events might occur e.g. to claim an estimated amount of £6,000 plus VAT every five years. If a claimant lives in a constant state of crisis this should be reflected in the annual management charges.

16. On the application for a deputy in the course of ongoing litigation much of the information needed to make the application will be readily available so the costs incurred are likely to be lower than those incurred in a later application. However, if the new deputy is in another practice, the costs may be greater and the retiring deputy will incur "handover" costs. A capacity report will be required and the cost for that may be significantly more than one completed at the time of the litigation. The schedules below reflect the current charges applied by a specialist mental capacity assessor. They do not reflect the charges which may be rendered by a psychiatrist.

17. The deputyship will come to an end on the claimant recovering their capacity or on their death. There will be winding-up costs associated with accounting to the claimant or to the representatives of the claimant's estate. An application for discharge or final directions requires a court application and a supportive capacity assessment.

18. No provision has been made in the accompanying breakdown for incidental applications for additional or special authority, but each will cost £408.00 in terms of an application fee, with a further £494.00 payable in the event of an attended hearing to which must be added professional fees and VAT. A capacity report may also be needed.

19. A professional deputy's annual management costs are assessed by the Senior Court Costs Office (SCCO) on the anniversary of each deputyship year. The bill will need to be prepared by a costs draftsman whose fees are often between 5.5 per cent and 7 per cent of the profit costs claimed plus VAT. In addition, there will be an SCCO assessment fee of £96.00.

20. Bills are also submitted for assessment on the appointment of the first deputy and any replacement and on completion of a Statutory Will application.

J3: Deputyship costs

IMPORTANT

The professional costs figures within these tables are based on the current Guideline Hourly Rates at National Band 1.

One-off cost of an application for a deputy to be appointed and modest amounts of pre appointment work

1	Solicitors' costs	£4,275.00 - £5,345.00
2	Cost Draftsman's fees—6.5 % of item 1	£277.88 - £347.43
3	+ VAT @ 20% on items 1 and 2	£910.56 - £1,138.49
4	Capacity report—assumes an expert within the litigation can provide the report	£660.00 including VAT
5	Court of Protection Application fee	£408.00
6	OPG fee for appointment of the Deputy	£100
7	Security Bond Premium—use the most cost effective option by a preferred provider when full details are known.	
8	SCCO Assessment fee	£96.00
	Total set up cost	£6,727.36 – £8,094.92 + Bond premium

Estimated annual costs for the first deputyship year during which funds become available for the purchase of a property and the commencement of adaptations

9	General management costs	£32,100.00
10	Cost Draftsman's fees—6.5% of item 9	£2,086.50
11	+ VAT @ 20% on items 9 and 10	£6,837.30
12	SCCO Annual Assessment fee	£96.00
13	Security Bond Premium—use the most cost effective option by a preferred provider when full details are known	
14	OPG Annual General Supervision fee	£320.00
	Total first year	£41,439.80 + Bond premium

Estimated annual costs for the second deputyship year, during which property adaptations are completed and a care regime implemented

15	General management costs	£23,520.00
16	Cost Draftsman's fees—6.5% of item 15	£1,528.80
17	+ VAT@ 20% on items 15 and 16	£5,009.76
18	SCCO Annual Assessment fee	£96.00
19	Security Bond Premium—use the most cost effective option by a preferred provider when full details are known	
20	OPG Annual General Supervision fee	£320.00
	Total second year	£30,474.56 + Bond premium

Estimated annual costs for year 3 (and possibly year 4, depending on progress made during the first two years)

21	General management costs	£19,245.00
22	Cost Draftsman's fees—6.5% of item 21	£1,250.93
23	+ VAT@ 20% on items 21 and 22	£4,099.19
24	SCCO Annual Assessment fee	£96.00
25	Security Bond Premium—use the most cost effective option by a preferred provider when full details are known	
26	OPG Annual General Supervision fee	£320.00
	Total each year	£25,011.12 + Bond premium

Ongoing years

27	General management costs	£17,100.00
28	Cost Draftsman's fees—6.5% of item 27	£1,111.50
29	+ VAT@ 20% on items 27 and 28	£3,642.30
30	SCCO Annual Assessment fee	£96.00
31	Security Bond Premium—use the most cost effective option by a preferred provider when full details are known	
32	OPG Annual General Supervision fee	£320.00
	Total each year	£22,269.30 + Bond premium

Other future costs

Applications for the appointment of a new deputy—per application

33	Professional fees	£3,000.00 - £4,810.00
34	Cost Draftsman's fees—6.5% of item 33	£195.00 - £312.65
35	+ VAT@ 20% on items 33 and 34	£639.00 – £1,024.53
36	COP application fee	£408.00
37	OPG fee for the appointment of the Deputy	£100.00
38	Capacity Report including VAT	£660.00
	Total	£5,002.00 - £7,315.18

Statutory will (non-contentious), per application

39	Professional fees	£8,000.00 - £10,700.00
40	Official Solicitor's Costs	£1,925.00 - £3,848.00
41	Costs of others to be notified (assumes all are adult and no contention)	£2,140.00**/***
42	+ VAT@ 20% on items 39, 40 and 41	£2,413.00 – £3,337.60
43	Application fee	£408.00
44	Capacity Report including VAT	£900.00
45	Costs draftsman fee—6.5% of items 39 and 40***	£645.13 – £945.63
46	+ VAT @ 20% on item 45	£129.03 – £189.13
47	SCCO detailed assessment fees: two bills at £96.00 each	£192.00
	Total	£16,752.16 – £22,660.36

* The Official Solicitor's office reports that the Official Solicitor is sometimes asked to give an indication of the likely total cost of a Statutory Will application. It is not really possible to give a reliable estimate at the commencement of the application when it is not known how much work will have to be done and the respondents approach to matters. However, they have found in practice that many applications are completed for less than £5,000 plus disbursements and VAT and generally fall within a range of £1,800.00 – £3,600.00 plus disbursements and VAT. In the case of an application that requires a hearing (a minority) the costs can be tens of thousands of pounds. The figures in the table above uplift the figures in this paragraph by the increase in National Band 1.

** Assumes advice is modest and a maximum of 2 – 3 persons requiring separate advice.

*** In practice the costs of others and the OS may on occasions be agreed without the need for cost drafting fees or assessment.

Contingency for additional deputy input or crisis, per crisis—this will need to be tailored to the client, paying particular attention to life expectancy and behaviour and risk issues and the following is by way of example

48	Professional fees for additional general management costs	£32,000.00 – £85,500.00
49	Costs draftsman fees—6.5% of item 48	£2,080.00 – £5,557.50
50	+ VAT@ 20%	£6,816.00 – £18,211.50
	Total	£40,896.00 – £109,269.00

Preparation of tax returns and associated work: cost per annum

51	Professional fees—average	£550.00
52	+ VAT@ 20% on item 51	£110.00
	Total	£660.00

Winding up: single payment

53	Winding up costs	£1,925.00*
54	+ VAT@ 20% on item 53	£384.84
	Total	£2,309.84

*If the Deputy is in the same practice as the appointed Executors this amount will be less.

IMPORTANT

The professional costs figures within these tables are based on the current Guideline Hourly Rates which were introduced on 01.10.2021. Costs incurred in earlier years will be based on different rates and the deputyship expert should identify the relevant rates within their report.

Group K

Carer Rates and Rehabilitation

K1: Care and attendance

Introduction

1. A series of cases since 2005 involving injuries of the utmost severity has led to highly developed claims for care and attendance, including case management.[1] This section aims to be a source of practical assistance to practitioners and courts setting about the task of assessing damages for care and attendance.

Past non-commercial care

2. Damages awarded in respect of non-commercial care, usually by family members, are governed by the following rules/practical advice.
3. The aim is to award the reasonable value of/proper recompense for gratuitous services rendered—*Hunt v Severs*.[2]
4. Accordingly, a claimant holds the damages on trust for those who provided the care.[3]
5. If a tortfeasor has himself provided the care, there can be no recovery of damages on that score.[4]
6. If a claimant has fallen out with the care provider so that the recovery on trust will not be honoured, again there will be no award in damages.[5]
7. There is no threshold requirement to be satisfied before an award can be made, whether in terms of severity of injury or level of care.[6] Extra domestic services are sufficient.[7]
8. While there is no threshold to satisfy, there must be actual care. So, when a claimant is still in hospital, damages are not to be awarded for *mere visiting*—only for any periods of care given during the course of the visit.[8] Companionship/emotional and practical assistance to a relative while in hospital has been found to amount to care on the facts.[9]

[1] Readers interested in the finer detail of big cases can find it set out in the third edition of the book "Serious Personal Injury Litigation—Quantum Updated to 2024" consolidating previous papers by James Rowley KC and the familiar tables. It is available at: www.byromstreet.com.

[2] [1994] 2 A.C. 350 at 363A ff. These are special damages. While not referred to expressly in the speeches, the rationale in *Daly v General Steam Navigation Co Ltd [1981] 1 W.L.R 120 CA*—awarding general damages in respect of past non-commercial domestic services—was overruled by the House of Lords through the result in *Hunt v Severs*.

[3] *Hunt v Severs* above also expressly over-ruled the line of authority derived from *Donnelly v Joyce [1974] QB 454* in favour of that derived from Lord Denning's judgment in *Cunningham v Harrison [1973] QB 942*. No longer is an award for services considered as a claimant's damages (based on his need for the care) for him then to make a present to the carer. Rather it is recompense to the carer and only held by a claimant on trust.

[4] *Hunt v Severs* at 363D. This is a common occurrence when passengers are suing a member of the family who was the negligent driver. Where liability is split, there is no known authority but no reason in principle why a tortfeasor carer cannot recover to the extent of another tortfeasor's share of the blame.

[5] See *ATH v MS [2003] P.I.Q.R. Q1* at [30] as to the principle; but in this case of fatal accident, the court was already ordering damages to be paid into court for investment on behalf of dependent children and felt able to enforce the trust through the investment control of the court. It would be otherwise if the monies were simply to be paid over to a claimant and the court really felt the trust would not be honoured.

[6] The Court of Appeal in *Giambrone v Sunworld Holidays Ltd [2004] P.I.Q.R. Q4* at Q36 decided that dicta in *Mills v British Rail Engineering Ltd [1992] P.I.Q.R. Q130* to the effect that there was a threshold of devoted care or care well beyond the ordinary call of duty (and similar phrases) were obiter and not to be followed.

[7] The Court of Appeal in *Mills* had overlooked a passage from Lord Denning in *Cunningham v Harrison*—quoted with apparent approval by Lord Bridge in *Hunt v Severs* above at 360E—"Even though she had not been doing paid work but only domestic duties in the house, nevertheless all extra attendance on him certainly calls for compensation." *[1973] QB 942* at 952B-C.

[8] *Havenhand v Jeffrey* (unreported 24 February 1997 CA); *Tagg v Countess of Chester Hospital Foundation NHS Trust [2007] EWHC 509 (QB)* at [85]; *Huntley v Simmons [2009] EWHC 405 (QB)* at [65].

[9] *Warrilow v Norfolk and Norwich Hospitals NHS Trust [2006] EWHC 801 (QB)*, Langstaff J at [157]-[160], followed in *Welsh v Walsall Healthcare NHS Trust [2018] EWHC 1917 (QB)* by Yip J at [109]-[115], where 14 hours a week were awarded for care while in hospital.

9. Compensable care must relate to the claimant himself or, under the rule in *Lowe v Guise*[10], another disabled member of the same household, usually cared for by the claimant but who, because of the claimant's injury, is cared for by another. Where the provision spreads out into non-commercial cover for the claimant in his business, different considerations apply; there is no compensable claim here for the hours provided by analogy with real care.[11]
10. Between the two positions, the sort of extra domestic services (see §7 above) usually allowed when a claimant is home from hospital have recently been invoked to allow an hour a week for relatives to collect post and monitor the home while the claimant was an in-patient.[12] By contrast, the additional ordinary domestic services sufficient to trigger compensation when aimed at the claimant were insufficient to trigger the rule in *Lowe v Guise* when aimed at others. So, where someone stepped in to cover for the household chores a claimant usually did for parents and a niece, it was not allowed.[13]
11. Claims are rarely put on the following footing but where a carer has lost earnings in the provision of services, the value can be assessed as the lost net earnings up to a ceiling of the commercial value of the care provided.[14] The usual reduction for the non-commercial element still stands to be applied from the ceiling: a submission to opposite effect was rejected in *Mehmetemin v Farrell*—it would amount to an artificial inflation and include an element that could never be paid to a relative.[15]
12. In the majority of cases the exercise is to examine the care and make a fair assessment of the number of hours in fact provided. (In doing this, one will in passing register if care has been given at anti-social hours or has been particularly demanding.) The assessment is easy in respect of discrete blocks of care; but calls for more subtle evidence/judgment when care is given in multiple short bursts over the course of day and night or constitutes more general supervision/support in the home while daily life continues.
13. Hourly rates are then applied to the determined number of hours.
14. Many different scales have been used in the past; but now there is near uniformity in taking rates derived from the National Joint Council Payscales—Spinal Point 2 (old Spinal Point 8).
15. The suggested starting points are the basic (daytime weekday) rate or the enhanced aggregate rate (which takes into account care in the evenings, at night and at weekends). Both are set out in the table below but they are only starting points.
16. The aggregate rate balances all the hours of the week by their relative number and appropriate rate. It is logically entirely apt only when care equivalent to home care is spread out evenly through the whole week and the hours of the day and night. The odd hour here and there in the evening will not justify an aggregate rate; but intensive care given only at night and not by day, seven days a week (for example when commercial daytime care has been purchased but a relative left to care at night), would logically justify more than the aggregate rate. Where a spouse has risen early to provide care before going to work and then carried on in the evenings on returning home, no care has been given when the daytime weekday rate is applicable.

[10] [2002] QB 1369 at [38]. The ratio of this case (and how widely or narrowly the rule established should be construed) is a fertile area for argument. Is it really confined to care of a disabled member or will care of a baby or child suffice? Is the element of provision being within the same household essential to the legal rule? Is it an important difference if a disabled mother has come to rely on her daughter's care while living in the next street; or in a self-contained granny-flat within the curtilage of the daughter's house; or in the spare room of her house? In *Rix v Stonegate Pub Co Ltd* unreported 7 May 2024, HHJ Duddridge interpreted *Lowe v Guise* more narrowly to exclude care of a relative that a claimant would have given after the accident during Covid but which had not become established before it.

[11] *Hardwick v Hudson [1999] 1 W.L.R 1770.*

[12] Yip J in *Welsh* above at [116].

[13] Ibid at [117]-[118].

[14] *Housecroft v Burnett [1986] 1 All E.R. 332* O'Connor LJ at 343e, albeit his view of the *Cunningham v Harrison* and *Donnelly v Joyce* debate was over-ruled in *Hunt v Severs.* The ceiling of the commercial rate has sometimes been criticised on the basis that it would have been enough simply to apply a wider test of reasonableness to the evaluation of the mother's claim for care of her daughter. However, that evaluation was at the very heart of the appeal and it would be difficult to contend that the invocation of the commercial ceiling was not part of the ratio.

[15] [2017] EWHC 103 (QB) Sir Robert Nelson at [33].

17. There is no reason in principle why different rates cannot be used in different periods—the aggregate rate during more intensive care in early convalescence and the basic rate afterwards; or a rate over the whole period averaged somewhere between the two. No doubt the exercise would have to be relatively broad brush but it may be none the worse for that.[16] The overarching aim is to attach a reasonable value to the actual care and award proper recompense.
18. Notwithstanding the logical attraction, however, of choosing a rate close to the circumstances of the actual provision, following *Fairhurst v St Helens & Knowsley Health Authority*[17] the basic rate was used for over a decade in reported cases, even those of maximum severity when the care was of an onerous nature and much of it provided at nights and at weekends.[18]
19. Even after *Wells v Wells*[19] and modernisation of the assessment of damages for personal injuries, it took until *Massey v Tameside*[20] for there to be a reported case at the aggregate rate. Since then, there has been a move away from using the basic rate as the universal starting point.
20. The position on choice of rate now stands as follows:
    a) In serious cases involving long-term, high quality care of a grievously injured claimant including care at anti-social hours (the *Massey* type case), nothing less than the full aggregate rate will provide reasonable value/proper recompense.[21] While no previous modern case went above the full aggregate rate (with a non-commercial reduction for tax and NI), in *CCC v Sheffield Teaching Hospitals NHS Foundation Trust* [2023] EWHC 1770 (KB), Ritchie J made no non-commercial discount, which was tantamount to increasing the net award to the mother by about a third. The main reason given was that even the full aggregate rate undervalued all that she had done. See the discussion at [146]–[147]. It remains to be seen if other courts follow this lead.
    b) Where care is found *not* to include a significant element at anti-social hours, the basic rate still forms the basis of reasonable value/proper recompense.[22]

[16] Averaging things with a broad brush appealed to Stuart-Smith J in *Ali v Caton & MIB [2013] EWHC 1730 (QB)* at [323b–d] and he effectively reached a rate between the aggregate and basic ones. He took the starting point of the claimant's expert's figures and discounted them by 25% on account of arguments over both rates and the number of hours. " ... Adoption of a basic rate throughout would lead to under-compensation while adoption of the enhanced rate would have the opposite effect." See below for more about this case. Cotter J awarded a mid-point between the day aggregate and basic rates in *Scarcliffe v Brampton Valley Group Ltd* [2023] EWHC 1565 (KB) after the first six months or so of convalescence—see [232]–[265].

[17] [1995] P.I.Q.R. Q.1.

[18] Many settlements were negotiated with an enhancement for a higher rate, but there was no reported case until *Massey v Tameside [2007] EWHC 317 (QB).*

[19] [1999] 1 A.C. 345.

[20] [2007] EWHC 317 (QB).

[21] This line started with *Massey* and moved through numerous cases including the landmark decision in *Whiten v St George's Healthcare NHS Trust [2011] EWHC 2066 (QB),* Swift J at [141] and [144], and was exemplified in *AB v Royal Devon & Exeter NHS Foundation Trust [2016] EWHC 1024 (QB),* Irwin J as he then was at [129]—care of a paraplegic at various times of the day and sometimes including travel. The *full aggregate rate* used in these cases includes attendance at night. It is to be contrasted with the more recently calculated aggregate day rate i.e. seven-day care without significant input at night, now shown in the tables below.

[22] Examples of use of the basic rate include three chronic pain cases: *Hayden v Maidstone & Tunbridge Wells NHS Trust [2016] EWHC 3276 (QB),* Jay J (general damages £37,500); *Maguire v Carillion Services Limited HHJ Main KC, Manchester County Court 31 March 2017 (unreported)* at [154] (general damages £26,500), where the judge referred to the *Massey* line as reflecting cases of an exceptional nature with extraordinary commitment; *Karapetianas v Kent and Sussex Loft Conversions Limited [2017] EWHC 859 (QB),* Mr Jonathan Swift KC sitting as a Judge of the High Court at [51] (general damages £29,000) with a finding that care was not needed at nights or weekends. In *Thorburn v South Warwickshire NHS Foundation Trust [2017] EWHC 1791 (QB),* a case of failed knee replacement surgery, HHJ Pearce sitting as a High Court Judge awarded [126] the basic rate with a 25% reduction, not the 33% argued for the defendant. In *Swift v Carpenter [2018] EWHC 2060 (QB),* an amputation case, Lambert J awarded the basic rate [67] with an agreed 25% reduction. In *Scarcliffe v Brampton Valley Group Ltd* [2023] EWHC 1565 (KB), Cotter J said at [234]: "The basic rate is appropriate when care is provided (or very largely provided) during what could be considered as ordinary working hours, whereas the aggregate rates balances out all the hours of the week and is appropriate when care is provided throughout the week i.e. across the hours of the day and night". David Allan KC, sitting as a Deputy High Court Judge, followed this statement in *PHJ v HMA* unreported 7 Dec 2023 at [80].

c) The area of interest lies in the hinterland where there is indeed some care at anti-social hours but the case is not at the most serious end of the spectrum. Here there is no uniformity of approach and the matter calls for judgment.[23]

21. It is common for experts in valuable cases to break the past down into many periods with minor fluctuations in hours and annual increases in rates. It is fine in that type of case, albeit use of properly considered averages would surely simplify things considerably at no significant cost in overall accuracy. In cases without experts, practical experience suggests focussing on fewer distinct periods of care and taking into account minor fluctuations through the reasoned choice of an average number of hours or average rate[24] rather than embarking on over-elaborate calculation. Where cases involve gradually diminishing care from a point on hospital discharge to recovery or a plateau of continuing need, looking to the level of care midway through that period has much to commend it as a starting point in picking an overall average.
22. Since personal injury damages are awarded net of tax and NICs, there was invariably (until *CCC v Sheffield supra*) an appropriate reduction in respect of past non-commercial care.[25] It is now almost always 25 per cent[26] but the bracket appears historically to have been between 20 per cent and 33 per cent.[27]

[23] Examples can be given of courts taking both the aggregate and basic rates in this group of cases, often without much in the way of detailed argument or reasoning, so reference is no longer made to them. The key is a finding as to what would constitute reasonable value/proper recompense in all the circumstances of the case. It will likely balance the severity of the disability, the commitment of the relative, the period required and the relative proportion of the care at anti-social hours. Having made that effort, a broad brush finding amounting to compensation somewhere between the two rates may well commend itself in this type of case. For those who prefer greater apparent accuracy, the aggregate *day* rate might be suggested.

[24] See also *Ali v Caton & MIB*, above.

[25] At a time when the basic rate was being used as the universal starting point, a few very serious cases emerged where it was felt that a deduction from such a low rate would leave a carer with inadequate recompense; and some Courts refused to make a deduction. Now that the quality and difficulty of care is beginning to be reflected through higher rates, this method of achieving a fair result is no longer required. Choose the appropriate rate for the quality/intensity of care; but then make the principled deduction for tax and NI. As with any rule, however, there is the odd reasoned departure to be found: in *AC v Farooq & MIB [2012] EWHC 1484 QB*) King J did not make deduction from the £7.11 rate used by one of the nursing experts since it already represented a compromise over what was the appropriate commercial rate [131].

In *Totham v King's College Hospital NHS Foundation Trust [2015] EWHC 97 (QB)*, the parties agreed the rate and the hours. Nevertheless, the claimant submitted that Mrs Totham had given up highly paid work and consequently there should be no discount at all for the non-commercial element. The submission was rejected by Laing J at [25]–[28]: the argument in respect of Mrs Totham's work did not go to the correct non-commercial reduction (principally to do with tax and NI), rather it went to the correct rate to be allowed for the hours (which had already been compromised).

In *CCC v Sheffield supra*, in a similar situation to *Totham*, Ritchie J came to an opposite conclusion and made no non-commercial reduction, effectively releasing the claimant from the agreed gross value of the care. (See the main text at §20a).

[26] This was the considered reduction in *Whiten* above from the already chosen aggregate rate—see [144]. It was described by Stuart-Smith J in *Ali v Caton & MIB* above, fn.16, as the "conventional 25% discount" and he refused to make more adjustment [323c]. 25% has been the reduction in *Loughlin v Singh [2013] EWHC 1641 (QB); Farrugia [2014] EWHC 1036 (QB); Tate v Ryder Holdings [2014] EWHC 4256 (QB); Ellison v University Hospitals of Morecambe Bay NHS Foundation Trust [2015] EWHC 366 (QB); Totham* above; *Robshaw v United Lincolnshire Hospitals NHS Trust [2015] EWHC 923 (QB), AB v Devon & Exeter*, above; *Mehmetemin* above and other cases too numerous to specify. 25% was agreed in *Swift v Carpenter [2018] EWHC 2060 (QB)* at [67]; *Stansfield v BBC [2021] EWHC 2638 (QB)* at [291]; in *Riley v Salford Royal NHS Foundation Trust [2022] EWHC 2417 (KB)* at [43]; 25% in *Scarcliffe v Brampton Valley Group Ltd* [2023] EWHC 1565 (KB) at [265].

[27] Evans v Pontypridd Roofing Limited [2002] P.I.Q.R. Q5 is the leading general authority on the non-commercial reduction. In *Zambarda v Shipbreaking (Queenborough) Ltd [2013] EWHC 2263 (QB)*, John Leighton Williams KC (sitting as a Deputy High Court Judge) made only a 20% discount [64] because the sum was so small that income tax would not be paid. It is a very long time since an argued and reported decision at 33%: *Nash v Southmead Health Authority [1993] P.I.Q.R. Q.156*, decided in late 1992, is the case usually cited. Ritchie J surveyed a few earlier cases in *CCC v Sheffield supra* at [134], mostly from over 20 years ago, to find a bracket from a zero reduction to a third; but he did not include the large number of modern serious cases taking 25% as the conventional reduction.

23. A sum equivalent to any Carer's Allowance received is to be deducted from an award for non-commercial care.[28]

Example schedule[29]

Care while an in-patient—2 weeks Average of 2 hours actual care at the bedside each evening (including Saturday and Sunday): 2 hours × 14 days @ the aggregate rate (£15.22)	426	
Care during 4 weeks intensive convalescence at home: 6 hours provided daily, including weekends and evenings: 6 hours × 28 days @ the aggregate rate (£15.22)	2,557	
Further 6 months of care gradually diminishing from 6 hours a day to nil, more during the evenings and weekends at the beginning than at the end: Average of 3 hours a day care × 365/2 × the average of the basic and aggregate rates (£15.22/£11.59 = £13.40)	7,336	
	10,319	
Non-commercial discount	×0.75	
		7,739
No continuing personal care but assistance still required in respect of heavier DIY, gardening etc. chores Making allowance from £2,650 p.a.[30] for the chores still possible: £1,500 p.a × 15 (discounted lifetime multiplier to say 70):		
		22,500
Total		£30,239

[28] Teare J in *Massey* above at [52]:

> "To the extent that the carer has received benefits in respect of his or her voluntary care the claimant does not need a sum of money to give proper recompense for that care. It therefore seems to me that the Defendant's contention is right in principle."

Where there has been a discount on liability for litigation risk, carers might well argue that the Carer's Allowance should be considered as filling in for that reduction and not taken off their already reduced claims for non-commercial care.

[29] The example will pick up the threads of the "logical" approach as outlined in the text. No doubt a counter schedule, as well as attempting to reduce the number of hours, would take a point that the basic rate only should be allowed in a case beneath that of maximum severity.

[30] Mackay J in *Fleet v Fleet [2009] EWHC 3166 (QB)*:

> "25. This is claimed based on a multiplicand of £1500 p.a. I do not understand the multiplier to be controversial. The defendant contends for between £750 and £1,000 per annum as a 'more conventional sum' than the £1500 sought by the Claimant. The evidence on this issue is that Mr Fleet did all the DIY in the house and had in the past installed a new bathroom according to his wife. He was a skilled man albeit he was busy and worked long days and sometimes long weeks. He also said that he had plans to redecorate the house, and Mrs Fleet said that the living room now needs redecoration; though she could do some of the preparatory work, and did do so when her husband did the work, she could not in my judgement be reasonably expected to fill the gap left by him.
> 26. Equally, there is considerable garden at the house which Mrs Fleet tends but she cannot manage the trimming of the trees a screen of which separates the house from its neighbours and which has to be kept in order, or cut the grass.
> 27. I believe I am justified in saying that I can take into account the general level of awards under this head of damage from past experience. It would be dismal if experts had to be called to say how much it costs to mow a lawn or paint a room; after all judges do have some experience of that kind of activity and what it cost to buy it in the market place.
> 28. I see nothing wrong with the figure of £1,500 per annum claimed by the plaintiff and I think that is the right sum."

Past commercial care

24. Where there has been actual expenditure in the past on commercial care, it should be capable of easy proof (or reasonably accurate estimation if records have not been kept.)
25. It will usually be awarded in full unless the defendant raises issues of unreasonable provision (or elements of separate causation leading to unrelated provision).[31]
26. The primary measure of damage against which to judge the claimed level of provision is one of reasonable care to meet a claimant's needs.[32]

John Leighton Williams KC (sitting as a High Court Judge) allowed £1,250 p.a. to age 77 in *Zambarda v Shipbreaking (Queenborough) Ltd* above at [88]. Contrast Stuart-Smith J in *Ali v Caton & MIB* above and below at [337] where he awarded £250 p.a. to a young man with no track record for DIY, decorating and gardening. In *McGinty v Pipe [2012] EWHC 506 (QB) HHJ Foster* KC (sitting as a High Court Judge) awarded a woman of 51 £750 p.a. for gardening and DIY with a multiplier of 16 (to just beyond 70.) Kenneth Parker J in *Tate v Ryder Holdings* above discounted the claim for a 24-year-old man heavily to a lump sum award of £15,000 because of the considerable uncertainty over whether he would have carried out such activities. HHJ McKenna (sitting as a High Court Judge) awarded [96] £900 p.a. between the ages of 25 and 70 in *FM v Ipswich Hospital NHS Trust [2015] EWHC 775 (QB)*. Foskett J [421] awarded £1,500 p.a. in *Robshaw* above from age 25 when life expectancy was reduced to 63. In *Irani v Duchon [2018] EWHC 2314 (QB)* at [59], Mr David Pittaway KC (sitting as a Deputy High Court Judge) would have awarded £1,200 p.a. for "some of the heavier domestic maintenance and gardening tasks at home" but the figure was reduced to £500 p.a. with the claimant's anticipated return to India in mind leading to c.£2,000. Yip J awarded [292] £750 pa with a multiplier to around age 70 in *Stansfield v BBC [2021] EWHC 2638 (QB)*, where the claimant was "handy" but would have been working hard with little time for DIY and could still manage lighter tasks.

It is over 14 years since Mackay J saw nothing wrong with £1,500 and, with recent inflation, an RPI increase on that figure leads to c.£2,650 p.a.

[31] In *O'Brien v Harris (Transcript 22 February 2001)* the BIRT rehabilitation costs (£21,860) significantly exceeded those originally estimated (£13,700) [191]. There was no evidence from BIRT explaining the difference or resiling from the estimate [192]. The case manager was not called to justify the additional case management costs (£10,834 v £6,461) [193]. Some increased costs were allowed based on inferences from the invoices to the effect that a higher quality of support worker had been provided than in the estimate [195]. There had, however, been inadequate management of cost [194] (but by whom?—see below) and Pitchford J made an overall award of £18,500 [196].

In the case of *Loughlin v Singh* above, Kenneth Parker J was invited [62] to disallow the costs of past care and case management on the basis that "the standard of such care and management fell significantly below that which could reasonably be expected to meet the exigencies of the claimant's condition and circumstances". The full submission was rejected as "wholly disproportionate and unjust"; but the claim was reduced by 20 per cent with a broad brush on account of the case manager's failure to address the claimant's need for a specific and effective sleep hygiene regime in timely fashion. Kenneth Parker J made a finding that

> "the efforts made on this fundamental aspect of the rehabilitation were simply not adequate [61] ... Principle requires that I should take due account of the fact, that I have found, that the standard of the care and case management services did, in an important respect, fall significantly below the standard that could reasonably have been expected. In other words, the objective value of what the Claimant received was less than the amount of the charges made for the relevant services" [62].

There was no finding in *Loughlin* that the claimant through his Financial Deputy had knowingly appointed an incompetent case manager. Kenneth Parker J made no finding of failure to mitigate against the claimant/Financial Deputy in the handling/funding of the case manager (although this may have been an under-current in the case). As long as Kenneth Parker J's findings amounted to *gross* negligence on the part of the case manager, his observations can be squared with wider principles of novus actus under *Rahman v Arearose Ltd [2001] QB 351* and *Webb v Barclays Bank [2001] EWCA Civ 1141*: insofar as the increased costs of failing to implement a sleep hygiene regime were caused by the gross negligence of a third party, they were separately caused. It is difficult to see, however, why a finding of mere as against gross negligence in the past on the part of a case manager should break the chain of causation and lead to the dis-allowance of part of the claim.

In the more recent case of *Ali v Caton & MIB* above and below, Stuart-Smith J awarded the full claim for past support workers, the regime having been set up in accordance with apparently competent third party advice.

> "The position of a significantly brain-damaged claimant who acts on the basis of apparently reasonable advice is strong, though not always impregnable, when seeking to recover the costs of doing so from a tortfeasor. On this item, the balance of the argument strongly favours the claimant" [323f–h].

This approach is in keeping with the writer's understanding of the real legal issue set out in the previous paragraph.

Laing J in *Totham* above conveniently ignored deciding whether the poor case management had been grossly negligent or merely negligent and awarded the whole claim on the basis that Mrs Totham "had acted reasonably in appointing [the case management company] in the first place, and in continuing to employ, and pay, them until they walked off the job." [39]

[32] The principle was put succinctly by Lord Lloyd in *Wells v Wells [1999] 1 AC 345* at 377F in just 17 words: "Plaintiffs are entitled to a reasonable standard of care to meet their requirements, but that is all." Stephenson LJ traced in *Rialis v Mitchell*

27. If, at first blush, the claim in the past appears to exceed the primary measure of damage, principles of mitigation of loss may yet come to a claimant's aid if some evidence is adduced to explain the apparent over-spend. Once a claimant raises such arguments, the burden of proof lies on a defendant to prove a failure in mitigation; and the standard against which to judge a claimant's actions is not a harsh one.[33]
28. The value of direct payments stands to be deducted.[34] There is no loss to the extent that there is NHS continuing care.

Future non-commercial care

29. If non-commercial care is to be carried on long into the future, the potential break down of the package is a contingency to be assessed. Where there is detailed expert evidence, there will often be an alternative package laid out drawing on greater commercial care. It will then be a matter for the judge to reach a fair balanced assumption in monetary terms between two or more packages, weighting the award according to the available evidence.[35]
30. Where the evidence is not so detailed and there is no provision elsewhere in the calculations for a break down in the non-commercial care package, it may well be appropriate to reflect adverse contingencies by refusing to apply the usual non-commercial discount. In this way some allowance is made with a broad brush for the possibility of more expensive commercial care on separation/ill health/death in the family member who is to supply the care.[36]

Future commercial care

Hourly rates

31. There is no "conventional" hourly rate for future commercial care, whether recruited through direct employment or an agency. All depends on the nature/difficulty of the required care; the level of need for continuity in carers; the prevailing rates local to a claimant's home (probably the

(Court of Appeal transcript, 6 July 1984) how the 100% principle was finessed through a series of Victorian cases involving fatal accidents on the railways to reflect the recovery of reasonable rather than perfect compensation. Reasonable compensation is now 100% compensation since it is the primary measure of damage. Recently, claimants and defendants are jousting, the one using the language of "full compensation" and the other "proportionality". It is far from clear what these ideas add if the primary measure of damage is "reasonable compensation": this test is infinitely flexible and requires no gloss; all the decisions are ultimately explicable applying a simple test of *reasonableness* to the very specific facts. Readers interested in seeing the development of this trend can look to *Whiten* above at [4]–[5]; *Totham* above at [12]; *Ellison* above at [9]; *Robshaw* above at [161]–[167]; and to Baroness Hale in *XX v Whittington Hospital NHS Trust [2021] AC 275* at [43], enunciating a qualification to the principle of Lord Blackburn in *Livingstone v Rawyards Coal Co.*, "A second qualification is that, in seeking to restore what has been lost, the steps taken must be reasonable ones and the costs thereby incurred must be reasonable." In *Muyepa v MoD [2022] EWHC 2648 (KB)* Cotter J reminded us of the orthodox approach and what it involves: "295. The evaluation of damages for care and equipment is not just a question of a requirement simpliciter, including on a theoretical and/or very limited or occasional basis, rather of a reasonable requirement. Damages will not be recoverable if the cost is disproportionate to the benefit. The requirement of reasonableness is used to qualify and filter suggested requirements and there is no entitlement to have funding for a wish list of all care and expenditure which could conceivably provide any benefits."

[33] This topic is beyond the scope of this chapter; an obvious source of assistance lies in McGregor on Damages, 21st edition, para. 9-079 and in the surrounding paragraphs.

[34] *Crofton v NHS Litigation Authority [2007] 1 W.L.R. 923.*

[35] In *C v Dixon [2009] EWHC 708 (QB)* King J assessed damages where the relationship between the claimant and his partner was far from assured in the long run. He took an assumed period of 10 years before break up as a fair reflection of the chances and proceeded to do the arithmetic from that starting point.

[36] In *Willbye v Gibbons [2004] P.I.Q.R. P15* at [12] and [16] in which, on a quality of evidence which was insufficient to warrant fine alternative contingency calculations in the event of breakdown in the non-commercial package, Kennedy LJ varied the sum awarded by removing the non-commercial discount allowed by the Recorder.

biggest factor). Evidence on all three scores is highly desirable.[37] Previous editions of *Facts & Figures* provided a table of hourly rates decided or agreed in big cases between 2008 and 2015. There has been such turmoil and increase in rates in recent years that earlier cases appear unreliable as a current guide. Accordingly, the table has been removed. Even more attention than usual will have to be taken in preparing the care evidence,[38] at least for a while. In *CCC v Sheffield (2023) supra* in a directly recruited package, the Court preferred £15 an hour (weekdays) and £17 (weekends) to £14 and £15 an hour [177].

32. Readers still tempted to look at past cases will bear in mind inflation and ASHE 6115 at the 80th Centile before the recent rises (not yet fully reflected in ASHE 6115).

Year	ASHE % change
2011-12	0.29
2012-13	0.39
2013-14	-0.78
2014-15	1.67
2015-16	3.58
2016-17	2.51
2017-18	4.0
2018-19	3.49
2019-20	5.31
2020-21	2.32
2021-22	6.6
2022-23	7.0

Case management—hourly rates

33. As with support worker rates there is no "conventional" hourly rate for case management; but the rate for this (as against the number of hours required) has proved mostly uncontroversial. The rate has crept up gradually and £90 an hour + travel time (£45 an hour plus mileage) was agreed in

[37] Jack J bewailed the lack of evidence of decent quality in *XXX [2008] EWHC 2727 (QB)* at [16].

[38] In early 2022, the best general evidence appeared from a survey carried out by BABICM, then on its website at https://www.babicm.org/2022/02/03/perfect-storm-survey-results/. Case managers were asked about the maximum rates (often close to the rates awarded at Common Law in big cases) that they had to pay and the responses in relation to directly recruited staff were between £13 and £21 an hour (the majority were at £14/£15 an hour); agency support worker rates were in a £20-£40 bracket; agency nurse rates between £40-£80. Scarcity of staff was a continuing problem, with spiralling pay demands. An end to the situation was not thought to be in sight. BABICM had not published any new survey as at the end of April 2024. £14/£15 an hour for directly employed support workers is already turning out (2024) to be a conservative rate. Higher rates still will surely be seen in cases where the work is onerous and in geographical locations where recruitment is especially difficult.

In *Riley v Salford Royal* supra, the agency care awarded was based on £22.11 an hour on weekdays and £26.90 at weekends, averaging out in the judgment (Sept. 2022) at about £23.65 an hour in [75], when an hour a day agency support cost £8,634 pa. Experience suggests there is a very wide range of agency rates and evidence justifying the type of provider—hence rates—will be required in each case.

Whiten in 2011. £95 an hour was awarded in 2013/14 in *Ali v Caton* [332], *Streeter* [217] (noting the agreement of Mrs Gough's costing) and *Farrugia* at [107], all above. £98 an hour was the rate allowed in *Tait v Gloucestershire Hospitals NHS Foundation Trust.*[39] Despite a claim for £107 an hour actually being paid for case management in *Manna,*[40] Cox J allowed [217] only £95 an hour, accepting the defendant's evidence that £107 an hour was beyond the normal range. Irwin J [142] awarded £98 an hour in 2016 in *AB v Royal Devon & Exeter.* Travel time and mileage are calculated/awarded generally on top. The upward trend in recent years has continued but without a specific decision as to what constitutes reasonable hourly rates; they currently (2024) appear to range between £110 and £130 an hour. In *CCC v Sheffield,* in 2023, the preferred [181] long term case management package was not broken down but totalled £22,860 pa (based on 180 hours a year with travel time and expenses added in).

34. The required number of hours varies greatly and will be lower where there is agency care as against direct employment.
35. In *Swift v Carpenter*[41] Lambert J disallowed most of the claim for case management on the basis that she was awarding care at agency rates (which involves payment already for supervisory/organisational elements) and the claimant did not really require the assistance of a case manager. She awarded, however, a "contingency" sum, to allow for case management, particularly in older age when her partner might not be on hand, based on 50 hours at an all-inclusive rate of £160 an hour = £8,000 [68]–[69].

Provision for holidays, sick pay etc.

36. Where future care is to be provided through direct employment rather than agency provision, it is now customary to take into account i) paid holidays ii) higher hourly rates paid on Bank Holidays iii) sick leave and iv) down time in the package for training days by adopting calculations based on a notional 60 weeks in the year.[42] While a few experts continue to use it, the alternative method of taking 52 weeks in the year and a percentage uplift to cover the required extras (which started at around 27 per cent and rose steadily[43]) has fallen out of favour in reported cases. Jay J in *Farrugia* above described [100] taking a 60-week year as "standard practice".

[39] [2015] EWHC 848 (QB) at [92].
[40] [2015] EWHC 2279 (QB).
[41] [2018] EWHC 2060 (QB).
[42] See: *XXX v A Strategic Health Authority* above at [24] and *Whiten v St George's Healthcare NHS Trust [2011] EWHC 2066 (QB)* at [167]–[168]. For the evolution of the 60-week calculation, see the book at fn 1. *Streeter* above is an exception, where the experts both adopted 59.6 weeks but made an additional allowance on Bank holidays—ruled on by Baker J in line with Mrs Gough at £1 an hour uplift.

It is clear that down time for training days, additional pay for bank holidays etc. are included in the 60-week calculation. Those care experts who take 60 weeks and routinely bill for training time and so on in addition might be said to be trying too hard. The taking of 60 weeks, however, might be distinguished up or down for the specific training etc. requirements of any case since it has evolved out of the bigger cases—it might be easier to distinguish down rather than up (or the attempt not worth the effort). See also the discussion below in the main text with regard to liaison and MDT meetings as within the 60-week calculation.

In *HS v Lancashire Teaching Hospitals NHS Trust [2015] EWHC 1376 (QB),* the claimant's care expert asked for a 5% contingency uplift (5% × 60 weeks = 3 more weeks) "in order to cover holidays, sickness and other unexpected and sudden absences on the part of employed carers". William Davis J rejected the argument at [31] on the basis that the 60-week calculation included holidays and sickness. He continued: "Any maternity leave will be funded from the public purse given the number of employees. Any other absences will almost certainly be accommodated with the carers' shift patterns."

[43] In *Martin v Salford [2022] PIQR Q2,* the preferred expert used this method and allowed 36 per cent as the uplift.

ERNIC

37. Calculation of ERNIC on carers' wages was often misunderstood but not now. It is currently (tax year 2024/25) payable at 13.8 per cent on wages above the secondary threshold[44] (£175 a week × 52 weeks = £9,100 p.a.) So, to reach the annual sum of ERNIC, calculate the annual wages bill and deduct from it (£9,100 × the likely number of carers in the package) to give the sum on which 13.8 per cent is likely to be paid. There is no longer real controversy over taking into account the uplifted £5,000 Employment Allowance; it is now routinely claimed by deputies and should offset the first £5,000 of ERNICs as previously calculated.

Auto enrolment pension contributions

38. NEST is but one of many providers of what are generically referred to as "auto enrolment" pensions.
39. If enrolled within such a scheme, employers pay a percentage of *qualifying earnings*: for tax year 2024/25 this remains between £6,240 and £50,270 p.a.
40. Enrolment is compulsory for all workers aged at least 22 but under State retirement age who earn at least £10,000 p.a. from that employer, who work (or normally work) in the UK and who are not already an active member of a qualifying scheme with that employer. If enrolled, workers can opt out if they do so within the first month, otherwise they cannot withdraw their money until aged at least 55.
41. Enrolment is at a worker's own option if aged at least 16, with the employer having to contribute if they have *qualifying earnings*, i.e. earn over £6,240 p.a.
42. The staged introduction of the duties is now completed.

	Minimum percentage of qualifying earnings that must be paid in total	Minimum percentage of qualifying earnings that ***employers*** must pay
April 2019 onwards	8 per cent	3 per cent[45]

Childcare

43. The possible costs of caring for children have been claimed in *Totham* and *Robshaw*, both above. They were cases of cerebral palsy and the claims were resisted on the basis that neither claimant would realistically have children. The defences succeeded with slightly different formulations in the rationale. In *Totham*, Laing J found [71] that she was "not satisfied that there is a more than fanciful chance that Eva will have children". In *Robshaw*, Foskett J [191] would not go so far as to say the chance was "merely speculative or fanciful" but nevertheless said that the discount for contingencies would have to be so significant that "it would reduce the figure to something that would bear no real relationship to that actual cost if the event itself materialised. An award of such a sum would, in my view, be wholly artificial." And he made no award at all [192].

[44] There is an upper ceiling; but no carer is ever paid enough to bring it into play.

[45] In *JR [2017] 1 W.L.R. 4847* [57], William Davis J followed Swift J in *Whiten* in adjusting the long term 3% contribution to about 2% for contingencies, the main one clearly being the chance of opt out. According to the experience of NEST, the largest of the Master Trust Corporations, however, opt out is comparatively rare, particularly among younger workers who will often be providing much of the required care: see the NEST Corporation Annual Report and Accounts 2018/19 at p.16 available at: *https://www.nestpensions.org.uk/schemeweb/nest/nestcorporation/library.html*. Later accounts have not provided comparable data.

44. Childcare claims in less serious cases are often raised but rarely pursued fully as strictly *child* care—often they are a facet of care of claimants themselves to enable them to provide their own childcare, adding only modestly or not at all to their underlying requirements. What is left may well amount to household services rather than *care*: see Jay J in *Hayden*—"The claim is for a nanny but I see him or her as being more by way of factotum, assisting the Claimant with the heavier aspects of cleaning and childcare ... "[46]
45. In *Swift v Carpenter* above the claimant was female, aged 43, worked, had a child of just two and was hoping to have another, with a below knee amputation of one leg and significant orthopaedic disability in the other. She was a resourceful woman and it was agreed [9] that she would remain self-caring until her late 70s and early 80s, with greater care in the last two years of life including assistance with transfers. It was also agreed that she was already compromised in terms of heavier housework, lifting, carrying and working/cleaning at ground level. The claim was split into six periods and Lambert J found for the *additional childcare and other care needs* (she would have been working) [51] as follows:
    1. First 18 months, one child of 2-3, before birth of a second child [54]–[55]: 15 hours a week commercial help at an agency mother's help rate of £16.50 with seven hours of non-commercial care (at the basic rate [67] which the parties agreed should be reduced by 25 per cent for the non-commercial element).
    2. During maternity leave [56]–[57]: a full-time nanny/housekeeper (£53,000) was neither reasonable nor would one be engaged; instead, 25 hours per week at the agency mother's help rate and non-commercial care at 14 hours a week (during the first six months) and seven hours a week (during the second six months).
    3. Then to the younger child reaching secondary school age [58]–[60]: 20 hours a week at the agency mother's help rate and 11 hours a week non-commercial care.
    4. Then to age 80 [61]–[62]: based on purely commercial care at seven hours a week giving a multiplicand of £3,778.32 p.a. (so based on c.£10.38/hour as an average, presumably privately engaged this rate.)
    5. From 80 to last two years [63]: 14 hours a week commercial care, leading to a multiplicand of £15,750 p.a. (now presumably at agency rates averaging at c. £21.63 an hour over weekdays, weekends and Bank Holidays).
    6. Last two years of life [64]–[66]: live-in care costing £1,250 per week or £65,000 p.a. The Parties had contended for £1,500 per week as against £900 per week; Lambert J chose to find in the upper middle of the range on the basis that the care would be at high London rates but *not of the most arduous.*
46. In contrast to the hourly rate of £16.50 allowed in *Swift v Carpenter* for an agency mother's help, Martin Spencer J awarded future nanny care in *Zeromska-Smith v United Lincolnshire Hospital NHS Trust [2019] EWHC 980 (QB)* at [129] over a two-year period while the mother recovered—15 hours a week in the first year and 10 hours a week in the second. This was awarded on the basis of the costings of the defendant's expert at £8.25 an hour, over 52 weeks in the year, with £135 p.a insurance cover.
47. In *Riley v Salford Royal [2022] EWHC 2417 (KB)*, a male lower limb amputee obtained a baseline package of an extra 3 hours per week of domestic assistance (£2,026 pa) [74], with an agency care package [75] beginning modestly at age 70 (1 hour a day); then 2 hours a day (75-80); 4 hours a day (80-83); finally a single live in carer (last 2-3 years of life costed at £362,199 overall). There were add ons, such as 14 hours a week for 5 weeks a year for life to cover the contingency of stump breakdown [76]. He obtained childcare over 6 years (for 2 presumed children to the age of 3), on a non-commercial basis—10.5 hours a week from his partner; and £1,351 pa, while children were under the age of 12, for extra help with cleaning and laundry.

[46] [2016] EWHC 3276 (QB) at [214]: "... I allow £9,082 per annum until the claimant's youngest child reaches the age of 5. Thereafter, I allow 4 hours a week at £12 per hour. The Parties have agreed a multiplier of 7.05."

Parental contribution to the future care package

48. The court's attitude to any fair offset from future commercial care of very severely damaged children on account of parental involvement has evolved since 2006. The seeds sown by Sir Rodger Bell in *Iqbal*[47] to the effect that parents are not to be presumed to take part in the care of grievously injured children requiring onerous care—have grown on strongly via Teare J in *Massey* [64], Lloyd Jones J in *A v Powys*[48] [57] and HHJ Collender KC (sitting as a High Court Judge) in *Crofts*[49] [120]. By the time of *Whiten* (2011) above the NHSLA was no longer apparently arguing for any real offset: the only point at which the parents' potential contribution was considered relevant was in allowing for a single night sleeper in the commercial package on the basis that they would be available in an emergency [205]. In *Farrugia* above [96], care was awarded for 14 hours a day × 2 commercial carers except when a family member would take the place of one commercial carer in outings spread over 10 hours each week. This modest adjustment to the rates for family provision covered only 48 weeks in the year up to the claimant's age of 49. While not arguing for any offset in *Robshaw* above (claimant 12 years old), the NHSLA renewed its fight in *HS v Lancs.*[50] (claimant only eight) but were again unsuccessful.

Pre-existing conditions—a matter of causation or deduction?

49. In *Huntley*[51] the claimant's pre-accident problems had not led to any prior requirement for care and attendance. In other cases, later negligence increases a pre-existing need for care, accommodation and therapies above those that would have been required anyway. How should the court approach the task? Is it a matter of *causation* so that, when damages are assessed, it is only in respect of the strictly increased elements satisfying the prior test of causation? Or, is it a matter of *quantification of damage* so that the whole of the reasonable needs are taken as the starting point and the pre-existing needs considered only as a matter of potential deduction? If the latter, a claimant can recover damages for the whole of his condition on a commercial basis and, if the pre-existing needs would have been satisfied at essentially no cost to him (family or local authority care), giving little or no credit.
50. In *Sklair v Haycock,*[52] the claimant (49 and looked after informally by his "Bohemian" father) had suffered with Asperger's Syndrome and Obsessive Compulsive Disorder. Edwards-Stuart J found that the claimant's elderly father would have continued to look after him for 5–10 years longer, when his wider family would have looked after him at a financial cost to them of £150–£200 per week for 5–10 years, after which a residential placement in local authority care would have been likely. The accident had turned the claimant's need for this lower level of care (as a matter of fact) into a reasonable need for 24-hour commercial care [80.] The findings of Edwards-Stuart J amounted to deciding the causation issue on the basis that the negligence had caused the whole of the need for care (awarding the full commercial cost) and he then made, as a matter of quantification of the damages, a small deduction only for the short period when modest financial cost would have been incurred.

[47] [2006] EWHC 3111 (QB) [20].
[48] [2006] EWHC 1178 (QB).
[49] Lawtel, Judgment 5.09.08.
[50] [2015] EWHC 1376 (QB).
[51] [2009] EWHC 405 (QB).
[52] [2009] EWHC 3328 (QB).

51. In *Reaney v Various Staffs NHS Trusts*,[53] the claimant's spinal cord condition had been made worse by clinical negligence: she would have needed some more modest care etc. anyway but now needed, on Foskett J's findings, an intensive commercial package. He too decided that the negligence had caused the whole of the need for commercial care etc. and made no real deduction in respect of the prior needs. He went so far as to say that the principle of *material contribution* would have led him to a similar result [71].
52. The defendant appealed in *Reaney* where the Master of the Rolls overturned the reasoning and remitted the case for further consideration. The essential question is one of *causation* not *deduction.* Where negligence increases a claimant's needs *quantitatively* (even if *significantly* or *substantially* so—"more of the same") [21], a defendant's negligence only *causes* the additional need, not the underlying one: *Performance Cars Ltd v Abraham*[54] followed, as applied in *Steel v Joy.*[55]
53. If, however, the negligence makes a *qualitative* difference—the needs are no longer of the same type—it has *caused* the whole of it in its different form. The Master of Rolls agreed with counsel for the appellant that the causation result in *Sklair* might be explained on the basis that the care need before and after the negligence was indeed qualitatively different—the difference between "personal support in a 24-hour care regime and general supervisory care of an essentially independent life" [32]. Nothing was said, in that event, as to the correctness of making even a small deduction at the quantification stage. In *Reaney,* however, despite the findings of Foskett J for very substantially increased needs, they did not go far enough to move the case across the line between the negligence having made merely a *quantitative* as against a *qualitative* difference.
54. Further he had been wrong to have recourse to ideas of *material contribution* and invocation of the principle (described by the MR as an "accurate distillation of the law") in *Bailey v MoD.*[56] Since there was no doubt as to the claimant's needs before and after the negligence, the principle could have no application. See the discussion at [36].
55. Whipple J distinguished *Reaney* and instead applied *Rahman v Arearose Ltd*[57] in the case of *XP v Compensa Towarzstwo SA & Przeyslaw Bejger.*[58] In *Reaney* the claimant was already paralysed before the clinical negligence and there was a clear baseline against which the Court could assess how much, if any, additional or different care was needed. Whipple J contrasted the *Reaney* position [93] with the one before her: two accidents on top of each other and no clear baseline to determine condition and prognosis after the first accident compared with the position after the second. She found the facts of the case not to be capable of such neat separation as envisaged in *Reaney* [95] on some heads of damage; she there applied the broader brush of the Court of Appeal in *Rahman,* coming to a "just conclusion" with a 75:25 split.
56. David Allan KC, sitting as a Deputy High Court Judge, in *PHJ v HMA* unreported 7 Dec 2023 found [74] that the claimant's needs were *qualitatively* different following severe brain injury compared with the sort of anxiety and depression she is likely to have suffered. He made no offset and commented that there is at least an evidential burden on a defendant seeking an offset to provide some evidence to enable an appropriate estimate [75]. The broad brush 25% discount sought in that case was insufficient.

Resident carers

56. The old arguments for residential agency care have almost completely fallen away in the most serious cases. There may still be a place for such a provision, however, in cases requiring a lighter

[53] [2014] EWHC 3016 (QB).
[54] [1962] 1 QB 33.
[55] [2004] 1 W.L.R 3002. How the need would have been/will now be supplied (whether at commercial cost or free) is irrelevant to the causation question [33].
[56] [2007] EWHC 2913 (QB).
[57] [2001] QB 351.
[58] [2016] EWHC 1728 (QB).

touch, as with care of the partial tetraplegic claimant in *Davies*[59] (between the ages of 70 and 75, after which extensive top up for double up hours was added.) The last gasp of the argument for residential care in the most serious cases came when the NHSLA in *Whiten* above tried to run a *Davies*-post-75-style argument in the case of a grievously injured child with mixed spastic-dystonic, severe, quadriplegic cerebral palsy. It suggested the bedrock of a care package through a residential agency carer with extensive hourly top up. Swift J rejected that potential solution without hesitation [204].

57. Nevertheless, in the unusual case of *AB v Devon & Exeter NHS Foundation Trust*[60]—a high paraplegic with severe spasm—a single resident carer was the answer to age 55 and two resident carers, overlapping and doubling up sensibly, from that age onwards. The annual multiplicands for the packages, including case management, were £79,420 [142] and £150,140 [145].
58. See also the award of £65,000 p.a. for live in agency care in *Swift v Carpenter* during the final two years of life, set out above under child care. Contrast *Riley v Salford* when a single live in carer was allowed for the final 2-3 years, but with £362,199 allowed overall (so presumably on an agency hourly paid basis).

Risk/benefit applied to care regimes

59. *Davies* and *C v Dixon*, both above, have also been interesting in the detailed way in which Wilkie J and King J balanced risk and benefit to the claimant in reaching the appropriate care package. In each case the defendant argued that the package suggested by the claimant's experts amounted to substantial over-provision and would be stifling of the claimant. In *Davies* some risk of falling was found to be acceptable without a resident carer always on hand before the age of 70: a resident carer package before that age did not take into account the contribution which a degree of self-reliance has to a person's sense of worth and well-being [110]. In *C v Dixon* the claimant was not to be wrapped in cotton wool [35] with unnecessary commercial and double-up provision—he could have the required 24-hour care in a looser sense, including some down time in the package as long he had someone to contact in an emergency. Since his partner was assumed to be with him for the next 10 years, there was no need for commercial overnight care during that period.
60. In the moderate (general damages £147,500—July 2013) brain injury case of *Ali v Caton & MIB* above Stuart-Smith J described the scope of the care package there allowing 15 hours a week of support as follows [331ii]:

> "The purpose of the future care regime should be to provide sufficient support to enable [the claimant] to pursue a structured and constructive existence so far as possible, reinforcing constructive routines and being available to assist when he is confronted by the new, the unfamiliar or the complex."

Two carers throughout the day

61. Until *Manna* above in 2015, whether two carers are required throughout the day had not been litigated for a while to a formal decision—it was common ground in the 2014 case of *Farrugia* above (severe brain injury) that it was necessary and in *Streeter* above in 2013 (C5/6 motor tetraplegia) that it was not. In *A v B*[61] two carers were required throughout waking hours (essentially in respect of transfers for toileting which could not be forecast as to timing) in a case of severe compromise in dystonic athetoid tetraplegic cerebral palsy. A similar result ensued in *XXX*.

[59] [2008] EWHC 740 (QB) Wilkie J.
[60] [2016] EWHC 1024 (QB) Irwin J.
[61] [2006] EWHC 1178 (QB).

In both cases the claimants had little or no appreciation of their predicament but swift availability of changing was necessary for their health and comfort. The result was the same in *Massey* for a different reason: here the claimant had substantially retained intellect in a grossly malfunctioning body: for him the availability of two carers was essential for transfers and transport so that he could exercise autonomy and make decisions to act on impulse rather than live in the strait-jacket of double-up provision which was less than continuous and at fixed hours of the day.

62. In *Farrugia* above, while awarding care based on two carers in attendance during waking hours, Jay J said this when considering whether two commercial carers had to be present throughout:

> "I do not accept ... that Jack should, in effect, be free to do whatever he wishes at the spur of the moment. I do not consider that Jack's personal autonomy is overridden, or the dictates of spontaneity are unreasonably quelled, by providing for a regime which presupposes a modest degree of pre-planning and organisation. This, after all, reflects the realities of ordinary life."

63. The case for two carers in respect of a sentient adult who can give basic cooperation with hoisted transfers (in the sense of not lashing out or being subject to spasm) has not yet been clearly made out for transfers within the home. While the NHS commonly uses two nurses for such transfers even with a hoist on hospital wards, that appears to be at least partly because two nurses are available in such a setting and the use of two speeds things up.

64. *Manna* above saw the principal dispute at trial focus on the amount of double up care for an ambulant young man with profound cognitive problems and prone to outbursts: 14+14 hours per day—total daytime double-up—was found to be reasonable because of the unpredictability of outbursts [209]; it would simply be too much for one person alone to provide the required structured care all day [211]; 28 hours of double-up per week was rejected.

Day centre provision

65. The argument for offset from a commercial care package for down time while an adult claimant attends a local authority day centre was never strong. With its lack of forensic success, coupled with further funding cuts and closure of day centres, the argument is not currently being aired.

Team leaders

66. Although the payment of a higher rate to a member of the support worker team did not find favour over 15 years ago now in *Crofton* or *Iqbal*, the allowance of a team leader (reducing the amount and cost of case management intervention) has become pretty standard in really serious cases. An extra £2 an hour was conceded in *XXX*. In *Whiten* the principle was disputed; and as a fall back it was suggested by the defendant that any provision could be by reference to a small proportion of the hours worked by the team leader, i.e. only those hours when in fact engaged on team leader duties. Swift J [164] rejected that line and allowed 30 hours a week at a weekday rate enhanced by £3 an hour (London). The whole point was to attract someone to the post with experience and ability: the defendant's suggestion would not achieve the aim. Contrast *Farrugia*, in which Jay J awarded an increase of £5 an hour (Hants.) [104] but over only 22 hours a week [103], commenting that he simply could not accept that a full week's work was required for the combination of tasks required of the team leader. In *Streeter*, Baker J allowed an increment of £2 an hour over 15 hours a week.[62] In *Robshaw*, Foskett J [183]–[184] allowed an enhanced rate of £4 an hour for 30 hours a week to age 19; £5 an hour (the gap being said to grow over time) for 25 hours a week from that age onwards. In *HS v Lancs.* William Davis J awarded 33.5 hours a week at unspecified

[62] See fn.41.

team leader rates. In *Manna* Cox J awarded £5 an hour uplift but the number of hours is unclear. In *JR v Sheffield,*[63] the parties compromised at £4 an hour uplift [55]. In *Martin v Salford [2022] PIQR Q2,* the team leader award [58] was at £5 an hour for 36 hours a week. In *CCC v Sheffield (2023) supra,* the award was £7,800 pa as claimed [175] and almost certainly based on £5 an hour uplift x 30 hours a week x 52 weeks in the year.

67. Much appears to depend on the precise nature of the case, the experts, and the judge as to how things are expressed.

Waking or sleeping night rates?

68. In *JR v Sheffield* above there was detailed discussion [51]-[54] concerning how often a sleeping night carer might be made to get up more than twice a night on an occasional basis (then paid for a waking night). The evidence was that those taking on responsibilities for sleeping night care often have commitments the next day and will not tolerate frequent additional interference in their sleep. The absolute maximum was said to be six to eight weeks in total in a year. Care diaries suggested in *JR* that the total would exceed ten weeks so the second night carer post had to be one for waking rather than sleeping night care in the first place. A similar analysis appears in *CCC v Sheffield (2023) supra* at [178].

Hand over meetings

69. Claiming hand over periods of up to half an hour at the conclusion of each shift has never appeared an attractive argument and is not generally being run at the moment unless in unusual circumstances.

Liaison/team meetings

70. These were not contended for in *Whiten* or *Farrugia*; allowed as to merely one hour a month in *C v Dixon,* and substantially conceded in *XXX*—all cases referred to above. There may have been oversight when these allowances have been made or conceded: as the "60 weeks in the year" evolved, it was supposed to take into account a routine allowance for training and team meetings—see the discussion of the evidence in the judgment of Penry-Davey J in *Smith* above.
71. The result was more complicated in *Robshaw* above, where Foskett J allowed for the costs of therapists attending multi-disciplinary meetings but decided—in line with the above discussion—that the attendance of the case manager, team leader and support workers should be funded out of the normal working time already awarded within the 60-week year. He allowed five meetings in the first year; four per annum then until age 18; three per annum then to age 25; the claim was limited to one per annum then for life but he would have awarded two per annum. All meetings were said to require two hours allocated to them and should not be rushed. See [474]–[479].

The status of family choice on behalf of a claimant

72. The issue of the status of a future family choice on behalf of a claimant raised its head in the case of *Harman v East Kent Hospitals NHS Foundation Trust.*[64] The claimant, aged 13 and suffering severe autism with significant cognitive impairment, was being cared for in a specialist placement

[63] [2017] EWHC 1245 (QB).
[64] [2015] EWHC 1662 (QB).

funded by the LEA but spending eight weeks a year at home. The issue was where the claimant would live when his education came to an end in 12 years at age 25: the parents wanted him then to come home. Turner J found in favour of that course, following expert evidence that a care package which met with the aspirations of the parents would be more likely to succeed than one which did not [38]. As to the underlying point of law, however, the parents' choice did not trump the view of the court of the primary measure of damage in the future:

> "[36] Care must be taken in cases such as this not to equiparate the preferences of relatives with the regime of care and support the cost of which should be the basis of reasonable compensation. Each case must be looked at on its own facts. There may well be circumstances in which, however strong and genuine the desire of the parents or a spouse or partner may be to have the claimant home, there are good reasons for taking a contrary course. The purpose of damages in a personal injury claim is to compensate the victim and not to accommodate the wishes of his family whatever the extent of the inevitable personal sympathy one might have for those who are left to pick up the pieces and suffer the inevitable and sustained emotional impact of serious injury to someone dear to them."

Chance contingencies and PPOs for care

73. *Huntley* above illustrates that the essential chance assessment of damages for future loss has survived the new PPO regime, which purports to trace everything back to a claimant's needs. There the claimant, who had suffered a frontal lobe injury and whose rehabilitation had not gone well up to trial, contended for 24 hours of care per day as the long-term solution: the defendant submitted for 21 hours per week. Underhill J (as he then was) approached matters by evaluating first of all the hard-core minimum level that he thought was reasonable, which he assessed at six hours a day [109]. This hard-core cost he would have put within a PPO [114] but not the full chance reasonable amount that he went on to evaluate as follows. He uplifted the package by 50 per cent from six hours to nine hours a day with a broad brush for all the possibilities of needing greater care. He then discounted that back by one hour to eight hours a day for the chance that the claimant would not in fact engage all the care that he might reasonably require. There was a real chance that he would reject care (as he would if he entered a stable relationship) and small chances of imprisonment and detention under the Mental Health Act. The resulting additional two hours a day beyond the core six hours Underhill J would have provided within an additional lump sum award; but the whole PPO submission was withdrawn when the claimant did not recover for 24-hour care.
74. For a further example taking contingencies into account, see the decision of Kenneth Parker J in *Tate v Ryder Holdings* above [38]–[42] where he averaged the cost of caring for the claimant in his own and residential accommodation, catering for different times in his life, and adjusted further for the chances of non-compliance by 20 per cent for reasons similar to those set out by Underhill J in *Huntley*. As in *Huntley*, the adjustments led to a lump sum award rather than PPO.
75. In *Martin v Salford No.1 [2022] PIQR Q2* and *No.2 [2022] EWHC 532 (QB)* there was an interesting use of the rarely used power to order a variable PPO. At [61] of the first judgment there was the following finding as to the balance in the awarded multiplicand for care:

> "There is a risk that an award of damages on a lifetime multiplier basis in the amounts I have set out might over-compensate Miss Martin if she is hospitalised for long periods, or her night time care needs increase [sic], or because (contrary to the view I have already expressed, and although the possibility is in my view small) at some point in the future she seeks section 117 assistance. Equally there is a prospect that an award might under-compensate if her physical needs increase over time, but she can be cared for at home. Such an award in my judgment

takes account of the small potential that she will be required to pay residential care in later life."

76. By the end of the consequential argument following the second judgment, however, and when a PPO had been the Claimant's preferred disposal rather than a lump sum award, the Defendant argued for and obtained an order for a variable PPO, with the trigger for variation being if the Claimant deteriorated to the extent of requiring care in a nursing home rather than care in her own home.[65] This was a novel idea in using a *deterioration* in a claimant's condition to justify what was hoped would lead to a *saving* in care costs. The Claimant's response was to apply for an earlier trigger for variation—should she need increasing levels of night care at home precisely to avoid having to go into a nursing home—but it was refused. Neither side appealed.
77. This case is far from straightforward and there are wide-ranging considerations if courts are to consider going down this route again. Discussion of this important first instance decision and how it fits within the wider regime of lump sum once and for all assessment, PPOs generally, and provisional damages is a topic beyond the scope of Facts & Figures.[66]

[65] The precise wording of the trigger in the Order was: "The serious deterioration specified for the purpose of variation is that the Claimant's mental and/or physical condition deteriorates as a result of an aggravation of her psychiatric illnesses and/or increasing spasticity of the Claimant's left limbs and/or increasing problems with her right hip resulting in a level of nursing care that can only be provided in a nursing home or similar institution providing nursing care, on a permanent basis."
[66] Readers interested in knowing more can consult Serious Personal Injury Litigation—Quantum Updated to 2024 by James Rowley KC, which had a new chapter in 2023 discussing the issues.

National Joint Council Payscales – Spinal Point 8 / Spinal Point 2 from April 2019

Year	Time of day	Hourly rate £	Hours pw	Cost pw £	Divided by hours pw	Aggregate rate	Day (9am to 8pm) aggregate rate (i.e. inc. w/ends)
Apr 1998 to Mar 1999	Basic Evening Saturday Sunday	£4.98 £6.22 £7.47 £9.96	55 65 24 24	£273.90 £404.30 £179.28 £239.04	168	£6.53	£6.05
Apr 1999 to Mar 2000	Basic Evening Saturday Sunday	£5.13 £6.41 £7.69 £10.26	55 65 24 24	£282.15 £416.65 £184.56 £246.24	168	£6.72	£6.23
Apr 2000 to Mar 2001	Basic Evening Saturday Sunday	£5.29 £6.61 £7.93 £10.58	55 65 24 24	£290.95 £429.65 £190.32 £253.92	168	£6.93	£6.42
Apr 2001 to Mar 2002	Basic Evening Saturday Sunday	£5.49 £6.86 £8.23 £10.97	55 65 24 24	£301.95 £455.90 £197.52 £263.28	168	£7.19	£6.66
Apr 2002 to Sep 2002	Basic Evening Saturday Sunday	£5.65 £7.06 £8.47 £11.30	55 65 24 24	£310.75 £458.90 £203.28 £271.20	168	£7.41	£6.86
Oct 2002 to Mar 2003	Basic Evening Saturday Sunday	£5.71 £7.14 £8.56 £11.42	55 65 24 24	£314.05 £464.10 £205.44 £274.08	168	£7.49	£6.93
Apr 2003 to Mar 2004	Basic Evening Saturday Sunday	£5.90 £7.37 £8.85 £11.80	55 65 24 24	£324.50 £479.05 £212.40 £283.20	168	£7.73	£7.16
Apr 2004 to Mar 2005	Basic Evening Saturday Sunday	£6.06 £7.57 £9.09 £12.12	55 65 24 24	£333.30 £492.05 £218.16 £290.88	168	£7.94	£7.36
Apr 2005 to Mar 2006	Basic Evening Saturday Sunday	£6.24 £7.80 £9.36 £12.48	55 65 24 24	£343.20 £507.00 £224.64 £299.52	168	£8.18	£7.58
Apr 2006 to Mar 2007	Basic Evening Saturday Sunday	£6.43 £8.04 £9.65 £12.86	55 65 24 24	£353.65 £522.60 £231.60 £308.64	168	£8.43	£7.81
Apr 2007 to Mar 2008	Basic Evening Saturday Sunday	£6.59 £8.24 £9.88 £13.18	55 65 24 24	£362.45 £535.60 £237.12 £316.32	168	£8.64	£8.00
Apr 2008 to Mar 2009	Basic Evening Saturday Sunday	£6.75 £8.44 £10.13 £13.50	55 65 24 24	£371.25 £548.60 £243.12 £324.00	168	£8.85	£8.20
Apr 2009 to Mar 2012	Basic Evening Saturday Sunday	£6.85 £8.56 £10.28 £13.70	55 65 24 24	£376.75 £556.40 £246.72 £328.80	168	£8.98	£8.32

Year *NB Change to day hours & evening enhancement*	**Time of day**	**Hourly rate £**	**Hours pw**	**Cost pw £**	**Divided by hours pw**	**Aggregate rate**	**Day (6am to 8pm) aggregate rate (i.e. inc. w/ends)**
April 2012 to March 2013	Basic Evening Saturday Sunday	6.85 9.13 10.28 13.70	70 50 24 24	479.50 456.50 246.72 328.80	168	9.00	8.32
April 2013 to Dec 2014	Basic Evening Saturday Sunday	£6.90 £9.20 £10.35 £13.80	70 50 24 24	£483.00 £460.00 £248.40 £331.20	168	£9.06	£8.38
Jan 2015 to 31 Mar 2016	Basic Evening Saturday Sunday	£7.19 £9.59 £10.79 £14.38	70 50 24 24	£503.30 £479.50 £258.96 £345.12	168	£9.45	£8.73
April 2016 to 31 Mar 2017	Basic Evening Saturday Sunday	£7.66 £10.21 £11.49 £15.32	70 50 24 24	£536.20 £510.50 £275.76 £367.68	168	£10.06	£9.30
April 2017 to 31 Mar 2018	Basic Evening Saturday Sunday	£7.90 £10.53 £11.85 £15.80	70 50 24 24	£553.00 £526.50 £284.40 £379.20	168	£10.38	£9.59
April 2018 to 31 Mar 2019	Basic Evening Saturday Sunday	£8.62 £11.49 £12.93 £17.24	70 50 24 24	£603.40 £574.50 £310.32 £413.76	168	£11.32	£10.47
April 2019 to 31 Mar 2020 **NB NOW SPINAL POINT 2**	Basic Evening Saturday Sunday	£9.18 £12.24 £13.77 £18.36	70 50 24 24	£642.60 £612.00 £330.48 £440.64	168	£12.06	£11.15
April 2020 to 31 March 2021	Basic Evening Saturday Sunday	9.43 12.57 14.15 18.86	70 50 24 24	660.10 628.50 339.60 452.64	168	12.39	11.45
April 2021 to 31 March 2022	Basic Evening Saturday Sunday	9.60 12.80 14.40 19.20	70 50 24 24	672.00 640.00 345.60 460.80	168	12.61	11.66
April 2022 to 31 March 2023	*Basic* *Evening* *Saturday* *Sunday*	10.60 14.13 15.90 21.20	70 50 24 24	742.00 706.50 381.60 508.80	168	13.92	12.87
April 2023 to 31 March 2024	*Basic* *Evening* *Saturday* *Sunday*	11.59 15.45 17.39 23.18	70 50 24 24	811.30 772.50 417.36 556.32	168	15.22	14.07
April 2024 to 31 March 2025 NOT DECIDED	*Basic* *Evening* *Saturday* *Sunday*	11.59 15.45 17.39 23.18	70 50 24 24		168	15.22	14.07

National Joint Council for Local Government Services

The hourly rate is calculated by dividing the annual salary by 52.143 (which is 365 days divided by 7) and then divided by 37 hours (the standard working week in the National Agreement Green Book). (10/04/2018, Letter to Chief Executives in England, Wales & N Ireland, Re 2018 and 2019 Payscales and Allowances.)

Bank holiday pay is not incorporated into the above as the LGA provision is for staff to be paid at the normal rate for the period in question and to take either a half or full day time off in lieu, according to time worked. Specific calculation is therefore difficult and is likely to make minimal difference at 0.03 per cent overall.

Source for the above rates: National Joint Council for Local Government Services

Year commencing April 2023/24

The National Joint Council pay scales have been updated to 31 March 2024. An award of 9.42% was agreed.

Year commencing April 2024/25

The National Joint Council Payscales have been updated to 31 March 2024.

Negotiations remain ongoing in respect of the Payscales for 2024/25. The NJC claim for 2024–25 has been submitted by the Joint Trade Union Side (comprising UNISON, GMB and UNITE) for an increase of £3,000 or 10% (whichever is the greater).

The rising cost of future care provision

As a combined consequence of Brexit, the Covid-19 Pandemic and the cost of living crisis, there has been an unprecedented shortage of carers and commercial care costs have significantly increased in many geographical areas throughout the UK.

These costs have been driven by the increasing demand for care due to the ageing population at a time when the care sector faces its highest turnover rates, coupled with poor staff retention issues. This has been further fueled by the increased difficulty in recruiting and retaining EU nationals, who prior to Brexit filled many of these care worker roles.

In February 2022, the British Association of Brain Injury and Complex Case Management (BABICM) published the results of their "Perfect Storm" survey which confirmed that over 90 per cent of case managers had had difficulties recruiting staff. There were reports of carers seeking significant increases in rates and the payment of extortionate fees in desperation to get cover for unfilled shifts. It is unknown how long these conditions will continue, however, at the time of going to press there is no sign that the problems are abating; accordingly, where possible, claimants may wish to consider seeking periodical payments for future care and case management so that the costs keep pace with inflation.

K2: Nannies, cleaners and school fees

The death or incapacity of a spouse frequently involves incurring the costs of a nanny or a housekeeper or of sending a child to boarding school so that the surviving parent can continue working. Also, with some employments, typically when they involve overseas postings or frequent moves, school fees are part of the remuneration and will be lost if the employee dies or is disabled from that particular employment.

Nannies

	Live-out	
	Weekly gross	**Annual gross**
Central London	£889	£46,228
Outer London/Home Counties	£847	£44,018
Other areas	£776	£40,326

The figures are derived from the 2023/24 survey by *Nannytax*. During the pandemic lockdowns some nannies switched temporarily to a Live-in role; their salaries will not be representative of the usual terms for Live-in nannies. Nannytax has therefore not published updated figures for Live-in nannies since then. The total cost to the client will be more than the gross wage as it is necessary to pay for holidays, sickness, employer's national insurance contribution, agency fees and so on. (See the discussion in the notes to Table K1: Care and attendance.)

Cleaners

The services of cleaners in London are currently (May 2024) advertised at the following rates. These are commonly for three or more hours a week: one-off visits usually cost more.

Housekeep	£18.50 per hour	(Minimum visit: two hours)
Amy Cleaning	£16.00 per hour	(Varies. The cleaner is paid separately, avoiding VAT; there is also an agency fee).
Happy House Cleaning	£19.00 per hour	

School fees

Annual school fees for a three-term year are as follows.

Public school		**Independent Schools Council (average)**	
Boarders (Upper school)	£52,488	Boarder	£42,459
Day pupils (Upper school)	£36,873	Day pupil (boarding school)	£24,861
Day pupils (Under school or preparatory school)	£26,523	Day pupil (day school)	£19,089
		Day pupil (day junior school)	£16,503

Notes:

1. Fees for pupils entering in the sixth form may be higher.
2. Fees for weekly as opposed to full-time boarders may be lower.

The information has been obtained from the websites of Nannytax, Happy House Cleaning, Housekeep, Amy Cleaning, Westminster School, and the Independent Schools Council.

K3: DIY, gardening and housekeeping

1. The sort of injury which limits one's capacity to earn will often also limit one's capacity to do jobs around the house. Depending on the kind of injury and the claimant's pre-accident talents, these may range from the skilled, such as plumbing or electrical work, to the mundane, such as washing up and putting out the bins.

2. It is well established that these skills have a monetary value[1] and that "the loss of ability to do work in the home is a recoverable head of damages and includes 'services' such as general housekeeping, gardening and maintenance".[2]

3. The Court of Appeal decided in *Daly v General Steam Navigation Co (The Dragon)*[3] that *special* damages for past loss must comprise actual expenditure (or presumably the value of gratuitous care actually provided by others). Absent actual expenditure or gratuitous care, loss of capacity before trial is reflected in enhanced *general* damages. With regard to future loss, however, the court held that the claimant need not prove an actual intention to employ replacement services (paid or unpaid). Bridge LJ said:

   "... it seems to me that it was entirely reasonable and entirely in accordance with principle in assessing damages, to say that the estimated cost of employing labour for that time, ..., was the proper measure of her damages under this heading. It is really quite immaterial, in my judgment, whether ... the plaintiff chooses to alleviate her own housekeeping burden ... by employing the labour which has been taken as the estimate on which damages have been awarded, or whether she continues to struggle with the housekeeping on her own and to spend the damages which have been awarded to her on other luxuries which she would otherwise be unable to afford."

4. One difficulty is finding an appropriate rate and working out a number of hours per week which these tasks take. People in rented accommodation may do little maintenance, and older people often, though not invariably, find their appetite for such tasks diminishes. The claimant will need evidence that he or she would be carrying out the work personally if it had not been for the injury. The evidence may include (in addition to witness statements) photographs, estimates from those providing such services locally (for labour only), and reports from a local surveyor and/or an independent agency. There are however differences of judicial opinion as to the utility of expert evidence: some judges accept it[4], whilst Mackay J in *Fleet v Fleet*[5] derived his own figure from experience, saying, "It would be dismal if experts had to be called to say how much it costs to mow a lawn or paint a room."

5. The courts have made a range of awards, sometimes using a multiplier/multiplicand approach and sometimes making a global award.[6] Cases in Kemp & Kemp show (adjusted for inflation to 2024) multiplicands for DIY and gardening of the order of £1,850–£3,000, and global awards of some £22,500–£30,500.

[1] *Phipps v Brooks Dry Cleaning Services Ltd* [1996] P.I.Q.R. Q100.
[2] "Damages for Personal Injury: Medical, Nursing and Other Expenses", Law Commission, Law Com. No.262 (1999), para.2.34.
[3] [1981] 1 W.L.R. 120, 127.
[4] e.g. *Smith v East & North Hertfordshire Hospitals NHS Trust [2008] EWHC 2234 (QB).*
[5] [2009] EWHC 3166 (QB).
[6] See the analysis in Kemp & Kemp Vol.1, Ch.17.

Handyman, gardening and housekeeping services are being advertised in May 2024 at the following rates:

	London	Home Counties	Rest of country
Handymen per hour	£79 per hour	£39 per hour	£30 per hour
Handymen half-day	£256 per half-day	£149 per half-day	£90 per half-day
Handymen day rates	£456 per day	£282 per day	£170 per day
Gardening— (for team of two)	£68 per hour	£79 per hour	£51 per hour
Cleaning and housekeeping	£18 per hour	£17.50 per hour	£14 per hour

Notes to the table:

- The figure in the table is generally the median.
- Charges for handymen and gardeners vary with the type of work. Plumbing and electrical work is usually dearer than decorating and putting up shelves. Garden design and planting may cost more than garden maintenance such as mowing the lawn and trimming the hedge.
- There is often a minimum period or a supplemental charge for the first hour.
- Charges are generally higher in the evenings and at weekends.
- Some firms prefer to quote for a specified job and do not advertise an hourly rate.
- Some firms provide services at a reduced rate for pensioners and those on a low income. These are not reflected in the table.

K4: Hospital self-pay (uninsured) charges

The following figures are inclusive of hospital charges and surgeons' and anaesthetists' fees. The charges are approximate, as certain factors affecting cost, such as length of stay or prosthesis used, vary from patient to patient.

	London average	Outside London average
Arthroscopy (hip)	7,600	7,600
Arthroscopy (knee)	4,500	4,400
Arthroscopy (shoulder)	6,125	5,900
Arthroscopy (ankle)	6,500	6,400
Carpal tunnel release	2,100	2,100
Cataract removal	2,900	2,800
Circumcision	2,800	2,500
Colonoscopy	2,300	2,200
Cruciate knee ligament repair	7,700	7,400
CT scan	550	540
Cystoscopy	2,100	2,200
Epidural injection	1,800	1,800
Facet joint injection	2,500	2,500
Gall bladder removal—laparoscopic	7,175	6,900
Gastric banding	8,000	7,800
Gastric balloon insertion	5,400	5,300
Gastric bypass	12,500	11,600
Gastroscopy	1,900	1,900
Grommets insertion	3,200	2,800
Haemorrhoids removal	3,000	3,000
Hernia repair (inguinal)	3,200	3,400
Herniated disc removal	8,200	8,000
Hip replacement—total	13,700	13,400
Hip replacement—revision	20,000	19,250
Hysterectomy	8,800	8,000
Hysteroscopy	2,200	2,700
Knee replacement—total	14,900	14,000
Knee replacement—revision	23,175	23,175
Laparoscopy	4,000	4,000
MRI Scan	570	570
Prostate resection	6,900	6,900
Rotator Cuff Repair	7,000	6,600
Flexible Sigmoidoscopy	1,800	1,700
Vaginal prolapse repair	6,200	5,800
Varicose vein ablation (one leg)	3,200	3,200
Vasectomy	1,600	1,600
Vasectomy reversal	4,000	3,800

These charges are drawn from around the country. Charges vary from hospital to hospital and between different areas of the country. They are generally higher in London than elsewhere. All figures are correct as of April 2024.

K5: NHS charges

NHS prescriptions (from 1 May 2024)

Charge per prescribed item		£9.90
Prescription prepayment certificate:	three months	£32.05
	12 months	£114.50

For items dispensed in combination (duo) packs, there is a charge for each different drug in the pack.

NHS dental treatment (from 1 April 2024)

If patients are not exempt from charges, they should pay one of the following rates for each course of treatment they receive:

Course of treatment	Cost	Scope
Band 1	£26.80	This covers an examination, diagnosis and advice. If necessary, it also includes X-rays, a scale and polish (if clinically needed), and planning for further treatment.
Band 2	£73.50	This covers all treatment included in Band 1, plus additional treatment, such as fillings, root canal treatment and removing teeth (extractions).
Band 3	£319.10	This covers all treatment included in Bands 1 and 2, plus more complex procedures, such as crowns, dentures and bridges.

Notes

1. These are the only charges for NHS dental treatment.
2. A patient only has to pay one charge for each course of treatment, even if it takes more than one visit to the dentist to finish it.
3. If the patient needs more treatment within the same or lower charge band (e.g. an additional filling), within two months of completing a course of treatment, there is no extra charge.
4. There is no charge for repairing dentures or for having stitches removed or if your dentist has to stop blood loss.
5. Children under 19, and many adults, do not have to pay NHS charges. (See "Help with Health Costs", which can be found on NHS website: *https://www.nhs.uk/nhs-services/help-with-healthcosts/*).

K6: The 2015 Rehabilitation Code

(Code of Best Practice on Rehabilitation, Early Intervention and Medical Treatment in Personal Injury Claims)

INTRODUCTION

The Code promotes the collaborative use of rehabilitation and early intervention in the compensation process. It is reviewed from time to time in response to feedback from those who use it, taking into account the changing legal and medical landscape.

The Code's purpose is to help the injured claimant make the best and quickest possible medical, social vocational and psychological recovery. This means ensuring that his or her need for rehabilitation is assessed and addressed as a priority and that the process is pursued on a collaborative basis. With this in mind, the claimant solicitor should always ensure that the compensator receives the earliest possible notification of the claim and its circumstances whenever rehabilitation may be beneficial.

Although the objectives of the Code apply whatever the clinical and social needs of the claimant, the best way to achieve them will vary depending on the nature of the injury and the claimant's circumstances. The Code recognises that the dynamics of lesser-injury cases are different to those further up the scale. A separate process is set out for claims below £25,000 (in line with the Civil Procedure Rules definition of low value). Separate provision is also made for soft tissue injury cases as defined in paragraph 1.1(16A) of the Pre-Action Protocol for Low Value Personal Injury Claims in Road Traffic Accidents.

It is important to stress, however that even low value injuries can be life-changing for some people. The projected monetary value of a claim is only a guide to the rehabilitation needs of the injured person. Each case should be taken on its individual merits and the guidelines for higher- value injuries will sometimes be more appropriate for those in the lowest category.

Sections 1 to 3 set out the guiding principles and the obligations of the various parties, and apply to all types of injury. After that, the sections diverge significantly depending on the size of claim.

Although the Code deals mainly with the Immediate Needs Assessment it encourages all parties to adopt the same principles and collaborative approach right up until the case is concluded. In doing so it does not stipulate a detailed process. Rather, it assumes that the parties will have established the collaborative working relationships that render a prescriptive document unnecessary.

Ten 'markers' that can affect the rehabilitation assessment, and therefore the treatment are to be found in the Glossary at the end of the Code. They should be considered in all cases.

With the more serious injuries, it is envisaged that Case Managers will have an essential role to play in assessing the claimant's needs and then overseeing treatment. This Code should be read in conjunction with the Guide for Case Managers and those who Commission them published separately.

1. ROLE OF THE CODE

1.1 The purpose of the personal injury claims process is to restore the individual as much as possible to the position they were in before the accident. The Code provides a framework for the claimant solicitor and compensator to work together to ensure that the claimant's health, quality of life, independence and ability to work are restored before, or simultaneously with, the process of assessing compensation.

1.2 Although the Code is recognised by the relevant CPR Pre-Action Protocols, achieving the aims are more important than strict adherence to its terms. Therefore it is open to the parties to agree an alternative framework to achieve the early rehabilitation of the claimant.

1.3 Where there is no agreement on liability the parties may still agree to use the Code. The health and economic benefits of proceeding with rehabilitation at an early stage, regardless of agreement on liability may be especially strong in catastrophic and other severe cases. Compensators should consider from the outset whether there is a possibility or likelihood of at least partial admission later on in the process so as not to compromise the prospects for rehabilitation.

1.4 In this Code, the expression "the compensator" includes any person acting on behalf of the compensator. "Claimant solicitor" includes any legal representative acting on behalf of the claimant. "Case Manager" means a suitably qualified rehabilitation case manager.

2. THE CLAIMANT SOLICITOR

2.1 The claimant solicitor's obligation to act in the best interests of their client extends beyond securing reasonable financial compensation vital as that may be. Their duty also includes considering as soon as practicable, whether additional medical or rehabilitative intervention would improve the claimant's present and/or longer-term physical and mental well-being. In doing so, there should be full consultation with the claimant and/or their family and any treating practitioner where doing so is proportionate and reasonable. This duty continues throughout the life of the case but is most important in the early stages.

2.2 It is the duty of a claimant solicitor to have an initial discussion with the claimant and/or their family to identify:

1) Whether there is an immediate need for aids, adaptations, adjustments to employment to enable the claimant to perform their existing job obtain a suitable alternative role with the same employer or retrain for new employment. They should, where practical and proportionate, work with the claimant's employers to ensure that the position is kept open for them as long as possible.
2) The need to alleviate any problems related to their injuries.

2.3 The claimant solicitor should then communicate these needs to the compensator by telephone or email, together with all other relevant information, as soon as practicable. It is the intention of this Code that both parties will work to address all rehabilitation needs on a collaborative basis.

2.4 The compensator will need to receive from the claimant solicitor sufficient information to make a well-informed decision about the need for rehabilitation assistance including detailed and adequate information on the functional impact of the claimant's injuries. There is no requirement for an expert report at this early stage. The information should, however include the nature and extent of any likely continuing disability and any suggestions that may have already been made concerning rehabilitation and/or early intervention. It should be communicated within 21 days of becoming aware of those injuries or needs once the compensator is known.

2.5 Upon receiving a rehabilitation suggestion from the compensator, the claimant solicitor should discuss it with the claimant and/or their family as soon as practical and reply within 21 days.

2.6 Many cases will be considered under this Code before medical evidence has actually been commissioned or obtained. It is important in these situations that rehabilitation steps are not undertaken that might conflict with the recommendations of treating clinical teams. It is equally important that unnecessary delay is avoided in implementing steps that could make a material difference to the injured person or their family. Early engagement with the compensator is crucial to discuss such issues.

2.7 Whilst generally in catastrophic and other particularly severe cases, it is recommended that an appropriately qualified Case Manager should be appointed before any rehabilitation commences, this may not always be possible even though it should be a priority. Methods of selecting Case Managers are described in paragraphs 7.3 and 7.4. The aim when appointing a Case Manager should be to ensure that any proposed rehabilitation plan they recommend is appropriate and that the goals set are specific and attainable. The Case Manager should before undertaking an Immediate Needs Assessment (INA) as part of the claims process, make every attempt to liaise with NHS clinicians and others involved in the claimant's treatment, and to work collaboratively with them, provided this does not unduly delay the process. If possible, they should obtain the claimant's rehabilitation prescription discharge summary or similar, including any A&E records and/or treating consultant's report and medical records.

3. THE COMPENSATOR

3.1 It is the duty of the compensator from the earliest practicable stage, to consider whether the claimant would benefit from additional medical or rehabilitative treatment. This duty continues throughout the life of the case but is most important in the early stages.

3.2 If the claimant may have rehabilitation needs, the compensator should contact the claimant solicitor as soon as practicable to seek to work collaboratively on addressing those needs. As set out in paragraph 2.5, the claimant solicitor should respond within 21 days.

3.3 Where a request to consider rehabilitation has been communicated by the claimant solicitor, the compensator should respond within 21 days, or earlier if possible, either confirming their agreement or giving reasons for rejecting the request.

3.4 Nothing in this Code modifies the obligations of the compensator under the Protocols to investigate claims rapidly and, in any event within the relevant liability response period.

LOWER-VALUE INJURIES

4. THE ASSESSMENT PROCESS—LOWER-VALUE INJURIES

4.1 Different considerations apply for soft-tissue injury cases compared to other lower-value cases of £25,000 or below. In all cases, the claimant's solicitor should consider, with the claimant and/or the claimant's family, whether there is a need for early rehabilitation. The results of that discussion should be recorded in section C of the electronic Claims Notification Form, which will be transmitted through the Ministry of Justice Claims Portal to commence the claim. That form requires details of any professional treatment recommendations, treatment already received (including name of provider) and ongoing rehabilitation needs.

4.2 For lower-value injuries generally this might involve physiotherapy diagnostics and consultant follow-up, psychological intervention or other services to alleviate problems caused by the injury. In soft-tissue injury cases, in particular, it is understood that there is not always necessarily a requirement for a rehabilitation intervention. It is considered likely that, where there is an initial intervention it will focus on treating any physical need, for example through physiotherapy.

In all cases, the claimant solicitor should communicate with the compensator as soon as practical about any rehabilitation needs, preferably by electronic means. The mechanism of completion and transmission of the Claims Notification Form should facilitate this process and should take place before any significant treatment has been commenced, subject always to any overriding medical need for urgent treatment.

4.3 Nothing in this Code alters the legal principles that:

1. Until there has been a liability admission by a compensator (through the Compensator's Response in the Claims Portal), the claimant can have no certainty about the prospect of recovery of any treatment sums incurred.
2. Until the compensator has accepted a treatment regime in which the number and price of sessions have been agreed, the level of recovery of any such sums will always be a matter for negotiation (most likely through exchange of offers in the portal system) unless the subject of a Court order.
3. Where a claimant has decided not to take up a form of treatment that is readily available in favour of a more expensive option the reasonableness of that decision may be a factor that is taken into account on the assessment of damages.

4.4 Unless there is a medico-legal report containing full recommendations for rehabilitation, which both parties are happy to adopt, an initial Triage Report (TR) should be obtained to establish the type of treatment needed. In most cases, the Triage Report will be the only report required Where both the claimant's solicitor and the compensator agree that further reports are required, the assessment process is likely to have two further stages:

(i) A subsequent Assessment Report (AR) provided by the healthcare professional who is actually treating the claimant;
(ii) A Discharge Report (DR) from the treating healthcare professional to summarise the treatment provided.

It is, however, understood within the Code that a treatment discharge summary should routinely be included within the claimant's treatment records.

It is always possible for the Assessment Report (AR) and Discharge Report (DR) to be combined into one document.

4.5 The Triage Report (TR) assessment should be undertaken by an appropriately qualified and experienced person who is subject to appropriate clinical governance structures Guidance on this may be obtained by reading the British Standards Institute standard PAS 150 or the UKRC Standards. It is permissible under the Code that the assessor providing the Triage Report could also be appointed to implement the recommendations.

4.6 The person or organisation that prepares the Triage and, if appropriate, Assessment and Discharge Reports and/or undertakes treatment should, save in exceptional circumstances, be entirely independent of the person or organisation that provided any medico-legal report to the claimant. In soft-tissue injury cases, the parties are referred to Part 4529I of the Civil Procedure Rules.

4.7 The Triage and the preparation of any subsequent Assessment and Discharge Report and/or the provision of any treatment may be carried out or provided by a person or organisation having a direct or indirect business connection with the solicitor or compensator only if the other party agrees. The solicitor or compensator will be expected to reveal to the other party the existence and nature of such a business connection before instructing the connected organisation.

4.8 The assessment agency will be asked to carry out the Triage Report in a way that is appropriate to the needs of the case, which will in most cases be a telephone interview within seven days of the referral being received by the agency. It is expected that the TR will be very simple, usually just an email.

4.9 In all cases, the TR should be published simultaneously or made available immediately by the instructing party to the other side This applies also to treatment reports (AR and DR) where the parties have agreed that they are required Both parties will have the right to raise questions on the report(s), disclosing such correspondence to the other party.

4.10 It is recognised that, for the Triage Report to be of benefit to the parties, it should be prepared and used wholly outside the litigation process Neither side can rely on the report in any subsequent litigation unless both parties agree in writing. Likewise, any notes, correspondence or documents created in connection with the triage assessment process will not be disclosed in any litigation. Anyone involved in preparing the Triage Report or in the assessment process shall not be a compellable witness at court This principle is also set out in the Protocols.

4.11 The compensator will usually only consider rehabilitation that deals with the effects of the injuries that have been caused in the relevant accident. They will not normally fund treatment for other conditions that do not directly relate to the accident unless these conditions have been exacerbated by it or will impede recovery.

5. THE REPORTS—LOWER-VALUE INJURIES

5.1 It is expected under the Code that all treatment reporting described in this section will be concise and proportionate to the severity of the injuries and likely value of the claim.

5.2 The Triage Report should consider, where relevant, the ten 'markers' identified at the end of this Code and will normally cover the following headings:

1. The injuries sustained by the claimant;
2. The current impact on their activities of daily living, their domestic circumstances and, where relevant, their employment;
3. Any other relevant medical conditions not arising from the accident;
4. The past provision and current availability of treatment to the claimant via the NHS, their employer or health insurance schemes;
5. The type of intervention or treatment recommended;
6. The likely cost and duration of treatment;
7. The expected outcome of such intervention or treatment.

5.3 The Triage Report will not provide a prognosis or a diagnosis.

5.4 The assessment reports (TR, or any AR or DR) should not deal with issues relating to legal liability and should therefore not contain a detailed account of the accident circumstances, though they should enable the parties to understand the mechanism by which the injury occurred.

5.5 Where agreed as needed, any Assessment Report (AR) will normally have the following minimum headings:

1. Nature, symptoms and severity of injury(ies);
2. Relevance of any pre-existing conditions or injuries;
3. Primary rehabilitation goal and anticipated outcome;
4. Expected duration, number, type and length of treatment sessions;
5. Impact of injuries upon work and or activities of daily living and barriers to recovery and return to work.

5.6 Where agreed as needed, such as where a treatment discharge summary is considered inadequate, any Discharge Report (DR) will normally have the following minimum headings:

1. Current nature, symptoms and severity of injury(ies);
2. Whether the primary rehabilitation goal has been attained;
3. Number, type and length of treatment sessions/appointments attended or missed/DNAs (Did Not Attend);
4. Current impact of injuries on work or activities of daily living;
5. Whether the claimant has achieved, as far as possible, a full functional recovery;
6. Whether additional treatment is required to address the claimant's symptoms.

In cases where no AR or DR has been agreed, it is expected that the notes and discharge summary of the treatment provider will contain the necessary information.

5.7 The provision as to the report being outside the litigation process is limited to the Triage Report and any notes or correspondence relating to it Any notes and reports created during the subsequent treatment process will be covered by the usual principle in relation to disclosure of documents and medical records relating to the claimant.

5.8 The compensator will normally pay for the TR within 28 days of receipt Where the claimant's solicitor and the compensator have agreed that such reports are required, the compensator will also pay for any AR and DR within 28 days of receipt. In either case, the compensator may challenge bills that they believe to be excessive or disproportionate.

5.9 The reporting agency should ensure that all invoices are within reasonable market rates, are clear and provide the following detail:

1. Type of treatment provided, eg. telephonic CBT, face-to-face physiotherapy;
2. Dates of treatments/sessions attended and DNAs of treatment sessions;
3. Total number of treatments delivered and whether those treatments were provided remotely or in person;
4. Total cost and whether this is for treatment provided or an estimate of future cost.

5.10 Where any treatment has been organised prior to notification to or approval by the compensator, any invoice submitted to the compensator will also need to be accompanied by a discharge summary recording treatment outcome in addition to the information contained in paragraph 5.9 The need for the discharge summary to be included in the treatment records is covered in paragraph 44.

5.11 The parties should continue to work together to ensure that the recommended rehabilitation proceeds smoothly and that any further rehabilitation needs continue to be assessed.

6. RECOMMENDATIONS—LOWER-VALUE INJURIES

6.1 The compensator will be under a duty to consider the recommendations made and the extent to which funds will be made available to implement the recommendations. The claimant will be under no obligation to undergo intervention, medical or investigation treatment Where intervention treatment has taken place, the compensator will not be required to pay for treatment that is unreasonable in nature, content or cost.

6.2 The compensator should provide a response to the claimant's solicitor within15 business days from the date when the TR is disclosed. If the Insurer's Response Form is transmitted via the portal earlier than 15 business days from receipt of the CNF and the TR, the response should be included in the Response Form. The response should include: (i) the extent to which the recommendations have been accepted and rehabilitation treatment will be funded; (ii) justifications for any refusal to meet the cost of recommended rehabilitation and (if appropriate) alternative recommendations. As stated in paragraph 4.3, the claimant may start treatment without waiting for the compensator's response, but at their own risk as to recovering the cost.

6.3 The compensator agrees that, in any legal proceedings connected with the claim, they will not dispute the reasonableness or costs of the treatment they have funded, provided the claimant has undertaken the treatment and it has been expressly agreed and/or the treatment provider has been jointly instructed. If the claim later fails, is discontinued or contributory negligence is an issue, it is not within the Code to seek to recover such funding from the claimant unless it can be proven that there has been fraud/fundamental dishonesty.

6.4 Following on from implementation of the assessment process, the parties should consider and agree at the earliest opportunity a process for ensuring that the ongoing rehabilitation needs of the claimant are met in a collaborative manner.

MEDIUM, SEVERE AND CATASTROPHIC INJURIES

7. THE ASSESSMENT PROCESS—MEDIUM, SEVERE AND CATASTROPHIC INJURIES

7.1 The need for and type of rehabilitation assistance will be considered by means of an Immediate Needs Assessment (INA) carried out by a Case Manager or appropriate rehabilitation professional, eg. an NHS Rehabilitation Consultant. (For further information about Case Managers, refer to the Glossary and The Guide for Case Managers and those who Commission them, published separately).

7.2 The Case Manager must be professionally and suitably qualified, experienced and skilled to carry out the task, and they must comply with appropriate clinical governance. With the most severe life-changing injuries, a Case Manager should normally be registered with a professional body appropriate to the severity of the claimant's injuries. The individual or organisation should not, save in exceptional circumstances, have provided a medico-legal report to the claimant nor be associated with any person or organisation that has done so.

7.3 The claimant solicitor and the compensator should have discussions at the outset to agree the person or organisation to conduct the INA, as well as topics to include in the letter of instruction. The INA should go ahead whether or not the claimant is still being treated by NHS physicians, who should nonetheless be consulted about their recommendations for short-term and longer-term rehabilitation. A fundamental part of the Case Manager's role is to make immediate contact with the treating clinical lead to assess whether any proposed rehabilitation plan is appropriate.

7.4. The parties are encouraged to try to agree the selection of an appropriately qualified independent Case Manager best suited to the claimant's needs to undertake the INA The parties should then endeavour to agree the method of instruction and how the referral will be made. When considering options with the claimant, a joint referral to the chosen Case Manager may maximise the benefits of collaborative working Any option chosen by the parties is subject to the claimant's agreement In all situations, the parties should seek to agree early implementation of reasonable recommendations and secure funding. In circumstances where trust has been built, it is recommended that the parties agree to retain the Case Manager to co-ordinate the implementation of the agreed rehabilitation plan.

7.5 With catastrophic injuries, it is especially important to achieve good early communication between the parties and an agreement to share information that could aid recovery. This will normally involve telephone or face-to-face meetings to discuss what is already known, and to plan how to gain further information on the claimant's health, vocational and social requirements The fact that the claimant may be an NHS in-patient should not be a barrier to carrying out an INA.

7.6 No solicitor or compensator may insist on the INA being carried out by a particular person or organisation if the other party raises a reasonable objection within 21 days of the nomination. Where alternative providers are offered, the claimant and/or their family should be personally informed of the options and the associated benefits and costs of each option.

7.7 Objections to a particular person or organisation should include possible remedies such as additional information requirements or alternative solutions. If the discussion is not resolved within 21 days, responsibility for commissioning the provider lies ultimately with the claimant as long as they can demonstrate that full and timely co-operation has been provided.

7.8 A rehabilitation provider's overriding duty is to the claimant Their relationship with the claimant is therapeutic, and they should act totally independently of the instructing party.

7.9 The assessment may be carried out by a person or organisation having a direct or indirect business connection with the solicitor or compensator only if the other party agrees The solicitor and compensator must always reveal any business connection at the earliest opportunity.

7.10 The assessment process should provide information and analysis as to the rehabilitation assistance that would maximise recovery and mitigate the loss. Further assessments of rehabilitation needs may be required as the claimant recovers.

7.11 The compensator will usually only consider rehabilitation that deals with the effects of injuries for which they are liable. Treatment for other conditions will not normally be included unless it is agreed that they have been exacerbated by the accident or are impeding the claimant's recovery.

8. THE IMMEDIATE NEEDS ASSESSMENT (INA) REPORT—MEDIUM, SEVERE AND CATASTROPHIC INJURIES

8.1 The Case Manager will be asked to carry out the INA in a way appropriate to the case, taking into account the importance of acting promptly. This may include, by prior appointment, a telephone interview. In more complex and catastrophic cases, a face-to-face discussion with the claimant is likely.

8.2 As well as the ten 'markers' identified in the Glossary at the end of this Code, the INA should consider the following points, provided doing so does not unduly delay the process:

a. The physical and psychological injuries sustained by the claimant and the subsequent care received or planned;
b. The symptoms, disability/incapacity arising from those injuries. Where relevant to the overall picture of the claimant's rehabilitation needs, any other medical conditions not arising from the accident should also be separately noted;
c. The availability or planned delivery of interventions or treatment via the NHS, their employer or health insurance schemes;
d. Any impact upon the claimant's domestic and social circumstances, including mobility, accommodation and employment, and whether therapies such as gym training or swimming would be beneficial;
e. The injuries/disability for which early intervention or early rehabilitation is suggested;

f. The type of clinical intervention or treatment required in both the short and medium term, and its rationale;
g. The likely cost and duration of recommended interventions or treatment, their goals and duration, with anticipated outcomes;
h. The anticipated clinical and return-to-work outcome of such intervention or treatment.

8.3 The INA report will not provide a medical prognosis or diagnosis, but should include any clinically justifiable recommendations for further medical investigation, compliant with NICE guidelines and, where possible, aligned to the NHS Rehabilitation prescription, discharge report or similar. Where recommendations are in addition to or deviate from the NHS recommendations, these should be explained with appropriate justification provided.

8.4 The INA report should not deal with issues relating to legal liability, such as a detailed account of the accident circumstances, though it should enable the parties to understand the mechanism by which the injury occurred.

8.5 The Case Manager will, on completion of the report, send copies to the claimant solicitor and compensator simultaneously. Both parties will have the right to raise questions on the report, disclosing such correspondence to the other party. It is, however, anticipated that the parties will discuss the recommendations and agree the appropriate action to be taken. Subject to the claimant's consent, their GP and/or treating clinical team will also be informed of the INA and its recommendations once funding to proceed has been obtained. In most cases, the INA will be conducted, and the report provided, within 21 days from the date of the letter of referral to the Case Manager.

8.6 For this assessment report to be of benefit to the parties, it should be prepared and used wholly outside the litigation process, unless both parties agree otherwise in writing.

8.7 The report, any correspondence related to it and any notes created by the assessing agency will be deemed to be covered by legal privilege and not disclosed in any proceedings unless the parties agree. The same applies to notes or documents related to the INA, either during or after the report submission. Anyone involved in preparing the report or in the assessment process will not be a compellable witness at court. (This principle is also set out in the Protocols.)

8.8 Any notes and reports created during the subsequent case management process post-INA will be covered by the usual principle in relation to disclosure of documents and medical records relating to the claimant. However, it is open to the parties to agree to extend the provisions of the Code beyond the INA to subsequent reports.

8.9 The compensator will pay for the INA report within 28 days of receipt.

9. RECOMMENDATIONS—MEDIUM, SEVERE AND CATASTROPHIC INJURIES

9.1 When the Immediate Needs Assessment (INA) report is received, the compensator has a duty to consider the recommendations and the extent to which funds are made available to implement them. The compensator is not required to pay for treatment that is unreasonable in nature, content or cost. The claimant will be under no obligation to undergo treatment.

9.2 The compensator should respond to the claimant solicitor within 21 days of receiving the INA report. The response should include: (i) the extent to which it accepts the recommendations and is willing to fund treatment; and (ii) justifications for any refusal, with alternative recommendations.

9.3 The compensator will not dispute the reasonableness or costs of the treatment, as long as the claimant has undertaken the treatment and it was expressly agreed in advance (or the treatment provider had been jointly instructed). Where there is disagreement, general interim payments are recommended to provide continuity of services with an understanding that recovery of such sums is not guaranteed and will always be a matter for negotiation or determination by a court. Where a claimant has decided not to take up a form of treatment that is readily available in favour of a more expensive option, the reasonableness of that decision may be a factor that is taken into account on the assessment of damages. If the claim later fails or is discontinued or contributory negligence is an issue, the compensator will not seek to recover any agreed rehabilitation funding it has already provided unless it can be proven that there has been fraud/fundamental dishonesty.

9.4 Following implementation of the INA, the parties should consider and attempt to agree, as soon as possible, a collaborative process for meeting the claimant's ongoing rehabilitation needs.

9.5 The overriding purpose of the INA should be to assess the claimant's medical and social needs with a view to recommending treatment rather than to obtain information to settle the claim.

GLOSSARY—THE TEN 'MARKERS'

The ten 'markers' referred to in this Code that should be taken into account when assessing an injured person's rehabilitation needs are summarised below:

1. Age (particularly children/elderly);
2. Pre-existing physical and psycho-social comorbidities;
3. Return-to-work/education issues;
4. Dependants living at home;
5. Geographic location;
6. Mental capacity;
7. Activities of daily living in the short-term and long-term;
8. Realistic goals, aspirations, attainments;
9. Fatalities/those who witness major incidence of trauma within the same accident;
10. Length of time post-accident.

September 2015
The working parties that drew up the 2015 Rehabilitation Code included representatives of ABI, APIL, CMSUK, FOIL, IUA, MASS and PIBA. Although it is for the parties involved in personal injury claims to decide when and how to use the Code, it is envisaged that it should become operational from December 1, 2015.

A Summary Version of the Rehabilitation Code*

The 2015 Rehabilitation Code 96 Making a real difference to injured people

The Rehabilitation Code provides an approved framework for injury claims within which claimant representatives and compensators can work together. Whilst the Code is voluntary, the Personal Injury Pre- action Protocol provides that its use should be considered for all types of personal injury claims. The objective is to ensure that injured people receive the rehabilitation they need to restore quality of life and earning capacity as soon as possible and as much as possible. Although the principles are the same throughout, the Code recognises significant differences between the handling of lower value injuries (<£25k) and medium or catastrophic injuries.

* Although this document provides a summary, it should always be read in conjunction with the entire Code.

The important features of the Code are:

1. The claimant is put at the centre of the process.

2. The claimant's lawyer and the compensator work on a collaborative basis to address the claimant's needs, from first early notification of the claim and through early exchange of information.

3. The need for rehabilitation is addressed as a priority. Time-frames are set out in the Code.

4. Rehabilitation needs are assessed by independent professionals with appropriate qualifications, skills and experience.

5. Initial rehabilitation assessments can be conducted by telephone or personal interview, according to the type of case. The resulting report should deal with matters specified in the Code.

6. The parties may consider whether joint instruction of rehabilitation assessor and provider would aid collaborative working and be in the claimant's best interests.

7. The claimant has the ultimate say in choice of case manager, and is not obliged to undergo treatment or intervention that is considered unreasonable. A guide to appointing and working with case managers accompanies this Code, but is not part of it.

8. The case manager should seek proactively to co-operate with treating NHS clinicians.

9. The compensator will pay for any agreed assessment of rehabilitation needs, and must justify a refusal to follow any of the rehabilitation recommendations.

10. Initial assessment (including the Triage Report for lower value injuries) is outside the litigation process.

11. Where rehabilitation has been provided under the Code, the compensator will not seek to recoup its cost if the claim later fails unless fraud or fundamental dishonesty can be proven.

12. The Code recognises that lower value claims (typically < £25k) have different dynamics, and that there will sometimes be a medical need for claimant solicitors to arrange treatment before getting agreement from the compensator. In these circumstances, the compensator is not obliged to pay for treatment that is unnecessary, disproportionate or unduly expensive.

13. In the interests of streamlining the process, most lower value claims will require a Triage Report only.

14. It is the intention that the parties adopt the principles of the Code beyond the Immediate Needs Assessment and throughout the rehabilitation process.

The working parties that drew up the 2015 Rehabilitation Code included representatives of ABI, IUA, APIL, FOIL, MASS, PIBA and CMS UK.

For enquiries, please email deborah.finch@iua.co.uk

Timescales (calendar days unless indicated otherwise)

Claimant solicitor	• Duty of every claimant solicitor to consider the need for rehabilitation from the earliest practicable stage in consultation with the claimant/their family and, where appropriate, treating physicians. • Give the earliest possible notification to compensator of the claim and need for rehabilitation. • Where the need for rehabilitation is identified by the compensator, consider this immediately with the claimant and/or their family.
Compensator	• Shall equally consider and communicate at earliest practicable stage whether the claimant will benefit from rehabilitation. • Where the need for rehabilitation is notified by the claimant solicitor, the compensator will respond within 21 days.
Both parties	• Consider choice of assessor and object to any suggested assessor within 21 days of nomination.
Immediate Needs Assessor	• Assessment to occur within 21 days of referral letter (but see below for smaller injuries). • Provide report simultaneously to parties.
Compensator	• Pay for report within 28 days of receipt. • Respond substantively to recommendations to the claimant solicitor within 21 days of receipt of report.
Lower value injuries (<£25k)	• As above, save that in the interests of speeding up the process, there will sometimes be a medical need for the claimant and/or their solicitor arrange treatment before the compensator has had time to approve it. In these circumstances, the compensator is not obliged to pay for treatment that is unnecessary, disproportionate or unduly expensive. • The claimant solicitor should communicate any rehabilitation needs to the compensator as soon as practical using the Claims Notification Form in the MoJ Portal. • The Triage Report, which will normally form the basis of treatment, should be made available simultaneously to both parties. • The compensator will respond to the report within 15 working days and pay for it within 28 days of receipt.

K7: Serious Injury Guide

The Serious Injury Guide
Last updated 4 May 2023

INTRODUCTION

This best practice Guide is designed to assist with the conduct of personal injury cases involving complex injuries, specifically cases with a potential value on a full liability basis of £250,000 and above and that are likely to involve a claim for an element of future continuing loss. If the parties agree, the Guide can also be followed – in spirit if not to the letter – in lower value multi track cases with an element of future continuing loss. The Guide excludes clinical negligence and asbestos related disease cases.

The Guide has been developed following years of collaborative work between APIL, FOIL and a number of major insurers. The Guide is specifically referenced in the Pre-action Protocol for Personal Injury claims. Whilst the protocol is designed primarily for claims likely to be allocated to the fast track, its spirit is expected to be followed in multi-track cases. In keeping with that spirit, paragraph 1.1.2 of the Pre- action Protocol states that: "All parties are expected to consider the Serious Injury Guide in any claim to which that Guide applies."

The Guide is intended to help parties involved in these multi track claims resolve any/all issues whilst putting the claimant at the centre of the process. It puts in place a system that meets the reasonable needs of the injured claimant whilst ensuring the parties work together towards resolving the case by cooperating and narrowing the issues.

This Guide creates an environment that encourages positive collaborative behaviour from both sides, and will work in parallel with the Civil Procedure Rules.

Nothing within this document affects a solicitor's duty to act in the best interests of the client and upon their instructions.

It is recognised that there will be occasions when the defendant[1] insurer and or agent cannot commit a commercial client for whom they are handling agents to comply with the Guide. The claimant representative will be notified of this issue immediately.

It is recognised that there will be occasions where either the claimant or the defendant insurer /and or the claims handling agent are unable to comply with the Guide. Where this occurs it is expected that notification of this fact to the opposing party should be made immediately.

This Guide comprises the following:

- A. Objectives
- B. Guidance
    1. Collaboration
    2. Early notification
    3. First contact
    4. Claims involving multiple defendants

[1] [1981] W.L.R. 120,127.

5. Ongoing review and case planning
6. Rehabilitation
7. Escalation
8. Dispute resolution
9. Costs

A. OBJECTIVES

The principal aims are as follows:

1. to resolve liability as quickly as possible;
2. where beneficial to the claimant to provide early access to rehabilitation to maximise their recovery;
3. to resolve claims in a cost appropriate and proportionate manner;
4. to resolve claims within an appropriate agreed time frame;
5. resolution through an environment of mutual trust, transparency and collaboration.

To achieve the above the parties agree to work collaboratively bringing tangible benefits to all parties.

The key objectives are:

i. Notification

Early notification of claims to defendants and their insurers when known, with a view to achieving resolution of the case as quickly as possible and where liability is admitted or established, providing compensation.

ii. Case planning

Collaboration and dialogue are a central objective to achieve efficient case progression through an agreed action plan, dealing with but not limited to liability resolution, rehabilitation, quantum evidence and overall settlement.

iii. Liability

In all cases handled under the Guide a commitment to resolve liability by agreement, with a view to this being finalised within a maximum period of six months from the date of first notification. Where this is not possible, to identify the barriers that are stopping liability being resolved and to agree an action plan to conclude the issue at the earliest opportunity. The plan can include trial or alternative dispute resolution as appropriate.

For cases handled in accordance with this Guide the withdrawal of an admission would only be in exceptional circumstances and an admission made by any party may well be binding on that party in the litigation. The rules concerning admissions at CPR 14.1A continue to apply.

iv. Considerations on resolution of liability

A commitment to an early interim payment of disbursements (the subject matter of which has been disclosed) in addition to base costs related to liability once resolved. If the parties are unable to agree the amount of contribution an action plan will be developed to conclude the issue at the earliest opportunity.

The objectives and processes set within the Guide do not prevent the parties agreeing to additional items such as payment of interest on general damages, stay of proceedings or on any other issue in the course of the claim, all such discussions being in the spirit of the Guide.

v. Rehabilitation

Discussion at the earliest opportunity by all parties to consider effective rehabilitation where reasonably required.

Appointment, where necessary, of an independent clinical case manager instructed by the claimant, or subject to the claimant's agreement, on a joint basis.

vi. Interim damages

A willingness to make early and continuing interim payments where appropriate.

vii. Part 36/Calderbank offers

No Part 36/Calderbank offers unless or until the parties have tried to agree an issue through dialogue and negotiation but cannot do so.

viii. Documents

Commitment by all parties to obtain and disclose promptly all relevant documents, such as:

a. liability documents;
b. police reports in road accident cases (police guidance on disclosure of information to third parties in relation to civil claims can be found at *www.seriousinjuryguide.co.uk* and at National Police Library Online);
c. accident report documentation;
d. medical notes and records;
e. documents relating to past loss;
f. case manager records;
g. other relevant non-privileged material.

Where possible, all parties are to obtain evidence in such a way as to avoid duplication of effort and cost.

B. GUIDANCE: ACHIEVING THE OBJECTIVES

1. COLLABORATION AND CASE PLANNING

1.1. The aims and objectives of this Guide will be achieved through the parties working together, allocating tasks where appropriate, narrowing the issues throughout the claim, leading to resolution at the earliest time.

1.2. Collaboration begins with a commitment to early notification of a claim to the potential defendant.

Collaborative working between the parties should continue throughout the life of the claim with the objective of achieving:
a. early liability resolution
b. maximising rehabilitation opportunities
c. making provision for early interim payments
d. emphasising restitution and redress, (rather than just compensation)
e. early identification of issues not in dispute
f. flexible approaches to resolution of issues in dispute

1.3. The parties should aim to agree a framework/timetable for engaging on a regular basis in order to bring the case to conclusion.

2. EARLY NOTIFICATION

2.1. The claimant's solicitor should ensure that the defendant and their insurers/handling agents are given early notification of the claim. The recommended contents of the early notification letter are set out below. The early notification point for each insurer can be found at *www.seriousinjuryguide.co.uk.*

2.2. A full formal detailed letter of claim is not expected (in the first instance). The aim is to alert the proposed defendant and insurer/handling agent to the potential claim, applicability of this Guide and to enable:

a. an initial view for the purpose of understanding the nature of the claim and severity of injuries;
b. allocation of the case to an appropriate level of file handler within their organisation;
c. liability to be resolved promptly without further investigation by the proposed claimant.

2.3. The claimant's solicitors should aim to send a written notification within 7 calendar days of instruction. This should include where available but not be limited to:

a. Name, address, date of birth and NI number of claimant (Such personal data should not be sent in one letter because of the risk of fraud.)
b. Date, time and place of accident or date of onset of condition giving rise to the claim.
c. Factual outline of accident and injury if available.
d. Who is said to be responsible and relationship to claimant.
e. Any other party approached.
f. Occupation and approximate income.
g. Name and address of employer if there is one.
h. Current medical status in summary form (e.g. inpatient or discharged).
i. Any immediate medical or rehabilitation needs if known.
j. The identity of the firms' escalation point of contact (see escalation section) and email address.
k. Protected party status on a without prejudice basis.
l. A reference to the claim being conducted within the Guide.

2.4. In the notification letter, the name of file hander with conduct at the claimant's solicitor's firm and immediate line manager/supervisor should be identified. Relevant e-mail addresses and telephone numbers should also be included.

2.5. The solicitors representing the claimant should take all reasonable steps to locate and notify the appropriate insurer/handling agent. Where known the letter should be sent to an established address to enable the file to be allocated at the correct handling level within the insurance company/handling agents.

2.6. If an insurer or handling agent is unknown, a short notification letter should be sent to the proposed defendant with a request to pass it on to any relevant insurer. In RTA cases, the MIB should be approached in the absence of an alternative insurer.

2.7. In the event that more than one potential defendant is identified details should be communicated to all other defendants (see section 4 below).

2.8. The reasonable costs of the solicitor in complying with this section will not be challenged for the lack of a retainer at this point in time.

3. FIRST CONTACT

3.1. At the earliest opportunity but no later than:

3.1.1. 14 calendar days of receipt of the notification letter, the defendant insurer / handling agent must acknowledge the correspondence in writing and confirm it is with the correct handler, confirming the name of the file handler, escalation contact point, as well as e-mail addresses and telephone numbers of the same.

3.1.2. 28 calendar days of receipt of the notification letter, the defendant insurer shall make contact with the claimant solicitor. The purpose of this first contact is to establish lines of communication between the parties, to include but not limited to:

a. the parties' views on liability
b. update on injuries
c. any rehabilitation needs identified
d. other potential defendants
e. agreement as to when to hold further discussions.

4. CLAIMS INVOLVING MULTIPLE DEFENDANTS

4.1. The claimant solicitor must be kept informed in the event that additional defendants are identified.

4.2. In the event that there is more than one potential defendant it is expected that one defendant will coordinate correspondence with the claimant representatives. The identity of the coordinating party in such cases ought to be communicated within 28 calendar days of the last letter of claim where more than one is sent.

4.3. Where a coordinating contact point is offered the claimant representative shall restrict communication to that party, save that in the event that they consider there is a failure to make satisfactory progress in accordance with this Guide, all other known defendants should be alerted to the concern(s) raised. It is expected that this step will not be taken unless the escalation procedure has been tried first.

4.4. The defendants should confer within a maximum of 28 days in order to agree a response or to appoint a replacement coordinating defendant.

4.5. It may be that a coordinating defendant cannot be agreed between the defendants. In such cases the claimant must be notified of the fact immediately. However, there is a continuing expectation that the defendants will, as soon as possible, agree a coordinating defendant.

5. ONGOING REVIEW AND FORWARD PLANNING

5.1. Regular on-going dialogue should take place between the parties with a view to agreeing the next steps required to progress the case. Material changes in circumstances should be communicated immediately (e.g. death of the claimant, loss of capacity, significant medical deterioration, material change in care regime costs, risk of loss of employment etc).

5.2. The claimant solicitor should give reasonable access for medical facilities when requested by the defence insurer. The parties should liaise on the issue of selection of any expert and the status thereof as part of the planning process.

6. REHABILITATION

6.1. One of the overriding aims of the Guide is to help claimants to access rehabilitation when appropriate. At the earliest practical stage the parties should, in consultations with the claimant and/or the claimant's family, consider whether early intervention, rehabilitation or medical treatment would improve the present or long term situation. Defendants should reply promptly to any request to rehabilitation, and in any event within 21 days.

6.2. Further guidance can be found in the following material:

6.2.1. APIL's Best Practice Guide on rehabilitation *https://www.apil.org.uk/publications/rehabilitation-965858111.pdf*

6.2.2. The **Guide to Best Practice at the Interface Between Rehabilitation and the Medico-legal Process** endorsed by BSRM, APIL and the Royal College of Physicians published November 2006, *https://www.apil.org.uk/files/members/pdf/ApilDocuments/86.pdf*

6.2.3. The Rehabilitation Code 2015 (official implementation 1 December 2015) *http:// iual.informz.ca/IUAL/data/images/2015%20Circular%20Attachments/067%20REHAB%20CODE.pdf*

6.2.4. The Guide to Case Managers 2015 (official implementation 1 December 2015) *http://iual.informz.ca/IUAL/data/images/2015%20Circular%20Attachments/067%20CM%20GUIDE%20MASTER2.pdf*

6.3. The parties are encouraged to try to agree the selection of an appropriately qualified case manager best suited to the claimant's needs.

6.4. The insurer and/or appointed solicitor will be kept up to date with rehabilitation progress as part of the case planning process, by whatever means is agreed between the parties or generally.

6.5. Rehabilitation reports and case management material should be provided to the insurer on a regular basis.

6.6. The parties should seek to agree the frequency with which records and documents should be disclosed.

6.7. The parties should seek to agree the frequency of meetings or conference calls with the case manager (if such meetings or calls are appropriate).

7. ESCALATION PROCEDURE

7.1. In the event that either party feels that the opposing handler is not acting in accordance with the spirit of the Guide the first step must always be to exhaust attempts to resolve the point of concern by dialogue or a meeting.

7.2. If such dialogue still fails to allay the concerns, contact should be made with the nominated contact point at the firm/insurer/handling agent (see notification stage above) in order to try to deal with the issue.

7.3. In circumstances where a defendant solicitor has been instructed, the signatory insurer escalation point will remain the nominated contact point for the purposes of the Serious Injury Guide. The claimant solicitor should contact the signatory insurer escalation point directly with any escalation procedure issues, and in doing so, there will be no issue raised in relation to the Code of Conduct. The defendant solicitor should be notified of the intention to escalate, and should be copied into the correspondence sent to the insurer escalation contact point.

7.4. All parties are expected to adhere to the objectives set out above.

8. DISPUTE RESOLUTION

8.1. Ongoing dialogue is fundamental to the process. The parties will continue to discuss the case on a regular basis and at the times agreed. Disagreement on one or more issues, however important, should not limit dialogue or discourage the parties from seeking agreement on those issues that might be agreed upon or narrowed. The aim in each case should be to reduce the areas and scope of any disagreement so far as dialogue permits.

8.2. There may be occasions when issues arise that cannot be resolved through discussion. Here, the parties should consider and agree if possible how they will approach such disputes. Such an approach should be adopted when any dispute emerges in the case, whether it relates to a discrete issue or resolution of the dispute generally.

8.3. All methods of dispute resolution should be considered. Including:

a. Stocktake/cooling off period before the parties re-engage
b. Early Neutral Evaluation
c. Joint Settlement Meeting
d. Mediation
e. Arbitration

8.4. Considering other methods of dispute resolution does not prevent the parties from starting legal proceedings including Detailed Assessment if needed.

9. COSTS

9.1. Where the stage has been reached in the case where it looks like there stands a good prospect of resolution, the parties should also consider how to resolve costs promptly. For example, if there is a Joint Settlement Meeting, then the defendants are entitled to expect the claimant to provide cost details to be served seven days prior to the JSM; the parties should agree the manner in which the cost details will be given (by way of a schedule, some other form or draft Bill of costs). The parties should agree whether cost lawyers need to be available at the meeting in order to facilitate resolution of costs. If it is not possible to resolve costs at the meeting, the parties should agree a 28 day period following the meeting to enable without prejudice discussions with a view to finalising the costs issues.

9.2. Where the case is resolved by acceptance of written offer, the parties should be prepared to engage immediately in discussion concerning costs. Agreement should focus on the information that is to be provided by the receiving party to the paying party, and a without prejudice timescale established, normally 28 days after acceptance of offer, to try and resolve costs once and for all prior to commencing the costs procedure.

9.3. Following resolution of liability, the Guide recognises an early commitment to pay an interim payment towards disbursements and a contribution towards base costs. See objective (iv) above.

Serious Injury Guide Appendix – what can be achieved?

"Open book" rehabilitation best practice

Effective dialogue concerning rehabilitation progress and related challenges are a central part of case planning under the SIG.

The defence insurer / lawyer should be encouraged to attend periodic meetings/ conference calls with the case manager and claimant lawyer to provide an oral update on rehabilitation progress and current rehabilitation goals and objectives.

What are the benefits of such a level of access and transparency?

1. Improved dialogue around rehabilitation may serve to control the amount of case reporting obligations on the case manager, over and above what is clinically required on good rehabilitation practice.
2. Interim funding requests can be discussed and understood (or even volunteered by the defence insurer) and agreed promptly.
3. Delays in funding can be avoided.
4. The environment encourages fact to replace perception and the case manager gains first-hand experience understanding of any areas of concern.
5. Medico legal assessments can be planned and programmed to dovetail with the rehabilitation work.
6. Medico legal driven case manager reporting time can be minimised.
7. A forum is created that enables views and suggestions from experienced medical legal experts can be fed into the case manager in a timely manner to the benefit of the claimant.

Insurers who are given this high level of access to the rehabilitation should always act in the best interests of the rehabilitation; if they disagree with the plans or actions the meetings are a perfect opportunity to air these in an open and transparent manner in order to try to resolve the concerns by dialogue.

This approach improves the way the rehabilitation process dovetails with the claim process and is just another example of the way that route mapping and collaborative working has developed over time as the Guide has been applied in practice.

Many claimant lawyers and defence insurers successfully progress cases on this basis. At the Serious Injury Guide participant workshop on 21 November 2018 there was universal support for this approach to rehabilitation, if it could be achieved.

4 May 2023

Steering Group

Matthew Stockwell (APIL)
Marcus Weatherby (APIL)
Ann Allister (APIL)
Brett Dixon (APIL)
Raquel Siganporia (APIL)
Jeffrey Wale (FOIL)
Andrew Hibbert (FOIL)
Steven King (FOIL)
Jon Ramsay (Munich re)
Ben Hibbs (LV)

APIL contact:

Alice Taylor
Alice.taylor@apil.org.uk

FOIL contact:

Jeffrey Wale
Jeffrey.Wale@foil.org.uk

Signatories

A list of general insurers, claimant firms and professional organisations who have agreed to follow this Guide are listed at www.seriousinjuryguide.co.uk. All named firms commit that all handlers within their organisations will follow the Guide in all respects including the escalation process.

L

Group L

Motoring and Allied Material

L1: Motoring costs

Illustrative vehicle running costs

RAC Motoring Services, in conjunction with Emmerson Hill Associates (Vehicle Management Consultants), have compiled the following illustrative vehicle running costs. The figures represent a guide to the cost of running, from new, a privately-owned petrol or diesel car for a period of three years with an annual mileage of 10,000 miles. See note on updating on p.439.

Petrol cars

Engine size (cc)	**1000**	**1200**	**1400**	**up to 1800**	**2000**	**2500**	**3000**	**over 3000**
Assumed fuel consumption	58	50	46	40	36	31	27	25
CO 2 emissions level g/km	Under 120	121-150	151-165	166-185	186-225	226-255	226-255	255 plus
New cost incl. first year VED	8450	9650	10950	14750	16950	21750	24950	29750
Average value at 3 years	3450	3950	4250	4950	5750	6500	7250	9500
Projected depreciation	5000	5700	6700	9800	11200	15250	17700	20250
Finance charge @4.8% APR	625	714	810	1092	1254	1610	1846	2202
Servicing and maintenance	550	575	600	700	880	1070	1200	1375
Tyres and replacement parts	340	370	415	500	600	760	790	835
Insurance premiums 3 years	1005	1185	1230	1500	1860	2775	3150	3600
Excise licences next 2 years	280	280	280	280	280	280	280	280
RAC membership 3 years	495	495	495	495	495	495	495	495
Total cost over 3 year period excl. petrol	8295	9319	10530	14367	16569	22240	25461	29037
Annual cost	2765	3106	3510	4789	5523	7413	8487	9679
Cost per mile in pence excl petrol	**27.65**	**31.06**	**35.10**	**47.89**	**55.23**	**74.13**	**84.87**	**96.79**
Fuel cost pence per mile @ 1.10/litre	**8.59**	**9.97**	**10.83**	**12.46**	**13.84**	**16.07**	**18.46**	**19.93**
Standing cost per mile	**24.68**	**27.91**	**31.72**	**43.89**	**50.30**	**68.03**	**78.24**	**89.42**
Running cost per mile	**11.56**	**13.12**	**14.22**	**16.46**	**18.78**	**22.17**	**25.09**	**27.30**
Adjustment for change in fuel price of 1p +/-	**0.08**	**0.09**	**0.10**	**0.11**	**0.13**	**0.15**	**0.17**	**0.18**

Diesel cars

Engine size (cc)	**Up to 1400**	**Up to 1400**	**1401-2000**	**2001-2200**	**2001-2200**	**2201-2500**	**2501-3000**	**over 3000**
Assumed fuel consumption	60	58	53	42	40	39	36	34
CO 2 emissions level g/km	Under 120	121-150	151-165	166-185	186-225	226-255	255 plus	255 plus
New cost incl. first year VED	9750	9950	13750	20450	22500	25950	31650	33000
Average value at 3 years	3950	4250	5750	7950	8250	9450	11250	12250
Projected depreciation	5800	5700	8000	12500	14250	16500	20400	20750
Finance charge @4.8% APR	722	736	1018	1513	1665	1920	2342	2442
Servicing and maintenance	520	520	760	1075	1075	1440	1520	1650
Tyres and replacement parts	350	350	475	595	595	625	650	750
Insurance premiums 3 years	1185	1185	1500	1860	1860	2850	3600	4200
Excise licences next 2 years	280	280	280	280	280	280	280	280
RAC membership 3 years	495	495	495	495	495	495	495	495
Total cost over 3 year period excl. diesel	9352	9266	12528	18318	20220	24110	29287	30567
Annual cost	3117	3089	4176	6106	6740	8037	9762	10189
Cost per mile in pence excl diesel	**31.17**	**30.89**	**41.76**	**61.06**	**67.40**	**80.37**	**97.62**	**101.89**
Fuel cost pence per mile @ 1.10/litre	**8.31**	**8.59**	**9.40**	**11.86**	**12.46**	**12.78**	**13.84**	**14.66**
Standing cost per mile	**28.27**	**27.99**	**37.64**	**55.49**	**61.83**	**73.48**	**90.39**	**93.89**
Running cost per mile	**11.21**	**11.49**	**13.52**	**17.43**	**18.02**	**19.66**	**21.08**	**22.66**
Adjustment for change in fuel price of 1p +/-	**0.08**	**0.08**	**0.09**	**0.11**	**0.11**	**0.12**	**0.13**	**0.13**

Note to the RAC vehicle running figures above:

The standing and running costs per mile and the adjustment for changes in fuel price have been calculated by the editors from the RAC figures.

Standing costs include Vehicle Tax, insurance, finance charges, depreciation and RAC membership.

Running costs include fuel, tyres and replacement parts, service and maintenance.

Illustrative motorcycle running costs

RAC Motoring Services, in conjunction with Emmerson Hill Associates (Vehicle Management Consultants), have compiled the following illustrative motorcycle running costs. The figures represent a guide to the cost of running a privately-owned motorcycle for a period of three years with an annual mileage of 6,000 miles. See note on updating on p.439.

Motorcycles

Engine size (cc)	100	125	250	400	up to 600	750	1000	over 1000
Assumed fuel consumption	80	68	56	48	45	43	37	33
Average cost new	1,950	2,150	2,950	4,250	4,500	5,250	6,150	7,750
Average value at 3 years	950	1,250	1,850	2,150	2,650	3,100	3,500	4,450
Projected depreciation	1,000	900	1,100	2,100	1,850	2,150	2,650	3,300
Finance charge @4.8% APR	144	159	218	315	333	389	455	574
Fuel cost @ 1.10/litre	1,125	1,323	1,607	1,875	2,000	2,094	2,432	2,727
Insurance and repairs 3 years	715	910	1,075	1,155	1,460	1,475	1,710	1,790
Servicing and maintenance	250	295	525	550	600	725	795	825
Tyres and replacement parts	350	450	650	690	740	820	820	900
Excise licences 3 years	54	54	123	123	186	255	255	255
RAC membership	150	150	150	150	150	150	150	150
Protective clothing and helmet	425	425	525	525	525	525	525	525
Total cost over 3 year period	4,213	4,666	5,973	7,483	7,844	8,583	9,792	11,046
Annual cost	1,404	1,555	1,991	2,494	2,615	2,861	3,264	3,682
Cost per mile in pence	**23.41**	**25.92**	**33.18**	**41.57**	**43.58**	**47.68**	**54.40**	**61.37**
Standing cost per mile	**13.82**	**14.43**	**17.73**	**24.27**	**25.02**	**27.47**	**31.92**	**36.63**
Running cost per mile	**9.58**	**11.49**	**15.46**	**17.31**	**18.56**	**20.22**	**22.48**	**24.73**
Adjustment for change in fuel price of 1p +/-	**0.06**	**0.07**	**0.08**	**0.09**	**0.10**	**0.11**	**0.12**	**0.14**

Note to the RAC motorcycle figures above:

The standing and running costs per mile and the adjustment for changes in fuel price have been calculated by the editors from the RAC figures.

Standing costs include Vehicle Tax, insurance and repairs, finance charges, depreciation, protective clothing and RAC membership.

Running costs include fuel, tyres and replacement parts, service and maintenance.

Note on updating

The RAC illustrative running costs in these tables have not been updated since 2016. The RAC Foundation has however produced figures showing the general changes in motoring costs over the last 10 years. The editors recommend that the figures in the tables should be multiplied by the following factors, which update the costs from January 2016 to March 2024:

All motoring costs generally	1.56	Tax and insurance	3.20	Maintenance	1.43
Petrol and oil	1.45	Purchase	1.22		

Vehicle Tax

Vehicles registered before March 2001

If the engine capacity is 1,549 cc or less the duty is £210; if it is over 1,549 cc the duty is £345. (Vehicles registered more than 40 years before 1 January in the current year are entitled to exemption from Vehicle Tax.)

Vehicles registered between 1 March 2001 and 31 March 2017

The tax depends on the fuel type and the emissions of carbon dioxide in the legislated Type Approval tests. In the tables, averages for the price groups are used for the tax rate.

Bands	**CO_2 Emission (g/km)**	**Petrol or Diesel Car Standard Rate £**
Band A	Up to 100	0
Band B	101–110	20
Band C	111–120	35
Band D	121–130	160
Band E	131–140	190
Band F	141–150	210
Band G	151–165	255
Band H	166–175	305
Band I	176–185	335
Band J	186–200	385
Band K*	201–225	415
Band L	226–255	710
Band M	Over 255	735

* Band K includes cars with a CO_2 figure over 225 g/km which were registered before 23 March 2006.

An alternative fuel car has a discount of £10 for all bands. A fully electric vehicle is exempt from tax.

The CO_2 emission of a particular vehicle can be found at a website provided by the Vehicle Certification Agency (VCA): *www.carfueldata.direct.gov.uk*. It is also on the V5 registration document.

Vehicles registered on or after 1 April 2017

Only vehicles with zero emissions will benefit from zero tax.

Standard rate, from year 2 onwards

	Zero emissions	Alternative fuel car	Petrol or diesel car
£	0	180	190

Premium rate, in years 2–6 on all cars costing over £40,000; the premium depends on list price, not the actual purchase price. £410 (on top)

First year rate

CO_2 Emission (g/km)	First year rate £
Zero	0
1–50	10
51–75	30
76–90	135
91–100	175
101–110	195
111–130	220
131–150	270
151–170	680
171–190	1,095
191–225	1,650
226–255	2,340
Over 255	2,745

New diesel vehicles registered after 1 April 2018 that do not meet the real driving emission step 2 (RDE2) standard are charged a supplement on their First Year Rate to the effect of moving up by one VED band.

L2: Taxation of car and fuel benefits

Car benefit 2013/14 to 2022/23

CO_2 emissions (g/km)							Percentage of car's price taxed if car does not run solely on diesel	Percentage of car's price taxed if car does run solely on diesel		From 2020/21 those electric and hybrid vehicles producing between 1 and 50 g/km of CO_2 were further subdivided based on the maximum number of miles they could travel on electricty alone. For diesel vehicles add 4% to each group.				
								Up to and including 2017/18	From 2018/19 to 2019/20					
2013/14	**2014/15**	**2015/16**	**2016/17**	**2017/18**	**2018/19**	**2019/20**	(%)	(%)	(%)	CO_2 (g/km)	miles	**2020/21**	**2021/22**	**From 2022/23**
1-75	1-75	1-50					5	8	9	0	n/a	0	1	2
			1-50				7	10	11	1-50	>130	0	1	2
		51-75		1-50			9	12	13	1-50	70-129	3	4	5
76-94							10	13	14	1-50	40-69	6	7	8
95-99	76-94		51-75				11	14	15	1-50	30-39	10	11	12
100-104	95-99						12	15	16	1-50	<30	12	13	14
105-109	100-104	76-94		51-75	1-50		13	16	17	51-54		13	14	15
110-114	105-109	95-99					14	17	18	55-59		14	15	16
115-119	110-114	100-104	76-94				15	18	19	60-64		15	16	17
120-124	115-119	105-109	95-99		51-75	0-50	16	19	20	65-69		16	17	18
125-129	120-124	110-114	100-104	76-94			17	20	21	70-74		17	18	19
130-134	125-129	115-119	105-109	95-99			18	21	22	75-79		18	19	20
135-139	130-134	120-124	110-114	100-104	76-94	51-75	19	22	23	80-84		19	20	21
140-144	135-139	125-129	115-119	105-109	95-99		20	23	24	85-89		20	21	22
145-149	140-144	130-134	120-124	110-114	100-104		21	24	25	90-94		21	22	23
150-154	145-149	135-139	125-129	115-119	105-109	76-94	22	25	26	95-99		22	23	24
155-159	150-154	140-144	130-134	120-124	110-114	95-99	23	26	27	100-104		23	24	25
160-164	155-159	145-149	135-139	125-129	115-119	100-104	24	27	28	105-109		24	25	26
165-169	160-164	150-154	140-144	130-134	120-124	105-109	25	28	29	110-114		25	26	27
170-174	165-169	155-159	145-149	135-139	125-129	110-114	26	29	30	115-119		26	27	28
175-179	170-174	160-164	150-154	140-144	130-134	115-119	27	30	31	120-124		27	28	29
180-184	175-179	165-169	155-159	145-149	135-139	120-124	28	31	32	125-129		28	29	30
185-189	180-184	170-174	160-164	150-154	140-144	125-129	29	32	33	130-134		29	30	31
190-194	185-189	175-179	165-169	155-159	145-149	130-134	30	33	34	135-139		30	31	32
195-199	190-194	180-184	170-174	160-164	150-154	135-139	31	34	35	140-144		31	32	33
200-204	195-199	185-189	175-179	165-169	155-159	140-144	32	35	36	145-149		32	33	34
205-209	200-204	190-194	180-184	170-174	160-164	145-149	33	36	37	150-154		33	34	35
210-214	205-209	195-199	185-189	175-179	165-169	150-154	34	37	37	155-159		34	35	36
215+	210+	200-204	190-194	180-184	170-174	155-159	35	37	37	160-164		35	36	37
		205-209	195-199	185-189	175-179	160-164	36	37	37	165-169		36	37	37
		210+	200+	190+	180+	165+	37	37	37	170+		37	37	37

Notes

1. From 6 April 2002, although the benefit of a company car is still to be calculated as a percentage of the price of the car (normally list price), the percentage is graduated according to carbon dioxide (CO_2) emissions and adjustments for business mileage and older cars no longer apply.
2. There are discounts for certain cleaner alternatively-propelled cars, which may reduce the minimum charge to that shown in the table.
3. The diesel supplement and the discounts for cleaner alternatives apply only to cars first registered on 1 January 1998 or later.
4. Cars without an approved CO_2 emissions figure are taxed according to engine size. This includes all cars registered before 1998 but only a tiny proportion of those registered 1998 and later.
5. Except where otherwise indicated, the exact CO_2 figure is rounded down to the nearest five grams per kilometre when using the above table.
6. From 6 April 2008 there was a new lower rate of 10 per cent (13 per cent for diesel) for cars with CO_2 emissions of 120 grams per kilometre or less.
7. From 6 April 2010 cars and vans with zero CO_2 emissions were exempt from company car tax for five tax years.
8. From 6 April 2010 an ultra low carbon cars band was introduced for five years.
9. From 6 April 2018 the differential between petrol and diesel cars was increased to 4 per cent (previously a 3 per cent differential). However, a maximum taxable value of 37 per cent applies to both petrol and diesel cars.
10. From 2020/21 those electric and hybrid vehicles producing between 1 and 50 g/km of CO_2 were further subdivided based on the maximum number of miles they could travel on electricity alone. For diesel vehicles add 4% to each group.
11. There has been no increase in the percentage of a car's price taxed since 2022/23, although the current proposal is to increase all percentages by 1% a year over the course of the next 3 tax years i.e. 2025/26 to 2027/28.

Car fuel benefit — petrol and diesel — cash equivalent 2003/04 to 2024/25

Notes

1. From 6 April 2003, the car fuel benefit is, like the car benefit, linked directly to the CO_2 emissions of the company car.
2. There are the same diesel supplement and discounts for cleaner alternatively-propelled cars as there are in calculating the car benefit.
3. To calculate the car fuel benefit the percentage in the table used for calculating car benefit is multiplied against a set figure for the year:

2003/04 to 2007/08	£ 14,400
2008/09 to 2009/10	£ 16,900
2010/11	£ 18,000
2011/12	£ 18,800
2012/13	£ 20,200
2013/14	£ 21,100
2014/15	£ 21,700
2015/16	£ 22,100
2016/17	£ 22,200
2017/18	£ 22,600
2018/19	£ 23,400
2019/20	£ 24,100
2020/21	£ 24,500

2021/22	£ 24,600
2022/23	£ 25,300
2023/24	£ 27,800
2024/25	£ 27,800

Hence if the car produced between 100 and 104 g/km of CO_2 emissions, the benefit percentage for 2024/25 is 25%, so the fuel benefit would be £25,300 × 25% = £6,325.

4. For cars registered before 1 January 1998 and cars with no approved CO_2 emissions figure, the percentage to be applied is the same as that used to calculate the car benefit.

Authorised Mileage Allowance Payments — tax-free rates in pence per mile 2002/03 to 2024/25

	Annual mileage	*Pence per mile*
Cars and vans	Up to 10,000 10,001 +	45p* 25p
Motorcycles		24p
Bicycles		20p
Business Passengers		5p

* For 2002/03 to 2010/11 (inclusive) this rate was 40 pence per mile

L3: The Motability Scheme

Disabled people who need a motor vehicle may obtain one by utilising most if not all of the Higher Rate component of the Disability Living Allowance, the Enhanced Rate Mobility Component of Personal Independence Payment or their Scottish equivalent, the War Pensioner's Mobility Supplement or the Armed Forces Independence Payment. However, to lease a car you must have at least 12 months of any award left. Motability is only available to those in receipt of any of these benefits who assign all or some of them to the scheme for the duration of the contract. Because of the very wide range of physical and mental disabilities of those in receipt of them the scheme does not require the person seeking to use it to be a driver: anyone in receipt of one of these allowances who is over three is entitled to use it. Under the Scheme there are three available options:

1. A new car can be obtained on a three-year lease hire contract.
2. A wheelchair accessible vehicle (WAV) can be obtained on a five-year lease hire contract or three-year for a secondhand one.
3. A powered wheelchair or scooter may be taken on a three-year contract hire.

A national network of some 4,500 dealers provides a wide range of suitably adapted new and used cars. In the case of any option, the scheme requires a capital sum and a monthly payment which is provided for by the assignment of the relevant state benefit to the scheme. As well as the adapted vehicle, all maintenance is provided to include the cost of tyres, as is insurance for three named drivers of whom two must be over 25, annual road fund tax and roadside recovery. Fuel, oil and other incidentals are the responsibility of the driver. For electric vehicles the scheme arranges and covers the cost of a home charging point. There is a 60,000 mile limit on use over a three-year contract or 100,000 miles over a five-year contract. Any mileage over that limit attracts a penalty of 5p per mile. At the end of the contract period the car reverts to the scheme. Hire purchase is no longer available.

When costing, care must be taken to distinguish between the three elements of any claim:

(i) the capital cost of both purchase and adaptation which recur every three years;
(ii) the monthly running costs covered by the Motability Scheme; and
(iii) running costs not covered by the scheme such as oil, fuel and electric charging.

Not all cars are available and advice must be obtained as to whether what is available adequately meets the needs of the disabled person. When experts have recommended that a car be obtained under the scheme practitioners should ensure that they are clear which option is being recommended and ensure that they compare like for like.

The condition precedent for using the Motability Scheme is that the beneficiary is in receipt of a state benefit which falls within the Second Schedule of the Social Security (Recovery of Benefits) Act 1997. It is now clear, following *Eagle v Chambers (No.2)* [2004] EWCA Civ 1033, that s.17 of the Act precludes a court from insisting that the mobility component of the Disabled Living Allowance should be used by any recipient to mitigate her loss. Henceforth no defendant can insist that a claimant use the mobility allowance to participate in the Motability Scheme.

DLA, hitherto the gateway into Motability, is being replaced by the Personal Independence Payment (PIP). When this is fully implemented only those receiving the enhanced rate of the mobility component of PIP will be eligible to use the Motability Scheme. During the transitional period those with the higher rate of the mobility component of DLA continue to be eligible although the requirement of having a year remaining will prevent many from taking on a new lease. PIP is assessed in a less generous way than DLA and it is likely that as the shift occurs to PIP some will cease to be eligible for Motability.

Further reading and assistance in specific cases can be obtained at:
http://www.motability.co.uk and Customer Services (0300) 456 4566.

L4: The costs of buying and replacing cars

There are a number of commonly encountered calculations involving the cost of cars. This section contains tables and examples of calculations dealing with the following and should be read along with the table of Motoring costs in section L1:

1. Cost of future replacements.

2. Cost of more frequent replacement.

3. Cost of automatic cars.

4. Cost of additional mileage.

5. Cost of professional servicing.

6. Cost of Assessment.

We have classified cars as follows:

Mini:	Most cars of 1.1 litre or under, such as Toyota Aygo 1.0, Vauxhall Corsa 1.0
Super mini:	Similar cars between 1.1 and 1.4, Ford Fiesta 1.25, Suzuki Swift 1.2
Small:	Cars of the smaller Ford Focus, VW Golf type, mostly 1.3–1.6 litre
Medium:	The Ford Mondeo, VW Passat type, mostly cars from 1.6–1.9 litre
Executive:	The larger Passat, Volvo S60 type, mostly 2.0–2.8 litre
Prestige:	The BMW 330d, Jaguar 3.0, mostly up to 3.5 litre
Luxury:	The Jaguar XJ, Audi A8 4.2, mostly over 3.5 litre and expensive
Estate etc:	Self-explanatory

Notes:

1. Depreciation: Different cars, even produced by the same manufacturer, depreciate at different rates. As a model of car may change after a few years even if the same name is retained, losses over a long period cannot be calculated for individual models but only by reference to the general position.

2. Automatics: The comparison of manual and automatic cars is similarly a generalisation. The calculation for depreciation assumes that the new price of the automatic is higher than for the manual model. There is considerable variation, even among cars of similar type with similar new prices, in the rate at which the premium for the automatic version is eroded. With some cars the gap disappears very quickly: with some the premium for the automatic version is actually greater for used cars than for new ones.

3. Where the current new price of the manual and automatic versions is the same, which is often the case with expensive cars, the used automatic tends to retain its value better than the manual model. It may nevertheless have higher fuel consumption but whether it will be more expensive overall may depend on the mileage.

1. Cost of future replacements

Table 1 below has representative trade-in values of used *manual* cars expressed as a proportion of the current new price (calculated from material in Parker's Car Price Guide). Automatic cars may depreciate faster. Where the new price of an automatic car is higher than that of the corresponding manual car, there is a tendency for the automatic to depreciate by about one per cent more (altogether, not per year).

Table 1 Trade-in values of used manual cars

Age of car	Residual value	Loss of value	Equivalent annual depreciation
1	0.64	0.36	0.360
2	0.50	0.50	0.256
3	0.41	0.59	0.204
4	0.36	0.64	0.168
5	0.33	0.67	0.143
Adjustment for automatics	–0.01	+0.01	

The table can be used to calculate the future net costs of replacements where the replacements will be second hand as well as where they will be new.

Example 1: The claimant is 54 and needs a people carrier such as a Chrysler Grand Voyager 3.3 LE Auto 5d, automatic version. He will need to replace it every four years, the final replacement being when he is 70. He would not otherwise have had a car (or the car is additional to whatever vehicle would have been bought in any event).

Initial price of people carrier, say		£32,995.00
Proportion of price lost at each replacement (Table 1 above, + 0.01)	0.65	
Cost of each replacement	0.65 × 32,995 = 21,446.75	
Multiplier for 16 years (table A5, -0.25%, four-yearly)	4.10	
Cost of future replacements	4.10 × 21,446.75 =	£87,931.68
Total		£120,926.68

Example 2: The same claimant currently runs a manual Volvo S80 2.4 SE and will replace it with the Chrysler people carrier. The additional cost is the future cost of the Chryslers *minus* the corresponding figure saved on Volvos. (If either both cars are manual or both automatic the calculation is simpler.)

Initial price of Volvo saved, say		£28,245.00
Proportion of price saved at each replacement (Table 1 above, manual)	0.64	
Cost of each replacement	0.64 × 28,245.00 = 18,076.80	
Multiplier for 16 years (table A5, -0.25%, four-yearly)	4.10	
Cost of future replacements saved	4.10 × 18,076.80 =	£74,114.88
Total		£102,359.88
Net future cost of Chryslers instead of Volvos (120,926.68 - 102,359.88)	=	£18,566.80

2. Cost of more frequent replacement

Claimants are sometimes advised that because of their condition they need a more reliable car and should therefore replace it more often than they needed to do before the injury. Table 2, which is derived from Table 1, shows the additional annual cost, expressed as a proportion of the new price. Find the row corresponding to the new interval in years and the column corresponding to the old interval.

Note that the table expresses the multiplier as an *annual* cost, not the cost *on each exchange*. Thus in row 2, column 4, the figure 0.088 means that the additional expense of replacing a car every two years, instead of every four years, is 8.8 per cent of the price of the car per year for however long the claimant continues to drive.

Table 2 Multipliers for additional annual cost of replacing car more frequently

		Old interval in years				
		1	**2**	**3**	**4**	**5**
	1	0	0.104	0.156	0.192	0.217
New	**2**		0	0.052	0.088	0.113
interval	**3**			0	0.036	0.061
in	**4**				0	0.025
years	**5**					0

Example: The claimant is 40 and drives a car currently costing £11,995 new. She has just bought one. She can continue to drive a similar car, with modifications. She has been advised that because of her disability she should now change it every three years rather than every five as she has until now. She should stop driving at about 73, so the last change will be at about age 70.

Multiplier for additional annual cost from table above – new frequency three years, old frequency five years	0.061	
Multiplier for woman of 40 until age 70 (Table A1)	30.24	
Multiplier for additional cost of more frequent replacement	0.061 × 30.24	= 1.84
Current cost of car		£11,995.00
Additional cost of replacing car more frequently until age 70		£22,070.80

3. Cost of automatic cars

Claimants' injuries sometimes make it necessary for them to have an automatic car which they would not otherwise have needed. Generally this involves additional costs in three respects: the automatic car is more expensive to buy, is more expensive to run and tends to depreciate faster than the corresponding manual model (but see the notes in the introduction).

Table 3 Added cost of automatic cars

		Mini and Super Mini	Small	Medium and Executive	Prestige and Luxury	Estate, 4 × 4 and MPV
Added cost of new car in £		850	1,075	1,145	1,275	1,245
Added cost of **Petrol** in pence per mile	At 129.0p per litre	3.42	1.73	1.42	0.41	–
	For every penny more/less, add/subtract	0.030	0.015	0.012	0.004	–

Greater depreciation

Where the new price of an automatic model of a car is *higher* than that of the corresponding manual car, there is a tendency for the automatic to depreciate by about one per cent more (altogether, not per year)—see Table 1 above. Thus:

New manual model	£11,000	three-year-old manual	11,000 × 0.41 = £4,510
New automatic	£12,000	three-year-old automatic	12,000 × 0.40 = £4,800

Example: The claimant is 48. He drives a manual car of medium type whose price new is about £16,000. He drives about 10,000 miles a year and changes his car every three years. Because of his injury he now needs an automatic at a cost of £17,145. He is likely to stop driving in about 30 years.

Extra cost of automatic car:			
On first purchase (from Table 3, column 3 above):			£1,145.00
Cost at each replacement of automatic (Table 1, row 3): 17,145 × 0.60 =		10,287.00	
less cost at each replacement of manual 16,000 × 0.59 =		9,440.00	
Additional cost at each replacement			£847.00
Crude multiplier for replacements (Table A5, 27 years, three-yearly)	9.35		
Multiplier for 27 years certain (Table A5, cont's loss)	27.93		
Multiplier for man of 48 until age 75 (Table A1)	26.00		
Multiplier discounted for mortality (9.35 × 26.00/27.93) =		8.70	= £7,368.90
Extra cost per mile, petrol at 135.7 p/litre (Table 3, column 3) = 1.42 + (6.7 × 0.012) = 1.50 pence			
Extra running cost 10,000 miles p.a		£150.00	
Crude multiplier (Table A5, 30 years, cont's loss)	31.16		
Multiplier discounted for mortality (31.16 × 26.00/27.93) =		29.01	£4,351.50
Total extra cost:			£12,865.40

4. Cost of additional mileage

The RAC figures for running costs at Table L1 do not include depreciation. Mileage reduces the value of a car by a factor which varies with the type of car and its age on resale. Age on resale is not necessarily the length of time the claimant had the car. The categories A, B, C, etc. are derived from Parker's Price Guide.

The table may not be appropriate for mileages below 1,000 miles a year or above 30,000 miles a year.

Table 4 Adjustment for depreciation for extra mileage

Age on resale	Depreciation in pence per mile							
	A	B	C	D	E	F	G	H
1	3.00	4.00	5.00	6.00	7.00	8.50	10.50	13.50
2	2.50	3.50	4.50	5.50	6.50	7.50	9.00	11.00
3	2.00	3.00	3.50	4.50	5.00	6.00	7.50	10.00
4	1.20	2.00	2.50	3.50	4.00	5.00	6.00	8.00
5	1.00	1.50	2.00	2.50	3.00	4.00	5.00	7.00
6	0.70	1.20	1.50	2.00	2.50	3.00	4.00	6.00
7	0.50	0.90	1.00	1.50	2.00	2.50	3.50	5.00
8	0.40	0.60	0.90	1.00	1.50	2.00	2.50	4.00

Example: The claimant would have had a car anyway. His mileage is increased by 4,000 miles a year because of his injury. He buys a one-year-old car and changes it after four years, with a 1.3 litre engine, in category C in the mileage adjustment table.

Running cost per mile from RAC figures (Table L1)		14.22 pence
Adjustment for increase since RAC figures	× 1.45 =	20.60
Adjustment for mileage (category C, Four years old)		2.50
Total per mile		23.10 pence
Total annual cost (4,000 × 23.10)		£ 924.00

5. Cost of professional servicing

Some claimants will have carried out the routine servicing of their cars themselves, but their injury may make that impracticable and they will in future need to have the car serviced professionally.

The resulting increased cost consists essentially in the labour element in the cost of servicing. Costs such as the cost of the Ministry of Transport test itself will remain the same and will not form an element of the loss. There will be some increase in the cost of materials such as replacement parts and oil, as these may be less expensive online or at a supermarket rather than at a garage. On the other hand, particularly with newer models, the more complex servicing tasks may not be feasible without specialised equipment, and so even mechanically minded car owners may be unable to do these jobs themselves. This section therefore takes the loss as equivalent to the cost of labour and treats these other factors as neutral overall.

Labour costs vary between main dealers and independent garages, and between different parts of the country. They are generally cheaper in the north and away from London, but do not conform to any clear pattern. In a 2011 survey Gwynedd was one of the most expensive areas, but Clwyd, not far away, was one of the cheapest. Also, as will be seen from the figures in *Table L1: Motoring Costs*, the most powerful cars involve higher labour costs but the least powerful are not particularly cheaper to service than those with slightly larger engines. For those reasons it is not straightforward to try to produce figures independently on the basis of time estimates and hourly labour charges, and the editors recommend using the following figures derived from Table L1, updated as suggested there.

Table 5 Additional cost of professional servicing

	Additional cost in pence per mile							
Engine size (cc)	**1000**	**1200**	**1400**	**1800**	**2000**	**2500**	**3000**	**over 3000**
Petrol cars	2.61	2.74	2.85	3.32	4.18	5.09	5.70	6.53
Engine size (cc)	**up to 1400**	**up to 1400**	**1401-2000**	**2001-2200**	**2001-2200**	**2201-2500**	**2501-3000**	**over 3000**
Diesel cars	2.47	2.47	3.61	5.10	5.10	6.84	7.23	7.84
Engine size (cc)	**100**	**125**	**250**	**400**	**600**	**750**	**1000**	**over 1000**
Motorcycles	1.98	2.34	4.16	4.36	4.75	5.74	6.30	6.53

Example: The same claimant as in section 4 used to do his own servicing and because of his injury is now unable to do so. His car has a 1.3 litre engine. Before the accident he drove 12,000 miles a year, but because of the accident he must now drive a further 4,000 miles, making 16,000 miles in all. He incurs the additional cost of professional servicing, as well as the additional cost of extra mileage.

Extra cost of professional servicing per mile		2.85 pence
Annual cost (for 12,000 miles)	12,000 × 2.85 pence	£342.00
Cost of additional 4,000 mileage (from section 4 example)		£924.00
Total annual cost		£1,266.00

Note that the figure for running costs used to calculate the cost of additional mileage already includes service labour costs. The extra cost of servicing must therefore be based on the pre-accident 12,000 miles: there will be double counting if it is calculated on the basis of the post-accident 16,000 miles.

6. Cost of assessment

At the QEF Mobility Centres, the Queen Elizabeth Foundation for Disabled People conducts a variety of driving assessments, such as car adaptation assessments, for people with disabilities, and will provide a report. The centre also provides advice and training but does not provide costings or carry out adaptations itself.

The cost of an assessment for litigation purposes is £1,080 (including VAT).

There is a lower, subsidised, rate for individuals not requiring the report for litigation, but the Centre will then deal only with the client personally, and not with others such as solicitors or case managers.

Sections 1–4 are based on figures in Parker's Car Price Guide and from the websites of the Vehicle Certification Agency and the United States Department of Transportation.

L5: Time, speed and distance

Table of speeds and distances

Speeds				Distances in yards																			
mph	**km/h**	**yd/sec**	**m/sec**	**5**	**10**	**15**	**20**	**25**	**30**	**40**	**50**	**60**	**75**	**100**	**125**	**150**	**175**	**200**	**225**	**250**	**300**	**400**	**500**
5	8.0	2.44	2.24	2.0	4.1	6.1	8.2	10.2	12.3	16.4	20.5	24.5	30.7	40.9	51.1	61.4	71.6	81.8	92.0	102.3	122.7	163.6	204.5
10	16.1	4.89	4.47	1.0	2.0	3.1	4.1	5.1	6.1	8.2	10.2	12.3	15.3	20.5	25.6	30.7	35.8	40.9	46.0	51.1	61.4	81.8	102.3
15	24.1	7.33	6.71	0.7	1.4	2.0	2.7	3.4	4.1	5.5	6.8	8.2	10.2	13.6	17.0	20.5	23.9	27.3	30.7	34.1	40.9	54.5	68.2
20	32.2	9.78	8.94	0.5	1.0	1.5	2.0	2.6	3.1	4.1	5.1	6.1	7.7	10.2	12.8	15.3	17.9	20.5	23.0	25.6	30.7	40.9	51.1
25	40.2	12.22	11.18	0.4	0.8	1.2	1.6	2.0	2.5	3.3	4.1	4.9	6.1	8.2	10.2	12.3	14.3	16.4	18.4	20.5	24.5	32.7	40.9
30	48.3	14.67	13.41	0.3	0.7	1.0	1.4	1.7	2.0	2.7	3.4	4.1	5.1	6.8	8.5	10.2	11.9	13.6	15.3	17.0	20.5	27.3	34.1
35	56.3	17.11	15.65	0.3	0.6	0.9	1.2	1.5	1.8	2.3	2.9	3.5	4.4	5.8	7.3	8.8	10.2	11.7	13.1	14.6	17.5	23.4	29.2
40	64.4	19.56	17.88	0.3	0.5	0.8	1.0	1.3	1.5	2.0	2.6	3.1	3.8	5.1	6.4	7.7	8.9	10.2	11.5	12.8	15.3	20.5	25.6
45	72.4	22.00	20.12	0.2	0.5	0.7	0.9	1.1	1.4	1.8	2.3	2.7	3.4	4.5	5.7	6.8	8.0	9.1	10.2	11.4	13.6	18.2	22.7
50	80.5	24.44	22.35	0.2	0.4	0.6	0.8	1.0	1.2	1.6	2.0	2.5	3.1	4.1	5.1	6.1	7.2	8.2	9.2	10.2	12.3	16.4	20.5
60	96.6	29.33	26.82	0.2	0.3	0.5	0.7	0.9	1.0	1.4	1.7	2.0	2.6	3.4	4.3	5.1	6.0	6.8	7.7	8.5	10.2	13.6	17.0
70	112.7	34.22	31.29	0.1	0.3	0.4	0.6	0.7	0.9	1.2	1.5	1.8	2.2	2.9	3.7	4.4	5.1	5.8	6.6	7.3	8.8	11.7	14.6
80	128.7	39.11	35.76	0.1	0.3	0.4	0.5	0.6	0.8	1.0	1.3	1.5	1.9	2.6	3.2	3.8	4.5	5.1	5.8	6.4	7.7	10.2	12.8
90	144.8	44.00	40.23	0.1	0.2	0.3	0.5	0.6	0.7	0.9	1.1	1.4	1.7	2.3	2.8	3.4	4.0	4.5	5.1	5.7	6.8	9.1	11.4
100	160.9	48.89	44.70	0.1	0.2	0.3	0.4	0.5	0.6	0.8	1.0	1.2	1.5	2.0	2.6	3.1	3.6	4.1	4.6	5.1	6.1	8.2	10.2

Seconds

Notes:

1. The table shows the time taken to cover a given distance at a given speed, to the nearest $\frac{1}{10}$ second.

2. The table can also be used to ascertain the approximate speed of a vehicle, if the time and distance are known.

3. As an example, to find how long it would take to cover 125 yards at 35 mph, follow the vertical column down from the figure 125 and follow the horizontal row across from the figure 35: they meet at the figure 7.3, which is the number of seconds taken to cover the distance.

4. A speed of z miles per hour approximately equals [0.5z] yards per second.

5. The general formula for the number of seconds to cover a given distance at a given speed is approximately:

$$\frac{\text{distance in yards} \times 2.04545}{\text{speed in miles per hour}}$$

Typical Stopping Distances (average car length = 4 metres)

Speed (mph)	**Thinking Distance** (metres)	**Braking Distance** (metres)	**Total Stopping Distance** (metres)	(car lengths)
20	6	6	12	3
30	9	14	23	6
40	12	24	36	9
50	15	38	53	13
60	18	55	73	18
70	21	75	96	24

Extracted from *The Highway Code*, published by The Stationery Office.

Group M

Other Information

M

M1: Senior Court Costs Office Guideline Rates

SCCO 2010 Guidelines Rates

Band One	A	B	C	D
2010–Sept 2021	217	192	161	118

Aldershot, Farnham, Bournemouth (including Poole), Birmingham Inner, Bristol, Cambridge City, Harlow, Canterbury, Maidstone, Medway and Tunbridge Wells, Cardiff (Inner), Chelmsford South, Essex and East Suffolk, Chester, Fareham, Winchester, Hampshire, Dorset, Wiltshire, Isle of Wight, Kingston, Guildford, Reigate, Epsom, Leeds Inner (within two-kilometres radius of the City Art Gallery), Lewes, Liverpool, Birkenhead, Manchester Central, Newcastle—City Centre (within a two-mile radius of St Nicholas Cathedral), Norwich City, Nottingham City, Oxford, Thames Valley, Southampton, Portsmouth, Swindon, Basingstoke, Watford.

Band Two/Three	A	B	C	D
2010–Sept 2021	201	177	146	111

Bath, Cheltenham and Gloucester, Taunton, Yeovil, Bury, Chelmsford North, Cambridge County, Peterborough, Bury St E, Norfolk, Lowestoft, Cheshire and North Wales, Coventry, Rugby, Nuneaton, Stratford and Warwick, Exeter, Plymouth, Hull (City), Leeds Outer, Wakefield and Pontefract, Leigh, Lincoln, Luton, Bedford, St Albans, Hitchin, Hertford, Manchester Outer, Oldham, Bolton, Tameside, Newcastle (other than City Centre), Nottingham and Derbyshire, Sheffield, Doncaster and South Yorkshire, Southport, St Helens, Stockport, Altrincham, Salford, Swansea, Newport, Cardiff (Outer), Wigan, Wolverhampton, Walsall, Dudley and Stourbridge, York, Harrogate, Birmingham Outer, Bradford (Dewsbury, Halifax, Huddersfield, Keighley and Skipton), Cumbria, Devon, Cornwall, Grimsby, Skegness, Hull Outer, Kidderminster, Northampton and Leicester, Preston, Lancaster, Blackpool, Chorley, Accrington, Burnley, Blackburn, Rawtenstall and Nelson, Scarborough and Ripon, Stafford, Stoke, Tamworth, Teesside, Worcester, Hereford, Evesham and Redditch, Shrewsbury, Telford, Ludlow, Oswestry, South and West Wales.

London City [EC1–4]	A	B	C	D
2010–Sept 2021	409	296	226	138
London Central [W1, WC1, WC2, SW1]	**A**	**B**	**C**	**D**
2010–Sept 2021	317	242	196	126
London Outer [N, E, SE, W, SW, NW, Bromley, Croydon, Dartford, Gravesend and Uxbridge]	**A**	**B**	**C**	**D**
2010–Sept 2021	229–267	172–229	165	121

A – Solicitors and Fellows of CILEx with over eight years' post-qualification experience including at least eight years' litigation experience.
B – Solicitors, legal executives and costs lawyers with over four years' post-qualification experience including at least four years' litigation experience.
C – Other solicitors and legal executives, costs lawyers and fee earners of equivalent experience.
D – Trainee solicitors, paralegals and fee earners of equivalent experience.
Note "Legal Executive" means a Fellow of the Institute of Legal Executives.

The SCCO Guideline Rates were reviewed but not increased in **July 2014**.

The SCCO Guideline Rates were updated as from **1 October 2021**

SCCO 2021 Guideline Rates

	Grade A	Grade B	Grade C	Grade D
London 1	**£512**	**£348**	**£270**	**£186**
London 2	**£373**	**£289**	**£244**	**£139**
London 3	**£282**	**£232**	**£185**	**£129**
National 1	**£261**	**£218**	**£178**	**£126**
National 2	**£255**	**£218**	**£177**	**£126**

The SCCO Guideline Rates were updated as from **1 January 2024**

SCCO 2024 Guideline Rates

	Grade A	Grade B	Grade C	Grade D
London 1	**£546**	**£371**	**£288**	**£198**
London 2	**£398**	**£308**	**£260**	**£148**
London 3	**£301**	**£247**	**£197**	**£138**
National 1	**£278**	**£233**	**£190**	**£134**
National 2	**£272**	**£233**	**£189**	**£134**

The banding for the **2021** & **2024** Guideline rates is as follows:

Band	Area	Postcodes
London 1	Very heavy commercial and corporate work by centrally based London firms	
London 2	City & Central London – other work	EC1-EC4, W1, WC1, WC2 and SW1
London 3	Outer London	All other London Boroughs, plus Dartford & Gravesend

National 1:

i. The counties of Bedfordshire, Berkshire, Buckinghamshire, Dorset, Essex, Hampshire (& Isle of Wight), Kent, Middlesex, Oxfordshire, East Sussex, West Sussex Suffolk, Surrey and Wiltshire
ii. Birkenhead, Birmingham Inner, Bristol, Cambridge City, Cardiff Inner, Leeds Inner (within 2km of City Art Gallery), Liverpool, Manchester Central, Newcastle City Centre (within 2m of St Nicholas Cathedral), Norwich City and Nottingham City.

National 2:

All places not included in **London 1-3** and **National 1**

The **Guide to the Summary Assessment of Costs 2021** provides useful assistance. It states:

- *"Guideline rates are not scale figures: they are broad approximations only" and "are intended to provide a starting point for those faced with summary assessment. They may also be a helpful starting point on detailed assessment."*
- *"The guideline figures have been grouped according to locality by way of general guidance only. Although many firms may be comparable with others in the same locality, some of them will not be."*
- *"In any particular case the hourly rate which it is reasonable to allow should be determined by reference to the rates charged by comparable firms. For this purpose the statement of costs supplied by the paying party may be of assistance. The rate to allow should not be determined by reference to locality or postcode alone."*
- *" Many High Court cases justify fee earners at a senior level. However, the same may not be true of attendance at pre-trial hearings with counsel. The task of sitting behind counsel should be delegated to a more junior fee earner in all but the most important pre-trial hearings. The fact that the receiving party insisted upon the senior's attendance, or the fact that the fee earner is a sole practitioner who has no juniors to delegate to, should not be the determinative factors. As with hourly rates the statement of costs supplied by the paying party may be of assistance. What grade of fee earner did they use?"*
- *"In substantial and complex litigation an hourly rate in excess of the guideline figures may be appropriate for **Grade A, B and C** fee earners where other factors, for example the value of the litigation, the level of the complexity, the urgency or importance of the matter, as well as any international element, would justify a significantly higher rate."*

Entitlement to VAT on Costs

DATE	VAT RATE
1 April 1991–30 November 2008	17.5%
1 December 2008–31 December 2009	15%
1 January 2010–3 January 2011	17.5%
4 January 2011 to date	20%

Costs PD 44 para.2.3 deals with entitlement to VAT on Costs. It provides:

> *"VAT should not be included in a claim for costs if the receiving party is able to recover the VAT as input tax. Where the receiving party is able to obtain credit from HM Revenue and Customs for a proportion of the VAT as input tax, only that proportion which is not eligible for credit should be included in the claim for costs."*

Costs PD 44 para.2.7 deals with the form of a Bill of Costs where the VAT Rate changes. It provides:

> *"Where there is a change in the rate of VAT, suppliers of goods and services are entitled by ss.88(1) and 88(2) of the VAT Act 1994 in most circumstances to elect whether the new or the old rate of VAT should apply to a supply where the basic and actual tax points span a period during which there has been a change in VAT rates."*

Costs PD 44 para.2.8 provides:

> *"It will be assumed, unless a contrary indication is given in writing, that an election to take advantage of the provisions mentioned in paragraph 2.7 and to charge VAT at the lower rate has been made. In any case in which an election to charge at the lower rate is not made, such a decision must be justified to the court assessing the costs."*

Costs PD 44 para.2.9 deals with apportionment. It provides:

> *"Subject to 2.7 & 2.8 all bills of costs, fees and disbursements on which VAT is included must be divided into separate parts so as to show work done before, on and after the date or dates from which any change in the rate of VAT takes effect. Where, however, a lump sum charge is made for work which spans a period during which there has been a change in VAT rates, and paragraphs 2.7 and 2.8 above do not apply, reference should be made to paragraphs 30.7 or 30.8 of the VAT Guide (Notice 700) (or any revised edition of that notice) published by HMRC. If necessary, the lump sum should be apportioned. The totals of profit costs and disbursements in each part must be carried separately to the summary."*

M2: Conversion formulae

	To convert	Multiply by	To convert	Multiply by
Area	square inches to square centimetres	6.452	square centimetres to square inches	0.1555
	square feet to square metres	0.0929	square metres to square feet	10.7638
	square yards to square metres	0.8361	square metres to square yards	1.196
	square miles to square kilometres	2.590	square kilometres to square miles	0.3861
	acres to hectares	0.4047	hectares to acres	2.471
Length	inches to centimetres	2.540	centimetres to inches	0.3937
	feet to metres	0.3048	metres to feet	3.281
	yards to metres	0.9144	metres to yards	1.094
	miles to kilometres	1.6093	kilometres to miles	0.6214
Temperature	Fahrenheit to Celsius	$-32 \times 5 \div 9$	Celsius to Fahrenheit	$\times 9 \div 5 + 32$
Volume	cubic inches to cubic centimetres	16.39	cubic centimetres to cubic inches	0.06102
	cubic feet to cubic metres	0.02832	cubic metres to cubic feet	35.31
	cubic yards to cubic metres	0.7646	cubic metres to cubic yards	1.308
	cubic inches to litres	0.01639	litres to cubic inches	61.024
	gallons to litres	4.545	litres to gallons	0.22
Weight	grains to grams	0.0647	grams to grains	15.43
	ounces to grams	28.35	grams to ounces	0.03527
	pounds to grams	453.592	grams to pounds	0.0022
	pounds to kilograms	0.4536	kilograms to pounds	2.2046
	tons to kilograms	1016.05	kilograms to tons	0.0009842
Speed	miles per hour to kilometres per hour	1.6093	kilometres per hour to miles per hour	0.6214
Fuel cost	pence per litre to pounds per gallon	0.045	pounds per gallon to pence per litre	22.00
USA measures (dry)	USA pint to UK pint	0.9689	UK pint to USA pint	1.032
	USA pints to litres	0.5506	litres to USA pints	1.816
	USA bushel to UK bushel	0.9689	UK bushel to USA bushel	1.032
	USA bushels to litres	35.238	litres to USA bushels	0.0283

	To convert	Multiply by	To convert	Multiply by
USA measures (liquid)	USA pint to UK pint	0.8327	UK pint to USA pint	1.2
	USA pints to litres	0.4732	litres to USA pint	2.113
	USA gallon to UK gallon	0.8327	UK gallon to USA gallon	1.2
	USA gallons to litres	3.7853	litres to USA gallons	0.2641

Clothing

Shirts

UK/USA	14	14½	15	15½	16	16½	17	17½
Europe	36	37	38	39	40	41	42	43

Ladies clothes

UK							
Size code	10	12	14	16	18	20	22
Bust/hip inches	32/34	34/36	36/38	38/40	40/42	42/44	44/46
Bust/hip cm	84/89	88/93	92/97	97/102	102/107	107/112	112/117
USA							
Size code	6	8	10	12	14	16	18
Bust/hip inches	34½/36½	35½/37½	36½/38½	37½/39½	38/40	39½/41½	41/43

European sizes vary from country to country

Footwear—Men							
British	6	7	8	9	10	11	12
American	6½	7½	8½	9½	10½	11½	12½
Continental	40	41	42	43	44	45	46

Footwear—Women							
British	3	4	5	6	7	8	9
American	4½	5½	6½	7½	8½	9½	10½
Continental	36	37	38	39	40	42	43

Children's clothes

UK												
Age	1	2	3	4	5	6	7	8	9	10	11	12
Height/inches	32	36	38	40	43	45	48	50	53	55	58	60
Height/cm	80	92	98	104	110	116	122	128	134	140	146	152
USA												
Boys' size code	1	2	3	4	5	6	8		10		12	
Girls' size code	2	3	4	5	6	6x	7	8	10		12	
Europe												
Height/cm	80	92	98	104	110	116	122	128	134	140	146	152

M3: Perpetual calendar

The number opposite each of the years in the list below indicates which of the calendars on the following pages is the one for that year. Thus the number opposite 2000 is 14, so calendar 14 can be used as a 2000 calendar.

Leap years

Years divisible by four without remainder are leap years with 366 days instead of 365 (29 days in February instead of 28). However, the first year of the century is not a leap year except when divisible by 400.

Year	Calendar	Year	Calendar	Year	Calendar	Year	Calendar	Year	Calendar	Year	Calendar
1980	10	1992	11	2004	12	2016	13	2028	14	2040	8
1981	5	1993	6	2005	7	2017	1	2029	2	2041	3
1982	6	1994	7	2006	1	2018	2	2030	3	2042	4
1983	7	1995	1	2007	2	2019	3	2031	4	2043	5
1984	8	1996	9	2008	10	2020	11	2032	12	2044	13
1985	3	1997	4	2009	5	2021	6	2033	7	2045	1
1986	4	1998	5	2010	6	2022	7	2034	1	2046	2
1987	5	1999	6	2011	7	2023	1	2035	2	2047	3
1988	13	2000	14	2012	8	2024	9	2036	10	2048	11
1989	1	2001	2	2013	3	2025	4	2037	5	2049	6
1990	2	2002	3	2014	4	2026	5	2038	6	2050	7
1991	3	2003	4	2015	5	2027	6	2039	7	2051	1

1

	January	February	March	April
M	2 9 16 23 30	6 13 20 27	6 13 20 27	3 10 17 24
T	3 10 17 24 31	7 14 21 28	7 14 21 28	4 11 18 25
W	4 11 18 25	1 8 15 22	1 8 15 22 29	5 12 19 26
T	5 12 19 26	2 9 16 23	2 9 16 23 30	6 13 20 27
F	6 13 20 27	3 10 17 24	3 10 17 24 31	7 14 21 28
S	7 14 21 28	4 11 18 25	4 11 18 25	1 8 15 22 29
S	1 8 15 22 29	5 12 19 26	5 12 19 26	2 9 16 23 30

	May	June	July	August
M	1 8 15 22 29	5 12 19 26	3 10 17 24 31	7 14 21 28
T	2 9 16 23 30	6 13 20 27	4 11 18 25	1 8 15 22 29
W	3 10 17 24 31	7 14 21 28	5 12 19 26	2 9 16 23 30
T	4 11 18 25	1 8 15 22 29	6 13 20 27	3 10 17 24 31
F	5 12 19 26	2 9 16 23 30	7 14 21 28	4 11 18 25
S	6 13 20 27	3 10 17 24	1 8 15 22 29	5 12 19 26
S	7 14 21 28	4 11 18 25	2 9 16 23 30	6 13 20 27

	September	October	November	December
M	4 11 18 25	2 9 16 23 30	6 13 20 27	4 11 18 25
T	5 12 19 26	3 10 17 24 31	7 14 21 28	5 12 19 26
W	6 13 20 27	4 11 18 25	1 8 15 22 29	6 13 20 27
T	7 14 21 28	5 12 19 26	2 9 16 23 30	7 14 21 28
F	1 8 15 22 29	6 13 20 27	3 10 17 24	1 8 15 22 29
S	2 9 16 23 30	7 14 21 28	4 11 18 25	2 9 16 23 30
S	3 10 17 24	1 8 15 22 29	5 12 19 26	3 10 17 24 31

2

	January	February	March	April
M	1 8 15 22 29	5 12 19 26	5 12 19 26	2 9 16 23 30
T	2 9 16 23 30	6 13 20 27	6 13 20 27	3 10 17 24
W	3 10 17 24 31	7 14 21 28	7 14 21 28	4 11 18 25
T	4 11 18 25	1 8 15 22	1 8 15 22 29	5 12 19 26
F	5 12 19 26	2 9 16 23	2 9 16 23 30	6 13 20 27
S	6 13 20 27	3 10 17 24	3 10 17 24 31	7 14 21 28
S	7 14 21 28	4 11 18 25	4 11 18 25	1 8 15 22 29

	May	June	July	August
M	7 14 21 28	4 11 18 25	2 9 16 23 30	6 13 20 27
T	1 8 15 22 29	5 12 19 26	3 10 17 24 31	7 14 21 28
W	2 9 16 23 30	6 13 20 27	4 11 18 25	1 8 15 22 29
T	3 10 17 24 31	7 14 21 28	5 12 19 26	2 9 16 23 30
F	4 11 18 25	1 8 15 22 29	6 13 20 27	3 10 17 24 31
S	5 12 19 26	2 9 16 23 30	7 14 21 28	4 11 18 25
S	6 13 20 27	3 10 17 24	1 8 15 22 29	5 12 19 26

	September	October	November	December
M	3 10 17 24	1 8 15 22 29	5 12 19 26	3 10 17 24 31
T	4 11 18 25	2 9 16 23 30	6 13 20 27	4 11 18 25
W	5 12 19 26	3 10 17 24 31	7 14 21 28	5 12 19 26
T	6 13 20 27	4 11 18 25	1 8 15 22 29	6 13 20 27
F	7 14 21 28	5 12 19 26	2 9 16 23 30	7 14 21 28
S	1 8 15 22 29	6 13 20 27	3 10 17 24	1 8 15 22 29
S	2 9 16 23 30	7 14 21 28	4 11 18 25	2 9 16 23 30

3

	January	February	March	April
M	7 14 21 28	4 11 18 25	4 11 18 25	1 8 15 22 29
T	1 8 15 22 29	5 12 19 26	5 12 19 26	2 9 16 23 30
W	2 9 16 23 30	6 13 20 27	6 13 20 27	3 10 17 24
T	3 10 17 24 31	7 14 21 28	7 14 21 28	4 11 18 25
F	4 11 18 25	1 8 15 22	1 8 15 22 29	5 12 19 26
S	5 12 19 26	2 9 16 23	2 9 16 23 30	6 13 20 27
S	6 13 20 27	3 10 17 24	3 10 17 24 31	7 14 21 28

	May	June	July	August
M	6 13 20 27	3 10 17 24	1 8 15 22 29	5 12 19 26
T	7 14 21 28	4 11 18 25	2 9 16 23 30	7 14 21 28
W	1 8 15 22 29	5 12 19 26	3 10 17 24 31	6 13 20 27
T	2 9 16 23 30	6 13 20 27	4 11 18 25	1 8 15 22 29
F	3 10 17 24 31	7 14 21 28	5 12 19 26	2 9 16 23 30
S	4 11 18 25	1 8 15 22 29	6 13 20 27	3 10 17 24 31
S	5 12 19 26	2 9 16 23 30	7 14 21 28	4 11 18 25

	September	October	November	December
M	2 9 16 23 30	7 14 21 28	4 11 18 25	2 9 16 23 30
T	3 10 17 24	1 8 15 22 29	5 12 19 26	3 10 17 24 31
W	4 11 18 25	2 9 16 23 30	6 13 20 27	4 11 18 25
T	5 12 19 26	3 10 17 24 31	7 14 21 28	5 12 19 26
F	6 13 20 27	4 11 18 25	1 8 15 22 29	6 13 20 27
S	7 14 21 28	5 12 19 26	2 9 16 23 30	7 14 21 28
S	1 8 15 22 29	6 13 20 27	3 10 17 24	1 8 15 22 29

4

	January	February	March	April
M	6 13 20 27	3 10 17 24	3 10 17 24 31	7 14 21 28
T	7 14 21 28	4 11 18 25	4 11 18 25	1 8 15 22 29
W	1 8 15 22 29	5 12 19 26	5 12 19 26	2 9 16 23 30
T	2 9 16 23 30	6 13 20 27	6 13 20 27	3 10 17 24
F	3 10 17 24 31	7 14 21 28	7 14 21 28	4 11 18 25
S	4 11 18 25	1 8 15 22	1 8 15 22 29	5 12 19 26
S	5 12 19 26	2 9 16 23	2 9 16 23 30	6 13 20 27

	May	June	July	August
M	5 12 19 26	2 9 16 23 30	7 14 21 28	4 11 18 25
T	6 13 20 27	3 10 17 24	1 8 15 22 29	5 12 19 26
W	7 14 21 28	4 11 18 25	2 9 16 23 30	6 13 20 27
T	1 8 15 22 29	5 12 19 26	3 10 17 24 31	7 14 21 28
F	2 9 16 23 30	6 13 20 27	4 11 18 25	1 8 15 22 29
S	3 10 17 24 31	7 14 21 28	5 12 19 26	2 9 16 23 30
S	4 11 18 25	1 8 15 22 29	6 13 20 27	3 10 17 24 31

	September	October	November	December
M	1 8 15 22 29	6 13 20 27	3 10 17 24	1 8 15 22 29
T	2 9 16 23 30	7 14 21 28	4 11 18 25	2 9 16 23 30
W	3 10 17 24	1 8 15 22 29	5 12 19 26	3 10 17 24 31
T	4 11 18 25	2 9 16 23 30	6 13 20 27	4 11 18 25
F	5 12 19 26	3 10 17 24 31	7 14 21 28	5 12 19 26
S	6 13 20 27	4 11 18 25	1 8 15 22 29	6 13 20 27
S	7 14 21 28	5 12 19 26	2 9 16 23 30	7 14 21 28

5

	January	February	March	April
M	5 12 19 26	2 9 16 23	2 9 16 23 30	6 13 20 27
T	6 13 20 27	3 10 17 24	3 10 17 24 31	7 14 21 28
W	7 14 21 28	4 11 18 25	4 11 18 25	1 8 15 22 29
T	1 8 15 22 29	5 12 19 26	5 12 19 26	2 9 16 23 30
F	2 9 16 23 30	6 13 20 27	6 13 20 27	3 10 17 24
S	3 10 17 24 31	7 14 21 28	7 14 21 28	4 11 18 25
S	4 11 18 25	1 8 15 22	1 8 15 22 29	5 12 19 26

	May	June	July	August
M	4 11 18 25	1 8 15 22 29	6 13 20 27	3 10 17 24 31
T	5 12 19 26	2 9 16 23 30	7 14 21 28	4 11 18 25
W	6 13 20 27	3 10 17 24	1 8 15 22 29	5 12 19 26
T	7 14 21 28	4 11 18 25	2 9 16 23 30	6 13 20 27
F	1 8 15 22 29	5 12 19 26	3 10 17 24 31	7 14 21 28
S	2 9 16 23 30	6 13 20 27	4 11 18 25	1 8 15 22 29
S	3 10 17 24 31	7 14 21 28	5 12 19 26	2 9 16 23 30

	September	October	November	December
M	7 14 21 28	5 12 19 26	2 9 16 23 30	7 14 21 28
T	1 8 15 22 29	6 13 20 27	3 10 17 24	1 8 15 22 29
W	2 9 16 23 30	7 14 21 28	4 11 18 25	2 9 16 23 30
T	3 10 17 24	1 8 15 22 29	5 12 19 26	3 10 17 24 31
F	4 11 18 25	2 9 16 23 30	6 13 20 27	4 11 18 25
S	5 12 19 26	3 10 17 24 31	7 14 21 28	5 12 19 26
S	6 13 20 27	4 11 18 25	1 8 15 22 29	6 13 20 27

6

	January	February	March	April
M	4 11 18 25	1 8 15 22	1 8 15 22 29	5 12 19 26
T	5 12 19 26	2 9 16 23	2 9 16 23 30	6 13 20 27
W	6 13 20 27	3 10 17 24	3 10 17 24 31	7 14 21 28
T	7 14 21 28	4 11 18 25	4 11 18 25	1 8 15 22 29
F	1 8 15 22 29	5 12 19 26	5 12 19 26	2 9 16 23 30
S	2 9 16 23 30	6 13 20 27	6 13 20 27	3 10 17 24
S	3 10 17 24 31	7 14 21 28	7 14 21 28	4 11 18 25

	May	June	July	August
M	3 10 17 24 31	7 14 21 28	5 12 19 26	2 9 16 23 30
T	4 11 18 25	1 8 15 22 29	6 13 20 27	3 10 17 24 31
W	5 12 19 26	2 9 16 23 30	7 14 21 28	4 11 18 25
T	6 13 20 27	3 10 17 24	1 8 15 22 29	5 12 19 26
F	7 14 21 28	4 11 18 25	2 9 16 23 30	6 13 20 27
S	1 8 15 22 29	5 12 19 26	3 10 17 24 31	7 14 21 28
S	2 9 16 23 30	6 13 20 27	4 11 18 25	1 8 15 22 29

	September	October	November	December
M	6 13 20 27	4 11 18 25	1 8 15 22 29	6 13 20 27
T	7 14 21 28	5 12 19 26	2 9 16 23 30	7 14 21 28
W	1 8 15 22 29	6 13 20 27	3 10 17 24	1 8 15 22 29
T	2 9 16 23 30	7 14 21 28	4 11 18 25	2 9 16 23 30
F	3 10 17 24	1 8 15 22 29	5 12 19 26	3 10 17 24 31
S	4 11 18 25	2 9 16 23 30	6 13 20 27	4 11 18 25
S	5 12 19 26	3 10 17 24 31	7 14 21 28	5 12 19 26

7

	January	February	March	April
M	3 10 17 24 31	7 14 21 28	7 14 21 28	4 11 18 25
T	4 11 18 25	1 8 15 22	1 8 15 22 29	5 12 19 26
W	5 12 19 26	2 9 16 23	2 9 16 23 30	6 13 20 27
T	6 13 20 27	3 10 17 24	3 10 17 24 31	7 14 21 28
F	7 14 21 28	4 11 18 25	4 11 18 25	1 8 15 22 29
S	1 8 15 22 29	5 12 19 26	5 12 19 26	2 9 16 23 30
S	2 9 16 23 30	6 13 20 27	6 13 20 27	3 10 17 24

	May	June	July	August
M	2 9 16 23 30	6 13 20 27	4 11 18 25	1 8 15 22 29
T	3 10 17 24 31	7 14 21 28	5 12 19 26	2 9 16 23 30
W	4 11 18 25	1 8 15 22 29	6 13 20 27	3 10 17 24 31
T	5 12 19 26	2 9 16 23 30	7 14 21 28	4 11 18 25
F	6 13 20 27	3 10 17 24	1 8 15 22 29	5 12 19 26
S	7 14 21 28	4 11 18 25	2 9 16 23 30	6 13 20 27
S	1 8 15 22 29	5 12 19 26	3 10 17 24 31	7 14 21 28

	September	October	November	December
M	5 12 19 26	3 10 17 24 31	7 14 21 28	5 12 19 26
T	6 13 20 27	4 11 18 25	1 8 15 22 29	6 13 20 27
W	7 14 21 28	5 12 19 26	2 9 16 23 30	7 14 21 28
T	1 8 15 22 29	6 13 20 27	3 10 17 24	1 8 15 22 29
F	2 9 16 23 30	7 14 21 28	4 11 18 25	2 9 16 23 30
S	3 10 17 24	1 8 15 22 29	5 12 19 26	3 10 17 24 31
S	4 11 18 25	2 9 16 23 30	6 13 20 27	4 11 18 25

8

	January	February	March	April
M	2 9 16 23 30	6 13 20 27	5 12 19 26	2 9 16 23 30
T	3 10 17 24 31	7 14 21 28	6 13 20 27	3 10 17 24
W	4 11 18 25	1 8 15 22 29	7 14 21 28	4 11 18 25
T	5 12 19 26	2 9 16 23	1 8 15 22 29	5 12 19 26
F	6 13 20 27	3 10 17 24	2 9 16 23 30	6 13 20 27
S	7 14 21 28	4 11 18 25	3 10 17 24 31	7 14 21 28
S	1 8 15 22 29	5 12 19 26	4 11 18 25	1 8 15 22 29

	May	June	July	August
M	7 14 21 28	4 11 18 25	2 9 16 23 30	6 13 20 27
T	1 8 15 22 29	5 12 19 26	3 10 17 24 31	7 14 21 28
W	2 9 16 23 30	6 13 20 27	4 11 18 25	1 8 15 22 29
T	3 10 17 24 31	7 14 21 28	5 12 19 26	2 9 16 23 30
F	4 11 18 25	1 8 15 22 29	6 13 20 27	3 10 17 24 31
S	5 12 19 26	2 9 16 23 30	7 14 21 28	4 11 18 25
S	6 13 20 27	3 10 17 24	1 8 15 22 29	5 12 19 26

	September	October	November	December
M	3 10 17 24	1 8 15 22 29	5 12 19 26	3 10 17 24 31
T	4 11 18 25	2 9 16 23 30	6 13 20 27	4 11 18 25
W	5 12 19 26	3 10 17 24 31	7 14 21 28	5 12 19 26
T	6 13 20 27	4 11 18 25	1 8 15 22 29	6 13 20 27
F	7 14 21 28	5 12 19 26	2 9 16 23 30	7 14 21 28
S	1 8 15 22 29	6 13 20 27	3 10 17 24	1 8 15 22 29
S	2 9 16 23 30	7 14 21 28	4 11 18 25	2 9 16 23 30

9

	January	February	March	April
M	1 8 15 22 29	5 12 19 26	4 11 18 25	1 8 15 22 29
T	2 9 16 23 30	6 13 20 27	5 12 19 26	2 9 16 23 30
W	3 10 17 24 31	7 14 21 28	6 13 20 27	3 10 17 24
T	4 11 18 25	1 8 15 22 29	7 14 21 28	4 11 18 25
F	5 12 19 26	2 9 16 23	1 8 15 22 29	5 12 19 26
S	6 13 20 27	3 10 17 24	2 9 16 23 30	6 13 20 27
S	7 14 21 28	4 11 18 25	3 10 17 24 31	7 14 21 28

	May	June	July	August
M	6 13 20 27	3 10 17 24	1 8 15 22 29	5 12 19 26
T	7 14 21 28	4 11 18 25	2 9 16 23 30	6 13 20 27
W	1 8 15 22 29	5 12 19 26	3 10 17 24 31	7 14 21 28
T	2 9 16 23 30	6 13 20 27	4 11 18 25	1 8 15 22 29
F	3 10 17 24 31	7 14 21 28	5 12 19 26	2 9 16 23 30
S	4 11 18 25	1 8 15 22 29	6 13 20 27	3 10 17 24 31
S	5 12 19 26	2 9 16 23 30	7 14 21 28	4 11 18 25

	September	October	November	December
M	2 9 16 23 30	7 14 21 28	4 11 18 25	2 9 16 23 30
T	3 10 17 24	1 8 15 22 29	5 12 19 26	3 10 17 24 31
W	4 11 18 25	2 9 16 23 30	6 13 20 27	4 11 18 25
T	5 12 19 26	3 10 17 24 31	7 14 21 28	5 12 19 26
F	6 13 20 27	4 11 18 25	1 8 15 22 29	6 13 20 27
S	7 14 21 28	5 12 19 26	2 9 16 23 30	7 14 21 28
S	1 8 15 22 29	6 13 20 27	3 10 17 24	1 8 15 22 29

10

	January	February	March	April
M	7 14 21 28	4 11 18 25	3 10 17 24 31	7 14 21 28
T	1 8 15 22 29	5 12 19 26	4 11 18 25	1 8 15 22 29
W	2 9 16 23 30	6 13 20 27	5 12 19 26	2 9 16 23 30
T	3 10 17 24 31	7 14 21 28	6 13 20 27	3 10 17 24
F	4 11 18 25	1 8 15 22 29	7 14 21 28	4 11 18 25
S	5 12 19 26	2 9 16 23	1 8 15 22 29	5 12 19 26
S	6 13 20 27	3 10 17 24	2 9 16 23 30	6 13 20 27

	May	June	July	August
M	5 12 19 26	2 9 16 23 30	7 14 21 28	4 11 18 25
T	6 13 20 27	3 10 17 24	1 8 15 22 29	5 12 19 26
W	7 14 21 28	4 11 18 25	2 9 16 23 30	6 13 20 27
T	1 8 15 22 29	5 12 19 26	3 10 17 24 31	7 14 21 28
F	2 9 16 23 30	6 13 20 27	4 11 18 25	1 8 15 22 29
S	3 10 17 24 31	7 14 21 28	5 12 19 26	2 9 16 23 30
S	4 11 18 25	1 8 15 22 29	6 13 20 27	3 10 17 24 31

	September	October	November	December
M	1 8 15 22 29	6 13 20 27	3 10 17 24	1 8 15 22 29
T	2 9 16 23 30	7 14 21 28	4 11 18 25	2 9 16 23 30
W	3 10 17 24	1 8 15 22 29	5 12 19 26	3 10 17 24 31
T	4 11 18 25	2 9 16 23 30	6 13 20 27	4 11 18 25
F	5 12 19 26	3 10 17 24 31	7 14 21 28	5 12 19 26
S	6 13 20 27	4 11 18 25	1 8 15 22 29	6 13 20 27
S	7 14 21 28	5 12 19 26	2 9 16 23 30	7 14 21 28

11

	January	February	March	April
M	6 13 20 27	3 10 17 24	2 9 16 23 30	6 13 20 27
T	7 14 21 28	4 11 18 25	3 10 17 24 31	7 14 21 28
W	1 8 15 22 29	5 12 19 26	4 11 18 25	1 8 15 22 29
T	2 9 16 23 30	6 13 20 27	5 12 19 26	2 9 16 23 30
F	3 10 17 24 31	7 14 21 28	6 13 20 27	3 10 17 24
S	4 11 18 25	1 8 15 22 29	7 14 21 28	4 11 18 25
S	5 12 19 26	2 9 16 23	1 8 15 22 29	5 12 19 26

	May	June	July	August
M	4 11 18 25	1 8 15 22 29	6 13 20 27	3 10 17 24 31
T	5 12 19 26	2 9 16 23 30	7 14 21 28	4 11 18 25
W	6 13 20 27	3 10 17 24	1 8 15 22 29	5 12 19 26
T	7 14 21 28	4 11 18 25	2 9 16 23 30	6 13 20 27
F	1 8 15 22 29	5 12 19 26	3 10 17 24 31	7 14 21 28
S	2 9 16 23 30	6 13 20 27	4 11 18 25	1 8 15 22 29
S	3 10 17 24 31	7 14 21 28	5 12 19 26	2 9 16 23 30

	September	October	November	December
M	7 14 21 28	5 12 19 26	2 9 16 23 30	7 14 21 28
T	1 8 15 22 29	6 13 20 27	3 10 17 24	1 8 15 22 29
W	2 9 16 23 30	7 14 21 28	4 11 18 25	2 9 16 23 30
T	3 10 17 24	1 8 15 22 29	5 12 19 26	3 10 17 24 31
F	4 11 18 25	2 9 16 23 30	6 13 20 27	4 11 18 25
S	5 12 19 26	3 10 17 24 31	7 14 21 28	5 12 19 26
S	6 13 20 27	4 11 18 25	1 8 15 22 29	6 13 20 27

12

	January	February	March	April
M	5 12 19 26	2 9 16 23	1 8 15 22 29	5 12 19 26
T	6 13 20 27	3 10 17 24	2 9 16 23 30	6 13 20 27
W	7 14 21 28	4 11 18 25	3 10 17 24 31	7 14 21 28
T	1 8 15 22 29	5 12 19 26	4 11 18 25	1 8 15 22 29
F	2 9 16 23 30	6 13 20 27	5 12 19 26	2 9 16 23 30
S	3 10 17 24 31	7 14 21 28	6 13 20 27	3 10 17 24
S	4 11 18 25	1 8 15 22 29	7 14 21 28	4 11 18 25

	May	June	July	August
M	3 10 17 24 31	7 14 21 28	5 12 19 26	2 9 16 23 30
T	4 11 18 25	1 8 15 22 29	6 13 20 27	3 10 17 24 31
W	5 12 19 26	2 9 16 23 30	7 14 21 28	4 11 18 25
T	6 13 20 27	3 10 17 24	1 8 15 22 29	5 12 19 26
F	7 14 21 28	4 11 18 25	2 9 16 23 30	6 13 20 27
S	1 8 15 22 29	5 12 19 26	3 10 17 24 31	7 14 21 28
S	2 9 16 23 30	6 13 20 27	4 11 18 25	1 8 15 22 29

	September	October	November	December
M	6 13 20 27	4 11 18 25	1 8 15 22 29	6 13 20 27
T	7 14 21 28	5 12 19 26	2 9 16 23 30	7 14 21 28
W	1 8 15 22 29	6 13 20 27	3 10 17 24	1 8 15 22 29
T	2 9 16 23 30	7 14 21 28	4 11 18 25	2 9 16 23 30
F	3 10 17 24	1 8 15 22 29	5 12 19 26	3 10 17 24 31
S	4 11 18 25	2 9 16 23 30	6 13 20 27	4 11 18 25
S	5 12 19 26	3 10 17 24 31	7 14 21 28	5 12 19 26

13

	January	February	March	April
M	4 11 18 25	1 8 15 22 29	7 14 21 28	4 11 18 25
T	5 12 19 26	2 9 16 23	1 8 15 22 29	5 12 19 26
W	6 13 20 27	3 10 17 24	2 9 16 23 30	6 13 20 27
T	7 14 21 28	4 11 18 25	3 10 17 24 31	7 14 21 28
F	1 8 15 22 29	5 12 19 26	4 11 18 25	1 8 15 22 29
S	2 9 16 23 30	6 13 20 27	5 12 19 26	2 9 16 23 30
S	3 10 17 24 31	7 14 21 28	6 13 20 27	3 10 17 24

	May	June	July	August
M	2 9 16 23 30	6 13 20 27	4 11 18 25	1 8 15 22 29
T	3 10 17 24 31	7 14 21 28	5 12 19 26	2 9 16 23 30
W	4 11 18 25	1 8 15 22 29	6 13 20 27	3 10 17 24 31
T	5 12 19 26	2 9 16 23 30	7 14 21 28	4 11 18 25
F	6 13 20 27	3 10 17 24	1 8 15 22 29	5 12 19 26
S	7 14 21 28	4 11 18 25	2 9 16 23 30	6 13 20 27
S	1 8 15 22 29	5 12 19 26	3 10 17 24 31	7 14 21 28

	September	October	November	December
M	5 12 19 26	3 10 17 24 31	7 14 21 28	5 12 19 26
T	6 13 20 27	4 11 18 25	1 8 15 22 29	6 13 20 27
W	7 14 21 28	5 12 19 26	2 9 16 23 30	7 14 21 28
T	1 8 15 22 29	6 13 20 27	3 10 17 24	1 8 15 22 29
F	2 9 16 23 30	7 14 21 28	4 11 18 25	2 9 16 23 30
S	3 10 17 24	1 8 15 22 29	5 12 19 26	3 10 17 24 31
S	4 11 18 25	2 9 16 23 30	6 13 20 27	4 11 18 25

14

	January	February	March	April
M	3 10 17 24 31	7 14 21 28	6 13 20 27	3 10 17 24
T	4 11 18 25	1 8 15 22 29	7 14 21 28	4 11 18 25
W	5 12 19 26	2 9 16 23	1 8 15 22 29	5 12 19 26
T	6 13 20 27	3 10 17 24	2 9 16 23 30	6 13 20 27
F	7 14 21 28	4 11 18 25	3 10 17 24 31	7 14 21 28
S	1 8 15 22 29	5 12 19 26	4 11 18 25	1 8 15 22 29
S	2 9 16 23 30	6 13 20 27	5 12 19 26	2 9 16 23 30

	May	June	July	August
M	1 8 15 22 29	5 12 19 26	3 10 17 24 31	7 14 21 28
T	2 9 16 23 30	6 13 20 27	4 11 18 25	1 8 15 22 29
W	3 10 17 24 31	7 14 21 28	5 12 19 26	2 9 16 23 30
T	4 11 18 25	1 8 15 22 29	6 13 20 27	3 10 17 24 31
F	5 12 19 26	2 9 16 23 30	7 14 21 28	4 11 18 25
S	6 13 20 27	3 10 17 24	1 8 15 22 29	5 12 19 26
S	7 14 21 28	4 11 18 25	2 9 16 23 30	6 13 20 27

	September	October	November	December
M	4 11 18 25	2 9 16 23 30	6 13 20 27	4 11 18 25
T	5 12 19 26	3 10 1 24 31	7 14 21 28	5 12 19 26
W	6 13 20 27	4 11 18 25	1 8 15 22 29	6 13 20 27
T	7 14 21 28	5 12 19 26	2 9 16 23 30	7 14 21 28
F	1 8 15 22 29	6 13 20 27	3 10 17 24	1 8 15 22 29
S	2 9 16 23 30	7 14 21 28	4 11 18 25	2 9 16 23 30
S	3 10 17 24	1 8 15 22 29	5 12 19 26	3 10 17 24 31

M4: Religious festivals

	2023	
☬	Birthday of Guru Gobind Singh	5 January
✝	Ash Wednesday	22 February
✡	Purim	7 March
ॐ	Holi	8 March
☬	Hola Mohalla	8 March
☪	Ramadan begins	23 March
✡	Passover	6 April
✝	Good Friday	7 April
✝	Easter/Pascha/Resurrection Day	9 April
✝	Easter Monday	10 April
☬	Vaisakhi Day	14 April
☪	Eid al Fitr	22 April
✝	Ascension	18 May
✡	Shavuot	26 May
✝	Pentecost	28 May
☪	Eid al Adha	29 June
☪	Hijra – New Year	19 July
☪	Ashura	28 July
✡	Rosh Hashanah	16 September
✡	Yom Kippur	25 September
☪	Mawlid al-Nabi	27 September
✡	Sukkot	30 September
ॐ	Dussehra	24 October
ॐ	Diwali	12 November
☬	Birthday of Guru Nanak	27 November
✡	Chanukah	8 December
✝	Christmas	25 December

	2024	
☬	Birthday of Guru Gobind Singh	17 January
✝	Ash Wednesday	14 February
☪	Ramadan begins	11 March
✡	Purim	24 March
ॐ	Holi	25 March
☬	Hola Mohalla	25 March
✝	Good Friday	29 March
✝	Easter/Pascha/Resurrection Day	31 March
✝	Easter Monday	1 April
☪	Eid al Fitr	10 April
☬	Vaisakhi Day	13 April
✡	Passover	23 April
✝	Ascension	9 May
✝	Pentecost	19 May
✡	Shavuot	12 June
☪	Eid al Adha	17 June
☪	Hijra – New Year	8 July
☪	Ashura	17 July
☪	Mawlid al-Nabi	16 September
✡	Rosh Hashanah	3 October
✡	Yom Kippur	12 October
ॐ	Dussehra	12 October
✡	Sukkot	17 October
ॐ	Diwali	1 November
☬	Birthday of Guru Nanak	15 November
✝	Christmas	25 December
✡	Chanukah	26 December

	2025	
☬	Birthday of Guru Gobind Singh	6 January
☪	Ramadan begins	1 March
✝	Ash Wednesday	5 March
✡	Purim	14 March
ॐ	Holi	14 March
☬	Hola Mohalla	14 March
☪	Eid al Fitr	31 March
✡	Passover	13 April
☬	Vaisakhi Day	14 April
✝	Good Friday	18 April
✝	Easter/Pascha/Resurrection Day	20 April
✝	Easter Monday	21 April
✝	Ascension	29 May
✡	Shavuot	2 June
☪	Eid al Adha	7 June
✝	Pentecost	8 June
☪	Hijra – New Year	27 June
☪	Ashura	5 July
☪	Mawlid al-Nabi	5 September
✡	Rosh Hashanah	23 September
✡	Yom Kippur	2 October
ॐ	Dussehra	2 October
✡	Sukkot	7 October
ॐ	Diwali	20 October
☬	Birthday of Guru Nanak	5 November
✡	Chanukah	15 December
✝	Christmas	25 December

✝ Christian
ॐ Hindu
✡ Jewish
☪ Muslim
☬ Sikh

Note: all Islamic and Jewish holidays begin at sundown on the preceding day.

M5: Medical reference intervals and scales

Haematology—reference intervals

Measurement	Reference interval
White cell count	4.0–11.0 × 10^{9}/l
Red cell count – Male: Female:	4.5–6.5 × 10^{1}2/l 3.9–5.6 × 10^{1}2/l
Haemoglobin – Male: Female:	130–180g/l 115–165g/l
Platelet count	150.0–400.0 × 10^{9}/l
Erythrocyte sedimentation rate (ESR) – Male: Female:	Up to age in years divided by two. Up to (age in years plus 10) divided by two.
Prothrombin time (factors II, VII, X)	10–14 seconds
Activated partial thromboplastin time (VIII, IX, XI, XII)	27–41 seconds

Target INR (international normalized ratio) for acute venous thromboembolism (British Society for Haematology Guidelines on oral anticoagulation with Warfarin, 4th edition, 2011)

First episode of venous thromboembolism (VTE)	INR target 2.5
Recurrent VTE whilst anticoagulated within the therapeutic range	INR target 3.5

Cerebrospinal fluid—reference intervals

Opening pressure (mmCSF)	Infants: < 80; children: < 90; adults: < 210

Substance	Reference interval
Glucose	3.3–4.4 mmol/l or ≥ 2/3 of plasma glucose
Chloride	122–128 mmol/l
Lactate	< 2.8 mmol/l

Biochemistry—reference intervals

Substance	Specimen	Reference Interval
Albumin	P	*35–50 g/l
Amylase	P	30–118 U/l
Bicarbonate	P	*24–30 mmol/l
C reactive protein (CRP)	P	< 6 mg/l
Calcium (ionised)	P	1.0–1.25 mmol/l
Calcium (total)	P	*2.12–2.65 mmol/l
Chloride	P	98–107 mmol/l
Cholesterol	P	3.3–6.2 mmol/l
Creatinine	P	*58–110 mmol/l
Glucose (fasting)	P	3.5–5.5 mmol/l
Glycosylated haemoglobin	B	5–8%
Phosphate	P	0.8–1.45 mmol/l
Potassium	P	3.6–5.0 mmol/l
Protein (total)	P	60–80 g/l
Sodium	P	*137–145 mmol/l
Urea	P	*2.5–7.5 mmol/l

Key: P = plasma; B = whole blood

* Reference intervals for these substances differ in pregnancy. Reference intervals in pregnancy are not reproduced here.

Arterial blood gases—reference intervals

pH:	7.35–7.45
PaO^2:	>10.6 kPa
$PaCO^2$:	4.7–6.0 kPa
Base excess	±2 mmol/l
NB: 7.6 mmHg = 1 kPa (atmospheric pressure = 100 kPa)	

Apgar scoring chart

A baby's condition is assessed at one and five minutes after birth by means of the Apgar score. This system observes five signs. A score of nought, one or two is awarded for each sign.

Sign	0	1	2
Heart rate	absent	slow (below 100)	over 100
Respiratory effect	absent	weak cry, hypoventilation	good cry
Muscle tone	limp	some flexion of extremities	well flexed
Reflex irritability	no response	some motion	cry
Colour	blue, pale	body pink, extremities blue	completely pink

NB: An Apgar score of 10 represents optimal condition. A score of three or less indicates a markedly asphyxiated infant.

Glasgow coma scale

Three types of response are assessed:

	Score	
Best motor response	6	Obeys commands
	5	Localises to pain
	4	Flexion/withdrawal to pain
	3	Abnormal flexion
	2	Abnormal extension
	1	None
Best verbal response	5	Oriented
	4	Confused
	3	Inappropriate words
	2	Incomprehensible sounds
	1	None
Eye opening	4	Spontaneously
	3	To speech
	2	To pain
	1	None

The overall score is the sum of the scores in each area, e.g. no response to pain + no verbal response + no eye opening = three.

In severe injury the score is eight or under.
In moderate injury the score is nine–12.
In minor injury the score is 13–15.

PULHHEEMS rating

This is a "qualitative" system of physical and mental assessment and grading for Armed Forces Personnel. It is taken from the joint Services publication JSP950 and is issued to all Service and Civilian medical practitioners who are required to examine applicants for entry to the Armed Forces. It is carried out on new recruits, and repeated at five-yearly intervals after the age of 30. After the age of 50, it is performed at two-yearly intervals. Service Medical Boards are also conducted throughout service to "assess and re-grade personnel following changes in their functional capacity and medical employability resulting from illness and/or injury, either on a temporary or permanent basis".

PULHHEEMS is an abbreviation for the qualities to be tested. These include:

P	Physique/Age/Strength/Stamina
U	Upper limbs; Strength/Range of Movement
L	Lower limbs, pelvis and back; Strength/ROM [range of movement]
H	Hearing in the left ear
H	Hearing in the right ear
E	Visual acuity—left eye
E	Visual acuity—right eye
M	Mental Capacity
S	Stability (emotional)

Interpretation of a value in each field describes function and determines the grading used. In general, a "lower" number indicates a "higher" level of physical prowess in all areas. For example "P2" equates to satisfactory level of ability in all areas, whereas a score of P7 would indicate "medical fitness but with major employment limitations". A score of S8 renders the individual unfit for service—*i.e.* "defect of emotional stability such that the individual is below P7 criteria". In the form this appears in a table as follows (Lord Nelson taken as an example):

P	U	L	H	H	E	E	M	S
2	7	3	2	2	2	8	2	2

FDI World Dental Federation notation

FDI Two-Digit Notation

Permanent Teeth

			upper right								upper left				
18	17	16	15	14	13	12	11	21	22	23	24	25	26	27	28
48	47	46	45	44	43	43	41	31	32	33	34	35	36	37	38
			lower right								lower left				
							Deciduous teeth (baby teeth)								
			upper right								upper left				
			55	54	53	52	51	61	62	63	64	65			
			85	84	83	82	81	71	72	73	74	75			
			lower right								lower left				

Codes, names and usual number of roots

Codes		Names	Usual number of roots
11	21	maxillary central incisor	1
41	31	mandibular central incisor	1
12	22	maxillary lateral incisor	1
42	32	mandibular lateral incisor	1
13	23	maxillary canine	1
43	33	mandibular canine	1
14	24	maxillary first premolar	2
44	34	mandibular first premolar	1
15	25	maxillary second premolar	1
45	35	mandibular second premolar	1
16	26	maxillary first molar	3
46	36	mandibular first molar	2
17	27	maxillary second molar	3
47	37	mandibular second molar	2
18	28	maxillary third premolar	3
48	38	mandibular third premolar	2

How the codes are constructed

Syntax: <quadrant code><tooth code>

Quadrant codes

1	upper right
2	upper left
3	lower left
4	lower right

Tooth codes

1	central incisors
2	lateral incisors
3	canines
4	1st premolars
5	2nd premolars
6	1st molars
7	2nd molars
8	3rd molars